ISBN 978-1-330-37553-2
PIBN 10043966

For support please visit www.forgottenbooks.com

1 MONTH OF
FREE
READING

at

www.ForgottenBooks.com

By purchasing this book you are eligible for one month membership to ForgottenBooks.com, giving you unlimited access to our entire collection of over 1,000,000 titles via our web site and mobile apps.

To claim your free month visit:
www.forgottenbooks.com/free43966

English
Français
Deutsche
Italiano
Español
Português

www.forgottenbooks.com

Mythology Photography **Fiction**
Fishing Christianity **Art** Cooking
Essays Buddhism Freemasonry
Medicine **Biology** Music **Ancient
Egypt** Evolution Carpentry Physics
Dance Geology **Mathematics** Fitness
Shakespeare **Folklore** Yoga Marketing
Confidence Immortality Biographies
Poetry **Psychology** Witchcraft
Electronics Chemistry History **Law**
Accounting **Philosophy** Anthropology
Alchemy Drama Quantum Mechanics
Atheism Sexual Health **Ancient History**
Entrepreneurship Languages Sport
Paleontology Needlework Islam
Metaphysics Investment Archaeology
Parenting Statistics Criminology
Motivational

PUBLICATIONS OF THE CALIFORNIA STATE LIBRARY,

No. 1.

HISTORY

OF

POLITICAL CONVENTIONS

IN

CALIFORNIA, 1849—1892.

BY

WINFIELD J. DAVIS,

Historian of the Sacramento Society of California Pioneers.

SACRAMENTO:

1893.

AUTHOR'S PREFACE,

Of necessity a work of this character must contain imper-fections, as no record of political conventions has been pre-served, save in newspaper reports. Yet it is believed the text of this work embraces as accurate a history of the pro-ceedings of state political bodies as can be compiled from the material available.

The register of state officers has been drawn from various sources; primarily, the official records of the state. The dates of deaths have been supplemented from newspaper and other data. It is as complete as possible, after painstaking research.

Acknowledgment is due for the furnishing of important data to Judges John H. McKune and A. P. Catlin, and Hon. W. A. Anderson.

WINFIELD J. DAVIS.

TRUSTEES' PREFACE,

It has been the object of the authorities of the California State Library to collect all obtainable matter relating to the history of California and of the Pacific coast. While pursuing this object, the librarian learned of the valuable manuscript in the hands of Winfield J. Davis, from which this book is printed. Believing that it contained matter which should be preserved and made accessible, a proposition for its purchase was made. Mr. Davis finally offered to transfer the copyright to the library provided the trustees would publish the book. This was considered very liberal, and was accepted. A limited number of copies have been printed, and will be sold to cover the cost. We think the work a valuable one, and hope the reception accorded it by the public will justify our action in printing it in this form.

Sacramento, January, 1893.

CORRECTIONS. *Corrected JBR.*

Read Amerman *for* Ammerman, *page* 310.
" Brunson *for* Bronson, *pages* 314, 326.
" Curry *for* Currey, *pages* 26, 34, 43, 92, 94, 95, 102, 108, 196, 201, 249, 268.
" Eagon *for* Eagan, *page* 409.
" Gwinn *for* Guinn, *page* 328.
" Kalloch *for* Kallock, *pages* 420, 421.
" Meloney *for* Maloney, *page* 79.
" Owen *for* Owens, *page* 61.
" Reardon *for* Rearden, *page* 79.
" Reardon *for* Reardan, *page* 418.
" Shattuck *for* Shuttuck, *page* 472.
" Spreckels *for* Spreckles, *pages* 313, 318, 321, 430, 455.
" Sweasey *for* Swasey, *page* 248.
" Sweasey *for* Sweasy, *pages* 452, 453, 468.
" Wilcoxon *for* Wilcoxson, *pages* 316, 421.
" Wilcoxon *for* Wilcoxen, *pages* 419, 438.

History of Political Conventions in California.

CHAPTER I.

1849. First Political Mass Meeting in California—Primary Effort for the Organization of the Democratic Party—First State Election.

The first political mass meeting in California assembled at San Francisco, October 25, 1849. It was composed of democrats, and was called in view of the election to be held November 13th following, to vote on the question of the adoption of the constitution, and for the selection of governor, lieutenant-governor, members of congress and of the legislature. John W. Geary was the presiding officer. The attendance was so large that the meeting was compelled to adjourn from a hall to the public square. Dr. McMillan, O. P. Sutton, E. V. Joice, Thomas J. Agnew, John McVicker, Annis Merrill, and W. H. Jones were vice-presidents, and Joseph T. Downey, J. Ross Browne, Daniel Cronin, and John A. McGlynn, secretaries. William Van Voorhies delivered an address, and the following preamble and resolutions were adopted:

WHEREAS, The people of California are taking steps, preparatory to an application for admission into the union, to organize their system of state government in accordance with the provisions of a constitution adopted in convention by delegates chosen from amongst themselves; and, whereas, in furtherance of this great object, elections are soon to be holden to fill the various executive, legislative, and judicial offices provided for by that instrument; and, whereas, also, it becomes the duty of the people of California, through their representatives in the state legislature, to select from amongst their fellow-citizens senators and delegates to represent their interests in the national councils; and, whereas, we, the democratic citizens of the district of San Francisco, feel a natural and deep interest in the general welfare of our adopted home, and are anxiously solicitous that its career shall continue to be upward and onward; *therefore be it resolved,*

1. That there are certain great cardinal principles handed down to us by the framers of the charter of our liberties, as the very founda- tion of republican institutions, which neither distance, time, nor place can change, destroy, or materially modify; and that we will use every honorable effort and resort to all legitimate means to engraft upon such laws and regulations as shall be hereafter established for the government of the people of California the spirit of those principles.

2. That there are certain principles of public policy under the constitution of the United States, and in respect to their operation upon the general interests of the country, contended for and sus- tained by our democratic brethren of the Atlantic states, which we hold to be essential and important, and not to be overlooked in our organization nor disregarded in our selection of senators and repre- sentatives.

3. That a "union of Californians for the sake of California" is well, but that a "union of Californians for the sake of California and the union," is better.

4. That we owe to the policy which acquired and developed our territory an earnest and ardent support, and that we will not permit ourselves to be beguiled into the support of any other opposed to this; that in the selection of our senators and representatives to the congress of the United States we will vigilantly guard against any misrepresentation of our views and opinions, as well in respect to measures affecting the union at large, as our immediate state in- terests.

5. That we will meet at the threshold, and, if possible, defeat any and all attempts, emanating from whatever source they may, to place California in a mere local, sectional and therefore false position before the union, mindful of no interests but her own, and aiding in the support of no measure which has not for its object her imme- diate and exclusive aggrandizement.

6. That *partyism* for the sake of party merely we totally reject, but the support of principles, which have for their object the pre- servation of our glorious constitution inviolable, resistance to and defeat of all powerful and chartered monopolies by the general gov- ernment, opposition to all enactments intended to benefit the few at the expense of the many, a zealous support of that course of policy

which preserves the honor of the country when menaced, punishes the offender when her rights are invaded, and ever looks to an honorable extension of the "area of freedom"—of such *principles* we are the ardent and decided supporters.

7. That we cannot consistently elevate to positions of trust and confidence any man who voted that the war with Mexico was unholy and iniquitous, that it was unnecessary and unjust in its inception, wicked and murderous in its prosecution, or who, by his political connections or otherwise, directly or indirectly *denounced* every life destroyed on the fields of Mexico to have been an *unmitigated murder*.

8. That we cannot consistently support for any public station he who did or would have refused to vote supplies for our gallant little army, when gloriously engaged in grappling with the enemies of its country upon the ensanguined fields of Mexico; that to do so we should outrage the gallant spirits engaged in that conflict, and pay tribute to a factions opposition, scarcely less inimical to their success than the foreign enemies whom they encountered.

9. That we are for our country first, our country last, and our country all the time; not a section, not a circumscribed locality, not a limited interest, but the *whole country*.

A nominating committee was appointed, consisting of Stephen R. Harris, E. V. Joice, L. Stowell, Edmund Randolph, J. A. McGlynn, F. P. Tracy, and others.

On October 27th, an adjourned meeting was held at Portsmouth square for the purpose of receiving the report of the committee. Paul K. Hubbs stated that the committee had not been legally appointed, that its appointment was not in accordance with the time-honored usages of the democratic party, and suggested the propriety of selecting primary election officers by ballot, and to hold an election on the Monday following for delegates to select a ticket to be recommended to the party. He offered the following resolution, which was unanimously adopted :

"That this meeting recognize and will maintain the democratic doctrine, that the people are all true sovereigns of political power, and from the people only shall emanate the nomination of candidates for office. In accordance, therefore, with the time-honored usages of the democratic party, resolved that eleven delegates be elected by party vote to select a ticket to be recommended to the democratic party."

Under the resolution, the election officers selected were M. Fallon, judge; Dr. S. R. Harris, A. Johnson, J. A. McGlynn and Myron Norton, inspectors. It was resolved that the candidates be pledged to vote for no man for United States senator unless he would "uphold exemption of household for debt, and would vote for the formation of a railroad through our own territory in preference to any other." It does not appear that any further action was taken towards making nominations.

On October 25th, a meeting was held at Sacramento to "talk about the new constitution," and the candidates to be voted for at the November election. A motion was made to appoint a committee to report at a future meeting the names of candidates. A substitute was offered and accepted to call a nominating convention, but during the discussion a motion was carried unanimously to submit the whole subject of selecting candidates to the people, on the day of election.

On October 29th, a large political meeting, called "without distinction of party," was held at Sacramento, "to hear the report of the delegates to the constitutional convention, and to consider matters connected with the approaching election." S. C. Hastings was chairman. A committee was selected to nominate a legislative ticket for the district, and that being done, no further action was taken.

A public meeting of citizens was held at Monterey, on October 30th, and a nominating committee of seven was appointed. The committee tendered the nomination for governor to General Bennet Riley, but he declined to run, and W. S. Sherwood was named for the office. Francis J. Lippitt was nominated for lieutenant-governor, and Edward Gilbert and James L. Ord for congressmen.

The other candidates who ran at the election were independent, and no particular attempt was made to draw party lines.

The election was held on November 13th, and the constitution was ratified by a vote of 12,061 in its favor to 811 against it.

The San Francisco *Alta*, in its issue of November 15th, said, in referring to this election:

"The election held throughout the state of California on Tuesday last was an important era in the history of this remarkable country. From its results are to come the weal or woe of the new state, not only for a year, but possibly for ten years, and it is to be hoped that the men then chosen to carry into effect the constitution, which was at the same time adopted, will prove themselves the patriots which the country has the right to expect.

"The day of the election was very disagreeable. Several showers of rain fell, and the mud, which was unfathomable before, suddenly disclosed a 'lower deep.' It is not strange, therefore, that, instead of 5,000 votes, as was generally expected, only 3,169 were polled in San Francisco.

"All, or nearly all, the candidates were independent nominees. In some instances they have been indorsed or recommended by public meetings in different parts of the state; but in only one district (San Francisco) was an attempt made to organize a party, or fight the battle upon the old issue of democrat and whig. We have no doubt that, had time permitted, there would have been a state convention held, at which a 'regular democratic ticket,' would have been nominated; and, had such been the fact, we are well satisfied that its complete triumph would have been the result."

On December 10th, following, Henry W. Halleck, the military secretary of state; P. Ord, a judge of the superior tribunal; David Spence, prefect; Mariano Malarin, judge of first instance, and Y. Esquar, alcalde of Monterey, met at that place pursuant to the provisions of section six of the schedule to the constitution, and canvassed the vote of the state. In their report they stated that "after three days of continuous labor, we have not been able to complete the list of scattering votes for the districts of Sacramento and San Joaquin;" but they said their report " is believed to be sufficient for the purposes intended." They reported the vote of the various candidates as follows:

For Governor—Peter H. Burnett, 6,783; W. S. Sherwood, 3,220; John A. Sutter, 2,201; W. M. Steuart, 619; John W. Geary, 1,358; with 32 scattering.

For Lieutenant-Governor—John McDougal, 7,374; Richard Roman, 2,368; F. J. Lippitt, 1,127; John B. Frisbie, 1,558; A. M. Winn, 802; Pablo de la Guerra, 129; with 363 scattering.

For Congressmen—George W. Wright, 5,451; Edward Gilbert, 5,300; Rodman M. Price, 4,040; Lewis Dent, 2,129; W. M. Sheppard, 1,773; P. A. Morse, 2,066; E. J. C. Kewen, 1,826; Pet Halstead, 1,271; W. E. Shannon, 1,327; L. W. Hastings, 215; with 750 scattering.

On December 18th, the state legislature met in joint convention and canvassed the votes that had been cast at that election, and the result as then ascertained, differed from the Monterey canvass, in that for governor, Burnett was shown to have received 6,716 votes; Sherwood, 3,188, and Geary, 1,475; for lieutenant-governor, Lippitt, 1,060; and for congressmen, Gilbert, 5,100; Dent, 2,029; Kewen, 1,806; Halstead, 593; P. B. Reading, 171; W. H. Russell, 92; K. H. Dimmick, 41; and J. Thompson, 86.

The convention declared that Burnett had been elected governor; McDougal, lieutenant-governor; and Wright and Gilbert, Congressmen.

CHAPTER II.

1850. Call for an Organization of the Whig Party—First County Election—General Election.

The first state legislature passed an act providing for the holding of an election on April 1, 1850, to elect county officers and a clerk of the supreme court. Early in that year efforts were made to organize the democratic and whig parties. In San Francisco a partial organization of the democratic party had been kept up from the year before, but there was no general organization of any political party in the state.

Late in January, a democratic meeting was held at San Jose, where the legislature was then meeting, with the object to effect a State organization of that party, and on February 2d an adjourned meeting was held in the assembly chamber. David C. Broderick was the presiding officer. A series of resolutions were adopted, but they were not published.

On February 9th the whig members of the legislature and a number of citizens of San Jose held a mass meeting in the senate chamber in that city. David F. Douglass was the chairman. The following preamble and resolutions were adopted :

WHEREAS, the organization of the democratic party of the state of California has been commenced and is about being completed, and the broad, proscriptive doctrine has been publicly declared and adopted 'that no whig shall hereafter receive a democratic vote for any office in the gift of the people ,' and, whereas, however much as Californians we deprecate the present organization of mere political parties, and the promulgation of doctrines calculated to arouse all the acuity of party spirit, whilst our infant state requires the united energies of all her sons to secure to her that position which her wealth and population entitle her, yet as whigs we feel called upon to indicate not only our principles as a party, but our rights as freemen; *be it therefore resolved,*

1. That the whigs of California are invited to unite with us, by a prompt and efficient organization, in repelling the assertion that a whig is unworthy to possess the rights and incompetent to perform the duties of a freeman.

2. That in order to further the objects of this meeting a committee of five be appointed by the chair to draft resolutions for the action of this meeting.

In accordance with the second resolution, the chair appointed a committee, consisting of Jones, Tingley, Heydenfeldt, Allen and Dimmick, and they submitted the following report, which was adopted :

1. That liberty, equality and justice are the fundamental principles of whig faith.

2. That the veto power, the great monarchial feature of our republic, should be restrained in its exercise to the clear violations of the constitution, or manifest want of consideration on the part of congress, and that the frequent exercise of this kingly prerogative by late democratic presidents from motives of professed expediency, whereby the will of the people has been made subservient to the will of the man, should excite the alarm and arouse the vigilance of every true republican.

3. That commerce, agriculture and manufactures constitute the wealth of a nation, and equally require the fostering hand of government; and that a tariff, whilst it should produce no greater revenue than is necessary to the economical administration of the government, should contain such just and moderate discriminations as will enable these great sources of our wealth to compete with foreign nations in our own markets.

4. That the declaration of James K. Polk, the great exponent of democratic principles, contained in his veto of the river and harbor bill, that "there is no middle ground between an absolute d nial of the power of the government to make appropriations for these objects (improvements of rivers and harbors) and the establishment of

a wide and general system, in accordance with that power," is a doctrine false in theory, unstatesmanlike in policy, and especially ruinous to the interests of our infant state. That California, destined hereafter by the wealth and enterprise of her citizens, by the vast extent of her sea coast, and by her spacious ports and great inland seas, to command the commerce of the entire Pacific, peculiarly requires the fostering hand of the government in the erection of light-houses and the improvement of her harbors. That her isolated position demands that a speedy means of internal communication be established with the older states; and that the party or the man who denies the power of congress to accomplish these great and necessary objects, is unworthy the support of a true Californian.

5. That it is a cardinal principle of the whigs of California, that her mines should be free to all American citizens. That we regard it as practically impossible to parcel and sell the public lands contained in the mining districts. That immigration would be thereby greatly lessened, and that the richest portions of those lands would inevitably fall into the hands of speculators and monopolists, whilst a vast multitude of laboring classes would be compelled to hire their services, to abandon the country, or to violate a law unfounded in justice and unsupported by public opinion.

6. That the interests of agriculture, the most solid foundation of national prosperity, require that the actual settler should be protected in his possession of the public lands, when it does not interfere with private rights; and congress should extend the preëmption laws over California at the earliest possible moment.

A central committee was appointed, consisting of J. M. Jones, J. D. Hoppe, Charles Campbell, Pedro Sansevaine, R. M. May, C. E. Allen, E. Heydenfeldt, B. F. Moore, S. E. Woodworth, G. B. Tingley, and A. W. Hope.

Shortly before, in San Francisco, the whigs had elected Heydenfeldt to the senate at a special election, and this success had inspired them with confidence. On February 10th, a whig mass meeting was held in that city to nominate a candidate for sheriff, and it was resolved "that the whigs of San Francisco and California at large have had enough of the cry 'no party,' 'union of California for the sake of California,' and that from and after this time they solemnly pledge themselves to each other that they will, under no political necessity, confer office on or vote for a man who is not an open, undisguised whig; and further, that they will sanction on all occasions the nominee of the party and no other candidate."

On the 26th, the whig general committee of San Francisco, composed of Alfred Wheeler, Levi Parsons, L. R. Lull, S. Flower, R. H. Taylor and others, issued a lengthy address to the people, indorsing the San Jose resolutions as the basis for the organization of the party.

On the same day a mass meeting was held in the same city, and Alfred Wheeler was nominated as the whig candidate for the assembly, to fill a vacancy.

The democrats also named a candidate, and the attempt was made to draw party lines closely, but it did not succeed. Local dissensions had been engendered among the democrats of San Francisco, and on March 1st the leading members of the party issued an address to the party urging them to support the democratic candidate for the assembly. The address asked the members of the party "to take no exceptions to the mode of proceeding in making the nomination, as the respective committees of the party are about effecting a reconciliation, and are reorganizing the heretofore discordant elements of the party."

At the special election held on March 2d, Wheeler was elected by a vote of 876, to 738 for the democratic candidate.

On March 8th, a call was issued at San Francisco for a democratic mass meeting, to be held on the following evening, to act upon the report of a committee of conference that had been appointed, to select a general committee, and take such steps "as may be necessary for harmoniously organizing the party," in view of the county election.

At the appointed time, a large meeting was held at the plaza. Wilson Shannon was the chairman. Resolutions were adopted, and a committee was appointed to complete the organization. A primary was called for the 25th, at which J. J. Bryant was nominated for sheriff, John A. McGlynn for recorder, J. E. Addison for clerk, S. B. Marye for county judge, J. C. Smith for county attorney, D. M. Chauncey for assessor, R. G. Berford for treasurer, Alexander Wells for district attorney, E. H. Tharp for clerk of the supreme court, W. M. Eddy for surveyor, and Ed. Gallagher for coroner.

The whig committee also called a primary election, which was held on March 22d. Seventeen hundred and sixty-four votes were cast, and the following ticket was nominated: County judge, R. N. Morrison; district attorney, Calhoun Benham; county attorney, Louis R. Lull; recorder, Orrin Bailey; clerk, R. G. Crozier; surveyor, W. P. Humphreys; assessor, J. G. Gould; treasurer, George Endicott; coroner, G. P. Ogden; sheriff, J. C. Hays. The following day Hays withdrew and came out as an independent candidate, and the committee nominated John E. Townes for that office. W. E. Shannon received 1,432 votes for clerk of the supreme court.

On March 6th Ellison Dickey announced himself as an independent candidate for that office, and on the 20th William G. Marcy came out for the same position. Marcy withdrew, however, in favor of Tharp. At the county election Tharp was elected.

On March 23d an act was passed by the legislature providing for the holding, on the first Monday of October of each year, of a general election throughout the state, for members of the legislature, and such other state officers as might be required by law to be elected. Under this law the first election was held October 7, 1850.

The first legislature by statute provided that at this first general election a superintendent of public instruction and a clerk of the supreme court should be elected; and Attorney-General Kewen having resigned, it became necessary to select his successor at the same election. Although there were several state officers to be elected, no general conventions were held, and less attention was paid to politics than at the county election.

On September 14th, at a democratic meeting in San Jose, a legislative ticket was nominated; and on the 19th the democracy of San Francisco placed a ticket in the field, with Eugene H. Tharp as the candidate for clerk of the supreme court, Frederick P. Tracy for superintendent of public instruction, and James A. McDougall for attorney-general.

The whigs held a primary at San Francisco on the 28th, and nominated John D. Munford for attorney-general, Dr. John F. Morse for clerk of the supreme court, and James Nooney for superintendent of public instruction. R. Townsend Huddart, B. Brierly, C. W. Butterfield, E. B. Bateman, John G. Marvin, S. H. P. Ross, J. Stratman and H. W. Carpentier were independent candidates for school superintendent; John Jack and W. C. Sharron for clerk of the supreme court, and E. B. Cone, T. W. Sutherland, A. P. Crittenden and George Rowe for attorney-general. The canvass of the votes cast at the election showed this result:

For Attorney-General—McDougall, 10,405; Munford, 5,227; C. T. Botts, 154; Sutherland, 203; Crittenden, 36; Cone, 2,722; S. P. Weller, 25; Blackburn, 52; scattering, 87.

For Clerk of the Supreme Court—Tharp, 13,873; Morse, 6,040; S. S. Burt, 24; T. Higgins, 15; Jack, 46; scattering, 75.

For Superintendent of Public Instruction—Nooney, 3,144; Tracy, 2,414; C. W. Butterfield, 3,262; Huddart, 1,151; Bateman, 2,227; Brierly, 2,204; Marvin, 3,823; Ross, 84; Bandini, 82; scattering, 237.

McDougall was, therefore, elected attorney-general, Tharp clerk of the supreme court, and Marvin superintendent of public instruction.

CHAPTER III.

1851. Democratic Convention. Whig Convention.

The first democratic convention that was held in California met in the Episcopal church, at Benicia, at 11 o'clock on Monday, May 19th, and was called to order by James M. Estell. Thomas J. Henley was chosen temporary chairman, and on permanent organization ex-Governor Smith of Virginia was president, and Patten of El Dorado, Alvarado of Contra Costa, Southerland of San Diego, Joshua Ralden of Tuolumne, Bright of Yuba, Ralston of Sacramento, Lowe of Butte, Sutter of San Francisco, and A. C. Bradford, vice-presidents. In the evening addresses were delivered by William M. Gwin, John B. Weller, T. J. Henley, Governor John McDougal, and others.

On the 20th, John B. Weller, John Bigler, Richard Roman, W. S. Sherwood, T. J. Green, Samuel Brannan and John McDougal were placed in nomination for governor. Bigler was nominated on the sixth ballot, the results of the different ballotings being as follows:

First Ballot—Weller, 18; Roman, 35; Bigler, 25; Green, 12; Brannan, 1; McDougal, 44; Sherwood, 40.

Second Ballot—Weller, 21; Roman, 35; Bigler, 35; Green, 5; Brannan, 1; McDougal, 41; Sherwood, 37.

Third Ballot—Roman, 43; Bigler, 46; Green, 7; Brannan, 1; McDougal, 45; Sherwood, 34.

Fourth Ballot—Roman, 40 ; Bigler, 47 ; Green, 7 ; McDougal, 42 ; Sherwood, 40.

Fifth Ballot—Roman, 40; Bigler, 79 ; Green, 14 ; McDougal, 43 ; Sherwood, withdrawn.

Sixth Ballot—Roman, 39 ; Bigler, 129 ; Green, 4 ; Brannan, 1 ; McDougal, 2.

On the 21st, the following additional nominations were made: Samuel Purdy, for lieutenant-governor, on the second ballot, over Murphy of Calaveras and B. F. Keene.   Solomon Heydenfeldt, for justice of the supreme court, on the first ballot, over W. D. Fair. Richard Roman, for treasurer, on the first ballot, over W. W. Gift. Winslow S. Pierce, for controller, without opposition.   S. O. Hastings, for attorney-general, without opposition.   William M. Eddy, for surveyor-general, without opposition.   J. W. McCorkle and E. C. Marshall, for congressmen, over E. D. Hall (withdrawn), J. D. Van Voorhies (declined), M. F. Hoit, D. W. Murphy, and T. B. Van Buren (declined).

The convention adopted a lengthy address to the people, and a series of resolutions, but they were not published in the newspapers.

The whig state convention met at Rev. Mr. Taylor's M. E. church, on Powell street, San Francisco, at 12 o'clock on Monday, May 26th.   It was called to order by P. W. Shepherd, and Dr. John F. Morse was the temporary chairman.   Delegates were present from the counties of San Francisco, Sacramento, San Diego, Santa Clara, Contra Costa, Santa Cruz, Solano, El Dorado, Calaveras, Sutter, Tuolumne, Yuba, Placer, San Joaquin, Trinity, Nevada, Butte, Shasta, Yolo, Marin, and Mariposa.

On permanent organization, Gen. John Wilson was president, and G. R. Griffin, Captain Rush, J. M. Burt, Alfred Morgan, and James Fitton, vice-presidents.

On the 27th and 28th, the following nominations were made:

Pearson B. Reading, for governor, on the first ballot, by a vote of 43, to 35 for William Waldo; David F. Douglass withdrawing. D. P. Baldwin, for lieutenant-governor, on the first ballot, over W. D. Fair.   E. J. C. Kewen and B. F. Moore, for congressmen, over Jesse O. Goodwin (withdrawn), R. N. Wood, John C. Fall, G. T. Martin (withdrawn), and Dr. Peter Smith.   Tod Robinson, for justice of the supreme court, on the first ballot, over D. O. Shattuck, R. N. Morrison, and A. F. Wilson.   W. D. Fair, for attorney-general, on the first ballot, over J. O. Goodwin, Horace Smith, and Lorenzo Sawyer. J. M. Burt, for treasurer, on the first ballot, over Albert W. Bee. Alexander G. Abell, for controller, on the first ballot, over George O. McMullin and James B. Devoe. Walter Herron, for surveyor-general, on the first ballot, over William H. Graham and F. R. Loring (withdrawn).

A state central committee was appointed, consisting of General John Wilson, R. Hampton, P..W. Tompkins, Jesse D. Carr, D. H. Haskell, R. N. Wood, William Robinson, Judge Chambers, and James E. Wainwright.

On the 29th, the following resolutions, reported by J. Neely Johnson, were adopted:

1. That we are opposed to the sale or lease of the mineral lands of California, but are in favor of the same being held by the general government, for the benefit of the miners, to be worked by them, free from any tax or toll whatever.

2. That in the adjustment of disputed land titles in this state we are in favor of the same being referred to the decision of commissioners, under authority of the general government, with the right of appeal from such decision, by any party interested, to the proper United States courts.

3. That the dictates of good policy, and the simple demands of justice, require at the hands of the general government the early extension of the pre-emption laws over the public domain not embraced within the mineral lands of this state; the adoption of such laws as shall secure to actual settlers a donation of such public lands, not exceeding one hundred acres, to each head of a family, and also to provide grants of the same to be made to such persons as have settled upon private lands within this state, and made valuable improvements upon them, in good faith, supposing the same to be a part of such public domain.

4. That we are in favor of the general government granting to this state, for the purposes of education and works of internal improvement, a quantity of public lands, at least equaling the grants heretofore made, or hereafter to be made, to the most favored states of the union, in this respect.

5. That we are in favor of liberal appropriations by the general government for works of a public character, especially the improvement of our rivers and harbors.

6. That we are in favor of the adoption of such proper measures

by the general government as shall most speedily tend to foster and aid the construction of a railroad, connecting this state with the Mississippi valley.

7. That the establishment of steam communication between this state, the Sandwich Islands, and China, is of the utmost importance, and will tend greatly to the advancement of the commercial and political condition of the whole union, and especially of California; therefore, we approve of the adoption of a liberal policy by the general government in aid of such an enterprise.

8. That the failure of congress to make provision for a mint in California has been greatly detrimental to the interests of the people of the state, and our present condition and wants urgently demand that early and ample appropriations be made for that object.

9. That we have a just and equitable claim on the general government for such moneys as were collected by her officers, as revenue on imports in this state, prior to our admission into the union.

10. That it is the duty of the general government to assume the indebtedness of this state necessarily contracted in the protection and defense of her citizens, from Indian warfare.

11. That we will ever maintain the due execution and supremacy of the laws, and, that the people may not be subjected to onerous and oppressive taxation, we are in favor of the strictest economy in the administration of the state and general governments.

12. That the recent compromise measures adopted by congress receive our cordial approbation, and in defense of the constitution and the union we will ever be found faithful and true.

The democratic candidates were early on the stump, and the campaign soon became exciting and interesting. The whigs had the greater number of newspapers supporting their ticket, but the democrats had the better speakers. A large portion of the people deprecated the formation of parties upon the basis of Atlantic politics, with the plea that California was not interested in those questions, and at first they were apathetic, but before the close of the campaign almost every voter had taken sides. In the southern portion of the state some dissatisfaction was manifested with both tickets, because there was no representative from that section, and a movement was made to put an independent ticket in the field. Captain Elisha K. Kane (U. S. A.), who was then stationed on this coast, was nominated for governor by the people of the south, but he published his withdrawal in the early part of August.

On April 26th the legislature passed an act amending the election law of March 23, 1850, and changing the time for the holding of the general state election from October to the first Wednesday in September, of each year.

Accordingly, the election of 1851 was held on September 3d, at which the entire democratic ticket was elected.

The official canvass of the votes developed this result:

For Governor—Bigler, 22,613; Reading, 21,531.

For Lieutenant-Governor—Purdy, 23,373; Baldwin, 19,656.

For Judge of Supreme Court—Heydenfeldt, 24,428; Robinson, 20,670.

For Treasurer—Roman, 24,666; Burt, 19,777.

For Controller—Pierce, 22,996; Abell, 20,675.

For Attorney-General—Hastings, 23,016; Fair, 21,044.

For Surveyor-General—Eddy, 22,678; Herron, 21,473.

For Congressmen—Marshall, 23,604; McCorkle, 23,624; Kewen, 20,407; Moore, 19,071.

On January 8, 1852, the legislature met in joint convention and canvassed the election returns for governor and lieutenant-governor. The whig members objected to considering the returns from some of the counties, on the ground that they had been opened by parties other than the speaker of the house, and, as they claimed, unlawfully. An animated discussion followed, when a motion to throw out the returns alleged to be irregular was laid on the table—65 to 16. The convention then declared Bigler and Purdy to have been elected. The whigs always claimed that their ticket had been elected, but that it had been defeated on the count of the votes. While the convention was in session Governor McDougal sent in his resignation, but it was not accepted. About an hour afterward the legislature again met in convention, and Bigler was inaugurated governor.

CHAPTER IV.

1852. First Presidential Campaign—Whig Convention, February 19th—Democratic Convention, February 23d—Whig Convention, June 7th—Democratic Convention, July 20th—Free Soil Convention—First Presidential Election.

Preparations for the first presidential campaign in California were early commenced, and each of the great parties had active organizers in the field. There was a pride in the result of the first presidential election in the state that gave energy to the work, and it soon became apparent that the campaign would be full of life.

Unfortunately for the democrats, a division occurred in their party in San Francisco, between the adherents of Stephen A. Douglas and the friends of the other presidential candidates. The Douglas party was considerably in the minority, but it made up in tact what it lacked in strength, and the feud that was engendered partook of all the bitterness that characterized the subsequent dissensions in the democratic party in this state.

On December 23, 1851, a primary election of that party was held in San Francisco, and two sets of delegates to the county convention claimed the election. The general committee gave credentials to one set, and the other delegation went in without certificates. A double convention was the result, and each branch elected delegates to the state convention. One set was designated the "general committee" delegates, while the other was called the "protest" delegates.

The whigs were united all over the state.

The whig state convention met on Thursday, February 19th, at Rev. Mr. Benton's church, Sacramento. George O. McMullin was chosen temporary chairman, and afterwards president; and G. A. Shurtleff, W. R. Hopkins, A. Hinchman and others, vice-presidents.

On the 20th, the convention proceeded to select delegates to attend the national convention. On the first ballot 113 votes were cast, of which W. Heath had 1, J. H. C. Mudd 22, A. A. H. Tuttle 3, Isaac Davis 5, R. N. Morrison 2, B. F. Whittier 7, William M. Stewart 39, A. C. Monson 10, A. J. Ellis 17, John A. Lyle 6, and Gregory Yale 1. There was no choice, and the name of Morrison was withdrawn.

On the second ballot Stewart had 102 votes, and was elected.

On the third ballot Jesse O. Goodwin received 64 votes, and was elected.

On the fifth ballot Mudd was elected, having received 57 votes.

On the seventh ballot Heath was elected, having received 68 votes.

On the last ballot John H. Moore and E. T. Wilson were among the unsuccessful candidates.

A. Morgan was selected as the substitute delegate for Mudd, J. A.

Lyle for Goodwin, Isaac Davis for Stewart, and B. F. Whittier for Heath.

On the 21st, a determined but unsuccessful effort was made to nominate presidential electors, instead of having a subsequent convention for that purpose. A great deal of feeling was engendered by the discussion, and a number of the delegates retired from the hall when it was announced that the proposition had been defeated.

A state committee was selected, composed of Dr. John F. Morse, E. J. C. Kewen, Tod Robinson, I. N. Hoag, John Wilson, H. A. Crabbe, Thos. Robinson, and R. H. Taylor.

The whig state platform of 1851 was re-adopted.

The democratic state convention met on Monday, February 23d, at Sacramento. The two sets of delegates from San Francisco appeared—one headed by David C. Broderick, and the other by Elcan Heydenfeldt, and they created a serious disturbance in the convention.

On simultaneous motions J. W. Coffroth and Walker of Yuba sprang upon the stage, and each endeavored to act as temporary chairman. For a time there was the greatest excitement, when a motion was made requesting each aspirant to withdraw from the stand, that it might be decided who was the choice of the convention; but Broderick was too quick for the other side, and when the question on the motion was about to be put, he sprang to his feet and named T. B. Van Buren as chairman *pro tem.*, and decided that that gentleman had been chosen. Amidst great confusion Van Buren reached the chair.

When something like order was restored another disagreement arose upon the chairman refusing to put the question when a division was called for on the vote for secretary.

Isaac B. Wall then moved "that the chairman be respectfully requested to leave the stand;" he put the motion himself, and declared that it had carried, but Van Buren refused to vacate the stand.

M. S. Latham moved, in order to quell the disturbance, that both sets of delegates from San Francisco be requested to leave the room. The motion prevailed, and the parties retired. A debate then sprang up, which consumed the remainder of the day, upon the claims of the delegates from San Francisco to seats in the convention. This debate was resumed on the 24th, when counsel for the competing sets of delegates addressed the convention; Judge Heydenfeldt and ex-Governor Smith of Virginia representing the protesting delegates, and Alexander Wells and Edmund Randolph representing the general committee delegates.

At the evening session the convention decided, by a vote of 100 to 64, to admit the protesting delegates.

On the 25th, a permanent organization was effected, by the election of Milton S. Latham as president, by a vote of 169, to 116 for James W. Coffroth. B. H. Williams, Joseph Walkup, William S. Patterson, S. R. Harris, Andres Pico, R. B. Buchanan, Dr. S. A. McMeans, Juan B. Alvarado, J. L. Warner, Isaac B. Wall, S. Fleming, and R. Ashe were elected vice-presidents. William H. Richardson, J. M. Covarrubias, Joshua Holden, and Henry A. Lyons were elected delegates to attend the national convention, over Thomas J. Green, C. C. Hornsby, J. J. Bryant, Jacob Frye, James Schofield, M. M. Wombough, John Middleton, E. W. Roberts, Harrison Olmstead, J. J. Warner, S. C. Foster, E. D. Wheeler, W. McDaniels, Charles Loring, E. D. Hammond, and M. Miller. E. D. Hammond, Amos T. Laird, Charles Loring, and M. M. Wombough were elected substitute delegates.

The convention did not adopt resolutions. The following resolution was offered:

That, in the opinion of this convention, it is unwise, and by no means necessary, to instruct our delegates for whom they shall cast their votes in the national convention. That, in the opinion of the democratic party of California, it is not at this time our best policy to discriminate between the many prominent citizens of our party whose names are spoken of for president and vice-president of the United States. That the democratic party of California have full and entire confidence in the integrity and democratic principles of Lewis Cass, Stephen A. Douglas, W. R. King, James Buchanan, W. O. Butler, R. J. Walker, and Sam Houston, and that the democracy of this state will cheerfully support either of them or any other good democrat for president or vice-president, if selected by the national democratic convention.

Denver moved to amend and instruct the delegates to vote for Douglas for president; and a substitute was offered declaring in favor of any "union compromise candidate," but the whole matter was laid on the table. Subsequently another resolution in favor of Douglas for president was offered, but after discussion it was withdrawn.

On the 25th, the San Francisco general committee delegates published a protest against the action of the state convention, by which they said they had been deprived of their rights. They claimed that they had been regularly chosen. The protest was signed by Edmund Randolph, Eugene Casserly, D. C. Broderick, F. P. Tracy, Herman Wohler, John A. McGlynn, Alexander Wells, W. M. Eddy, Edward McGowan, James A. McDougall, Henry H. Haight, H. H. Byrne, Geo. McDougal, David Scannell, and others.

Another whig state convention met at Sacramento, on June 7th. It organized by electing J. Neely Johnson, president, and D. F. Douglass, T. D. Johns, E. W. Gemmill, S. S. Brooks, E. C. Bell, C. McDonald, Robert Tevis, Orrin Bailey, L. Sawyer, and others, vice-presidents.

On the 8th, the following nominations were made :

J. M. Huntington, for justice of the supreme court (long term), over Stanton Buckner and David O. Shattuck.

Stanton Buckner, for justice of the supreme court (short term), over John Chetwood.

Geo. B. Tingley and P. L. Edwards, for members of congress, over H. A. Crabbe, Calhoun Benham, Johnson Price, J. T. McCarty, R. N. Wood, E. F. W. Ellis, Frank Soule, D. O. Shattuck, E. J. C. Kewen, Tod Robinson, and John C. Fall.

John C. Fall, D. H. Haskell, T. D. Johns, and James E. Hale, for presidential electors.

Thos. Robinson, A. Maurice, William A. Robinson, and Samuel Barney, for alternate electors.

Wm. W. Hawks, for clerk of the supreme court.

The following resolutions were adopted :

1. That as congress has donated lands to actual settlers in Oregon, we do insist that it is but a simple act of justice that the same liberality should be extended to every actual settler in California, for we do not recognize the justice of the rule that would grant such boon to the one, and refuse it to the other.

2. That in all cases where American citizens have in good faith, settled upon lands, believing the same to be a part of the public domain, but which shall prove to be private property, in every such instance the general government should give such settler at least one hundred and sixty acres of public land, as a compensation for improvements and loss sustained by reason of such settlement.

3. That we respectfully insist that congress shall donate an amount of public lands to the state of California, equal to that

hitherto granted to any other new state. On no just ground could they grant to us less, and, owing to our peculiar situation, we could reasonably demand more.

4. That we are opposed to the sale or lease of the mineral lands of California, and as whigs we now, as heretofore, hold the doctrine that they shall be left free to the industry and enterprise of American citizens, native or adopted, subject to such laws, rules, and regulations as may be from time to time prescribed by those interested therein.

5. That common justice demands at the hands of congress, the prompt establishment of a branch of the United States mint in California—a subject recommended by a whig president to congress—in order to give to gold its full value in the hands of the miner; a recommendation which a so-called democratic congress has hitherto refused to carry out—preferring to add to the coffers of foreign bankers rather than aid in giving full value to the daily toil of California miners.

6. That congress should speedily establish a weekly mail communication between the Atlantic and Pacific, and should make liberal appropriations to establish a line of steamers between San Francisco and China, Japan, and the intermediate islands of the Pacific, giving the citizens of California a preference in extending aid to accomplish this great national object.

7. That we most heartily approve the whig doctrine of internal improvements, knowing, as we do full well, that the prevalence of this doctrine as advocated and carried out by the whig party, has been one of the great leading causes of the rapid rise, growth, and unexampled prosperity of our common country.

8. That it is a paramount duty that congress owes to California, as well as to the whole union, to speedily undertake and promptly prosecute to completion a railway from the valley of the Mississippi to the Pacific ocean.

9. That we hold it as one of the paramount duties of congress to make liberal appropriations for the improvement of the harbors, bays, and navigable rivers of California; likewise for the erection of custom houses, light-houses, docks, fog-bells, and all other improvements tending to protect and facililate trade and commerce.

10. That it is the imperative duty of congress to refund without delay, to California, the large sums extorted from her citizens before her admission into the union, under the disguise of custom-house dues or public revenue, but which were in fact only military exactions, levied without color of law, the enormity of which has no par-

allel in the history of our government, unless it shall hereafter be found in the adoption of a proposition recently introduced into the senate of the United States by a distinguished representative of the democracy of California, to rob the *bona fide* lawful owner of his lands under the pretense of law, whilst the validity and justice of his title is confessed.

11. That with the vast capabilities of California, it is indispensible that her legislation should be especially directed to the speedy development of her agricultural resources, the building up of manufactures, the extension and protection of her commercial interests, and the encouragement of domestic industry in all its branches. Such, in the opinion of this convention, has not been the character of its legislation under democratic rule.

12. That we concur with the self-styled democratic convention that assembled at Benicia, in their resolution declaring that the general government, in the hands of a so-called democratic senate and house of representatives, "have been guilty of the most culpable neglect of the higher interests of California, and have utterly disregarded the wants and demands of the people."

13. That we regard the series of measures recently adopted by congress, denominated the compromise measures, as a settlement of those questions on a basis alike just and honorable, and we will strictly maintain and support them as such.

14. That it is the duty of the general government to assume the indebtedness of this state necessarily contracted in the protection and defence of her citizens in warfare.

15. That we will support the doctrines set forth in the foregoing resolutions, for the reason that they are whig doctrines, and if carried out will not only promote all the great leading interests of California, but of the whole union; and as whigs, we pledge our united and individual advocacy of the same, before the people.

John M. Huntington, the nominee for justice of the supreme court, resigned his place on the ticket on August 21st, and on September 8th the whig central committee nominated John Chetwood for the office, over David O. Shattuck; but Chetwood died at San Francisco on the 17th of that month, and on the 25th the committee filled the vacancy on the ticket by nominating E. W. F. Sloan.

A second democratic convention met at Benicia, on Tuesday, July 20th, with 258 delegates present. The San Francisco delegates represented by proxies four other counties, and a motion to rule out proxies created a commotion, but was defeated.

The convention was called to order by F. P. Tracy, and Wm. H. Lyon was chosen temporary chairman. On permanent organization, W. T. Barbour was president, and E. Allen, A. Ludlow, C. Culledge, W. Robinson, C. T. Ryland, A. Randall, R. H. Deering, and Col. Thorne, vice-presidents.

On the 21st, the following nominations were made:

Milton S. Latham, for congressman from the northern district, on the first ballot, having received 193 votes, to 78 for Joseph W. McCorkle and 27 for James W. Denver; B. F. Keene withdrawing.

James A. McDougall, for congressman from the southern district, on the first ballot, receiving 165 votes, to 130 for R. P. Hammond, 2 for E. C. Marshall, and 1 for A. C. Peachy; Thos. B. Van Buren withdrawing.

Hugh C. Murray, for justice of the supreme court (long term), by acclamation; J. Churchman withdrawing.

Alexander Wells, for justice of the supreme court (short term), on the fifth ballot, over Seth B. Farwell, Alexander Anderson, James Churchman, and A. P. Crittenden.

P. K. Woodside, for clerk of the supreme court, on the fifth ballot, over E. H. Tharp, James G. Stebbins, Wm. Haskins, W. G. Marcy, L. B. Mizner, and James L. Trask.

On the 22d, the following additional nominations were made:

W. S. Sherwood, J. W. Gregory, Thos. J. Henley, and Andres Pico, for presidential electors, over Blanton McAlpin, John Y. Lind, J. L. Brent, J. C. Palmer (withdrawn), F. P. Tracy (withdrawn), Wm. Smith, and Wm. McDaniel.

J. L. Brent, L. B. Mizner, J. A. Watson and S. B. Farwell, for alternate electors

The following resolutions were reported:

1. That we cordially approve of the nominations for president and vice-president of the United States, made at the recent democratic national convention, and that we also approve of the general resolutions adopted as a platform by that body; and we pledge ourselves to give General Franklin Pierce and Wm. R. King, the nominees, our united, hearty and enthusiastic support.

2. That the democratic party is in favor of the donation of the public lands to American citizens, whether native or naturalized, who become actual settlers, in quantities not exceeding one hundred and sixty acres to each settler.

3. That we view the project of a great national railroad from the Atlantic states to the Pacific ocean as a measure of great impor-

tance, believing that its completion will tend to cement the bonds of the American union; that it will not only connect the various local interests of this country, but will give us the control of a large share of the trade and commerce of the world, and increase our influence and power with other nations.

4. That we recommend to our delegation in congress to use every exertion in their power to have some measure adopted to secure the early commencement and completion of this work.

After a discussion, the second resolution was laid on the table, and the following was adopted as a substitute:

2. That all public lands of California ought to be reserved by the government from sale, and granted to citizens and actual settlers.

The balance of the resolutions were then adopted.

John Conness offered a resolution that all contracts for labor made outside of the state, either in any of the other states or in foreign countries should not be deemed valid, and it was laid on the table.

A resolution was unanimously adopted declaring " that we do not approve of the bill offered by Tingley, in the legislature, providing for the introduction of serfs or coolies into California to compete with white laborers, who at the same time constitute the democracy and aristocracy of this state."

The free soil democrats held a convention on October 15th, at San Francisco, and nominated for presidential electors, Joseph Lloyd, Asa Walker, Asa D. Hatch and J. Bryant Hill. No nominations were made for state officers. A state central committee was appointed, and an address was issued earnestly inviting " the friends of the cause to unite in using every lawful means, morally and politically, to free our country from the foul stain and curse of slavery."

The election was held on November 2d, and the democratic ticket was successful.

For President—Scott, 34,971 ; Pierce, 39,665 ; Hale, 100.

For Congressmen—Edwards, 31,814 ; Tingley, 31,774 ; Latham, 36,961 ; McDougall, 35,685.

For Justices of the Supreme Court—long term—Sloan, 32,160 ; . Murray, 36,420. *Short term*—Buckner, 32,859 ; Wells, 35,453.

· *For Clerk of the Supreme Court*—Hawks, 32,859 ; Woodside, · 35,627.

The democratic presidential electors met at Vallejo on December 1st, and cast the vote of the state for Pierce and King. On the eighth ballot Henley was selected to convey the returns to Washington.

CHAPTER V.

1853. Democratic Convention—Whig Convention—Result of the Election.

On April 20th, the democratic state committee issued a call for a state convention of that party, to consist of 238 delegates, and pursuant to that call the convention met at Benicia, on Tuesday, June 21st. It was called to order by David C. Broderick, the chairman of the state committee, and James W. Coffroth was called to the chair temporarily. A permanent organization was effected by the selection of A. C. Bradford, as president; and Richard Irwin, I. S. K. Ozier, John Nye, J. Warner, B. Bryant, A. W. Goodwin, Wm. H. Smith, John H. McKune, and W. H. Endicott, as vice-presidents.

On the 22d, John Bigler was nominated for governor on the first ballot—receiving 134 votes, to 58 for Richard Roman, and 47 for Henry P. Haun.

On the 23d, the following additional nominations were made:

Samuel Purdy, for lieutenant-governor, on second ballot, over Jesse Brush, Joseph C. McKibben, John J. Warner, A. C. Bradford, and Charles F. Lott; W. H. Lyons, J. M. Covarrubias, C. H. Bryan, F. Yeiser, A. M. Winn, and Philip Moore withdrawing.

Alexander Wells, for justice of the supreme court, without opposition.

John R. McConnell, for attorney-general, without opposition.

S. A. McMeans, for treasurer, without opposition.

Samuel Bell, for controller, on the fourth ballot, over B. F. Lippincott and W. S. Pierce; W. C. Kibbe withdrawing.

Paul K. Hubbs, for superintendent of public instruction, on the first ballot, over John G. Marvin, Judge Watson, and Isaac Bragg.

S. H. Marlette, for surveyor-general, on the second ballot, over F. McDonald.

The following resolutions were adopted:

1. That the true interests of the state demand that the public

lands be disposed of in limited quantities to actual settlers, and that it is unwise to adopt any policy that may tend to encourage a landed monopoly, but at the same time we cherish as a right, guaranteed by the consitution, that every citizen shall be protected by law to the fullest extent, in his person and in his property.

2. That the surest and most speedy method of developing the resources of the state, promoting industry, and elevating society, is to encourage, by the enactment of proper laws, the ownership and cultivation of the soil in limited quantities by actual settlers.

3. That the democratic party cherishes as among the best features in the constitution of this state, those which protect the laborer from degradation and oppression; that special legislation, and particularly the formation of special corporations, is at all times dangerons; and that general incorporation laws, while they should protect the honest and legitimate application of associated capital, should not allow the irresponsible contraction of debts or a monopoly of privileges.

4. That we recognize to the fullest extent, the principle that all political power exists in the hands of the people, and that constitutions and laws are but the expressions of the popular will; therefore, we deprecate any change of the constitution of this state, other than by amendments, until such an amendment shall have been incorporated in it as shall guarantee to the people that the constitution prepared by a convention for its revision shall be submitted to the people for their ratification or rejection.

5. That the increasing permanent population of our state demands a more complete organization of our common school system, under such enactments as will best preserve the property of the state set apart by the constitution for this purpose, and apply the proceeds exclusively to such a system of education for the children of the state as will make them intelligent and independent citizens.

6. That, in the democratic state conventions hereafter to be held in this state, each county shall be entitled to one vote, and one additional vote for every 200 democratic votes cast at the general election next preceding the time of holding the convention, taking the highest vote cast for any state officer, and also one vote for a fraction of no less than 100 votes.

7. That we reaffirm the resolutions adopted by the democratic state convention of last July, to wit: (Quoting the third and fourth resolutions adopted by the convention of July 20, 1852.)

8. That we recommend to our delegates in congress to use every exertion in their power to secure the early completion of the work.

The following central committee was appointed : D. C. Broderick, J. Middleton, D. Scannell, M. E. Flannagan, D. Mahoney, M. J. Swasey, J. T. Hall, J. H. McKune, G. W. Colby, H. P. Haun, and R. P. Hammond.

The whig convention convened at Sacramento, on Wednesday, July 6th, and was composed of 384 delegates. Madison Walthall was chosen president *pro tem.* On permanent organization, S. P. Mulford, was president, and H. C. Malone, W. G. Brown, A. Farns-worth, D. Sheppard, J. C. Hawthorne, A. W. Bee, Horace Smith, James McVicker, E. S. Lathrop, and A. M. Rosborough, vice-·presidents.

On the 7th, the following nominations were made :

William Waldo, for governor, on the first ballot, receiving 345 votes, to 39 for P. B. Reading; D. O. Shattuck withdrawing.

Henry Eno, for lieutenant-governor, on the first ballot, over Jesse O. Goodwin, William Blackburn, David F. Douglass, James M. Warner, and Frank Soule.

Tod Robinson, for justice of the supreme court, on the fourth ballot, over Calhoun Benham, Lorenzo Sawyer, R. N. Wood, W. R. Turner, John Currey, and D. O. Shattuck.

D. K. Newell, for attorney-general, on the first ballot, over J. Neely Johnson, W. S. Spear, and Elcan Heydenfeldt.

Gilbert F. Winters, for controller, on the fourth ballot, over C. I. Hutchinson, R. B. Hampton, J. Brewster, J. McPherson, C. J. Brenham, and Samuel Knight.

Samuel Knight, for treasurer, over M. Walthall, Beverly C. Saunders, W. A. Robertson, and Geo. Pendleton.

S. E. Woodworth, for surveyor-general, over W. A. Eliason, and Sherman Day.

Sherman Day, for superintendent of public instruction, over T. J. Nevins, John M. Howe, William Taylor, A. G. McCandlass, O. C. Wheeler, T. C. Crouch, and M. C. Briggs.

The following preamble and resolutions were adopted :

WHEREAS, the dominant party of the state have, by mismanagement and corruption, bankrupted the treasury, and loaded us with a debt too grievous to be borne, and which sits like an incubus upon all our energies ; and whereas, by caucussing and pipe-laying management, the most honest portion of the democracy have been out-generaled, and honor and office withheld from them, giving us nothing to hope for the future from the party in power but con-

tinued corruption and misrule, and the concomitant evils of tyranny
and oppression; therefore, we, the whig convention of California,
believe that a crisis has arisen in our affairs of state that loudly
demands the exercise of the highest patriotism, and a united concert
of action to reform the state, on the part of all those who believe
with us that public plunder is the object of the dominant party, is
of more importance than the discussion of national issues.

To particularize, let us submit facts to a candid and oppressed
people: the dominant party of the state has, in its short but *fast*
career, collected and disbursed one million five hundred thousand
dollars of the people's money, and fixed a debt upon our labor, property, and energy of three millions of dollars more. The enormous
sum of $4,500,000 has in three short years been expended—not for
public buildings, public improvements, or public works, but to fatten
and strengthen official cormorants, and make their power for evil
greater than before. The party in power has passed "stamp acts,"
notarial, port warden, and other laws and edicts more oppressive
than the stamp act which excited our forefathers to arms.

It has neglected to pass laws for the protection of property, or
common welfare of the people, but on the contrary has oppressed our
citizens with the most grievous taxation; it has created useless
offices, and given large salaries to sinecures in office, to strengthen
the hands that oppress us, and render us less able to resist oppression. For these and many other reasons, *Resolved,*

1. That we most heartily disapprove and condemn the administration of the government of the state since the organization thereof,
the results of which have eventuated in squandering $1,500,000, by
the official cormorants who have been a constant curse upon the
state.

2. That the annual expenditures of the state should never in time
of peace exceed its revenues, and that any administration not capable of so limiting the expenditure is unworthy the support of the
people.

3. That in creating the enormous debt of the state that is now
oppressing us, article eight of the state constitution, in the opinion
of this convention, was disregarded, and the violators of it are
unworthy the suffrages of the people.

4. That the law confining the publication of legal notices to certain specified *pet papers,* is an offensive monopoly, not in accordance
with the spirit of the constitution and laws of a well regulated free
government; and that the members of the legislature who voted for

it, and the governor who approved it, are alike unworthy of the sup
port of a free people. ˙

5. That we hereby pledge our sacred honor to vote for no candidate who does not unconditionally advocate a most thorough
retrenchment of expenditures in every department of state; and
for this reform we invoke the aid of all good citizens.

6. That to overthrow a dynasty so incompetent and corrupt as
that which has cursed California, is of more importance to the state
than the discussion and support of any issues of a national character
which have hitherto divided parties.

7. That the number of officers should be diminished; the number
of judicial districts lessened; the salaries of state officers materially reduced; and in all those offices of fees, where the revenue
shall exceed a liberal salary, the excess shall pass into the treasury
of the state.

8. That the *bona fide* settlers upon lands (supposed public lands at
the time of settlement) deserve our warmest sympathy, and every
protection in their improvements that can legally be given them.

9. That we as whigs (always conservative) will concede anything
but *principle*, for the overthrow of corruption, and the salvation of
the state.

10. That holding these sentiments we cordially invite all good
citizens opposed to the nominees of the Bigler dynasty, and in favor
of reform, and who believe that the redemption of the state is of
more importance than the triumph of party, to aid us in electing an
opposition ticket, noted for its competency, purity, and fidelity to
the best interests of the state.

11. That we reaffirm our ancient doctrine in favor of the most
liberal preëmption laws, donation of lands to actual settlers, homestead exemption, the perfection of our common school system, opposition to all land monopolies, and in favor of the location and early
completion of the great overland railroad.

12. That the extension bill (of the last legislature) which passed
the assembly and was indefinitely postponed in the senate was, in
effect, a proposition to squander the valuable property of the whole
people of California, for the benefit of a few scheming political
speculators.

The election was held on September 7th, and the entire democratic ticket was elected. The official canvass exhibited this result:

For Governor—Bigler, 38,090; Waldo, 37,454.

Lieutenant-Governor—Purdy, 44,498; Eno, 32,968.

Controller—Bell, 41,843 ; Winters, 34,912.

Treasurer—McMeans, 41,465 ; Knight, 35,250.

Superintendent of Public Instruction—Hubbs, 41,553; Day, 35,465.

Attorney-General—McConnell, 40,729 ; Newell, 34,899.

Surveyor-General—Marlette, 42,100 ; Woodworth, 34,663.

Justice of the Supreme Court—Wells, 41,882; Robinson, 34,212.

CHAPTER VI.

1854. Democratic Convention—Whig Convention.

The democratic convention of 1854 met at the First Baptist church, Sacramento, at 3 o'clock P. M., on Tuesday, July 18th. Sometime before the hour for meeting, the doors of the church were surrounded by a large assemblage of persons, many of whom were not delegates ; and as soon as the doors were opened the church, which was estimated to afford accomodation for about 400 persons, was filled to its utmost capacity. D. C. Broderick, the chairman of the state committee, ascended the platform, and was received with loud and long-continuing cheering. Instantly on his calling the convention to order several delegates sprang to the floor for the purpose of nominating candidates for temporary chairman. Broderick recognized T. L. Vermule as having the floor, but before the announcment was made, John O'Meara proposed ex-Governor John McDougal for chairman *pro tem.* Vermule nominated Edward McGowan for the position. Broderick stated that he could not recognize O'Meara's motion, and put the question on McGowan's election, and declared that it had carried McGowan instantly mounted the stand, closely followed by McDougal, whose friends insisted that he had been selected, although his name had not been submitted to the convention in regular form. The two chairmen took seats side by side, and a scene of indescribable confusion and tumult ensued. When something like order was restored, McDougal read the names of Major G. W. Hook and John Bidwell, as vice-presidents ; and McGowan announced J. T. Hall and A. T. Laird as his appointees for those offices. Again a scene of extreme confusion occurred, but the gentlemen named seated themselves with their respective leaders. Two sets of secretaries and committees were then appointed, and reports were made to each side recommending that the temporary officers be declared permanently elected. Motions were made to adopt the reports, and, amid the greatest excitement, they were declared carried. The double-headed convention sat until about 9 o'clock in the night. No further business was transacted, but each side tried to sit the other out. Two sickly candles—one in front of each president—lighted up the scene. The trustees of the church finally relieved both sides by stating that they could not tolerate the riotous crowd longer in the building, and the delegates left without a formal adjournment. The session throughout was like pandemoniun let loose. Soon after the organization, a rush was made by the crowd to the stage. One of the officers was seized, and at that instant a pistol exploded in the densely crowded room. A mad rush was made for the doors, and a portion of the delegates made a precipitate retreat through the windows to the ground—a distance of some fifteen feet. Towards night, Governor Bigler was called to the stand, and he made a conciliatory speech, but it had no effect for good.

On the 19th, the wing presided over by McDougal, and which represented the chivalry or southern element of the party, met at Musical Hall; and the McGowan or Tammany branch, representing the northern element, met at Carpenter's building. The officers of the chivalry wing resigned, and Major Hook was elected president, and H. P. Barber, William A. Mannerly, A. W. Taliaferro, and J. G. Downey, vice-presidents. A committee on address and resolutions was appointed, consisting of B. F. Washington, James M. Estell, William Van Voorhies, H. P. Barber, and John McDougal. A communication was received from the other convention asking that a committee of conference be appointed, with a view of settling the disagreement, but the language of the communication was regarded as offensive, and it was withdrawn for the purpose of changing the phraseology. Afterwards a second note almost similar to the first was sent in, but it was flatly rejected. The following nominations were then made:

James W. Denver, for congressman from the northern district, and Philip T. Herbert from the southern district, over J. T. Crenshaw (withdrew), Charles L. Scott, Blanton McAlpin, and A. C. Bradford.

Charles A. Leake for clerk of the supreme court, over Sarshall Bynum.

On the 20th, the following resolutions, offered by McAlpin, were adopted :

1. That we view the construction of the Atlantic and Pacific railroad as one of the most important matters for the welfare of our common country that has agitated the public mind since the formation of our national government; and we but echo the sentiments of nine-tenths of the people of California when we declare that congress should do all and everything consistent with the constitution in aiding the commencement and completion of the same.

2. That while we renew the oft-expressed views of the democracy of California in favor of the donation to actual settlers in limited quantities of the public domain, we nevertheless believe and recommend that liberal donations should be made, in accordance with the well established policy of the general government in similar cases, to aid in the construction of the greatest national work of the age— the building of the Atlantic and Pacific railroad.

3. That we most cordially approve and sustain the passage of the Nebraska bill, and the vote thereupon shows most clearly that it was a democratic measure—one of principle, that should have enlisted in its favor every true lover of republican principles, and we only regret that among the names of those who opposed its passage we notice some few who claim to be democrats.

4. That we reassert and maintain the principles of the democratic platform adopted at Baltimore in 1852, and we endorse to the fullest extent the administration of General Franklin Pierce.

An assessment of five dollars per delegate was collected to repair the damages to the church building. A state committee was appointed, consisting of B. F. Washington, Blanton McAlpin, Wilson Flint, James O'Meara, W. A. Mix, J. R. Hardenbergh, W. T. Sexton, V. E. Geiger, J. H. Ralston, S. A. Booker, C. S. Fairfax, J. H. Baker, C. L. Scott, and others.

The McGowan wing met at 9:30 A. M. on the 19th, that gentleman continuing to act as the presiding officer. A committee of seven was appointed to invite the McDougal convention to attend, and the committee were empowered to arrange the difficulties. A recess was taken until 1 o'clock to give the committee time to act. On the convention reassembling, the committee reported that they had sent the following communication to the chivalry convention, and that the proposition contained in it had been rejected :

John McDougal, Esq., chairman of democratic delegates convened at Musical Hall—Sir: The undersigned have been this morning constituted a committee, with full powers, by and on behalf of the democratic state convention, at Carpenter's hall, for a conference with our fellow democrats at Musical Hall, for the purpose of harmonizing and uniting the democracy of California. You will be pleased to announce this to your body, and any communication may be addressed to the chairman of this committee, at Jones' hotel. We are, sir, very respectfully your fellow citizens, William Walker, John Burke Phillips, James Churchman, Eugene Casserly, R. T. Sprague, Thos. L. Vermule, John M. McBrayer.

The committee was discharged, and the convention proceeded to nominate a ticket.

Milton S. Latham and James A. McDougall were unanimously nominated for congress; W. T. Wallace, J. W. Coffroth, B. F. Myers, C. H. Bryan, and E. C. Marshall, withdrawing.

P. K. Woodside was nominated for clerk of the supreme court, over Humphrey Griffeth, William S. Long, Martin Rowan and D. A. Enyard.

The following address was adopted :

To the democracy of California : The democratic party of this state is necessarily composed of more heterogeneous elements than those which constitute the party in other states of the union. Coming as our people do from all parts of the world, bringing with them a thousand differences of feeling and opinion, it is to be expected that all aggregations of party shall be less accordant here than elsewhere.

This has been apparent from the first organization of the democratic party in California. But there has always been a portion of the party—and this the masses of it—who have desired to sink all sectional issues, and unite on the great principles of the party of the union. Others have as long and as certainly manifested a desire to divide the party and sectionalize its principles.

These two motives have always influenced, to a great extent, the action of the party within itself. It was not until last year, and after the nominations of the Benicia convention, that there was open rupture between the two branches of the democracy.

The same diversity of prejudices and opinions divided the party during the last session of the legislature. It moved the democracy in the recent election of delegates to the state convention.

When the delegates to the Sacramento convention assembled, the same radical division was apparent. One portion of the democracy organized under the laws and usages of the party, and placed officers over the convention who had supported the action of previous state conventions. The portion of the delegates who seek to make the party sectional, placed at their head men who repudiated a nominee of the last state convention. By their acts and declarations these latter evinced a desire to agitate in this state social questions of the most disturbing character; and discussion of these subjects can only tend to schismatize the party.

On the other hand, we, the representatives of men who wish to maintain the catholicity of the party, sought to harmonize the divisions of the democracy. Our proposals for compromise were treated with disdain, and scorn was the only reward they were willing to bestow on our conciliatory efforts. In this emergency the convention has nominated for members of congress men whom the whole democracy has approved. Let the party bear witness to the zeal with which we have labored to maintain the unity of the party. Let the future prove the wisdom with which we have deliberated and decided.

We present the ticket we have nominated to the democracy of California. We ask the masses of the party to strive for its welfare with as much singleness of purpose as have their delegates in the state convention; and if they do, victory will again perch on the eagles of the democracy.

The platform of the democratic convention of June 21, 1853, was readopted *verbatim*, with the exception that to the end of the second resolution were added the words, "and of guaranteeing to such settlers the value of all improvements *bona fide* made." The following additional resolutions were adopted:

9. That one of the cardinal principles in the usages and practice of the democratic party for the last half century has been, that all differences of opinion upon questions of party policy, expediency, or men, are to be settled by convention, or caucus of members of the party for that purpose assembled, and that at such conventions or caucuses, a majority shall rule, and that it is the duty of every democrat, cheerfully to submit to a decision of such questions thus made, and that any violation or departure from this usage, is subversive of party organization, and destructive of the harmony and dangerous to the success of the party.

10. That we cordially approve and endorse the resolutions adopted by the democratic national convention assembled at Baltimore, which nominated Franklin Pierce for the presidency.

The following state committee was selected: David Mahoney, B. S. Lippincott, F. A. Kohler, Thos. Brannan, Edw. McGowan, J. T. Hall, G. W. Colby, J. H. McKune, A. T. Laird, J. W. Coffroth,

3

and others. A collection of $400 was taken up to repair the damages that had been done to the Baptist church on the previous day, a committee having reported that the building had been injured to that extent.

Shortly after the adjournment of the conventions, Judge Heydenfeldt declined the nomination for Latham, and Judge Murray published a card withdrawing McDougall's name from the canvass. On August 31st, Latham arrived from Washington, and on September 2d telegraphed his withdrawal from the ticket to the state committee. On the same day James Churchman was nominated for congress to supply the vacant place on the Tammany ticket. It was pretty generally understood throughout the campaign that McDougall was not a candidate, but he did not formally withdraw from the fight after his return from Washington. After the election the Tammany party ascribed the defeat of their ticket to Latham's withdrawal.

The whig convention met at the theater in Sacramento, on Tuesday, July 25th. It was called to order by Frank Soule, chairman of the state committee, and Joshua P. Haven was elected temporary chairman. In the evening J. Neely Johnson was elected president; and A. D. McDonald, J. A. Lewis, R. Tevis, J. M. Stewart, J. C. Hawthorne, J. H. Moore, and others, vice-presidents. A committee on resolutions was selected, consisting of W. S. Spear, B. Peyton, D. K. Newell, Louis R. Lull, H. T. Huggins, John Currey, and others. The candidates for the congressional nominations were George W. Bowie, Edward P. Fletcher (withdrawn), J. E. Hale (withdrawn), R. N. Wood, Frank Soule (withdrawn), Edward Woodruff (withdrawn), P. H. Harris, W. W. Stow (withdrawn), T. H. Williams (withdrawn), J. M. Crane, P. B. Reading (withdrawn), E. D. Baker (withdrawn), D. K. Newell (withdrawn), W. W. Hawks (withdrawn), and Calhoun Benham. On the 26th, on the second ballot, Bowie was nominated from the northern district; and on the fifth ballot Benham was successful from the southern district. Joseph R. Beard was nominated on the second ballot for clerk of the supreme court, over Horace Smith, General Allen, and Josiah Gordon. The following address and resolutions were adopted :

The condition of your state demanding reformation, calls upon you to inaugurate the rule of honesty, and to put an end to abuses and evils which are the parisitical and withering results of mal-

administration and bad government. From Washington to Clay—
we refer to an unserried line of patriotism, alike in adversity and in
prosperity, the protectors of our country. The union can only be
advanced by the preservation of principles, and the advancement of
measures that in their *nationality* command the support of every
American. We point to the whig administrations, from Washington
to Fillmore, as having exemplified devotion to the constitution,
fidelity to the union, and paternal care for the honor, happiness and
prosperity of the country. The welfare of California and its imper-
illed integrity require a revolution of public affairs. In such
change will be insured good government, economy in its exercise,
rigid adherence to the laws, and strict accountability of all in authority
to the tribunal of public opinion. Aid us to reduce the taxes; to
unshackle commerce; to remove the anti-republican restrictions to
trade imposed by venal legislation; above all, join us in the effort
to restore the purity of the ballot box, and the freedom of elections;
to make secure the life, liberty, and property of every citizen. We
proclaim the building of the Pacific railroad to be the paramount
duty of the government of the United States, as furnishing, when
completed, the best and surest means of national defense. We desire
the adoption and perfection of the best system of common school
education, and to yield aid in all possible ways to learning and
science. We demand a purification of the judgment seat, and
a revision of the statutes. It is, *therefore, resolved,*

1. That we, the whigs of California, in common with the whigs
of the union, regard the building of the Atlantic and Pacific railroad as of paramount national importance, believing its construction
strengthens and perpetuates the bond linking this continent together;
marvelously increases the general prosperity, and forever removes
from this immense travel all and every danger—rendering secure
the lives of myriads, and the immense property which will pass over
its lines—demand from the congress of the United States and every
branch of the general government that instant action which a blessing so vast and immeasurable to our own and every other land,
requires at their hands.

2. That for these reasons, as well as regarding it the foremost—
as it is the surest—means of a perfected national defense, and a
vindication of the great and vital American principle for which
whigs have always contended, we will never cease to implore the
national legislature and urge upon the executive the pursuit and
furtherance of this measure, as one of the first duties they owe to
their country.

3. That we regard the public domain as the property of the people of the United States, and insist that California shall receive her full and entire share thereof, to aid in the construction of her railroads, the fostering of education, the diffusion of knowledge, and the endowment of common schools, colleges, and universities.

4. That we hold as a changeless whig principle the duty of the law to protect inviolate the property of all classes—the miner, the mechanic, the agriculturist, and the trader—and we denounce every measure or system of measures, the effect of which would be to rob industry of its natural reward, and to deprive honest labor of its hardly acquired earnings.

5. That California demands from congress and the executive such prompt action as will ensure the immediate completion of the survey of the public lands, and put a period to the vexatious delays of the land commission.

6. That the whigs of California hold the right of the people of the territories of the United States to determine and legislate for themselves, to be inherent; and, as such, whenever the population entitles them to frame a state constitution, they possess the authority to do so without the interference of, and independent of any other power.

7. That it is the true interest of the government to secure to every actual settler upon the public lands of the United States a competent homestead.

8. That in reference to the mineral lands of the state, the property of the United States, and the disposition of mining privileges, we regard the miners as the first parties whose interest and proper wishes should have greatest weight in settling and determining these important matters.

9. That the revenue collected by the general government in California, prior to her admission into the union, of right belongs to her and should be promptly refunded.

10. That the "Farewell Address of Washington" is the undeviating chart of American freedom; the whig party coherent in and supporting all its principles, look to its maxims when adhered to by the people, as the surest reliance of the constitution and the union.

11. That we are admonished that the time approaches when the nation, tired with the imbecility of an irresponsible and vacillating administration, turns with trusting hope and confidence to the whig party—obeying that high summons, from the shores of the Pacific, we shout to our Atlantic brethren "union of the whigs for the sake of the union."

A state committee was appointed, consisting of Baillie Peyton, Frederick Billings, S. W. Holliday, G. H. Hossefross, A. C. Monson, J. Price, J. W. Winans, A. B. Nixon, G. W. Crane, S. Buckner, J. C. Fall, D. F. Douglass, H. A. Crabbe, D. K. Newell, and others.

In the latter part of July, the state committee of the chivalry wing of the democracy appointed three of its members—B. F. Washington, Blanton McAlpin, and William G. Ross—to arrange terms for a compromise with the other faction of the party, and they submitted to the central committee of the Tammany side, the following conditions upon which to base a settlement of the existing difficulties.

1. The withdrawal of McDougall and Latham.

2. The withdrawal of Leake, by his consent.

3. That the two state committees act jointly, upon an equal footing.

4. That the county nominations which had been made be allowed to remain, and that the people would be asked to support them.

5. That, in the counties of San Francisco and Sacramento, the nominations to be made should be equally divided between the wings.

6. That they would jointly recommend to the democracy of El Dorado and Placer to harmonize upon some fair basis.

B. F. Lippincott, George Wilkes, and John H. McKune, representing the Tammany committee, submitted these propositions:

1. We propose to meet you by each relinquishing one-half of our several claims, making a joint congressional ticket of one member nominated at your late convention, and one member of ours—say Denver and Latham.

2. We propose to draw lots to decide which of us shall be entitled to the nomination of clerk of the supreme court.

3. We propose to form a new state committee by equal numbers drawn from the two present committees, and to draw lots for chairman.

4. We propose to issue an address on the part of the new committee, urging the new ticket upon the adoption of the democracy of the state, such address to be signed by all the members of the committee.

The propositions were both rejected.

Early in 1854, American or "know nothing" organizations were formed in the state, and it was not long before an association existed in almost every town and mining camp.

On May 27th, the San Francisco *Alta,* in referring to the new movement, said :

The mysterious association called the "know nothing," appears to have spread its branches until one of them has cast a shadow on the Pacific shore. The "know nothings," as near as they can be understood, or their doctrines or intentions fathomed, are a secret political organization, strongly native American in its feelings, and organized for the purpose of acting politically, with the intention of curtailing the political privileges of persons of foreign birth or descent. They are, in fact, a reorganization of the native American party in a new form, and adopting all their principles, intend making a secret application of them.

On August 30th, the same paper said :

From all the papers in every portion of the state we gather the fact that the mysterious associations of "know nothings" have spread themselves until a branch is formed in almost every mining town and village of any importance throughout the country. That they will have a great influence, if not an entire control, over the ensuing election in this state, there can now be but little doubt, although from the entire secrecy of their operations it is impossible to form an idea of how that influence will be used.

In San Francisco, the "know nothings" ran a local ticket in 1854, and it was successful. The organization did not openly take part in state politics, but its influence on the election was doubtless important.

The election was held on September 6, 1854, and the result in the state was as follows :

For Congressmen—Denver, 36,819 ; Herbert, 36,542 ; Bowie,. 34,734 ; Benham, 34,411 ; McDougall, 9,968 ; Churchman, 10,006;. Latham, 1,843 ; scattering, 448.

For Clerk of the Supreme Court—Leake, 33,700 ; Beard, 35,133 ;. Woodside, 11,721 ; scattering, 47.

Denver and Herbert were consequently elected to congress, and Beard was elected clerk of the supreme court.

CHAPTER VII.

1855. Gubernatorial Election—Democratic Convention—Convention of the American Party—Settlers' and Miners' Convention—Temperance Conventions.

The whig party virtually disbanded in 1855, and the secret American party took its place as a prominent political organization. This new faction originated in 1852, and its animating spirit was hostility to the exercise of political power in this country by foreigners, and more especially by Roman catholics. Its members were popularly termed "know nothings," because they were required when interrogated with respect to the order to declare that they knew nothing about it. The new party had figured somewhat in California politics in 1854, but it was not until 1855 that it assumed an aspect so formidable as to be considered worthy of the steel of the democracy. At the spring municipal elections, the success of the know nothing tickets so aroused the democrats that their organs devoted most of their thunder to attacks upon the secret organization.

On March 5th, at a municipal election in Marysville, the Americans carried everything, although their nominations had not been made public until the morning of the election. At the Sacramento city election, on April 2d, the entire "know nothing" ticket was elected ; and in the smaller towns their successes had been as marked. The democratic papers called upon the divided wings of their party to unite and make a common enemy of the new party, but it was soon apparent that the secret association had captured nearly all of the whigs and a goodly number of the democrats.

On May 23d, the state committees of the two wings of the democratic party met and harmonized, and issued a joint call for a state convention. The call recited that "the undersigned, members of the two democratic state committees, respectively presided over by B. F. Washington and B. S. Lippincott, as chairmen, feeling the necessity of a united action on the part of the democratic party in the ensuing state election, and for the purpose of insuring an unbroken front against the common enemy, have mutually agreed upon the above call for a convention." Pursuant to this call the democratic convention met at Sacramento, on Wednesday, June 27th. Charles S. Fairfax was selected president *pro tem.*, and afterwards permanent president. About the first business before the convention was the consideration of the following resolution

That the secretary of this convention shall propose the following interrogatory to each and every candidate who shall present himself for an office in this convention, to wit: Are you a member of a secret political organization known and generally called "know nothings"? All who answer affirmatively or refuse to answer shall be excluded from any nomination.

The following was offered as a substitute:

That all candidates for nomination in this convention, shall, previous to balloting for such candidate, sign the following pledge, and any member of this convention nominating a candidate, shall deliver to the officers of this convention the aforesaid pledge, signed by such candidate: We, the undersigned, pledge the democracy of California, that we do not belong to the secret political society known as "know nothings,' or American party, or to any secret political association whatever; and that whether members or not, we will hereby support and use all honorable means to secure the election of the nominees of this convention.

After considerable discussion, the resolutions were referred to the committee on resolutions.

On the 28th, the following resolutions were adopted:

(The first five resolutions of the democratic national convention of June, 1852, were adopted.)

6. That the democrats of this state feel that the best and highest interests of California are involved in the speedy construction of the great Pacific railroad; and that we, as a party, will, by legislation or otherwise, give our earnest and hearty support to the accomplishment of this truly glorious enterprise.

7. That we are in favor of just legislative action, securing, as far as possible, the rights of actual settlers and miners, who in good faith are occupying lands in this state.

8. That all secret political organizations, bound together by pledges and oaths, having for their object the proscription of any American citizen, are contrary to the spirit of our free institutions, treasonable in appearance, if not in design, and should receive, as they deserve, the just animadversion of all good citizens.

9. That the democracy of California abhor and repudiate as un-American and anti-republican, the proscription of a man for the accident of his birth, or for his religious opinions; and in this crisis of American liberties, institutions, and ideas, they re-affirm and proclaim in full force the universal democratic doctrine of "equal rights

to all under the constitution and laws "—and declare in the immortal words of the greatest of American patriots, that "any man conducting himself as a good citizen is accountable to God alone for his religious opinions, and ought to be protected in worshiping the Deity according to the dictates of his own conscience."

10. That we do now cordially invite all our former political brethren who may have strayed from us for a time, attracted by curiosity or otherwise, and who have joined themselves to secret political orders, to return to us and with us defend the principles of their former faith, and abandon institutions which the daily current of events is developing to be founded on intolerance, and controlled by men dangerous to the permanency and welfare of our government.

11. That we will neither nominate nor support any man for office who will not pledge himself, and subscribe to the foregoing platform and resolutions.

In view of the agitation of the temperance question in the state, the following additional resolutions were adopted :

12. That, in the opinion of this convention, the time has come when sober men, and sober men only, should be presented for the suffrages of moral and intelligent freemen.

13. That, as a convention, we will respect the moral sentiment of the state, in the nominations which we are about to make.

The following nominations were made on the 29th and 30th :

John Bigler, for governor, on the second ballot, receiving 157 votes, to 125 for Milton S. Latham, 1 for J. W. McCorkle, and 2 for Richard Roman.   On the first ballot, Bigler had 128 votes ; Latham, 115 ; James Walsh, 39, and C. A. Clark, 3. Walsh withdrew before the second ballot was taken, and H. P. Haun, whose name was proposed, declined to be a candidate.

Samuel Purdy, for lieutenant-governor, on the first ballot, over Frederick Yeiser and I. S. K. Handy.

Myron Norton (full term) and Charles H. Bryan (to fill vacancy), for justices of the supreme court, over Charles T. Botts, Lewis Aldrich, Alpheus Felch, Eugene Casserly, and R. T. Sprague.

Thomas C. Flournoy, for controller, on the first ballot, over Benjamin Hall and I. N. Dawley.

B. F. Keene, for treasurer, on the first ballot, over William A. Mix ; Thomas Payne declining.

B. C. Whiting, for attorney-general, on the second ballot, over Allen P. Dudley, S. B. Axtell, H. W. Carpentier, G. E. Montgomery, Augustus Redman, W. S. Spear, and W. S. Long.

S. H. Marlette, for surveyor-general, without opposition.

George H. Crossette, for printer, on the first ballot, over H. C. Patrick, Vincent E. Geiger, and S. H. Dosh.

C. F. Powell, W. H. Bell, and Samuel C. Astin, for state prison directors, over R. N. Snowden, Geo. Langdon, Jas. Creighton, Jas. T. Ewing, and W. J. Burnside.

The candidates for nominations were required to specifically declare themselves before the convention on the question of know nothingism. A state committee was selected, consisting of B. F. Washington, B. S. Lippincott, Thos. Kendall, Edw. McGowan, T. W. Taliaferro, J. L. Brent, W. S. Long, J. H. McKune, M. E. Cooke, F. Forman, T. W. Sigourney, V. E. Geiger, Jos. Walkup, J. W. Owen, Nelson Taylor, W. A. Mix, C. S. Fairfax, J. W. Mc-Corkle, E. O. F. Hastings, P. T. Herbert, Alex. Hunter, and others.

The American state convention met at Sacramento, on Tuesday, August 7th, with 379 delegates, and organized temporarily by selecting Samuel B. Smith, as chairman *pro tem.* In the evening, a permanent organization was effected by the election of James W. Coffroth, as president ; and Robt. McCall, James Churchman, S. A. McMeans, Isaac Davis, William Thornburg, Henry Bates, J. Tooker, Chas. Ford, T. W. Robertson, L. H. Bascom, S. C. Hastings, E. L. Bond, and H. B. Lathrop, vice-presidents.

The following platform was adopted :

The American party of California, in convention assembled, declare the following as the principles of their association :

1. The maintenance and support of the union against all attempts to overthrow or undermine it.

2. The supremacy of the constitution and laws of the republic.

3. A judicous revision of the laws regulating naturalization.

4. Universal religious toleration.

5. No union of church and state.

6. Inflexible opposition to the appointment or election to offices of trust, honor, or emolument, of all who are not truly national in feeling, and especially of all who acknowledge allegiance to any foreign government.

7. A stern and unqualified opposition to all corruption and fraud in high places.

8. The preservation of the purity of the-ballot box, and with a view thereto, the early adoption of a judicious registration law in the cities, so as entirely to prevent the fraudulent multiplication of votes.

9. The immediate appropriation by congress of either money or land, or both, in sufficient quantities to secure the early establishment of a railway from the Pacific ocean to the Mississippi river.

10. The most liberal and just legislation in favor of that portion of our population known as "settlers."

11. Eligibility to office, both in the states and nation, should be restricted to persons born on some part of the territory included within the jurisdiction of the United States.

12. The firmest and most enduring opposition to the agitation of all questions of a merely sectional character.

13. Retrenchment and reform in the civil administration in California, by reducing the expenses of government, and lessening the burthens of the taxpayers.

14. To apply in all cases, the Jeffersonian test in selecting men for office, viz.: Is he honest? Is he capable? Will he support the constitution?

15. Utter disregard of ancient party names and worn-out party issues, and cordial confraternity with all who are willing to coöperate with us in support of the principles herein set forth.

On the 8th, it was resolved, by a vote of 185 to 62, "that this convention approve of the temperance reform now going on throughout the state, and that we will nominate none for office but men of high moral character and known habits of temperance."

The following nominations were made on the 8th and 9th:

J. Neely Johnson, for governor, on the fourth ballot, over Drury P. Baldwin, J. W. Coffroth (declined), B. C. Whitman, James H. Wade, W. W. Stow, J. H. Ralston, Jesse O. Goodwin, General John Wilson, James L. English, C. T. Ryland, and Geo. B. Tingley.

Robert M. Anderson, for lieutenant-governor, on the first ballot, over T. J. White and D. R. Ashley.

Hugh C. Murray, for justice of the supreme court (full term), on the first ballot, over Lorenzo Sawyer and Green T. Martin.

David S. Terry, for justice of the supreme court (to fill vacancy), on the second ballot, over L. Sawyer, R. N. Wood, G. N. Mott, D. O. Shattuck, and John Curry.

George W. Whitman, for controller, on the fifth ballot, over

Samuel Bell, J. H. Miller, N. Carroll, E. A. Rowe. John Gray, and W. B. May.

Henry Bates, for treasurer, on the second ballot, over J. B. Laforge, Thos. Paine, N. C. Cunningham, A. H. Murdock, J. C. Curtis, R. Chenery, and H. H. Means.

W. T. Wallace, for attorney-general, on the sixth ballot, over William M. Stewart, G. B. Tingley, H. Lee, Alex. Ely, A. B. Dibble, Horace Allen, and Henry Meredith.

John A. Brewster, for surveyor-general, on the second ballot, over Lansing Tucker, A. S. Easton, and T. D. Judah.

James Ailen, for printer, on the second ballot, over John K. Lovejoy, Paul Morrill, W. R. Butte, and John A. Lewis.

E. Wilson, F. S. McKenzie, and Alex. Bell, for prison directors.

On July 5th, a call was issued for a state convention of the settlers and miners, to be held at Sacramento, on August 8th, for the purpose of nominating a state ticket and to organize a separate party. The call was signed by William J. Shaw, G. W. Colby, I. W. Underwood, R. D. Ferguson, H. Amyx, and others, and recited :

The great magnitude and importance of this movement cannot be overrated. The necessity of immediate and timely action on the part of the settlers and miners of this state must be apparent to all. No good citizen can fail to foresee the public injury which must result from the sweeping and indiscriminating confirmation of Mexican grants to lands, which have been purchased as speculations, without ever having been located, or in possession of the pretended grantees. According to the recent extraordinary decision of the supreme court of the United States, neither boundaries, nor possession, nor location of the lands, prior to our acquisition of this country, is necessary to insure the confirmation of these claims. No equities are exacted which a just people would recognize; and claims which neither justice, law, nor our national honor require us to respect, are to be pronounced valid and obligatory. Consequently, thousands of our fellow citizens in all parts of the state, in possession of a lot, a homestead, a mining claim, or a farm, are liable to have a floating grant located upon the very places which they occupy. Indeed, justice to the people is being forgotten, and the object of government seems to be the success of speculations alone. Notwithstanding this impending crisis between the people and mere speculations, no party has hitherto done anything to shield the producing portions of our population from the impending storm. Indeed, without immediate constitutional legislation to protect the just rights of our fellow citizens as far as possible, he must be blind to actual experience who does not see that scenes of bloodshed and open resistance to the decisions of our courts, will be the painful result of longer neglect. We make no appeal to party, but directly to the people themselves, for the nomination and election of men from our own ranks to carry out these reforms. They have already too long trusted to the lead of mere politicians, who have no aim but personal success, and no principles which are of any practicable moment to the country.

Pursuant to this call, the convention met on the day named and was called to order by I. W. Underwood. On the 9th, David F. Douglass was elected president, and a lengthy platform touching the subjects referred to in the call was adopted, but no nominations were made It was resolved to support no man who did not indorse the platform, and whose previous word, act, and deeds did not show the sincerity of his pledge. A state committee was selected, composed of B. R. Nickerson, W. T. Barbour, A. A. Sargent, W. Holden, G. W. Colby, J. McClatchy, J. H. Ralston, H. Amyx, W. J. Shaw, and others.

On June 20th, a state temperance convention met at Sacramento. James Churchman was temporary chairman, and John Wilson was permanent president. Delegates were present from San Francisco, Sutter, Nevada, Yolo, Sacramento, Alameda, and Yuba. The following resolution was adopted :

That it is inexpedient for this convention, as the voice of the temperance people of the state, to make nominations for state officers for the coming general state election.

On the 21st, the committee on resolutions presented the following report :

WHEREAS, the highest social, moral, commercial, and political well-being of our beloved state is involved in the triumph of the principles of temperance reform, *therefore, resolved,*

1. That the most vigorous efforts should be made in every appropriate way to secure the speedy and entire destruction of the liquor traffic in our state.

2. That the time has fully come when the friends of temperance in California should use all their influence at the ballot box to secure the election to office of sober men, and sober men only.

3. That we deem it highly improper for the friends of prohibition to vote for any man who is not willing to give his support to a stringent prohibitory liquor law for this state.

4. That we hereby disclaim for ourselves, and the men we represent, all intention to using the temperance strength to aid any party or set of candidates, to secure office for any other reason than that they may be with us in the vital issue of the rule or ruin of the liquor traffic.

5. That we urgently request the political parties, which may be in the field, to nominate men characterized by the sobriety of their habits, and their willingness to aid us in our work to the full measure of legal prohibition.

6. That a state central committee be appointed to propound the following questions to the candidates who may be nominated for the state offices, by the respective political parties :   1. Do you practice total abstinence ?   2. Will you, if elected, give your influence in favor of a prohibitory liquor law in California ?

7. That when said committee have received responses, it shall proceed to nominate a ticket taken from the various candidates. Should two or more respond satisfactorily, who are seeking the same place, they should both be presented as acceptable, and should not enough respond favorable to constitute a ticket, the committee shall then take measures to nominate men who may not be in the list of any other party.

8. That we request our friends in the various counties to hold conventions as soon as possible, and adopt a plan in relation to the local tickets similar to the one proposed in the preceding resolution.

9 That we urge all who wish the salvation of the country, to vote in favor of prohibition at the next election.

The first and second resolutions were adopted.   The following substitute for the third resolution was adopted :

3. That we deem it to be the solemn duty of every temperance man in our state to withhold his political support from all candidates for office who are not in favor of a stringent prohibitory liquor law for California.

The fourth, fifth, eighth, and ninth resolutions were adopted; the first question in the sixth resolution was stricken out, and the following was adopted as a substitute for the seventh resolution:

7. That the state central committee provided for in a previous

resolution be instructed to publish and circulate extensively through-out the state the interrogatories addressed to the respective candidates for state offices, together with the replies of those candidates, so that the temperance men of the state may know who of the candidates are true to our cause, and may vote at the polls accordingly.

A state committee was appointed, consisting of Gen. John Wilson, Annis Merrill, D. W. Welty, S. J. May, James Allen, J. T. McLean, J. M. Buffington, James E. Hale, and others.

The following additional resolutions were adopted:

That it is expressly understood by this convention that the state committee shall have no power to make any nominations for state or county officers.

Whereas, The last legislature of this state provided for a vote of the people in relation to the question of prohibition, which vote is to be reported by the secretary of state to the next legislature; and, whereas, a neglect to vote will be construed against the temperance reform and retard prohibition; *therefore, resolved,*

That we earnestly solicit all the temperance organizations of the state to act vigorously until and at the election to secure as large a majority for prohibition as possible.

Another state temperance convention met at Sacramento August 22d, for the purpose of taking some action toward nominating a new state ticket. About one hundred persons attended. Rev. S. D. Simmonds called the convention to order, and A. M. Winn was elected president.

The following resolution was offered:

That all gentlemen present who will register their names as independent of the two great political parties of the day, and as pledged to the object of this convention, shall be and they are hereby constituted the true convention of the people of California for the purpose of nominating two supreme judges, and the transaction of such other business as may be deemed advisable by the convention.

E. B. Crocker offered the following substitute:

That this convention has met for the purpose of nominating new and independent candidates for the supreme court of the state, and we invite all moral, religious, and temperate men who are in favor of such nominations to co-operate with us, and take such further action as may be proper.

That the orders of Sons of Temperance and Templars are hereby relieved from all responsibility for the action of this convention, as it is a meeting of citizens opposed to the present nominees for the supreme court.

The substitute was adopted.

On permanent organization, B. Hayward was president and D. W. Welty vice-president.

The following resolutions were reported:

WHEREAS, The legislature at its last session proposed certain amendments to the constitution of the state; and whereas, according to the provisions of the said constitution amendments must be approved by two consecutive sessions of the legislature before they can be submitted to the people; and whereas, the failure of the legislature, at its next session, to pass these amendments or to pass an act providing for a vote of the people upon them, will render void the action of the last legislature on the subject, and defer the action of the people upon the said amendments for three years; *therefore, resolved*:

1. That we recommend to the people in their respective counties in selecting members of the legislature to select such as are known to be in favor of submitting the said amendments to a vote of the people.

2. That we recommend the enactment of a registry law, as indispensible to the purity of the ballot-box.

3. That the present condition of political affairs in this state demands a political organization of the moral, religious and temperate citizens of the state; and in order to perfect such an organization, this convention will appoint a state committee, to be composed of thirteen persons, who shall have power to call future conventions and take such other action as the interests of the organization may require.

4. That in order that our organization may be properly designated, we hereby style ourselves "The Independent Democracy" of the state of California. Inasmuch as we have no legally elected representatives in congress from this state, that the citizens of the counties of San Francisco, Contra Costa, San Joaquin, Calaveras and all the counties south of the same, forming the southern or first congressional district, and the citizens of all the counties north of San Francisco, Contra Costa, San Joaquin and Calaveras, forming the northern or second congressional district, be requested and advised to elect suitable persons to fill said offices at the coming election.

5. As a cardinal principle of our organization, that we shall oppose the election of all duelists to office.

The resolutions were temporarily laid on the table.

For justice of the supreme court (long term), Chas. H. S. Williams was nominated on the first ballot, over Myron Norton, H. C. Murray, J. H. Ralston, G. B. Tingley, and R. T. Sprague (withdrawn).

On the 23d, John B. Harmon was nominated for justice of the supreme court (short term), David S. Terry, Cornelius Cole, and J. M. Howell withdrawing. Shortly afterward, Harmon telegraphed his declination, and H. O. Beatty was nominated.

For congressman from the southern district, Annis Merrill was nominated on the first ballot, over J. H. Purdy, B. Haywood, P. H. Burnett, and P. T. Herbert.

John H. McKune was nominated from the northern district, but he declined the next day, after the convention had adjourned.

It was understood that the regular party candidates for the other offices were sound on the temperance question, and were therefore acceptable. A state committee was chosen, consisting of Rev. S. D. Simmonds, E. B. Crocker, J. M. McDonald, J. T. McLean, J. R. Crandall, and others. The resolutions presented on the 22d were adopted, except that in the fourth resolution, the name of the party was changed to the "People's Party of California."

The following additional resolutions were adopted:

That the *bona fide* settlers on private land claims in this state, under the belief that they are on public property, are justly entitled to compensation for all permanent improvements; and we will favor the passage of any suitable law on that subject.

That we are in favor of a donation of a reasonable quantity of the public lands to actual settlers.

A resolution was adopted asking the people to vote for a prohibitory liquor law.

Towards the close of August, an effort was made in San Francisco to reorganize the whig party, and an attempt was made to get the state committee of that party together, but the movement was not successful.

The election was held on Wednesday, September 5th, and the entire American ticket was elected. Following are the totals:

For Governor—Johnson, 50,948; Bigler, 45,937.

Supreme Judge (long term)—Murray, 48,141; Norton, 47,734.

Supreme Judge (short term)—Terry, 49,677; Bryan, 46,892.

Lieutenant-Governor—Anderson, 49,385; Purdy, 47,669.

Controller—Whitman, 49,911; Flournoy, 46,691.

Treasurer—Bates, 49,947; Keene, 46,941.

Attorney-General—Wallace, 50,113; Whiting, 46,685.

Surveyor-General—Brewster, 49,994; Marlette, 46,977.

Printer—Allen, 50,060; Crossette, 46,696.

Prison Directors—A. Bell, 49,789; McKenzie, 49,644; Wilson, 50,550; W. H. Bell, 46,818; Powell, 46,132; Astin, 46,785.

CHAPTER VIII.

1856.   Presidential Election—American Council—Democratic Conventions—Republican Conventions—American Convention—Vigilance Committee.

The first movement toward preparing for the presidential campaign of 1856 was made by the American party. The state council met in secret session at Sacramento, on Tuesday, November 13, 1855, with 109 delegates present. Dr. T. J. White called the council to order, and, on the 14th, Dr. S. A. McMeans was elected president and Silas Selleck, vice-president, for the ensuing term. For delegates to attend the national council, to meet on February 22d, 1856, to nominate a presidential ticket, Johnson Price, S. H. Brooks, R. N. Wood, C. N. Hitchcock, N. T. Gough, E. P. Brown, Louis Teal, Thomas D. Johns, Samuel D. Smith, Louis R. Lull, E. P. Bowman, and Silas Selleck were named, and Brooks, Wood, Price, and Smith were elected. Teal, Hitchcock, Bowman, and Johns were elected alternates. Hitchcock, John Skinker, S. W. Brockway, and Theodore Winters were elected delegates to the national council, to meet at Philadelphia, on June 5, 1856; and John C. McKellum, S. C. Evelett, G. W. Leihy, and John M. Batson were elected alternates.

On the 15th, the following address and platform was adopted:

To the American party of California—Brothers: California has been the best taxed and the worst governed country of which there is any record. In vain have the onerous. exactions of government been paid without stint. In vain have thus far all the sources of peaceful reformation been exhausted. Long suffering has not propitiated our rulers, nor has indignant remonstrance been able to inspire terror. Evil has followed evil—calamity has been heaped upon calamity, until the young state which yesterday filled the world with her renown, to-day lies bankrupt, crime ridden, and abject. Much—very much of our misfortunes is the result of accidents and contingencies which no human foresight could have prevented, but that crime, fraud, and infamy should have aggravated our sorrow, we must blame ourselves and a reckless public policy. But there is always a limit to passive endurance of flagrant wrongs by a free and enlightened people. The history of the election campaign of 1855 in our state is ample testimony that the people united to inaugurate a stronger, wiser, and better government. Let it be our fervent hope, brothers, that this time they have not been deceived.

What have been the issues thrust upon us heretofore, in the political world? Not our home interests—the political sanhedrim of California has uniformly kept them from the view of the people, and has cunningly fomented discord on issues foreign to this state. In our legislative halls, and in our cabinet councils, the interests of California have been subordinate topics to the political issues which have convulsed the old states since 1798. What are these issues to us? California has asked for reform, and she has been answered by a clamor about the annexation of Cuba. She has asked for a railroad, and the response has been a howl upon the Nebraska bill. She has asked for protection against lynch law, judicial corruption, and imbecility. She has asked for a speedy settlement of our land titles, and for a proper and just protection of the *bona fide* settlers, and disunion is thundered upon our ears in reply. Have we not a mission in the world—a separate duty to perform, and a distinct destiny to work out? The broad Pacific lies before us to bring into commercial subjection, and a wilderness behind us in hardly diminished wealth invites the enterprise of the pioneer and capitalist. Intemperance and corruption banquet in the high places in the land, and bold and bloody crime stalks unchecked in our midst.

While these home duties are before us to perform, these domestic wrongs to redress, are we ever to hang loosely on the skirts of remote scrambling factions over the mountains, kicked and trodden on by all, suffering all the heat and dust of the turmoil without the hope of receiving any of the trophies of the contest? Neither the success nor defeat of the Nebraska bill—neither American nor Spanish dominion in Cuba—neither the cotton spinners in Massachusetts, nor the cotton planters of Alabama, could or would at the cost of a dollar advance the interests of California one jot. The main duty of California at this juncture is to act for herself.

The questions which have caused such serious agitations in the old states are the ones which we wish to ignore and discard from this state. Let us rest assured that the union is safe—that liberty strikes its root too deep and strong in American soil to be so easily and suddenly uprooted. But even did danger impend, it is not in the power of California to rescue the continent from its imminent doom. Yet, we too, owe a duty to the confederacy in this question, and our sectional isolation enables us to take a noble and impressive stand upon it. Removed, as we are, by position and actual interest from its baneful influence, we should allay instead of precipitating its agitation.

Analyze this slavery question. It has no proud principle; it is the mere ebullition of sectional antipathies. Side by side, in friendly contact, repose the historic states of Pennsylvania and Maryland— the one a free and the other a slave state—the border lines of the hotspur state of Kentucky come flush up to those of the young giant Ohio, and the pioneer of the western plains, the Missourian, has only to stretch his arms across an imaginary line to shake hands with his friend from the granary of the west, Illinois. Here, at the very line of contact between the free and slave states, there is comparatively little feeling on the subject of their different domestic institutions, and there would be none at all were they let alone, but exactly in proportion as we recede from this line, where, were the question one of principle, we would see a deadly border warfare, do we find the antagonism growing stronger and stronger, and instead of Pennsylvania finding fault with her neighbor, Massachusetts and Mississippi are at loggerheads. Why should we, therefore, lend our voices to swell the clamor? Why enlist in a cause so senseless and unprofitable in itself, which, while it divides us to our own destruction, is valueless to those with whom we sympathize? Our true course to the confederacy and ourselves, is to mind our own business, and let that question sink to that insignificance its unprofitableness deserves.

The enunciation of abstract political theories is perhaps expedient whensoever there is a necessity for promulgating doctrines upon the subject of our international policy, but at present there is no such necessity. The agitation of such questions at present, to the exclusion of our state affairs, would fall short of the point to which it is our duty to address ourselves.

Discarding, therefore, all sectionalities, and while our allegiance to the fatherland is the foundation and corner stone of our political faith, and while we earnestly hope to see all sectional animosities there allayed, and are convinced that silence and indifference are the true means of accomplishing anything toward that end, we cannot forget that we have nearer and more pressing home duties required of us. For the purpose, therefore, of more clearly defining and of re-affirming those doctrines, which the people have heretofore so clearly endorsed through the ballot-box—we deem it expedient at this juncture to address you.

We demand a careful revisal of our criminal code, an expurgation of its errors and a reconcilement of its inconsistencies; that the means of enforcing its penalties be made more certain, so that while the guilty shall not escape trial, the convicted shall not escape punishment. We demand the enactment of laws for the protection of our votes against the tricks and frauds of bullies and knaves. We demand that the fountains of both civil and criminal jurisprudence be purified. We demand that a more urgent effort be made for the settlement of our land titles, and also for the protection of *bona fide* settlers. We demand a more economical, responsible, and systematic administration of our state government. We demand that laws be enacted which, independent of a healthy commercial intercourse, will check the exhausting drain from our pockets to those of eastern capitalists and speculators, and protest against making the state, either a divided political or financial dependency of New York or Louisiana. We demand that our legislators shall direct their attention to the passage of laws for the support and maintenance of *only that* system of common schools for the education of our children which shall be wholly uncontrolled by sectarian influence. We ask that immediate steps be taken to urge successfully upon the general government the enlargement of the plan, and the hastening of the completion of our coast defenses, their present condition leaving our sea ports exposed to blockade and bombardment, and our communication with the rest of the world liable to be interrupted at any time. We insist upon the establishment amongst us of a United States arsenal of sufficient resources, in variety and quantity, to arm and equip all our citizens for any emergency which our ever-varying foreign relations may at any time create. We demand that the general government shall cease to tax this people for government purposes beyond those of our sister states.

We believe that the general government has the power to lend her aid in the building of works of internal improvement which, in the event of war, would become vitally important to the proper defense of our people.   The Pacific railroad being such, we urge the united effort of our representatives in congress to expediate its building.

We pledge ourselves to the support or"every measure which has for its object the facilitating means of transit to and from our state.

While we advocate either the repeal of great modification of our naturalization laws, we demand that all who have or will comply with our terms, be allowed the privileges guaranteed to them.

We believe in the doctrine of "Americans ruling America," and' that the boon held out to foreigners and secured to our naturalized citizens by our constitution and laws is *protection* in the enjoyment of life, liberty, and the pursuit of happiness.

We believe that all white native born citizens of good moral character, who acknowledge no allegiance superior or equal to their allegiance to the constitution and laws of the United States, are a common brotherhood and entitled to the same privileges, without reference to sect or religion, and drawing ourselves out of all sectional agitation upon the subject of southern rights as distinguished from the northern, we demand that our congressional delegation shall vote "*nay*" upon every proposition, coming from whatever quarter it may, to continue or renew it.

These are some of the more prominent measures and doctrines which we believe it becomes our party to carry out, and though there may be others which should demand the attention of our representatives in both state and general government, yet we have sufficient confidence in the integrity, ability, and statesmanship of those who have received our suffrages, to believe that they will lend all their energies to making our people happy as well as intelligent,. and give us wise and beneficent laws.

A democratic paper, in referring to the meeting, indignantly said:

Its proceedings only furnish additional proof that the "know nothing" is nothing but a whig movement in California.   We should like to know how democrats could sit quietly in that body and allow their former professions to be buried—how they could allow whigs to pass over their heads an endorsement of a policy against which they have been warring during the early stages of their lives.

The democratic convention, to select delegates to attend the national convention, met at the Congregational church, Sacramento, on Wednesday, March 5, 1856. It was called to order by B. F. Washington, chairman of the state committee, and Humphrey Griffith was selected temporary chairman. There were two sets of delegates from San Francisco, and the entire day was consumed in a discussion as to which of them should be admitted. On the 6th, the convention received the report of the committee on credentials. All went on smoothly until San Francisco was reached. The committee reported in favor of admitting the delegates who had been elected under the direction of the general committee, acting for the democracy of the city, and a struggle followed for the floor. It was secured by E. D. Sawyer, the spokesman for the "reform" wing, and he earnestly protested against the action of the committee. At the close of his remarks, the report of the committee was adopted, and the delegation, he represented, retired. While the discussion was pending, H. P. Haun stated that the question of the election of a United States senator had been sprung in the legislature, and that it was then being debated. Many of the democratic senators were in the convention as delegates, and hardly had the announcement escaped his lips, when the convention rose en masse, and the delegates rushed pell mell to the capitol. In half an hour, however, the matter was adjusted in the legislature, and the session of the convention was resumed. A permanent organization was effected by electing James W. Mandeville, president; and J. R. Gitchell, Samuel McConnell, W. A. Mix, and Frank Tilford, vice-presidents.

The following resolution was intoduced and laid on the table:

That we entertain for General Joseph Lane, of Oregon, as a national democrat, unbounded confidence, and should he receive the nomination of the democratic national convention for vice-president, California will extend to him a most cordial support.

A committee on resolutions was appointed, consisting of W. Van Voorhies, J. W. McCorkle, W. L. Dudley, D. P. Durst, W. W. Gift, J. C. Zabriskie, John Bigler, J. L. Brent, B. F. Myers, H. C. Patrick, J. M. Covarrubias, J. R. Gitchell, Pablo de la Guerra, C. T. Ryland, J. B. Frisbie, M. E. Cooke, T. N. Cazneau, H. Griffith, C. E. Lippincott, and others.

In the evening, the committee reported the following platform:

WHEREAS, The prosperity and progress of the United States have resulted in a great degree from the principles and action of the democratic party; and, whereas, the preservation and perpetuation of those principles are essential to the security of liberty and the integrity of the union of these states; it is, therefore, fitting and proper that the cardinal principles of the democratic party, by the influence of which our country has advanced with such unparalelled rapidity to power and greatness, should be clearly set forth, not only to guide the party in its future action, but to exhibit the wisdom, the patriotism, and the exalted love of liberty in its broadest sense of the illustrious founders of our faith. *Therefore, resolved,*

1. That we inscribe on our banner the following principles of our political faith, which were proclaimed by the immortal Jefferson, sustained and enforced by the illustrious Jackson, and which have been adhered to by friends of liberty and humanity to the present period, to-wit: First—A strict construction of the constitution, that the honest will of the people may be carried out. Second— Equal justice to all men, of whatever state or persuasion, religious or political. Third—Strict economy and rigid accountability in all the departments of the government. Fourth—To secure which we are in favor of the prompt arraignment and punishment of all public officers convicted of peculation. Fifth—An undeviating adherence to the universal standard of value of gold and silver, that honest industry may receive its just reward, and the general interests of the country be securely and permanently established. Sixth—*Univer-sal suffrage, unrestricted by property qualifications,* that every citizen may enjoy the highest prerogative of a free man, on the basis of his manhood, and not of his property. Seventh—*Liberal natu-ralization laws,* that the oppressed of every nation may speedily secure the blessings of liberty guaranteed by our national constitu-tion, after reaching "the land of the free, and home of the oppressed." Eighth—The support of the state government in all their rights as the most competent administrations for our domestic concerns and the surest bulwarks against anti-republican tendencies. Ninth.—The preservation of the general government in its whole constitutional vigor, as the sheet-anchor of our peace at home, and safety abroad. Tenth—A jealous care of the right of election by the people, and prompt and exemplary punishment of all frauds upon the elective franchise. Eleventh—Absolute acquies-cence in the decisions of the majority, the vital principle of repub-lics, from which there is no appeal but to force, the vital principle and immediate parent of despotism. Twelfth—*Universal educa-tion,* and the prompt arraignment of all abuses at the bar of public reason. Thirteenth—The honest payment of our debts, and the sacred preservation of the public faith. Fourteenth—Freedom of

religion, freedom of the press, freedom of person, under the protection of the habeas corpus, and trial by juries impartially selected. Fifteenth—That although democrats may have differed in opinions upon the expediency of the Missouri compromise, yet, as that question is now a by-gone issue, we are ready to resist its restoration as inexpedient and unwise, and recognize in the principle of "popular sovereignty," as embraced in the compromise measures of 1850, and the Baltimore platform of 1852, and subsequently embodied in the Kansas-Nebraska bill, as the one great issue before the American people as this time ; and we will cherish and maintain such principle as the sheet-anchor of our hopes, and will uphold it as the only sure means of perpetuating our government through all time to come. Sixteenth—The prompt construction of the Atlantic and Pacific railroad. And, as a means of accomplishing this great result, an appropriation by the general government, of land sufficient to secure its speedy completion. Seventeenth—We are in favor of "union and liberty, now and forever, one and inseparable." Eighteenth— We demand of the general government the prompt construction of the necessary fortifications upon this coast, to afford protection to the great interests of this state ; the establishment of a United States arsenal, with such supplies and munitions of war, as will enable the citizens of this state to protect themselves against Indian aggressions or foreign invasions. Nineteenth—We are opposed to all secret political organizations, regarding them as subversive of the great principles upon which our institutions are based, and dangerous to liberty. We are opposed to that party (falsely called American) which recklessly assails the sacred rights of conscience, proscribes naturalized American citizens, assails all the great doctrines secured by the heroism of the revolution, and established by the wisdom and patriotism of the founders of the republic; and yet hypocritically professes attachment "to the purer days of the republic, and invokes the spirit of heroism, patriotism, and virtue that precipitated the revolution," and declares that "Americans shall rule America." Twentieth—We are opposed to all sectional organizations ; the formations of parties upon geographical divisions, and the agitation of the question of slavery.

2. That we approve of the principles and policy of the administration of President Pierce, and urge their adoption and enforcement upon all succeeding administrations.

3. That we are in favor of the most liberal appropriation by the general government of the public lands in California for the benefit of actual settlers, and that the same should be donated to said

settlers in limited quantities; and that we are in favor of protecting the actual settler in all his just, equitable and legal rights.

4. That in common with a large majority of the people of California, the members of this convention have unbounded confidence in the integrity, great ability, sterling democracy and ardent devotion to country of the Hon. James Buchanan; that we have not forgotten the distinguished services by him rendered as secretary of state, under the lamented Polk, during the war with Mexico, which resulted in the acquisition of the territory we now occupy; nor have we failed to appreciate his fearless bearing and discreet action as our minister to Great Britain during the discussion of questions highly important to the interests as well as the honor of his country; *therefore, be it resolved*:

5. That the members of this convention, in expressing our ardent desire for the nomination and triumphant election of the Hon. James Buchanan as president of the United States, do but give utterance to the wishes of an immense majority of the democracy of California.

6. That the delegates elected by this convention to the democratic national convention be and they are hereby instructed that it is the earnest and unanimous desire of the democracy of California that the nomination for president of the United States shall be given to the Hon. James Buchanan.

7. That the democratic party still adheres to that policy which has already filled our mountains with hardy and prosperous miners, and built up for our state that prosperity which has so wonderfully marked her brief history: To the miners belongs the regulation of the mines.

The resolution to instruct the delegates excited a prolonged discussion, and several substitutes were offered and defeated. The platform was adopted as a whole, by a vote of 225 to 41. On the 7th, the following additional resolutions were adopted:

8. That our delegates be, and they are hereby instructed to support no man for president or vice-president who is not a sound national democrat, in favor of preserving the union at all hazards, and of protecting the constitution against all assaults, coming from whatsoever quarter they may.

9. That the election of N. P. Banks to the very responsible position of speaker of the house of representatives of the congress of the United States, is dangerous to the peace and harmony of the people of the United States and the integrity of the union, because

the known and avowed opinions of that gentleman on the subject of slavery, if carried into operation by the election of a president and a majority of the two houses of congress entertaining similar opinions on this question, would have a tendency to dissolve the union.

The following gentlemen were placed in nomination for delegates to attend the national convention: P. C. Rust, Samuel H. Dosh, D. E. Buel, J. H. Hill, P. L. Solomon, J. L. Brent, I. N. Dawley, S. W. Inge, Michael Gray (withdrawn), B. F. Marshall, Daniel Aldrich, R. H. Bowlin, B. S. Lippincott, E. F. Beale, Jesse Brush, Volney E. Howard, W. H. Endicott (withdrawn), Nelson Taylor, W. D. Farren, C. F. Lott, A. Redman and W. J. Ford. On the first ballot Rust, Dosh, Brent, Hill, Buel, Solomon, Dawley and Inge were elected. W. J. Ford, Jas. M. Wilson, R. H. Boring, Jesse Brush, Nelson Taylor, John L. Chipman, A. Redman, J. B. Frisbie, Jefferson Hunt, Samuel T. Leake, W. D. Farren, Thomas McConnell, W. Lowe and W. H. Graham were nominated for alternates, and Ford, Taylor, Wilson, Hunt, Frisbie, Lowe, McConnell and Chipman elected. Immediately before the adjournment the following resolution was adopted:

That the convention does hereby most fully approve of the action of the senate and assembly in preventing the election to a seat in the senate of the United States of a "know nothing;" that in so doing they have fully done their duty and expressed the wishes of the entire democratic party, and the wishes of a majority of the people.

On the evening of April 19th, the first mass meeting of republicans in California was held at Sacramento. E. B. Crocker, who was the leader of the new party in that county, opened the meeting and was granted a fair hearing. Geo. C. Bates was then introduced, but the general disturbance raised by the Americans and democrats present prevented his voice from being heard. Henry S. Foote then took the stand and begged the disturbers to desist and allow the meeting to proceed, but he was not heeded. The republican speakers again attempted to talk, when suddenly a rush was made for the stand by the crowd and it was overturned and the meeting broken up.

On April 30th, the first state convention of republicans met in the Congregational church at Sacramento. E. B. Crocker was temporary chairman, and the permanent officers were Nathaniel Bennett, president; and Thos. Hill, H. Wade, John Dick, H. Robin son, Jonathan Phelps, Thos. Bartlett, and E. P. Flint, vice-presidents. The convention was slimly attended, but thirteen counties being represented, and several by but one delegate. Of the 125 delegates present, 66 were from San Francisco and Sacramento.

The following resolutions were adopted :

1. That the republican party is organized to preserve the liberties of the people, the sovereignty of the states, and the perpetuity of the union, by administering public affairs upon the principles established by our forefathers at the organization of our federal government.

2. That we adopt as the cardinal principle of our organization, the prohibition of slavery in all the national territories—a principle derived from the ordinance of 1787, adopted at the formation of the republic, and which was applied to all the territory then the property of the nation.

3. That we are in favor of "preventing the increase of the political power of slavery" in our federal government.

4. That the prohibition of slavery in the territories of the union, is properly within the control of congress, and all the people of the union are, therefore, directly responsible should it be permitted to extend over such territories.

5. That slavery, in the several slave states, depends solely upon state laws for its existence, and that congress has no power to modify or repeal such laws, and we are not, therefore, responsible therefor. We are therefore opposed to all interference with slavery in the slave states.

6. That slavery is a sectional institution, in which only about 350,000 slave holders are directly interested, while *freedom* is a national principle, by which 26,000,000 of American freeman are secured in their rights. The republican, being the only party opposed to the extension of slavery, and in favor of free institutions for our territories, is therefore the only *national* party now seeking the support of the American people.

7. That we heartily welcome to our country the honest and industrious immigrants, who seek our shores to escape from European despotism, and we deprecate all attempts to embitter their feelings against our free institutions by political persecution on account of their foreign birth.

8. That the speedy construction of a national railroad, by the most central and eligible route, from the Missouri river to the bay of San Francisco, is demanded by the military, postal, and commer-

cial necessities of the republic, and should command the direct and immediate aid and support of the federal government; and the only hope of its construction is in the success of the republican party.

9. That the future growth and prosperity of our state depends upon the speedy settlement of land titles; and we regard a law, judiciously framed, for securing to the *bona fide* settler the improvements he may have made upon private lands, in ignorance of the title, as peculiarly required in the present uncertainty of boundaries and titles. We are also in favor of a free grant to actual settlers, of reasonable portions of the public lands; and also of the present system of free mining established in our state.

10. That it is the duty of the people to select as candidates for office in this state, only such men as are permanently located here, and who, by their moral character and correct business habits, give assurance that a rigid economy, as well as an energetic enforcement of the laws, will govern in the administration of public affairs.

The following resolution was offered by Mr. Crocker, and withdrawn after a discussion:

That the repeal of the Missouri compromise utterly absolves us from all support of any of the compromises respecting slavery, not embraced in the federal constitution; and we are therefore opposed to the admission of any more slave states into the union.

The platform of the Pittsburg convention was adopted unanimously.

The following were selected, as delegates, to attend the national convention: From San Francisco, Francis B. Folger, O. A. Washburn, Jas. A. Wells; Sacramento, Eben Owens; Alameda, W. H. Chamberlain; Santa Clara, Jas. M. Pierce; Sutter, Geo. M. Hanson; Butte, John Dick; Yuba, John O. Fall, S. M. Judkins; Nevada, John Phelps; Yolo, John M. Reed.

A state committee was selected, consisting of E. B. Crocker, George Rowland, Cornelius Cole, Annis Merrill, Charles Watrous, James Churchman, and others.

Owens offered a resolution to the effect that the delegation be instructed to cast their first vote for John O. Fremont for president.

Crocker offered the following substitute:

That this convention declines to instruct its delegates to the national convention as to their votes in that convention for the respective candidates for president and vice-president of the United States; that we leave this matter entirely to the good sense and discretion of our delegates, being well satisfied that, after consultation with their republican brethren of the other states of our union in convention assembled, they will act with a clear and decided purpose to insure the success of the national republican party in the coming presidential election.

The substitute was adopted.

Among the delegates to the convention, other then those mentioned in the proceedings, were George C. Bates, Samuel Soule, J. W. Foard, C. P. Huntington, P. Coggins, Dr. A. B. Nixon, E. H. Miller, Mark Hopkins, and O. C. Wheeler.

Early in May, a public discussion was announced to take place at Sacramento, between Geo. C. Bates (rep.) and J. C. Zabriskie (dem.), but when the appointed time arrived no location could be secured on account of the anticipated disturbance, and the meeting was postponed until the evening of the 10th of that month. At that time, the discussion was commenced. Rotten eggs were thrown and fire crackers burned to create a disturbance, but the police made several arrests, and order was restored. After the meeting closed, outsiders took possession of the stand, and a resolution was adopted declaring "that the people of this city have been outraged by the discussion of treasonable doctrines by a public felon, and that we will not submit to such an outrage in the future."

A few days later the Sacramento *Tribune* (Amer.), referring to the meeting, said:

The fact that a public discussion was permitted to take place in a public street in the heart of our city, in the presence of a large concourse of citizens, mostly all of whom disapprove of the doctrines advocated by the speakers, and this, too, when it is the firm conviction of a large majority of the persons assembled that the agitation of the slavery question as the basis of political party organization, is against the true interest of the state and the nation, speaks volumes in favor of the public morals in Sacramento.

On May 13th, the semi-annual session of the state council of the American party commenced at Sacramento. It was presided over by S. A. McMeans, the grand president; and 140 delegates were present, representing twenty-five counties. On the 14th, McMeans was unanimously elected president, and Silas Selleck, vice-president.

The following resolutions were adopted :

1. That the people of the territories of the United States have the sole right to regulate their own domestic institutions, and that congress has no constitutional power, either directly or indirectly, to interfere with slavery either in the states or territories.

2. That we heartily indorse the nomination of Millard Fillmore for president and of Andrew J. Donelson for vice-president, as *national men*, and in that their former course of policy guarantees to California their favorable action upon the construction of the Atlantic and Pacific railroad by the general government as a national work, and for the benefit of the union as a whole.

3. That we consider the construction of the Atlantic and Pacific railroad as paramount to every other interest of California in our relations to the general government, and that our safety, prosperity, and well being, in a great measure, require that it be built with all reasonable speed.

4. That we cordially indorse the platform adopted by the national council assembled at Philadelphia, on February 22, 1856.

5. That the American party of this state cannot view with indifference the evil that must naturally grow out of the large amount of our mineral lands, which are covered by Spanish grants, which must ultimately result in immense monopolies, that will endanger the peace and quietude of our state; and that we will, to prevent such evils, as well as to protect generally the mining interest (which is one of such paramount importance to this state), use all our strength and influence as a party to procure the purchase of all such domain by the general government, that the same may be left free and open for mining purposes to all our citizens.

The following resolutions were offered, and tabled :

WHEREAS, The time has arrived when it becomes the right of every member of the American party to know how that party, as a party, stands upon the one great issue which now divides the people of the states, east of the Rocky mountains, and which, contrary to the wishes of the people, has been thrust into the politics of this state ; *therefore, resolved,*

1. That, in the opinion of the state council of California, the measure known as the " Kansas-Nebraska bill " should be regarded as a finality, so far as congressional action on the subject of slavery is concerned ; said bill only guaranteeing to the people of the territories the same privilege of deciding for themselves, with regard to

their domestic institutions, that the people of California claimed and exercised.

2. That the republican movement in this state is regarded by this council as mischievous and treasonable—the doctrines advocated by said party, if carried into effect, disfranchising entirely those citizens born in a particular section of the republic ; and, therefore, having a direct tendency to build up sectional parties, and to encourage sectional strife, against which we were solemnly warned by George Washington himself, and which, if carried to any extent, must inevitably procure the disruption of the confederacy.

3. That the American party will oppose with all its power, the success of said republican movement, and we pledge ourselves to each other to wage an uncompromising war upon it.

Thos. J. Oxley offered the following, which was tabled :

That this state council will not express any opinion in regard to the principles embodied in the measure known as the " Kansas-Nebraska bill."

McCallum offered the following :

The recognition of the right of the native born and naturalized citizens of the United States permanently residing in any territory thereof, to frame their constitution and laws, and to regulate their domestic and social affairs in their own mode, subject only to the provisions of the federal constitution, with the right of admission into the union whenever they have the requisite population for one representative in congress ; *provided, always,* that none but those who are citizens of the United States, under the constitution and laws thereof, and who have a fixed residence in any such territory, ought to participate in the formation of the constitution, or in the enactment of laws for said territory or state.

The whole matter was laid on the table, and afterward the resolution numbered one, in the series adopted, was passed. On the 17th, a lengthy address was issued to the people signed by a committee, composed of James T. Farley, W. W. Hawks, B. C. Whitman, and others.

The republican convention, to nominate presidential electors and congressmen, met at Sacramento, on August 27th, and was called to order by E. B. Crocker, chairman of the state committee. Joseph A. Nunes was elected temporary chairman. On permanent organization, Gen. C. H. S. Williams was president; and Daniel Olds, W. F. Curtis, C. G. Lincoln, E. Fitzhenry, J. R. Clark, C. Wadhams, C. G. Boerman, L. T. Wilson, J. C. Harmer, Thos. Cox, P. H. Sibley, James Cathers, T. O. Larkin, A. B. Nixon, J. W. Jones, C. S. Haswell, S. W. Brown, S. Overmeyer, Antonio M. Pico, J. W. Kelsey, Wm. Page, Julius Smart, and Lewis Cunningham were vice-presidents.

On the 28th, the following nominations were made :

Cornelius Cole, for clerk of the supreme court, on the first ballot, over R. A. Perkins, Thos. Cox, George A. Runk, Wm. S. Cooper, Herman Camp, and E. Giddings.

Alex. Bell, F. P. Tracy, C. N. Ormsby, and L. C. Gunn, for presidential electors, by acclamation—the other candidates, T. O. Larkin, John N. Turner, W. W. Shepard, A. M. Pico, G. B. Tingley, Warner Oliver, F. B. Murdock, Chas. G. Lincoln, and John Dick, withdrawing.

J. M. Buffington, for school superintendent, on the first ballot, over John M Howe, Wm. Sheldon, Wm. Sherman, A. H. Myers, and S. S. Johnson.

Ira P. Rankin, for congressman from the southern district, on the first ballot, over C. H. S. Williams, F. P. Tracy, E. D. Baker, and C. A. Washburn.

Thos. Cox, for congressman from the northern district, on the first ballot, over C. A. Tuttle, L. Cunningham, J. C. Brown, J. T. McLean, E. B. Crocker, D. W. Cheesman, and C. N. Ormsby.

Moses Arms, for state prison director, over J. O. Wheeler, Geo. Goodrich, Chas. Brown, and H. S. Gates.

A state committee was selected, consisting of Trenor W. Park, B. W. Hathaway, Samuel Soule, J. T. McLean, E. B. Crocker, C. Cole, and L. C. Granger.

The following resolutions were adopted :

1. That we cordially endorse the resolutions adopted by the national republican convention, and in them we recognize the principles which governed the political course of the fathers of the republic.

2. That we heartily ratify the nomination of John C. Fremont and Wm. L. Dayton, and we will give them an enthusiastic support, as the standard bearers of republicanism in this presidential campaign.

3. That we inscribe on our banner " Freedom, Fremont and the

5

Railroad," and under it we will fight on until victory shall crown our efforts.

4. That slavery in the slave states depends solely upon state laws for its existence; that congress has no power to modify, change or repeal such laws, and is not responsible therefor. We are, therefore, opposed to all interference with slavery in the slave states.

5. That the speedy construction of a national railroad, by the most central and eligible route, connecting the Atlantic states with California, is demanded by the military, postal, and commercial necessities of the republic; and we recognize the power of congress, under the constitution, to appropriate money, as well as land, to aid in building this great work, and the only hope of its construction is in the election of John O. Fremont.

6. That P. T. Herbert, by the murder of an humble laborer, has rendered himself unworthy of a seat as our representative in congress; and the democrats in the federal legislature, by refusing to investigate the facts, have sanctioned the bloody deed; and Senator Weller, in attempting to screen him from public odium, merits the severest condemnation. (This resolution referred to the killing of Thos. Keating, a waiter at Willard's Hotel, Washington, by Congressman Herbert, on May 8, 1856.)

7. That the time has fully come for a thorough and radical reform in our state affairs, and the complete overthrow of political parties who have encouraged and sustained a host of cormorants in their schemes for plundering the people.

8. That the practice of electing to important public offices immoral and unprincipled men, and those who have no permanent interest in the welfare of the country, has disgraced our state, and is an evil which demands an immediate remedy.

9. That we are in favor of the speedy settlement of land titles in this state, of a free grant to actual settlers of reasonable portions of the public domain, and of free mining upon the public lands.

On October 7th, Cox, one of the nominees for congressman, withdrew from the ticket, on account of personal attacks which had been made upon him by the opposition press. In his letter of withdrawal, he stated that the charges were " in the main false," but as he had not time before election to disprove them by obtaining testimony from the east, he would not become a stumbling block by remaining on the ticket. The state committee immediately nominated J. N. Turner for the place.

The new party continued to be the object of most bitter attacks by both of the old parties, on account of its tendency toward aboli-tionism. The feeling that was entertained toward it may be imag-ined from the following allusion to the last convention, that appeared in the Sacramento *State Journal*, of August 28th :

The convention of nigger worshipers assembled yesterday in this city. *Ecce Signum!* This is the first time that this dangerous fanaticism has dared to bare its breast before the people of Califor-nia. Heretofore, it has skulked in dark corners, denied its own identity, and kept in the background; but the success which attended the "know nothing" party in its efforts to abolitionize con-gress, and inaugurating a reign of anarchy in the northern and western states of the confederacy, has emboldened these political des-peradoes to attempt the work of abolitionizing California. A year ago no such a scene as we now witness in this city would have been tolerated or thought of ; a year ago the fanatics would have been ashamed to acknowledge allegiance to the party founded by Hale, Wilson, Chase, Sumner, *et id omne genus.* We tell our readers there is dangerous meaning in the spectacle of political degradation now before us, and that it is high time all national men should unite in saving California from the stain of abolitionism—high time that we should, for the present, at least, cast aside our personal pre-ferences for men, and our little personal rivalries, and unite upon the party which is the strongest and truest exponent of conserva-tism and unionism—which is neither propagandist nor abolitionist, but which arrays itself in support of the sacred guarantees of the constitution. * * * The "know nothings," it is clearly demon-strated, are "down amongst the dead men." They do not under-stand their own position in respect to the great issue now in contro-versy. Ask one of them how he stands on the Kansas-Nebraska question, and he will be unable to reply.

On September 2d, the American state convention met at the Congregational church, Sacramento. It was called to order by S. A. McMeans, president of the state council. The first day was con-sumed in settling contests among delegates. On the 3d, on perma-nent organization, J. G. McCallum was elected president, and Thos. J. Oxley, J. H. Harris, B. G. Weir, Eben Niles, and Alex. G. Abell, vice-presidents.

The following nominations were made :

B. C. Whitman and A. B. Dibble, for congressmen, on the second ballot, over D. R. Ashley, O. C. Hall (withdrawn), W. W. Upton (withdrawn), Jesse O. Goodwin (withdrawn), J. M. Williams (withdrawn), Jas. W. Coffroth (withdrawn), W. S. Sherwood, Jas. T. Farley (withdrawn), George H. Cartter, A. P. Catlin, J. D. Cosby (withdrawn), Wm. H. Culver (declined), J. G. McCallum (declined), and John M. Howell (declined).

John Skinker, for supreme court clerk, on the third ballot, over G. W. Gilmore, E. C. Gillette, Oliver Wolcott, Dr. J. Powell, D. T. Bagley, Louis Teal, J. D. Scellen, W. H. Taylor, and H. R. Hawkins.

Horace P. Janes, for school superintendent, on the first ballot, over J. C. Cook, Dr. F. W. Hatch, N. Slater, O. C. Wheeler, R. H. Tibbetts, M. M. Noah, Dr. W. W. Stevenson, M. Walthall, and C. F. Linn.

Bailey Peyton, Jesse S. Pitzer, R. N. Wood, and O. C. Hall, for presidential electors, over W. W. Upton, W. W. Sefton, D. R. Ashley, James W. Coffroth, Caleb Dorsey, J. G. McCallum, A. M. Rosborough, R. H. Daly, Geo. H. Rhoades, E. Garst, and Henry S. Foote.

Manuel A. Castro, Chas. D. Semple, Jos. Winston, and J. Milton Williams, for alternate electors.

The convention decided not to nominate a candidate for state prison director, considering that the office had been abolished by the legislature. At this stage of the proceedings, a resolution was handed to the secretary to read, but as soon as that officer had proceeded far enough to enable the convention to conjecture what was coming, a storm was raised which beggars description. The first manifestations of opposition were the hisses from fifty lips at once, and then cries came from all parts of the house of "kick it under the table," etc. The reading was discontinued, and the offensive document was hurried out of sight. The "bombshell" was in the following words:

That the American party recognize the constitution and the laws of this state as the supreme authority; that such laws should be maintained in every part, and that we repudiate the heretical higher-law doctrine lately promulgated by many newspapers of this state; that we, as a party, condemn the acts and doctrines of the organization known as the vigilance committee of San Francisco, as destructive of the prosperity of this state and dangerous to the rights and liberties of her citizens; that this question cannot be treated as merely local, affecting only the citizens of San Francisco, but it is one in which every citizen of California is vitally interested ; the question being, practically, whether the constitution and laws, instituted by the people, and the rights of citizens under them, shall be maintained, or whether the majority of any town or precinct may, at their own option, nullify the laws and abrogate the constitution.*

The following platform was adopted :

That the American party, being essentially a reform party, they pledge themselves, in laboring to elect Fillmore and Donelson, the nominees of the convention; to lend their energies in the aid of the

---

*This resolution referred to the action of the Vigilance committee in San Francisco in 1856. In that city crime had been frequent and its punishment rare. Wm. H. Richardson, the United States marshal for the northern district of the state, was shot and killed on the street by a gambler named Charles Cora, on November 17th, 1855, and while the murder was unprovoked, it was evident that Cora could never be convicted in the courts because of the money and influence that was being used in his behalf. The culmination came, however, with the assassination of James King of William, by James P. Casey, on May 14th, 1856. King was the editor of the San Francisco Bulletin, and Casey was the proprietor of the Sunday Times, and a political manager. A communication appeared in the Times, signed "Caliban," which reflected on Thomas S. King, a brother of James, and another appeared in the Bulletin relative to one, Bagley, who had been indicted for attempting to kill Casey. On the evening of the 14th, King in an editorial said :

It does not matter how bad a man Casey had been, nor how much benefit it might be to the public to have him out of the way, we cannot accord to any one citizen the right to kill him, or even beat him, without justifiable personal provocation. The fact that Casey has been an inmate of Sing Sing prison in New York is no offense against the laws of this state ; nor is the fact of his having stuffed himself through the ballot-box as elected to the Board of Supervisors from a district where it is said he was not even a candidate any justification for Mr. Bagley to shoot Casey, however richly the latter may deserve to have his neck stretched for such fraud on the people.

Two hours after the Bulletin appeared that evening, King was fatally shot by Casey. The latter was arrested, but it was with difficulty that Mayor Van Ness and the officers kept him from the mob. That evening the old vigilance committee of 1851 met and reorganized, and on Sunday they took Casey and Cora from the jail to the committee rooms. On the 20th King died, and, when the bells tolled forth the sad intelligence, a deep gloom overspread the city. His remains were interred in Lone Mountain cemetery on the 22d, and on the same day Casey and Cora were hanged by the committee, they having previously been secretly tried and convicted. Two other men who were charged with murder, Joseph Hetherington and P. Brace, were afterward, on July 29th, hanged by the committee, and a number of objectionable characters were banished from the state. On June 21st Sterling A. Hopkins, one of the committee's policemen, was sent for Reuben Meloney, who was required as a witness. Meloney was found in the office of R. P. Ashe, the U. S. naval officer, where also was David S. Terry, a justice of the state supreme court. Ashe and Terry interfered for Meloney, and when Hopkins returned with assistance they had procured arms and were escorting Meloney to the Dupont-street armory. In the collision which ensued Terry stabbed Hopkins severely in the neck. Terry was captured by the committee and was kept by them in close confinement until August 7th. During this period no business was transacted in the supreme court, as Judge Heydenfeldt had departed for the east and Europe on March 3d, and was still abroad, and there was no quorum of the judges at liberty in the state. The court resumed its sessions on August 25th, with Justices Murray and Terry on the bench. Heydenfeldt did not return until in October. The committee disbanded in August.

great and essential reform movements of the day—the Pacific railroad, the purity of the ballot-box, the elevation of none but pure
men to positions as local officers, and that we recognize all persons
advocating the election of Fillmore and Donelson, as co-laborers
with us in the glorious cause of union and regeneration.

Another democratic convention met in the Congregational church,
at Sacramento, on September 9th. It was called to order by B. F.
Washington, the chairman of the state committee.' On the 10th,.
Jos. P. Hoge was elected permanent chairman, and Geo. P. Porter,
Wm. McClure, D. B. Milne, John M. O'Neill, A. T. Laird, and.
Andres Pico, vice-presidents.

The following nominations were made:

Chas. L. Scott, for congressman from the southern district, on the
third ballot, over Frank Tilford, Wm. L. Dudley, and Pablo de la.
Guerra.

Jos. C. McKibben, for congressman from the northern district, on
the first ballot, over John Conness, Royal T. Sprague, John T. Crenshaw, Jas. W. Denver, P. T. Herbert, and F. J. McCann.

On the 11th, Chas. S. Fairfax, for supreme court clerk, on the
third ballot, over Humphrey Griffith, Geo. S. Evans, Moses E.
Flannigan, D. W. Gelwicks, P. K. Woodside, and Thos. H.
Coombs.

Andrew J. Moulder, for school superintendent, on the second
ballot, over E. A. Theller, Wm. G. Wood, A. C. Baine, Paul K.
Hubbs, W. H. Graham, Sherman Day, and W. M. Gwin.

Augustin Olvera, George Freanor, P. dé la Torre, and A. C. Brad-
ford, for presidential electors, over P. de la Guerra, P. H. Clayton,
Wm. McClure, G. W. Colby, W. S. Long, C. J. Lansing, Alex.
Hunter, Geo. Pearce, J. P. Hoge, Chas. Precht, Wm. McDaniels,
H. Griffith, and John B. Frisbie.

J. M. Covarrubias, C. Precht, J. C. Palmer, and W. S. Long were
selected as alternates.

No nomination was made for state prison director.

On the 12th, the following address and resolutions were adopted:

To the people of California—Your convention, in closing its
labors, congratulates the democracy of California on its present position and its future prospects. At our late national convention,
held at Cincinnati, a platform was adopted replete with sound.

sense, distinctly defining the course of that great political party to which we belong, and clearly enunciating that foreign and domestic policy which it has ever been the great aim of the democratic party to uphold and maintain, and to which we invite a cordial and unanimous assent. At that convention were nominated, respectively, as candidates for the president and vice-president of the United States, James Buchanan and John C. Breckinridge; the former a statesmen who has grown gray in the service of his country, well acquainted with the policy of foreign powers, perfectly conversant with the machinery of European cabinets, and to whose experienced hands we may safely trust the destinies of the republic in its various and complicated relations with the other powers of the globe. The latter, John C. Breckinridge, though a younger laborer in the political field, a man of unquestionable ability, well calculated to assist in the administration of the government, and both possessing a private character and public reputation which may safely challenge the investigation of a world. At a time, like the present, when fanaticism and intolerance are rearing their hydraheads in various sections of the union, we calmly and confidently invite attention to the doctrines of the democratic party, as expressed in the Cincinnati platform, believing, as we do, these doctrines fully calculated to sustain the integrity of our national union in the time of difficulty and danger. Guaranteeing to every state its respective privileges, they trample on the rights of none, they broach no new and dangerous political heresies calculated to subvert the original articles of confederacy and endanger the safety of the union; they strive by no mercenary appeals to array one section of the country in hostile attitude against another, but in the true spirit of the original compact, declare the perfect integrity of the union in its fullest and most ample sense. We seek not to prescribe to any man the mode in which he shall worship his Creator, nor will we drive by intolerance from our shores the oppressed of any clime or nation. We welcome, as an addition to national wealth and strength, the honest industry of other lands, guaranteeing to those who may choose to become willing and worthy citizens of the republic "equal rights, equal privileges, and exact justice to all." In conclusion, we congratulate the gallant democracy of California on the perfect unanimity which has pervaded our councils. Difficult and delicate questions of national and domestic policy have been met and argued in the happiest spirit of compromising unanimity. "Bear and forbear" has been our motto, and we now present in favor of our national and state nominees an unbroken array, an undivided front, an impenetrable pha-

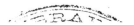

lanx, against which our foes may spend their shafts in vain.   In the full confidence that those time-honored principles for which we have so long contended are again about to assert their proud supremacy over the factional "isms" of the day, we bid you a kind farewell until on the ides of November, when we shall meet again once more to celebrate a democratic triumph in this El Dorado of the western world.   *Resolved,*

1. That the democracy of California unanimously endorse and cordially approve the platform of the democratic party, as adopted in the Cincinnati convention.

2. That the democracy of California decidedly and unequivocably advocate and approve the construction of the Pacific railroad, as a measure of the greatest importance, not only to California, but to the union at large, and hereby urge upon the federal government and our national representatives of the state at Washington the necessity of using their most united exertions and utmost endeavors to secure the construction of this truly important work.

3. That the liberal and enlightened policy of our democratic government, in opening to the hardy pioneer the broad field of our public lands, as an invitation to his industry and enterprise, has already secured the affection of our early settlers; and that we regard an extension of that policy, so far as to secure a homestead to every honest settler, free of charge, against vicissitudes of fortune, as the wisest, most just and reasonable course which the general government can pursue; and we earnestly recommend it to the serious attention of our representatives at Washington.

4. That the democracy of California are in favor of guaranteeing to every state and territory the rights and privileges secured to them by the constitution and laws of the country—that for them there is neither north, south, east, nor west; and that duly regarding the importance of the whole as a union, they, as a unit of the confederacy, will jealously guarantee the rights of each individual state.

5. That we recommend the utmost economy in the appropriation and disbursement of all public moneys; that we hold all public officers strictly accountable for the administration of the public funds; that we regard it as a cardinal principle of the democracy to preserve unimpaired the credit and resources of the state; and that he who commits the slightest defalcation in this respect, is unworthy the support, and has justly forfeited the respect and confidence of the democratic party.   •

6. That we cordially welcome to the ranks of the democracy, and receive into full brotherhood and communion, those old-line

whigs and members of other parties, who, regarding the democratic party as the great conservative party of the union, now join with us in the existing struggle to preserve the constitution.

7. That in James Buchanan and John C. Breckinridge, the democracy recognize leaders of whom they may well be proud, of unsullied public character, and unspotted private reputation; and that they will use all honorable endeavors to secure for them a triumphant majority in the El Dorado of the Pacific.

8. That, in the nominees of this convention, we recognize men worthy of our implicit confidence and deserving of our undivided support, and hereby pledge to them the undivided vote of the democracy of this state.

9. That we are in favor of, and recommend the party to vote for, at the coming election, the proposed amendment of section two, article ten, of the constitution; which amendment provides that no new state constitution shall be adopted without a direct vote of the people.

10. That we do now adjourn to meet again at the polls in the month of November next, and add our efforts to swell the triumph which then awaits the democracy of the union.   •

Immediately after the platform was reported by the committee, McConnell offered the following:

That the writ of habeas corpus and the right of trial by jury are sacred, and that the democracy of this state will ever guarantee those sacred privileges to the humble citizen.

This resolution referred to the vigilance committee question. After a lengthy discussion, the chairman announced that the church in which the convention was sitting must be vacated by two o'clock, as it was then needed by its trustees. A motion was then carried to adopt the resolutions reported by the committee, and the chairman declared that by virtue of the tenth resolution the convention was adjourned *sine die.*

The convention selected a state committee, consisting of C. E. Thom, R. Heath, P. K. Woodside, H. A. Higley, C. Benham, J. J. Hoff, J. P. Hoge, H. P. Barber, G. W. Dent, A. Redington, D. J. Thomas, J. B. Frisbie, J. Temple, W. A. Mix, G. H. Crossette, Jas. Walsh, A. T. Laird, B. F. Myers, and others.

The deliberations of the convention were by no means harmonious. It was divided into the old factions—Broderick and anti-Broderick —and the latter party was in the ascendency. Tilford and Conness were the candidates for congress on the Broderick side. No nomination was made for state prison director.

Intelligence of the nomination of Fillmore and Donelson reached California on March 21st, and of Buchanan and Breckenridge and Fremont and Dayton, on July 14th. Early in July, a movement was instituted in San Francisco to organize a people's party for the purpose of making nominations for the legislature and local officers, on the vigilance committee issue. On August 11th, a public meeting was held, which was attended by about 3,000 persons, for the purpose of consummating that object. Ira P. Rankin was chairman, and a committee to nominate a ticket was appointed. After passing resolutions approving the action of the vigilance committee, the meeting adjourned. The ticket, that was subsequently nominated, was elected by a large vote.

At the election held on November 4th, the democratic electoral and state tickets were elected, and at the official canvass, the following result was exhibited :

For President—Buchanan, 51,935; Fillmore, 35,113; Fremont, 20,339.

For Congressmen—Scott, 49,429; McKibben, 49,529; Whitman, 34,681; Dibble, 34,159; Rankin, 21,519; Turner, 20,595.

For Supreme Court Clerk—Fairfax, 50,579; Skinker, 33,396; Cole, 20,536.

For School Superintendent—Moulder, 50,174; Janes, 35,609; Buffington, 20,616.

Moses Arms received a number of votes for state prison director, but they were disregarded.

The democratic electors met at the state capitol, on December 3d, and cast their votes for Buchanan and Breckinridge. On the first ballot, Freanor was chosen as the messenger to convey the returns to Washington.

CHAPTER IX.

1857. Gubernatorial Campaign—Republican Convention—Democratic Convention—American Convention—Settlers' and Miners' Convention—Result of the Gubernatorial Election.

The republican state convention met in the Congregational church, at Sacramento, on July 8th, and was composed of 300 delegates.

It was called to order by G. W. Parr, and on permanent organization F. P. Tracy was president; and Richard Rowe, G. C. Grammar, Smith Herrick, J. A. Quimby, G. M. Hanson, and A. B. Nicholson, vice-presidents. The committee on resolutions consisted of T. W. Park, E. B. Crocker, C. A. Tuttle, L. C. Gunn, and G. W. Baldwin, and they made the following report, which was adopted :

WHEREAS, The issue upon which the republican party has been formed is of a national character, we forbear to express any opinion in reference to questions of state policy, leaving republicans free to act and vote on all questions; therefore, we adopt the following resolutions as the basis of our organization:

1. (Same as the first resolution of the republican convention of August 27, 1856.)

2. (Same as the fourth resolution of the republican convention of April 30, 1856.)

3. (Same as the fourth resolution of the convention of August 27, 1856.)

4. (Same as the fifth resolution of the convention of August 27, 1856, omitting all after the words "this great work.")

5. (Same as the ninth resolution of the convention of August 27, 1856, omitting all after the words "the public domain.")

6. (Same as the seventh resolution of the convention of April 30, 1856.)

7. That the opinion rendered by Chief Justice Taney, and concurred in by other judges, in the late "Dred Scott" case, is a palpable violation of the principles of the declarations of independence, a falsification of the history of our country, subversive of state rights, and a flagrant injustice to a large portion of the people of the United States, and, as such, merits the indignant reprobation of every freeman.

8. That, as citizens of the free state of California, we deprecate the introduction of the institution of slavery on the Pacific coast, and therefore do extend to the freemen of Oregon an earnest desire for their success in the establishment of free principles as the basis of their state government.

The following nominations were made on the 8th and 9th :

Edward Stanly, for governor, on the first ballot, by a vote of 163, to 9 for E. D. Baker, 6 for D. R. Ashley, 1 for T. W. Park, 1 for I. P. Rankin, and 1 for R. Chenery; J. A. Nunes, Samuel Bell, E. B. Crocker, F. P. Tracy, and J. N. Turner withdrawing.

D. W. Cheesman, for lieutenant-governor, on the first ballot, over Ashley, Dr. A. J. Spencer, and Leland Stanford.

Nathaniel Bennett, for justice of the supreme court, on the first ballot, over O. L. Shafter and F. M. Haight.

L. C. Gunn, for controller, on the first ballot, over Wm. L. Newell.

Leland Stanford, for treasurer, without opposition; J. N. Turner declining.

Aaron A. Sargent, for attorney-general, without opposition; F. P. Tracy and C. J. Hillyer withdrawing.

P. M. Randall, for surveyor-general, without opposition; Wm. Mott withdrawing.

F. B. Murdock, for state printer, without opposition.

A state committee was selected, consisting of E. B. Crocker, Mark Hopkins, J. T. McLean, J. R. Clark. T. W. Park, F. P. Tracy, Cyrus Palmer, F. F. Fargo, H. Cummings, J. C. Birdseye, C. A. Tuttle, C. Cole, J. E. Benton, Curtis Baird, J. A. Quimby, C. S. Haswell, J. F. Houghton, C. H. Chamberlain, and others.

Nunes offered the following, which was laid on the table:

That the numerous imperfections existing in our state constitution render it necessary that a constitutional convention should be convened to make such changes in it as may be deemed advisable, and it is therefore recommended to republicans throughout the state to vote in favor of the convention.

The democratic state convention, with 312 delegates, met in the Congregational church, Sacramento, on July 14th, and was called to order by A. Redington, chairman of the state committee. A. C. Bradford was elected temporary president. The committee on credentials reported a resolution that no delegate be entitled to a seat in the convention who had voted in opposition to Buchanan.

Wm. Van Voorhies offered the following substitute:

We pledge ourselves to support the nominees of the democratic state convention, and to use our utmost exertions to secure their election, and for this purpose we not only now urge upon the democracy the necessity of harmonious and vigorous action in the approaching campaign, but cordially invite all national men, of whatever party heretofore, to unite with us in finally and forever destroying within the limits of our state the fell spirit of disunion and sectionalism which has threatened the existence of our beloved institutions; and we recognize all those who co-operate with us in the approaching campaign as co-laborers with the democracy of this state.

The substitute was adopted by a vote of 224 to 81.

A committee on resolutions was appointed, consisting of John Boggs, P. T. Herbert, James Anderson, V. E. Geiger, Jefferson Hunt, R. McGarvey, H. T. Huggins, J. B. Devoe, J. M. Hudspeth, John C. Burch, G. W. Patrick, C. H. Bryan, and others. On permanent organization, Bradford was president, and S. A. Merritt, N. E. Whiteside, Philip Moore, W. M. Lent, J. C. James, C. J. Couts, F. J. Hoover, F. D. Kohler, B. F. Varney, J. A. Putney, D. W. Connelly, and U. Edwards, vice-presidents.

The following nominations were made on the 14th and 15th :

John B. Weller, for governor, on the first ballot, receiving 251 votes, to 61 for J. W. McCorkle; John Nugent withdrawing.

Joseph Walkup, for lieutenant governor, on the first ballot, over J. R. Hardenbergh and J. J. Warner; E. T. Beatty withdrawing.

Stephen J. Field, for justice of the supreme court, on the first ballot, over Peter H. Burnett and John H. McKune.

Thos. H. Williams, for attorney-general, on the first ballot, over R. Aug. Thompson; W. Gouverneur Morris withdrawing.

James W. Mandeville, for controller, on the first ballot, over J. T. Paine, Geo. W. Dent, and S. H. Brooks (withdrawing).

Thos. Findley, for treasurer, without opposition.

John O'Meara, for printer, on the first ballot, over H. C. Patrick and T. A. Springer.

Horace A. Higley, for surveyor-general, on the first ballot, over Rowland Shea.

The majority of the committee reported the following resolutions, which were all adopted, after a debate :

1. (Same as the first resolution adopted by the democratic convention of September 9, 1856.)

2. (Same as the second resolution in the series above referred to.)

3. That we hail with pleasure the commencement of the wagon roads, believing that they will bring within the state a hardy, enterprising and laborious class of citizens, and we call upon the government to hasten their completion by liberal appropriations.

4. (Same as the third resolution in the series above referred to.)

5. (Same as the fourth resolution in the series above referred to.)

6. (Same as the fifth resolution in the series above referred to.)

7. (Same as the sixth resolution in the series above referred to.)

8. (Same as the eighth resolution in the series above referred to.)

9. That there is a radical defect in our laws regulating preëmptions, whereby the owner of a floating Mexican grant is enabled to prevent the settlement of a tract of land much larger than he claims.

10. That the rights of preëmptions in this state ought to be as liberal as obtained in other new states, and these rights ought to be secured to settlers on all lands not actually segregated as private property.

11. That the policy of government which is sought to be established by the present chief magistrate of the United States, is eminently entitled to our most hearty and cordial approbation, as truly democratic, and calculated to secure the promotion of the best interests of our common country.

12. That this convention acknowledge a moral obligation to liquidate the existing debt of the state, and that its payment is hereby recommended.

13. That political associations, whether secret or otherwise, based upon religious intolerance, or exclusion from the exercise of political privileges, guaranteed by the constitution as it is, on account of personal rank or the accident of birth, are at once inconsistent with the spirit of our institutions, and a slander upon the liberty-loving and freedom-disseminating people of this union.

14. That we consider the present naturalization laws of the United States in accordance with our free and liberal institutions, and will resist their abrogation or amendment, as uncalled for, illiberal and unjust.

The minority of the committee reported the following:

1. That this convention recognizes the time-honored principle of instructions, and feel it a duty to condemn the conduct of our recent delegates to the democratic national convention at Cincinnati for their unpardonable disobedience in voting against that sterling patriot and honored statesman, Jas. Buchanan, now president of the United States.

2. That the perpetuity of our democratic form of government is based upon the respect of the people for the laws they themselves create.

3. That, inasmuch, as under our form of government all power comes from the people, and constitutions and laws are but the expressions of the popular will; therefore, the late violations of our con-

stitution and laws, by a portion of the people organizing themselves into armed bodies, and exercising legislative, judicial, and executive functions, is a direct repudiation of the principles upon which our government is founded, and can but tend to debase us in the estimation of the people of other countries, and postpone the day when a republican form of government will be the only one known among civilized nations.

The first minority resolution was indefinitely postponed. The second and third resolutions were offered by P. T. Herbert and had reference to the action of the vigilance committee of 1856. They gave rise to an exciting and stormy debate, when finally the following was adopted as a substitute, by a vote of 181 to 104, and it was incorporated in the platform, by a vote of 242 to 51.

15. That the democracy of California will ever support the constitution and laws of their state, and of the United States, and will ever use their utmost endeavors to preserve as sacred and inviolate that priceless legacy of our fathers contained in the bill of rights and the writ of habeas corpus.

A state committee was selected, consisting of V. E. Geiger, F. Forman, H. B. Truett, R. C. Page, J. P. Hoge, D. W. Gelwicks, W. S. Smith, S. H. Chase, W. A. January, S. S. Lewis, J. Anderson, T. B. Reardon, E. Steele, H. T. Huggins, J. A. Turner, T. A. Springer, A. R. Maloney, and others.

Early in 1857, the idea of abandoning the organization of the American party was earnestly considered by prominent members of that faction, and many were in favor of disorganization. On March 31st, Henry S. Foote, who had been the caucus nominee of the party for United States senator in 1856, published a letter addressed to the members of the party in the state, in which he gave his opinion touching the expediency of continuing the party organization. He said that he had no desire to dictate the course to be pursued by others, but simply desired that there might be no mistake as to his individual attitude on the question; that the party was originally organized mainly for the purpose of securing the faithful execution of the compromise measures of 1850, of suppressing the agitation of the slavery question, and of preserving the union from the dangers which seemed to menace it from the prevalence of feelings of fierce sectional hostility in two opposite quarters of the confederacy; that the party in California had been at all times wholly untainted either with the heresy of abolitionism or with that of secession; that universal religious toleration had been with them a cardinal principle, and that with regard to the naturalization laws they had contented themselves with simply insisting upon their judicious revision; that the presidential contest had passed, and a new and bright era had dawned; and that there was much promise in the administration of President Buchanan. He concluded by saying:

Such a cabinet as Buchanan has formed, and such political views as are announced in the inaugural, should command universal confidence, and give most gratifying assurance that for the next four years, at least, the republic will be in the enjoyment of complete repose; that its great domestic interests will be carefully guarded and assiduously promoted, and the honor of the American nation be wisely and fearlessly maintained in every quarter of the globe. I have, therefore, no hesitation in declaring that I can see no propriety in attempting to keep up the distinctive organization of the American party, either in California or elsewhere. At any rate, whatever may be the action of others, I shall myself yield to Buchanan and his administration as hearty and true a support as it would have been possible for me to accord to them had I ever so actively participated in elevating them to the high official places which they hold.

On April 29th, a meeting of the leading members of the party was held at Sacramento for the purpose of advising upon the best course to be pursued as to the future position of the party. Among those present at the conference were Jesse O. Goodwin, J. G. McCallum, W. T. Ferguson, A. J. Stevenson, James T. Farley, D. F. Douglass, Jesse D. Carr, Frank Hereford, W. C. Wallace, G. W. Bowie, and John C. Barr. It was unanimously resolved that it would be useless to attempt to keep up a distinctive organization on the old issues. The meeting fully endorsed the principles laid down in Buchanan's inaugural address, and it was declared that they would stand upon that platform so long as those principles were maintained by the president. In May, the county councils of the party were held and in several of them resolutions to disband were voted down. On June 26th, the state council met at Sacramento. A resolution to abandon the organization was defeated, and it was determined to reorganize the party in the state, and abolish all tests, obligations of secresy, etc. The council issued an address calling a state convention to nominate a full ticket and recommended that an energetic campaign be made.

The American state convention met in the assembly chamber,. Sacramento, on July 28th. Dr. Joseph Powell was elected temporary chairman, and on permanent organization, O. C. Hall was president, and J. M. Day, F. Knox, T. L. Reed, and R. S. Mesick, vice-presidents. In the evening, an interesting debate sprang up on the proposition to adjourn without making nominations. The delegates who advocated that course favored the election of Stanly, but the convention determined to present a straight ticket to the people. On the 29th, the following nominations were made:

George W. Bowie, for governor, without opposition; James H. Ralston and Bailey Peyton withdrawing.

Dr. J. A. Raymond, for lieutenant-governor, without opposition; James W. Coffroth, O. C. Hall, and Hiram R. Hawkins withdrawing.

Geo. W. Whitman, for controller, without opposition; Wm. H. Taylor, F. M. Proctor, D. K. Newell, and E. F. Burton withdrawing.

T. B. McFarland, for attorney-general, without opposition; John J. Musser, A. P. Catlin, and R. M. Briggs withdrawing.

Lucien B. Healey, for surveyor-general, without opposition; J. L. Brown withdrawing.

B. H. Monson, for printer, on the first ballot, over N. P. Brown, H. A. Appleton, and H. R. Hawkins.

J. R. Crandall, for treasurer (long and short terms), on the first ballot, over Jas. L. English, W. K. Lindsey, W. H. Howard, F. M. Proctor, and J. Powell.

Jas. H. Ralston, for justice of the supreme court (long and short terms), without opposition; H. C. Gardiner withdrawing.

The following resolutions, reported by a committee consisting of T. B. McFarland, M. M. Noah, J. R. Crandall, R. M. Briggs, L. Tooker, A. P. Catlin, and others, were adopted:

1. That we cordially endorse the platform of principles adopted by the national American convention at Louisville, Ky., on the 4th day of June, 1857.

2. That we have an abiding faith in the truth of our political creed, and that we will struggle in the future, as we have struggled in the past, to engraft the policy of our party upon the legislation of the country.

3. That we still hold to the fundamental principle of our party, that "Americans shall rule America," and that our naturalization

6

laws should be so amended as to insure, on the part of the applicant, a just appreciation of the rights and duties of an American citizen.

4. That the American party is in no way responsible for the recent intense excitement of national issues; and that a restoration of the brotherly feelings that should actuate one great national people, can only be accomplished by the permanent success of the national American party.

5. That the main objects of the American party being to promote American interests, and to cherish American nationality, the con-struction of a Pacific railroad—thus bringing the extreme portions of the country into close contact, and promoting the welfare of all— would be a natural and certain consequence of the triumph of the American party.

6. That the American party of California acknowledge it as a duty paramount above all others of a local character to protect set-tlers upon Spanish grants in their just rights and claims. We believe that laws designed to protect the *bona fide* settler in his improvements are not only absolutely necessary in order to insure confidence and prosperity, and to encourage agriculture and trade, but are also constitutional and just. The wants of the people require, and equity and good conscience demand such laws, and while the past history and recent actions of the democratic party in this state exhibit a record of broken faith, we refer for the sincerity of our professions to our past efforts in this behalf, and to the character of the men whom we present for the suffrages of the people.

7. That we consider it our duty to recommend to the electors of this state to vote in favor of paying the state debt; that while we have the utmost abhorrence for the party corruptions which saddled this onerous burden upon us, we yet would find it still more grievous to bear the load of obloquy and shame which repudiation of the claims of innocent creditors would earn for us and our posterity.

8. That the democratic party of California is responsible for the long course of improvident legislation and official corruption which has finally brought the state to the verge of bankruptcy, and is not fit longer to be in power.

9. That the American party of California, during its partial suc-cess in 1856, did more, by way of legislation, for the protection of the state from corrupt officials, than the democratic party has done during all the years of its misrule; and that the recent discovery of official unworthiness has been the result of stringent laws passed by an American legislature.

10. That we will use every possible effort to select none but

honest men for office, and the fact that we have, in some instances, been deceived, will only make us the more vigilant in this behalf hereafter.

11. That while the salaries and fees of some offices, both county and state, are sufficiently low, yet in many instances, they are so extravagant as to amount to a heavy burden upon the people, and we pledge the influence of the American party to effect still further reductions in the fees of office, with a view of making such offices less desirable to the incumbents thereof, and of removing motives for corruption in obtaining them.

A state committee was selected, consisting of A. P. Catlin, J. Powell, W. C. Wallace, B. Peyton, M. M. Noah, D. P. Talmadge, D. K. Newell, R. S. Mesick, A. McDonald, E. F. Burton, H. R. Hawkins, R. M. Briggs, O. C. Hall, A. R. Andrews, and others.

Shortly before adjourning, a resolution was adopted that the organization of the party in the state, thereafter, be under the direction of the state committee; that the state and subordinate councils should be abolished; that no obligation of secrecy should be required of the members of the party, and that all American citizens should be eligible to membership.

On July 3d, the state committee of the settlers' and miners' party met at Sacramento, issued an address calling a state convention, and recommended the nomination of a ticket from the candidates nominated by the other parties. The convention met in the assembly chamber, Sacramento, on August 4th, and about 40 delegates were present. The convention was called to order by Dr. A. B. Nixon, and I. W. Underwood was elected president. Delegates were present from the counties of San Francisco, Solano, Sacramento, Alameda, Yolo, Butte, Yuba, and Sutter.

The following ticket was made up:

For governor, Edward Stanly; justice of the supreme court, N. Bennett; lieutenant-governor, Joseph Walkup; controller, J. W. Mandeville; treasurer, Thos. Findley; attorney-general, A. A. Sargent; surveyor-general, P. M. Randall; printer, J. O'Meara.

A lengthy set of resolutions was adopted.

The sessions of the convention were stormy. At an early stage in the proceedings, a resolution was adopted to exclude the full vote of such counties as were but partially represented, and as San Francisco and Sacramento counties constituted the mass of the convention, and acted in concert, they controlled the deliberations of the body. At the close of the first day, most of the delegates from without those counties withdrew in a body.

The democratic and republican conventions neglected to nominate candidates for the offices of justice of the supreme court and treasurer for the short terms which were then filled by Burnett and English, respectively, and to avoid difficulty, the democratic state committee nominated those two gentlemen to fill the offices until the time when their successors would take office. News reached California, on August 17th, of the appointment of Mandeville, the democratic candidate for controller, to the office of United States surveyor-general for California, but he was not officially notified of his selection to that place until a few days before the election—too short a time to substitute another nominee on the state ticket.

The election was held on September 2d, and the official canvass developed the following result :

For Governor—Weller, 53,122 ; Stanly, 21,040 ; Bowie, 19,481.

Lieutenant-Governor—Walkup, 57,336 ; Cheesman, 16,800 ; Raymond, 19,718.

Justice of the Supreme Court (long term)—Field, 55,216 ; Bennett, 18,944 ; Ralston, 19,068.

Justice of the Supreme Court (short term)—Burnett, 54,991 ; Bennett, 10,550 ; Ralston, 7,710.

Controller—Mandeville, 57,048 ; Gunn, 16,398 ; Whitman, 19,-842.

Treasurer (long term)—Findley, 57,641 ; Stanford, 16,529 ; Crandall, 19,348.

Treasurer (short term)—English, 55,236 ; Stanford, 4,390 ; Crandall, 7,271.

Surveyor-General—Higley, 55,858 ; Randall, 18,205 ; Healey, 19,703.

Attorney-General—Williams, 55,561 ; Sargent, 18,418 ; McFarland, 19,701. ·

Printer—O'Meara, 57,274 ; Murdock, 16,365 ; Monson, 19,797.

Pay the state debt—Yes, 57,661 ; No, 16,970,

Constitutional Convention—For, 30,226 ; against, 17,680.

The entire democratic ticket was consequently elected, and the people ratified the act to provide for the payment of the state indebtedness. On December 2d, a writ of injunction was sued out from the sixth district court, at the instance of Thos. S. Fiske, and served on the governor, controller, and treasurer, restraining them from issuing the bonds provided for in the act. The case was an agreed one, and was designed to test the constitutionality of the proceeding. It was carried to the supreme court, and on Jannary 4th, 1858, that tribunal rendered an opinion declaring that the law and the action of the people upon it were constitutional. The proposition to call a constitutional convention was lost, not having received a majority of all the votes which had been cast at the election.

CHAPTER X.

1858. Division of the Democratic Party—Convention of the Lecompton Wing of the Party—Convention of the Anti-Lecompton Wing—Republican Convention.

Kansas had been erected into a territory by act of congress, of May, 1854, by the terms of which the question of slavery was to be determined by the vote of her citizens. Shortly afterward, an extensive immigration flowed into the new territory from both the free and the slave states, and election disturbances ensued, which were finally quelled by the United States militia. Two legislatures were chosen—one composed of free-states men, and the other of pro-slavery men. The free-state legislature met on Jannary 6th, 1857, but was dispersed by the United States marshal. Soon afterward, the pro-slavery legislature convened and provided for a constitutional convention, which met at Lecompton, in September, and framed a pro-slavery constitution. The election for delegates to this convention was held June 15th, but the free-states men did not participate, as they claimed that the legislature which made the call was an illegal body. The convention provided for the submission of the direct slavery clause separately to the people, but no votes were to be counted unless they read "for the constitution with slavery" or "for the constitution without slavery," and of course it could not well happen that the constitution would be defeated.

The election was held on December 21st, and with the colonization of pro-slavery men from Missouri and the refusal of the anti-slavery men to vote, the constitution "with slavery" was carried by a vote of 6,266 to 567. Meanwhile, in October, an election had been held for members of a territorial legislature, under a law enacted by the pro-slavery legislature; and at this election most of the free-states men, trusting to the assurances of the territorial governor, had voted. Over 11,000 votes were polled, of which 1,600 were taken at a little precinct known as Oxford, on the Missouri border, where there were but forty-three voters; and 1,200 were returned from McGee county, where no poll had been opened. But, notwithstanding these enormous frauds, the free state preponderance was so decided that it carried the legislature. An act was passed by this legislature to submit the Lecompton constitution to a vote of the people on January 4th, and at the election then held, in which the pro-slavery men declined to participate, the full poll returned was—for the Lecomton constitution, with slavery, 138; without slavery, 24; against the constitution, 10,226.

President Buchanan, in his annual and also in a special message of February 2d, urged congress to accept and ratify the Lecompton constitution (which meant to make Kansas a slave state), but Senator Stephen A. Douglas took strong ground against it. The senate, on March 23d, passed a bill accepting this constitution, by a vote of 32 to 25; but the house, on April 1st, adopted a substitute requiring a resubmission of the constitution to the people of Kansas, by a vote of 120 to 112. This amendment was rejected by the senate, but a bill was finally passed by both houses, on the 30th, which indirectly allowed the people of the territory to again vote upon the instrument. Under this bill, on August 3d, the people rejected the Lecompton constitution by an overwhelming majority. Senator Broderick and Congressman McKibben sustained the course of Douglas in his opposition to the Kansas policy of the president; Senator Gwin and Congressman Scott sided with the administration.

On May 10th, the democratic state committee met at Sacramento and called a state convention to consist of 324 delegates to meet at that place on August 4th. It soon became evident that a serious division was growing in the party on the Kansas question, and the bitterness of feeling that was evinced augured a wider difference than had ever before existed in the party. The commencement of the storm was not until June 23d, when the democratic convention of Del Norte county adopted the following resolutions:

1. That the democracy of Del Norte county, through their delegates in convention assembled, cordially and entirely approve and endorse the administration of President Buchanan.

2. That David C. Broderick, by his opposition to the administra-

tion, manifested as well in his degrading and disreputable language in relation to it, as by his votes; by his treachery to the party which elected him, his refusal to obey instructions, and by his league with the republicans, has placed himself beyond the pale of the democratic party, and should only receive at its hands the scorn and contempt which he so justly merits.

Soon after, conventions were held in other counties, and in most cases, they divided, and two sets of delegates were elected to the state convention—one representing the Lecompton and the other the anti-Lecompton sentiment.

Early in July, the Sacramento *Mercury* said, in commenting upon the action of the various county conventions:

For our part, we should not consider ourselves any more bound by the action of a convention, composed of Broderick (anti-Lecompton) men, than we would by a convention of republicans; and now, at the risk of being called "bolter," we have no hesitation in proclaiming here, in advance of the state convention, that if it should be a Broderick one, of which, however, we have no fears, that we will not support its nominees.   *   *   *   We had rather be beaten with a good set of true democrats, than to succeed with a set of men who are democrats in nothing but the name.   *   *   *   Let the Stanly and Broderick men go over to the black republicans, where they properly belong; let us cleanse our party of this rubbish; let us wipe off this incubus that has been festering and eating out the very life and substance of our party in this state since its first organization, now while we have the opportunity, and our word for it, we shall never regret it.

The Sacramento *Union*, of July 10th, said:

We have expressed the opinion that if the Douglas popular sovereignty democrats succeeded in electing a majority of the delegates to the state convention, the Buchanan Lecompton wing would   *   *   *   withdraw from the convention, and organize one of their own.   *   *   *   An effort is made to avow a distinction between Broderick and Douglas, but the object is too transparent.   *   *   *   The Buchanan leaders are determined to rule the convention or divide it; that the Kansas policy of the administration shall be sustained, or there shall be two democratic parties.   It may be added that they declare they will not admit the possibility of a man's being a democrat who does not sustain the policy of the administration.   *   *   *   We may conclude that if the Buchanan men elect a majority of the convention, they will force the Douglas democrats to endorse the administration in full, or withdraw from that body.

The same paper said, on the 28th :

Accounts come from all sides of a breaking up of the democratic party, and that two sets of delegates are likely to be elected from most of the counties, and two tickets run for the county officers and legislature on that side. The bonds of party were never so much set at defiance in California before, and we predict a political improvement in the future in consequence. One great reason why there is so much splitting among the democracy is, that the state election this year is not important, as there are no political offices of consequence to fill; hence, the pressure is not sufficient to keep the elements of the party together. It is by no means a clear question which of the contending divisions of the great democratic party is to gain the ascendency.

The division had increased to such an extent that by the time appointed for the meeting of the state convention there was no thought of a joint session, and each wing selected its own time and place for meeting.

The administration state convention met in the Congregational church, Sacramento, on August 4th, and was called to order by V. E. Geiger, chairman of the state committee. Chas. R. Street was selected temporary chairman, and after some dispute in relation to the membership of certain delegates, a permanent organization was effected by the election of James H. Hardy, as president; and and H. P. Haun, A. T. Laird, C. Kerrins, A. French, B. M. Henry, G. R. Ayers, James Osborne, W. T. Gough, J. B. Carr, T. Foley, George Coulter, W. C. Stratton, B. F. Mauldin, J. C. Hinkson, and A. Magee, as vice-presidents. A committee on resolutions was appointed, consisting of W. H. Glascock, A. C. Adams, D. W. Gelwicks, G. W. Hook, J. G. Downey, A. Deering, Henry Meredith, V. E. Geiger, E. Casserly, J. P. Hoge, Rasey Biven, C. T. Ryland, C. R. Street, J. R Kittrell, Z. Montgomery, H. P. Barber, Chas. Lindley, and others.

On the 5th, the following resolutions were reported by the committee :

1. That the democracy of California maintain, with unfaltering faith, their attachment to the wise, just and liberal principles announced in the Cincinnati platform; and, among others, they most

cordially approve and will most faithfully sustain the doctrine of popular sovereignty and its inseparable guarantee, non-intervention of the federal government with the domestic institutions of a state or territory.

2. That the act of congress known as the "English compromise bill," having referred the whole subject of the admission of Kansas to the decision of the people thereof, we do, without regard to former differences of opinion, accept and abide by that reference, and cannot but deem any attempt to revive the agitation of that subject in national politics as a violation of the spirit and intent of the Kansas-Nebraska law, and dangerous to the peace and integrity of the union.

3. That we have undiminished confidence in the wisdom, patriotism and democracy of the chief magistrate of the United States, and pledge to him and his administration the earnest support of the people of California in maintaining the honor and integrity of the union, both at home and abroad.

4. That we deem the passage of the Pacific railroad bill as of vital importance, not only to the interests of California, but to those of the union at large; and that whilst we deeply regret the postponement of that measure, and the unfortunate causes which led to it, we congratulate our people upon the establishment of a complete system of overland mail lines upon all the main northern, central and southern routes to the Pacific coast.

5. That American ships at sea under the American flag, in time of peace, are subject to the jurisdiction of the United States, and to that of no other power on earth, whether for search, visitation or any other purpose whatever; and we rejoice in the promptitude, energy and success with which this great principle has just been maintained by a democratic administration.

6. That the present democratic administration of this state is entitled to and receives our cordial approval.

7. That we cordially invite the co-operation of all national men, without regard to former political associations, to unite with us in the present and prospective struggles against sectionalism and its attendant evils.

Immediately when he had concluded the reading of the resolutions, Hoge moved their adoption, and also for the previous question on his first motion. The previous question was ordered by a vote of 117 to 49; and the resolutions were adopted as reported by a vote of 287 to 2. Montgomery then offered the following additional resolutions:

8. That we recognize the right of the people of each state and territory, when so desired by them, to vote upon the adoption or rejection of their fundamental law; but we hold that it belongs not to the congress of the United States, but to the people themselves, speaking through their own representatives, to say whether they do or do not desire to exercise such right.

9. That, in the opinion of this convention, the formation of and adherence to the so-called Topeka constitution by the abolition party of Kansas was, in the language of Stephen A. Douglas, "an act of rebellion, which ought to have been put down by force."

10. That it is the will of those who adhere to the government, and not the will of those who array themselves in rebellion against the government, that should be looked to and carried out, both in the formation of state constitutions and the admission of states into the union.

After a lengthy discussion the convention refused to consider the resolutions, by a vote of 122 to 178 ; but afterward, just before the adjournment, they were taken up and adopted, by a vote of 202 to 65, and made a portion of the platform. The following nominations were then made :

Joseph G. Baldwin, for justice of the supreme court, without opposition ; John M. Howell, S. K. J. Handy, Henry P. Barber, P. H. Burnett and W. T. Barbour withdrawing.

A. R. Meloney, for controller, without opposition ; S. H. Brooks and S. C. Tompkins withdrawing.

A resolution was introduced to proceed to make nominations for congressmen, but it was withdrawn after a debate. A state committee was chosen, composed of J. R. Hardenbergh, W. S. Long, E. Aubrey, V. E. Geiger, J. P. Hoge, M. D. Sweeney, R. C. Page, H. C. Patrick, W. J. Hooten, C. R. Street, L. Magruder, N. E. Whiteside, D. T. Loufbourough, A. Deering, J. G. Doll, C. J. Lansing, J. N. Doak, H. P. Barber, W. C. Stratton, and others.

The anti-Lecompton (Douglas) state convention also met on August 4th, in the Baptist church, Sacramento. J. A. Turner, a member of the state committee, called it to order, and Wm. I. Ferguson was elected temporary chairman. A committee on resolutions was appointed, consisting of J. W. McCorkle, C. H. Bryan, H. Griffith, J. Powell, B. S. Lippincott, John Conness, and others. On the 5th, a permanent organization was effected by electing H. Griffith, president; and G. W. Colby, E. McGarry, R. Irwin, W. N. Anderson,

Robert Bell, Chas. Kent, H. Fitzsimmons, J. Allen, C. F. Lott, and J. C. Davis, vice-presidents.

The following resolutions, reported by the committee, were unanimously adopted :

1. That all just powers of government are derived from the people; that this principle is recognized as fundamental by all American constitutions, and by the democratic party.

2. That the right of the people to form and regulate their political institutions in their own way, subject only to the constitution of the United States, as guaranteed to Kansas and Nebraska by their organic law, belongs alike to the people of all other territories of the United States.

3. That while we adhere to the fundamental democratic principles embraced in the Cincinnati platform of 1856, we especially renew and reaffirm that principle contained in the resolution known as "the popular sovereignty resolution," declaring the true intent and meaning of that resolution to be, that the people of a state or territory are invested with the right of ratifying or rejecting, at the ballot-box, any constitution that may be framed for their government; and all attempts by the administration and congress to coerce and bribe the people into the adoption of a particular constitution, not thus ratified by them, are subversive of the principles of pure democracy, and destructive of the equality of the states under the constitution.

4. That the recent attempts of the executive and congress to force upon the people of Kansas a constitution which they have rejected at a legal election, are in violation of the principles of the party which placed them in power, derogatory to the positions they occupy, and destructive of our form of government.

5. That we regard with detestation the passage by congress, at its last session, of the bill known as the "English bill," and look upon it as an attempt to bribe a free people into the indorsement of an odious constitution; as calculated to create sectional feelings and cause sectional jealousies; as a violation of the federal compact, a breach of the compromises of the constitution, and a blow at the equality of the states, in that it proposes to make large donations of land, and admit Kansas into the union as a state without reference to her population, if she adopts the Lecompton constitution, which establishes slavery, while it refuses her people admission until they obtain a population of 90,000 or 120,000, if they prefer any other than the Lecompton constitution.

6. That we heartily endorse the action of those members of con-

gress who sustained the " Crittenden-Montgomery bill," and who opposed the English bill, at the last session of that body.

7. That it is the right of the people of the states to regulate, in their own way, their political affairs ; that federal office holders are servants of the people, and the constant interference by those servants with the primary affairs of party, whether by menaces of dismissal from office, by forced levies, or by the distribution of promises and moneys at the polls and elsewhere, is incompatible with the spirit of our constitutions, state and federal, subversive of popular liberty, and calculated to destroy the sovereignty of the states and centralize power at the federal capital.

8. That the immediate action of congress in securing the construction of a railroad to the Pacific is a recognized feature in our party policy; indispensible to our safety in war and prosperity in peace, and we call upon the administration to redeem its pledges, and devote its energies to the consummation of this great work.

9. That we regard with favor the bill before congress, at its past session, known as the " homestead bill," which proposes to donate to each actual settler upon the public lands of the United States one hundred and sixty acres, and earnestly recommend the passage of the same.

10 That, relying implicitly upon the soundness and integrity of the principles above set forth, and upon the justice and intelligence of the masses, we present this platform to the people of the state, and earnestly invoke the active support of all in its vindication and success, cordially inviting to a full and equal communion all those of whatever creed who recognize the justice of our cause in the doctrines we profess, and who desire to participate in their triumph.

The following nominations were then made :

John Curry, for justice of the supreme court, on the first ballot, over H. O. Beatty.

Isaac N. Dawley, for controller, without opposition; Thomas O'Brien withdrawing.

H. U. Jennings, for clerk of the supreme court, without opposition ; Moses E. Flannagan withdrawing.

Joseph C. McKibben and Wm. L. Dudley, for congressmen, without opposition.

A state committee was chosen, consisting of B. B. Redding, W. S Manlove, G. W. Colby, J. F. Morse, Josiah Johnson, E. McGarry, Edmund Randolph, H. Wohler, W. J. Knox, Geo. Pearce, C. F. Lott, Wm. Higby, Thos. Eager, and others.

The republican convention met in the theater at Sacramento on August 5th, and was called to order by F. P. Tracy, chairman of the state committee. M. Frink, Jr., was temporary chairman; and on permanent organization S. B. Bell was president, and S. H. Parker, L. Stanford, J. McKinstry Smith and E. Harkness, vice-presidents. A committee was appointed on order of business, and when it met it was found that its members were divided as to the policy of making nominations—standing 5 in favor to 3 against. When the report was presented by the majority, A. A. Sargent moved to strike out the portion relative to making nominations. After a lengthy discussion the report was adopted, and the convention determined to make nominations. A committee on resolutions was appointed, consisting of E. D. Baker, T. W. Park, E. B. Crocker, J. E. Benton, A. A. Sargent, F. P. Tracy, A. H. Myers, C. A. Tuttle and D. W. Cheesman. On the 6th, the following resolutions, reported by the committee, were unanimously adopted:

1. That we hereby again declare our adherence to the resolutions adopted by the national republican convention held at Philadelphia in 1856.

2. That we do now, and always have maintained the doctrine of popular sovereignty, when interpreted to mean the people of a territory in forming a state government had a right to·regulate their political institutions in their own way, and to vote for or against any proposed constitution.

3. That this sacred principle, dear to freemen and formidable˜ only to despotism, has been most ruthlessly violated by the present democratic administration in its course upon the Kansas question.

4. That the "English bill," pressed through congress by the administration party, is a flagrant violation of the great principle of popular sovereignty, a bold attempt upon the freedom of the ballot-box, and a most insulting sectional discrimination in favor of slavery in Kansas.

5. (Same as the sixth resolution of the democratic [anti-Lecompton] convention of August 4, 1858.)

6. That the speedy construction of a national railroad, by the most central and eligible route, connecting the Atlantic states with California, is demanded by the military, postal and commercial necessities of the republic; and we recognize the power of congress, under the constitution, to appropriate money as well as land to aid in building this great work. That the people of California will

never consent to the termination of such road at Guaymas, or at any other point on the Gulf of California.

7. That the course of the administration, in relation to the Pacific railroad and other modes of communication between the Atlantic and Pacific states, conclusively demonstrates the insincerity of the administration party, and the existence of a bitter hostility to the interests and welfare of California among its leaders.

The following nominations were made:

John Currey, for justice of the supreme court, on the first ballot, by a vote of 171, to 62 for O. L. Shafter. Currey had already been nominated for the office by the democratic (anti-Lecompton) convention, and Shafter was the candidate of the straight republicans.

L. C. Gunn, for controller, without opposition; L. Stanford and G. W. Baldwin withdrawing.

The following additional resolutions were introduced and adopted:

8. That the conduct of the Hon. D. C. Broderick, senator in congress from California, during the late session of congress is worthy of approval, and evinces a regard for the interests of free labor and free men equally becoming the state which he represents and the station he occupies.

9. That the course of the Hon. J. C. McKibben during the late session of congress has been manly, courageous and just, and that he deserves the highest praise for his opposition to the administration in its attempts to destroy the purity of elections and defeat popular rights.

A resolution was adopted instructing the state committee to place on the ticket the names of F. P. Tracy and J. C. McKibben as candidates for congressmen in case a majority of the committee should deem it advisable to run candidates for those offices; and on August 9th the announcement was formally made by the committee that those gentlemen had been nominated. No nomination was made for clerk of the supreme court. A state committee was selected, consisting of F. B. Higgins, E. B. Crocker, A. A. Sargent, J. T. McLean, C. Cole, Mark Hopkins, P. H. Sibley, S. H. Parker, S. W. Holladay, E. L. Sullivan, L. R. Lull, F. P. Tracy, R. Matheson, Samuel Bell, D. W. Cheesman, G. M. Hanson, and others.

In view of the action of the legislature in changing the time for electing members of congress and clerk of the supreme court, Governor Weller did not include in his election proclamation the selec- • tion of persons to fill those offices, and it was generally understood that the votes that might be cast for candidates to fill those positions would not be considered in the count. The election was held on September 1st; and it was developed by the official canvass that for justice of the supreme court Baldwin had received 44,599 votes and Curry 36,198; for controller, Meloney 44,285, Dawley, 27,759, and Gunn, 7,481 ; for clerk of the supreme court, Jennings 27,221 ; and for congressmen, McKibben 31,833, Dudley 22,910, Tracy 9,293. The votes that were cast for clerk of the supreme court and congressmen were not considered. The Douglas democrats and the republicans had confidently expected the election of Curry, but in the remote counties the anti-Lecompton party had not organized, and in a number of the counties no ticket of that party was in the field. The influence of the federal and state officers was used in favor of the Lecompton ticket. Very curiously, in Butte county a fusion was made between the administration democrats and the republicans, and the former actually voted for the republican candidates for the legislature. Another curiosity developed in the returns from Santa Barbara county, where it appeared that Baldwin had 313 votes, Curry 6, McKibben 287 and Tracy 286.

On September 6th, the Sacramento *Union* said, in referring to the result :

Had the anti-Lecomptons organized a month earlier, they would, judging from the result, have carried the state. They contested the election without having an organization in a goodly number of counties. The leading Douglas men were timid ; they hesitated about acting until it was too late to secure a thorough organization. Ground was thus lost which they could not recover. * * * Had the naked question of Lecompton been presented, without the English bill, we believe it would have been voted down by an overwhelming majority. But the English bill, as President Buchanan hoped, assisted to save the democratic party in one of the free states. In fact, the question has not been fairly met by the administration advocates. They have insisted that the question was settled ; that Douglas had so declared, and that there ought not to be any issue upon Kansas, among democrats. In some portions of the state, the administration democrats were as strong Douglas-popular-sovereignty democrats as their opponents. In this way, the real issue was evaded.

CHAPTER XI.

The anti-Lecompton democrats began early to prepare for the fall campaign, and on February 21st, the leading members of that party held a meeting for consultation at Sacramento. It was there determined to effect a thorough organization in every county before the time for holding the primary elections. The previous year the party had not been organized in some fourteen counties, and that fact was regarded as an important factor which had tended to its defeat. On the 26th, another meeting was held, at which it was resolved that there should be no affiliation with the Lecompton democracy. Gwin, Broderick, McKibben, and Denver arrived in San Francisco from the east, on April 17th, and almost immediately the political pot began to boil energetically. McKibben spoke in San Francisco, on May 11th, and took a firm stand against the Buchanan administration, and in favor of the position which had been assumed by Douglas. During the same month, anti-Lecompton mass meetings were held elsewhere in the state, and the party succeeded in carrying the municipal elections at Marysville, Stockton, Santa Cruz, and Nevada, and in consequence, confidence was felt in their ability to carry the state in the fall.

The republicans were almost without hope, but they felt that it was necessary to keep up their party rganization in view of the presidential election in 1860. They spurned the advice of the independent press to unite their fortunes with the anti-Lecompton democracy and to make the administration party the common foe. In May, the candidates for the Lecompton nomination for governor commenced the usual tour to the principal points in the state with a view of shaping the election of delegates to the state convention. Governor Weller was a candidate for re-nomination, and his principal opponents were Latham, Nugent, and Denver. The governor evidently suspected that the political convention workers were against him, for on May 13th, he issued a lengthy appeal to the democratic masses to insist on expressing themselves at the primaries directly on the gubernatorial question, and not to suffer him to be sacrificed by the politicians. The administration party organs charged that the anti-Lecompton party had its inception through the influence of Senator Broderick, and that he instigated its every movement; and the anti-Lecompton press retorted by assigning to Senator Gwin, the dictatorship of the Lecompton wing.

In its issue of April 23d, the Sacramento *Union* said, when reviewing the political situation of the state:

The policy which governed the anti-Lecompton central committee in setting the time for the meeting of their state convention a week before the Lecompton convention was probably to take the initiative, and present the issues which the popular sovereignty wing of the party intend to maintain in the canvass. Both sides appear to be sanguine of success. The Lecompton wing relies greatly upon its position and prestige; the anti-Lecompton upon the strength of their cause with the people. The former have the state and national administrations with them; the latter must rely upon the principles they advocate, the qualities of the men they nominate, and the esthusiastic feelings of the masses in favor of popular sovereignty and non-intervention. An exciting canvass is in prospect. The anti-Lecompton Douglas democrats manifest a deep interest in coming events, and a strong confidence in the popularity of the platform they stand upon. As an evidence of the zeal and promptness of its members where party duty is to be performed, we refer to the fact that only two of the central committee were absent when the roll was called.

The republican state convention met in the Congregational church, Sacramento, on June 8th, with about 150 delegates present. It was called to order by F. P. Tracy, chairman of the state committee, and Ira P. Rankin was elected temporary chairman. The body organized by electing O. A. Tuttle, president; and E. D. Harkness, Guillermo Castro, M. Frink, Jr., A. W. Blair, D. J. Staples, Samuel Soule, Thos. Fallon, A. W. Rawson, and D. W. Cheesman, vice-presidents. A motion was made to adjourn until the 21st, and to then proceed to endorse the anti-Lecompton nominees. The motion aroused a warm discussion. The straight-out republicans were in favor of nominating a square party ticket, while others rather favored the policy of uniting the opposition vote in the state upon one ticket. F. M. Pixley led off for the "straights," and E. D. Baker championed the liberal wing. The motion to adjourn was lost. A committee on resolutions was appointed, consisting of A. W. Blair, E. D. Baker, Samuel Bell, M. Frink, Jr., C. Cole, D. J. Staples, J. F.

Kennedy, D. W. Cheesman, P. H. Sibley, G. A. Grant, J. T. Mc-Lean, G. M. Hanson, A. A. Sargent, and others.

They· reported the following resolutions, which were unanimously adopted :

1. That the republican party of Californa are now, as formerly, unalterably opposed to the introduction of slavery into the territories now free, and will use all just and constitutional means to prevent it.

2. That we repudiate the modern dogma that slavery exists in all the territories of the United States by force of the constitution, and view it as the entering wedge for the enslavement of the free states.

3. That the intervention of congress for the extension and protection of slavery in the territories, recently announced in congress by leading democrats as a cardinal element of democratic faith and practice, is an alarming evidence of the advance in the demands of the slave power, and a gross infraction of popular rights.

4. That the corruptions and errors of the national administration demand the sternest rebuke which can be administered by a free people.

5. That the welfare of the whole country, and particularly the welfare and political influence of California, depend upon cheap and easy communication between the Atlantic and Pacific states; and while patriotism and philanthropy, no less than interest, conspire to impel the national republican party to facilitate such communication, the interest of the "democratic" party lies in a different direction, and its entire energies are devoted to other and sectional measures; and it is, therefore, the deliberate opinion of this convention that the dependence of the country for a Pacific railroad is upon the republican party, and in no sense upon their opponents.

6. That California demands for the central mail route from St. Joseph, via Pike's Peak, Salt Lake and Carson Valley, to Placerville, the same protection and encouragement as is extended by government to the southern, or Butterfield mail route.

7. That we approve of the homestead bill, giving a home, free of cost, to every landless man who will occupy and improve it; and also favor Grow's land bill, providing by law that none of the public lands shall be sold, except to actual settlers, until the plots of the surveys of these lands shall have been in the land office ten years from the time of the survey.

8. That we are opposed to any unjust discrimination against naturalizing citizens, which shall require any length of residence after naturalization before they can vote.

The following nominations were made

Leland Stanford, for governor, without opposition; E. D. Baker, D. R. Ashley, T. G. Phelps, Samuel Bell, and F. M. Pixley withdrawing.

James F. Kennedy, for lieutenant-governor, without opposition; D. W. Cheesman, F. M. Pixley, C. A. Tuttle, L. Cunningham, J. T. McLean, A. M. Crane, C. Watrous, and James Patterson withdrawing.

O. L. Shafter, for justice of the supreme court, on the first ballot, over F. M. Haight.

S. D. Parker, for clerk of the supreme court, without opposition; Cornelius Cole withdrawing.

P. P. Caine, for treasurer, without opposition; M. Frink, Jr., C. T. H. Palmer, and Charles Crocker withdrawing.

J. R. Clark, for controller, on the first ballot, over P. H. Sibley, A. M. Blair, J. N. Turner, G. C. Haven, R. N. Mattheson, and B. T. Bachman.

A. W. Randall, for surveyor-general, without opposition; C. T. Thomas withdrawing.

S. W. Brown, for superintendent of public instruction, on the first ballot, over T. J. Nevins, W. Sherman, Jacob Moore, and N. Slater.

F. B. Murdock, for printer, without opposition; C. A. Washburn, J. Hancock, W. B. Ewer, L. R. Lull, and H. Arms withdrawing.

H. S. Love, for attorney-general, by acclamation; R. A. Jones, C. J. Hillyer, J. McM. Shafter, and A. A. Sargent withdrawing.

P. H. Sibley, for congressman (northern district), without opposition; D. W. Cheesman, A. A. Sargent, J. C. McKibben, H. Cummings, and Charles A. Tuttle withdrawing.

E. D. Baker, for congressman (southern district), on the first ballot, over F. M. Pixley, A. W. Blair, F. P. Tracy, Ira P. Rankin, J. A. Nunes, Thomas Fallon, C. P. Hester, and A. M. Crane.

On the 9th a state committee was appointed, consisting of H. H. Haight, C. Watrous, J. G. Stebbins, E. B. Crocker, A. B. Nixon, J. T. McLean, L. Cunningham, Samuel Bell, A. M. Crane, R. N. Mattheson, F. B. Higgins, A. A. Sargent, D. W. Cheesman, and others. Thirty-two counties were represented in the convention.

The anti-Lecompton state committee met on April 21st, and called a state convention, to consist of 240 delegates, to meet on June 15th. On the day last named, the convention met in the Congregational church, Sacramento, and delegates were present from all but six of the counties. The body was called to order by B. B. Redding, chairman of the state committee, and H. Fitzsimmons was chosen temporary chairman. A committee on resolutions was appointed, consisting of H. W. Carpentier, James Denman, Wilson Flint, George Pearce, S. W. Raveley, C. H. Bryan, James Johnson, Alex. Campbell, H. T. Huggins, John Caldwell, and others. On the 16th, the convention permanently organized, with Joseph W. McCorkle as president; and J. B. Frisbie, A. G. Gould, D. H. Hanrahan, I. N. Underwood, and O. L. Bridges, as vice-presidents.

The following resolutions were reported by the committee :

1. That we reaffirm the principles set forth in the Cincinnati platform, and recognize it as an authoritative exposition of the democratic creed.

2. That in order to preserve the peace and harmony of the union, and prevent the frequent recurrence of sectional agitation, it is essential that the people of the territories should be allowed to legislate or omit to legislate upon the subject of slavery, as well as upon other matters of domestic policy, according to their own will, without any interference, direct or indirect, on the part of either congress or the executive.

3. That the administration of James Buchanan, by its outrages upon the rights of the people of Kansas ; its unrelenting proscription of tried and worthy democrats for the offense of adhering to democratic principles ; its constant violation of the pledges which brought it into life ; its attempts to render the legislative subject to the executive department, and its gross extravagance, mismanagement, and corruption, has forfeited the respect and lost the confidence of the American people.

4. That the immediate construction of the Pacific railroad ought to be encouraged by the federal and state governments by all means in their power, and that, meanwhile, the mail service by the overland routes should be sustained and increased.

5. That our state judiciary system needs a thorough and complete revision, and that the constitution should be so changed as to increase the number of judges of the supreme court, and insure a speedy, honest, and faithful administration of justice.

6. That, in the opinion of this convention, congress should enact a law to protect actual *bona fide* settlers upon the public lands in their just rights.

7. That we, as a convention representing the true democracy of

California, adhere with unfaltering firmness to the principles of democracy, as taught by Thomas Jefferson, and which guided the councils of the immortal Jackson.

8. That, when this convention adjourn, its members adjourn to meet, as citizens, at the polls in the ides of September, and that by our labors and our voices they will show to the world that the free-men of California are unbought by federal patronage, are unawed by federal power, and will stand by the sacred principles of democracy, in defiance of treacherous presidents and their cabinets.

On motion of John Conness, the resolutions as reported were adopted.

The following resolution was then offered, and it was laid on the table, by a large majority:

9. That freedom, as the natural or normal condition of the human race, is a proposition lying at the foundation of our free system of government, and that maintaining, as we do, the natural freedom of man, we hold it to be a fundamental truth that his natural condition can only be changed by local law and as punishment for crime whereof he shall first have been duly convicted; holding, as we do, firmly and unalterably, to these fundamental truths, we, therefore, repudiate the dicta of the supreme court in the Dred Scott case, which dicta has become the platform of Lecompton democracy.

The following preamble and resolutions were then offered, and after a lengthy discussion were withdrawn:

10. WHEREAS, The rights of man have been invaded, and popular sovereignty entirely set at naught by the action of the general government of the United States, at Washington city—particularly and especially in regard to its action on the Kansas question, as well as in other matters pertaining to the welfare of the people and the perpetuity of the union—of that union which has been, and still is, looked to as an asylum for the oppressed of the whole earth—and that we believe this government, instead of being progressive as its founders intended it to be, is retrograding, and tending towards anarchy; and, whereas, the action of the last legislature of this state, by the passage of certain resolutions in regard to D. C. Broderick, indorses the opinions set forth in the above first preamble; that said resolutions were passed by a factions spirit, and in opposition to a large majority of the people of this state, and should by all means be expunged from the journals of the said legislature, for the following reasons: First—That he had advocated in the senate the

rights of man to its fullest and original intent. Second—That he has honestly and fearlessly labored to retrench the expenses of the government. Third—That he has, in all cases, in the senate, endeavored to suppress fraud and fraudulent contracts, and particularly so in regard to the Lime Point swindle ; *therefore, resolved:*

1. That we use our best exertions to have the resolutions referred to in the second preamble expunged from the journals of the legislature of this state.

2. That all power is vested in, and consequently derived from the people ; that magistrates are their trustees and servants, and at all times amenable to them.

3. That government is, or ought to be, instituted for the common benefit of the whole people, and that government is the best which produces the greatest degree of happiness, and is the best protected against maladministration.

4. That the freedom of the press is one of the great bulwarks of liberty, and can never be restrained but by despotic governments.

5. That the people have a right to uniform government.

6. That no free government or the blessings of liberty can be preserved to any people but by a firm adherence to justice, moderation, temperance, frugality, and virtue.

7. That religion can be directed only by reason and conviction— not by force or violence ; and that it is the duty of all to practice christian forbearance, love, and charity towards each other.

The following nominations were then made :

John Curry, for governor, on the first ballot, receiving 139 votes, to 69 for Humphrey Griffith ; Alfred Redington, D. R. Ashley, and J. W. McCorkle withdrawing.

John Conness, for lieutenant-governor, on the first ballot, over Richard Irwin.

Jos. C. McKibben, for congressman (northern district), without opposition.

S. A. Booker, for congressman (southern district), on the first ballot, over Jas. W. Coffroth.

Royal T. Sprague, for justice of the supreme court, without opposition.

Jos. Powell, for clerk of the supreme court, on the second ballot, over M. D. Boruck, H. U. Jennings, and A. R. Baldwin.

D. R. Ashley, for treasurer, without opposition ; D. K. Porter withdrawing.

Geo. Pearce, for controller, without opposition.

E. K. Steele, for attorney-general, without opposition.

James O'Meara, for printer, on the second ballot, over John R. Ridge.

On the 17th, the following additional nominations were made :

Jas. S. Long, for surveyor-general, on the first ballot, over W. S. Watson and Sherman Day.

A. H. Myers, for superintendent of public instruction, without opposition ; A. R. Jackson and J. C. Pelton withdrawing.

The words "be allowed to" were stricken from the second resolution of the series adopted, and the following additional resolutions were adopted :

11. That the right of the people of the territories to form all their domestic institutions in their own way is absolute and complete, and that we are unalterably opposed to any interference with such right, either by the legislative or executive department of the general government.

12. That the doctrine of "intervention" by congress to establish a slave code for the territories, assumed by the administration adherents, is a gross departure from the principles of the true democracy, as laid down in the platform made at Cincinnati, and we repudiate it as the heresy of a faction, and condemn it as an outrage upon the great charter of American liberty.

13. That the chief executive of the nation has broken his pledges to the people of California in regard to the Pacific railroad, which pledges were announced in his ill-timed letter of 1856, two weeks previous to the election in this state, and that we condemn the administration for its refusal to place the central overland mail on the same footing, as to compensation, etc., as the southern route.

A state committee was selected, consisting of J. Middleton, Wilson Flint, A. Redington, H. U. Jennings, Edward McGarry, C. E. De-Long, Wm. H. Lyons, L. B. Arnold, and others. On June 21st, D. R. Ashley, the nominee for treasurer, declined ; and on the 24th, Elijah K. Steele, the nominee for attorney-general, also withdrew. On July 7th, the state committee nominated Edmund Randolph, for attorney-general, and J. W. Jewett for treasurer. Jewett declined to be a candidate, and on the following day the committee nominated Josiah Johnson for the office.

The Lecompton democratic state convention met in the Congregational church, Sacramento, on June 22d, and was composed of

269 delegates. Every county, except Fresno, was represented. The body was called to order by J. P. Hoge, chairman of the state committee, and R. P. Hammond was chosen temporary chairman. A great deal of time was consumed in deciding contests for seats. On the 23d, a permanent organization was effected by electing Hammond, president; and Jasper O'Farrell, Chas. R. Street, W. R. Garrison, W. C. Stratton, and F. M. Smith, vice-presidents.

The following nominations were then made:

Milton S. Latham, for governor, on the second ballot, receiving 136 votes, to 104 for John B. Weller, and 29 for John Nugent; A. P. Dudley and James W. Denver withdrawing. First ballot—Weller, 111; Nugent, 29; Latham, 129.

John G. Downey, for lieutenant-governor, without opposition; James A. Johnson withdrawing.

On the 24th, a committee on resolutions was appointed, consisting of C. T. Ryland, J. P. Hoge, O. C. Hall, A. French, L. R. Bradley, H. P. Barber, C. J. Lansing, W. S. Long, D. P. Durst, W. S. Wells, P. H. Harris, R. M. Anderson, Chas. Lindley, C. R. Street, Myron Norton, and W. C. Stratton.

The following additional nominations were made:

John C. Burch, for congressman (northern district), on the first ballot, over Vincent E. Geiger, N. E. Whiteside, Z. Montgomery, and Henry Meredith.

Chas. L. Scott, for congressman (southern district), on the first ballot, over Samuel A. Merritt, Wm. Van Voorhies, E. W. McKinstry, and Calhoun Benham.

W. W. Cope, for justice of the supreme court, on the first ballot, over Lewis Aldrich and David S. Terry.

Thos. H. Williams, for attorney-general, on the first ballot, over R. Aug. Thompson.

Chas. S. Fairfax, for clerk of the supreme court, on the first ballot, over W. J. Hooten, John S. Robberson, and Wm. A. Johnson.

Thos. Findley, for treasurer, on the first ballot, over R. P. Ashe and C. Reese.

Samuel H. Brooks, for controller, on the first ballot, over P. A. McRae, A. R. Meloney, Archibald McNeill, and J. M. Haven.

Horace A. Higley, for surveyor-general, on the first ballot, over William Holden.

Andrew J. Moulder, for school superintendent, without opposition; W. C. Stratton withdrawing.

Chas. T. Botts, for printer, on the first ballot, over H. C. Patrick and L. Magruder.

The following resolutions, reported by the committee, were unanimously adopted:

1. That the democracy of California, in convention assembled, again reiterate their firm determination to stand by, and maintain in all their integrity, the wise, just and liberal principles enunciated in the Cincinnati platform, by the democratic party of the union.

2. That the organized territories of the United States, although not endowed with *all* the attributes of sovereignty, are yet justly entitled to the rights of self-government, and the undisturbed regulation of their domestic and local affairs, subject to the constitution of the United States; and that any attempt by congress, or any of the states, to establish or maintain, prohibit or abolish the relation of master and slave in a territory, would be a departure from the original doctrines of our American institutions; and that we adhere immovably to the principle of "non-intervention" by congress, with slavery in the states and territories, as declared in the "Kansas-Nebraska bill," and openly disclaim fellowship with those, whether at the south, the north, or the west, who counsel the abandonment, limitation, or avoidance of that principle.

3. That the vigor and efficiency of the present democratic administration, manifested in the adjustment of our difficulties with Great Britain, in regard to the right of search; in the prompt and successful redress of wrongs inflicted upon us by the government of Paraguay; the decisive suppression of the rebellion in Utah; in the enforcement of the neutrality laws; in the impartial execution of the acts of congress for the suppression of the African slave trade, and for the rendition of fugitive slaves, commands our cordial approbation, and we have full confidence in its ability and inclination to protect the rights of our citizens and uphold the honor of our flag.

4. That the republican party of Massachusetts have, by incorporating in their constitution a provision requiring of the naturalized citizens a residence of two years after naturalization, in order to enjoy the right of suffrage, or the privilege of holding office; and yet, at the same time, allowing those privileges even to the fugitive slaves upon a residence of one year, attempted to degrade the foreign white man below the level of the negro and the mulatto, and that we, the democracy of California, utterly repudiate such infamous doctrine.

5. That the persistent effort to fix upon the national democracy

the stigma of a design to legislate through congress a "*slave code*" for the territories, is but a desperate trick of unprincipled and ren-egade politicians to divert popular attention from their own base and disorganizing purposes.

6. That we deem the speedy construction of the Pacific railroad a national necessity, and again earnestly urge upon congress and the states their duty of co-operation for that purpose.

7. That it is the duty of the general government to stand by and sustain the overland mails, so successfully put in operation by a democratic administration.

8. That the democracy of California again tender to the administration of James Buchanan our renewed pledge of support in maintaining the honor and integrity of the union, at home and abroad.

9. That we again extend to the present democratic administration of this state our most cordial and unqualified approval.

On the 25th a state committee was appointed, consisting of W. S. Long, Frank Powell, Myron Norton, C. T. Ryland, R. P. Hammond, B. F. Langford, W. J. Hooten, J. P. Hoge, E. Casserly, Thomas Hayes, Calhoun Benham, D. W. Gelwicks, S. A. Merritt, A. T. Laird, I. N. Quinn, W. Van Voorhies, W. H. Parks, W. C. Stratton, J. A. Watson, A. H. Rose, Charles Lindley, B. E. S. Ely, and others. On motion the word "maintain" was stricken from the second resolution. The following preamble and resolution, offered by Horace Smith, was laid on the table, by a vote of 163 to 95:

10. WHEREAS, It is the sense of this convention that the organic law of this state is defective, and needs a thorough remodeling; and whereas, it is the opinion of this convention that the democracy of California are in favor of calling a constitutional convention; therefore, *resolved*, that we recommend to the various county committees throughout the state to order and cause to be printed upon the tickets to be voted at the coming election the words "for a constitutional convention."

The following resolution was also adopted:

11. That it is the duty of every branch of our state government to enforce and practice the most rigid economy in conducting our public affairs, and that no more revenue shall be raised than is actually required to defray the expenses of the state government and provide for the gradual extinguishment of the state debt.

It was soon apparent that the opposition to the administration party would be defeated at the election unless a union of their forces could be effected, and a strong effort was made to have the republican party—the weaker organization—withdraw its ticket and join hands with the anti-Lecompton faction. On July 30th Horace Greeley arrived at Placerville, by the overland route from the east, and there and elsewhere in the state he met with an enthusiastic reception by the opponents to the administration. He delivered several political speeches, and on August 20th addressed a letter to the republicans of the state advising them to unite with the anti-Lecomptons on a joint ticket. On August 10th a letter was addressed to Stanford, inquiring if it was his purpose to withdraw from the canvass on the eve of the election in favor of Currey—as it had been rumored. Stanford replied on the 13th that he would not withdraw, but that his party would maintain an unbroken front throughout the campaign. On the 22d Frank M. Pixley issued a novel three column address, denouncing both Gwin and Broderick severely, and urging the republicans to stand together by their ticket. The republican committee on the 29th issued the following address to the members of that party:

The rumors which have been afloat for the past few days relative to a union upon the congressional ticket between the republican and the anti-Lecompton parties, make it proper and necessary for the republican state central committee to state that no such arrangement will be made, as the leaders of the anti-Lecompton party, after making the first advances for this purpose, and after a favorable response on our part to their proposition, have failed to come to any understanding with us upon the subject. It is, therefore, the duty of all republicans to use every effort for the election of the whole republican ticket.

The candidates in a measure effected the end which the committees could not attain, but at so late a day in the canvass as to help matters very little, if any. On August 24th, F. B. Murdock, the republican nominee for printer, published a card of withdrawal, and asked his friends to support O'Meara. On September 1st, the republican committee accepted the resignation, and made no nomination to fill the vacancy on the ticket. P. H. Sibley, the republican candidate for congress, withdrew on September 2d in favor of Baker and McKibben; and on the 3d, Samuel A. Booker, the anti-Lecompton candidate for the same office, followed Sibley's example. About the same time, S. W. Brown, the republican candidate for school superintendent, declined the nomination. On August 31st, the state committee of the settlers' party issued an address, in which they said that they deemed it unnecessary to call a state convention of that party when such men as Curr*y, Sprague, Randolph, Baker, McKibben, and O'Meara had been nominated by the regular parties. Curr*y published a letter to Latham on June 29th, inviting him to canvass the state with him, and to speak from the same platform. The proposition was accepted by Latham on July 1st, and both gentlemen lived up to the agreement during the entire campaign. The campaign of 1859 was the most exciting and remarkable in the history of California. The interest centered upon Senators Gwin and Broderick, who spoke in favor of the Lecompton and anti-Lecompton tickets, respectively. Their speeches were intensely personal, and in them was given the inside history of the famous Broderick-Gwin fight for the United States senatorship. When it was announced that Broderick intended to make a stumping tour through the state, his opponents raised a shout of derision. For many years they had represented him as a man of low instincts, immoral habits, and ungovernable temper, and it was their pleasure to describe the sorry appearance he would make before the people as a public speaker. It was asserted as above dispute that he was entirely incapable of composing and delivering a sentence which should possess any of the qualities of directness, perspicuity, or grammatical accuracy, and it was prophesied that his first effort at stumping would be a sad failure; and even some of his best friends caught the infection of the oft-rehearsed disparagement, and trembled for his success. His first speech, however, covered his enemies with chagrin and disappointment and elated his friends with confidence and hope, and his subsequent efforts but confirmed him as a speaker of ability. Broderick delivered his first speech at Placerville, on July 9th.

The election was held on September 7th, and it developed upon the official canvass of the returns, that

For Governor—Latham had received 62,255 votes; Curr*y 31,-298, Stanford 10,110.

Lieutenant-Governor—Downey 59,051; Conness 31,051; Kennedy 11,148.

Congressmen—Scott 56,998 ; Burch 57,665 ; McKibben 43,474 ; Booker 2,969; Baker 41,438 ; Sibley 301.

Justice of the Supreme Court—Cope 59,357 ; Sprague 30,978 ; Shafter 11,799.

Treasurer—Findley 62,889 ; Johnson 28,889 ; Caine 10,290.

Controller—Brooks 59,712 ; Pearce 31,238 ; Clark 10,855.

Attorney-General—Williams 59,292 ; Randolph 33,166 ; Love 9,-403.

Surveyor-General—Higley 60,127; Long 31,073; Randall 10,676.

Superintendent of Public Instruction—Moulder 60,787 ; Myers 32,033 ; Brown 9,431.

Printer—Botts 57,381 ; O'Meara 44,048 ; Murdock 494.

Supreme Court Clerk—Fairfax 60,179 ; Powell 31,179 ; Parker 10,104.

Constitutional Convention—For, 46,129 ; against 10,060.

New Territory—For 1,202 ; against 2,156.

The entire Lecompton ticket was consequently elected.

CHAPTER XII.

1860. Presidential Campaign — Republican Convention, February 22d—Efforts to Combine the Democracy—Democratic Convention, February 29th—The Breach of 1858 in the Democratic Party made Wider—Republican Convention, June 29th—Meetings of the Democratic State Convention—Convention of the Douglas Democrats, September 5th—Convention of the Breckinridge Democrats, September 11th—Convention of the Union Party—Result of the Election —Secession of the Southern States—Efforts to Set Up a Pacific Republic.

On January 21st, the republican state committee met at San Francisco, and called a state convention to meet at Sacramento, on February 22d, to select delegates to attend the national convention which was to meet at Chicago, on June 15th, to nominate a presidential ticket. The convention assembled at the appointed time, and was called to order by H. H. Haight, chairman of the state committee. P. H. Sibley was temporary chairman, and on permanent organization, Samuel H. Parker was president; and J. F. Chellis, T. G. Phelps, J. T. McLean, W. W. Belshaw, and G. W. Towle, vice-presidents. The following were nominated for delegates to the national convention : F. P. Tracy, Leland Stanford, Samuel Bell, A. A. Sargent, Chas. A. Sumner, D. J. Staples, S. F. Johnson, D. W. Cheesman, Chas. Watrous, R. N. Mattheson, J. C. Hinckley, Isaac M. Baldwin, J. A. Nunes, J. C. Wycker, F. C. Haven, W. H. Pratt, B. M. Hance, Chas. A. Tuttle, Geo. M. Hanson, P. Whit-beck, Chas. McDonald, and Geo. Stacey.   Tracy, Stanford, Sargent, Cheesman, and Staples were elected.   Hinckley, Baldwin, John B. Yan, Francis Snyder, and James Churchman were elected alternates. The convention adopted no resolutions.

Early in 1860, a movement was inaugurated to bring together the two wings of the democratic party in view of the presidential election, but the anti-Lecompton faction preferred, before consummating the union, to await the result of the national convention.   Douglas was the presidential candidate of the northern democrats, but to the Lecompton wing, he was about as obnoxious as any republican nominee could be, and many of the southern democrats openly announced that in the event of his nomination they would not support him.   An air of trouble surrounded the democratic camp, and the apparent disinterestedness of the northern democracy was but as the lull before a great storm.   On January 18th, the two democratic state committees met separately at Sacramento, and the Lecompton wing called a democratic state convention of 359 members, to select delegates, and to meet on February 29th, at Sacramento.

The anti-Lecompton committee adopted the following resolutions and adjourned:

1. That the recent re-enunciation of James Buchanan of his federal heresies demands from us that we should renew our adherence to our old principles, believing, as we do, that upon those principles only can our government be safely conducted, and the union of the states preserved.

2. That we reaffirm the Cincinnati platform and the great principles contained therein; and that we declare our unalterable adherence to the great doctrines of popular sovereignty, as understood and expounded in 1856.

3. That we deem it inexpedient to recommend the election of delegates to the Charleston convention, but that it is of the greatest importance to cherish the principles of our party, and we desire our friends in the different counties to sustain them at all times and under all circumstances, as their wisdom may best suggest.

Soon afterward, the county conventions were held, and the anti-Lecompton democrats generally participated in the primaries, but the majority of the conventions returned Lecompton delegates to the state convention.   The generally expressed preference for the presidential nominee was in favor of Daniel S. Dickinson, J. C. Breckinridge, or Joseph Lane.

The democratic state convention to select delegates to attend the national convention to meet at Charleston on April 23d, met in the Fourth-street Baptist church, Sacramento, on February 29, 1860. The majority of the delegates had arrived in the city as early as the morning of the 28th, and the legislature adjourned over for a day to allow its members to attend the convention. The church was filled with delegates and spectators the instant the doors were opened, and it was found that sufficient room was not afforded in the building. Immediately after the body was called to order by J. P. Hoge, the chairman of the state committee, an adjournment was had to the Forrest theater, but that building also was not sufficiently commodious, and at 4 o'clock another removal was made to the Congregational church. During the day there was a stormy session, and in the evening a partial compromise was effected by choosing Philip Moore for temporary chairman, by a vote of 180 to 176 for N. Kilpatrick. Immediately afterward Moore was elected permanent president. On March 1st, Wm. Glaskin, John Bidwell, J. C. Hunsaker, John P. Haynes, S. G. Whipple, W. Neely Johnson, B. F. Mauldin, Peter Donahue, Thos. W. Lane, Walter Murray, C. W. Tozer, Thos. Baker, John P. Jones, C. F. Reed, and others were elected vice-presidents ; and a committee on resolutions was appointed, consisting of William Van Voorhies, P. H. Harris, John Boggs, D. E. Buel, D. J. Johnson, J. T. Ryan, Andres Pico, S. A. Merritt, T. J. Henley, B. E. S. Ely, W. W. Caperton, J. W. Coffroth, S. A. Sharp, Thos. Laspeyre, D. W. Connelly, E. Garter, H. I. Thornton, Jr., J. Temple, V. E. Geiger, I. N. Quinn, H. Griffith, and others. The committee reported the following resolutions :

1. That the democracy of California most unhesitatingly declare their adherence to the principles laid down in the Cincinnati platform of 1856, believing that those principles can alone secure the prosperity and perpetuity of our glorious Union.

2. That we recognize the decision of the supreme court of the United States in what is known as the Dred Scott case, to be the true construction of the law of the land ; that the courts are invested with ample powers, under the laws and constitution of the United States, for the protection of the person and property of the citizen ; and that any intervention of federal power in controlling the policy of the territories is highly impolitic and subversive of the fundamental principles of self-government, except in cases of unlawful resistance to the laws and the mandates of the courts.

✗ 3. That we most earnestly recommend the immediate passage by Congress of a Pacific railroad and telegraph bill, regarding the construction of such a road and telegraph to be the only method by which the federal government can extend to the state of California that protection in time of war which is guaranteed by the federal compact to each state.

4. That we regard it a matter of the first importance to California that the overland mail lines should be fostered by the government, and that we urge upon our senators and representatives in congress the necessity of using all honorable means to that end.

5. That we approve and endorse the administration of James Buchanan, and commend it entirely.

6. That we approve of the policy of the present and the preceding state administrations.

7. That Daniel S. Dickinson is the first choice of the democracy of California for the next President of the United States.

The following additional resolution was offered by B. F. Mauldin, and laid on the table:

8. That we, the people democratic, while we deprecate all efforts at disunion, are prepared to maintain the independence of California.

The seventh resolution provoked considerable discussion, and the following was offered as a substitute for it:

That this convention, having an abiding faith in the democracy and integrity of those delegates who shall be elected to represent California in the national democratic convention, to convene at Charleston, emphatically refuse to trammel them with instructions for any man for the offices of president and vice-president of the United States.

The substitute was lost by a vote of 21 to 317, and the platform as reported by the committee was adopted. The following were placed in nomination for delegates to the national convention: Wm. G. Easton, Austin E. Smith, G. W. Patrick, Jas. D. Terrill, D. S. Gregory, Jas. E. Torrey, Newell Gregory, John S. Dudley, L. R. Bradley, John Raines, Charles M. Creaner, John A. Driebelbiss, John H. Seawall, H. P. Haun, Myron Norton, J. W. Osborn, John Bidwell, T. J. Henley, Volney E. Howard, and John F. McCauley. On the first ballot Patrick, Dudley, Bradley, Newell Gregory, Bidwell, Driebelbiss, Smith and Raines were elected. The following resolution was offered by V. E. Geiger, and laid on the table by a vote of 282 to 65:

That Stephen A. Douglas is the last choice of the democracy of California for president of the United States.

The news of the split in the democratic national convention, and of the nominations of Breckinridge and Douglas for president, was received in California on July 15th. It produced the greatest excitement. The northern democrats generally went to the support of Douglas, claiming that he was the regular presidential nominee of the party, and they set about immediately with enthusiasm to organize for the purpose of conducting the campaign. The southern democrats, who supported Breckinridge, did not claim for him the regular nomination, but they urged that as neither of the candidates had received a two-thirds vote of all the delegates who had been elected to attend the national convention, the party was without a regular nominee, and therefore its members could support either candidate with propriety. Governor Downey immediately declared himself for Douglas, and ex-Governor Weller took stand for Breckinridge. Twenty-six of the members of the democratic state committee were Breckinridge men, and ten were for Douglas; and of the democratic newspapers in the state twenty-four were for Douglas and twenty-two for Breckinridge. The federal office holders supported Breckinridge almost to a man. During July democratic clubs were organized throughout the state. The Douglas clubs resolved to repudiate the action of the national delegates from the state who had supported Breckinridge, and to support Douglas at the election. The Breckinridge clubs declared in their resolutions that the platform upon which their leader stood embodied principles which they cherished, and which for years had been endorsed by the regular democratic conventions of California. On July 25th, it was announced in the dispatches that Senators Gwin and Latham had determined to support Breckinridge. A lengthy address to the democracy was published in the San Francisco *Herald* on July 27th. It was signed by sixty-five persons—twenty-two of whom were federal officers, and eight or nine were interested in governmental contracts. Among the signers were O. L. Weller, J. P. Haven, R. Aug. Thompson, R. R. Provines, A. C. Peachy, Jas. H. Wade, Frank Tilford, J. R. Snyder, S. Heydenfeldt, B. F. Washington, C. J. Brenham, J. W. Mandeville, V. E. Howard, R. P. Ashe, O. C. Pratt, J. H. Wise, Hall McAllister, O. C. Hall, J. B. Haggin, Lloyd Tevis, D. W. Perley, and J. D. Thornton. The address defended the action of

8

the seceding branch of the national convention and ended by saying :

In the absence, then, of any candidate who can properly claim to be the nominee of the democracy of the whole union, no alternative is left but for the democratic party of each state to determine for itself which of the two tickets presented most truly represents the views and opinions of the party, and which would be most likely to carry out and perpetuate its long-cherished principles. * * * It is scarcely necessary to add that we shall give our cordial and earnest support to Breckinridge and Lane; and in doing so we feel that we are standing upon the ancient principles of our party, and maintaining the consistency of our former political action.

On July 28th, a large Breckinridge ratification meeting was held in San Francisco, at which addresses were delivered by R. Aug. Thompson, V. E. Howard, J. B. Weller, Calhoun Benham, and Frank Tilford. Resolutions were adopted endorsing the nomination of Breckinridge and Lane, and the platform upon which they had been nominated. It was also resolved:

That the attempt to fasten upon the national democracy the purpose of enacting a slave code for the territories is but a trick of designing demagogues to divert the attention of the people from their own departure from national principle.

That Stephen A. Douglas, in ignoring the decision of the supreme court, by which he was pledged to abide, has not only proved false to his promises, but by his consistent advocacy of the doctrine of a law higher than the constitution as interpreted by that august tribunal, has caused the unhappy divisions which now distract the democratic party.

That a faithful adherence to the principles enunciated and decided by the supreme court in the Dred Scott case, is essential to the peace and harmony of the union, and we hereby accept them as a final solution and adjustment of the vexed question of slavery in the territories.

Another address to the democracy was published in the San Francisco *Herald* on July 31st, to which 150 names were signed, including those of John G. Downey, J. P. Hoge, J. Mora Moss, W. M. Lent, John Parrott, R. P. Hammond, James T. Ryan, H. W. Halleck, J. A. McDougall, W. S. Long, James Denman, Frederick Billings, E. Casserly, A. Hayward, S. M. Wilson, S. A. Sharp, L. B.

Mizner, J. J. Papy, R. H. Lloyd, L. McLane, H. A. Cobb, A. J. Bryant, Elisha Cook, E. D. Sawyer, T. N. Cazneau, D. J. Oliver, P. B. Cornwall, O. T. Ryland, M. Norton, T. W. Freelon, R. H. Sinton, Samuel Purdy, E. B. Mastick, and others. The address was in response to the Breckinridge document, and stated, among other things :

There is disunion at the bottom of the Charleston and Baltimore secession movement. The dissolution of this government is the ultimate object proposed by the great champion and leaders of this faction. To this the true men of the south and the north, the east and west will object. They will not only object—they will resist. They will do more than this—they will overwhelm the disunionists. The movement is yet in its infancy ; let it be crushed before it obtains a larger and more vigorous growth. We call upon the democracy everywhere, and upon all true, union-loving patriots, to join us in giving them one effective and final blow, by placing at the head of this nation the true representative of the national and union-loving democracy. In November next our country will expect every man to do his duty by sustaining and voting for Douglas and Johnson, as the only regular candidates of the national democratic party. Let no man shrink from its performance.

On August 4th, James W. Denver published a lengthy letter, defining his political position. He declared for Douglas, and took the ground that California was not interested in the territorial controversy. He characterized the Breckinridge wing as a disunion faction that was striving to divide the democratic party, and finally to dissolve the union. Senator Latham, on August 16th, published a lengthy address to his party. After lamenting on the differences in the democracy, and reviewing the claim of Douglas to be the regular nominee, and deciding adversely to it, he said :

Neither do I claim for Breckinridge that he is the "regular nominee" of the national democracy. He is presented to the people just as Douglas is, as the exponent of a principle. It is upon a difference as to the correctness of a political proposition that the party is divided, and has taken position under two distinguished leaders. The question of mere regularity, in comparison with its settlement, sinks into the most wretched insignificance. The democratic party has always boasted with pride and exultation its adherence to principle. Let not now its followers, who can cast their eyes back upon a long series of yearly triumphs of principle, mar that reputation by a beggarly and miserable scramble among themselves as to mere party machinery or regularity, irrespective of principle. I support Breckinridge, not because he is the regular nominee, but because I agree with him and those who nominated him as to what is correct as a political principle—as to what, under the constitution, is just to all the states of this nation. I oppose Douglas because I do not agree with him, and for no other reason. The point at issue involves the right of the people in the territories, while under a territorial form of government. * * * From a sense of duty and honest conviction, I shall vote for Breckinridge, believing that the platform upon which he is nominated is right, and the only one upon which our institutions can be maintained, and the peace, unity, and happiness of our country secured. There has been no peace to the democratic party since the doctrine of "squatter sovereignty" was promulgated. The effulgence of Douglas' giant intellect has concealed its true form from the eye of the party. It has been a gift from him of a political Pandora's box.

Intelligence of the nomination of Lincoln and Hamlin was received in California on June 10th, and the republican state convention to nominate presidential electors met at Sacramento on the 20th of that month. It was composed of 240 delegates, and was called to order by F. B. Folger. James Churchman was elected temporary chairman, and a committee on resolutions was appointed, consisting of J. S. Love, G. A. Grant, W. H. Weeks, and others. On permanent organization, J. A. Nunes was president, and C. C. Burbank, F. S. Dexter, G. W. Baldwin, and L. H. Foote vice-presidents. A. W. Blair, C. A. Washburn, W. H. Weeks, and Charles A. Tuttle were nominated for presidential electors, over George M. Hanson, Edward Stanly, G. W. Baldwin, J. F. Polton, C. W. Reed, S. D. Parker, J. Churchman, F. M. Haight, John C. Fremont, A. H. Myers, A. A. DeLong, P. H. Sibley, William Rabe, Antonio M. Pico, and Abel Stearns. Afterward, the vote by which Blair was nominated was reconsidered, and Antonio M. Pico was nominated in his place.

The following resolutions were adopted :

1. That with a just and patriotic pride we endorse the action of the national convention held at Chicago, on May 16th.

2. That the broad, comprehensive, and national sentiments expressed in the platform adopted at that convention meet with our heartiest approval, and, standing by them, we earnestly invite all opponents of the present corrupt administration to join with us in .

hurling it from power, and in bringing back the government to the principles of the fathers of the republic.

3. That Abraham Lincoln, of the great west, is the appropriate representative of the great principles of the republican party; the fit opponent of the sectional, factional, dissonant, and disordered "democracy;" known at home as "Honest Old Abe"—the sturdy champion of freedom and justice—we commend him to the free voters of this state as a man possessing alike the genius to will and the courage and determination to maintain, at all hazards, the integrity of the union, and the honor of the government.

4. That in Hannibal Hamlin we have an honest, courageous, and talented statesman ; one who had the courage and honor to desert a mighty and triumphant party to which he had long been attached, at the first moment when it became the assailant of the constitutional principles of the government.

5. That the great republican, Wm. II. Seward, ever the warm and judicious friend of California, is the object of the unalterable love and admiration of the republicans of this state ; and whether in office or in retirement, our affections will follow and surround him. And to him, constantly, will our pride and patriotism point as one of the wisest men and greatest statesmen of any country or of any age.

The democratic state committee met at San Francisco, on July 30th. It was understood beforehand that a split was inevitable. A strong effort was made, however, to bring about a compromise to run but one electoral ticket. All of the members of the committee were present. A. H. Rose offered a resolution recommending an adjustment of the differences existing between the two wings of the party by nominating an electoral ticket with two electors from each side, the tickets to be headed indifferently for Breckinridge or for Douglas, and the electors to be pledged to vote for the democratic candidate who should receive the majority of the democratic votes in the state. After a great deal of debate, the resolution was defeated—22 to 14. It met with no favor from the Douglas party. Chas. Lindley then offered a resolution calling a state convention to nominate four electors for Breckinridge. Eugene Casserly offered a substitute that the convention nominate Douglas electors. The substitute was lost by a vote of 26 to 6—four declining to vote. An adjournment was then taken until the 31st. On that day, separate meetings were held, the ten Douglas members—J. P. Hoge, A. H.

Rose, B. M. Henry, Myron Norton, A. D. Rightmire, W. S. Long, C. T. Ryland, R. P. Hammond, Geo. F. Price, and S. D. Krider— withdrawing.

The Breckinridge members sent the following message to Hoge, the chairman :

SAN FRANCISCO, July 31, 1860.

Hon. Joseph P. Hoge, chairman of the democratic state central committee :

Sir—At a meeting held pursuant to adjournment, at 10 o'clock A. M., to-day, the undersigned were appointed by the state central committee to inform you that they are now assembled and ready to proceed to business, and desire your attendance, which we accordingly do.

Hoge's reply was as follows :

I have your note notifying me, as the chairman of the democratic state committee, that you are a committee from a portion of that body to desire my attendance. This is my reply : The action of yourselves and your friends, in the state committee, on yesterday, in rejecting every proposition for maintaining the harmony and organization of the democratic party of this state, and in repudiating the regular national democratic convention of Charleston and Baltimore, and its candidates for president and vice-president—Douglas and Johnson—has, in my judgment, placed you and them outside of the regular democratic party of the state and union. I cannot, therefore, any longer recognize you or them as members of the democratic state committee, and must respectfully decline to accede to your request. I shall continue to act with the regular democratic committee, and the organization of the party in this state, as I have done all my life, here and elsewhere.

Upon the receipt of this reply, the Breckinridge members adopted the following preamble and resolution :

WHEREAS, The democratic state committee of California, met on Monday, July 30th, 1860, there being present Joseph P. Hoge, chairman, and 36 members of the committee ; and whereas, after due organization and discussion of the business, the committee, by resolution regularly passed, adjourned to meet again on Tuesday morning, July 31st, at 10 o'clock ; and whereas, on the said July 31st, the committee having assembled at 10 o'clock, the chairman not being present, a committee of three was appointed to inform him that the committee was assembled and ready to proceed to business and desired his attendance; and the committee, in writing, informed the chairman thereof; and whereas, the said Hoge, in answer, addressed a note to the said committee, designating the said state committee as "a portion" of the state committee, and declining further to act with said committee; now, therefore, be it resolved by the democratic state committee of California, that the place of chairman of the state committee is vacant, by the refusal of the said Hoge to act as such, and that this committee do elect a chairman.

The Breckinridge members adopted also the following resolutions:

1. That the platform promulgated by the convention at Baltimore, which nominated Breckinridge and Lane, meets with our cordial approval, and that we accept it as the true exposition of democratic principles.

2. That we regard Breckinridge and Lane, for president and vice-president, as the representatives of the true national democracy.

3. That the democracy of California meet by delegates in state convention, at Sacramento, on Tuesday, September 11th, to choose electors, who shall support Breckinridge and Lane.

The Douglas committee adopted the following resolutions on the 31st:

1. That we recognize and sustain the regular candidates of the national democratic convention—Douglas and Johnson—and approve the platform of principles there adopted.

2. That a democratic convention be held at Sacramento, on Wednesday, September 5th, to nominate four electors of president and vice-president, to cast the vote of California for the regularly nominated candidates of the national democracy.

The committee recommended the adoption of a test at the primaries which should admit all national and union-loving men who would support Douglas. The county committees followed the example of the state committee, and the machinery of both wings was in perfect working order in most of the counties by the middle of August.

The Douglas state convention met in the Sixth street M. E. church, Sacramento, on September 5th, and was composed of 359 delegates. It was called to order by J. P. Hoge, chairman of the state committee, and I. N. Quinn was elected temporary, and afterward permanent, president. The vice-presidents were Alfred Redington, Myron Norton, John Middleton, J. N. Hill, J. W. Denver, S. S. Lewis, and R. T. Sprague. The committee on resolutions consisted of G. F. Price, J. W. Denver, John Conness, E. Garter, E. Casserly, J. W. McCorkle, E. D. Wheeler, George S. Evans, Alex. Deering, W. S. Long, and others. On the 6th the following resolutions were reported and adopted :

1. That the democracy of California, in convention assembled, relying upon the justice and patriotism of the people, reiterate their firm determination to stand by, and maintain in all their integrity, the wise, just, and liberal principles enunciated in the Cincinnati platform by the democratic party in 1856, and reaffirmed by it at Charleston in 1860 ; and also the following resolutions, adopted at Charleston and Baltimore by the national democratic organization, to-wit :

a. That it is the duty of the United States to afford ample and complete protection to all its citizens, at home or abroad, and whether native or foreign born.

b. That one of the necessities of the age, in a military, commercial, and postal point of view, is speedy communication between the Atlantic and Pacific states, and the democratic party pledge themselves to such a constitutional enactment as will ensure the construction of a railroad to the Pacific coast at the earliest practicable period.

c. That the democratic party are in favor of the acquisition of the island of Cuba, on such terms as shall be honorable to ourselves and just to Spain.

d. That the enactments of state legislatures to defeat the faithful execution of the fugitive slave law are hostile in character, subversive of the constitution, and revolutionary in their effect.

e. That it is in accordance with the Cincinnati platform that, during the existence of territorial governments, the measures of restriction, whatever they may be, imposed by the federal constitution on the power of the territorial legislature over the.subject of the domestic relations, as the same has been or shall hereafter be finally determined by the supreme court of the United States, should be respected by all good citizens, and enforced with promptness and fidelity by every branch of the general government.

2. That we recognize and sustain the action of the national convention in nominating Stephen A. Douglas, of Illinois, and Herschel V. Johnson, of Georgia, for the offices of president and vice-president of the United States, as in accordance with the usages and

discipline of the democratic party; and, as such nominees, they are entitled to the support of all good democrats; and believing the platform adopted by the convention which nominated them to be patriotic, national and sound—being the same, in fact, as that upon which the great political battle of 1856 was fought and won by the democracy of the whole nation—we will give them a hearty support at the next November election.

3. That the compromise measures of 1850 were intended as a full and final settlement of the slavery question in congress, as is fully evidenced by the endorsement given them, in 1852, by the whig and democratic national conventions, and we deprecate any interference calculated to disturb that settlement; and we repeat with renewed energy the following resolution adopted by the state convention of 1859, which nominated Milton S. Latham for Governor, to-wit: (Here followed the second resolution adopted by the Lecompton convention of June 22, 1859.)

4. That we repudiate and disavow the action of that portion of the California delegation which withdrew from the late national convention at Charleston and Baltimore (excepting from this censure Major John Bidwell, the only one among them who has as yet disavowed that act), and that we never can and never will acknowledge the right of a minority of the members of a convention to break up and destroy the democratic party organization.

5. That we are opposed to all sectionalism which would tend in any way to disturb the harmony of our federal union, no matter whether it comes in the shape of northern congressional intervention for the prohibition of slavery in the territories, or of southern congressional intervention for the maintenance of slavery in the territories.

6. That we are in favor of a homestead bill, the establishment of a daily overland mail, the building of an overland telegraph, and a Pacific railroad, and that there is no constitutional objection to congress extending such aid as will ensure the speedy construction of such road.

7. That in the judgment of this convention the title of the United States to the island of San Juan, on our northwest coast, is as good as it is to the District of Columbia; that the recent history of our territorial relations with England in that quarter may well make us fear that the delays of diplomacy are full of danger to our rights. That the man or the administration that will allow a grasping power a second time to overreach us on that coast will merit and receive the lasting indignation of the American people.

8. That excessive, wasteful, and special legislation has been the bane of California, and has imposed upon the people a burden of taxation which is almost intolerable. That these evils should be corrected, and the business of legislation be restored to the democratic basis of inflexible opposition to a large public debt; to the granting of special privileges to the few at the expense of the many; to the extravagant expenditure of the public moneys; that this much needed reform cannot be withheld without wrong to the state and a violation of the plain duty of the representative to the constituent, and of the true policy and cardinal principles of the democratic party.

9. That it is imperatively necessary for the true interests of the state that the legislature should use all constitutional power to increase the public school fund and advance the interests of education, believing, as we do, that upon the education of the people depends the advancement and honor of the state.

10. That we cordially endorse the administration of Governor John G. Downey, as eminently calculated to advance the true interests of California.

11. That we heartily endorse the action of the democratic state central committee, presided over by J. P. Hoge, and recognize their action in calling this convention as right, proper, and democratic.

The following resolution was offered by George S. Evans, and laid on the table:

12. That, in the opinion of this convention, it is the imperative duty of our state legislature to exercise all its constitutional power to prevent the further immigration of coolies or Chinese to our state.

The following preamble and resolution was also laid on the table:

WHEREAS, the time has arrived in the affairs of our state for a decided expression of the democratic party regarding the propriety and necessity of a bulkhead for the city and county of San Francisco; and whereas, the whole and every part of the state is equally interested with the city of San Francisco upon this subject; therefore,

Resolved, That this convention deem it expedient and proper to express its opposition to any and all plans for a bulkhead for the harbor of San Francisco until such time as a legal and scientific survey by proper engineers can be made.

George F. Price, Humphrey Griffith, Richard P. Hammond, and Pablo de la Guerra were nominated for presidential electors, over

John R. McConnell, Jesse S. Pitzer, S. H. Dosh, and O. T. Ryland. No alternate electors were nominated. A state committee was appointed, consisting of J. W. McCorkle, T. B. Shannon, P. E. Conner, B. Shurtleff, George F. Price, J. G. McCallum, A. St. C. Denver, John Conness, J. T. Ryan, M. Norton, A. B. Dibble, John Caldwell, R. C. Poland, A. Redington, W. B. Hunt, D. D. Colton, J. P. Hoge, J. Middleton, L. Haskell, R. C. Page, P. W. Keyser, I. N. Quinn, T. B. Reardon, C. E. DeLong, and others.

The Breckinridge state convention met at Sacramento on September 11th, and was called to order by Charles Lindley, of the state committee. Thomas J. Henley was elected temporary chairman. A committee on resolutions was appointed, consisting of John B. Weller, D. W. Gelwicks, W. C. Wallace, Niles Searls, James Anderson, J. F. Montgomery, T. Hayes, E. C. Winchell, O. C. Pratt, J. S. Dudley, W. J. Hooten, Z. Montgomery, H. Gwinn, C. L. Weller, C. Benham, D. E. Buel, T. L. Thompson, W. F. Goad, C. Lindley, and P. L. Edwards. On the 12th, John B. Weller was elected president, and J. L. Brent, J. C. Duncan, S. B. McKee, O. C. Hall, J. P. Hardy, D. Fairchild, F. L. Aud, Joseph Walkup, D. W. Connelly, E. C. Winchell, A. T. Laird, and others vice-presidents. Senators Gwin and Latham, who were present, were invited to seats on the platform. Antonio F. Coronel, Vincent E. Geiger, Zach. Montgomery, and A. P. Dudley were nominated for presidential electors, over Jackson Temple, Horace Smith, Frank Ganahl, W. Matthews, and D. B. Hoffman; and H. P. Barber, Smith, Ganahl, and Hoffman were named for alternate electors. The following resolutions were unanimously adopted:

1. That the democracy of California, in convention assembled, endorse and cordially approve the platform adopted by the convention which nominated John C. Breckinridge and Joseph Lane, as a just exposition of the true principles of the true national democracy.

2. That the administration of James Buchanan has met the just expectations of the country by its patriotism, firmness and loyalty to the constitution.

3. That we congratulate the people of this state upon the passage through the Senate of the United States of a bill to establish a daily overland mail on the central routes; and respectfully, but earnestly, request Scott and Burch to urge its passage through the house of representatives at an early day in the next session of congress.

4. That we earnestly recommend to the county committees of the several counties of this state to have ballots prepared favoring the calling of a constitutional convention.

5. That this convention do most cordially endorse and approve of the action of the state democratic central committee, presided over by Chas. Lindley, at its recent meeting in San Francisco.

6. That we enter into the present contest with an enthusiasm worthy of our cause, and the watchwords "Pacific Railroad," "Daily Overland Mail," "Mail Steamships to China and Japan," and the "Annexation of all the Territory we can Honorably Acquire" inscribed upon our banner.

A state committee was selected, consisting of H. C. Smith, J. E. N. Lewis, D. W. Gelwicks, John Daggett, E. J. C. Kewen, J. A. Watson, C. H. Mitchell, W. J. Hooten, Chas. Lindley, H. C. Patrick, R. A. Redman, John H. Wise, T. L. Thompson, J. J. Kendrick, Z. Montgomery, Thos. Hayes, J. P. Haven, C. Benham, Jas. Haworth and others.

On May 21, 1860, information was received of the nomination of John Bell and Edward Everett by the union convention, but no action was taken to organize the party in California until July 26th, when a meeting for that purpose was held at Sacramento, which was presided over by A. P. Catlin. A county committee was chosen, and resolutions adopted recommending that the friends of the union party organize and send delegates to a state convention to be held at Sacramento on September 5th, to nominate an electoral ticket. Similar meetings were held elsewhere in the state shortly afterward, and on August 10th a call was issued, signed by citizens of the counties of San Francisco, Placer, Nevada, Tulare, Santa Cruz, Alameda, Napa, Solano and Sacramento, also calling the state convention for September 5th. Among the signers to this call were D. O. Shattuck, T. H. Selby, J. B. Crockett, H. R. Hawkins, W. B. Lyon, J. D. Carr, E. Gibbons, R. D. Hopkins, J. M. Dudley, G. W. Bowie, J. Neely Johnson, A. P. Catlin, H. O. Beatty and David Meeker. Pursuant to these calls the union state convention met in the M. E. church (south), Sacramento, on September 5th. Twenty six counties were represented, and 309 delegates had been elected. The convention was called to order by D. O. Shattuck, and W. R. Longley was elected temporary chairman. On permanent organization, Shattuck was president; and S. B. Woodin, John Anderson, J. W. Smith, J.

W. Porter and E. Gibbons vice-presidents. The committee on resolutions consisted of H. R. Hawkins, H. O. Beatty, J. E. Wainwright, A. P. Catlin and others. The following resolutions were unanimously adopted :

1. That we cordially endorse, and will earnestly support the nominations of John Bell, of Tennessee, and Edward Everett, of Massachusetts, for the offices of president and vice-president of the United States.

2. That we reaffirm and endorse the resolutions adopted at the national union convention, held at Baltimore, on the 10th day of May, 1860, which are as follows :

WHEREAS, Experience has demonstrated that platforms, adopted by the partisan conventions of the country, have had the effect to mislead and deceive the people, and at the same time to widen the political divisions of the country, by the creation and encouragement of geographical and sectional parties ; therefore, *resolved*, that it is both the part of patriotism and of duty to recognize no political principles other than the constitution of the country, the union of the states, and the enforcement of the laws ; and that, as the representatives of the constitutional union men of the country, in national convention assembled, we hereby pledge ourselves to maintain, protect, and defend, separately and unitedly, these great principles of public liberty and national safety against all enemies, at home and abroad, believing that thereby peace may once more be restored to the country, and the just rights of the people and of the states reestablished, and the government again placed in that condition of justice, fraternity, and equality, which, under the example and constitution of our fathers, has solemnly bound every citizen of the United States, to maintain a more perfect union, establish justice, insure domestic tranquillity, provide for the common defense, promote the general welfare, and secure the blessings of liberty to ourselves and our posterity.

3. That the above resolutions are suggestive of the whole duty of every citizen and patriot, and we cordially invite conservative men of all parties to unite with us in their support.

4. That this convention recommend a complete organization of the union constitutional party throughout the state, and the nomination of full legislative tickets in the several counties and districts.

J. B. Crockett, G. W. Bowie, Phineas L. Miner, and James H. Lander were nominated for presidential electors, without opposition. On the 6th, A. M. Rosborough, Dr. E. Gibbons, R. H. Daly, and

W. R. Longley were nominated for alternate electors. A state committee was selected, consisting of J. E. Wainwright, G. H. Hossefross, M. M. Noah, A. P. Catlin, David Meeker, James Queen, R. H. McDonald, E. Gibbons, C. E. Filkins, Jesse D. Carr, A. M. Stevenson, H. R. Hawkins, A. M. Rosborough, and others.

The campaign was conducted with great vigor by the advocates of Lincoln, Douglas, and Breckinridge, but the Bell men cut very little figure, as it was evident from the outset that there was no hope for them. Wideawake clubs, in the interest of the republican ticket, and little giant clubs, in the interest of the Douglas ticket, were organized, and their parades with torches in the cities lent much to the general enthusiasm. The principal campaign speakers were: for Breckinridge—W. M. Gwin, S. Heydenfeldt, W. C. Stratton, Z. Montgomery, M. S. Latham, A. P. Dudley, H. P. Barber, Horace Smith, J. B. Weller, B. F. Washington, and Frank Tilford; for Douglas—J. G. Downey, John Nugent, J. R. McConnell, J. A. McDougall, J. W. McCorkle, H. Griffith, R. P. Hammond, and G. F. Price; for Lincoln—Thos. Fitch, C. A. Tuttle, L. Stanford, George Cadwalader, W. H. Weeks, Nathan Porter, G. B. Tingley, C. Cole, A. A. Sargent, Alex. Campbell, F. M. Pixley, J. A. Nunes, Wilson Flint, and I. P. Randall. Early in September a movement was inaugurated in San Francisco to nominate a people's independent ticket for the local offices, and a committee was appointed at a public meeting to make selection of the candidates and in October the ticket was announced. On the 20th of that month the republican county convention endorsed the people's ticket, and two days later the Bell convention followed the same course; but some of the straight-out republicans, being dissatisfied with the action of their convention, nominated a full local ticket for the party. This action engendered bad blood, and on October 31st the republican county committee held a meeting which broke up in a row, growing out of an attempt by the straights to oust from their seats such committeemen as had endorsed the people's movement. The intervention of the police was necessary to quell the disturbance. On October 26th, the Breckinridge and Douglas democrats in that city fused on the local nominations. The division in the republican party did not extend beyond San Francisco, and a thorough and effective organization was early effected in all parts of the state. In October an imposing display was made by the republicans at San Francisco in honor of the election of E. D. Baker to the United

States senate from Oregon. The new senator arrived in that city on the 18th, on his way to Washington, and a grand reception was given him under the auspices of the republican state committee. On the 21st intelligence was received of republican successes in Pennsylvania, Indiana, and Ohio, and it resulted in numerous accessions to the ranks of that party. The Douglas organs charged that the Breckinridge strength was to be given to elect Lincoln, as the only means of carrying the state against their candidate, and there is little doubt that the Breckinridge leaders preferred the election of the republican rather than that of Douglas, in what they regarded as a choice between two evils. That they were not admirers of Lincoln is evidenced by a speech delivered in San Jose in October, by ex-Governor Weller, when he said :

I do not know whether Lincoln will be elected or not; but I do know that if he is elected, and attempts to carry out his doctrine, the south will surely withdraw from the union; and I should consider them less than men if they did not.

The election was held on November 6th, and the official canvass of the votes, made on December 4th, exhibited the following result:

For Presidential Electors—Lincoln—Washburn, 38,733; Weeks, 38,720; Tuttle, 38,734; Pico, 38,699. Douglas—Hammond, 37,-999; Griffith, 38,023; de la Guerra, 37,957; Price, 37,959. Breckinridge—Coronel, 33,969; Geiger, 33,970; Montgomery, 33,970; Dudley, 33,975. Bell—Crockett, 9,111; Bowie, 9,110; Miner, 9,136; Lander, 9,098.

Constitutional Convention—For, 59,732; against, 12,481.

State Debt—Pay, 62,514; repudiate, 8,763.

The proposition to call a constitutional convention was therefore again defeated. The republican electors met in the capitol, in Sacramento, on December 5th, and cast the vote of the state for Lincoln and Hamlin, and after four ballotings, selected Weeks, as the messenger, to convey the returns to Washington.

CHAPTER XIII.

1861. Secession of the South—Union Resolutions—Condition of the Democratic Party—Union Mass Meeting—Breckinridge Convention—Republican Convention—Douglas Convention.

On November 14th, the intelligence arrived from the east of the election of Lincoln, and the southern sympathizers in the state regarding the secession of the south as inevitable, talked boldly of the possibility of erecting a Pacific republic from California, Oregon, and the adjoining territories. The San Francisco *Herald,* on November 28th, editorially suggested the establishment of such a republic. The advocates of a Pacific republic were, however, few in California, and they were confined to the extreme secession sympathizers in the ranks of the Breckinridge party. Senator Latham saw the handwriting on the wall in the result of the election in the state, and made haste to retract his declaration that California would leave the union, in a speech which he delivered in the United States senate, in December, 1860, and which was published in this state, on the 31st of that month. In the course of his remarks on that occasion, he said :

I arise to correct a false impression upon the public mind, as I have seen it published in several leading journals of the country, as to the attitude of California in the present crisis. It has been said, and by many believed, that, in the event of the secession of several of the states of the union, California would avail herself of the opportunity to declare her own independence, and in conjunction with the other territories of the United States on the Pacific, would form a Pacific republic. There is not a word of truth in this idea, and it does great injustice to the people of that state. The union has no more loyal subjects than the people of California ; and out of her half million population, I believe there are not many who are for disunion in any shape. California will remain in the union as it is and as it may be. And if, as seems now to be conceded, the cotton states withdraw from the union, and are eventually followed by all the southern states, California, I am certain, will still remain with the great west and the north, with whom she is identified. In addressing this body, on April 16th, 1860, I foreshadowed the idea of a Pacific republic upon the dissolution of the existing union. I am satisfied, upon more mature reflection, to say the least, I was premature. For, whatever may be my own opinion of the right or

wrong of the present agitating question—a question in which California has no present or vital interest—I feel it my bounden duty
to thus give, not only my own opinion, but, as one of her representatives, to state what I believe to be the voice of her majority. There
is but one thing which will or can alienate the affections of the
people of the Pacific from the union as it is, or as it may be, and
that is, a failure to give them a Pacific railroad, and, until that is
completed, overland mail facilities. Upon this question, they are
clamorous, urgent, unanimous ; and, since the great west and north
are thoroughly committed to this material idea, their loyalty cannot
be questioned.

It was understood that Senator Gwin favored the establishment
of a Pacific republic in the event of the secession of the south. On
January 3d, the San Francisco *Herald* published a lengthy letter
from Congressman Burch, addressed to Chas. R. Street, and dated
at Washington, on November 22d, 1860. In the letter, Burch
said :

Our government has fallen upon strange times. The dissolution
of the union, which but a short time ago seemed to be too far away
in the future for me to give it even a passing thought, is now
regarded not only with gravity and seriousness, but it is looked upon
by many wiser heads than mine as a fixed fact. * * * It is
not unreasonable to conclude that they (the southern leaders) may
possibly prosecute successfully the work of disunion in which they
are so earnestly engaged.

He hoped they would recede from the position they had taken, and
said he would lose no opportunity to restore peace to the country,
and to reconcile and reunite our estranged and maddened brethren
of the north and south. He held that it was the duty of the representatives of the Pacific coast, who were removed from the scene of
strife to use their utmost exertions to prevent disunion, and suggested that it would be well for the people of California, Oregon,
New Mexico, Washington, and Utah to seek refuge for themselves
from the blighting effects of disunion and civil war by retiring and
establishing a prosperous, happy, and successful republic on the
Pacific slope, to which they and our brethren here may look for
peace and quiet for themselves and their children when such blessings are no longer tolerated near the Atlantic, along the Ohio, nor
even in the broad valley of the Mississippi. He pictured the prospective republic in these glowing terms :

9

The people of California and her neighbors should be of one mind on this subject, and be prepared for the emergency; and if the "fates" should *force* us to this last sad resort, let us, with a disposition to welcome all who come to us from our "old homes" seeking an asylum, raise aloft the flag of the "bear," surrounded with the hydra-pointed cactus of the western wilds, and call upon the enlightened nations of the earth to acknowledge our independence, and to protect us, the only "waif" from the wreck of our once noble union, the youthful but vigorous *Cæsarian* republic of the Pacific.

On January 18th, a letter from Congressman Scott, dated at Washington, December 21, 1860, and addressed to Charles Lindley, chairman of the democratic state committee, was published in the *Herald*. It was very lengthy, and urged the formation of a Pacific republic for self-preservation, in case of disunion and civil war. The people of the state were generally in favor of standing by the federal government in the event of the secession of the south, and "union" clubs were immediately organized in every town. These clubs passed resolutions declaring the loyalty of the people to the union, and their opposition to any form of secession.

An important part of the history of the legislature of 1861, was the numerous resolutions on the state of the union that were introduced, and the debates upon them.

On January 18th, in the senate, C. E. DeLong (Douglas) introduced the following resolutions:

1. That it is proper that the legislature of California should, at this time, give expression to the sentiments with which the people of the state are inspired by the unhappy events which are occurring within these United States.

2. That California cherishes a loyal devotion to the union. Our honor and our pride are in its flag. Our safety and our prosperity depend upon its continuance. Through a glorious and beneficent history we trace our rights and liberties to the founders of the union, and with its destruction would go down our hopes of their preservation.

3. That California will never despair of the union.

4. That, remote from the scenes and unaffected by the causes of the strife of sections, with a population drawn from every state, who entertain all opinions, and yet upon her soil are bound together by a common allegiance, California, by her position, by the feelings of her people no less than by her interests, is called to assume the part

of a peacemaker, and to labor to restore harmony to the states from which she has sprung, and of whose might in union she is the noblest monument.

5. That California, with an unbroken faith in the power of reason and justice, and in the efficacy of peaceful measures, will recognize no policy but the preservation of the union in all its parts, and the enforcement of all its laws. To the wisdom and patriotism of those to whom the people of the United States have committed the powers of government she entrusts the selection of the means necessary to the accomplishment of those ends, and pledges them her support.

6. That the governor be requested to transmit a copy of these resolutions to our congressional delegation, to apprise them of the true sentiments of their constituents, to serve as their instructions and guide in all questions that may arise for their consideration, and that they may be informed that California *repudiates* the suggestion of a Pacific republic, and of any other confederacy than our present union, as fraught with all the dangers and mischiefs of *treason.*

Senator Henry Edgerton (Douglas) offered the following substitute:

1. That this legislature, and the people whom they represent, have witnessed with sentiments of the profoundest sorrow the political events which have occurred and are in progress of development in the Atlantic states of the union; and that this alarming crisis in our public affairs demands the exercise of moderation, patience, justice, and wisdom upon the part of the people of these states and their representatives.

2. That the people of California are devoted to the union of these states; that they regard that union as the source of our prosperity, happiness, and power; that it has assured us peace at home and respect abroad; that it has brought to us and secured for us all the blessings of civil and religious freedom; that under the government formed by that union the fondest anticipations of the fathers of the republic have been realized in a confederacy already advanced to the rank of a first-class power in the world, in the greatest progress ever made by any nation in the same period in population, wealth, and material resources and achievements, and in the rare union of the largest liberty ever accorded to the citizen, with sufficient energy in the government for national defense and self-preservation, and with the security to minorities and individuals of all rights of person and property.

3. That this union and the constitution which establishes it, were framed in the spirit of compromise, conciliation, and concession; minor advantages and considerations being wisely surrendered in order to secure the greater benefits of a good and efficient government for all sections of the confederacy; that in the nature of things, and from the constitution of men, it must have been expected that collisions and disagreements would arise, as they have occasionally arisen in all countries; and that to avoid or to remedy these disturbances, we must invoke the same spirit of justice, moderation, and conciliation to which the union owes its origin.

4. That we look upon the dissolution of this union with feelings of horror; that we prize this union above all sordid standards of pecuniary interest; that we love it and cherish it with the unselfish affection of freemen loving and cherishing the most valued institution of their country, and the sacred heritage of their fathers. That if disunion could be peaceably accomplished, it would be unwise, imprudent and impolitic, a rash experiment, because exchanging happiest political institutions for other and untried schemes of government; and, if not peaceably effected, it would bring in its train a multitude of evils too horrible to contemplate. That we regard, therefore, the disruption of the union as one of the greatest calamities which could ever fall upon the world; as blighting the hopes of freedom and free men everywhere; as impairing the confidence of patriots in the capacity of man for self rule; as overturning the freest and best of all governments, and destroying the most prosperons of the nations of the earth, and as putting back for years, perhaps for centuries, the cause of civilization itself, and of rational liberty regulated by law.

5. This legislature—composed themselves, and representing a constituency made up of men born and reared in every part of the union and of the civilized world, of men of diverse origin, yet meeting as brethren in daily political and social relations with each other—do utterly repudiate the notion, sometimes expressed, that between the citizens of different sections or states of the American union there is any natural or other inequality; but, on the contrary, neither here nor elsewhere should there be made any discrimination or distinction, political or social, founded upon the birthplace or residence in a given state of any American citizen; and we do emphatically repudiate the idea that, from a difference of interest or character between the people of the northern and those of the southern sections of the confederacy, there is any such incompatibility or antagonism as to prevent a continuance of the union, or a just and

mutually beneficial central government over the whole; that, on the contrary, the happy frame of our system of state and federal governments, if faithfully carried out, would make of those very circumstantial diversities elements of national strength and civil order.

6 That the union of these states is founded upon the principles of justice and equality, upon the equal right of every member of the confederacy, and of every citizen of every state; that the government instituted for the whole should be administered upon the same principles, and that the union can only be preserved by a faithful adherence to this rule, and by a prompt and cheerful discharge by every state of the constitutional duties and obligations which she owes to her confederates.

7. That California has ever been national in character and feeling; that she has resisted all encroachments upon the just rights of her sister states, because she deemed it national to conserve the rights of every part of the nation; that we have seen with regret acts and proceedings in and of other states, the tendency of which was to alienate the affections of the southern states from the union, and to produce the deplorable condition of affairs now existing; that in the passage of certain acts called liberty bills, by several of the northern states, the southern states have just cause of complaint, as of acts of hostility to them, in plain violation of the constitution, and tending directly to revolution and disunion; that in the interference by states, or citizens of states, with the domestic affairs of other states, we recognize a plain and unwarrantable intrusion, which is not only wrong in itself, but calculated to enfeeble the sacred ties which bind the members of the confederacy together.

8. That in the deliberate judgment of this legislature, there is no matter, cause, or thing between the southern and northern states which cannot be settled, and which ought not to be settled and adjusted, in a spirit of fair and just compromise; and that we approve of such settlement. That the exigency of the danger now impending over us demands prompt, decided, and patriotic action; that this settlement should be thorough, complete, and radical. That the northern states that have passed unconstitutional "liberty bills" should repeal them; that the fugitive slave law should be made effectual to secure its objects, if any amendment be necessary; that the south should be relieved of any apprehensions in respect to the abolishing or interference with slavery in the states or the District of Columbia.

9. That we approve of, and will abide by the plan of adjustment of the present difficulties in which the country is involved, as sub-

mitted by the Hon. Stephen A. Douglas in the United States senate on the 24th of December, 1860.

10. That this confederacy of co-equal states, so seriously divided upon these exciting questions, can only be preserved, as we believe, by a prompt and patriotic union of all conservative and loyal men, sincerely acting in concert, and patriotically sacrificing sectional prejudices and mere pride of opinion upon the altar of their common country.

11. That whatever may be, or may be supposed to be, the wrongs and grievances of any of the members of the confederacy, such wrongs should be redressed within the union, and by the means the constitution has provided for that purpose.

12. That it is the sense of this legislature, and of the constituency it represents, that the constitution is the fundamental law of the land, sovereign and supreme within its own sphere, operating directly upon each individual citizen of the republic, and justly exacting an implicit obedience to all its provisions and requirements. That the union of these states, under the constitution as it now exists, or may be hereafter amended, must be preserved; and that the people of this state will steadfastly stand by the general government in the exercise of every constitutional power to uphold and sustain both in all their integrity, and in the enforcement of the federal laws.

13. That our representatives in congress have not, nor have they ever had, the right to commit the people of this state to any other policy than that of strict adherence to the union.

14. That the governor be requested to forward a copy of these resolutions to each of our representatives in congress, and to each of the governors of our sister states.

In the assembly, on January 19th, G. W. Patrick (Breckinridge) introduced the following:

1. That we most heartily concur with his excellency, John G. Downey, in his late annual message transmitted to the general assembly of California, wherein his excellency speaks in that eminently union, conservative spirit of our federal relations.

2. That "the nullification of the fugitive slave law, and the passage of personal liberty bills by many of the sovereign states, cannot be viewed in any other light than subversive of all amicable relations between those states and that portion of the confederacy interested in slave property; that these enactments are unconstitutional,

are founded upon injustice and bad faith, and are in violation of the federal compact."

3. That "the estimation in which California is held by both of the contending sections, her citizens, as it were, being a congress of the whole confederacy, fits her for a mediator, and this is the position she desires to occupy."

4. That while anything exists worthy of being called an American union, California will cling to it with patriotic devotion at all hazards.

Zach. Montgomery (Breckinridge) offered the following substitute:

WHEREAS, Events which have recently transpired, and which are daily transpiring in the Atlantic states, leave too little room to doubt that the American union, if not already dissolved, is on the verge of dissolution; and whereas, the people of California regard such dissolution as a most direful calamity; and whereas, we look upon the remodelling of the federal constitution by a national constitutional convention as the surest means of restoring peace and harmony to our distracted country; therefore, be it resolved:

1. That the congress of the United States be, and is hereby urged to take steps for the calling of such convention, in accordance with the 5th article of the federal constitution.

2. That we do most earnestly invite the several states of the union, as well as such state or states as may deem themselves to have withdrawn from the union, to co-operate with us through their respective legislatures, in urging upon congress the immediate necessity of calling said convention.

3. That the present excited state of public feeling, both north and south, engendered by reciprocal violations, or threatened violations, of the federal laws, calls for like reciprocal forbearance, in order that reason may resume her sway and that patriotism may regain her wonted place in the hearts of the people.

4. That the wilful refusal on the part of certain of our sister states to surrender fugitives from labor, and the strenuous and persistent efforts on the part of said states to prevent the enforcement of the fugitive slave law, are palpable infringements of the constitution of the United States.

5. That we deprecate any attempt on the part of the general government to maintain by force of arms the federal union, as against such state or states as may deem themselves to have withdrawn, or as may hereafter attempt to withdraw from the union on account of

continued and flagrant violation of their constitutional rights by other states; and we hold that any such attempt, without first affording to such aggrieved state or states adequate protection against a continuation of said grievances, is to light the fires of civil war and crush forever the last hope of reconciliation between the opposing sections.

6. That the people of California acknowledge neither the north nor the south, but the whole American union, as their common mother, to whom they are united not merely by the considerations of interests, but by the more enduring ties of blood and filial affection.

7. That, as Californians, we are willing to stand by the whole union, hazarding, if necessary, our lives and our fortunes for her defense; but we are not prepared to pledge our allegiance to either a northern or a southern fragment of a dismembered confederacy, nor will we ever consent to become the ally of one section in waging a fratricidal war against another section of our common country.

Charles Crocker (republican) offered the following substitute for the substitute:

1. That the constitution of the United States is not a mere confederacy or compact between the several states, but is the organization of the government proper, and creates direct relations between the federal government and the people of all the states; that no state, either by convention or otherwise, has power to dissolve those relations, and therefore any attempt by a state to secede from the union is unconstitutional and revolutionary.

2. That it is the duty of the president of the United States to take care that the laws be faithfully executed, and to preserve, protect and defend the constitution of the United States, and to preserve the public ports, arsenals and other property from all attempts to wrest them from the general government; and it is his duty to use all the power vested in him to accomplish these purposes.

3. That while we would rejoice to have the state of South Carolina withdraw from the union, should her citizens on a free and fair vote elect so to do, yet, as such withdrawal cannot be effected without a breach of the constitution and a revolution subversive of this glorious fabric of our national union, we are, therefore, opposed to all acts and proceedings sanctioning such a withdrawal.

4. That the election of any person as president of the United States, in accordance with the provisions of the constitution, affords no just ground of complaint on the part of those defeated in such

election; and this state will oppose all attempts of such defeated minority to subvert and destroy the federal union.

5. That California will stand by the constitution framed by the fathers of our republic and union, and cemented by the blood of our revolutionary sires, so long as any state will unite with her in its support. In the words of our heroic Jackson : "the federal union— it must be preserved."

On Jannary 22d, Oaleb Burbank (republican) offered the following resolutions in the senate :

1. That the people of California regard the present as a fitting time, and a proper occasion, to avow their sentiments clearly, boldly, and respectfully, upon the extraordinary and unprecedented attempts to destroy the integrity of the American union.

2. That in the judgment of the people of California, our national government has in it the vested power to enact laws, and also the rightful power and authority to carry into complete execution the laws it may make, and that without such power of enactment and execution, there can be no national government.

3. That no state in the confederacy has the right to secede from the union or to nullify any law duly enacted by the congress of the United States.

4. That no nation can be entitled to respect among the nations of the earth, or be worthy of the love and confidence of its own citizens, without a due observance of its laws is required and maintained:

5. That the multiplied blessings enjoyed by the people of this union, from the beginning of our government to the present time, show most clearly to us and to the civilized world, the wisdom and foresight of our fathers who ordained this government, and the statesmanship and patriotism of their descendants, who through successive generations have nobly sustained their government and transmitted its blessings to the present generation of thirty millions of people, now the most happy and prosperous of any nation of people upon the habitable globe.

6. That it is the imperative duty of the chief executive of the general government to require of the people a due and proper observance of the laws thereof in every part and portion of our common country, and that it is the reasonable duty of every citizen, in his individual capacity, and the duty of all the citizens in each and every state, in their collective and organic position as a state of the confederacy, to yield a ready and willing compliance with the laws

of the general government; and that upon the faithful performance of such duty by the executive, as well as upon such compliance by the people and the states, depend the integrity of the union, and the happiness of this great and glorious nation, whose high destiny can be realized only through a patriotic devotion to the principles of self-government—kindred indeed, to the devotion which gave to our fathers a just, a glorious and an immortal renown.

7. That the people of California look with deep regret and with unqualified disapprobation upon the antagonism of South Carolina to the constitution, union, and laws of the United States.

8. That the people of California are firmly attached to the union; that they believe our general government to be the best form of government known among men, and that, with this full belief, they will honor it, uphold it, and maintain it, at all times, under all circumstances, and in every contingency, against any and all attempts to weaken, distract or to dissolve it—whether such attempts are made by a foreign power, by domestic insubordination, or by treasonable infidelity and usurpation.

9. That the people of California are not so lost to self-respect, so blind to their present and future interest and security, or so unpatriotic and disloyal as to entertain a wish or a thought favorable to the unwise, imprudent, suicidal and disloyal idea of a Pacific republic.

10. That our congressional representatives are warranted by their constituents in asserting and declaring on all proper occasions that all the sentiments contained in these resolutions are the sentiments of the people of California.

On the same day J. H. Watson (Douglas) offered the following in the Senate:

1. That this legislature approves and affirms the patriotic recommendations and suggestions of his excellency the governor, for the settlement of this vexed and dangerous question of disagreement between the northern and southern sections of the union.

2. That in order that a settlement may be effected, it is indispensable that no attempt be made to coerce any state or states by force of arms into submission to federal authority, since, upon the exhibition and exertion of force, though directed only against a single state, in the present temper of parties north and south, and under existing circumstances, the inevitable effect would be to array the whole north and south as two hostile nations, against each other; that civil war would ensue between the sections—civil war, the most

deplorable and cruel of all wars at the best, but the horrors and
enormities of which in this case would be aggravated by circumstances peculiar to this controversy and the causes of it; that the
commencement of hostilities will close the door forever to a peaceful solution of this difficulty, whether to be effected by a renewal
by the discontented states of the connection with the other states,
or by a satisfactory adjustment of questions between the sections
or states, upon an agreement to separate ; that this war would be,
in all probability, of long duration, withdrawing all the energies of
the contending sections from the peaceful pursuits of industry to
the dreadful trade of fratricidal strife, in which the wealth of the
north would be taxed and exhausted in the vain attempt to desolate
the south ; and if successful, the result would be scarcely less deplorable, by reducing freemen to slaves, sovereign states to subjugated
provinces, and a fertile land to desolation. That federal force, thus
producing civil war, can secure no single purpose for which it is
offered—since it is chimerical to suppose the general government,
represented, in that contingency, only by the northern states, have
the ability to conquer the southern states. And if this could be
done, the conquest must be preserved and maintained by immense
standing armies, quartered in the south, which the northern states
have neither the power nor the wealth to maintain. And if this
last purpose could be effected, the states so conquered and disgraced
would not be elements of strength, dignity, or power to the confederacy, but discontented and disgraced colonies, burdening their con-
querors with unremunerated and intolerable expenses, and exposing
them to destruction whenever assailed by foreign enemies. The
conquest of a state would change the whole theory of the government, and destroy the principle of state equality which is the corner
stone of the confederacy. The prosecution of such a war would
change the whole genius of our people, corrupt the public morals,
introduce into every neighborhood the vices of the camp, withdraw
enterprise, industry, and intellect from trade, commerce, and agriculture, to war, and thus introduce the evils of martial domination
and ambition as controlling influences in both sections, to end at
last in the establishment of a military despotism. That a union of
states, held in enforced combination by the sword, could answer
none of the purposes and fulfill none of the promised blessings of a
free and pacific confederacy, uniting the energies of its members in
peace for a wise and fraternal government, and in war for mutual
protection and national glory ; and that no evils likely to arise from
a peaceable separation can equal the evils flowing from an attempt

to compel a union by force of arms — in which vain effort, every evil of a disordered commerce, a divided people, of trade destroyed, and of prosperity reversed, of bankruptcy, civil war, famine and insurrection would succeed. And, besides all this, it is as little consistent with the pride, as with the interest, of the free states, to endeavor to maintain a connection, as brethren and equals, with an unwilling people, if a union with them can only be secured and maintained by the sword; therefore, *resolved :*

3. Because we are in favor of the preservation of this union, we are opposed to the attempted coercion by arms of any southern state, since such attempt must necessarily cause and perpetuate disunion and superadd to disunion the evils of an interminable, unchristian and unnatural civil war.

4. That this legislature do not and will not despair of the union of these states. We believe that too much patriotism and too enlightened a sense of self-interest exist in the intelligent people who compose the American states to permit the destruction of thousands of millions of material wealth—the diversion to war of energies, that, employed as now exerted, would produce thousands of millions more; and to see, without an opposing effort worthy of the stake, the destruction of the best government in the world. We rejoice to see that the conservative sentiment of the whole country is now being aroused, and we are unwilling to believe that the efforts now made to adjust this difficulty will be fruitless; but it is our solemn conviction that those efforts must all prove unavailing if force be employed by the federal government before the loyal, just, and patriotic sentiments of the people shall have been invoked, and respond to the appeal.

5. That these views derive additional strength from these considerations; that this action of the southern states is taken by one and threatened by others in their sovereign capacity; that these states claim, under the sanction of high, though it may be mistaken authority, the right so to act; that the sentiment of the southern people and of a large proportion of all the people of the United States is, that the southern states have been grievously oppressed and imposed upon by a large portion of the people of the northern states; that apprehensions have been justly excited by the action of certain states, and by the formation and success of a sectional party, as to the safety of their domestic institutions; that under the circumstances, they are entitled to be guaranteed in their just and equal rights; that it is conceded that several of the northern states have themselves openly defied a constitutional law of congress, by

the passage of so-called liberty bills; that these acts, still unrepealed, exhibit those states in open and flagrant disobedience to the constitution, the offense of opposing and nullifying one law, and that of nullifying all laws, being the same in kind and only differing in degree; that a delay, until justice be done the south, to attempt to enforce the federal authority against the resisting southern states by arms could be productive of no injury; and that such an attempt would be fruitless of good, arbitrary, impolitic, partial, and unjust, and productive only of the worst possible sentiments.

6. That it is the deliberate sense of this legislature that an appeal to force should not be made by the federal government, until at least every effort be made in good faith to settle and adjust the unhappy difficulties now existing between the two sections; and that the offending northern states that have passed the unconstitutional acts before referred to, be respectfully requested to set an example of loyalty to the constitution and laws by immediately repealing these obnoxious statutes.

In the assembly, on Jannary 22d, J. Dougherty (Douglas) offered the following:

1. That the people of California, drawn from the different states, from the north, from the south, from the east, and from the west, cherish a loyal attachment to the union; that they regard it, and the constitution by which it was established, as the cause of the unexampled prosperity of the country, the source of its power and influence abroad, and of its peace and security at home, and as furnishing the only assurance of the perpetuation of the government and the blessings of free and republican institutions.

2. That no state has the right, under the constitution, to secede from the union; that secession can only be justified upon the ground of revolution; and that in the judgment of the people of California, there are no evils endured by any members of the confederacy that cannot be remedied in the union under the constitution, whilst those evils, whatever they may be, would be immeasurably increased by dissolution, and accompanied by calamities of the most appalling nature.

3. That the people of California, with poignant feelings of indignation and horror, utterly repudiate and repel the suggestion of secession on the part of this state as well as the formation of a separate Pacific republic; and that their true policy is to recognize and sustain a permanent adherence to the union.

4. That California is peculiarly fitted for, and imperatively called upon to act the part of pacificator between the contending sections and alienated states of the union. She is removed from the strife, and is not interested in the causes from which it originated, except so far as they may impair the integrity of the confederacy. Her population is bound together by a common attachment for the union, and by a like determination that the state of their adoption shall remain, with the states from which they emigrated, members of the same great confederacy. In assuming the part of a peace-maker she will eminently respond to the warmest feelings of her people.

5. That while the people of this state have unshaken confidence in the peaceful solution of all questions at present exciting and estranging from each other the citizens of other states, they expect the general government to see that the republic suffers no detriment, and to exercise all necessary constitutional power for the preservation of the union in its integrity, and the enforcement of the federal laws.

In the assembly on January 23d, P. Munday (Douglas), offered the following:

WHEREAS, One of the southern states of this union, in consequence of alleged grievances for which she could obtain no redress from the hands of the federal government, has declared herself out of the confederacy of states; and whereas, other states, for like causes, complain of hostile legislation against and unjust treatment by their brethren of the north, have evinced an unmistakable determination to secede; and whereas, the people of California, composing citizens of all portions of the union, and all nations of the earth, possess interests in common with all the states and own no special bias to or affiliation with any section, loving the union for its own sake, sustaining it as the great ark of safety for the liberties of the people, and looking upon its destruction as the death-blow to freedom everywhere, *resolved,*

1. That we have viewed with extreme sorrow the sectional agitations which have for many years disturbed the peaceful and harmonious relations that should always exist between the different states of the confederacy.

2. That whatever may have been the provocation given by the unwholesome agitation of the question of negro slavery by evil-disposed persons at the north, we most earnestly deplore the hasty action of our sister state of South Carolina, in the adoption of meas-

ures for her separation from the confederacy ; and we indulge the earnest hope that, upon reflection and friendly consultation, she will reconsider a resolve that cannot fail to result in disaster to herself, and the most deplorable consequences to the whole union, and in the retardation of the cause of human freedom all over the world.

3. That we urge upon each of the free states, having passed laws inimicable to the interests, or calculated to wound the feelings of the southern people, an immediate repeal of such laws, and a decent and becoming abstinence from all such action or language as may agitate the present excited condition, and thus precipitate the impending evil.

4. That we are unalterably attached to the union as it is ; and as that union was in the beginning based upon compromise and conces- sion by the various sections, so, in view of the alarming dangers that now for the first time seriously threaten its existence, a spirit of compromise and conciliation should guide the federal and state councils to all means productive of harmony, good feeling, and broth- erly love ; and that these should be exhausted before abandoning hopes for the perpetuation of the republic.

5. That while a withdrawal of even one state is to be regarded by us all as a grievous calamity, yet more than all is to be deprecated the shedding of brother's blood by brother's hand ; that if the union cannot be preserved by peaceful means, it cannot be perpetuated by force of arms ; that any attempt to compel a. sovereign state to remain in the confederacy will only result in civil war, the end of which cannot be foreseen ; that even if the attempt should result in the subjugation of the seceding state, the condition of the state would be that of a conquered province, and not that of an equal ; and that such compulsory fealty would be degrading to the people on whom it would be imposed, and inconsistent with the whole spirit and design of the union of the states.

6. That the people of California, equal inheritors with their brethren at the east, in this glorious republic, while they cannot contemplate without grief and horror a dissolution of the union, yet they reserve to themselves the right to act as their own interests may require in the deplorable event of a dismemberment of the states. They now reiterate solemnly and fervently through their representa- tives, their earnest devotion to the union loving-citizens throughout the confederacy, and their hearty co-operation for its preservation.

7. That our congressional delegation be directed to act as far as practicable in accordance with the spirit of these resolutions.

On January 24th, the majority of the committee on federal relations of the senate reported favorably, with amendments, the series of resolutions introduced by Edgerton. John H. Watson, of the minority, concurred with the amendments except so far as related to the twelfth resolution, and, as a substitute for that resolution, he recommended the resolution introduced by himself.

The amendments proposed were as follows, to add to the seventh resolution :

That in the acts of personal violence and outrages perpetrated in the southern states upon northern citizens, which acts have been entirely unpunished, and almost wholly unrebuked in said states, there is just cause for reproach and exasperation on the part of the north towards the south.

To strike out in the ninth resolution all after the word "abide," and insert "by the plan proposed by Senator Stephen A. Douglas, as a compromise and adjustment of the difficulties between the north and south or some similar plan."

On January 24th, in the senate, T. G. Phelps (republican) offered the following as a substitute for the union resolutions reported by the committee :

1. That the people of California look with troubled apprehension upon the condition of our national affairs.

2. That our government was formed to be perpetual, and cannot be dissolved except by revolution.

3. That there is sufficient power in the constitution of the United States to maintain the integrity of the union, and enforce the laws of Congress.

4. That secession is but another term for treason against the government.

5. That California will aid the general government with the entire strength of her militia in maintaining the integrity of the union and enforcing the laws of congress, in whatever quarter the one may be assailed or the other impeded.

6. That to apologize for the present secession movement is to aid and abet treason.

7. That the idea of a Pacific republic is repudiated by our entire people.

These resolutions were made the special order for the 31st.

On Jannary 26th, in the assembly, John White (democrat) introduced the following :

1. That the union of these states under the constitution was the result of a compromise, and a just regard for the rights and interests of all sections, and that these are the only conditions upon which it can be perpetuated.

2. That, in the judgment of the people of California, the right of secession finds no warrant in the constitution; but that we would regard with disfavor and alarm an attempt to compel by force a state to remain in the federal union.

3. That, in our judgment, the best mode of meeting the present difficulty is to call a convention of the states for the purpose of adjusting the present unhappy differences, and of making such amendments to the constitution of the union as may be thought necessary to secure the rights of all sections of the country, and to preserve the union for all time to come.

On the same day, Assemblyman A. W. Blair (republican) offered the following:

1. That while we deeply deplore the unfortunate state of political affairs that now disturbs the peace and prosperity of our common country, we clearly trace its cause to the false political doctrines of the party and men now having the control of the administration of the general government; and that we deem the administration of James Buchanan an unfortunate national calamity, and that the same has our unqualified condemnation.

2. That any person or persons, state, community or association of individuals whomsoever, who raise their hands or voices against the union of these states or the constitution thereof, or the due execution of the laws therein, should be held and treated by the people of California as enemies of the republic, false to their country, false to us, false to the federal constitution, and false to the cause of freedom, humanity, and civilization everywhere.

3. That the people of California are true to the union of these states, and unalterably and unqualifiedly opposed to the secession of any state or states from the federal union, and deny the right of secession or to dismember the government of these states in any way; and that they will with their lives, their fortunes, and most sacred honor support the federal government in the due exercise of all constitutional power necessary to preserve the union of these states, maintain inviolate the federal constitution, and enforce the due execution of the laws of the federal government.

10

On January 28th, in the senate, J. McM. Shafter (republican) made the following report from the minority of the committee on federal relations, to whom the various sets of resolutions had been referred :

1. That this legislature, and the people they represent, have witnessed with profound sorrow the political events which have been initiated, and are in progress of development in the federal union, and that the present crisis in our public affairs demands the exercise of firmness, justice, and wisdom upon the part of the people of these states and their representatives.

2. That the federal constitution was fully considered at the time of its adoption; that its provisions were the most just that would have been then generally acceptable, and now, when properly executed, furnish an adequate protection to all portions of the common union.

3. That the binding force of the constitution is in no way dependent upon the present volition of any citizen or state, and that the right of withdrawing from such union by such citizen or state exists under no circumstances nor pretenses whatever.

4. That the act of seizing upon the public property, the actual and forcible occupation of public vessels, forts, arsenals, and revenues with the intent of denying the right, and an actual resistance of the power of the constitution and of government organized under it, are acts of war, and if persisted in by organized bodies of men, will amount to a levying of war against the states of the union, within the constitutional definition of treason.

5. That so long as the constitution is recognized, the executive created by it should inflexibly enforce its provisions; and that the punishment of crimes, treason included, is one of those provisions which cannot be disregarded.

6. That California entirely repudiates the idea of a Pacific republic; that she will adhere with unalterable firmness to the government exercising its functions under the constitution, and that as its prosperity and triumphs have been hers, so in whatever perils that government may be placed, she pledges to its aid her fortune and her sacred honor.

In the assembly, on January 30th, Johnson (republican) offered the following :

1. That duty demands and justice requires our senators and repre-

sentatives in congress not to compromise the people of this state by declaring that in the event of a dissolution of the union California will go with the north or with the south, or will form a separate government of her own.

2. That our only aim is the preservation of the union of all the states, and that our devotion to the constitution of the union is unalterably fixed.

On February 1st, in the senate, S. H. Chase (Douglas) offered the following :

1. That the people of a state cannot absolve themselves from their allegiance to the national government, or from their obligations to support the constitution of the United States, and all laws made in pursuance thereof ; that this union was designed to be perpetual, and that the provisions of the constitution are ample to perpetuate the union ; that secession is not a constitutional right, nor a power reserved to the states, but a revolutionary remedy, to be resorted to only as a last mode of redress against continued wrong and oppression, when all constitutional remedies have failed.

2. That it is the duty of the executive to uphold the constitution and enforce the laws ; to see that the revenue is collected ; that the property of the United States is protected, and by prudence, moderation and forbearance to endeavor to preserve the public peace and maintain the union.

3. That whenever any state or states shall deliberately determine and undertake to secede from the union, it is for the national government to decide how far it will resist such revolutionary action ; that such decision is one of state policy alone, and based upon considerations of life, liberty, property, and prosperity; that until such a time as the national government shall recognize such seceding state or states as an independent nation, the laws should be respected and executed, and the honor, dignity, and power of the government sustained.

4. That the secession of any state or states from the union does not relieve other states from their obligations to abide by the national constitution and laws ; that no rights are acquired by revolution, and there is no dissolution of existing relations beyond the limits conceded by the government to a revolutionary people.

5. That California has no grievances originating in the union that should cause her to seek an existence out of the union, and that any

attempt to establish an independent Pacific republic would be impolitic and revolutionary, and condemned by and offensive to the sense and sentiment of the state.

6. That a faithful fulfillment of all the obligations that the constitution imposes, both by the national and state governments, an exclusion from the halls of congress of the subject of slavery in all its relations, except in those cases specified in the constitution, and the same spirit of concession and compromise, in which the government was established, are the only sure guarantees of liberty and union, peace and prosperity.

7. That the preservation of this union from impending danger should be a paramount consideration with every patriot; that there is no just cause to sever the social and political relations of the people of these United States, and no insurmountable obstacle to a satisfactory and permanent adjustment of all our political difficulties; that California, anxious to restore harmony and cement by affection this union, would come to the settlement of these difficulties in a spirit of the most liberal concession; that she would sanction either of the following modes of adjustment (not intending, however, to assert that she would not sanction other modes):

a. The plan submitted to the senate by Senator Crittenden, being certain amendments to the constitution, restoring the Missouri compromise, and making further provisions in relation to slaves and slavery; or,

b. An immediate admission of several states into the union, embracing all the territory of the United States, with some fair provision for the formation out of them of future states, when necessary; preferring, however, that plan which would most effectually and readily dispose of all controversy as to slavery in the territories, and contribute most "to form a more perfect union, establish justice, and insure domestic tranquillity."

8. That our congressional delegation be instructed to carry out the foregoing views, so far as applicable to their official action.

On February 3d, the assembly committee on federal relations submitted the following majority report :

WHEREAS, The obligations of the constitution, which bind each state as a member of the union of these United States, were voluntarily assumed; and whereas, an attempt is being made by the people of one or more of the states forcibly to dissolve this union and subvert this constitution ; and whereas, in the furtherance of this treasonable purpose, forts and other property of the people of all the states are being taken from the possession of the constitutional agents of the United States government; and whereas, the people of said states are preparing to resist the enforcement of the laws of the United States; and whereas, the people of California, by their representatives in the legislature, desire to express their loyalty to the constitution and the union, and to instruct their congressional representatives to support and sustain in all their integrity, the union and the constitution as they were bequeathed to us by our fathers ; therefore, resolved :

1. The withdrawal of a state from its membership and obligations in the federal union, in defiance of the general government, can only be accomplished by a successful resistance to the whole power of the United States.

2. Decent respect to the opinions of the people of the civilized world, and the instinct of self-preservation, demand that the United States government should use all the power necessary to enforce obedience to its laws and to protect its property.

3. The people of California will sustain and uphold the constitutionally elected officers of the United States government in all constitutional efforts to preserve the integrity of the union and to enforce obedience to the acts of congress and the decisions of the courts. After the laws have been enforced, and the power and authority of the constitution and the government of the United States recognized and acknowledged, every feeling of nationality and brotherhood demand that such compromises as are consistent with justice shall be made, for the purpose of restoring that harmony which should characterize the people of a common country.

The minority of the committee reported the following :

WHEREAS, Events which have recently transpired, and which are daily transpiring in the Atlantic states, leave but little room to doubt that the American union, if not already dissolved, is on the verge of dissolution ; and whereas, the people of California regard such dissolution as a most direful calamity ; and whereas, we look upon a remodeling of the federal constitution by a national constitutional convention as the surest means of restoring peace and harmony to our distracted country ; therefore, resolved :

1. That the congress of the United States be, and is hereby urged

to take steps for the calling of such convention, in accordance with·
the fifth article of the federal constitution.

2. That we do most earnestly invite the several states of the union,
as well as such state or states as may deem themselves to have with–
drawn from the union, to co-operate with us through the respective
legislatures, in urging upon congress the immediate necessity of calling said convention.

3. That we deprecate any attempt on the part of the general government to maintain, by force of arms, the union of these states,
since to do so would light the fires of civil war and crush forever the
last hope of reconciliation between the opposing sections.

4. That the people of California acknowledge neither the north
nor the south, but the whole American union as their common
mother, to whom they are united not merely by considerations of
interest, but by the more enduring ties of blood and filial affection.

5. That as Californians we are willing to stand by the whole union,
hazarding, if necessary, our lives and fortunes for her defense ; but
we are not prepared to pledge our allegiance to either a northern or
a southern fragment of a dismembered confederacy, nor will we ever
consent to become the ally of one section in waging a fratricidal war
against another section of our common country.

In the assembly, on February 2d, O. W. Piercy (Douglas) offered
the following :

As the sense of this house, that the troubles existing in the Atlantic states are justly chargeable to the sectional doctrines advocated
by the republican party.

A motion to lay on the table was lost—28 to 41.   John Conness
(Douglas) offered the following amendment:

And that the United States forts and arsenals recently taken at
Charleston and elsewhere have undoubtedly been taken by black
republicans in disguise.

The amendment was lost—22 to 37.   Thomas O'Brien (Douglas)·
offered the following amendment :

Strike out republican party and insert "republican and Breckinridge parties."

N. Greene Curtis (Douglas) offered the following substitute :

That we have an abiding confidence in the justice and patriotism
of the people of the United States, and that the unhappy domestic·

difficulties now existing between the north and the south are not chargeable to the great masses of the people of the United States, but are justly chargeable to the abolitionists of the north and the secession leaders of the south.

The whole matter was laid on the table.

On February 5th, in the assembly, William Childs (Douglas) offered the following, which was laid on the table—43 to 29:

That we do most cordially approve the patriotic, conservative and humane sentiments enunciated by the Hon. Stephen A. Douglas, senator from Illinois, in the United States senate on January 3, 1861, inasmuch as in his view of the present fearful crisis in the destinies of our beloved country, that eminent senator repudiates as unwise, fratricidal, barbarous and inexpedient any attempt to make war upon any one or more states for the purpose of forcing them to remain in the union.

In the senate, on February 12th, Jas. T. Ryan (Douglas) gave notice that he would, at an early day, introduce a bill authorizing the governor to order an election of delegates to represent California in a convention of all the states that may be called by the joint action of the states, or by the action of congress, to take into consideration the present unfortunate condition of national affairs, and devise a plan by which the preservation of the union may be insured, provided such convention may be called. The bill was not introduced, however.

On February 12th, A. Wood (Douglas) introduced the following in the assembly:

1. That we fully and cordially endorse the plan proposed by the Hon. John J. Crittenden, for a settlement of the existing troubles in the Atlantic states, which is as follows. (Then followed at length what is known as the Crittenden compromise.)

2. That our congressional delegation are instructed to do all in their power to procure the adoption by congress, of the foregoing, or some similar plan.

The previous question was ordered, and the resolutions were referred to the committee on federal relations by a vote of 38 to 34. On the same day, P. H. Harris (Douglas) offered the following in the house:

That we heartily endorse the plan of settlement for existing diffi-culties in the Atlantic states, as proposed by the Hon. John J. Crit-tenden, in the United States senate, on January 3d, 1861 ; and that we approve and commend the patriotism and wisdom of the Hon. Ste-phen A Douglas and the Hon. John C. Breckinridge, manifested by them in their endorsement of the same, and in their condemning the use of military force to coerce the southern people, recommending conciliation and concession rather than war, and compromise rather than disunion.

The author said that he introduced the resolution for the purpose of affording the members an opportunity " to show their hands." E. W. Councilman (republican) offered the following substitute :

WHEREAS, Treason, as defined by the constitution of the United States, exists in several of the states of the union; *therefore, resolved:*

1. That the legislature of California, profoundly impressed with the value of the union, and determined to preserve it unimpaired, hail with patriotic gratitude the recent firm and dignified special mes-sage of the president of the United States ; and we cheerfully tender to him, through the chief magistrate of our own state, whatever aid in men and money may be required to enable him to enforce the laws and uphold the authority of the federal government, and in defense of the more perfect union, which has conferred prosperity and happiness on the American people. Renewing the pledge given and redeemed by our fathers, we are ready to devote our fortunes, our lives, and our sacred honors in upholding the union and the con-stitution.

2. That the union-loving citizens and representatives of Delaware, Maryland, Virginia, Kentucky, Missouri, and Tennessee, who have labored with devoted zeal and courage to withhold their states from the vortex of secession, are entitled to the warmest gratitude and admiration of the people of the whole country.

After an animated discussion, the substitute was lost by a vote of 5 to 69, and amid considerable feeling and disorder the Harris reso-lution was adopted—44 to 29. A motion to reconsider the last vote was lost on the following day.

On February 13th, J. Logan (Douglas) offered the Harris resolu-tion in the senate, and on the 14th, it was laid on the table. The resolution was subsequently taken from the table, and considered on the 16th. J. T. Ryan moved to amend by striking out all after "1861;" and R. C. Clark (Douglas) moved to amend the amendment by striking out all after the word "commend," and inserting the following "the position of all those who insist upon a peaceful adjustment by compromise of pending difficulties with the south." The Clark amendment was accepted.

S. A. Merritt (Breckinridge) offered the following substitute:

That we heartily endorse the plan of settlement for existing differences in the Atlantic states, as proposed by Senator John J. Crittenden in the senate of the United States, January 3d, 1861; and that we condemn the use of military force to coerce the southern people, and recommend conciliation and concession rather than war, and compromise rather than disunion.

The substitute was accepted.

Mr. DeLong moved to strike out all after "1861," and the motion was lost—15 to 15. Mr. Clark moved to strike out the words "and that we condemn the use of military force to coerce the southern people." On the 27th, the Clark amendment was lost—14 to 15. Mr. DeLong moved to amend by inserting after the words "southern people," the words "except such as may be by the constituted authorities of this union deemed absolutely necessary for the safety and perpetuity of the same, after all attempts to effect a reconciliation by compromise have failed." The amendment was lost—10 to 17. Several other amendments were proposed and lost, when T. G. Phelps offered the following substitute:

That the people of California are in favor of adjusting any and all difficulties, and causes of dissensions that do, or may hereafter exist between different sections of the country, or between any section thereof and the general government, so far as the same can be done without acknowledging the right of secession, or compromising the dignity and integrity of the general government.

That the people of California are loyal to the constitution and union, and will adhere to them under any circumstances, and will uphold the general government in any constitutional action.

The Phelps substitute was lost, as was also the Merritt substitute. Mr. Clark moved to amend by inserting after the word "force," the words "under existing circumstances," and it was adopted—16 to 10. The resolution, as amended, was adopted—21 to 6.

In the senate, on March 12th, S. H. Chase (Douglas) offered the following substitute for the union resolutions :

1 That the withdrawal of a state from its membership and obligations in the federal union, in defiance of the general government, can only be accomplished through successful revolution.

2. That self-respect and self-preservation demand that the government of the United States should use all its constitutional power, so far as may be necessary, to protect its property and maintain the union, and that we will sustain the executive department in all constitutional efforts for such purpose.

3. That for the sake of harmony and union, and to avoid the horrors of civil war, California would give her assent to either of the following propositions :

a. The Crittenden compromise, as originally offered in the senate.

b. The proposition known as that of Mr. Rice, of Minnesota, being substantially to enlarge the boundaries of several of the states, and to admit at once into the union two states, embracing all the remaining territory.

c. The plan known as the border states plan.

Regarding that as the best and wisest measure of pacification which will most speedily and permanently settle the pending difficulty.

4. That California will scrupulously observe all the obligations imposed upon her by the constitution of the United States, and earnestly desires that her sister states may observe the same obligations.

5. That while we recognize no constitutional right of any state to withdraw from the union, yet when it is satisfactorily ascertained to be the will and determination of the people of the several seceding states to depart from this union, we would sanction some fair and honorable arrangement on the part of the nation by which such states could be released from existing obligations to the union.

In the senate, on May 7th, Caleb Burbank (republican) introduced the following :

1. That California will cheerfully respond to such requisition as the president of the United States may make upon this state for men, money, and means to aid in maintaining the supremacy of the constitution and laws of the United States.

2. That the people of California are a loyal and union-loving people, and will hold themselves in readiness at all times to aid our

general government in upholding and defending the constitution, laws, and property of the United States against all insubordination, treason, or rebellion that may threaten to disturb domestic tranquillity, or to endanger the integrity and permanency of the constitution of the United States.

In the assembly, on May 18th, O. H. Kungle (Breckinridge) introduced the following, which was laid on the table—45 to 11.

WHEREAS, A number of the states have withdrawn from the federal union, and after asserting their independence have established a new government, which is known as the Confederate States of America, and it being evident to the world that the people of those states are able to maintain their independence and determined to do so; and whereas, to refuse to recognize their independence and to attempt, by making war upon them, to conquer and reduce them into subjection to the other states would be wrong, and violative of the spirit of our institutions and destructive of our liberties, since the attempt would require the raising of vast armies, the increase of taxation, and the creation of enormous debts to burthen the people, and since no object can be attained by making war upon those states, for if conquered they would be ruined and desolated, and inhabited by a dissatisfied population, ever seeking an opportunity to throw off the yoke, and as we are not yet ready to give up our free system of government, based upon the assent of the governed, and establish in its place those arbitrary military forms necessary for the prosecution of aggression and conquest; therefore, resolved :

That the independence of the Confederate States of America ought to be at once recognized by the United States government, and that all questions between the two governments should be settled by negotiation and treaty.

The resolution was laid on the table—45 to 11. In the assembly, on May 13th, Johnson (Breckinridge) offered the following :

WHEREAS, Our common country is in danger of being distracted with civil war; and whereas, the people of California are mainly from every section of the union, and deeply deplore the unnatural sectional war in which our brothers in the east are now about entering; and furthermore, we are interested in preserving intact the union of all the states that made the union when it was established by our fathers, and those added them to won by her sons; therefore, resolved :

That our congressional delegation be instructed to offer the state of California, by her representatives at Washington, as mediator between the general government and the confederate states, to the end that peace may be restored, and that provision may be made for the calling of a constitutional convention of all the states, for the purpose of reconstructing the federal union on a firm and imperishable basis.

On the 24th, Kungle introduced the following in the assembly, which was adopted:

WHEREAS, It is provided in the fifth article of the constitution of the United States, that congress, upon the application of the legislatures of two-thirds of the several states, shall call a convention for proposing amendments to the constitution; and whereas, it has now become necessary that the states should meet in convention, for the purpose of devising means for the settlement of our present interstate troubles; therefore, resolved:

That the congress of the United States be, and is hereby urged to take steps for the calling of a convention of the states, for the purpose of revising and changing the constitution of the United States, in accordance with the fifth article of the federal constitution.

Early in the session of the legislature a movement was inaugurated by the Breckinridge members to effect an alliance of the Douglas party of the state with their party, and on February 18, 1861, a caucus was held by the members of that party and some disaffected Douglas men for the purpose of initiating action towards uniting the parties. The call was addressed to all democratic members of the legislature who were in favor of the plan proposed in the United States senate by Senator Crittenden for the settlement of the difficulties existing in the Atlantic states. Thirty-five members were present—19 Breckinridge and 10 Douglas democrats. A committee was appointed to draft resolutions to be reported at a subsequent meeting. On the following evening another meeting was held, at which there were accessions from the Douglas party. The members of that party who participated in the proceedings of the caucus were adherents to J. W. Denver and John Nugent in the contest for the United States senatorship, and it was understood that they favored the Crittenden compromise resolutions that had been passed by the assembly. The committee on resolutions reported the following, which were adopted:

1. That we, the undersigned, democratic members of both branches of the California legislature, feeling the necessity of uniting the two wings of the democratic party of the state preparatory to the coming general election, do most urgently request the state central committees representing the Douglas democracy and the Breckinridge democracy of the state, to speedily call meetings of conference of their respective bodies to ascertain, on consultation, whether some general plan cannot be adopted by which all the democracy of California can be united on one common platform, in opposition to the disorganizing and destructive principles of republicanism.

2. That in the event that said committee shall determine to pursue the course we have respectfully suggested, that they be requested to make known to us, the democratic members of the legislature, at as early a day as possible, the result of their joint deliberations.

3. That should it be found impossible for the committees to agree upon any satisfactory platform, and they shall so report to the members of this body, that in such event a general call shall be made of all the democratic members of both branches of the present legislature, to adopt in joint council such measures as will ultimately lead to the end so necessary for the future success of the democratic party in California.

4. That the chair appoint a committee of —— to call on every democratic member of both branches of the present legislature, to notify and request them to be present at an adjourned meeting of this body to be held in this chamber on Friday next, the 22d inst., to confer upon such matters as may be then and there suggested, in order to obtain a speedy, permanent and satisfactory organization of the entire democracy of California.

F. Sorrell (Breckinridge) introduced the following, which was declared out of order :

That in the opinion of the democratic members of this legislature, in convention assembled, the course recently pursued by Lieutenant-General Scott, in connection with the preservation to the general government of forts and other property appertaining to the late union, is in contravention to the constitution, which guarantees to each state all rights not delegated to the general government.

Another meeting was held on the 26th, with 44 members present. Lloyd Magruder (Breckinridge) offered the following resolutions, which were referred to a committee with instructions to report at a subsequent time :

WHEREAS, The republican party has, by advocating and supporting sectional doctrines, placed itself in an attitude of hostility to the constitutional rights of the people of fifteen of our sister states, and thereby, notwithstanding the oft repeated warning of the democracy, have brought the union to the very verge of destruction; and whereas, the interpretation which the democracy have always placed on the federal constitution is, in our opinion, the only one which is in accordance with the true spirit and intent of that instrument, and which alone will secure equal rights to every portion of our confederacy, while the republicans occupy a position antagonistic to, and destructive of that equality of rights; and whereas, the demand now being made by the republican party under the specious pretext of upholding the constitution and enforcing the laws, after misconstruing that instrument first, and then grossly violating its spirit and intent, is in fact nothing but a declaration of war against the southern people, for the purpose of coercing them either to the adoption of republican doctrines, or the loss of their equality as states in the union, to assist in doing which the democracy would have to abandon its time-honored principles, those which have been reiterated time and again; therefore, *resolved*:

1. That we cherish the warmest attachment for our federal union, and that we contemplate with the most profound sorrow the troubles and difficulties at present existing in the Atlantic states, which threaten to destroy the unity of our government.

2. That the true attitude of the people of California at this time of trouble is that of fraternal kindness towards the people of all the states, and her honor and interest alike demand of her to do all in her power to bring about harmony and reunion among the people of the whole country.

3. That we are in favor of amending the federal constitution in such a manner as will specifically secure to every portion of the confederacy equal rights under the government, and leave nothing to implication or doubtful construction.

4. That it is as much the duty of every good citizen to adhere to and uphold the spirit and obvious intent of the constitution as of the mere words thereof; and, therefore, no good citizen who entertains a just appreciation of the blessings conferred on the whole people by our present form of government, will advocate doctrines which are hostile to the intendments of the constitution, and in opposition to the rights of any portion of our common country.

5. That we heartily endorse the plan of settlement for existing difficulties in the Atlantic states, as proposed by the Hon. John J. Crittenden, of Kentucky, or of another plan which may be adopted by the great border states, north and south, which is in accordance with the spirit of our federal constitution, as expounded by the supreme court of the United States, and as construed by the democratic party in convention assembled, provided the same does not commit the government to the use of military force to coerce the southern people, recommending conciliation and concession rather than war, and compromise rather than disunion.

6. That we will now unite for future political action, and recommend all democrats throughout the state to do the same, and rally as one party for the preservation of our common country and the maintenance of the federal union.

The Sacramento *Union*, on February 28th, in speaking of the attitude of the political parties in the state, said :

Parties in California are in a transition state. The events of the past few weeks indicate a reconstruction, which will offer to the people of the state but two parties to unite with and vote with. But up to this time, men who aspire to be leaders exhibit such a want of confidence in the future that they hesitate to advance much beyond present positions. They are waiting the course of events in the Atlantic states.

The Breckinridge file leaders, however, have ventured to make one positive move towards the presentation of a platform upon which they claim the two wings of the democratic party may unite and act together. The plank they offer is the Crittenden compromise, upon which there was no particular difference.   *   *   *   But the Douglas members did not vote for it directly in the legislature. They voted to refer it, and that vote gave the Breckinridge wing the advantage of voting directly for a resolution which simply endorsed the compromise. The failure of that resolution opened the door for the introduction of one by a Douglas member, endorsing the compromise, and also the sentiments of Douglas and Breckinridge against coercion. Enough of the Douglas wing voted with the Breckinridge members to secure the passage of that resolution through the assembly, and that resolution was offered as the basis upon which it was proposed to unite the two wings of the democracy. The intention of the Breckinridge leaders is, if possible, to place themselves and their party in the position of the democratic organization of the state and the only antagonist of the republicans. They are determined there shall be but two parties, and that they shall lead one of them. When the legislature convened, the Douglas party had a working majority in each house, but it sunk through mismanagement into a minority; and so confident were its opponents that it was about being dissolved, that each calculated its chances for gathering up a majority of the fragments. The leaders of the Douglas wing, however, looked upon the Breckinridge party as the minority party before the people, and preferred rather to cling to their own organization than cast their lot with it.

On February 28th, the chairman of the Breckinridge state committee, Charles Lindley, issued a call for a meeting of the committee at Sacramento on March 20th, "to consider the perilous crisis in our national affairs, and to arrange for the state convention." In the call he said:

The convention which conferred upon us the trust as state central committee, received from each of us a solemn pledge not to do the very thing which the recent Breckinridge-Denver-Nugent caucus requests us to do; thus impliedly *reserving to future conventions* the question of amalgamation of parties, and the adoption of platforms.

The call also contained the following remarkable series of questions and declarations:

Let us have union if we can; *peaceable* dissolution if we must; but conflict, never.

If peaceable dissolution comes, why should not California remain with the free states?

If a bloody separation, why should she not establish a Pacific nationality?

Is she willing to be dragged into a war against a southern confederation of her sisters, should such confederation be irrevocably established.

Ought not she to demand of the other free states to consent to a peaceable separation, if any must come, as an unyielding condition of her remaining with them?

Does not Lincoln's foreshadowed policy of executing the laws over seceded states, imply force, cocercion, war?

Are ou people ready to be plunged into anarchy, and suffer the ravages of such a war?

These are the momentous questions to be considered, and which, it is feared, will too soon require action.

On March 15th the same gentleman wrote a letter, in which he reconsidered that portion of his call which was adverse to the proposition of fusing the two parties; and after admitting that a strong desire for such a union existed in his party, he intimated that by the 20th of March, when Lincoln's policy would be known, there would be little difficulty in effecting the union. He suggested that the two committees call a convention, which by concurrent action could agree upon a principle and a platform upon which the parties could unite. The Breckinridge committee met at Sacramento on the 20th with twenty-eight members present, but nothing was done beyond the appointment of a committee on resolutions, who were instructed to report to the central committee at San Francisco, on April 2d. On that day a call was issued for a state convention, to meet at Sacramento on June 11th, to nominate a state ticket, and a very elaborate address to the democracy was adopted. The address acknowledged all as democrats who would subscribe to the Crittenden compromise, and who were opposed to coercion. It drew the following doleful picture of the horrors of civil war:

What will be the consequences of war? No mortal man can fully foretell. By the experience of nations, and the light of history, we can see conscript laws dragging the sons of toil into military service, families decimated, industry paralyzed, commerce destroyed, individuals and states bankrupt, ruin, gloom, and desolation in the land —the civil yielding to the martial law—military spirits and military chiefs rising, millions of lives sacrificed, finally ending the despotism, with liberty lost forever. For what purpose are we to have war? Is it to preserve a union by force? Will you make the south love the north at the point of the bayonet, and consent to live with her as a family of states? It is madness! Madness!! Madness!!! After a hundred victorious battles in favor of the north, she would need an immense standing army to hold her conquered possessions.

The committee adopted the following resolutions:

WHEREAS, We are desirous of co-operating with all democrats upon the present political issues, regardless of the divisions which existed at the presidential election last fall; *therefore resolved,*

That the several county committees be recommended to direct, in

11

view of such co-operation, that the votes of all citizens be received at the primary elections for delegates to the democratic state convention, who endorse the Crittenden, or similar amendments to the constitution, and are opposed to coercion, and any and all attempts on the part of the administration to enforce, by military or naval power, the federal laws within the jurisdiction of any of the seceding states.

Late in April, papers were circulated for signatures among the Breckinridge legislators and their Douglas allies, requesting the Breckinridge state committee to meet at the same time and place as the Douglas committee, and on the 29th, the chairman issued a call for a meeting to be held in San Francisco, on May 7th. The two state committees held meetings at that city on that day, but without any joint arrangement from the Douglas committee. The news of the attack on Fort Sumter reached California, April 25th, and it created an intense excitement. Men who had been weak-backed before, and who had acted with the Breckinridge party deserted it and attached themselves to the parties that were more loyal. The Breckinridge party lost strength every day, and the principles of the Douglas and republican parties became more identical. The meeting of the Douglas committee was presided over by Joseph P. Hoge. A communication was received from a sub-committee of the Breckinridge committee asking for a conference with a view of uniting the parties, but the whole matter was laid on the table by a vote of 20 to 5, and the sub-committee was informed that no negotiations would be entered into.

On May 8th, the Douglas committee adopted the following preamble and resolutions :

a. WHEREAS, The democratic party has ever been the party of fealty to free government and fraternal devotion to the rights of the states of the union, and of unwavering fidelity to the laws, the constitution, the union, and the country—ready to maintain them by all proper means and at every sacrifice ; and

b. WHEREAS, The country is now defending itself against a war without justification, or decent excuse; waged upon it by certain seceded states—which is manifestly a war for the invasion of our national capital ; for the overthrow of our national government ; the oppression of the loyal states ; the subjugation of the union—a war to humble in the dust our national flag—to wrench from the American people their constitutional rights of determining for themselves their own policy, foreign and domestic, and to blot them out from the class of the great powers of the world; and

c. WHEREAS, Such war, so aggressive in its character, and so deadly in its purposes, forces upon the country an issue which can be met but in one way by any people having the common instinct of self-preservation, or worthy of an existence as a nation; *therefore, be it unanimously resolved by this committee :*

1. That, at this time, when the country is resisting with all its might a war of 'invasion and destruction, indifference is impossible to the patriot, and neutrality is cowardice, if not premeditated disloyalty.

2. That the people of California in the past have been most anxious for peace throughout the land, and will hail with joy an honorable adjustment in the future; at the same time, they are above all things for the union, the country, and the flag, against all assailants, no matter who they are, whence they come, or with what power armed.

3. That, in this great crisis of the American nation and name, our state will always, as heretofore, faithfully discharge her constitutional obligations to the union and the federal government, and, as in duty bound, will earnestly sustain the constituted authorities at Washington in all measures necessary to defend and protect either against this most unjustifiable and unnatural war.

4. That, in the name of the loyal people of California, we demand of the general government, by all its power, to protect their lives and property on the high seas, between this coast and the Atlantic, from the piratical flag which already threatens injury, and would inflict destruction on both.

5. That all former partisan differences are lost in the present overwhelming crisis; and he who would seek, by reviving them, to distract the people, or to wrest from their honest and patriotic devotion some sordid partisan advantage, is not true to the country nor worthy of the name of an American citizen.

6. That, as Californians, we appeal to the whole people of California, without distinction of party or reference to partisan issues, to stand with us by our country and our flag, that all may know that the great union democratic party of California is the overpowering majority of her citizens.

7. That with these views we cordially invite all patriotic men,

who hold these sentiments, to meet in grand mass convention at Sacramento, on the 4th day of July next, to nominate candidates to be supported at the ensuing election; and we recommend in the election of delegates, that the only test be approval of these resolutions and willingness to support the candidates nominated.

The Breckinridge committee was in session several days after the attempt at amalgamating the parties had so signally failed. The following modes of settling the difficulties in the east were approved :

A peaceful dissolution of the union, by recognizing the independence of such states as refuse to remain in the union without such constitutional amendments as will insure the domestic tranquillity, safety and equality of all the states, and thus restore the peace, unity and fraternity of the whole country, and the establishment of a liberal system of commercial and social intercourse with them by treaties of commerce and amity.

War, with a view to the subjugation and military occupation of those states which have seceded or may secede from the union.

E. E. Eyre introduced a resolution of unconditional loyalty to the union, but it was lost—receiving but 7 votes.

A grand union mass meeting was held at San Francisco, on May 11th, and loyal addresses were delivered by Senators Latham and McDougall and Generals Shields and Sumner. An invitation had been sent to Governor Downey to be present, and in reply, he sent a letter explaining that business prevented him from attending. In the letter, he said :

I believe that the only means of preserving the American union is honorable compromise and respect for the constitutional rights of every section. I believe in the government using all its constitutional powers to preserve itself and resist aggression. I did not believe nor do I now, that an aggressive war should be waged upon any section of the confederacy, nor do I believe that this union can be preserved by a coercion policy.

The meeting passed strong resolutions in support of the federal government.

In May, an anonymous address was published for a "union" state convention to be held June 13th, for the purpose of nominating a state ticket without regard to politics, and with a view of uniting the union vote. When the time came for holding the convention but a corporal's guard was present, and an adjournment was had to July 10th. On that day, very few persons were present, and the movement was abandoned. The republican and union democratic conventions had met and nominated their tickets, and the people who desired the election of loyal officers felt satisfied that the success of either of those tickets would secure that result.

The Breckinridge democratic state convention met at Sacramento, on Tuesday, June 11th. It was composed of men of talent, many of whom in former days had, to a great extent, led the democratic party in the state. The convention was rather a small body, and several of the counties were not represented. Charles Lindley, the chairman of the state committee, called the convention to order, and a temporary organization was effected. On the 12th, Tod Robinson was elected president, and Volney E. Howard, James T. Farley, J. E. N. Lewis, F. M. Warmcastle, Charles S. Fairfax, G. D. Roberts, Charles T. Botts, A. P. Crittenden, J. J. Franklin, James A. Johnson, S. Heydenfeldt, Charles Lindley, S. W. Sanderson, and others were appointed a committee on resolutions.

Mr. Sanderson submitted the following minority report

The undersigned, member of the committee appointed to draft resolutions expressive of the sentiments of this convention upon the political questions of the day, respectfully submits the following minority report:

1. That the democracy of California endorse and reaffirm the principles and doctrines contained in the Cincinnati platform, and that adopted at the national convention held at Baltimore, in 1860, (except so far as the same shadows forth the doctrine of secession), the same being a sound exposition of the constitution of the United States, and the rights of the several states under the same. That the allegiance of every citizen of the United States is due, first, to the federal government; and, second, to the state in which he resides.

2. That while we recognize the right of the people to change their form of government whenever the same has become oppressive, or failed to accomplish the end and object of all governments, to-wit: the happiness and prosperity of the governed, we emphatically deny the right—under the federal constitution—of any state to withdraw

from the union without the consent of three-fourths of the states thereof.

3. That in the judgment of this convention, secession is revolu-tion, and that the same should never be resorted to by the people except upon good and sufficient cause.

4. That while we believe that the south has had grievous and just cause of complaint against the north on account of the non-en-forcement of the fugitive slave law, and the denial to her, by the republican party, of equal rights in the territories, and that the actual enforcement of the principles of the Chicago platform, by the present or any subsequent administration, would be good and suffi-cient cause for revolution on the part of the south—it is the judg-ment of this convention that such cause did not exist at the time South Carolina seceded, and that the action of the seceded states in withdrawing from the union has been hasty and premature.

5. That it is the duty of every administration to uphold the federal constitution, maintain the integrity of the union, and, at all hazards, enforce the laws in every section thereof; and that it is the duty of every citizen, in these times of impending danger to popular govern-ment, to stand loyally and firmly by the constitution and laws of his country.

6. That California is unalterably attached to the union of the United States, and that she repudiates and spits upon the idea of a Pacific republic.

The majority of the committee submitted the following:

1. That the democracy of California endorse and reaffirm the principles and doctrines contained in the Cincinnati platform and that adopted at the national convention held at Baltimore, in 1860—the same being a sound exposition of the constitution of the United States, and the rights of the several states under the same.

2. That we are opposed to the employment of force by the general government against the seceded states for the purpose of compelling obedience and submission to federal authority.

3. That we are in favor of the preservation of the union upon constitutional guarantees which will be acceptable to both sections of the confederacy; but if that desirable consummation be impossi-ble, then we are in favor of the recognition of the independence of the confederate states, and a treaty of amity and peace between them and the United States government, as the only alternative

which will terminate the horrors of civil war and bring back peace and happiness to our distracted country.

4. That it is the duty of California, as a member of the union, to yield obedience to all constitutional acts of congress, and to all constitutional and legal acts of the federal executive.

5. That the president of the United States (Lincoln) has been guilty of the violation of the constitution, and usurpation of power, in borrowing and appropriating money, raising armies and increasing the navy without the authority of congress, and that such acts are dangerous to liberty, and tend to convert the government into a military despotism.

6. That we are opposed to the tariff passed by the late congress, known as the Morrill tariff, and that we here reiterate the doctrine of the democratic party—in favor of free trade and in opposition to any tariff which looks to the protection of particular interests at the expense of others, and that the principle here enunciated is of more importance to the people of the Pacific states and territories than to any other portion of the union.

The following were offered by Lindley, in open convention, as a substitute for both series :

1. That the avowal of Wm. H. Seward, in 1850, that "there is a higher law than the constitution," and his subsequent avowal that "the conflict is irrepressible"—the rapid growth of the republican party upon these sentiments—the repudiation by the state governments of the plain letter of the constitution, and of the decisions of the supreme court upon the slavery guarantees—the aggressions upon the institution of slavery through the medium of the republican press, orators, and pulpits, with a direct tendency to produce servile insurrections—the final concentration of republican will in the Chicago platform, culminating in the election of President Lincoln, and the appointment of the author of the "higher law" and "irrepressible conflict" theories as premier of his administration, carry with them, as a conclusion to the southern mind, the apparent final adoption, by a majority of states, of the doctrine that moral law and natural rights, as viewed from their standpoint, are paramount to the constitution ; the total disregard by the administration of the supplications of the conservative border states for a peace policy; all these things have alarmed the whole south, and have provoked and expanded into fearful proportions the present revolution. There-

fore, before God, the civilized world, and our country, we charge the republican party of the nation as being the primary cause of plunging the best, the happiest, the most powerful and prosperous nation on earth into what now promises to be the most terrible civil and sectional war ever known in the history of the world.

2. That we condemn the mode and manner adopted by the south for redress, seeking security for their rights out of, rather than in, the union, without heeding the sincere petitions of the border states. We affirm that our destinies are with the government in this struggle, and we love and revere the flag of our country and the constitution as our fathers made it, and stand pledged to protect and defend both, and preserve the integrity of that nation with whose destiny we are linked, and whose honor is our honor.

3. That California, as a state, cannot take a neutral position in this trying crisis of our country; that she must either remain in the union or go out of it ; that we intend she shall remain in it, loyal to the constitution and to the national flag.

4. That it is the solemn duty of our state to contend in the congress of the union, for peace, and urge the reception of commissioners with a view of agreeing upon a peaceful settlement of our difficulties by guarantees and reunion. If this should fail, then let California stand (in congress) on this sectional contest between her common parents, as did Burke and Pitt in the commons on the seven years' struggle between England and her colonies, deploring separation, but denying the policy of subjugation.

5. That the democratic party of this nation has ever recognized the constitution of our country as the highest law in the land, and, with the watchwords, the "union and the constitution," carried our country safely through all its trials, and, in view of the impending peril, it is the duty of all good citizens to rally to the standard of that party which has ever recognized the obligations of the constitution upon all, and the constitutional right of all under it, and rescue, if possible, our whole country and her institutions from both northern and southern fanaticism; and present or accept any plan of peaceful solution which can be honorably adopted by our government.

After a discussion, in which Sanderson addressed the convention at length, the minority report submitted by him was rejected—only two persons voting for it. The substitute resolutions were also lost. The report of the majority was then taken up. A motion to amend the first resolution by adding the words "provided the resolutions of 1798, referred to in this platform, should not be construed as declaratory of the right of secession," was lost, and the original resolution adopted. Thomas H. Williams offered the following substitute for the second resolution :

That we are opposed to the doctrine of the republican administration—a party which holds that the constitution of the United States must be maintained, and the union preserved by the exercise of the coercive powers confided to and assumed by the federal government within the several states, in opposition to the will of the people thereof.

The amendment was rejected, and the original resolution adopted. James T. Farley offered the following substitute for the third resolution :

That we are in favor of the preservation of the union upon constitutional guarantees which will be acceptable to both sections of the confederacy, and that we believe the plan of settlement proposed by the Hon. John J. Crittenden, of Kentucky, would meet with the entire approbation of the conservative men in all sections of the union.

F. M. Warmcastle offered the following substitute for the substitute :

That we are in favor of and will urge the adoption of the Crittenden resolutions, so called, or any other measures of peace and compromise which will restore harmony to our common country.

Both substitutes were rejected.   Lindley moved to amend by striking out all after the first proposition, and inserting the following instead :

Then, we are in favor of the reception of peace commissioners, for the purpose of obtaining a peaceful settlement of our difficulties, upon such terms as the surrounding circumstances and the honor of our country may require.

The amendment was rejected, and the original resolution adopted. The fourth resolution was agreed to.   Kittrell moved to amend the fifth resolution by adding : "and that his action in the premises deserves that he should be impeached before the next congress of the United States."   A delegate said that Lincoln deserved impeachment in hell and heaven as well as on earth, and the remark was received with applause.   The amendment was lost by a close vote, and the original resolution adopted.   The sixth resolution was agreed to.   Williams offered the following additional resolution :

That the speedy construction of a Pacific railroad is a national necessity; and that the democracy of California earnestly urge the use of the public money in aid of such work, instead of the prosecution of a war for the subjugation of the seceded states, so called, and the forcible emancipation of negroes held as property within those states.

After a discussion, all after the words "seceded states" was stricken out, and the resolution, as amended, adopted.   Farley offered the following which was adopted :

That we recognize the plan of settlement proposed by the Hon. John J. Crittenden, of Kentucky, in the senate of the United States, as being patriotic and just to all sections of the union, and it should have been adopted as a settlement of the difficulties existing between the contending sections.

On the 13th, Lindley offered the following :

That the Kentucky and Virginia resolutions of 1798, referred to and approved by us in the Cincinnati platform, and reaffirmed by our first resolution, are not construed by us as being declaratory of the right of secession.

Williams offered to amend by adding the following: "or any other specific mode of redress."   After a lengthy discussion, a motion to lay on the table was lost—131 to 137 ; the amendment was adopted, and the resolution, as amended, adopted.   The convention then adjourned until July 23d.   This adjournment, without making nominations, was the result of two causes :   First, the hope of uniting a large portion of the Douglas and Bell and Everett parties with them when they would meet again, upon the common basis of opposition to the administration—it being a general sentiment among the delegates that a reaction would take place in a few weeks in popular sentiment, which would array a powerful party in the north against the president's war policy; and, second, the inability to fix upon a standard bearer.   At the adjourned meeting, the following resolutions, offered by H. P. Barber, were adopted :

That this convention is unequivocably opposed to the bulkhead scheme, either directly or indirectly, and that we will use all honorable means to prevent and defeat a measure which is eminently calculated to create a moneyed monopoly for a few, at the expense of the best interests of the many.

That we tender the hand of cordial welcome and friendship to those old tried democrats in the eastern states who, regardless of threats or menaces, are standing unflinchingly at their posts, battling in defense of the old Anglo-Saxon rights of freedom of speech and person against executive usurpations and unauthorized assumptions of power, destructive to the liberties of the people and subversive of a free government.

Lindley then offered the following :

1. That the federal government has no powers except such as are delegated by the constitution, or clearly implied as necessary in executing the expressed powers. It is supreme within the powers delegated, and has the constitutional right to preserve itself intact, until changed or destroyed, by means provided in the constitution.

2. That the state governments have respectively all the general powers of sovereignty not delegated to the government, and are equally supreme within the limits of their reserved powers, and have also the right to preserve themselves intact. There is no "paramount allegiance" to either, but a separate and complete obligation to each within their respective limits.

3. That California, from her institutions, interests, associations, and patriotism, remains true to the union, and loyal to the constitution and flag of our country.

4. That we condemn both northern and southern agitators—abolitionists and secessionists—for plunging our country into sectional war. It should be the mission of California to aid in arresting this fearful strife, and restoring peace to our distracted people. But she must contend for peace as a question of *policy within* the government with whose destinies she is cast, and whose honor is our honor. She must contend for it to preserve the whole country. If she fails in this, then she must contend for it as a means of preserving from exhaustion, anarchy, or military despotism, those states with which our lot is cast.

These resolutions gave rise to a prolonged, and in some respects, bitter controversy, which lasted during the greater part of the day.

On the next day, they were referred to a committee, consisting of A. P. Crittenden, J. J. Franklin, T. H. Williams, P. L. Edwards, A. Montgomery, D. F. Douglass, and N. E. Whiteside.

The following report of the committee was adopted, on the 24th:

That convinced, as your committee are, that this convention did not, and does not intend in its platform to express any opinion whatever in favor of the right of secession, your committee do not consider it either necessary or proper to adopt any explanatory resolution upon the subject; and believing that the substance of the third and fourth resolutions presented by Mr. Lindley is already contained in our platform, we see no reason for any further declaration of our loyalty to the union. We, therefore, recommend that the resolutions be indefinitely postponed.

On the 24th, the following nominations were made:

John R. McConnell, for governor, without opposition.

Jasper O'Farrell, for lieutenant-governor, on the first ballot, over John A. Eagon and John C. Dudley.

W. C. Wallace, for justice of the supreme court, on the first ballot, over Sydney L. Johnson; H. P. Barber and J. G. Baldwin declining.

H. P. Barber and D. O. Shattuck, for members of congress, on the first ballot, over N. E. Whiteside, R. P. Hammond (declined), John C. Burch (declined), and John A. McQuade (declined).

Samuel H. Brooks, for controller, on the first ballot, over G. W. Hook.

Thos. Findley, for treasurer, on the first ballot, over John Q. Brown; R. G. Mesick declining.

Tod Robinson, for attorney-general, by acclamation; John Nugent, Humphrey Griffith, and Edmund Randolph withdrawing.

Horace A. Higley, for surveyor-general, without opposition; W. S. Green withdrawing.

M. D. Carr, for printer, on the first ballot, over S. W. Ravely and D. Fairchild.

Chas. S. Fairfax, for clerk of the supreme court, on the first ballot, over Tabb Mitchell and John R. Kittrell.

At the second meeting of the convention, some eight or nine counties, not represented at the first meeting, had delegates present. Several secession speeches were made in the convention, the most remarkable of which was delivered by Edmund Randolph, who declined to be a candidate for attorney-general against Robinson, and after announcing that he was opposed to the policy of President Lincoln and the war, said :

If that be the democratic party represented by yourselves, then I am with you (applause). If it be any other party, under any other name, represented by anybody else under God's heaven, then I am with them. My thoughts and my heart are not here to-night in this house. Far to the east, in the homes from which we came, tyranny and usurpation, with arms in its hands, is this night, perhaps, slaughtering our fathers, our brothers, and our sisters, and outraging our homes in every conceivable way shocking to the heart of humanity and freedom. To me, it seems a waste of time to talk. For God's sake, tell me of battles fought and won. Tell me of the usurpers overthrown; that Missouri is again a free state, no longer crushed under the armed heel of a reckless, and odious despot. Tell me that the state of Maryland lives again; and oh! let us read, let us hear, at the first moment that not one hostile foot now treads the soil of Virginia (applause and cheers). If this be rebellion, then I am a rebel. Do you want a traitor, then am I a traitor? For God's sake speed the ball; may the lead go quick to his heart, and may our country be free from this despot usurper that now claims the name of president of the United States (cheers).

A state committee was appointed, consisting of Wm. H. Glascock, A. C. Hinkson, J. E. N. Lewis, Jas. H. Hardy, O. D. Semple, J. O. Hunsaker, D. W. Gelwicks, T. H. Williams, D. E. Buell, G. W. Hook, John Daggett, J. L. Brent, S. A. Merritt, J. W. Bost, Geo. D. Roberts, S. B. Wyman, John Q. Brown, C. T. Botts, W. J. Hooten, T. L. Thompson, A. P. Crittenden, T. Hayes, J. H. Wise, J. B. Haggin, V. E. Geiger, J. C. Burch, J. B. Lamar, O. S Witherby, J. L. Ord, W. W. McCoy, C. Lindley, P. L. Edwards, E. J. C. Kewen and others.

The republican state convention met at Sacramento on Tuesday, June 18, 1861, and was called to order by B. W. Hathaway, chairman of the state committee. About 250 delegates were present. J. McM. Shafter was chosen temporary chairman, and on permanent organization A. A. Sargent was president; and C. P. Hester, Alfred Barstow, L. Hamilton, G. W. Granniss, L. Cunningham, Hart Fellows, Jas. Collins and others vice-presidents. A committee on resolutions was appointed, consisting of E. B. Crocker, C. J. Hillyer, E. G. Waite, A. L. Rhodes, G. W. Granniss, A. H. Myers, H. Cummings, J. A. Banks, G. W. Tyler and others. On the 19th the following resolutions were adopted :

1. That the union of all the states must be preserved, the federal constitution sustained, and the national flag respected wherever it waves.

2. That we heartily endorse and approve the firm, bold and energetic course of the present administration in its defense of the national territory and property from the attacks of rebels and traitors, and we pledge ourselves and all that we have, to sustain the federal government, in the use of all its powers in maintaining the constitution, enforcing the laws, recapturing and preserving the national forts, arsenals and other property, punishing traitors, and in defending union men in all parts of the country.

3. That the doctrine that a state is superior to the federal government, and that the former has a paramount claim to our allegiance, and the consequent assumption of the right of secession, is repugnant to the constitution, and to every principle of our system of government, and can only result in the destruction of the union and the establishment of a general anarchy.

4. That we point with pride to the general uprising of the people of all classes and all parties, both native and foreign-born, in support of the federal administration, as giving assurance to the world that we have a government fixed in the hearts of the people, and which is able to withstand all shocks, whether from domestic traitors or foreign foes, and as giving further assurance of a speedy return of peace by a thorough crushing out of rebellion.

The words "and all parties" were stricken out of the above resolution in the convention.

5. That we invite all who love the union and the constitution, and who favor the enforcement of the laws, to unite with us in one great adminstration party, in the support of the federal government, and the defense and vindication of the national flag.

. 6. That our present public school system should be sustained in all its essential features, and every effort should be made to extend its benefits and efficiency, and keep it free from all sectarian influences.

7. That under our present administration we look forward with hope to the speedy completion of a Pacific railroad, and the adoption of the free homestead system in the disposition of the public lands.

8. That we are opposed to the granting of valuable franchises to private parties unless clearly required by the public good; and the opinions and interests of the local communities, whose rights are thereby affected, should always be consulted, and when it is clearly requisite that such franchises should be confided to individuals or incorporated companies, the right to enjoy them should be opened to free, public competition, and under suitable restrictions, awarded to those who will accept their use for the shortest period, or pay into the public treasury the largest annual, or other compensation·

The original resolution read "shortest period and pay," but the "and" was changed to "or" in the convention.

9. That in this hour of our country's peril, the death of the Hon. Stephen A. Douglas, whose course in the present unfortunate crisis of our affairs is so honorably in contrast with that of some of his late competitors and coadjutors, is a national calamity; and that in rising above party for the good of his country he proved himself a true patriot.

A. H. Myers offered the following, which was laid on the table :

That in the opinion of this convention the interference of federal officials in local conventions and elections is a fruitful source of corruption, and should be discontinued.

A. M. Crane offered the following, which was indefinitely postponed—135 to 108 :

That the treasonable conclave who recently assembled in this place, and under the name of a democratic convention, put forth to the people a platform announcing in substance their sympathy for traitors, and in condemnation of the federal administration in its attempts to preserve, defend and vindicate the constitution and laws, meets with the most unqualified condemnation of this convention, and, as we believe, of a vast and overwhelming majority of the people of this state.

The following candidates were nominated on the 19th and 20th:

Leland Stanford, for governor, on the first ballot, having received 197 votes, to 104 for T. G. Phelps, and 24 for D. J. Staples; Samuel B. Bell withdrawing.

John F. Chellis, for lieutenant-governor, on the first ballot, over Alex. G. Abell and Hiram Cummings; A. M. Crane withdrawing.

T. G. Phelps and Aaron A. Sargent, for congressmen, over Chas. A. Tuttle, S. B. Bell, F. F. Fargo, Alex. Campbell, Frank M. Pixley, D. R. Ashley, and D. J. Staples.

Edward Norton, for justice of the supreme court, on the first ballot, over Oscar L. Shafter.

Frank M. Pixley, for attorney-general, without opposition.

Frank F. Fargo, for clerk of the supreme court, on the first ballot, over A. L. Rhodes, John L. Sykes, and James Green.

George R. Warren, for controller, on the first ballot, over W. Jones, Louis Jazinsky, T. C. Boucher, George C. Hough, and F. F. Low.

J. F. Houghton, for surveyor-general, on the first ballot, over A. B. Bowers, J. E. Whicher, and D. T. Hall.

Benjamin P. Avery, for printer, without opposition; F. Eastman, James W. Towne, F. Blake, George Amerige, and H. S. Crocker withdrawing.

Delos R. Ashley, for treasurer, on the first ballot, over William Jones, A. E. Hooker, and M. B. Clute.

It is a matter of curiosity that, with one exception, the nominees were from either New York or Massachusetts. A state committee was selected, composed of A. B. Nixon, F. F. Low, B. W. Hathaway, A. Barstow, C. L. Taylor, A. G. Abell, L. R. Lull, William Sherman, Charles Maclay, and others.

The union democratic state convention met in Sacramento on Thursday, July 4th, with about 650 delegates present. All of the counties were represented, and it was the largest convention of a party character that had assembled in the state. Jos. P. Hoge, chairman of the state committee, called it to order, and Leander Quint was chosen temporary chairman. On the 5th, James W. Coffroth was elected president, and A. B. Dibble, Charles E. Allen, A. Redington, C. B. Fowler, J. G. Wickersham, P. E. Conner, C. V. R. Lee, T. N. Cazneau, A. Deering, A. C. Brown, and others, vice-presidents. The committee on resolutions consisted of M. Fallon, A. C. Brown, H. J. Tilden, D. P. Durst, John Hume, H. U. Jennings, J. T. Ryan, A. Deering, E. McGarry, J. K. Byrne, J. E. Hale,

T. B. Shannon, A. Redington, A. J. Bryant, W. F. White, A. Schell, C. E. Fisher, J. H. Lawrence, O. Wolcott, C. I. Hutchinson, C. E. DeLong, and others. On the 6th, the same preamble that had been adopted by the Douglas state committee on May 8th was adopted by the convention, except that in paragraph "*b*" the words, "treasonable combinations in certain states claiming to have seceded from the union," appeared in place of the words, "certain seceding states" (p. 162). The following resolutions were agreed to:

1. (The same as the first resolution of the committee, except that the words, "with all its might," were omitted—p. 163.)

(Resolutions 2, 3, and 4 were the same as the resolutions of like numbers adopted by the committee.)

5. That in the present overwhelming crisis, he who would seek by reviving past partizan issues—(The balance of the resolution was the same as the fifth resolution of the committee, after the words, "reviving them"—p. 163.)

6. That we hold our paramount allegiance is due to the federal government; that the right of state secession is a dangerous heresy, inevitably destructive of our form of government.

7. That obedience to the constitutional will of majorities is the only safeguard of republican governments; that we will uphold the constitutional authorities, under all circumstances and at all hazards, in maintaining federal jurisdiction in its sphere, regardless of what party may be in power.

8. That governments are political organizations, armed with coercive power, without which they cannot exist. That it is not only no assumption of authority upon the part of governments, but their positive duty, to exercise such coercive power in order to maintain themselves against either foreign invasion or domestic rebellion.

9. That we trace the causes through which the present rebellion has been accomplished to the existence of · sectional political parties in the country; one, founded upon anti-slavery, the other pro-slavery —both equally anti-democratic, and destructive of the peace, harmony, and prosperity of the country; that it is the duty of the union democratic party to take a strong conservative position in this the hour of our country's trial, and rallying around our national flag, present an unbroken front to all sectional agitation.

10. (The same as the sixth resolution adopted by the committee.)

11. That in the death of Stephen A. Douglas, the democratic party has lost a great and mighty leader; the country a true pa-

12

triot, and our nation one of its brightest ornaments and noblest benefactors, and that in his dying words he has left us an imperishable legacy which will constitute in history the highest tribute to his memory.

D. D. Colton offered the following, which were laid on the table :

1. That California has too long suffered from special, excessive and wasteful legislation; that we are unalterably opposed to all lawmaking for private profit at the the public expense, and especially to all schemes for giving up the water front and commerce of the state at San Francisco to private parties or companies under the pretext of a bulkhead, seawall, wharf, combination, or any other name or semblance whatever. And we recommend that candidates for the legislature be pledged to this resolution.

2. That it is the duty of the legislature, by all proper means, to increase, maintain, and preserve the common school fund of the state, the general education of the people being its practical power, prosperity and greatness.

On the 8th and 9th, the following nominations were made :

John Conness for governor, on the fourteenth ballot, over John G. Downey, J. W. McCorkle, Eugene Casserly, John Bidwell, and Samuel Platt. The various ballotings were as follows :

	1	2	3	4	5	6	7	8	9	10	11	12	13	14
Conness	212	227	231	237	240	239	231	233	235	238	261	282	297	336
Downey	178	171	179	169	172	174	176	178	180	183	170	179	184	123
Casserly	160	157	152	148	147	150	150	147	147	148	163	162	164	183
Bidwell	52	49	40	47	39	32	34	35	40	39	40	81	1	—
McCorkle	52	50	52	52	55	57	62	61	52	46	withdrawn.			

Richard Irwin, for lieutenant-governor, on the first ballot, over Thomas B. Shannon, J. H. Hill, and O. K. Smith.

Henry Edgerton and Joseph C. McKibben, for congressmen, over James W. Coffroth, J. I. Pitzer, David Mahoney, R. M. Briggs, and Charles E. DeLong.

B. C. Whitman, for justice of the supreme court, without opposition.

George S. Evans, for clerk of the supreme court, on the second ballot, over M. D. Boruck, W. A. Gard, James D. Ryan, and Wm. Hayden.

George W. Bowie, for attorney-general, without opposition, Frank Hereford, W. G. Morris, C. T. Ryland, S. W. Brockway, S. G. Clarke, and F. B. Higgins, withdrawing.

J. T. Landrum, for treasurer, on the first ballot, over I. N. Dawley and Thomas Findley.

James E. Nuttman, for controller, on the first.ballot, over Austin W. Thompson and M. Gray.

J. J. Gardiner, for surveyor-general, on the first ballot, over W. S. Watson, John Doherty, J. J. Cloud, and John Allen.

John R. Ridge, for printer, on the third ballot, over John White, W. J. Forbes, Thomas A. Springer, James H. Lawrence, Andrew Black, and Wm. Biven.

A state committee was selected, consisting of A. C. Brown, John Hume, Wm. Higby, W. G. Morris, J. T. Ryan, A. Deering, E. McGarry, L. Quint, J. K. Byrne, L. B. Arnold, J. W. Coffroth, C. V. R. Lee, J. C. Davis, J. B. Southard, W. J. Forbes, L. N. Ketchum, J. P. Hoge, D. D. Colton, P. Donahue, C. E. DeLong, L. D. Latimer, S. H. Chase, J. J. Green, A. Redington, Frank Denver, W. B. Hunt, M. Walden, and others.

On July 31st an attempt was made to hold a Breckinridge ratification meeting at San Francisco, but the people refused to hear the speakers. The candidate for governor endeavored to make himself heard, but he only partially succeeded. Other meetings of the same party, held elsewhere in the state, were also disturbed and broken up.

Under the congressional apportionment, based on the census of 1860, California became entitled to three representatives in congress, and the several state committees agreed to place on each ticket another candidate for congress. On August 20th, the republican committee nominated Frederick F. Low ; on the 22d, the union democratic committee nominated Joseph R. Gitchell ; and on the 27th, the Breckinridge committee nominated F. Ganahl.

Towards the close of the campaign, a settlers' ticket was placed in the field, but it cut no particular figure in the fight. It was made up from the other tickets, and endorsed Conness for governor, Irwin for lieutenant-governor, Phelps and McKibben for congressmen, Norton for justice of the supreme court, Fargo for clerk of the supreme court, Bowie for attorney-general, Ashley for treasurer, Nuttman for controller, and Gardiner for surveyor-general.

The election was held on Wednesday, September 4th, and resulted in a complete triumph for the republican ticket. It was attended with considerable excitement, and at San Francisco a few prominent secessionists were driven from the polls. Weapons were drawn, but no person was hurt. In a private conversation during the campaign, McConnell had stated, it was said, that as Kentucky would go so he would go, and that Kentucky would go out of the union. This remark was used with effect against him, and on the eve of the election he published a letter, in which he stated that if he should be elected he would obey the federal requisitions for troops, etc.; but his profession of loyalty came too late to save him from defeat.

An effort was made late in the campaign to consolidate the union democratic and republican parties and tickets, but it failed of consummation.

The vote of the state was officially canvassed on October 17th, and the following result was exhibited:

For Governor—Stanford, 56,036; Conness, 30,944; McConnell, 32,751.

Lieutenant-Governor—Chellis, 52,593; Irwin, 34,479; O'Farrell, 32,356.

Congressmen—Phelps, 51,651; Sargent, 50,692; Low, 39,060; Edgerton, 35,449; McKibben, 35,401; Gitchell, 22,550; Barber, 31,591; Shattuck, 31,712; Ganahl, 24,036.

Justice of the Supreme Court—Norton, 53,652; Whitman, 34,034; Wallace, 31,970.

Attorney-General—Pixley, 48,664; Bowie, 37,615; Robinson, 31,880.

Treasurer—Ashley, 51,868; Landrum, 34,116; Findley, 33,153.

Controller—Warren, 51,658; Nuttman, 35,186; Brooks, 31,239.

Surveyor-General—Houghton, 51,373; Gardiner, 35,439; Higley, 32,179.

Clerk of the Supreme Court— Fargo, 51,017; Evans, 36,487; Fairfax, 32,314.

Printer—Avery, 52,160; Ridge, 34,849; Carr, 32,300.

After the election, a number of southern sympathizers left the state to join the confederate army, and not a few citizens of California enlisted in the federal army. On August 3d, Austin E. Smith, a son of "Extra Billy" Smith, and who had been prominently connected with state politics, was arrested for treason in New York, on the arrival of the California steamer, on which he was a passenger. Senator Gwin, Calhoun Benham, and J. L. Brent were also arrested on board of a steamer for the east by General Sumner, for the same offence, and placed in a New York jail. None of the parties were detained long. D. Showalter and a party who were making their way south overland, were overhauled and brought back and imprisoned for a time. Congressman Scott did not return to the state, but went south and joined the confederate army. Ex-congressman Herbert also fought against the union, and was killed in action. Late in November, controller Brooks privately placed his resignation in the hands of the governor, and after disposing of his property, left the state and enlisted in the southern army.

CHAPTER XIV.

1862. Union Resolutions—Union Convention—Douglas Convention—Breckinridge Convention.

Early in the session of the legislature of 1862, resolutions on the state of the union were introduced, and, as in the session of 1861, they gave rise to lengthy debates. On April 4th, a preamble and series of resolutions were adopted by both houses, which recited that the federal government was, at that time, struggling to put down a formidable rebellion, and to preserve the integrity of the union, under which, by the blessing of heaven, we had grown to be a great and prosperous nation; and that the people of this state, as a part of the common government, whose existence had become endangered by such a rebellion, could not, with honor or propriety, remain silent or passive. Therefore, it was resolved, that the attachment of the people of California to the union of the states in one undivided nation is firm and unalterable; that the rebellion was without justification or decent excuse, and was but the result of a wicked conspiracy long since formed by designing and ambitious men to overthrow our republican form of government, and subvert the liberties of the American people; that they favored the most thorough and vigorous prosecution of the war; that they viewed with pride and admiration the conservative and patriotic course pursued by the president, and denounced as enemies of the country all those who sought to divide the executive councils or embarrass the government either by captious criticism or by efforts to convert the war into a means for carrying out ultra political doctrines; that the people of the state pledged their cordial and earnest support to the federal government; that the questions which had in the past divided the people into different political organizations had either become obsolete or were for the time being in abeyance, and that the only vital issue before the country was the one of loyalty or dis- loyalty. While the resolutions were under consideration in the senate, on March 6th, R. F. Perkins offered an amendment recom- mending that the slaves in the south be armed, but it received but one vote—his own.

F. F. Low, who had been elected a third member of congress in 1861, proceeded to Washington and presented his credentials, but was not admitted to a seat in the house of representatives, until June 3d.

The subject of uniting the republican and union democratic par- ties continued to be agitated in 1862, and many of the prominent members of those parties favored abandoning both party organiza- tions and forming a new party, the foundation principle of which should be the support of the union and of the administration of President Lincoln. A considerable number of union democrats, however, desired that no change should be made. They disliked the abolition doctrine of the republicans and the secession sentiment of the Breckinridge democracy, and preferred to occupy the middle ground. It was very evident, however, that their party was rapidly approaching dissolution, and that portions of it would go to each of the other parties.

On April 6th, several of the state officers addressed a letter to Governor Stanford, in which they stated that much discussion had arisen as to the propriety of calling a republican state convention to nominate a party candidate for the only state office to be filled that year, and asked his opinion as to the expediency of calling such a convention. The governor replied, on the 9th, and advised that a republican convention be called, and that a strict party organization be maintained. The letter was the subject of considerable comment, and was criticised by some of the papers as being at variance with the views of a majority of the party.

A meeting of republican and union democratic members of the legislature, who were of a liberal turn, was held on the 26th of April, for consultation, and it was resolved that the state committees of the two parties be requested to jointly call a union administration convention.

On April 28th, the republican committee issued a call for a state convention of the people who were in favor of sustaining the national administration, and of maintaining the constitution of the United

States, and preserving the union entire. The name "republican" was dropped from the call, which was issued in response to a numerously signed request directed to the committee, asking it to take the step as the initial move towards forming a new party.

An adjourned meeting of the legislative caucus was held on the same evening, which was attended by twenty-nine members. Resolutions were unanimously adopted endorsing the republican committee call, and recommending that the loyal voters of the state respond by the election of delegates to the convention. They also declared that the call sunk party designations and issues, and that instead of being a call for a party convention, it appealed to those who sustained the administration and the union. It was suggested that a more specific invitation be extended to the union democrats to co-operate in the election of delegates, by a call from their state committee.

In the meantime, in San Francisco, efforts were being made to effect a fusion of the Breckinridge and union democracy upon the basis of opposition to Lincoln's administration.

On May 6th, David D. Colton, the chairman of the union democratic state committee, addressed a letter to Senator W. Van Dyke, chairman of the legislative caucus, in response to the request that had been made for the committee to unite in the call for the union administration convention. In the letter, Colton said that he endorsed the union sentiments in the caucus resolutions; that he had neither the disposition nor the power, acting as chairman of the committee, to abandon the party organization and assist in the construction of a new party; that a union of union men was not necessary; that as true and loyal men as there were in California had voted for McConnell, as the most available candidate to defeat the republican nominee; that there was not then any considerable secession element in the state; that more than half of the federal soldiers in the field were democrats; that the democratic patriots at home should pray for the absent, and keep up the old democratic party; that that party alone could administer the government properly; that the best of a hundred good reasons why the democratic party should neither fuse with the republicans nor aid in building up a new party, was that when peace was restored, the people would as instinctively look to the democratic party to guide and control them, as would the mariner, after a frightful storm, turn his eyes to the compass to direct his course; that the dismemberment of the democratic party at Charleston was but temporary, and that the war would soon be ended, and the nation and the democracy would be restored to their original strength and purity. The letter was regarded as a strong bid for the peaceful adjustment of the differences in the democratic party.

On the 7th, the republican committee again met and extended a specific invitation to the union democratic committee to co-operate with them in the call for the union convention.

Pursuant to the call issued by the republican committee, the union administration state convention met at Sacramento on Tuesday, June 17th. The attendance of delegates was quite large, and the majority of them were republicans. The convention was called to order by William Sherman, chairman of the republican state committee, and G. W. Tyler was chosen temporary chairman over Alex. G. Abell. In the evening a committee on resolutions was appointed, consisting of Delos R. Ashley, C. B. Porter, T. J. Keyes, C. I. Hutchinson, Warner Oliver, Benj. P. Avery, Thos. Fitch, Nathaniel Holland, T. W. Park, R. H. Farquhar, William Higby and others. On permanent organization, Walter Van Dyke was president; and C. P. Hester, B. W. Hathaway, Dr. C. Duncombe, George C. Gorham, B. R. Nickerson, Wm. Sherman, and others, vice-presidents. A motion was made to appoint a committee to select a state committee, to be composed of one member from each senatorial district, and it was agreed to after some debate. On the 18th, the committee on resolutions made the following report which was unanimously adopted :

1. That we heartily endorse the present national administration, and hereby pledge ourselves to sustain it in all its efforts to preserve the union.

2. That we are in favor of a vigorous prosecution of the war, without regard to cost or sacrifice, until the last armed rebel is disarmed and the supremacy of the national government acknowledged in every state and territory of the union.

3. That we have no sympathy with any party or person who advocates a peace on any terms while there is an enemy of the union in open rebellion against the government; and that such a peace would prove to be but a hollow truce, leading again to rebellion and war, and would be a lasting disgrace to us and to our country.

4. That every citizen of the United States owes an allegiance to the national government which is paramount to his allegiance to

any state, and that any other doctrine would be repugnant to the constitution and to every principle upon which our government is founded.

5. That since the inauguration of the present national administration, all issues heretofore dividing the loyal people of the different political parties have been settled, and the only issue now before the nation is union or disunion.

6. That we call upon all loyal citizens of this state to unite with us in a union party, which shall place California where she of right belongs—high in the rank of states, ready to sacrifice all to preserve the rich heritage of liberty bequeathed to us by our forefathers.

The committee appointed on the preceding day reported the following names of gentlemen to constitute the state committee, and the report was adopted : Wm. Sherman, Alfred Barstow, A. G. Abell, James de la Montanya, W. G. Still, Charles A. Dana, James F. Kennedy, N. Holland, A. E. Hooker, A. A. DeLong, T. K. Wilson, W. H. Pratt, George Oulton, B. P. Avery, Charles James, J. C. Birdseye, Thomas Campbell, and others.

John Swett was nominated for superintendent of public instruction, on the first ballot, over George W. Reed, T. N. Machin, Frank Soule, J. B. McChesney, and A. H. Myers.

The following additional resolutions were adopted :

7. That we congratulate the army and navy of the United States upon the recent brilliant victories which their valor has achieved, and bespeak for them, when their work shall have been accomplished and peace consummated in the restoration of the union, the warm gratitude of all true patriots.

8. That the thanks of California are due to the house of representatives of the United States, for their prompt action in the passage of the Pacific railroad bill.

The union democratic state committee met at San Francisco on July 2d, 1862, and was presided over by D. D. Colton. Resolutions were adopted endorsing the action of the chairman in refusing to disband the party at the request of the republican committee; and expelling from their committee William Higby, "who had betrayed the trust reposed in him, by counseling, advising and co-operating with the republican leaders and officeholders for the purpose of disorganizing the union democratic party." The various communications requesting the committee to sanction the union administration movement were laid on the table. A preamble and resolutions were adopted declaring it to be inexpedient to call a state convention to nominate a party candidate for school superintendent. James J. Green and L. B. Arnold resigned as members of the committee, and several other members were not present at the meeting, as they had ceased to act with the party. The following resolutions were adopted :

The union democratic state central committee, while it adheres to and acknowledges the binding form of the principles of our party platform, as established by the union democratic state convention of the 4th of July, 1861, deems it eminently proper, under the existing state of the country and of parties, to present to the union democratic party of the state, the following resolutions :

1. That the union democratic party of California adheres immovably to its distinctive organization, and recognizes no necessity in the existing condition of the country and of the state, calling upon us as democrats, or as patriots, to abandon or qualify that organization.

2. That the democratic party of California are now, as heretofore, for the whole country, without division or diminution, and for nothing less—for the union and the constitution, without conditions or higher law reservations—for peace with all men and all nations, when it can be honorably secured or preserved, and for war when peace is no longer consistent with national dignity or the preservation of the people's just rights—for a strict construction of the constitution of the country, and a sacred regard, at all times, and under all circumstances, by ruler as well as people, by servant as well as citizen, for all its guarantees and provisions—for the preservation of the freedom of speech and the liberty of the press—for an honest and economical administration of the government, the faithful guardianship of the public credit, and the prompt punishment of treasury plunderers.

3. That the present rebellion and the attempt to overthrow, by force, the best government which the sun ever shown upon, is both unreasonable and criminal—an indefensible violation of all the pledges which citizenship implies, and such an outrage against humanity and civilization as nothing in the past can justify or palliate.

4. That, while this civil war continues, it is our duty and the duty of all loyal citizens to render to the government a cheerful and earnest support ; to stand by it in the enforcement of all constitutional measures tending to the suppression of armed rebellion ; to give its officers, so far as they are true to the trusts reposed in them, the aid and comfort which may be derived from our moral influence and physical resources ; and that we extend to these gallant men of our own and other states who have responded to the call of the government for that protection which arms alone can give, our hearty commendation and warmest sympathies. (The balance of the reso-lution is the same as the seventh resolution adopted by the union administration convention, on June 18th.)

5. That the effort now being made by a fanatical faction, under the assumption of superior patriotism and loyalty, to divert this war from its original purpose, as proclaimed by the president and congress of the United States—the maintenance of the federal constitution and the preservation of the union's integrity—and to turn it into a war of abolition, is an effort against the union, against the constitution, against justice, and against humanity, and should be promptly frowned upon by all the friends of free institutions.

6. That to bring the present war to a final and happy conclusion, and secure a union of hearts as well as a union of hands, it is absolutely necessary to reassure the misguided masses in the revolted states that we mean no warfare upon their rights, and are actuated by no spirit of revenge ; to disavow any other wish than that of bringing together these now belligerent states, without the loss to any one of them of a single right or privilege which it has heretofore enjoyed. To show by our acts, as well as by our professions, that our whole purpose is to preserve our government just as it came to us from the hands of our fathers ; to regard all the guarantees of the constitution, whether to the states, or to the people of the states and to become once more a harmonious and happy people. And that, to this end, it is the duty of the union democratic party not only to preserve its distinctive organization, but to demonstrate by honorable and patriotic measures, both its determination and its power, to withstand and render harmless the assaults of northern or southern sectionalists upon constitutional liberty.

Jonathan D. Stevenson was nominated, without opposition, for superintendent of public instruction.

On August 5th, L. B. Arnold, James J. Green, John B. Knox, Wm. Higby, John Hume, E. Willow, A. C. Brown, and P. E. Drescher, members of the union democratic state committee, published a letter in which they repudiated the action of the other members of the committee, and declared themselves in favor of abandoning the old party organization and adhering to the union administration party.

The Breckinridge state convention met at Sacramento, on Wednesday, August 6th. It was called to order by A. P. Crittenden, chairman of the state committee. Humphrey Griffith was elected temporary chairman. A committee on resolutions was appointed, consisting of W. H. Glascock, James T. Farley, Tod Robinson, Charles D. Semple, D. W. Gelwicks, A. P. Crittenden, W. C. Wallace, B. F. Myers, T. H. Williams, S. Heydenfeldt, D. S. Terry, W. J. Hooten, H. P. Barber, J. F. Linthicum, and others. On permanent organization, Griffith was elected president; and Colonel Haraszthy, H. P. Barber, W. C. Wallace, David Fairchild, and S. B. Wyman, vice-presidents.

On the 7th, the following resolutions were reported by the committee :

WHEREAS, In the earliest years of the republic, a controversy arose concerning the powers granted to the federal government, the federalists claiming the power to enact the alien and sedition laws, and the democrats denying that such power was delegated, and insisting that all powers not expressly delegated were reserved to the states or to the people. The democratic party was then formed upon the principles enunciated in the Kentucky and Virginia resolutions of 1798, and in the report of Mr. Madison to the Virginia legislature of 1799, and have ever since been the distinctive feature of democracy. The federal party became extinct, and the American people sustained the equality and all the reserved rights of the states until the inauguration of the present chief magistrate, who in his first address to the people denied that the states ever were independent sovereignties, and consequently had no right to judge of any infraction of the federal compact ; thus denying that the people are sovereign, or that they have a right to create a state government, and also a federal government, granting to the one and denying to the other any powers they may think best calculated to secure their safety and happiness; and whereas, the revival of the doctrines of the old federal party, destroying our former system of state govenment is dangerous to civil liberties and justly alarming to all lovers of free government; *therefore, resolved,*

1. That the democratic party of the present day is the true representative of the theory of the American revolution; that all just powers are derived from the consent of the governed, and that the people have the right to change their form of government and their political associations whenever they shall deem it essential to their happiness.

2. That the constitution of the United States was a compromise between conflicting sectional interests, and that the true construction of that instrument is the one which has always been maintained by the democratic party and enunciated by its statesmen, in the Virginia and Kentucky resolutions and the platform of the national democratic convention at Cincinnati.

3. That we agree with the present chief magistrate in one sentiment expressed by him, in substance, that the two sections of our union cannot fight always; that, after they had exhausted themselves by war, the same questions would arise, to be settled by negotiation, the same sentiment having been expressed by Mr. Douglas that *"war was disunion;"* and again reiterated by our state convention of last year, declaring that we preferred negotiations in the outset to war.

4. That the war now waged by the United States against the confederate states is unjust and unnecessary war, in which thousands of valuable lives and millions of treasure have been expended in vain, when, as we feel and believe, this vast destruction would have been avoided by wise diplomacy and temperate negotiation.

5. That the events of the past twelve months have convinced us that no compromise can be made between the republican party and the seceded states. Sectional hatred having constantly increased under republican obstinacy in adhering to the Chicago platform instead of the constitution, therefore, the democratic party must succeed, or the war will have no end.

6. That the democratic party is now the only true union party, because they now profess, and if in power would practice, the same principles which have governed their administrations from the foundation of the government, to-wit: equal rights to each state and to all sections, thus cutting off the possibility of sectional animosity.

7. That the military should be subordinate to the civil power of the government, and that we view with distrust the encroachments of the military upon the rights of the civil authorities.

8. That the privileges of the writ of habeas corpus, regarded for centuries as the greatest safeguard of the liberties of the people, and constituting a portion of our fundamental law, should, except as provided for by the constitution, remain inviolate to every citizen.

9. That the freedom of speech, and of the press, should remain unabridged; that to deprive the people of these rights, guaranteed to them by the constitution, would be rank usurpation; and that they are inestimable to the citizen, and formidable to tyrants only.

10. That no citizen should be arrested without just or reasonable cause, and the cause of his arrest should be made known to him, and a speedy trial granted.

11. That the rights of the several states, and state lines, and local state institutions, should remain unimpaired.

12. That the purpose avowed and advocated by *republican disunionists*—to liberate and arm the slaves—is revolting to humanity; a disgrace to the age; and meets our unqualified condemnation.

13. That we view with alarm the reckless extravagance which pervades every department of the federal government; that a return to rigid economy and accountability is indispensable to arrest the systematic plunder of the public treasury by favorite partisans, while the recent startling developments of frauds and corruptions at the federal capital, show that an entire change of administration is imperatively demanded.

14. That we rejoice that the democratic members of congress, from all the free states, have agreed upon the constitutional principles embodied in an address issued by them to the people of the United States, and that great victories have been won by our fellow democrats in the western states, upon principles which we can cordially endorse. (This resolution was stricken out in the committee.)

15. That we reaffirm and heartily endorse the sentiments contained in the resolutions adopted by the democratic state convention, in 1861, of California.

T. H. Williams moved to strike out the preamble and all the resolutions except the fifteenth. He said that there was much in the resolutions that would have a tendency to confuse the minds of the members of the convention, and that they would be made the subject for the severest criticism, if adopted. The motion prevailed, and the fifteenth resolution was adopted. C. D. Semple offered the resolution numbered 14 in the above series, and it was adopted.

O. P. Fitzgerald was nominated, without opposition, for superintendent of public instruction; Andrew J. Moulder withdrawing.

During the sitting of the convention, several leading members made speeches in favor of making no nominations, and leaving members of the party free to vote as they pleased, but a motion to that end was laid on the table by a vote of 226½ to 68½. About 108 delegates were present, although 295 votes were cast—nearly two-thirds of the votes being cast by proxy. A state committee was appointed, consisting of Harry Linden, C. R. Street, D. E. Buell, D. W. Gelwicks, George W. Hook, S. F. Hamm, J. Daggett, T. J. Henley, S. A. Merritt, J. W. Bost, D. S. Gregory, W. C. Wallace, James Anderson, P. O. Hundley, T. H. Williams, Thomas Hayes, J. H. Wise, P. L. Solomon, J. D. Thornton, D. S. Terry, J. L. Ord, L. Archer, T. L. Thompson, V. E. Geiger, H. P. Barber, H. Griffith, B. P. Hugg, W. J. Hooten, and others.

Towards the close of August, Senator Latham delivered several speeches from the stump, in which he took the inconsistent position of urging the prosecution of the war by the federal government to last extremity, and at the same time fiercely assailed the administration. He fixed the responsibility of the war upon the southern leaders, and declared that it was the most unjustifiable war recorded upon the pages of history, and that it was without apology or reason; that the federal government was compelled to fight in self-defense, and that, if it had not fought to vindicate itself, it would have merited and received the contempt of every government on the face of the earth; that it would have to be fought out, and that no settlement could be expected until the war was at an end; that the original object of the war, so far as the federal government was concerned, was legitimate and proper, but that that original object had been abandoned, and that it was then prosecuted for emancipation purposes; that the constitution had been violated in the passage of confiscation bills, and that men had been illegally and unconstitutionally imprisoned; that the law abolishing slavery in the District of Columbia was an outrage, and that the ultra abolitionists had obtained the control of the government; and he said that the world had never witnessed such corruption as had been developed in the conduct of the war by the federal government. Congressmen Sargent and Phelps delivered speeches in reply to Latham.

The election was held on September 3d, after a vigorous campaign, and the union administration ticket was successful. The official vote was published on November 3d, and exhibited that Swett had received 51,238 votes; Stevenson, 21,514; and Fitzgerald, 15,-817.

Shortly after the election, several prominent southern sympathizers, among whom were two members elect to the legislature, were arrested by the United States authorities and sent to Alcatraz, but on taking the oath of allegiance to the government, they were discharged.

CHAPTER XV.

1863. Union Resolutions—Union Convention—Democratic Convention.

In the senate, on January 6th, C. B. Porter, of Contra Costa, offered the following concurrent resolution :

That the loyal state of California receives with earnest favor the recent proclamation of freedom issued by the president of the United States and commander-in-chief of the army and navy, regarding the policy of the measure as necessary for the success of the efforts of the government for the suppression of a desperate and wicked rebellion, and the re-establishment of its authority, consistent with the spirit of our institutions, and full of promise for the future permanence, unity, and prosperity of the nation, and we hereby pledge to the measure the cordial and earnest support of the people of California.

B. Shurtleff offered a substitute, declaring in effect, that the people of California would continue to render the government their sincere and united support in the use of all legitimate means to suppress the rebellion, and "to restore the union as it was, and maintain the constitution as it is ;" that they believed that that sacred instrument, founded in the wisdom of our fathers, clothed the constituted authorities with full power to accomplish such purpose ; that the policy to which the government was pledged by a resolution passed by congress, in July, 1861, could not be departed from without violation of public faith, in which resolution it was declared that the war was not waged by the federal government in any spirit of oppression or for the purpose of conquest or subjugation, or for the purpose of overthrowing or interfering with the rights or established institutions of the seceded states, but to defend and maintain the supremacy of the constitution and to preserve the union; and that they viewed with disfavor the emancipation proclamation, believing that it was unwise, impolitic, and in direct contravention of the American doctrine as laid down by our fathers in the war of the revolution, and unanimously reaffirmed by the American people in the last war with Great Britain. The substitute was lost, and the original resolution adopted by a vote of 31 to 8. On the same day, E. B. Smith, of Sierra, introduced the following concurrent resolution in the assembly:

That we fully and heartily endorse the action of the president of the United States in issuing his proclamation of the 1st of January, declaring slaves, in certain states and parts of states in rebellion against the government, to be free; and that we believe with him that it is "an act of justice, warranted by the constitution as a military necessity"

The resolution was laid over. The next day, the senate resolution came up in the assembly, and it was laid over under the rule which required that resolutions concerning federal affairs should be treated the same as bills. On the 10th, the senate resolution was, after a lengthy discussion, amended on motion of Sanderson so as to indicate clearly that the measure was endorsed as a war policy, deemed proper and necessary by the commander-in-chief of the army and navy, and in that shape it was adopted by a vote of 64 to 11. The senate concurred in the amendments on the same-day. In the resolution, as thus finally passed, the words "policy of the" were omitted, and the words "laws of war" substituted for "spirit of our institutions."

The union state committee issued a call on April 10th, for a state convention, which was addressed "to all citizens who were willing to sustain the national administration in its efforts to suppress the rebellion." The party had greatly increased in strength since its success in 1862, and from the fact that national questions were kept prominently before the people through the action of union leagues, which had been organized in almost every town and precinct in the state. These leagues were in the nature of political clubs, in the interest of the union party. Stanford, Sargent, and Low were the leading candidates for the nomination for governor, and at first

13

the outlook was decidedly favorable to the renomination of the then incumbent of that office, but the friends of Low worked with system to secure the election of delegates pledged to his support, and with so much success that Stanford finally withdrew from the fight. On June 3d, the Sacramento county convention to elect delegates to the state convention met, and it was generally supposed that the friends of Stanford were in the majority. A resolution was introduced to instruct the state delegates to support that gentleman, but a substitute directing them to support Low was adopted by a majority of sixteen, to the great surprise of the Stanford men, who had been so confident of success that they had made no extra exertions to add to their strength. The defeated party charged bad faith and fraud, and a number of delegates seceded from the convention, but they cooled down the next day and, returning, assisted in nominating a county ticket. On the 10th, a primary election was held in San Francisco, and Low delegates were elected by a heavy majority, which assured that gentleman's success in the state convention.

The union state convention met at Sacramento, on Wednesday, June 17th, and the attendance of delegates was very large. N. Holland, chairman of the state committee, called it to order, and John H. Jewett was elected temporary chairman by a vote of 147 to 117 for W. H. Sears. This was regarded as a test vote, as Jewett was supported by the friends of Low. On permanent organization, W. L. Dudley was elected president; and Ramon Hill, J. J. Owen, W. W. Traylor, J. R. Watson, J. B. Frisbie, S. P. Wright, D. W. C. Rice, Jacob Deeth, J. N. Turner, J. Bidwell, R. M. Briggs, G. S. Evans, and others, vice-presidents.

D. O. McCarthy submitted the following resolutions to the convention:

1. That we cordially reaffirm the following resolutions adopted at the union state convention, of June 17th, 1862. (Then followed resolutions numbered 1, 2, 3, 4, and 5 of the series referred to.)

2. That we heartily endorse the president's proclamation of freedom, of January 1st, believing it to be a wise and proper war measure, and a step onward in the cause of civilization and human progress.

3. That the brave officers and men who are upholding the national flag on land and sea are worthy the admiration of mankind and the gratitude of the nation.

4. That we call upon all loyal citizens to unite with us in rebuk-

ing and defeating at the polls in September next the malignant tribe of copperheads, who, falsely claiming the name of democrats, seek on all occasions to discourage our armies in the field, and to corrupt the patriotic sentiment of the loyal people of the country.

The following additional resolution was offered :

5. That any means necessary to be made use of to preserve the union are constitutional.

The five resolutions were adopted, the vote on the last being very close ; and on the next day, on a motion to reconsider, it was rejected by a vote of 101 to 164, and the original resolutions offered by McCarthy were passed.

On the 18th, the following nominations were made :

Frederick F. Low, for governor, on the first ballot, having received 176 votes, to 93 for Aaron A. Sargent.

T. N. Machin, for lieutenant-governor, on the first ballot, by a vote of 164, to 47 for Alex. G. Abell, and 58 for J. F. Chellis ; Gen. James Collins withdrawing.

Thomas B. Shannon, for congressman from the northern district, without opposition ; William H. Parks withdrawing.

William Higby, for congressman from the middle district, without opposition.

Cornelius Cole, for congressman from the southern district, on the second ballot, over Caleb T. Fay and R. F. Perkins.

B. B. Redding, for secretary of state, on the first ballot, over A. B. Nixon,

Romualdo Pacheco, for treasurer, without opposition.

George Oulton, for controller, on the first ballot, over E. B. Vreeland, Wm. R. Robinson, and L. R. Lull ; T. M. Ames withdrawing.

John G. McCullough, for attorney-general, on the first ballot, over A. M. Crane, Jesse O. Goodwin, and F. M. Pixley.

W. D. Harriman, for clerk of the supreme court, on the second ballot, over Frank F. Fargo, Wm. G. Wood, E. F. Dunne, and James Green ; George S. Evans withdrawing.

O. M. Clayes, for printer, on the first ballot, over B. P. Avery and T. A. Springer.

J. F. Houghton, for surveyor-general, on the first ballot, over J. J. Gardner.

On the 19th, Charles L. Taylor was nominated, without opposition, for harbor commissioner.

A resolution was adopted endorsing the administration of Governor Stanford.

Silas W. Sanderson, John Currey, A. L. Rhodes, O. L. Shafter, and Lorenzo Sawyer were nominated for justices of the supreme court, on the first ballot, over Walter Van Dyke, George W. Tyler, H. O. Beatty, John B. Harmon, Walter Tompkins, and L. E. Pratt.

John Swett was unanimously nominated for superintendent of public instruction.

A state committee was selected, consisting of H. Robinson, F. Tukey, J. H. McNabb, S. G. Whipple, D. W. C. Rice, J. Bidwell, J. R. Buckbee, N. Holland, L. Shearer, H. S. Brown, J. McClatchy, and others.

The union democratic state committee issued a call on April 15th, for a state convention to meet on June 24th; and the Breckinridge committee also appointed a time and place for the meeting of their convention. The committees manifested no inclination to make any effort to unite the two wings, but some of the leaders and many of the rank and file felt that it was hopeless to go into a contest with the party under two banners, and they concluded that it would be advisable to unite the party without the instrumentality of the committees, and thus give it the character of a spontaneous movement of the people. To this end, democratic clubs were formed all over the state, the membership of which included adherents to both wings, and the proposition to reconstruct the democratic party was made the principal subject of discussion.

The Oroville club, on May 12th, adopted the following preamble and resolutions:

WHEREAS, the democratic clubs, a majority composed of the citizens of Butte county who have heretofore been divided between two organizations claiming superior legitimacy in the democratic party, now merging all past differences of opinion in the momentous issues involved in the present troubles of the country, periling alike its unity and its constitutional liberties, have unanimously agreed, by resolutions sent to this club, to call a state convention of the democracy, at a time and place set forth in their resolutions, and have asked us to concur with and join them in the same; we do, therefore, adopt said resolutions as follows:

1. That a state convention of the democracy be called to meet at the city of Sacramento, on Wednesday, the 8th day of July, for the

purpose of nominating candidates for the several state offices and for the transaction of such other business as may legitimately come before it.

2. That all legal voters be permitted to participate in the primary elections who are in favor, first, of adhering unalterably to the constitution of the United States, with all its guarantees of civil liberty unimpaired; second, of the restoration and preservation of the American union; third, of supporting the government in all constitutional and legal efforts to perpetuate its existence against all hostile forces arrayed in opposition to it; fourth, and who are opposed to the principles and present policy of the national administration.

3. That the democracy of all the counties in this state are requested to send delegates to said convention, and to make known their acquiescence in this call by publishing the action taken by them in their clubs, mass meetings, and county conventions, in the Sacramento *Republican*, Marysville *Express*, Butte *Record*, and other democratic papers.

The call was generally adopted by the various clubs, and the action of the state committees was ignored. On June 24th, no union democratic convention was held. The county of Placer alone sent delegates to it, and they met with Colton, the chairman, at the office of James W. Coffroth, at Sacramento, and after a short consultation, adjourned *sine die*. Thus it was that the union democratic party of California came to its end. The Breckinridge convention was not held, and the party passed out of existence in the same way.

On July 8th, the fusion democratic state convention met at Sacramento. John S. Berry called it to order, and read the Butte call, under which it assembled. James W. Coffroth was elected temporary chairman, and afterward president. While awaiting the report of the committee on credentials, speeches were made by Tod Robinson, H. P. Barber, Col. Hatch, J. B. Weller, James Johnson, W. H. Rhodes, and P. L. Edwards. A committee on resolutions was appointed, consisting of L. M. Shrack, D. Inman, D. W. Gelwicks, J. O. Crigler, W. Holden, W. S. Montgomery, J. D. Carr, W. C. Wallace, T. Findley, J. L. English, O. M. Wozencraft, C. L. Weller, R. T. Sprague, J. O'Farrell, Beriah Brown, H. P. Barber, Harrison Gwinn, F. L. Hatch, and others. On the 9th, J. W. Mandeville, J. L. English, T. N. Cazneau, James Johnson, L. M.

Shrack, J. S. Curtis, John Boggs, D. Mahoney, R. T. Sprague,. O. M. Wozencraft, L. R. Bradley and others were elected vice-presidents. A motion was made and lengthily discussed to strike from the order of business the nomination of justices of the supreme court, but it was lost.

The following resolutions, reported by the committee, were unanimously adopted:

1. That the democracy of California are in favor of an unalterable adherence to the constitution of the United States, with all its guarantees of civil liberty unimpaired.

2. That we are in favor of the restoration and preservation of the whole American union; that we recognize to its fullest extent the right and duty of the government to resist by every constitutional mode rebellion or insurrection against its lawful supremacy; but we recognize that right solely for the purpose of restoring its constitutional authority, and for no other purpose whatever.

3. That it is the duty of California, as a member of the union, to yield obedience to all constitutional acts of congress and the federal executive; and that any individual, of any party, who shall endeavor to incite insurrection or rebellion within her borders, or disaffection and discord among her people, is a traitor to her best interests.

4. That the aim and object of the democratic party is to preserve the federal union, and the rights of the several states unimpaired; and they hereby declare that they do not consider the administrative usurpation of extraordinary and dangerous powers not granted by the constitution—the subversion of the civil by military law in states not in insurrection or rebellion—the arbitrary military arrest, imprisonment, trial, and sentence of American citizens in such states where the civil law exists in full force and vigor—the suppression of freedom of speech and of the press—the open and avowed disregard of state rights—the fanatical attempt to place the negro on a social and political equality with the white race—and the employment of unusual test oaths—as calculated to preserve or restore a union of the several states or perpetuate a government deriving "its just powers from the consent of the governed."

5. That we are opposed to all secret political organizations and societies, as dangerous to the liberties of the people, and destructive of our republican form of government.

6. That we claim and demand as inalienable rights, freedom of

thought, freedom of speech, and freedom of the press; and further assert and declare that government agents should at all times be held to a strict accountability to the people, and that all errors of such agents should be liable to the full and free exercise of untrammeled popular discussion, for the purpose of correction by the ballot-box.

7. That we denounce and unqualifiedly condemn the emancipation proclamation of the president of the United States as tending to protract indefinitely civil war, incite servile insurrection, and inevitably close the door forever to a restoration of the union of these states.

8. That we disapprove of all congressional laws tending to substitute a paper currency in California in place of our own metallic circulating medium.

9. That the spirit and meaning of the democratic platform of this state are comprised in the words "The constitution as it is, and the union as it was."

The following nominations were made:

John G. Downey, for governor, on the first ballot, having received 200 votes, to 18 for Joseph W. McCorkle, 53 for John B. Weller, 56 for William M. Lent, and — for Royal T. Sprague.

E. W. McKinstry, for lieutenant-governor, on the second ballot, over William Holden, James L. English, and O. M. Wozencraft.

A. C. Bradford, for clerk of the supreme court, without opposition.

S. W. Bishop, for secretary of state, on the first ballot, over A. St. C. Denver.

R. O. Cravens, for controller, on the second ballot, over T. L. Barnes, William Ord, and William K. Lindsay.

Thomas Findley, for treasurer, without opposition. Findley afterwards declined the nomination, and moved that H. L. Nichols be nominated, but the convention refused to make the change.

L. C. Granger, for attorney-general, on the first ballot, over John M. Cochran, J. A. McQuade, and P. L. Edwards.

Presley Dunlap, for surveyor-general, on the second ballot, over J. Alexander, W. S. Green, and E. Twitchell.

Beriah Brown, for printer, without opposition; S. Addington, T. A. Brady, A. M. Kennedy, and J. R. Ridge withdrawing.

Michael Hayes, for harbormaster, without opposition.

John B. Weller, John Bigler, and Joseph W. McCorkle were

nominated, without opposition, for congressmen. McCorkle afterward declined the nomination, and on the second ballot, N. E. Whiteside was nominated in his stead, over James W. Mandeville, F. L. Hatch, C. M. Creaner, A. B. Dibble, E. J. Lewis, James T. Farley, and W. F. White.

Royal T. Sprague, William T. Wallace, J. B. Hall, Tod Robinson, and Henry H. Haight was nominated for justices of the supreme court, on the first ballot, over A. B. Dibble, W. H. Rhodes, H. H. Hartley, James L. English, J. P. Hoge, and Niles Searls.

A. J. Moulder, for superintendent of public instruction, without opposition.

A state committee was appointed, consisting of Murray Morrison, W. F. White, F. Tilford, C. L. Weller, T. N. Cazneau, H. A. Cobb, J. W. Mandeville, J. W. Coffroth, A. D. Patterson, A. B. Dibble, D. W. Gelwicks, J. A. McQuade, J. Daggett, W. Irwin, J. T. Farley, and others.

The convention was imposing so far as numbers were concerned; but few of the delegates were anti-war democrats. The disposition seemed to be for that element to keep in the background, and to allow the former members of the Douglas faction to occupy the conspicuous positions. Downey declined at first to accept the nomination, but the convention insisted that he should receive it, and he finally acquiesced. Sprague also declined, but the declination was not accepted. Shortly after the adjournment of the convention, Haight and Moulder resigned their nominations, and the state committee supplied their places with H. H. Hartley and O. M. Wozencraft.

On July 13th, Downey issued a lengthy address to the people, "as a means of recording in language which no one could fail to understand," his deliberate views on the constitutional rights and powers of the federal and state governments, and their relative powers, and also to outline his proposed policy in case of his election. On August 24th, Low issued an address, some three columns in length, which was devoted to national matters. The democracy made as warm a campaign as was possible under the circumstances, but the enthusiasm was mostly on the other side, and the result was apparently inevitable from the first that the union ticket would be successful by a large majority.

The election was held on September 2d, and the official count of the votes exhibited the following result:

For Governor—Low, 64,283; Downey, 44,622.

Lieutenant-Governor—Machin, 64,873; McKinstry, 43,923.

Congressmen—Shannon, 64,914; Higby, 64,881; Cole, 64,985; Weller, 43, 567; Bigler, 43,520; Whiteside, 43,693.

Secretary of State—Redding, 65,023; Bishop, 43,694.

Controller—Oulton, 65,039; Cravens, 43,730.

Treasurer—Pacheco, 64,984; Findley, 43,768.

Attorney-General—McCullough, 64,777; Granger, 43,615.

Surveyor-General—Houghton, 64,887; Dunlap, 43,760.

Printer—Clayes, 65,013; Brown, 43,789.

Clerk of the Supreme Court—Harriman, 64,954; Bradford, 43,-690.

Harbor Commissioner—Taylor, 63,614; Hayes, 43,111.

The judicial election was held on October 21st, under the amendment to the constitution, with the following result:

For Superintendent of Public Instruction—Swett, 44,791; Wozencraft, 18,902; Moulder, 606.

For Justices of the Supreme Court—Shafter, 45,102; Sawyer, 45,195; Currey, 45,216; Rhodes, 45,044; Sanderson, 45,065; Sprague, 20,768; Wallace, 20,776; Hall, 20,724; Robinson, 20,158; Hartley, 19,560; Haight, 944.

CHAPTER XVI.

1864. Union Resolutions—Union Convention, March 24th—Democratic Convention, May 10th—Union Convention, August 30th—Democratic Convention, September 7th.

On January 12th, Thompson Campbell introduced, in the assembly, a series of resolutions on the state of the union, and after a discussion, they passed that body by a vote of 59 to 8. They were sent to the senate on the same day, and were referred. On the 15th, they were reported back with amendments, and on the 20th, were amended and adopted by a vote of 27 to 4. The assembly, on the 21st, declined to concur in the amendments, and the senate refuse to recede. Committees on conference were appointed, but no agreement could be arrived at in committee. New committees were appointed on February 12th, and on the 17th, they agreed on a draft of the resolutions, and the series they reported was adopted by both houses.

The resolutions, as finally passed, were substantially as follows :

1. That the people of California are uncompromisingly loyal, and repudiate the political heresy of state supremacy when brought in conflict with federal authority, holding that each has its proper sphere—but that in all national affairs the constitution and laws of the United States are the supreme law of the land, and which no state, either by legislation, judicial decision, or otherwise, can disobey, controvert, or evade, without violating this great fundamental principle of our government, for the maintenance of which the people of this state are prepared to die rather than surrender.

2. That the rebellion is a war of the southern slave owning aristocracy against the democracy of the nation, and is a blow struck against all free governments.

3. That we endorse all the measures of the administration adopted for the purpose of subduing the present most wicked rebellion; and endorse the abolition of slavery in the District of Columbia, the act making free from slavery all the territory belonging to the United States, the confiscation act, the conscription law, the suspension of the writ of habeas corpus, the enlistment of negro soldiers, the noble stand taken by President Lincoln, that all who wear the union uniform shall receive the same protection, the financial policy of the government, and the legal tender act, as the great administrative measures for successfully carrying on the war and which we pledge ourselves to defend and uphold, the policy of establishing military governments in the revolting states, and the admission of West Virginia.

4. That we endorse the emancipation proclamation by the president, of January 1st, 1863.

5. That we endorse the plan of reconstruction as set forth in the proclamation of the president, and appended to his last message.

6. That the proposition of the copperhead members of congress, to send commissioners to Richmond to sue for peace from armed traitors, should consign their names to eternal infamy, and he who would treat with armed treason is himself a traitor, and deserves a traitor's punishment; California will accept no peace which is not based upon an unconditional surrender.

7. That we endorse the confiscation law which has for its object the unconditional forfeiture of the property of the rebels, and urge our federal representatives to secure its passage.

8. Thanking the army and navy, and guaranteeing to them civil rights while they are fighting.

9. Relating to the president's proclamation of pardon.

10. Condemning the barbarous treatment of union prisoners by the rebels.

11. Endorsing President Lincoln, and recommending his re-election.

The progress of the civil war so much absorbed the attention of the people that little attention was paid to local politics, and the decided majorities by which the union candidates had been elected in 1863, left no room for doubt that the presidential election would result in the election of that party. The existence of the war, and the feeling it engendered had the effect to sharply define party lines, and the adherents to the minority party labored under the stigma of secession, then so odious to the loyal majority of the people of the state. A number of those who had held high place in the democratic party of the state, had gone south and enlisted in the confederate army, notably, James Y. McDuffie, John T. Crenshaw, Daniel Showalter, Calhoun Benham, J. L. Brent, T. C. Flournoy, George W. Gift, Samuel H. Brooks, D. S. Terry, H. A. Higley, W. M. Gwin, R. Shoemaker, Philip Moore, and H. I. Thornton, and members of the democratic party at home made little effort to conceal the sympathy they felt for the confederate cause. A number of prominent democrats were arrested by the military authorities because of treasonable expressions, and confined in Fort Alcatraz. Their incarceration stirred up considerable indignation from the members of their party. On July 25th, Charles L. Weller, the chairman of the democratic state committee, was arrested by order of General McDowell, because of remarks he made in a political speech. This act, upon the part of the federal authorities inflamed the democracy to a high pitch, and meetings were held in various parts of the state and condemnatory resolutions passed. They threatened to carry arms to the polls and to get up an insurrection. Referring to the arrest of Weller, the Grass Valley *National* (democratic) said :

Scarcely any war was ever waged by England or any power in Europe during which there were not partisans of peace and partisans of war, the government not dreaming of visiting penalties for a mere difference of opinion upon public questions. It remained for the government of the United States—no, not the government, but the present infamous administration of it—to set the example in a country which bled from every pore to establish the very opposite principle. This state of things cannot last always. Several hundred thousand men in Ohio and Illinois are ready to defend their rights with their blood, and hundreds of thousands more are preparing to do the same thing in other states, or are already prepared. New York assumes the position to which she is entitled as a sovereign state, protecting the rights of her citizens, and the Lincoln power dares not lay its hand upon her. Let every democrat in California exercise the like determination, and all will be well.

On August 15th, a motion was made in the United States circuit court by Weller's counsel, to summon a grand jury for the purpose of investigating any charges against him that might be preferred. The motion was taken under advisement, and on the next day, it was withdrawn. On the 18th, Weller was released upon giving bonds in the sum of $25,000 to bear allegiance to the United States government.

Another affair occurred about the same time which created a great excitement in the state. On the night, of June 30th, the down stage from Virginia city was attacked about thirteen miles above Placerville, and a large amount of bullion belonging to Wells, Fargo & Co. stolen. The robbers gave to the stage driver a receipt in the following words : "June, 1864. This is to certify that I have received from Wells, Fargo & Co., the sum of $ cash, for the purpose of outfitting recruits enlisted in California for the confederate states' army. R. Henry Ingram, captain commanding company, C. S. A." It subsequently developed that the robbery was but the ramification of a scheme which had been set on foot in Santa Clara county to recruit and equip soldiers in this state for the confederate army. The robbers, after disposing of their booty, went to the Somerset house, where, about daylight the next morning, they were overtaken by deputy sheriff J. M. Staples and constable Ramsey, and a fight ensued in which Staples was killed. Some of the gang were arrested, and the balance scattered in the mountains. Subsequently, on July 15th, the rest of the party were found near San Jose, and several of them were killed in a fight with the sheriff's posse, and a number were taken. One of the captured robbers confessed fully, and his statement lead to the arrest of a number of conspirators in Santa Clara county. The grand jury of El Dorado county, for the July term, indicted Thomas B. Poole and nine others for the murder of Staples, and August 20th, they were arraigned before Judge Brockway, pleaded not guilty, and demanded separate trials. The trial of Poole commenced at Placerville, on August 24th, and on the 26th, he was convicted of murder in the first degree. On September 10th, he was sentenced to be hanged on October 28th, and another of the party was condemned to serve twenty years in state prison. The case of Poole was appealed to the supreme court, but the judgment was affirmed, and he was executed at Placerville, on September 29th, 1865. The rest of the parties were released because of legal technicalities.

The union state committee met at San Francisco, on November 30th, 1863, and called a state convention to meet at Sacramento, on March 24th, to select delegates to attend the national convention which was to meet at Baltimore. The test adopted for the primaries included all citizens who sustained the administration in all its efforts to suppress the rebellion, who favored the vigorous prosecution of the war to federal success, and who had voted for Low. Pursuant to this call, the convention met at the time and place set. About 350 delegates were present, representing every county except Fresno. The convention was called to order by Nathaniel Holland, chairman of the state committee. For temporary chairman, William H. Sears and William H. Parks were placed in nomination, and, on the first ballot, Sears was elected, receiving 201 votes, to 156 for Parks. There were evidently two powerful factions in the convention, but the causes of this division did not appear to be clearly and accurately understood, even by some of the delegates. The senatorial election for the successor of McDougall was supposed to cut a considerable figure in the matter. The greater portion of the first day was consumed in determining contests for seats among delegates. On permanent organization, Sears was president; and R. J. Hill, S. J. Clarke, W. E. Lovett, G. S. Evans, Amos Adams, C. Hartson, John P. Jones, R. Burnell, Timothy McCarthy, J. W. Wilcox, C. A. Tuttle, and others, vice-presidents. A committee on resolutions was appointed, consisting of W. L. Dudley, C. Hartson, M. M. Estee, E. W. Roberts, and others. On the 25th, the committee reported a resolution in respect for the memory of the late Rev. Thomas Starr King, which was unanimously adopted. The committee then submitted the following platform, which was adopted without opposition :

WHEREAS, The perils and distresses of civil war continue in this republic; and whereas, our national government is still assailed and sought to be overthrown by rebels in arms, and by traitors advocating peace at the sacrifice of the unity, dignity and power of our nation; and whereas, throughout this momentous and unparalleled struggle for national existence, it is the imperative duty of every citizen to unreservedly and earnestly sustain the national administration in the execution of all measures adopted by the government for the suppression of this unprecedented and iniquitous rebellion, and the restoration of the flag of our country over all the national domain; *therefore, resolved:*

1. That the union party of California re-affirms devotion to the union, and its determination to support and sustain the national administration in all its efforts to suppress this infamous rebellion, waged against our national existence, as long as a rebel is found in armed hostility to the laws and constitutional authorities of the country, or a copperhead is found to give him "aid and comfort."

2. That this convention, representing the union party of California, endorses the administration of President Lincoln, from the first hour of its existence to the present time; embracing a period in the history of our country more eventful, and fraught with more danger to the cause of constitutional liberty, than any like period in the history of the world; that we are unanimously in favor of his renomination to the presidency, believing it will contribute to the speedy triumph of our arms, the establishment of a permanent peace through victory, and will be a merited indorsement of a wise statesman and earnest patriot, who has earned and possesses the love and confidence of the American people. We therefore instruct our delegates to the national convention to vote for, and use all honorable means to secure his renomination.

3. That we are opposed to human slavery, as an institution condemned by God and abhorrent to humanity, a stain upon the nation's honor and a clog to its material progress; that as the rebels, by their own act, have brought destruction on this infernal system, we regard it as a just punishment for their crime against their government and the civilization of the age, and rejoice that such good results as its eradication will issue from our nation's tribulations.

4. That we take a just pride in the California volunteers, who have left the peaceful pursuits of life to go forth and battle for the maintenance of the flag of the republic against the polluting hands

of traitors ; they have proven their patriotism by their acts, and
have earned the gratitude and commendation of the loyal citizens of
their state. These brave soldiers of the union should be allowed to
exercise all the privileges and suffrages of freemen, and the legislature should, by suitable enactments, secure them in that right.

5. That we endorse the Hon. John Conness, our union senator in
congress, and believe that his official acts thus far have been fraught
with great good to the country and the people of this state, and
that in him we have a true representative and an able and patriotic
statesman.

6. That we recognize in the Hons. William Higby, Cornelius
Cole, and T. B. Shannon, our members in the house, able, faithful,
and patriotic representatives.

7. That the administration of Governor Low has been thus far
marked with wisdom and patriotism, and meets with the hearty
approval of the loyal citizens of this state.

8. That we regard the Pacific railroad as one of the most important measures of the national administration ; and the liberal donations by congress to aid in the construction of that great work entitles
it to the thanks and support of the American people.

Delegates to the national convention were then elected, as follows : From the third district—Nathan Coombs and Robert Gardner,
without opposition. Second district—O. H. Bradbury and William
Ritter, over John J. Sykes and C. C. Rynerson. First district—
James Otis and William S. McMurty, over Phineas Banning, Jacob
Deeth, Jerome Rice, and O. B. Crary. At large—Thompson Campbell, M. C. Briggs, John Bidwell, and Phineas Banning, over Frank
M. Pixley, S. H. Alley, O. Harvey, J. E. Benton, Alex. Hunter,
and Samuel Brannan. The following alternates were selected : Third
district—Andrew J. Snyder and A. W. Thompson ; second district—C. P. Huntington and C. C. Rynerson; first district—William
H. Culver and A. P. Jourdan ; at large—David Mahoney, Samuel
Brannan, John F. Neville, and Amos Kendall. George S. Evans
offered the following resolution, which was withdrawn after an animated discussion :

That during the calamity of civil war, when all true patriots are
united against the common enemy, the union party of California
should be undivided ; that the creation of local independent organizations, tending to impair or destroy the *one* union party of this
state, is wholly inexcusable by circumstance, pernicious in example,

and disastrous in consequences; and that henceforth the union men of California will disown and condemn every such faction as an auxiliary of disloyalists, and unworthy of recognition as friends of the country.

On March 9th, the democratic state committee met at San Francisco and called a state convention, to meet in that city on May 10th, for the purpose of selecting delegates to attend the national convention, to meet at Chicago on July 4th. The test adopted included all who were "opposed to the policy of the present national administration, which is subversive of the constitution, the laws, and the union of our fathers;" in "favor of a speedy and honorable peace that" would "secure equal and exact justice to every section of the American union;" and who would support the party nominees. On the day appointed, the convention met in Union hall, San Francisco, and was called to order by James W. Coffroth, chairman of the state committee. Every county was represented except Mono, San Mateo, and Santa Barbara. John B. Weller was elected temporary chairman. On permanent organization, Weller was president; and J. B. Crockett, C. M. Creaner, M. Whallen, P. W. S. Rayle, W. K. Lindsay, C. D. Semple, and Henry Hamilton, vice-presidents. On the 11th, the committee on resolutions reported the following platform, which was adopted:

1. (Same as the first resolution adopted by the democratic convention, of July 9th, 1863.)

2. (Same as the second resolution of the series above referred to.)

3. (Same as the third resolution of the series above referred to, except that the words "any individual of" were omitted.)

4. (Same as the fourth resolution of the series above referred to.)

5. (Same as the fifth resolution of the series above referred to.)

6. (Same as the sixth resolution of the series above referred to.)

7. (Same as the seventh resolution of the series above referred to.)

8. (Same as the eighth resolution of the series above referred to.)

9. (Same as the ninth resolution of the series above referred to.)

10. That, in the opinion of the convention, the war as at present conducted by the abolition party, is not prosecuted in a manner to restore the union, nor with any expectation that it will have that result. On the contrary, the object of those in power is simply to abolish slavery, and, in the event that they succeed in this, to revolutionize the government, and establish a centralized power utterly subversive of the rights of the states under the constitution,

and that we, therefore, hope and believe that the national convention will pledge the democratic party to a restoration of peace upon
just and honorable terms.

11. That the democratic party of this state is opposed to the
taxation of the mines by the general government, believing that it
will tend materially to repress the energy and enterprise with which
the mining population are now developing the resources of the country, be detrimental to the best interests of the state, and in many
instances will be simply an oppressive burden upon unproductive
labor.

12. That the increase of the state tax by the last republican
legislature, and their extravagant appropriations of public money,
when the people were already overburdened with national taxation,
is conclusive evidence of the unfitness of that party to control our
state legislation.

John B. Weller, John Bigler, John G. Downey, Thomas Hayes,
S. B. Stevens, J. S. Berry, C. Witheral, C. D. Semple, Charles L.
Weller, and S. G. Whipple were elected delegates to the national
convention; and a state committee was appointed, consisting of
J. J. Kendrick, W. F. White, R. R. Provines, J. S. Curtis, M.
Whallon, J. C. Burch, F. L. Hatch, D. W. Gelwicks, J. M. Bondu-
rant, William Watt, T. N. Cazneau, C. L. Weller, J. W. Coffroth,
J. C. Goods, and others. A resolution was unanimously adopted
instructing the ten delegates to cast the vote of the state as a unit.

Intelligence reached California, on June 9th, of the nomination of
Lincoln and Johnson by the national union convention, and salutes
were fired in honor of the event in the principal cities and towns.
The nominations were exceptionally acceptable to the union men of
California, who were to a man enthusiastic admirers of Abraham Lincoln. On June 4th, a call was issued by the state committee for a
union convention to meet on August 30th, for the purpose of nominating presidential electors. At that time, the convention met at
Sacramento and was called to order by Nathaniel Holland, chairman
of the state committee. J. G. McCallum was elected temporary
chairman on the first ballot, by a vote of 199, to 170 for William
L. Dudley On the 31st, a permanent organization was effected by
the election of McCallum, as president; and Walter Van Dyke,
T. R. Hooke, L. M. Foulke, J. M. Haven, and Charles Maclay, as
vice presidents. The committee on resolutions consisted of A. A.

14

Sargent, R. C. Gaskill, N. Hamilton, J. McM. Shafter, W. E. Lovett, W. H. Barton, and C. E. Greene, and they reported the following resolutions, which were unanimously adopted :

1. That this convention, representing the opinions and wishes of the union party of California, is fully conscious of the immensity of the struggle, and of its consequences, in which this nation and the government representing it are now engaged. We accept the contest with its crosses and triumphs, as the condition upon which treason has made our national existence to depend. This contest, by action now deemed humiliating, we have long avoided ; but when, at last, left no choice—attacked—peace and civilization, nation and home at once assailed—we have turned upon our enemies, resolved that this land shall hereafter be true to its professions of attachment to law, to justice and freedom.

2. That we firmly adhere to the platform and declarations of the national union convention recently held in Baltimore.

3. That we heartily and unreservedly approve the nominations of Abraham Lincoln and Andrew Johnson for president and vice-president of the United States, and we pledge to them that support which we tendered to them at our last union state convention.

4. That, in the nominations of candidates for presidential electors, it is upon the express condition that the votes of said electors be cast for the above named nominees of the national convention.

5. That John Conness, in the support which he has given to the present administration as senator from California, is heartily endorsed and approved, and the loyal people of this state will hail with lively satisfaction his further co-operation with the administration in its efforts to restore peace to the country by the destruction of the armed power of the states now in revolt against the government.

J. G. McCallum and Samuel Brannan were nominated, without opposition, for presidential electors at large.

Charles Maclay was nominated for elector from the first district, on the first ballot, over Andres Pico and E. D. Wheeler ; W. W. Crane, Jr., was nominated from the second district ; and Warner Oliver from the third district, all without opposition.

A state committee was selected, consisting of J. J. Warner, R. C. Gaskill, J. McClatchy, J. H. McNabb, S. Cooper, M. Boulware, J. W. Wilcox, A. A. Sargent, and others.

The first congressional district convention of the union party met at Sacramento, on August 31st, but no business was transacted on that day. On September 1st, another meeting was held. For member of congress, D. C. McRuer, Cornelius Cole, and Frederick Billings were named, and McRuer was nominated on the first ballot. On August 31st, William Higby was nominated for congress by the second district convention; and John Bidwell by the third district convention—both without opposition.

On August 31st, news was received of the nomination of McClellan and Pendleton by the national democratic convention. The state committee of that party had called the state convention to name presidential electors to meet at San Francisco, on August 16th, but on July 21st, the committee postponed the convention until September 7th, at which time the meeting was had. About 250 delegates were present. The convention was called to order by C. L. Weller, chairman of the state committee, and Beriah Brown was elected temporary chairman. On permanent organization, James W. Mandeville was president; W. S. Moss, J. C. McQuaid, W. Neely Johnson, S. Flemming, G. W. Crane, S. B. Axtell, D. O. Shattuck, J. R. Snyder, T. J. Henley, William Biven, W. W. McCoy,. and others, vice-presidents. The committee on resolutions consisted of E. J. Lewis, H. P. Barber, T. J. Henley, C. L. Weller, and Thos. Findley, and on the 8th, they reported the following platform, which was adopted :

1. That this convention do hereby reaffirm the political principles embodied in the platform of resolutions adopted by the democratic state convention of last May.

2. That this convention do most heartily endorse the nomination of George B. McClellan for president, and George H. Pendleton for vice-president of the United States; and also the platform of principles enunciated by the national democratic convention of the 29th of August last.

Presidential electors were nominated as follows: H. P. Barber and John T. Doyle from the state at large; William F. White from the first district; Jo Hamilton from the second ; and E. J. Lewis from the third. The defeated candidates for the nominations were Thomas Hayes, O. M. Wozencraft, William Watt, Beriah Brown, J. W. Mandeville, T. J. Henley and E. J. C. Kewen.

For members of congress John G. Downey was nominated from the first district, James W. Coffroth from the second, and Jackson

Temple from the third.   Shortly before the adjournment the follow-ing preamble and resolution was adopted :

WHEREAS, Citizens of this state, at various times, have been un-der military arrest by reason of entertaining and expressing senti-ments in opposition to the policy of the present administration; *now therefore be it resolved,*

That for the greater security of the citizen from arrest for the ex-pression of political opinion, either in speech or by pen, as guaran-teed to him by the constitution of the United States, the county democratic central committees of the various counties of the state be hereby requested, that when an arrest in their respective counties for opinion's sake, or for expression of such political opinion, shall be made, to immediately convene and inquire into the cause of such arrest; and if it shall appear to have been made without good cause, to take such immediate and proper action as shall be necessary to secure to the accused a speedy and impartial trial of the rights of a citizen under the constitution of the United States.

J. D. Hambleton was selected as alternate for White, S. B. Axtell for Hamilton, and W. Neely Johnson for Lewis.   A resolution was adopted recommending to the democrats throughout the state to hold mass meetings on September 17th, to commemorate the adoption of the constitution of the United States.

On September 25th, Downey declined to accept the nomination for congressman, and on October 15th, the congressional conven-tion of the first district met again at San Francisco, and nominated J. B. Crockett for the office and to fill the vacancy on the ticket.

The election was held on Tuesday, November· 8, 1864, and the official canvass of the vote on December 8th, exhibited the follow-ing result :

For Congressmen: First District—McRuer, 20,677; Crockett, 14,821.

Second District—Higby, 23,092 ; Coffroth, 14,557.

Third District—Bidwell, 18,018 ; Temple, 14,249.

For Presidential Electors: Lincoln—Brannan, 62,053; McCallum, 62,120; Crane, 62,134; Oliver, 62,131; Maclay, 62,117.   McClellan—Doyle, 43,839; Barber, 43,829; White, 43,833; Hamilton, 43,841; Lewis, 43,832.

On December 7th, the union electors met in the senate chamber in the state capitol and cast the vote of the state for Lincoln and Johnson ; and McCallum was appointed messenger to convey the re-turns to Washington.

CHAPTER XVII.

1865. Division of the Union Party—Union Convention—Democratic Convention.

Early in April, 1865, great excitement prevailed over the fall of Richmond, the surrender of Lee, and other successes of the union army, indicating the fall of the southern confederacy; and on the 13th the events were celebrated in various parts of the state by a general suspension of business, and by processions and the firing of salutes; but on the 15th a gloom was cast over the state by the reception of the intelligence of the assassination of President Lincoln. At San Francisco a mob organized on the afternoon of the 15th, and destroyed the printing material in the offices of the *Democratic Press*, the *Occidental, News Letter* and *Monitor*, and a French newspaper; and attempted to pay the same mark of respect to the *Ecco du Pacifique*, but desisted as the property of the *Alta* would be injured in the attempt. The newspapers against which these attacks were made were of the democratic school, and their destruction was excused by the mob upon the ground that their expressions had been disloyal to the government, and insulting toward the deceased president. During these scenes of violence the greatest excitement prevailed. In various parts of the state arrests were made of persons who rejoiced over the death of Lincoln, and the prisoners were confined in Fort Alcatraz, but were subsequently released upon taking oaths of allegiance.

In 1865 the first serious division occurred within the ranks of the union party since its organization. The wings of the party were styled the "long hairs" and the "short hairs," and in July, 1865, the Grass Valley *Union* gave the following account of the origin of the ridiculous distinctive designations:

The use of the terms "long hair" and "short hair," as now applied to the two sections of the union party, originated in the course of a debate in the assembly, at the last session of the legislature, upon a bill to re-district the city of San Francisco into wards, and the apportionment of the supervisor districts. It was charged upon those who claimed to be the particular friends of Conness, that they were endeavoring to "gerrymander" the city so that the control of its affairs might be thrown again into the hands of the "roughs" and "short hair boys." The term seemed so expressive that general opinion adopted it as the proper cognomen of that faction—and they have adopted it with a full knowledge of its literal and political significance. They desire power for its profit, and will rule or ruin.

Governor Low was a candidate for United States senator to succeed McDougall, and his claims were championed by Senator Conness. The short hair element of the party favored the election of Low, and the main split followed from the determined opposition of the long hairs, and the expression of preference by them for some other senatorial candidate. The first division occurred in Sacramento at the municipal election in March, 1865, but the long hair or regular candidate for city trustee was elected. The regular union primaries and county conventions were held in May, June, and July, and the main issue was on the senatorial election. Other than Low, the principal candidates for that office were A. A. Sargent, John B. Felton, and Cornelius Cole. Early in June the primary election was held in Nevada county, and the short hairs or Low men were defeated, the preference being expressed for Sargent. The county convention was held, and a union county ticket nominated. Soon afterward a call was issued for a "people's union" convention to assemble at Nevada City on July 1st, to nominate a ticket "without trickery and fraud," as it was alleged had been committed and resorted to in the regular convention. The call was issued by the short hairs, and it was the first signal for a general bolt in the other counties by the adherents of Low, wherever they met with defeat at the primary election polls. It was charged by the long hairs that the shorts resorted to frauds at the primary elections, and that they were aided in their scheme to disrupt the union party by the democrats. In July, 1865, the Placerville *Mirror* (long) said :

Every federal officer, every officer appointed by Governor Low, and two-thirds of the county officers, have been steadily at work for two months, trying to carry El Dorado county for Conness and Low ; and for the last week battalions of blowers and strikers from San Francisco, Sacramento, and San Quentin have been detailed here to operate at the primaries.

And on July 22d, the Sacramento *Union* said, in referring to the bolt :

In every county of the state where regular nominations have been made by union conventions, and the nominees have been anti-Low, the friends of that senatorial aspirant, when they have bolted, have sought affiliation with copperheads, and thus endeavored to destroy the integrity of the union organization, and give aid and comfort to the enemy. They have done this in Nevada, Placer, Plumas and Yuba counties, thus sacrificing principle for the political elevation of a favorite candidate, and it is said they will endeavor to pursue the same course in other counties under like circumstances.

The platforms adopted by the short hairs in their county conventions were generally framed in sentiment acceptable to the democrats, and it was generally understood that the latter would make no nominations, but would support the bolting tickets. In Yuba county the short hair convention adopted the following resolution :

That while we are willing to extend to the African or negro race upon the continent all their natural rights, and protect them in the enjoyment of the same, we still believe this to be a "white man's government," and that allowing or permitting the negro to vote would be the introduction of a system unnatural, impolitic, and degrading.

And that is a fair representation of the views expressed by that side upon this subject, upon which the democrats at that time were very sensitive. The short hairs contended that the union party at the commencement of the war, was formed of discordant materials; that men of all parties—whigs, democrats, republicans, and Douglas democrats—had united to sustain the national government; that they had responded nobly to the country's call; that as the war was over, the several elements of the party had again divided, and had ceased to treat each other with respect; that one class (the long hairs) claimed all the offices, to the exclusion of all other classes; and that as a consequence of this tendency on the part of the long-hair faction, the bolt had been projected by the short hair party as a measure in the direction of securing justice and a proper recognition. The Butte county regular union convention, on August 8th, adopted the following resolutions, directed against the bolters :

WHEREAS, In many counties of this state, certain union men have declared that the object for which the union party had been formed was now fully accomplished, and that they were therefore at liberty to dissolve and disorganize the party which had successfully sustained the government through years of rebellion against it; and whereas, new issues have been presented to the people of this state,

upon which union men of the union party may and will be called'
upon to act; and whereas, it is not only the privilege but the duty
of union men to make open avowal of their opinions upon such
issues; therefore, be it resolved by the union party of Butte county,
in convention assembled :

1. That the mission of the union party is not yet accomplished.

2. That the men and parties of men, who advocate the dissolution
or disorganization of that party can be successful in their desires
only by open affiliation with secessionists and copperheads.

3. That the union party propose to decide upon and settle the
new issues growing out of the rebellion and its suppression without
the advice of southern secessionists or northern doughfaces.

4. That we have unlimited confidence in the integrity, ability,
and patriotism of President Johnson and his cabinet, and in such
confidence we submit to the advice and the action of our national
congress all questions of reconstruction, and all action in regard to
the late seceded states of the union.

5. That the question of "negro suffrage," which the so-called democratic party is endeavoring to force upon the union party of the
union, and of this state, is one which belongs in the non-seceding
states, exclusively to the states themselves, and as yet in this state
is not an issue to be presented to the people for their action.

The union primaries and conventions were very exciting in consequence of the unfortunate division in the party, and much bitterness
of feeling was manifested. A feud had long existed between the old
line republicans and the Douglas democrats, and although events
had entirely erased the old party lines, issues long since dead had
been dragged into the political arena and had added to the feeling
of hostility produced by other causes. The only serious demonstration of this hostile feeling, however, occurred at Sacramento on July
25th, when the union county convention was held. The Low and
anti-Low delegates were about equally divided in numbers in the
body. The convention met in the assembly chamber in the then
state capitol. The desks which had ordinarily occupied the floor had
been removed, and a sufficient number of chairs had been placed in
their stead, to accommodate the 106 delegates who were expected to
participate in the proceedings. As the room filled up, it was a
noticeable fact that, almost without exception, the Low or short hair
delegates occupied the seats on the right of the speaker's chair, and
the anti-Low or long hairs those on the left. Immediately when the

convention was called to order, two persons were placed in nomination for temporary secretary, and voted for. The chairman of the county committee pronounced W. H. Barton, the long hair candidate, elected to the position on a viva voce vote. The convention was at once thrown into confusion, and the Low delegates insisted on a count of the votes. The scene that followed is thus described by the reporter of the Sacramento *Union:*

Barton advanced from the left toward the secretary's table, when the delegates from the right made a general rush to the left side of the house. Then ensued an indescribable and a terrible scene, such as was never before witnessed in Sacramento at any political convention. Barton was intercepted before reaching the secretary's table and told that he should not take his seat. The delegates on the left crowded up for the purpose of supporting him as those from the right formed a solid phalanx on the front to prevent him from advancing. In a moment, the two parties were engaged in a hand to hand fight. Solid hickory canes, which appeared to be abundant on both sides, were plied with vigor. Spittoons flew from side to side like bombshells on a battle field. Inkstands took the place of solid shot. Pistols were drawn and used as substitutes for clubs. The principal weapons, however, which were used by both sides were the cane bottomed arm chairs, which were of course within the reach of every one. These implements—not very well adapted to purposes of warfare—were swung in the air by the dozens and broken over the heads of the contending parties. In some instances, chairs were broken up for the purpose of procuring the legs to use as clubs. No firearms were discharged, and no knives were used. The fight took place exclusively on the left side of the room, and lasted probably five minutes. At the close, the anti-Low men or long hairs, who had rallied to the support of Barton, were driven from the field. Several jumped out of the windows, others who were badly hurt were assisted out of the building, while the greater portion passed into the ante-rooms and the main hall or to those portions of the assembly chamber which were regarded as neutral ground. The fight was stubborn and effective while it lasted on the part of the long hairs as well as the shorts.

After the fight, the long hairs retired in a body and organized in another hall, while the short hairs proceeded with business in the capitol. Each convention nominated a full local ticket, and elected a set of delegates to the state convention. Newton Booth was nominated for state senator by the long hairs, and E. H. Heacock by the shorts. The shorts attributed the trouble to an alleged partial ruling by the chairman of the committee in favor of Barton, and to the determination on the part of the longs to run the convention without regard to the rights or wishes of the opposition. The short hair convention instructed their nominees for the legislature to vote for Low for United States senator, but that gentleman, on August 2d, published the following card in the *Bulletin* withdrawing from the contest:

To the people of California—Some months since many personal and political friends in various portions of the state thought proper to put my name forward as a candidate for the United States senate, to succeed the Hon. James A. McDougall, whose term will expire March 4th, 1867. To their requests for authority to use my name, I replied that if I could be elected honorably I would accept the position. I expected, naturally enough, that the usual amount of partisan bitterness would be engendered by the contest, but hoped that the discussions would be conducted in a spirit of fairness and with due regard to the proprieties of life. My expectations have been more than realized in regard to the former, but my hopes of the latter have proved futile. As a citizen, I can bear attacks made in the excitement of political contests, calmly looking to the time when the heated passions shall have subsided for a just and considerate judgment and a complete vindication. As a public officer, I cannot longer remain silent and allow my usefulness to be impaired, or permit the attacks, directed at me personally, to bring odium upon the state. Occupying the position I do in the union party, I cannot longer permit the charge to go unrefuted that I am alone responsible for its threatened disruption to serve my personal ends, when the fact is, that never, by word or deed, have I assisted, counseled or advised a "split" or "bolt" in any county in the state, however much the circumstances of the case might seem to justify such action.

In view of these considerations, and desiring to settle at once and forever these and all other points of controversy, and not being aware of any other way of doing it so effectually, I desire that my name be no longer used in connection with the office referred to. Elect honest and capable men to the legislature, and let them select from among the numerous candidates, one as to whose integrity and ability there can be no question. Let him be a man of large and liberal views, devoid of meanness and partisan bigotry; one who has been faithful and true to the country during her years of darkness and peril; one whose past public record will be an ample assurance that he can safely be entrusted with the great work of reconstructing and readjusting the rebellious states in the union, having due regard to the great principles of liberty, humanity, and justice; one who will honestly endeavor to subserve the best interests of the state and the nation. To such a man, I will give my cordial support and co-operation. A consciousness of the rectitude of my purposes and actions, and a desire to allay rather than increase the bitterness of feeling at present existing, are my reasons for making this public announcement.

The withdrawal of Governor Low from the senatorial contest did not, however, heal the breach in the union party. In most of the counties bolting tickets were nominated, while the democratic conventions adjourned without making nominations, but with recommendations that the members of their party support the short hair tickets. The prospect of an election inspired the bolters to remain in the field. In San Francisco, early in August, a petition was circulated among the union voters, asking certain prominent citizens to constitute themselves a union county convention for the purpose of nominating a local ticket, electing delegates to the state convention, and appointing a county committee. This movement was excused upon the ground that the then union committee had no legitimate existence, because the terms for which its members had been elected had expired, and because the manner in which primary elections had been conducted in that city, and the means and appliances which had been notoriously used to influence their result had given no security that they would express the will of the real union men and lawful voters of the city as to the choice of the men they would have to represent them in the conventions and committees of the party. The petition was extensively signed, and the gentlemen designated met in convention and agreed upon a ticket and named delegates to the state convention. The "regular" union primaries were held in that city, on August 6th, and the short-hairs carried them by a large majority. The delegates so elected also held a convention and nominated a local ticket, and selected a set of delegates to attend the state convention. After the withdrawal of Low, the short-hairs generally transferred their support to Felton for United States senator.

The union state committee met at San Francisco, on June 28th, and called the state convention to meet at Sacramento, on August 16th, to nominate a candidate for justice of the supreme court. It was apprehended that the division that existed in the party would be carried into the convention, as double delegations had been elected from seven or eight counties, and each faction evinced a disposition to resort to any advantage that would have the effect to secure to it the control of the body. The convention met at the appointed time, at the Sixth-street M. E. church, and was called to order by A. J. Bryant, chairman of the state committee. J. G. McCallum (long-hair) was elected temporary chairman, without opposition—contrary to the general expectation. A committee on resolutions, consisting of J. W. Dwinelle, Ira P. Rankin, W. L. Dudley, I. S. Belcher, C. Hartson, W. S. Safford, and Henry Philip, was appointed. On the 17th, the committee on credentials reported that they had listened to a vast amount of evidence on the various contests, and had endeavored to determine in favor of the delegations which were the choice of the majority of the union voters of the counties. They decided in favor of admitting the long hair delegation from Sacramento, and the short-hair delegation from San Francisco. The minority of the committee favored the admission of the short hair delegation from Sacramento, but concurred in the majority report in the other particular. The defeated delegates from San Francisco waived their claims, and the lengthy discussion in the convention on the adoption of the majority report was confined entirely to the Sacramento case. The majority report was adopted. On permanent organization, McCallum was elected president; and W. L. Dudley and W. E. Hopping, vice-presidents.

For justice of the supreme court, Silas W. Sanderson, John H. McKune, W. T. Sexton, and S. W. Brockway were named. Sexton and Brockway withdrew. On the first ballot, Sanderson received 219 votes and McKune 88, and the former was declared nominated.

A state committee was appointed, consisting of W. Murray, S. J. Clarke, J. W. Dwinelle, H. S. Brown, A. B. Nixon, C. Hartson, Felix Tracy, W. H. Parks, John Yule, S. H. Parker, W. C. Ralston, A. Barstow, J. R. Hardenbergh, and others.

The following resolutions were unanimously adopted :

1. That representing the loyal union men, and the union party of California, we acknowledge our inestimable debt of gratitude to the brave men who on land and sea have fought the battles

of the republic through the varying fortunes of a desperate civil war; to the statesmen who have exercised the civil authority of the government and conducted its diplomacy; and above all, to Almighty God, whose gracious Providence in the affairs of men was never more signally manifest than in bringing our country—the hope and beacon light of humanity—triumphantly through so terrible a struggle.

2. That while we have reason to rejoice in the success which has attended union arms, and union principles, we recognize the fact that our work is not yet done; that great questions yet remain to be settled and great difficulties to be overcome by congress and the administration in bringing order, peace, and submission to law, out of the confusion and disorder in which the war has left the late rebel states; that there are still elements of disaffection to be restrained in the section lately in rebellion and to be combatted at the polls in California; and that consequently there is no less necessity than heretofore for maintaining the organization of the party in its full vigor and integrity, to the end that California may at all times be in a condition to render the most effective and loyal support to every measure of policy which may be found necessary by congress or the administration in order to maintain the authority of the union and to secure and perpetuate the just fruits of victory.

3. That in the life of Abraham Lincoln we recognize not only the eminent and lasting services which he rendered to our country as a patriot and a statesman, but also the brilliant and unstained example which he has left to his countrymen and to mankind. Hitherto our history has been wanting in our illustration of the stimulating energy and of the field of action bestowed by our republican institutions. But in the history of his life we have an actual instance of one born in the humblest condition of society, who surmounted the obstacles infused by poverty and want of education, rising successively from the lowest to the highest station in our country, equal to every position and superior to every trial, and everywhere and at all times, and for all time presenting to the world the ideal type of the representative republican, man, citizen, and patriot. On his tomb, we lay the offering of our gratitude and love.

4. That in Andrew Johnson we recognize the worthy successor of Abraham Lincoln; like him, the representative of the benefits of our free and beneficent republican institutions, and that to him we transfer, with undoubting faith, the allegiance of hope and love

which we bear to the beloved institutions of our country. That we approve the spirit of combined firmness and clemency which has thus far characterized his administration. We endorse his declaration "that the restoration of peace and order cannot be intrusted to rebels and traitors who destroyed the peace and trampled down the order that had existed more than half a century," and believe it to be the duty of all union men to oppose the restoration of civil power in the rebellious states until the president and congress shall be satisfied that it will be wielded by truly loyal majorities therein. We have the fullest confidence in the administration of President Johnson, and in his patriotism, wisdom, and judgment, and pledge him our earnest support.

5. That it is the duty and policy of California to adopt the amendment of the constitution of the United States prohibiting involuntary servitude, except on conviction for crime, throughout the United States.

6. That the Monroe doctrine is the traditional and well-established policy of the United States, and we cannot see with indifference the subversion of the liberties of a friendly republic by European arms, and the establishment of imperialism by the same means, on our immediate borders.

The following additional resolutions were offered by J. R. Buckbee, but they were lost by a large majority:

7. That California is unalterably pledged to maintain the plighted faith of the nation for the payment of the public debt; and that by no act, either direct or indirect, will she favor repudiation, nor pursue a state financial policy calculated to impair the national credit, either at home or abroad.

8. That we are in favor of collecting the state revenue on the national currency, and that a law making such provision should be enacted during the session of the next legislature.

9. That we are in favor of establishing the national banking system in this state, and that its introduction should be encouraged and promoted by all proper and necessary state legislation.

10. That it follows as a corollary from the three preceding propositions, that the law, known as the "specific contract law" should be repealed.

On August 24th, the union state committee issued an address to the members of the party, in which they recited:

It is useless for us to disguise the fact that there exists within the party, in the various counties of the state, much dissatisfaction. It has been said that there are now no issues before the people; that the mission and work of the union party are finished. It cannot be that this is the judgment of the loyal men of California. Never were there more momentous issues before any party. What more important issue could possibly be presented than the simple one of whether you shall be governed by loyal men or traitors? If no principle were involved, this alone should call forth your most earnest and enthusiastic exertions. * * * Losing sight of the work of reconstruction yet before the union party, ambitious men have allowed themselves to be drawn into a course of action which cannot be other than the destruction of the union party, and the triumph, not alone of its enemies, but of the deadly enemies of the country. Office acquired by the aid of traitor votes will only prove a legacy of shame. There is no middle ground. You must be for the country through the union organization, or against the country in company of traitors. Division can only result in disaster. No personal jealousy can justify it. Any success outside of the union organization will be, not the success of union men, but of traitors; for it will be the first step toward placing the latter in power. Defeat the regular nominations in any considerable number of counties at the approaching September election, and your state government will inevitably pass out of your hands at the next state election. Believing that this disaster can only be averted by union and harmony in our own ranks, we earnestly urge and implore the union men to stand firmly by the regular organization. If sacrifices of feelings are necessary, let them be made.

The general election for members of the legislature and county officers was held on September 6th. The democrats coalesced with the short hairs in most of the counties, upon the principle of opposition to negro suffrage, and of a paper currency in place of gold and silver. The fusion was made in Sacramento county two days before the election, but generally in the state the democrats made no nominations. The long hair ticket was successful in Shasta, Sierra, Sutter, Yuba, Butte, Tehama, Nevada, Placer, Alpine, Calaveras, San Joaquin, Santa Clara, Alameda, Los Angeles, Tuolumne, Mariposa, El Dorado, and several other counties; while the fusionists carried Sacramento, Amador, Yolo, Sonoma, and Stanislaus counties, and were partially successful in San Francisco. The long hairs secured the control of the legislature.

On August 16th, the democratic state committee called a state judicial convention of that party, to meet at Sacramento, on September 19th, at which time that body convened in the Seventh-street M. E. church. James C. Goods, chairman of the state committee, called the convention to order, and J. P. Hoge was unanimously elected temporary chairman. On permanent organization, Hoge was president; and John Bigler, W. McClure, James Johnson, W. F. White, George Pearce, Wm. Watt, John McDougal, Alex. Montgomery, W. T. Coleman, and others, vice-presidents. A committee on resolutions was appointed, consisting of P. A. Forrester, E. H. Vandecar, W. H. Glascock, Eugene Casserly, J. W. Coffroth, George Pearce, D. W. Gelwicks, C. D. Semple, W. T. Coleman, Thos. Findley, J. D. Hambleton, and others.

The committee reported the following resolutions :·

1. That we sincerely rejoice in the cessation of war and the return of peace throughout our whole country; and we trust that the momentous lessons of the past four years will inspire among all our fellow-citizens greater reverence for constitutional obligations, and those friendly and fraternal relations between the people of all the states, which are the most solid guarantee for the perpetuity of the union.

2. That the democracy of California will in the future, as in the past, give a cordial support to the national administration in the discharge of all its constitutional functions, and most especially in times of great national peril; that in the face of the manifold difficulties and embarrassments resulting from the late war, the democratic party will not withhold its support from the policy of the administration so far as the same tends to secure the rights and liberties of the states and of their citizens.

3. That upon every ground of justice and policy to the white people of the country, as well as of humanity to the negroes themselves, the democratic party is inflexibly opposed to negro suffrage, and its inevitable consequence : the political and social equality of the negro in every form, and especially to the unnatural and revolutionary scheme for thrusting universal suffrage, by action of congress, upon the negroes of the southern states.

4. That the welfare of California demands, imperatively, that her mining interests should be developed and fostered ; and her people are in the same degree opposed to any system for the sale or taxation of her mines.

5. That the whole history of California is a triumphant vindica-tion of her state policy of a gold and silver circulating medium; and that any change in this respect would be disastrous in the extreme; that unwritten contracts for work, labor, and services should by law, in all cases, be enforced in gold and silver coin.

6. That the Monroe doctrine is an essential part of the policy of the democratic party, and of the American people.

7. That when the civil authority is in full operation, there is neither warrant in the constitution or laws, nor even a pretext in any supposed necessity of state, for trials by military courts or arrests by military power. And that the writ of habeas corpus should be held inviolable under the provisions of the constitution.

The resolutions were unanimously adopted, except the sixth, for which John McHenry offered the following substitute:

That while we approve of the Monroe doctrine, we do not think that its enforcement either requires the United States of North America to give aid or assistance to, or to enter into any treaty, or alliance, offensive or defensive, or any compact or engagement, by which they shall be pledged to Mexico or any of the Spanish Ameri-can states, to maintain by force the principle that no part of the American continent is henceforward subject to colonization by any European power, nor does it bind them in any way, or to any extent, to resist interference from abroad with the domestic concerns of the aforesaid governments, or to adopt any measure which shall commit the present or future neutral rights or duties of these United States, as regards any other foreign state or nation whatsoever. This doc-trine being the enunciation of a right, to-wit: that each state on this continent which has achieved its independence is entitled to guard by its own means its own territory from future colonization, made with a view to establish a European form of government; and that the declaration of this doctrine was drawn from our govern-ment in 1823, in consequence of the promulgation of certain despotic principles by the allied powers, and which were immediately fol-lowed by certain military movements on the continent of Europe, among which principles were: "That the allied powers have an undoubted right to take hostile attitude in regard to those states in which the overthrow of the government may operate as an example;" "That useful and necessary changes in legislation and in the adminis-tration of states ought only to emanate from the free will and intelligent and well weighed conviction of those whom God has ren-

15

dered responsible for power;" "that all popular or constitutional rights are held not otherwise than as grants from the crown ;" "that there is henceforth but one policy in Christendom, which should be adopted both by people and kings, to protect religion and to secure the prevalence of those principles on which human society rests." The announcement of these principles, together with a then rumored combination of those European continental sovereigns against the newly established free states of South America, vindicated the wisdom of our government in adopting the policy it then pursued, and justified it in announcing in that crisis, the Monroe doctrine.

After a spirited discussion, the substitute was defeated, and the original resolution adopted.

For justice of the supreme court, Henry H. Hartley, Royal T. Sprague, William T. Wallace, and E. Steele were placed in nomination. Wallace withdrew, and Hartley was nominated on the first ballot, by a vote of 140, to 58 for Sprague, and 6 for Steele.

A state committee was appointed, consisting of P. A. Forrester, E. H. Vandecar, W. H. Glascock, T. W. Freelon, James W. Mandeville, J. S. Curtis, George Pearce, John Daggett, John Berry, A. Montgomery, D. W. Gelwicks, T. N. Cazneau, J. H. Lawrence, Thomas Findley, J. D. Hambleton, J W. Coffroth, J. C. Goods, W. Shattuck, W. T. Coleman, J. P. Hoge, E. Casserly, and others.

The judicial election was held on October 18th, and Sanderson was elected by a vote of 34,277, to 27,829 for Hartley.

On December 6th, George Pearce (democrat) introduced the following in the senate, and by a vote of 26 to 6, it was referred to the committee on federal relations :

WHEREAS, in the years 1860 and 1861, several of the states of the union passed acts through their legislatures professedly for the purpose of dissolving their relations to and connection with the federal government, which acts were and are wholly null and void, the people of which several states, however, took up arms in defense of their supposed right to so sever their relations, and after a sanguinary war, failed to maintain their avowed right so to sever their relations ; and whereas, in the bloody conflict through which they have just passed the local governments of the so-called seceded states were and now are suspended, which local state governments it is proper should now be restored, as well as their former relations to the federal government ; and whereas, President Johnson, since his inauguration has, by proclamation, in conferences and by message, declared that the governments of the so-called seceded states and their relations to the federal government should be restored by the friends and citizens of such states, and that the same should be effected by the friends and citizens aforesaid under the constitutions and local laws of each of such states in force at the date of the passage of the so-called secession acts or ordinances; and whereas, after the danger of dissolution has passed, we find a factious political element striving to thwart and defeat the humane efforts of the president to restore their relations to the union, and local state governments upon the principle so declared; *therefore, resolved,*

That we heartily approve the efforts of President Johnson to restore the social relations and governments, and upon the principle aforesaid, and hereby pledge him our undivided support in his said efforts upon the principles and plan so declared and promulgated by him, to the end that the said relations and local state governments may speedily be restored.

On December 8th, William Holden (democrat) introduced in the assembly the following resolutions, which were laid on the table by a vote of 50 to 16, but on the 12th, they were taken up by a vote of 41 to 38, and referred to the committee on federal relations, but were never reported :

1. That our senators in congress are instructed and our representatives requested to vote against and oppose any and all measure or measures having for its or their object the conferring upon the negro the right of suffrage in the District of Columbia, or any other territory belonging to the United States, over which congress has the exclusive power of legislation.

2. To vote against and oppose any measure in congress fixing or attempting to fix the qualifications of voters in any of the states or territories of the United States.

3. To vote against and oppose any and all measures the object of which may be to dispose of the mineral lands of California.

4. To vote for and sustain all measures of this administration which will tend to a complete and full restoration of the union, the constitutional authority of the federal government, the constitutional rights of the individual states, and that fraternal feeling that existed between the citizens thereof prior to the revolution.

5. To vote for the admission to seats in congress of all senators and representatives who have been elected by conventions or legisla-

tures, or by the people of states heretofore in rebellion, in pursuance of the proclamation of the president of the United States, provided they can take the oath of office required by the laws of the United States.

On December 9th, William J. Shaw (democrat) introduced the following in the senate, and they were referred to the committee on federal relations :

Inasmuch as the rebellion, and the peace which has ensued, present new issues and new measures for public consideration ; and inasmuch as legislation may be assisted and expedited by a prompt discussion and decision respecting some of them ; *therefore, resolved, as the sense of the senate :*

1. That we approve of "the reconstruction policy" of the president of the United States, Andrew Johnson.

2. That states admitted into the union become parts of it, and cannot commit treason against it; that states cannot be taken out of the union by separate acts of their own, nor by lawless acts of individuals acquiring temporary control. Secondly, that the states recently in rebellion are co-equal states of the union, as completely as though the late lawless control over them had not been acquired.

3. That the regulation of the elective franchise in the states appertains to the states severally and exclusively, and the same should not be extended, changed, nor interfered with by any act of the congress of the United States, or by either house thereof.

4. That every attempt to revive issues calculated to excite sectional hatred and maintain "parties by geographical discriminations" should be reprobated, because it tends unavoidably to embitter one section of the republic against another, to render a universal love of the union impossible, and thereby to impair its usefulness, lessen its strength and imperil its continuance; and that misfortunes such as these, and such as we have recently encountered from the same cause, are more serious to our country and to mankind than would be an utter neglect of all states and statesmen to interfere with the laws, customs, or people of the states not their own, however superior in virtue, humanity, and intelligence the intermeddlers might really be; consequently, that we will do no act to encourage any party which may seek to maintain itself through sectional issues and sectional prejudices.

5. That we are in favor of reducing the rate of interest of the war debt, and of taxing the holders thereof on the income therefrom as

:soon as the same can be constitutionally accomplished, without any violation of the national faith, credit, or honor.

6. That we are opposed to an irredeemable currency and the introduction of national banks into this state, unless provision be first made to insure the prompt redemption of their bills in gold and silver.

7. That we are opposed to the sale by government of the mines or mineral lands of this state, and in favor of an act of congress securing all mines to the discoverers and occupants.

On the same day, J. D. Goodwin (democrat) offered the following in the assembly, and they had the same reference :

WHEREAS, The military power of the states lately in rebellion against the constitutional authorities of the United States has been completely destroyed, and peace restored to the country; and whereas, it is indispensible to the future happiness, prosperity, and union of the American people that all the parties in the late terrible conflict shall work together in harmony, and that the said states shall assume without delay the exercise of all their functions as sovereign states in the union ; and whereas, the president of the United States has adopted, and is now urging upon the attention of the whole people, a wise and conciliatory policy to that end ; *therefore, resolved,*

That we heartily endorse the efforts of President Johnson to conciliate the southern people, and to restore their status to the union and the constitution.

On the 12th, S. L. Lupton (democrat) introduced the following in the assembly, and it was sent to the same committee :

That we heartly endorse the pardoning power conferred upon the chief executive of the United States as exercised by President Andrew Johnson toward the erring people of the southern states.

In the assembly, on the 14th, A. B. Hunt (union) offered the following, which were referred to the same committee :

WHEREAS, An armed and unauthorized resistance has been made to the national authority in certain states of this union, and a bloody civil war unequaled in the annals of the world for atrocity and cruelty has for the last four years been waged against the government of United States; and whereas, said war was instigated and carried on by men who were educated at the expense of the general government, and who have all their lives been the recipients of its favors and emoluments, and when by the constitutionally expressed will of the people the control of the government passed from their hands, resolved upon its overthrow and destruction, waged a bloody and unrelenting war to that purpose, filling the land with mourning and desolation, and as a fitting climax to so brutal and blood-thirsty a rebellion it culminated in the assassination of that great and good man, Abraham Lincoln, president of the United States, and the attempted assassination of that eminent American statesman, William H. Seward; and whereas, said rebellion has been met, combatted, and overthrown by the navy and armies of the United States, and the insurgent forces captured or dispersed, and their leaders are now within the control of the government, and peace and fraternal relations are being established within insurgent states; *therefore, resolved,*

1. That our hearty and sincere thanks are due, and are hereby extended to the president of the United States and his cabinet for the wisdom, devotion, and patriotism they have displayed in conducting the republic through difficulties such as never before environed a government, and that we still have full faith and confidence in the wisdom, integrity, and patriotism of the administration.

2. That our everlasting gratitude and thanks are hereby given to the soldiers and sailors of the armies and navy of the United States for their matchless courage, their unflinching devotion and the more than Spartan valor displayed by them, both in the storm of battle and the long continued sieges.

3. That we heartily concur and hereby approve of the declaration of his excellency, Andrew Johnson, president of the United States, that "treason must and shall be made odious."

4. That it is due to the martyred dead, to public justice and the majesty of law, and it is our most earnest desire that the leading conspirators, as soon as may be convenient, be brought to trial and convicted of the crime of treason—the highest crime known to our laws—and that they be made to suffer the penalty of their crimes.

CHAPTER XVIII.

1866. Union Resolutions—Policy of President Johnson.

On January 5th, 1866, John S. Hager (democrat) offered the following in the senate, and they were referred to the committee on federal relations :

1. That the sentiments of President Johnson in regard to maintaining the traditional policy of the nation by adhering to what is commonly known as the Monroe doctrine, so promptly disclosed in his first annual message, are eminently patriotic, and meet with the cordial approval of the people of California.

2. That we endorse and concur in the views entertained by the president, enunciated in his late annual message—that under the federal constitution all questions relating to an extension of the elective franchise to the freedmen of the south should be referred to the several states and determined and regulated exclusively by them—as just in principle, sound in policy, and best calculated to promote the future harmony and prosperity of the country.

On the same day, James Johnson (democrat) offered this resolution in the senate:

That the so-called confederate states are not out of the union.

Joseph Kutz moved to amend by adding, "but are emphatically out in the cold."

Horace Hawes offered the following substitute :

That the pretended right of secession on the part of any state, or the people thereof, is repugnant to the federal constitution, and subversive of the peace, order, and liberties of the country, and we rejoice that reason and the force of arms have forever overthrown the doctrine of the said pretended right of secession, and re-established the authority of the constitution and government of the United States, in all their plenitude, over the whole territories of the American union.

The Hawes substitute was adopted—26 to 5. It went to the house, and on the 9th, Holden (democrat) offered the following proviso :

Provided, however, that we recognize the right of any people, anywhere, being inclined and having the power and the right to rise up and shake off the existing government and form a new one that suits them better; that it is a valuable and a sacred right that any people who can, may revolutionize and make their own of so much territory as they inhabit.

The whole matter was referred to the committee on federal relations—49 to 12. On the 31st, the majority of the committee reported that the Holden amendment was "an extract from a speech on the Mexican war made by Lincoln in congress, and was a mere incidental remark intended doubtless to enunciate the right of revolution as that right is recognized in the declaration of independence, which extract is not as guarded in its terms as it would have been had the author sought to enunciate a principle in the form of a resolution, or had he supposed that his language might afterward be quoted for the purpose of justifying an attempt to overthrow a republican government with the intent of building on its ruins another government, the corner stone of which should be human slavery." The committee reported as a substitute for the Holden amendment that portion of the declaration of independence referring to the right of revolution. On February 1st, the resolution came up for discussion in the house, and after a heated debate the instrument reported by the majority of the committee was passed—47 to 7. It went to the senate again, but was not acted upon.

On January 11th, R. P. Mace (democrat) introduced the following in the assembly:

WHEREAS, The states lately in rebellion against the lawful authorities of the government of the United States have laid down their arms and have acknowledged as binding and unchangeable the authority of the federal constitution, and have submitted to the lawful power of every department of the general government; and whereas, peace once more blesses every portion of the national union; and whereas, reason and humanity dictate a course of leniency rather than violence toward those recently in armed rebellion against the lawful authority; and whereas, Jefferson Davis was only the visible representative of the feelings and sentiments of the southern people; *therefore, resolved,*

That our congressional representatives be instructed to use their influence to procure the unconditional pardon of said Davis.

T. J. Sherwood (union) offered the following substitute :

WHEREAS, Jefferson Davis, late president of the so-called confederate states, is now and has been for some months past in the custody of the United States, on the charge of treason against the government, and complicity in the assassination of the president; *resolved,*

That in view of the enormity of the crime, and the demands of the loyal people of this state, we respectfully request of the president that said Davis, for his alleged treason, be speedily brought to trial before a civil or military tribunal, and if convicted, that he be made to suffer the punishment prescribed by law.

The substitute was adopted and passed—58 to 20. It went to the senate on the 13th, when Johnson proposed the following substitute :

That in view of the fact that Jefferson Davis has been indicted for treason against the United States government, we are content to leave the question of his trial to the courts, and that of his pardon to the president.

On the 31st, the whole matter was indefinitely postponed.

The policy of President Johnson for the reconstruction of the southern states was much at variance with the views of the old line members of the union party, and toward the end of 1865, it received sharp criticism from the organs of that element. The democrats at first mildly approved the course of the president, but with his veto of the freedmen's bureau bill, on February 19th, he became their party hero, while the unionists declared open war against him, and they prosecuted it vigorously during the remainder of his term. The veto of the freedmen's bureau bill was endorsed in California by the members of the democratic party by torch-light processions, orations, and the firing of salutes. The democratic county committee of San Francisco adopted resolutions declaring their trust in the virtue, integrity, and intelligence of the American people, invoking the favorable judgment of the people in behalf of the president in his battle with congress (there being a union majority in each branch which was at war with the president and his policy), pledging their personal influence to strengthen his arm in the great work of restoration, declaring that the confederate states should be immediately admitted into the union to all the rights and privileges of states and upon such terms of perfect equality, pronouncing in opposition to negro suffrage in any form, and especially endorsing the president in his declaration that the question of suffrage is one peculiarly belonging to the states, and that for congress to attempt to interfere in the matter would be a gross violation of the federal compact. The committee called a mass meeting, to be held in that city, on February 27th. At the meeting, resolutions endorsing the policy of the president were adopted, and speeches were delivered by John B. Weller, Frank Hereford, and J. H. Hardy.

On February 23d, the executive committee of the union state committee met at San Francisco, and adopted the following resolutions :

1. That the present is a crisis in the closing of the war for the restoration of the union in which it becomes all union men to adhere firmly to the principles which have guided them through four years of rebellion, and to act with the greatest patience, discretion, and deliberation, and not be unwarily entrapped into any action or expression which shall seem to commit them to any co-operation with that party which for the last four years has sympathized with the rebellion.

2. That we do not yet perceive that there is an irreparable breach between the president and congress ; and that until such a breach shall conclusively appear to exist, we shall continue to hope that the fruits of the triumphs of the union armies are not to be lost ; and that it is the duty of all union men to avoid any entanglement with the Vallandighams, the Seymours, and the copperhead confederate sympathizers in California, by assisting at their public meetings or otherwise.

3. That when such men as Vallandigham and Seymour at the east, the notorious copperhead sympathizers of San Francisco, and those recreant Californians who have always denounced the suppression of the rebellion, openly avowed themselves traitors, sent their sons into the rebel army, and always rejoiced over the reverses of the union arms, unite together in a public endorsement of the policy of a president whom they have hitherto bitterly opposed, it is apparent that they do not fully understand that policy, or that they are endeavoring to seduce the president from his allegiance to the constitution.

4. That the abolition of slavery in the United States is one of the results of the late rebellion, and that it would be a most wicked, senseless, and dastardly act if the free and loyal people of the United States should now withdraw their protection from the four millions of freedmen and permit them to be reduced again into slavery under state laws enacted by men whose hands are red with the blood of patriots.

5. That we believe that President Johnson will remain true to the constitution and to his pledges, and that he will not suffer himself to be betrayed by the attempted seductions of men who were lately in arms against the union, or by those who in act and declared sentiment sympathize with rebellion.

In the assembly, on February 23d, Thomas Eager offered the following :

That we approve of the action of the majority of the United States senate in refusing to sustain the veto of the president of the freedmen's bureau bill.

That the Hon. John Conness, in acting with the majority of the United States senate on that question, represented the opinions and wishes of the people of California.

A motion to lay the resolutions on the table was defeated—28 to 40, and they went to the committee on federal relations. The next day the majority of the committee reported the following substitute:

That we heartily endorse the course of those of our delegation in congress who voted for the passage of the bill known as the "freedmen's bureau bill;" and that we endorse the course of the Hon. John Conness in voting against sustaining the president's veto of the same.

The minority of the committee recommended, that the original resolutions be indefinitely postponed, and that the following substitute be adopted :

That we do most heartily endorse President Johnson's recent veto of the freedmen's bureau bill, and his expressed views in relation to his restoration policy.

On the 28th, the majority substitute was passed—47 to 26. It was adopted by the senate, on March 2d—21 to 8.

On February 27th, John P. Jones (union) introduced in the senate a lengthy series of resolutions endorsing the position taken by congress on the question of reconstruction. W. J. Shaw offered a substitute endorsing the administration of President Johnson, and the matter came up for discussion and action on March 21st. Jones then offered an amended series of resolutions, which were finally passed—21 to 13, and they were adopted by the house, on the 30th—39 to 16.

The resolutions as finally adopted declared :

That in view of the present extraordinary condition of national affairs, it is proper that the legislature of the loyal state of California make the following declarations :

1. That although "indemnity for the past" has not been, and could not in the nature of things, be obtained by the recent triumph of our national arms in the great civil war, the late so-called confederate states ought not to be represented in congress, nor permitted the full exercise of civil power within their own limits, or to resume their positions as states of the union in full fellowship therein, until adequate guarantees of "security for the future" and of the maintenance of the nation's faith are incorporated in the United States constitution, and frankly, fully, and in good faith endorsed or adopted by the people of said so-called confederate states, and so made practically irreversible.

2. That the alarming pretense recently set up to the contrary of this by those in sympathy with the unsubdued spirit of the rebellion is incompatible with the course pursued by the president, and approved by the secretary of state, in instituting provisional or military governments in the rebel states (after the cessation of hostilities, and the surrender of the rebel armies), and in refusing to withdraw such temporary military governments until the ratification of the constitutional amendment abolishing slavery.

3. That while we agree with the position then taken by the president, that those states had no right to resume domestic civil power, or to send representatives to congress until they should fulfill certain conditions precedent, in determining the terms of which they should have no voice, we deny the right of the executive branch of the government to determine the nature or extent of such conditions.

4. That all questions pertaining to the status of the late rebel states, their just relations to the national union, and the time and method of their restoration thereto, belong to the legislative and not to the executive department of the federal government ; therefore, the measure of the guarantees which may be necessary for the future peace and security of the nation can be authoritatively determined only by the congress, and that any attempt by the national executive to control the questions, would be an invasion of the rightful authority of the people, and dangerous to republican liberty.

5. That because the second clause of the latest constitutional amendment, which empowers congress to carry into effect by federal enactment the first clause, abolishing slavery, would obviously be a dead letter with a congress composed of the enemies of liberty, and

because the present constitutional basis of representation is, under the new order of things, manifestly partial and unequal, we approve the spirit of the proposed constitutional amendment which has already received a two-thirds vote in the house of representatives, and which is now pending in the senate; and our senators are hereby requested to yield the same their full support, to the end that the late so-called confederate states may, when admitted, be reduced to an equality, as to representation, with the loyal states.

6. That the adoption of this and such other amendments to the constitution as congress may propose and the loyal states ratify, ought to be held as conditions precedent to the restoration of civil power in the late so-called confederate states, and the admission of their senators and representatives to seats in congress.

7. That we have full confidence in the wisdom, integrity, and moderation of the present congress; that the freedmen's bureau bill which recently passed that body appears to have been a well considered and constitutional measure, having only in view the maintenance of the pledged faith of the nation, and that the refusal of the president to give his assent, taken together with his implied purpose to veto all measures affecting the late rebel states unless their representatives are first admitted to vote for or against such measures, are totally indefensible, and an assumption of dictatorial power justly calculated to awaken the gravest apprehensions in the minds of a people jealous of their liberties.

8. That all fears for the future of the republic are silenced by an abiding faith in the patriotism, power, and purpose, the constancy, conscience, and courage of the loyal people, who have thus far proven equal to every emergency, and will continue so to the end.

On February 24th, a large union mass meeting was held at Sacramento, and it was addressed by Senator-elect Cole, who vindicated the action of the majority of congress on the subject of reconstruction. A lengthly set of resolutions was adopted which opposed the policy of the president. On March 2d, another meeting was held at the pavilion, at Sacramento, over which Governor Low presided, and similar resolutions were passed.

President Johnson vetoed the civil rights bill on March 27th, and the message met with the approval of the democratic party, but was severely condemned by the extreme unionists. The union congressional majority was now in open war with the president, and the conflict was carried on with much bitterness by both sides. On

June 25th, a call was issued by the executive committee of the national union club for a national union convention to be held, at Philadelphia, on August 14th, and to be composed of delegates chosen by citizens who endorsed and sustained the president's administration, and who were in favor of maintaining unbroken the union of the states under the constitution. On July 28th, a meeting of the Johnson administration club of Santa Clara county was held at San Jose, and a resolution was passed calling a state convention, to meet at San Francisco, on August 3d, of the friends of the administration, for the purpose of selecting delegates to represent California, in the Philadelphia convention. At the appointed time and place, the convention met. F. B. Murdock was chosen president; and A. J. Gunnison, J. Center, O. P. Sutton, W. H. Culver, C. P. Hester, B. P. Kooser, and G. W. Hagar, vice-presidents.

The following resolutions were passed :

1. That we recognize in Andrew Johnson, president of the United States, and his cabinet—at the head of which is William H. Seward, long tried and true—sterling patriots and wise and comprehensive statesmen, who have devoted their best energies to the welfare of the nation; and that we hereby approve of their plan for the speedy restoration of the states to their normal position in the national union.

2. That the rebellion has been crushed, that slavery has been destroyed, and that the rebels having laid down their arms and returned to their allegiance to the United States government and obedience to its laws; nothing now remains for the political power but to restore the states to their proper position.

3. That all the original states of the union are entitled to be represented in congress, providing that they select as representatives loyal men who are qualified by existing laws of the United States to serve as such.

4. That a spirit of wise and judicious forbearance, moderation and charity, should control the political action of the country, in order that the people of all sections may become thoroughly reunited in the bonds of national sentiment, common interest and industrial pursuits; that so long as one section of the country is unnecessarily kept out of its proper position in the union, its material interests cannot flourish; it cannot contribute its just quota to the general revenue, and thus onerous taxes must be levied upon other sections.

5. That we cordially endorse the spirit and principles embodied in

the call for a national convention to assemble in Philadelphia, August 14, 1866, and that we sincerely hope and trust that that convention will be guided by wise and patriotic counsels, so that all true patriots may endorse its action.

6. That the action of congress, in refusing to restore all the states of the union to their proper position in the union, is violative of the principles of the union party, and of the pledges made to the country by that party, which congress was in duty bound to fulfill.

7. That we do hereby call upon all citizens who have hitherto opposed the ruinous doctrine of the political right of secession, and who are still opposed to recognizing its principles in any shape, to rally, in connection with the national union party of this state, in support of the principles above set forth.

The following were elected delegates to the Philadelphia convention : First district—Cornelius Cole (who afterward published a letter repudiating the action of the convention) and Montgomery Blair. Second district—J. H. Riley and J. W. Wilcox. Third district—J. W. Simonton and J. P. Leese. At large—Senator Doolittle, Robert J. Walker, General Dix, and General Slocum. A state central committee was selected, consisting of M. S. Whiting, I. N. Thorne, W. H. Culver, Charles Maclay, J. Center, and Edw. Stanly.

On August 7th the democratic state central committee met at San Francisco, passed resolutions that the democracy of California should be represented in the democratic convention, and elected as delegates Jackson Temple, William T. Coleman, Jas. A. McDougall, and W. W. Cope, at large; Joseph P. Hoge and Samuel Purdy from the first district; John Bigler and Samuel Martin from the second district; and P. B. Reading and Thomas H. Hanson from the third district.

The Johnson union state committee, on September 26th, issued a lengthy address to the voters of California, urging the formation of clubs, and the appointment of county committees, in order that a vigorous support might be given to the policy of the president, but the movement never attained the dignity of a political party.

On August 1st, the union state central committee met at San Francisco, and adopted a resolution endorsing and approving the amendment to article fourteen of the federal constitution. The following resolutions were also adopted :

1. That until such amendment is adopted, those states lately in

rebellion should not be admitted to representation in congress; that by all laws the victor should not place political power in the hands of the vanquished until full and ample guarantees for future peace are given and accepted; that a people who have waged for four years an unjust war against the government cannot complain of injustice at being denied the opportunity to do in the halls of legislation what they were powerless to accomplish on the field of battle.

2. That the union party of California are opposed to any legislation or to any policy in congress, or by the president, which shall fall short of a full settlement of human slavery, in fact as well as name, throughout our whole country; and that any reconstruction, reorganization, or rehabilitation which does not assure to the whole people, white as well as black, "life, liberty, and the pursuit of happiness," will be mischievous in its results, and a full admission that the republic does not possess the genius to save what it had the valor to win.

3. That the work of reconstruction implies a moral regeneration of disloyal men and parties, and should be carried on among defeated and disorganized rebels and rebel states rather than in the ranks of the union party. That the Vallandighams, the Woods, and the Seymours, who are active in promoting a convention in Philadelphia, and who it is certain are to participate in it, are not fit associates for loyal men, and are not to be trusted in any degree with the destinies of the republic. That the party which has proved capable of carrying the country successfully through years of bloody war, may safely be trusted to finish, in time of peace, the work yet remaining to be done to insure the permanence of pure republican institutions in America.

4. That we approve the action of congress, and of our union delegation in congress, on the question of reconstruction, and that any course less "radical" would not have met the approval of the people of California.

The committee appointed Senators Conness and Cole, Congressmen McRuer, Bidwell, and Higby, and Frederick Billings, Richard Chenery, and Moses Ellis to attend the southern union convention, which was to meet at Philadelphia on September 3d, and to assure the members of that body that they had the sympathy of the loyal men of California.

CHAPTER XIX.

1867. The Chinese Question in Politics—Union Primaries—Union Convention—Bolt in the Union Party—Gorham's Appeal to the People—Revised Union Ticket—Republican Convention—Democratic Convention.

The Chinese issue was the most prominent one at the outset of the campaign of 1867. In San Francisco, anti-Chinese associations were formed, and they essayed to take a hand in the politics of the state. The officers of the anti-coolie association, on April 19, 1867, sent invitations to George C. Gorham, John Bidwell, Caleb T. Fay, and Frank M. Pixley, the candidates for the union nomination for governor, requesting their views on the Chinese labor question. Bidwell replied under date of May 3d, that "it ought not to be necessary for me to have to say that I am opposed to slavery in any form." Fay expressed himself as opposed to Chinese immigration and labor, and Gorham said in his letter:

If I understand the avowed object of the so-called anti-coolie movement, it is an attempt by men of the European race to prevent, by all lawful means, the employment, at the various industrial callings in California, of men of the Asiatic race. I am in favor of such a scheme. If, as some believe, ignorant Asiatics are improperly induced to make contracts with capitalists of their own race, by the terms of which they are to owe service or labor in this state for a term of years, without a good consideration, I will aid by any proper means to remedy the evil. I am opposed to human slavery, and to all its substitutes and aliases; coolieism, peonage, contract systems in which one side makes the bargain for both—these are all abhorrent. But because I am an anti-slavery man, I am also an anti-slave man. Because I detest the overreaching man who would grind the faces of the poor, I do not also detest the poor. Because I am opposed to the coolie system, I am not the enemy of its victims. I believe in the christian religion, and that rests upon the universal fatherhood of God and the universal brotherhood of man. The same God created both Europeans and Asiatics. No man of whatever race has any better right to labor, and receive his hire therefor, than has any other man. To controvert this is to contend with Him who said to man: "In the sweat of thy face shalt thou eat bread till thou return unto the ground." As a question, then, of right and wrong, I am as emphatically opposed to all attempts to deny the Chinese the right to labor for pay, as I am to the restoration of

16

African slavery whereby black men were compelled to labor without pay. This is with me an earnest conviction, the expression of which I have no desire to avoid.

As a question of policy, I am equally opposed to your movement. It is certain that the millions in Asia will, at no distant day, learn to consume some products of our own country. Imagine, if you can, a single article of American production, which, if it should come into general use in China, would not give employment to a greater number of our own race here than the whole immigration of Chinese can amount to for years. As we treat strangers in our land so will our countrymen be treated in the land whence those strangers came. We sought commercial intercourse with China and Japan. Now that we have succeeded in breaking down the Chinese wall let us not hasten to erect an anti-Chinese wall at home. The question of cheap labor I will not here discuss, but it seems certain to me that if we could have it in abundance, the state would go forward at such strides as would make prosperity general among all deserving classes. Principle and policy, then, both forbid the attempt to make war upon our Asiatic brethren.

In conclusion, let me suggest that the Chinese now in our midst, and those who may come hereafter, must either work, steal, beg or starve. It would be difficult to make an argument to show that the creation of so large a number of street beggars, or of thieves, would be compensated by the fact that none but men of the European race were permitted to earn a livelihood in California. As to starvation, the mere word makes us shudder. So, after all, if we would not have the Chinaman steal, beg, or starve, he must be allowed to work.

The first application of the Porter law was on the occasion of the municipal primary election of the union party, in Oakland, in February, and on March 2d, the second application was made at the Sacramento city primary. In both instances, the result was regarded as satisfactory, and it was hoped that a sufficient remedy had been found for the evils which had been attendant on elections of this character.

George C. Gorham early presented himself from the ranks of the short-hair or Douglas wing of the union party as a candidate for governor. Senator Conness had returned from Washington, in May, and had developed into an earnest supporter of Gorham, although the latter had some months before professed to be his bitter

·enemy. Conness was seeking a re-election to the senate, and he immediately inaugurated an active campaign in conjunction with the adherents of Gorham. It was not long when the long-hair or old-line element of the party assumed the attitude of antagonism toward the Conness faction which had characterized it in 1865, and it was evident from the first that the struggle within the ranks of the union party would be carried on with a bitterness almost unparalleled in the history of state politics. The long-hair element was supported by the leading newspapers, while the other wing comprehended the most active and experienced politicians. The antagonism to Conness was based by the long-hair journals upon the ground that at the most critical period of the union party he had figured as a disorganizer; that he had pursued his personal schemes regardless of the honor, integrity, or continued life of the party; and then he preferred to put its enemies in power rather than to aid the election of candidates who were not under his control.

The Sacramento *Union*, in explaining this feeling of hostility, said:

Before Senator Conness left our shores, in 1865, various circumstances had conspired to render him the most unpopular politician who claimed affiliation with the union party. The senator had done nothing at Washington to merit censure. If he had been content with the discharge of his legislative duties, no fault could have been found with him at that period. But a new senator was to be elected, to succeed McDougall, and Conness evinced a determination to prevent the choice of any other than a Conness man. He entered deeply into ward and county politics, superintended operations at the primaries, and made devotion to his personal fortunes a new test of promotion in the union party. The result of a fierce, distracting contest was a tremendous condemnation of the senator's dictatorial policy, a very large majority of the counties being carried by his opponents. What followed? Did the senator and his personal friends bow to the decision of the majority and give an honest or even a reluctant support to the regular ticket? This was the duty of the hour. The war was at an end, but the delicate work of reconstruction was yet to be performed. It was clear to men of average sense that if the union men of the country did not stand shoulder to shoulder and control this business the treason-tainted democratic party would return to power, and the fruits of a blood-bought victory would be lost. Yet at this critical period the record is that Senator Conness looked outside the union camp for the means of gratifying his personal spleen, and countenanced, if he did not actually assist in forming, combinations between his retainers and the copperheads in El Dorado, Sacramento, Nevada, and other counties for the defeat of the loyal ticket. In a speech delivered at Placerville, on the 12th of July, 1865, obviously designed to pave the way for an unholy alliance, he took pains to show that all important national issues had been settled, that there was no live question to prevent the people from acting together, without regard to past differences. "There is no question remaining upon which any considerable portion of the people now differ." Referring to the democratic party, he had the generosity to say: "Everywhere their organization is giving in its adhesion to the new order of things." And thereupon the Mountain *Democrat*, the organ of the El Dorado democracy, waxed gracious and flattering toward the senator. In Sacramento, the senator's lieutenants declared that the union party had lived long enough, had fulfilled its mission, and would now commit suicide by forcing Conness's friends into the ranks of the democracy. When the election day arrived, the unionists in El Dorado, Sacramento, and Nevada found themselves confronted by the threatened combination—Conness men and copperheads arrayed on the same ticket. This is why the senator, in 1866, went back to Washington with a dark shadow of repudiation resting upon his name.

It was announced by the long-hair press that a huge political combination had been effected looking toward the return of Conness to the senate, the election of Gorham as governor, and of others to other prominent offices; that this combination was backed by the large moneyed corporations in the state; and that money would be used at the primaries to influence the selection of delegates to the various conventions. However this may be, the Conness wing endeavored to have the primaries held without regard to the Porter law, but the long-hair faction resolutely insisted that that statute should be invoked as a protection against fraud. John Bidwell was the candidate for governor from the long-hair wing, and Frank M. Pixley and Caleb T. Fay were also in the field for the nomination, with an apparent willingness to accept the honor if tendered by either wing. Fay became a candidate at the published solicitation of a number of the prominent business men of San Francisco, and he promptly signified his willingness to run, "not feeling at liberty to decline, even if so disposed." The union state central committee had recommended in its call for the state convention that the primary elections be conducted in accordance with the provisions of the Porter law. The union county committee, at Sacramento, on May 15th, resolved to call the primary election for that county under the Porter law, except that all citizens, registered and unregistered should be entitled to vote. This action of the committee was regarded by the long-hair element as the opening act on the programme which had been arranged by the Conness side, and it was criticised with little regard for delicacy of expression. The call was addressed to "all union voters," who would endorse the test prescribed by the state committee, and it was contended that members of the democratic party could and would vote under it. Subsequently the reference to the Porter law in the call was annulled, leaving the call for an open primary. A few days later, a caucus of union men was held, and the old long-hair county committee were requested to call a "legal" primary and county convention. This was done, and it resulted in two union primaries, county conventions, and local tickets. Generally the division as to individuals was the same as in 1865. In San Francisco, on May 14th, the union county committee called a primary election for June 5th, to select delegates to the county convention to choose representatives in the state and congressional conventions, leaving it necessary to hold a subsequent primary to elect delegates to the county convention to nominate a local ticket. This primary was also called without the pale of the Porter law, and immediately petitions were circulated requesting the people's nominating committee of 1864–5, to again convene and nominate delegates to attend the union county, state, and congressional conventions. These petitions were signed by about 4,000 union voters, and the committee met on May 25th and organized. But two members declined to participate in the movement, and out of forty-eight members, thirty-eight were present. On May 31st, the county committee held another meeting, pursuant to a request of five of its members, for the purpose of considering the test questions, and a proposition to keep the polls open from 9 A. M. to 7 P. M., instead of from 11 A. M. to 5 P. M., as had been agreed on. Resolutions were read which had been adopted by the people's committee requesting the adoption of a test which would prevent any person from voting who had not theretofore acted with the union party, and an extension of the hours for voting. While discussing the proposition of amending the test, F. P. Dann stated that there was nothing before the meeting and moved to adjourn out of respect for the memory of the chairman (F. M. Pixley), who, he said, had recently deceased as a candidate for governor; that he was not dead in the body, but had suffered a political death from "too much card." Pixley stated that Dann had taken advantage of his position before the public to make a base, dirty, mean, and cowardly attack upon him, and that he would not have dared to talk in that manner had they met as men on a common plane. Dann declared that his remarks were intended as a joke, and not as an insult, but Pixley declined to entertain any apology. The meeting then adjourned without taking action upon the resolutions of the people's committee. As Pixley left the chair, Dann approached as if to explain, when the former told him not to speak, and said he would whip him as soon as he was out of the gubernatorial canvass. The other members of the committee and outsiders took sides in the difficulty, and in a few seconds, there was a general fight, which continued until the police interfered. This affair was seized upon by the press as an illustration of the character of the men who composed the committee, and the circumstance proved an effective weapon in its hands. No agreement being effected, the regular primary was held, but the supporters of the people's committee generally refrained from voting, and a Gorham delegation was selected. The people's committee went on with its work, and as a consequence two sets of state and congressional delegates, and two local tickets were selected in San Francisco. The press of the city was almost unanimous in the endorsement of the action of the people's committee. In the other counties, the primaries were generally held under the Porter law, and the conventions of Yuba and Butte counties exacted a pledge from their legislative nominees to support A. A. Sargent for the United States senate.

On April 10th, the union state central committee met at San Francisco and issued a call for a state convention, to assemble at Sacramento on Wednesday, June 12th, for the purpose of nominating a state ticket. The call was addressed to the union voters who were in favor of the adoption of the proposed constitutional amendments, and of the reconstruction of the late rebel states in accordance with the laws enacted by congress. Pursuant to this call, the convention met at the Sixth-street M. E. church, Sacramento. The body was called to order by W. H. Parks, chairman of the state committee, who advised cautious action as "owing to some little excitement in various parts of the state between contestants for the convention, there is some degree of feeling, and it is already whispered among our opponents that this convention is to be separated here to-day." For temporary chairman, W. W. Stow and T. B. McFarland, the caucus nominees of the adherents of Gorham and Bidwell, respectively, were placed in nomination. Stow was elected by a vote of 141, to 139 for McFarland. In taking the vote, the short-hair delegation from San Francisco was counted, and the rival delegation from Sacramento was not permitted to vote. In the evening, the committee on credentials reported that they had found no dispute except as to the counties of San Francisco and Sacramento, and they unanimously reported in favor of admitting the short-hair delegations from those counties. After a lengthy and exciting debate on the question of admitting that delegation from Sacramento county, the report of the committee was adopted. A permanent organization was then effected by the election of Stow, as president; and W. L. Dudley, S. G. George, Bernard Block, and George H. Riddell, vice-presidents. The order of business provided for the formation of a platform after all of the nominations should be made.

For governor, George C. Gorham and John Bidwell were placed in nomination, and Gorham was nominated on the first ballot, by a vote of 148, to 132 for Bidwell.

Gorham, in his speech accepting the nomination, said:

I am very free to say that I am much rejoiced to find that it has pleased this convention of the union party of the state of California to endorse the action of what I consider to be a majority of the union party. I have received, I am told, a majority of the votes of this convention as its nominee for the office of governor. I believe the union party to be invincible even with any load that may happen to be laid upon it through inadvertence. I shall be the governor of this state, and I hope I have great confidence that the duties that I will be called upon to discharge in the executive office of state will be discharged to the satisfaction of all; yet I am deeply sensible of the weight of my great responsibility to the state. I know that during the canvass a great many warm things have been said on both sides. I entertain no feelings of anger toward any, although I might complain a little perhaps at the want of fairness of some portions of the press toward me. They may be honestly mistaken in their incorrect impressions of me, but I hope to remove them all. I have said if anything could be pointed out in my life against my

private character—any failure to discharge the duties of my position in public places—then I would retire from the contest, and I
will still keep up the same proposition until September; if there is
anything brought against me I will give way.   For those who have
stood by me in this contest, I have a brotherly affection; for those
who opposed me, I have no feelings of ill-will, and I hope that no
state of animosity will exist hereafter.   I now ask for the united
support of the delegates in this convention.   I ask for the counsel
and aid of the leaders of the party in this convention, and that we
may place before the people of this state a ticket that shall be unex-
ceptionable.   I have no further ambition than to preserve the
interests of the state.

On the 13th, a committee on resolutions was appointed, consisting of David Belden, Walter Murray, Seneca Ewer, B. F. Ferris,
Nathaniel Holland, R. P. Johnson, L. Upson, J. B. Southard, W. J.
Swasey, E. Wadsworth, A. J. Batchelder, W. H. Leonard, T.
O'Brien, J. P. Dyer, A. J. Dyer, and J. C. Birdseye.   A communication was received from the president of the Central Pacific railroad
inviting the delegates to a free excursion by special train to Cisco, and
the invitation was accepted for the next day.   The committee on
resolutions reported the following, out of order, and the resolutions
were adopted :

1. That in the present, as in the past, we are irreconcilably opposed
to treason and to traitors, whether the same shall attempt to subvert our union and control our government by fraud and treachery
from within, or force from without; and that upon the loyalty of the
nation, tried and proved, we rely to re-establish, firmly and forever,
the bonds of our national union.

2. That in reconstructing the nation, its foundation should be
justice, and its architecture loyalty, and we are unwilling that those
so active to destroy should be the chosen and preferred builders to
erect it; and until it shall appear that in the states lately in rebellion loyal communities exist capable and ready to administer justice and enforce laws in accordance with the principles of a government of free men, and equals, it is our wish that the government be
administered and the laws enforced by the loyal agents of the federal
government.

3. That in the reconstruction plan of the late congress we recognize a policy as wise as it is magnanimous, and when the respective

states late in the rebellion shall bring themselves within its pro-visions, we will welcome them as sisters and receive them as equals in a reconstructed union.

4. That we deem the passage by the legislature of a law estab-lishing eight hours labor as a legal day's work, eminently just and proper.

5. That the importation of Chinese or any other people of the Mongolian race into the Pacific states or territories is in every respect injurious and degrading to American labor, by forcing it into unjust and ruinous competition, and an evil that should be restricted by legislation and abated by such legal and constitutional means as are in our power.

6. That the future primary elections of the union party in this state should be held under the provisions of the primary election law, and that such test should be prescribed and enforced as shall exclude all persons not members of the union party.

7. That we fully approve the amendment to the constitution of the state, presented by the legislature of 1866, and providing "that the legislature shall have no power to make an appropriation of money for any purpose whatever, for a period longer than two years;" that the same should be accepted by the legislature, adopted by the people, and become part of the constitution of the state.

The following additional nominations were then made:

John P. Jones, for lieutenant-governor, without opposition.

William H. Parks, for secretary of state, on the first ballot, by a vote of 162 to 140 for James E. Hale.

Josiah Howell, for controller, on the first ballot, by a vote of 177 to 120 for J. M. Avery; F. F. Lux withdrawing.

John Currey, for justice of the supreme court, on the fourth ballot, by a vote of 159 to 121 for S. W. Brockway, and 21 for J. H. Mc-Kune.

Charles F. Reed, for surveyor-general, on the first ballot, by a vote of 163 to 137 for J. H. Whitlock.

J. G. McCullough, for attorney-general, on the first ballot, by a vote of 222 to 80 for E. D. Wheeler.

Romualdo Pacheco, for treasurer, on the first ballot, by a vote of 196 to 99 for Antonio Pico and 28 for R. Ellis.

Charles Clayton, for harbor commissioner, on the second ballot, by a vote of 160 to 58 for C. L. Taylor; W. A. Holcomb and Marcus D. Boruck withdrawing.

R. H. Farquhar, for clerk of the supreme court, without opposition.

D. O. McCarthy, for state printer, on the first ballot, by a vote of 156 to 72 for T. A. Springer and 63 for J. J. Owen.

John Swett, for school superintendent, on the first ballot, by a vote of 170 to 131 for E. S. Lippitt.

The following additional resolutions were adopted:

8. That the union party of California cheerfully endorse the course of our senator and representatives in congress, who aided in making and consistently sustained the national policy known as the reconstruction policy of congress.

9. That the union party of California cheerfully endorse the present state officers for having honestly, faithfully, and economically conducted the state government during the past four years.

A state central committee was appointed, consisting of Walter Murray, Seneca Ewer, G. W. Ryder, W. B. Hunt, Charles Westmoreland, Felix Tracy, I. S. Belcher, M. D. Boruck, E. G. Waite, H. J. Tilden, J. P. H. Wentworth, and others.

On June 10th, the first district union congressional convention met at San Jose. Before the meeting, J. W. Wilcox, a candidate for the nomination, who had the support of the short-hair delegation from San Francisco, announced his withdrawal. He had also a strong support from the workingmen's organization, and they denounced his withdrawal as the result of a sale to the Pacific Mail Steamship Company. Wilcox declared that if nominated the capitalists would spend money to defeat him, and that with a defeat he would be ruined financially. The San Francisco short-hair delegation was admitted by a vote of 31 to 5, and T. G. Phelps was nominated for congress by acclamation. Wilcox, William E. Lovett, Frank Soule, George Barstow, C. C. Hickey, Rev. M. C. Briggs, and Harvey S. Brown were placed in nomination, but they all withdrew. The session of the convention was very animated.

The second district union congressional convention met at Sacramento, on June 11th, but adjourned without transacting any business. Another meeting was held on the 14th, at 2 A. M., immediately after the adjournment of the state convention. The first meeting had been held in the assembly chamber, and the adjournment was to meet at the same place, but the second session was held in the Sixth-street M. E. church, and a number of the delegates being absent, a determined effort was made to adjourn over until during business hours, but the motion to delay action was defeated, and several delegates withdrew. William Higby was renominated for congress by acclamation. The Sacramento *Union* subsequently supported Higby, but on the morning of his nomination it indignantly said :

The nomination of William Higby for congress was made under circumstances as discreditable as those which attended the nomination of Gorham. After the adjournment of the state convention, at the witching hour of two o'clock in the morning, the time for the meeting of the congressional convention was suddenly changed; the delegates could not be properly notified, and it was evident that the attendance of all of them was not desired. A convocation was got together at that unseasonable hour, and, the majority of those present being Higby men, the nomination was rushed through against the protest of the minority. The nominee has been taking lessons in the gophering tactics of Gorham. He may imagine that he is the regular candidate of the union party in the second district; but, from the indignation expressed by the minority, we judge he will be compelled to get a little more regular endorsement, in broad daylight, by a full convention to secure the votes of the union men of this district. The whole system of cheating the people out of a fair expression of their choice for public office must be crushed out, and now is the accepted time for accomplishing that result. Swindling is never regular, and when it is practiced in making nominations, revolt against it becomes the most consecrated regularity.

The third district union convention met at Marysville, on June 15th. After a protracted debate on the divided report of the committee on credentials, Chancellor Hartson and Jesse O. Goodwin were placed in nomination for congress. Goodwin withdrew, remarking that he had not money enough to recover the votes he had once controlled, and Hartson was nominated by acclamation. A few days later, Goodwin published a card announcing himself as an independent candidate, but in July he withdrew from the contest. In his card of announcement, he said :

To the free and independent voters of the third congressional district, state of California, who believe that nominations for office by conventions, conceived in fraud, put up in utter disregard of

public opinion, and shamelessly carried out according to the directions of a clique of politicians (so-called) acting under the mandates
of a few soulless corporations, I submit my name as an independent
candidate for congress.   Circumstances beyond my means to control,
together with the advice of prominent men from nearly half the
counties in the district concurring with me in this regard, have
induced me to this action.   Time and space will not allow me to discuss
the reasons here, but I shall take great pleasure in doing so in person
in every county in the district during the coming campaign; with
a full, firm, and abiding belief that the free yeomanry of California
have some rights left, even as against money and moneyed corporations, which may be made to appear on the fourth of September
next at the polls.   My platform is, equal and exact justice to all, to
accomplish which the government should be administered upon the
most economical basis that can be devised; unfaithful officers displaced and faithful ones put in their stead; taxation reduced to the
expenses of the government, including the interest of the national
debt, with only a nominal sinking fund for the present, and in the
collection of such tax that all money, property, or evidences of debt
should be taxed according to their real value, none to be excluded;
and that "the powers not delegated to the United States by the constitution, nor prohibited by it to the states, are reserved to the
states, respectively, or to the people."   Finally, for the present, having been brought up a laborer myself, I am in favor of all laws
tending to protect the white labor of the country, and am also in
favor of all that will kill or tend even to choke the soulless corporations now sucking the very life-blood of our young state.   I love and
venerate our common country and her flag, the starry emblem of our
nationality, and I am for all who will stand for the union of states,
and against all who are opposed to such union.   My motto is: God
and the right.

It was evident from the first that the nomination of Gorham
would alienate from the union party the support of the influential
newspapers of the state, and immediately on his nomination, an open
declaration of hostility to the ticket was made.   The San Francisco
Bulletin denounced the nomination of Gorham as the result of fraud,
saying that less than 1,500 union men had voted his ticket at the primaries, and that the democrats had done the rest of the work. · It
urged the people to compel Gorham to withdraw, and added, "We have
no means of knowing whether the respectable people of the city and

state will accept the yoke which has been fashioned to gall their necks. If they do quietly submit to the infliction, they will deserve the consequences." It was urged that Bidwell was the choice of a large majority of the union citizens of the state; that he had had the support of thirty-five newspapers of influence; and that he had been cheated out of the nomination by political trickery in the interest of Gorham. The opposition was directed against Gorham, Parks, Howell, and McCarthy. So far as the remaining nominees on the state ticket were concerned, they were entirely satisfactory, and the opposition, or "independent" press, as it styled itself, urged their support upon the party. The Sacramento *Union*, in explaining its hostility to Gorham, said:

The nomination of George C. Gorham by the union state convention for the high office of governor of California encounters the protest of thousands who have hitherto acted with the union party from considerations of patriotic duty and love of principle and without regard to the spoils of place. As a citizen, aside from his association with a gang of plunder seekers, Gorham is socially clever and is known to possess fair capacity. He has chosen to identify himself with a league of bad characters who have followed the union party, like the camp followers of an army, with a greedy eye for loot, to become their candidate and representative man, to adopt their peculiar tactics for preventing a free expression of the will of the people, and to give the state the most flagrant illustration of the power of such a crowd to wrest a nomination from an unwilling party that has been witnessed for years. Beginning with the state central committee, Gorham and his friends deprived the union men of the interior of their proper representation in the convention. Thence, they proceeded to secure the county committees and prescribe minor programmes of fraud, to get up primary elections which were palpable mockeries of free choice, and, with the money of scheming corporations to buy up delegates who were elected by interior constituencies to vote for a rival candidate. And, when the convention, thus fraudulently planned, had assembled, and it was found that a nomination depended upon the twenty-one votes of Sacramento county, the league determined to admit a delegation from that county which they knew did not represent five hundred legitimate voters out of forty-three hundred. A convention thus made up can have no valid title to be regarded as an exponent of the wishes of the union party, and the nomination of Gorham must be looked upon as a fraud, from its inception in San Francisco until it was consummated at the capital.

And now in what position does this action place those honest citizens who have hitherto affiliated with the union organization? They are not only asked to endorse with their votes the means by which the nomination of Gorham was procured, but to place in power at the state capitol, for four years, the whole league of spoils-men, schemers, and corruptionists with which he has chosen to identify himself, and for which he has been an active lobby-agent. We need not again do more than refer to the Western Pacific rail-road swindle, for which Gorham undertook to secure the sanction of the governor, as a fair sample of the sort of legislation which he would approve. In that instance, the gubernatorial veto saved the people from prolonged and grievous taxation, and the treasury of the state from depletion by a half dozen speculators who had clearly shown that they had no intention of building a railroad. Gorham's strength in seeking a nomination has consisted largely of the knowl-edge or belief that he would affix his signature to all similar bills, and they have many such, involving millions, at the bay. Now, elect Gorham and let a legislature as pliant as the last one be obtained—and that is, of course, the next object of the combination —and the state will be bled to bankruptcy within two years, while the pressure of taxation upon every interest will become intolerable to the people. It is quite clear that such an experiment would kill the union party, at any rate at the close of the Gorham administra-tion, if not before; and, with this view of the case, there are thou-sands of taxpayers and conscientious citizens who will respectfully decline to make an organization of which they have had reason to feel proud, responsible for the infliction or deserving of this unsavory end. As a last consolation, there is such a thing as dying with decency, leaving an honorable name. In any event, however, and whatever course partisans and their organs may see fit to pursue, the duty of the independent press in such emergencies as this is, to look after the interests of the state and the people. Protesting against the nomination of Gorham before it was consummated, we stated the considerations which would render the nomination a calamity to the party now dominant in the state. As the same reasons would make his election disastrous to the people, we repeat our protest, now that the convention has done its work. We find no pleasure in the performance of this task, It is, indeed, sorrowful to be compelled to witness the wreck of a party which has a bright record of service, and, if properly guided, might still lend potential aid to the cause of true progress and good government. But if the machinery of the organization is to be intrusted to wicked engineers, and the union party is to be run for the mere benefit of corrupt schemers, though we may regret the inevitable smashing up of the train and the consequent blighting of many cheering hopes, we must expect to see the people who don't want to go to ruin take passage in a safer political conveyance.

To stem the current of popular opinion, Gorham, on June 18th, issued the following address to the members of the union party:

As the nominee of the union party of the state for the office of governor, the welcome task is imposed on me of sounding the note of preparation for the impending contest. Previous to the nomination the usual efforts were made on behalf of the several candidates. The claims of all having been submitted to the state convention, and the choice having fallen upon me, I am gratified at being able to say that the representative men of the several elements of the party have warmly and enthusiastically assured me that they will now, as in the past, labor zealously for the success of the cause. They will soon be heard rallying the masses to the support of the union ticket. The party press, true to principle, have so far as I have heard, already entered upon the campaign.

After calling attention to the attitude of the democratic party toward the federal government and to the fact that the presidential election would be held in the succeeding year, he said:

But, notwithstanding the vital necessity at this time of the success of the union party principles and union party organization, murmurings of discontent are heard from quarters which have sometimes lent us aid from without the party lines. A portion of the independent press, refusing at all times to be bound by the action of the conventions of the party, has attempted to dictate its policy and its nominations, and failing to overawe its assembled representatives, has taken up arms against the organization. A persistence in this course will make them the allies of the democratic party, and as such they must be met as we meet all enemies of our cause. These papers forbade my nomination by the union state convention. They say I have been employed to urge upon the legislature schemes for the improper expenditure of public money. The charge is without foundation, and is utterly untrue. I never in my life aided in

the passage of any measure in the legislature for a consideration.
I never made use of nor advised any improper influences to reach
any legislator in behalf of any measure. It is well known that my
presence at the last legislature was at first for political purposes —
to aid in the elevation of another, not myself, to office; and subsequently, to urge party action on national subjects then of great
moment, and to solicit aid for the circulation of a little sheet called the
Free American, through which I was at my own expense, calling
public attention to the subject of reconstruction. I mean to be
clearly understood as giving a full and complete denial to all the
charges made against me, not one of which can for a moment stand
in the presence of the light of truth. But they go further, and say
that I am sure, if elected, to be under the control of schemers and
jobbers. To those who know me, so absurd a proposition needs no
denial. But I know I must address myself to those who do not
know me. Much has been said of measures for the disposal of property belonging to the state, and charges are made that those
interested have secured pledges from me that I will, if elected give
such measures my sanction. These charges are untrue; and so far
from their having any foundation in fact, I here emphatically declare
that no bill to dispose of state property anywhere without full and
just compensation, could ever have my sanction. If any have aided
in my nomination with expectations contrary to this declaration, let
them dismiss such hopes forever. It is also said that I would
approve heavy appropriations to aid public improvements. Let my
reply be explicit. I believe that the public improvements so necessary
to the building up of the material interests of the state must rely
mainly on private enterprise, and that public aid should only be
invoked after great outlays of private capital have already been
made; and I pledge myself to the tax payers of this state that no
measure to add to the burden of the public debt shall ever receive
my approval, in the event of my election, unless it is clearly in
obedience to the demand of public opinion, and clearly to the advantage of the commonwealth. No interest of private persons shall
ever be subserved through me at the expense of the state. I have
made no pledges, expressed or implied, to any corporation or individual, upon any proposed measure whatever. To an economical
administration of the state government; to firmness in the execution of the laws; to a watchful care in the examination of claims
against the state; to humane and thoughtful attention to the poor,
to the insane and the criminal; to the appointment of none but

trustworthy and competent men to office; to fidelity, at all times, to the cause of education; to boldness of speech in behalf of the right, when great issues shall arise; to all these I pledge myself most unreservedly. I trust I am on better terms with my Maker than I can believe my cruel calumniators to be, and in His presence I again asseverate the truth of all I have said. Let Him judge me. My heart is light, and my conscience is clear.

One of the journals of San Francisco affects to misunderstand a remark made by me to the state convention, and makes it the basis of an offensive suggestion. I will reproduce what was really said, and set the matter finally at rest. After alluding to the assaults made on me, I said that "if anything could be pointed out in my life against my private character, or if any failure to discharge my public duty could be shown, that I should cheerfully retire from the contest." Notwithstanding my name has been under discussion for a year, the utmost malignity of my enemies has been foiled in all efforts to fix a blemish upon me, and I now declare irrevocably that the party banner which has been intrusted to my keeping by the finally unanimous voice of the union state convention, shall be held aloft by me until the day of election; and that I would as soon think of surrendering it into the hands of those who rejoiced at the assassination of the martyred Lincoln, as of laying it down at the bidding of men who are eagerly whetting their knives to seek the life of the invincible union party.

For all who are union men I have the feeling of a fellow soldier in a sacred cause. Let us forget the bickerings of the last few weeks and resolve on victory. For open and manly political opponents I have the proper respect. For those who would, after time is given for the blood to cool, strike at the cause under a pretext 'of being dissatisfied with the nominations, I have nothing but defiance and scorn. At no time and under no circumstances will I desert the post of duty to which I have been legitimately assigned by my party. The union party has a charmed life, and nothing can destroy it until its great mission is fulfilled. I will do my whole duty during the canvass, visiting all accessible portions of the state. I shall thus meet you face to face, and we can come to good understandings.

In several counties a movement was immediately inaugurated to the end of a revision of the union state ticket by dropping the objectionable nominees, and in San Francisco it culminated in a call for a meeting to be held on June 17th. That meeting was presided

17

over by T. W. McColliam. The following resolutions were adopted, after a discussion :

WHEREAS, The machinery of the union party of California has been prostituted by unscrupulous demagogues to the support and advocacy of unworthy purposes, as has been evidenced by the late action of the union state central committee, of the county committees of Sacramento and San Francisco, and more recently by that of the union state convention excluding the legitimate representatives of the union party ; therefore be it resolved :

1. That we reorganize the republican party of California, and pledge ourselves to its support.

2. That a committee of five be appointed by the chair, who shall issue an address to the national republicans of this state and request their co-operation with us in reorganizing our party.

3. That said committee of five be authorized to act as members from the county of San Francisco of a republican state central committee.

4. That such state central committee, when organized, be requested to call a republican state convention, to assemble between the 15th and 25th days of July next, to nominate a state ticket for the support of the republicans of California.

5. That the republicans of the county of San Francisco be requested and urged to form a republican club in each election precinct in the county.

6. That said clubs, when so organized, appoint each two members to act as a republican county committee for the county of San Francisco.

Caleb T. Fay spoke in favor of the adoption of the resolutions, and a gentleman who desired to speak in opposition to the movement was prevented from proceeding by constant interruptions, and cries of "Put him out!" The chair appointed Joseph M. Wood, George Amerage, David N. Hawley, A. J. Snyder, and A. F. Scott to act on the committee provided for by the second and third resolutions. This committee afterward issued an address to the republicans of the state, urging them to reorganize their party.

A republican meeting was held at Sacramento on June 24th, and a committee was appointed to call a meeting for the 25th, of all union men who were opposed to or in favor of reconstructing the state ticket. A meeting was held pursuant to this call, but it was captured by the short hairs, and the long hairs retired to another hall, and after organizing, elected Charles H. Swift, Thomas Ross, and William Beckman members of the republican state central committee from that county, called a county convention, and adopted a lengthy set of resolutions. Similar meetings were held in other counties.

The republican state committee, composed of members chosen at these informal meetings, called a state convention, to assemble at Sacramento on July 16th, for the purpose of revising the union state ticket. The call was issued on July 3d. Accordingly, on the day named the union republican state convention met. It was called to order by J. M. Wood, chairman of the state committee. On motion of C. T. Fay, William Jones was elected temporary chairman. Delegates were present from the counties of Alameda, Amador, Contra Costa, El Dorado, Lake, Placer, Sacramento, San Francisco, Santa Cruz, Solano, Sutter, Tuolumne and Yuba. The committee on resolutions consisted of J. M. Wood, F. A. Hornblower, E. Judson, M. C. Tilden, A. Seavey, W. H. Reynolds and W. S. Coombs. On permanent organization, Jones was president, and William Kendall and George Amerage vice-presidents. A motion was carried heartily endorsing the nominations made by the union party, except for the offices of governor, secretary of state, controller and printer. On the 17th, by a resolution offered by Fay, John Bidwell was unanimously nominated for governor. The following nominations were also made without opposition : J. G. McCallum for secretary of state, William Jones for controller, and Edward G. Jefferis for printer. The following resolutions, reported by the committee, were unanimously adopted :

WHEREAS, Justice is essential to political peace, and patriotism should be exalted as a virtue, and it is the duty of the state to cherish all its people ; and, whereas, those who assert these principles are, throughout the nation, called republicans ; therefore be it resolved,

1. That the republican party of California declares itself a part of and in alliance with the national republican party of the union.

2. That we endorse the action of congress on the question of reconstruction, and will heartily endeavor to bring the same to a successful conclusion.

3. That we are the friends and advocates of free speech, a free press, free schools and the most liberal provision by the state for the purpose of educating the people thereof.

4. That we are opposed to any appropriation of the money or credit of the state for private purposes, or for the benefit of private corporations.

5. That we are in favor of such limit by law to the hours of labor as the sound judgment of laborers themselves shall fix, as for their best interests after mature deliberation in their own council.

＼ 6. That we are unqualifiedly opposed to coolie labor, but are in favor of voluntary immigration, and just protection to all free labor from whatever nationality it may come.

＼ 7. That we are in favor of impartial suffrage without distinction of color.

8. That we are in favor of the registry law and the law known as Porter's primary election law, and that we consider the honest and faithful enforcement of their provisions essential to the purity of the ballot box.

9. That we are in favor of rigid and strict economy in state, county and city governments, and the reduction of salaries of officers to the standard of industrial pursuits.

10. That the action of the late union county committees of San Francisco and Sacramento, by which democrats were allowed to take part in the late union primary election, was a fraud upon the union voters of this state, and disgraceful to all those who were concerned therein, and nominations obtained by such means have no binding obligation upon any member of the union party.

A state central committee was selected, composed of E. Judson, Samuel Soule, R. B. Torrence, J. M. Wood, B. R. Nickerson, Isaac E. Davis, J. H. Redington, C. H. Swift, W. Beckman, A. Leonard, George C. Perkins, D. Gordon, and others. After a debate, a resolution was adopted declaring it as the sense of the convention that no compromise could harmonize the union party while Gorham was retained as the gubernatorial nominee.

On July 26th, McCallum published a card declining the republican nomination for secretary of state, and on August 5th the state committee of that party substituted B. R. Nickerson as the candidate for that office.

Bidwell was nominated for governor without consultation, and it was not known if he would accept. On July 20th, a telegraphic

·dispatch dated on the 17th, from Bidwell to George S. Evans, was published, in which he stated: "Having been in the field once, I cannot consent to be a candidate again." The republican convention ᴍade no provision for officially notifying their candidates of their nominations, and therefore there was no opportunity for a formal de-·clination. Afterward, Bidwell was waited on by several prominent ᴍembers of the Gorham party, and on August 2d, the Marysville *Appeal* published the following correspondence :

MARYSVILLE, July 22, ·1867.

JOHN BIDWELL, Chico,— *Dear Sir:* Understanding that the late ·convention, which nominated you for the office of governor, do not intend to formally notify you of such nomination, and offer you an ·opportunity to formally accept or decline the same, and seeing that the paper published at your place favors the placing of your name as such nominee at the head of the ticket ; and feeling, like many other union men, anxious for the welfare of the union party, I address .you this note to inquire of you whether you approve or accept of such nomination ; or have authorized the Chico *Courant* to so use your name in placing it before the people as such nominee for the ·office of governor. Hoping an early reply, and one you may be willing to have published, I remain, your obedient servant,

G. N. SWEZY.

CHICO, July 24, 1867.

G. N. SWEZY,— *My Dear Sir:* Yours of the 22d inst. is received. In consequence of receiving so many letters, *pro* and *contra*, I am ·forced to abandon my original purpose to simply answer each letter in its turn and write nothing for publication, for it will consume all :my time. I, therefore, propose now, through this occasion, to speak ·to one and all. To those who congratulate me on my reported nom- ination for governor, I have promptly, but courteously, said that I could not possibly accept the honor. To those who urge me to de- ·cline the nomination in question and ·dictate the terms in which I .shall come out in favor of the regular ticket, I must kindly say that I have not been officially advised of such nomination, have accepted none, do not, under the circumstances, propose to accept any, prefer to employ my own language in making this formal declension, and that I have not abandoned, but still adhere unswervingly to the ·union party.

Some ask me to give an expression of sentiment, if consistent

with my views, favorable to a united effort in behalf of the union
state ticket. I answer, it certainly is consistent with my views, and
I proceed to do so. Having been a candidate before one convention,
I desire to say to those friends who adhered to me during the struggle for the nomination, and who labored earnestly for and were
favorable to my nomination, and to all others, that I feel profoundly
grateful to them, but that I cannot consent to enter the field again
and attempt to make the race for governor. To do so would be
tantamount to giving aid to the so-called democratic party, the success of which, at this juncture of affairs, would be a calamity both
to the state and nation, and ought not to be thought of by any loyal
man. As far as I am concerned, I am trying to lay aside all personal feelings and considerations; in fact, I have done so, so far as
human nature is capable under similar circumstances. I profess not
to be perfect. And I now ask, what can be done to restore harmony
to the union party of this state? In the pending contest we want
not only to win the battle for freedom and equal suffrage, but we
want to make the victory overwhelming. Being out of the race, I
am no longer a stumbling block in the way, and I think I can view
the scene from the standpoint of a tax payer and private citizen,
calmly, impartially. There is one question upon which all must
agree. Our public burdens are great and must not be increased.
There is a deep-seated apprehension pervading the minds of the
people, that the head of the state ticket, having been identified with
a measure vastly increasing the public debt or liabilities, and consequently the taxes of the people, would have the right to consider,
if elected, that his course in respect to the said measure had been
sanctioned, and that he would feel at full liberty to approve that
or any similar measure for the benefit of speculators, "as clearly
in obedience to the demand of public opinion;" also, that the tide-
lands belonging to the state, some of which are already valuable, and
which if safely guarded and properly managed can scarcely fail to
be more than ample to pay the entire state debt (for who can doubt
that a city is destined to rise from the waters of the bay of San Francisco, perhaps stretching from Goat Island to the Alameda shore, of
more than Venetian opulence and splendor?) will be recklessly
squandered for the benefit of speculators.

Now, there should be a cure for every ill. The only remedy that
suggests itself to my mind is this : Let the people everywhere exact
of the state ticket and candidates for the legislature pledges of the
most binding character upon these vital questions. Let candidates

pledge themselves to the people that no measure adding to the liabilities of the state or the taxes of the people, or squandering the
public property, shall be passed or approved; and, satisfactory
pledges having been given, let us vote the entire union ticket without
scratching a letter, syllable or name. No candidate can refuse to
accede to these reasonable demands. No person, in this time of
peace, can propose to favor oppressive measures and expect the
people to sustain him by their votes. A new ticket cannot be substituted, at this late hour, with any certainty of success. We must
then stand by this or let the copperheads take the state. I say,
therefore, to my friends everywhere, let us rally and prevent such a
calamity, by taking the only course that seems within our power.
Let us demand that the state indebtedness shall not be increased;
that the property of the state shall be preserved for the benefit of
the people; the state for the nation, and the nation for the cause
of freedom and humanity.   J. BIDWELL.

R. H. Farquhar, the union candidate for clerk of the supreme
court, was killed at Nevada City on July 27th, by the explosion of
gas in the record vault in the court house, and on August 4th the
state central committee nominated E. G. Waite for that office; and,
on the next day, the republican committee ratified the nomination.
On the same day the latter committee tendered the nomination for
governor to Caleb T. Fay (in place of Bidwell), and on the 6th he
published a lengthy letter of acceptance. The republican committee
construed Bidwell's letter to Swezy as placing him in a hostile attitude toward the revised ticket, and unanimously resolved to accept
the document as a withdrawal.

The democratic state committee met at San Francisco on April
19th, and called a state convention, to consist of 273 delegates, to
meet in that city on June 19th. The test adopted included all
voters who were opposed to the radical policy of congress, and who
were in favor of a constitutional administration of the government.
At the time appointed the convention assembled in Turn Verein hall,
on Bush street, and was called to order by James O. Goods, chairman of the state committee. Eugene Casserly was unanimously
elected temporary chairman, John Bigler declining the nomination.
On permanent organization, Casserly was president; and J. P. Hoge,
J. W. Coffroth, James Johnson, A. C. Adams, John C. Burch, A. G.
Stakes, James A. Johnson, E. D. Keyes and others, vice-presidents.

The committee on resolutions consisted of J. P. Hoge, A. C. Bradford, E. D. Keyes, Thomas Findley, W. W. Cope, P. B. Reading, A. H. Rose, E. T. Wilkins, and H. P. Barber. On the 20th, the convention met at Union hall, and adopted the following resolutions:

1. That the government of the United States is the paramount government of the country, and that the allegiance due from the citizens to such government is a binding and perpetual obligation, to be observed with fidelity and good faith.

2. That the questions involved in the late rebellion have been practically settled by the war, and it is the duty of all to acquiesce in this settlement and endeavor to restore friendly relations between the different sections of the country and re-establish the government in its constitutional authority throughout the union.

3. That, in order that our national difficulties may be speedily adjusted and the union restored on a permanent and satisfactory basis, the states lately in rebellion should be dealt with in a spirit of kindness and forbearance, and we regard the course of congress, in what are known as the reconstruction measures of that body, as harsh, illiberal, and oppressive, and more likely to result in a hollow truce than enduring peace

4. That the only way in which peace and concord can be re-established is by conforming to the requirements of the constitution and defeating the radical party, who spurn its provisions and imperil the union by their mad and seditious course.

5. That to effect this object we solemnly pledge our best and most untiring efforts, that the accomplishing of this end is the one grand question now pending, transcending all others in importance, and that the present imminent perils of the country demand the union of all conservative hearts and hands, irrespective of former or present party names, in a vigorous effort to maintain the federal constitution in its integrity and secure its operation according to the spirit and intent of its founders.

6. That the scheme of reducing a portion of the United States to territories, and stripping them of the rights enjoyed from the foundation of the government, is so absolutely opposed, not only to the dearest provisions of the federal constitution, but to any sound idea of practical statesmanship, so dangerous as a precedent and so thoroughly antagonistic to those principles of reserved rights and local self government which underlie our republican system, that it

is the duty of the people of California, without distinction of party, to set upon those measures the seal of their condemnation.

7. That we believe it impracticable to maintain republican institutions based upon the suffrages of negroes, Chinese, and Indians, and that the doctrines avowed by the radical leaders of indiscriminate suffrage, regardless of race, color, or qualification, if carried into practice, would end in the degradation of the white race and the speedy destruction of the government.

8. That we regard the right to regulate suffrage as belonging exclusively to the several states of this union.

9. That the payment of the public debt is a solemn duty resting upon the government, and that the people should cheerfully submit to any just system of taxation necessary to enable the government to discharge this duty; but no tax should be levied except to meet the necessary expenses of the government and sustain the public credit.

10. That all taxation should be equal and uniform, and the expenses of the government should be reduced to the smallest amount consistent with the proper administration of public affairs.

11. That in view of the enormous weight of state and national taxation, it is imperatively necessary to prevent any increase of the state debt, and to reduce our state and county expenses to the lowest standard compatible with good government; that we regard with serious apprehension the schemes which unprincipled men are now maturing for the people by corrupt legislation, and we hold it to be the duty of all good citizens to defeat the political schemers who, under the thin disguise of professed loyalty, are seeking an opportunity to deplete the public treasury and add to the burdens of taxation.

12. That the money and property of the public should be used for the public good and not wasted in reckless appropriations and private grants.

13. That the power to regulate foreign immigration being vested in congress, it is the duty of that body to protect the Pacific states and territories from an undue influx of Chinese and Mongolians, and it is the duty of the legislature of this state to petition congress to endeavor to obtain the adoption of such regulations as shall accomplish this object, and the legislature should use all its power to prevent the introduction of Mongolian laborers.

14. That labor is the basis of all material prosperity and the creator of wealth, and that its interests should always be favorably

regarded by the legislature; that the laborer should have time for mental and moral culture and for healthful recreation. We therefore heartily sympathise with the laboring classes in their endeavors to reduce the legal standard of a day's labor, and declare ourselves in favor of making eight hours a legal day's work, in the absence of any agreement to the contrary.

15. That the industrial interests of the country should be carefully guarded and nourished, and every effort made to improve the condition and protect the rights of the laboring classes will receive our hearty support.

16. That we regard the act known as the "Registry Law" of this state as unjust, oppressive, and tyranical, calculated to defeat the rights of the honest voters of the country, and should be immediately and unconditionally repealed.

The following nominations were made:

Henry H. Haight, for governor, without opposition; Gen. W. S. Rosecrans and William M. Lent withdrawing.

William Holden for lieutenant-governor, without opposition; William Irwin withdrawing.

H. L. Nichols for secretary of state, without opposition; J. A. McClelland withdrawing.

Robert Watt for controller, without opposition; Paul K. Hubbs and Jesse H. Craddock withdrawing.

Antonio F. Coronel for treasurer, without opposition; Joseph Roberts, Jr., withdrawing.

John W. Bost for surveyor-general, without opposition; C. D. Semple, A. G. Winn, and E. Twitchell withdrawing.

Jo Hamilton for attorney-general, without opposition.

Thomas H. Selby for harbor commissioner, without opposition; James H. Cutter, James C. Pennie, Thomas Boice, Charles McMillan, and Charles F. McDermott withdrawing. (Selby, on the 25th, declined the nomination, and J. H. Cutter was substituted by the state committee).

George Seckel for clerk of the supreme court, without opposition; S. L. Lupton withdrawing.

Daniel W. Gelwicks for printer, without opposition; P. B. Forster, T. L. Thompson, David Norris, W. S. Moss, John R. Ridge, and M. D. Carr withdrawing.

O. P. Fitzgerald for school superintendent, without opposition.

Royal T. Sprague for justice of the supreme court, on the first ballot, over William T. Wallace; J. B. Crockett and Eugene Casserly withdrawing.

On the 21st a state committee was selected, composed of T. J. Henley, William F. White, William Watt, Selden S. Wright, D. F. Douglass, John Daggett, P. B. Reading, E. T. Wilkins, A. H. Rose, C. J. Brenham, J. W. Roberts, S. T. Leet, John Bigler, H. H. Hartley, J. W. Coffroth, Eugene Casserly, J. P. Hoge, J. H. Baird, John Middleton, T. N. Cazneau, G. H. Rogers, J. O. Goods, and others.

The first district democratic convention met immediately after the adjournment of the state convention. S. B. Axtell was nominated for congressman, on the second ballot, over O. T. Ryland; Murray Morrison, W. S. Montgomery, Edward Stanly, and E. S. Tully withdrawing.

The second district democratic convention met at the same time, and nominated James W. Coffroth for congressman, without opposition; A. H. Rose and J. B. Crockett withdrawing.

The third district democratic convention also met on the 21st and nominated James A. Johnson for congressman, without opposition; W. W. Pendegast withdrawing.

The campaign which followed was vigorously prosecuted by the three parties, the independent press keeping up a persistent fire at Gorham and his ostracised associates on the union ticket. The election was held on September 4, and the union party met with its first defeat in the state since the breaking out of the war. The result was the election of the entire democratic ticket, and the official canvass exhibited the following result:

For Governor—Haight, 49,905; Gorham, 40,359; Fay, 2,088.
Lieutenant-Governor—Holden, 47,969; Jones, 44,584.
Secretary of State—Nichols, 48,573; Parks, 41,663; Nickerson, 2,019.
Controller—Watt, 48,841; Howell, 41,887; Jones, 2,001.
Treasurer—Coronel, 48,147; Pacheco, 45,243.
Attorney-General—Hamilton, 48,268; McCullough, 44,876.
Surveyor-General—Bost, 48,047; Reed, 45,039.
Clerk of the Supreme Court—Seckel, 48,237; Waite, 44,894.
Harbor Commissioner—Cutter, 48,155; Clayton, 44,853.
Printer—Gelwicks, 48,378; McCarthy, 39,072; Jefferis, 4,452.

Congressman: First District—Axtell, 18,793; Phelps, 13,989.
Second District—Coffroth, 14,786; Higby, 16,053.
Third District—Johnson, 14,767; Hartson, 14,394.

The judicial election was held on October 16th, and both of the democratic candidates were elected.

For Justice of the Supreme Court—Sprague, 38,113; Curr̶y, 34,706.

For Superintendent of Public Instruction—Fitzgerald, 37,074 Swett, 35,479.

CHAPTER XX.

1868. Reconstruction Measures—Impeachment of President John-son—Republican Convention, January 28th—Democratic Convention—Republican Convention, June 25th.

On December 14, 1867, George Pearce (democrat) offered the following resolution in the senate, and it was referred to the committee on federal relations :

That it is the sense and judgment of the people of California that the whole people of the United States owe it to themselves and posterity, as a sacred duty, to resist, by all honorable means, every effort and attempt to count an electoral vote of any state in the approaching presidential election cast under or by virtue of the reconstruction acts (so called) of congress.

On March 20th, the committee recommended the indefinite postponement of the resolution, but it was never reached on file.

On December 16, 1867, John M. James (democrat) introduced a resolution in the assembly to direct the congressional representatives "to use their exertions and all honorable means to restore the ten southern states, now governed by the military, to the same and equal constitutional rights with all the other states."

W. S. Green (democrat) offered the following, and both resolutions were referred to the committee on federal relations, but were never reported back :

WHEREAS, Some of our sister states, by their members of congress, claim the right to establish despotic military governments within the territory of ten of the states of this union, and to permit the negroes of those states not only to enact laws for the government of the white population, but to send members to congress, and to participate in the election of president; therefore resolved,

1. That such military governments are totally inconsistent with our free institutions and destructive of civil liberty.

2. That the negroes of the south are now incapable of self government, and therefore it would be unsafe and unwise to intrust them with political power or social equality.

3. That the action of congress in establishing pretended state governments in the said ten states, wherein the whites are disfranchised and the negroes enfranchised, is unconstitutional and void.

4. That the people of California will not recognize any state government established by force, nor members of congress, nor presidential electors elected therein.

5. That copies of these resolutions be transmitted by the governor to the president of the United States, to our senators and representatives in congress, and to the governors of all our sister states not controlled by military power.

On December 17, 1867, Charles Westmoreland (union) offered the following resolution in the assembly, which was laid on the table

That the recent elections in California and other states, resulting as they did in victories to the democratic party in some of the said states, and in an increase of the party vote in nearly all, is not in any way to be regarded as an indorsement of the doctrine of secession, nor as a rebuke to the conduct or result of the late civil war; but that, on the contrary, the said doctrine of secession is a pernicious heresy, unfounded in law, and the civil war named was maintained by the adhering of loyal states and people in strict response to the duties and instinct of patriotism.

The next day the resolution was taken from the table, when T. E. Farish (democrat) moved to amend by striking out the word "secession" wherever it occurred, and inserting "military reconstruction, Chinese and negro suffrage." After a discussion, the resolution and substitute were referred to the committee on federal relations, and it was not reported back until the last day of the session, when it was not considered. On December 19th, the house adopted a resolution that all motions and resolutions pertaining to the policy of the federal government toward the late confederate states and the people thereof, and to theories of reconstruction and suffrage therein, should be referred to the committee on federal relations without debate.

On January 9, 1868, A. H. Rose (democrat) offered the following resolution in the senate, which was referred to the judiciary committee, a previous motion to refer it to the committee on federal relations having been defeated by the casting vote of the president :

1. That the people of California are irreconcilably opposed to conferring the elective franchise upon negroes or Chinese; that congress has no constitutional power to regulate the elective franchise in the states of Virginia, North Carolina, South Carolina, Georgia, Florida, Alabama, Mississippi, Louisiana, Texas, Arkansas, or any other state or territory; that any attempt to make such regulation by congress is a usurpation of power against which this legislature, in the name of the people of California, doth solemnly protest.

2. That our senators in congress are instructed and our representatives requested to oppose and vote against all legislative action purporting to confer the elective franchise upon negroes or Chinese, and to vote for the repeal of all legislation of that character.

On March 27th the committee reported the resolution back among a mass of other business which had not been considered, and it was never afterward acted on by the senate.

On January 11th, Rose offered the following resolution in the senate, and it was referred to the committee on federal relations :

WHEREAS, The people of California having, in common with people of other states, and without distinction of party, declared their unalterable devotion to the federal union, and their conviction that the late war extinguished and settled forever all claims to the right of secession; therefore, resolved,

That, there being no difference of opinion between the people of California concerning the right of states to secede from the union, any discussion of that subject by this legislature is wholly unnecessary and improper.

The committee, on March 20th, reported against the resolution, and it was never reached on file.

On January 17th, Pearce offered the following resolution in the senate, which was referred to the committee on federal relations by a vote of 17 to 15 :

That the refusal of congress to admit to seats members elected to that body by the state of Kentucky, without any constitutional objection to their eligibility, is viewed with deep regret and anxiety, and is regarded by the people of California as wholly injurious and unjust, and exceedingly dangerous and revolutionary ; also, that the action of the United States senate in attempting to force ex-Secretary Stanton into the cabinet of constitutional advisors of the president, against the expressed wish and desire of that high functionary of the government, is equally injurious, dangerous and revolutionary, and tends to destroy the usefulness of the executive branch of the government.

This also met with an unfavorable report from the committee, on March 20th, and was not afterward considered by the senate.

The disagreement between the president and congress, which culminated in the passing of a resolution of impeachment of the chief magistrate of the United States, on February 24th, by the house of representatives, attracted a great share of public attention in California, and gave rise to many animated debates in the legislature. On February 20th, J. H. Moore (democrat) offered the following in the assembly, which was referred to the committee on federal relations :

WHEREAS, Measures are now pending before congress, the declared purpose of which is to extinguish ten states of the union, and establish in their stead a military dictatorship, in which the civil laws and public and personal liberty are to exist only at the pleasure of the military power; and whereas, the attempt is made to complete the scheme of usurpation by the degradation and subjection of the federal judiciary to the arbitrary will of a congressional majority ; therefore, be it resolved :

1. That the representatives of California, now assembled, reflecting the will of the people of the state, in obedience to their oaths to support the constitution, hereby pronounce these acts of usurpation treasonable, flagatious, and a crime against liberty and against the institutions of our fathers.

2. That our senators in congress be instructed and our representatives requested not only to vote against such measures, but to oppose and endeavor to defeat them by all the means in their power.

The resolution was reported back on the last day of the session, without recommendation, and it was not considered by the house.

On February 25th, Senator W. J. Shaw (democrat) introduced the following, which was referred to the committee on federal relations, by a vote of 11 to 10 :

That we view the recent action of members of congress seeking to force one of the bureaus of the executive department of the United States government from the control of the chief executive thereof, as inadvisable and as revolutionary in its tendencies ; and that our senators in congress are instructed and our representatives requested not to encourage, assist or advise said proceeding.

On March 20th, the committee recommended its indefinite postponement, and it was never reached on the file.

On February 25th, Westmoreland offered the following in the assembly, which was referred to the committee on federal relations, the house refusing to suspend the rules for the purpose of an immediate consideration of the resolution, by a vote of 17 to 31 :

1. That congress is the supreme law-making power of the United States of America, and that laws passed by such congress are binding upon every citizen and officer thereof, from the highest to the lowest, until repealed or set aside by competent lawful authority.

2. That the course of the acting president of the United States, Andrew Johnson, in removing Edwin M. Stanton from the place of secretary of war of the United States, as well as the course of that functionary—Andrew Johnson—in appointing General Lorenzo Thomas to the place or position named, are in direct, flagrant and undenied violation of the letter and spirit of the law of congress then and now in force, known as the tenure of office act.

3. That California disavows and denounces the said action of said acting president, Andrew Johnson, in the matter named herein as a gross and palpable violation of the laws of the nation, and an insult to its citizens, whose rights and privileges are destroyed thereby.

4. That the principles here announced the state of California will forever maintain and defend by all methods adequate to secure their supremacy.

The committee reported the resolutions back without recommendation on the last day of the session, and they were never considered in the house. On the same day, Asa Ellis (democrat) offered the following in the assembly :

WHEREAS, The radical majority of the congress of the United States are treasonably attempting to usurp the constitutional functions of the executive and judicial departments of the federal government, and to that end are endeavoring, in defiance of the laws and the traditions of our country, by violence, to remove from office the president of the United States ; therefore, be it resolved by the assembly of the state of California :

1. That the people of this state will now, as they have in the

past, bear true faith and fealty to the government of our fathers; that by all legal and just means they will sustain the president of the United States in the complete discharge of his duties.

2. That we urge the president of the United States, in the name of our people—the freemen of the state of California—and in the name and in the behalf of the cause of constitutional liberty, to be firm and unbending in the maintenance of the rights of the executive department of the government, and to that end we pledge him our undivided support.

3. That the radical majority in the congress of the United States have trampled upon and disregarded the great interests of the people, and instead of legislating to relieve the people from the burden of taxation, under which the entire industry of the country is suffering, are bending their united efforts to involve the country in the vortex of civil war, and, in the opinion of the assembly of the state of California, have proved themselves unworthy alike of the high positions they now occupy and of the confidence of the people.

4. That his excellency the governor be directed to send, telegraphically, a copy of the above resolutions to his excellency the president of the United States, Andrew Johnson.

The speaker *pro tem.*, A. J. Batchelder (union), decided that the resolutions were out of order, as they purported to give expression to the opinion of the assembly alone upon leading national questions, but this decision was not sustained by the house, by a vote of 10 to 38. A motion was carried to suspend the rules for the immediate consideration of the resolutions, when Paschal Coggins (union) offered the following substitute:

WHEREAS, The law-making power of the federal government is by the constitution exclusively vested in the congress of the United States; and whereas, repeated and flagrant attempts have been made by President Andrew Johnson to embarrass and overawe congress in the exercise of this power, and to violate laws constitutionally passed by that body; and whereas, the president has persistently opposed all efforts on the part of congress to reconstruct the governments of the southern states on a basis consistent with the issues determined and settled by the war; and whereas, the constitutional power of congress to create and regulate the office of secretary of war and other cabinet officers has never heretofore been denied; and whereas, the president has attempted to remove from that office the present incumbent, Edwin M. Stanton, during the session of the

18

senate, in open and direct violation of the tenure of office act; therefore, resolved :

1. That in the opinion of the assembly, the present unlawful attempt of the president to remove the secretary of war is deliberately
designed by him to re-inaugurate civil war for the purpose of overthrowing our republican form of government, and for the re-establishment of American slavery, the relic of barbarism recently abolished
by the conquest of arms, by presidential proclamation, and by an
amendment of the constitution of the United States.

2. That we regard the act of the president in attempting to remove the secretary of war, as a high crime and misdemeanor, for
which he should at once be impeached by congress.

The previous question was ordered, and the substitute was lost by
a vote of 18 to 30. The original resolutions were then adopted by a
vote of 32 to 18. The house immediately adjourned, before notice of
a reconsideration could be given.

On February 27th, E. H. Heacock (union) introduced in the senate a series of resolutions, the first three of which were identical
with resolutions 1, 2, and 3, offered in the assembly by Westmoreland on the 25th, and with the following in addition :

4. That his excellency, the governor, be directed to telegraph a
copy of the above resolutions to Hon. Benjamin F. Wade, president
of the senate, and the Hon. Schuyler Colfax, speaker of the house of
representatives of the congress of the United States.

The senate refused to postpone the special order for the consideration of the resolutions, and on the next day Heacock offered the
following in place of the series which he had offered on the 27th :

1. *Resolved, by the Senate of California,* That congress is the
supreme political and law-making power of the United States of
America, and that laws passed by such congress are binding upon
every officer and citizen thereof, from the highest to the lowest, until
repealed or set aside by competent legal authority.

2. That the course of the president of the United States, Andrew
Johnson, in removing Edwin M. Stanton from the position of secretary of war of the United States, and in appointing General Lorenzo
Thomas to such position, is in direct and flagrant violation of the
letter and spirit of the law of congress, then and now in force, known
as the " tenure of office act."

3. That we deem such removal and appointment as sufficient

cause of impeachment of the president, such removal and appointment being declared by said act to be a "high misdemeanor."

4. That his excellency the governor be directed to send by telegraph a copy of the above resolutions to the Hon. Benjamin F. Wade, president of the senate, and Hon. Schuyler Colfax, speaker of the house of representatives of the congress of the United States.

D. L. Morrill (democrat) offered the following as an amendment:

Provided, nevertheless, that as a total disavowal of the principles embodied in the foregoing resolutions was expressed by the people of California at the last general election, their adoption by this senate cannot in any manner be construed as reflecting the sentiments of the people of the state.

J. W. Mandeville (democrat) raised the point of order, that similar resolutions were already before the senate undisposed of, and thereupon the president ruled that the resolutions were out of order, but the senate failed to sustain the ruling. After a debate, and several roll-calls on collateral questions, the Morrill amendment was rejected, and the resolutions were adopted by a vote of 7 to 12. On the 29th, a motion to reconsider was made immediately on the opening of the session, and the entire day and evening was spent in the discussion of the questions which arose. On March 2d, the debate was resumed, and the senate refused to reconsider, by a vote of 12 to 15. Pending the discussion on the second, Maclay offered the following as a substitute, which, being declared out of order, were recommitted to him to be drawn up in the form of a protest on behalf of the democratic senators:

WHEREAS, The pending impeachment of the president is a proceeding of the most profound concern to the whole people of the United States, involving in its consequences the very existence of the government, and the perpetuity of free institutions; and whereas, the impeachment, conviction, and removal of the president from office on the charge of having violated, or attempting to violate the provisions of the "tenure of office act," before the supreme court of the United States shall have first decided that congress had the constitutional power to pass the said act, would be a measure not only of folly and of injustice and wrong to the president, for which no adequate atonement could be offered, but entail great reproach and odium on both congress and the country; therefore, resolved,

1. That, influenced by a sincere desire to preserve the peace, the

honor, and the dignity of our common country, that to this end for the present ignoring all questions of right and wrong, of constitutional law, and justice, as between the president and congress, we solemnly appeal to that honorable body to arrest at once all further proceedings touching the matter of impeachment until the supreme court shall have decided whether, in point of fact and of law, there is such a statute as the "tenure of office act."

2. That our representatives in the lower house are hereby earnestly requested and our senators instructed to use their influence and cast their votes in aid of the accomplishment of the purpose of these resolutions.

On March 5th, Maclay presented a protest against the action of the senate in passing the Heacock resolutions, but it was subsequently withdrawn. On March 4th, Governor Haight transmitted a message to the senate declining to send the resolutions to Washington, and setting forth his reasons at great length. A motion by Shaw that the reasons expressed by the governor for declining to send the resolutions as requested be declared satisfactory to the senate, was carried by the casting vote of the president. On the next day, this vote was reconsidered, when Heacock offered the following, which were adopted, by a vote of 20 to 16:

1. That the reason given by his excellency the governor in the following portion of his message, viz: "that body (meaning the senate of the United States) sits as a court to try the president upon the charge presented, and any attempt to forestall the judgment of that or any other judicial tribunal, before the accused is heard in his defence would be indelicate and improper," for not telegraphing the resolutions referred to therein, be deemed and accepted by the senate as a sufficient reason for his refusal to telegraph the resolutions to the Hon. Benjamin F. Wade, president of the senate of the United States, as directed by order of the senate.

2. Further, that such reason does not apply to that portion of the order of the senate which directs him to telegraph the resolutions to the Hon. Schuyler Colfax, speaker of the house of representatives, and that no sufficient reason or excuse is given or shown in his message for a failure to comply with such last-mentioned portion of the order of the senate; therefore, be it further resolved,

3. That the resolutions referred to in the governor's message be returned to him, and that he be respectfully requested to immediately telegraph the first three of such resolutions to the Hon. Schuyler

Colfax, speaker of the house of representatives of the congress of the United States.

On January 28th, an address was issued, which had been adopted on the 25th, at a meeting of the republican central club of San Francisco. It was addressed to the republicans of California, and urged them to at once organize clubs in harmony with that club with a view of facilitating the selection of delegates to the state convention which was to be called by the republican state committee to select delegates to attend the national convention, to be held in Chicago, in May. After urging the importance of selecting able and honest representatives, the address recited :

Republicans, friends—all who believe in the principles enunciated by the great national republican party: We cordially invite you to join with us in our efforts to again place ourselves upon the platform of our distinctive organization, that we may wisely profit by the disastrous results of the late political campaign and steer clear of the rocks upon which the late union party of this state was wrecked by a clique of selfish schemers who were thrust upon us during the rebellion, and who introduced and obtained control of the organization by the introduction of a system of tactics worthy only of our democratic opponents in their days of darkest degradation. The frauds through which the nominations of the union party were obtained are fresh in the minds of all, and the perpetrators are justly branded by your emphatic condemnation. We are now called upon again to meet the same influences, manipulated by the same class who led the union party into disgraceful defeat and buried it with themselves in hopeless oblivion. Let us not allow ourselves again to be led by scheming without honesty, policy without principle, or ambition without wisdom. There can be but two national parties in the coming contest : the one known as republican ; the other democratic. The one upholds the principles that carried us safely through the war; the other struggles to overturn them. Clad in our political armor, let us do battle for the living issues of the republican party, with all its wisdom, strength and prestige, its renown, its honored scars received in fierce contest in forum and on bloody fields for liberty and justice ; and, finally, its full and complete triumph over ignorance, barbarism, human degradation, false opinions, and vaulting ambition,

The republican state committee of 1867, however, did not issue a call for a convention, and the movement to infuse life into the party was signally unsuccessful.

On February 24th, a meeting of the union state central committee was held at San Francisco, and a state convention to choose delegates · to attend the national republican convention to be held in Chicago, on May 20th, was called to convene at Sacramento, on March 31st. The committee recommended that the primaries be held under the primary election law, and adopted a test to include all legal voters who would pledge themselves to support the national ticket. The following resolution was also adopted :

That the union state central committee earnestly urge upon all members of the union party of California unanimity of action in the approaching campaign, and that all differences of the past be forgotten.

Pursuant to this call, the state convention met at the Sixth-street M. E. church, at 2 o'clock, on the 31st of March. E. W. Casey, secretary of the state committee, called the convention to order, in the absence of the chairman, and Frank M. Pixley was unanimously chosen temporary chairman, Charles Westmoreland withdrawing in his favor. The committee on resolutions consisted of S. W. Brockway, C. Westmoreland, E. W. Roberts, L. R. Lull, W. H. Sears, C. A. Tweed, John F. Miller, O. B. Powers, and Chancellor Hartson. In the evening, the convention organized permanently by electing Pixley, president; and W. E. Lovett, Wm. Sherman, J. P. Dyer, L. H. Foote, G. W. Swan, H. G. Rollins, C. Westmoreland, Horace Beach, and J. A. Hutton, vice-presidents.

The following resolutions were reported, and unanimously adopted:

1. That the loyal masses of California are unalterably attached to the imperishable principles of the union republican party; that its history is the history of progress, of the advancement of civil, individual, and national liberty, of the war against rebellion, of the preservation of the union, of the delivery of four millions of people from bondage; and that its great mission will never end until the union of all the states shall be established on a foundation of justice and right, never again to be shaken, either by traitors at home or by their allies abroad.

2. That the constitution devolves upon the executive the duty to see that the laws are faithfully executed, and that when a law is

enacted in conformity with the prescribed constitutional forms, the executive is bound to execute the same.

3. That the house of representatives of the United States is entitled to the gratitude and thanks of the nation for its action in preferring articles of impeachment against Andrew Johnson; that his flagrant disregard of a positive enactment of congress, in the removal of the secretary of war, in direct violation of an expressed provision forbidding such act, was of itself a high crime, and, which added to the long series of his gross misdemeanors, would, if suffered to go unrebuked, subordinate all the other powers of government to the despotic will of the executive, and would end in the subversion of the constitution and the final destruction of representative government.

4. That the loyal masses of California, with one voice, approve of and pledge themselves to sustain all the reconstruction measures of congress; that in carrying out the principles involved in those measures congress is only executing that provision of the constitution which devolves upon the United States the obligation to guarantee to every state in the union a republican form of government.

5. That we have the most implicit confidence in the senate of the United States, before which august tribunal the highest officer known to the constitution and laws is now arraigned and on his trial, that they will fairly and impartially discharge the solemn duty imposed upon them according to the law and evidence, and they will, by their decision and judgment, maintain and vindicate the constitution and laws of their country, uninfluenced by either political or personal considerations.

6. That we are in favor of the strictest economy in the administration of our national, state, and county affairs; of reducing public taxation at once to the lowest limit allowable by the requirements of our public obligations.

7. That the payment of the public debt, and in which is involved the national honor, is a cardinal point in our political faith; that repudiation would be an abandonment of the principles upon which the war for the union was fought; a concession that the union was not worth defending; a breach of the public faith; a violation of plighted honor, and a crime against the loyal dead, who gave their lives on the battlefield in defense of the great cause for which it was incurred,

8. That it is the bounden duty of the national government, under all circumstances and at all hazards, so to use the national power in its fullest extent without hesitation and without delay, that the rights of every American citizen, native born and naturalized, shall be fully protected at home and abroad; and especially that no foreign nation should be permitted to arrest and punish any American citizen for any offense committed upon our own soil.

9. That in Ulysses S. Grant—the hero, the patriot, and statesman—we recognize the representative man of the times, one in whose keeping the destiny and honor of the nation will ever be safe, and therefore we name him as our unanimous choice for president of the United States.

Westmoreland offered the following additional resolution:

That the delegation elected by the convention are hereby advised to support Benjamin F. Wade, of Ohio, for the position of vicepresident of the United States.

G. A. Gillespie offered the following as a substitute:

That this convention now proceed to ballot, to indicate its choice for the office of vice-president, and select from the names of the following statesmen: · Benjamin F. Wade, Schuyler Colfax, Rueben E. Fenton, A. G. Curtin, and Henry Wilson, and that the person receiving the highest vote shall be deemed the preference of this convention, and the one receiving the next highest vote the second preference, and so on.

After a discussion, Westmoreland had leave to withdraw his resolution, and the Gillespie substitute was laid on the table.

On the first ballot, for four delegates at large to attend the national convention, General P. E. Conner, Colonel James Coey, J. J. Green, and John Stratman were elected, the vote being: for Conner, 211; Coey, 231; Green, 203; Stratman, 161; W. E. Lovett, 127; and William H. Sears, 111.

William H. Sears and W. E. Lovett were elected delegates from the first congressional district, on the first ballot, the vote being: For Sears, 159; Lovett, 175; Seth Wetherbee, 127; Josiah Belden, 32; and Henry Baker, 36. James L. Riddle, J. Benrimo, and T. T. Tidball were also placed in nomination before the convention, but no votes were cast for them.

Charles B. Higby and J. M. Days were elected delegates from the second district, by acclamation; John C. Byers withdrawing.

Thomas Spencer and J. S. Rogers were elected from the third district, by acclamation.

On April 1st, the following resolution was adopted :

That the firmness, consistency and devotion to principle exhibited by the union members of the legislature during its late session are entitled to the hearty commendation and grateful remembrance of the union party of California, and that this convention hereby acknowledges its obligations to those members for the thoroughness with which they were organized and their uncompromising devotion to the interests of the party and country.

Joseph Benrimo, J. C. Byers, B. N. Bugbey, and J. H. O'Brien were elected alternate delegates at large, over Henry G. Rollins, Benjamin Dore, Jerome C. Davis, C. E. Allen, Nathan Coombs, F. G. French, Charles F. Reed, and Walter Murray.

C. E. Allen and Benjamin Dore were elected alternates from the first congressional district; H. G. Rollins and Abijah Baker from the second district; and O. F. Reed and F. G. French from the third district—all by acclamation.

A state central committee was selected, composed of Samuel Merritt, J. R. Hardenbergh, T. K. Wilson, W. F. Huestis, J. C. Birdseye, J. S. Downes, A. N. Merrick, Robert McGarvey, J. M. Coghlan, E. W. Roberts, J. C. Boggs, John R. Buckbee, F. A. Gibbs, Harvey S. Brown, J. N. Chappel, J. M. Kelsey, Chas. E. Huse, A. Schell, O. B. Powers, Daniel E. Gordon, D. M. Kenfield, James A. Hutton, A. S. Smith, and others; and the state executive committee was composed of I. A. Amerman, J. G. McCallum, James Otis, Alpheus Bull, Jacob Deeth, Alfred Barstow, A. Seligman, E. N. Torrey, and Charles G. Thomas.

A resolution was adopted instructing the state central committee to call all primaries under, pursuant to, and in accordance with the pro-visions of the Porter primary election law of March 26, 1866 The convention adjourned with three cheers for General U. S. Grant.

It was universally recognized that Grant was the choice of the party in California for president, and that it was the business of the convention simply to record this choice. There was therefore a disposition to secure harmony.

On February 27th and 28th, meetings were held by the democratic state central committee at San Francisco, when it was resolved to hold the convention of the party in that city, on Wednesday, April 29th, to nominate 10 delegates to attend the national convention, and five candidates for presidential electors. The state convention was to consist of 304 delegates, and the test for the primaries was made to embrace "all voters opposed to the radical policy of congress, to negro or Chinese suffrage, and in favor of a constitutional administration of the government of the whole union." The committee recommended that the congressional conventions meet at the time and place fixed for the holding of the state convention and transact the business delegated to them; and the necessity for the formation of campaign clubs was urged upon the democratic and conservative voters of the state.

The following resolutions were unanimously adopted by the committee :

1. That the radical majority in congress, instead of seeking to lighten the burdens of taxation, disregarding the will of the people and their official oaths in an unnatural pursuit after negro equality, having been laboring to usurp the functions of the executive, degrade the judiciary, and after committing the indecency of forcing upon the executive a cabinet officer personally offensive to him, and making a military subordinate independent of the orders of the president, thus uniting in their own hands the purse and sword, they have for the first time presented to the world the disgraceful spectacle of an American president arraigned by a party vote, avowedly for party purposes, before a senate, more than two-thirds of which is composed of his political opponents, and placed on trial for no crime except that of having endeavored to preserve, protect and defend the constitution of the United States and the liberties of the people; that in these proceedings the radical party in congress have been manifestly actuated by a desire to perpetuate themselves in office, and merit the unqualified condemnation of all good citizens, without distinction of party.

2. That this committee view with sincere alarm the revolutionary action of the radical majority in congress, condemned in the foregoing resolution, believing the same calculated to create wide-spread distrust, and seriously derange the financial and other great interests of the country.

Pursuant to this call, the convention met in Union hall, San Francisco, at 12 o'clock M., on April 29th, and it was called to order by J. P. Hoge, chairman of the state committee. William Holden was elected temporary chairman, on the first ballot, by a vote of 199, to 92 for J. W. Mandeville. The committee on credentials reported that the county of Mono alone was unrepresented, and John Bigler moved that two gentlemen from that county who were then present be invited to act as delegates. This motion gave rise to a heated discussion and was finally carried—154 to 105. A permanent organization was then effected by the election of Holden, as president, and Thomas Findley, J. W. Mandeville, and N. E. Whiteside, as vice-presidents. The committee on order of business reported a programme calling for the election and nomination of one national delegate at large, and three from each congressional district; of two electors at large, and one from each district and of an alternate elector from each judicial district. A. H. Rose moved to strike out the portion providing for the nomination of electors and alternates, but the motion was lost—142 to 157. A committee was appointed on resolutions, consisting of John C. Burch, R. J. Betge, B. F. Myers, C. Howard, W. Z. Angney, H. P. Barber, T. J. Henley, A. B. Dibble, and S. A. Booker. About eight hundred spectators viewed the proceedings of the convention. On the 30th, a motion was made that before any man was selected as a national delegate he should declare his intention of devoting all his energies to procure the nomination of H. H. Haight, as president of the United States, but it was ruled out of order.

For delegates to attend the national convention, the following were elected :

Thomas Hayes, at large, over W. T. Coleman, E. Steele, Charles S. Fairfax, Henry H. Platt, and Eugene Casserly.

Charles S. Fairfax, E. Steele, and W. W. Woodward from the third congressional district, by acclamation; J. Berry and G. T. Crane withdrawing.

John Bigler, A. H. Rose, and Richard Heath from the second district, on the first ballot, over Joseph Dumont, Talbot of Nevada county, S. T. Leet, H. P. Barber, and Lewis R. Bradley.

Robert C. Page, Joseph R. Roberts, and A. Jacoby from the first district, on the first ballot, over James A. Couch, H. M. Black, John Middleton, James R. Lawrence, James C. Gallager, C. T. Ryland, and Dr. Sharkey.

A motion was made to reconsider the vote by which the convention had determined to nominate electors, and amid great confusion it was laid on the table—156 to 137. The convention then made the following nominations for presidential electors :

E. J. O. Kewen and Thomas J. Henley from the state at large, on the first ballot, by the following vote : Kewen, 212 ; Henley, 197; W. T. Wallace, 176 ; J. D. Hambleton and W. W. Pendegast withdrawing.

W. T. Wallace from the first congressional district, by acclamation ; W. F. White, Francisco Pico, and John R. Kittrell withdrawing.

A. B. Dibble from the second district, and George Pearce from the third—both by acclamation.

The following alternate electors were nominated :

Francisco Pico and John R. Kittrell, at large ; J. Burckhalter, from the first ; B. F. Myers, from the second ; and J. N. Martin, from the third congressional district.

On May 1st, a proposition to elect alternate delegates was discussed · and laid on the table. A state central committee was selected, composed of A. O. Bradford, William Watt, Robert Ferral, Charles A. Johnson, E. O. Tully, R. R. Provines, Jasper O'Farrell, P. H. Ryan, E. T. Wilkins, A. H. Rose, J. O. Maynard, P. H. Sibley, R. J. Betge, Thomas N. Oazneau, George Pen Johnston, Charles E. McLane, Creed Haymond, J. W. Coffroth, John Bigler, J. P. Hoge, and others.

After adopting the following resolutions, the convention adjourned:

1. That the expedients resorted to by the radicals in congress for the purpose of perpetuating their despotic power are such as to threaten the perpetuity of the government itself ; and it is, therefore, the duty of all good citizens to disregard minor considerations and local issues, and to combine in one grand and united effort to preserve the legacy left us by our fathers, to restore the industry of the country to its wonted condition of prosperity, and to relieve our people from the oppressive burden of taxation.

2. That the unanimous declaration of congress, made on the 23d day of July, 1861, "that the war is waged by the government of the United States, not in the spirit of conquest or subjugation, not for the purpose of overthrowing or interfering with the rights or institutions of the states, but to defend and maintain the supremacy of the constitution, and to preserve the union, with all the dignity, equality, and rights of the several states unimpaired," has been persistently falsified by its action, and the power of the government has been perverted to schemes of ambition and revenge.

3. That the impeachment of the president of the United States by

a radical congress (composed of those who assisted to elevate him to that high position) on the most frivolous charges, is only an additional evidence of party violence—not actuated by any solicitude for the common welfare, and which must tend to make the United States government ridiculous in the eyes of all civilized nations.

4. That Henry H. Haight, in all the elements of honesty, integrity, patriotic devotion to the best interests of the whole country, in elevated statesmanship and unswerving opposition to the disorganizing and destroying factions now threatening the permanency of constitutional government stands pre-eminent among the great men of the nation.

5. That the action of the radical house of representatives of the present congress of the United States, in refusing to make the necessary appropriation for the purchase of Alaska (a territory so important to the future welfare of the Pacific coast), after the purchase had been honorably consummated by the treaty-making power of the government, is an act of perfidy on the part of the representatives of the people, and the repudiation of a national obligation, which is entitled to and receives the hearty condemnation of the democracy of California.

6. That it is not only the patriotic duty, but the deliberate purpose of the democratic party *never to submit* to be governed by negroes, nor by those claiming to be elected by negro suffrage; and we do earnestly recommend the adoption of this resolution by the national convention of the democracy which shall assemble in July next.

7. That the eight-hour system of labor is a democratic measure, and ought to become a national principle—making eight hours a legal day's work on all public works in the United States; that our delegates to the national convention are requested to use their endeavors to incorporate this declaration in the national platform.

8. That the attention of the national convention, called to assemble at New York on the 4th day of July next, be directed to the question of coolie immigration into the United States, and respectfully asked by our delegation to devise some means to be recommended to congress to protect free industry against their incursions.

The democratic convention of the third congressional district met at San Francisco on May 1st—73 delegates being present. A. C. Bradford presided. On the 2d, S. B. Axtell was nominated for con-

gressman, by acclamation; W. D. Sawyer withdrawing while the roll was being called for the first ballot.

The democratic second district convention met at San Francisco, on May 1st, J. T. Farley presiding, but adjourned without action, to meet at Sacramento on August 19th. On the last named day, another meeting was held, and James W. Coffroth was nominated for congress, by acclamation.

The democratic third district convention met at San Francisco, on May 1st, and James A. Johnson was nominated for congress, by acclamation; A. Whalen and N. E. Whiteside withdrawing.

The "national union republican" state central committee, held a meeting at San Francisco on June 25th, and appointed August 5th as the time for the holding of the state convention at Sacramento, for the purpose of nominating an electoral ticket. The number of delegates was fixed at 275. The primaries were directed to be held in accordance with the provisions of the Porter election law, and the test embraced all legal voters who should pledge themselves to vote for the electors to be chosen by the convention. The committee recommended that a Grant and Colfax club be formed on the day of the primaries in every precinct where a union republican club did not then exist. At the time and place mentioned, the state convention met. It was called to order by James Otis, chairman of the state committee, and J. G. Eastman was unanimously elected temporary chairman. G. W. Tyler, H. J. Tilden, L. D. Latimer, E. G. Waite, and J. E. Wyman were appointed a committee on resolutions, and shortly afterward they reported the following, which were adopted:

1. That the platform of principles adopted by the national union republican convention, at Chicago, in May last, deserves and receives the approval and hearty endorsement of all the union republicans of California.

2. That the fearless chieftain, General Grant, and the pure statesman, Schuyler Colfax, were the first choice of the union republicans of California for president and vice-president of the United States for the ensuing four years, and that we rejoice in their nomination.

3. That General U. S. Grant and Schuyler Colfax, by their services to their country, by their devotion to principle, and by their unspotted reputation as men and as citizens, are deserving of the united and earnest support of all the loyal people of the United

States, and we pledge to them the electoral vote of California at the ensuing election, by an overwhelming majority.

The temporary officers were declared permanently elected. The convention made the following nomination :

Presidential Electors : First congressional district, David B. Hoff. man ; second district, Alfred Redington ; third district, Charles Westmoreland—all by acclamation. At large, John B. Felton and O. H. LaGrange, on the first ballot, over John F. Swift and Nathaniel Holland ; George W. Tyler withdrawing. The vote stood : Felton, 147 ; LaGrange, 225 ; Swift, 121 ; and Holland 24.

Alternate Electors : First congressional district, Louis Sloss ; second district, Charles A. Tweed ; third district, James H. Mc-Nabb. At large, Walter Van Dyke and George W. Tyler, on the first ballot, over James B. McQuillan.

On August 8th, the republican first district convention met at San Francisco, and on the first ballot, Frank M. Pixley was nominated for congress, by a vote of 72, to 18 for Soule. The republican convention of the second district convened at Sacramento, August 4th, and on the tenth ballot, Aaron A. Sargent received the nomination for congress, over S. W. Brockway, William Higby, J. G. McCallum, Charles A. Tuttle, and O. H. LaGrange.

The ballotings resulted as follows :

	1	2	3	4	5	6	8	10
Sargent	33	31	31	32	37	37	37	49
Brockway	13	16	23	20	21	20	18	15
Tuttle	11	11	11	10	10	10	10	....
Higby	28	28	22	....	....	....	....	....
McCallum	12	11	10	10	1	....	....	....
LaGrange	....	....	....	25	28	30	32	33

The third district republican convention met at Washington, Yolo county, on August 4th. Chancellor Hartson was nominated for congress, on the first ballot, by a vote of 47, to 32 for Charles Westmoreland, and 13 for H. L. Gear.

During the campaign a number of joint discussions were held, and in some instances the opposing candidates made the entire canvass in company. On July 13th, P. H. Sibley, a member of the democratic state central committee, published a card, announcing his resignation from that position, and assigning as the reason for the action that although he could conscientiously support Blair, because of his war record, he could not support Seymour, and that he did not approve of the 'democratic national platform. Under those circumstances, he felt it his duty to support Grant and Colfax. On August 12th, Alpheus Bull and A. Seligman resigned from the union state central committee, as was stated "on account of business arrangements," and Louis. R. Lull and Richard Chenery were elected to fill the vacancies.

The election was held on Tuesday, November 3d, and the official canvass, made in the following month, developed :

For Presidential Electors: Grant and Colfax—Felton, 54,588 ; LaGrange, 54,576 ; Hoffman, 54,565 ; Redington, 54,592 ; Westmoreland, 54,551. Seymour and Blair—Wallace, 54,069 ; Henley, 54,078 ; Kewen, 54,068 ; Dibble, 54,068 ; Pearce, 54,061.

For Members of Congress: First district—Pixley, 20,081 ; Axtell, 23,632. Second district—Sargent, 18,264 ; Coffroth, 15,124. Third district—Hartson, 15,528 ; Johnson, 15,792.

The republican electors were therefore elected, and Axtell, Sargent, and Johnson were elected to congress. Through a typographical error in a blank, the returns from seventeen counties, representing a vote of 13,047 for the republican electors, were for D. A. Hoffman, instead of D. B. Hoffman, and it became known that the secretary of state proposed to credit the D. A. Hoffman vote as if it had been cast for a distinct individual from D. B. Hoffman. This would of course elect Henley, but on November 30th, a writ of mandamus was issued by Judge McKune of the sixth district court, directing that officer to count the D. A. Hoffman votes the same as if they had been certified as having been cast for D. B. Hoffman. The question was submitted to the supreme court upon an agreed statement of facts, and that tribunal unaminously decided, on December 1st, that the returns should all be counted for D. B. Hoffman. Later in the day, the official canvass was made, and the republican electors were declared to be elected. On the 2d, the republican electors met in the office of the California steam navigation company, cast the votes of the state for Grant and Colfax, and appointed Charles Westmoreland messenger to carry the returns to Washington.

CHAPTER XXI.

1869. Democratic Convention—Republican State Convention.

The democratic state central committee met at San Francisco on May 12th, and it was resolved to hold the state convention at Sacramento on Tuesday, June 29th.

The following test was adopted :

That all voters in the state who are opposed to the radical measures of congress, including the proposed fifteenth amendment to the constitution of the United States; who are opposed to the appointment of negroes to office, and who pledge themselves to support the democratic ticket at the coming fall elections, shall be permitted to participate in primary elections.

On May 24th, the democratic committee of San Francisco resolved to appoint delegates to represent that county in the state convention, but this action produced so much disaffection that it was reconsidered, and primaries were held on June 17th.

The democratic state convention met in the assembly chamber, at Sacramento, on June 29th, and was called to order by J. P. Hoge, the chairman of the state committee, who was also elected temporary president. A committee on resolutions was appointed, consisting of C. T. Ryland, J. W. Mandeville, J. W. Coffroth, J. R. McConnell, W. P. Daingerfield, J. West Martin, H. P. Barber, J. G. Downey, and J. M. Burnett. On permanent organization, Hoge was president; and J. F. Williams, Charles Maclay, Joseph Powell, and R. O. DeWitt, vice-presidents.

The following resolutions were reported and adopted :

WHEREAS, Upon the eve of a political canvass, the time-honored usages of our party require that a platform of principles be announced for the government of those who may be elected to political office; and, whereas. new questions have arisen since the meeting of the last democratic convention, making such action eminently proper; therefore, resolved,

1. That the democracy of California now and always confide in the intelligence, patriotism, and discriminating justice of the white people of the country to administer and control their government without the aid of either negroes or Chinese.

2. That the democratic party view with alarm the action of an

19

unscrupulous majority in congress in their attempts to absorb the powers of the executive and judicial departments of the federal government, and to annihilate the rights and functions reserved to the state governments.

3. That the subjection of the white population of the southern states to the rule of a mass of ignorant negroes, their disfranchisement, and the denial to them of all those sacred rights guaranteed to every freeman, is an outrage and a wrong for which the history of free governments in modern times may be searched in vain for a parallel.

4. That the democratic party is opposed to the policy of lending the credit of the state and squandering the state property upon railway or other corporations to the detriment of the public interests and the overwhelming increase of the state debt and taxation.

5. That the democratic party ever has been, is now, and ever will be, the champion of the rights of the mechanic and working man; that all the reforms having for their.object the reduction of the hours of his labor, the enlargement of his privileges and the protection of his personal liberty, have ever been demanded, enacted and enforced by the democracy; that we point with pride to the fact that in California it was the democratic element in the legislature that passed, and a democratic governor that approved, the eight hour law, and that we pledge ourselves to use our utmost exertions to carry the provisions of that law into full force and effect, as well as to labor in other directions for the cause of the sons of toil.

6. That we are opposed to the adoption of the proposed fifteenth amendment of the United States constitution, believing the same to be designed, and, if adopted, certain to degrade the right of suffrage; to ruin the laboring white man, by bringing untold hordes of Pagan slaves (in all but name) into direct competition with his efforts to earn a livelihood; to build up an aristocratic class of oligarchs in our midst, created and maintained by Chinese votes; to give the negro and Chinaman the right to vote and hold office; and that its passage would be inimical to the best interests of our country, in direct opposition to the teachings of Washington, Adams, Jefferson and the other founders of the republic; in flagrant violation of the plainest principles upon which the superstructure of our liberties was raised; subversive of the dearest rights of the different states, and a direct step toward anarchy and its natural sequence, the erection of an empire upon the ruins of constitutional liberty.

7. That the democracy of California believe that the labor of our

white people should not be brought into competition with the labor of a class of inferior people, whose living costs comparatively nothing, and who add nothing to the wealth of our state, and who care and know nothing about our churches, schools, societies, and social and political institutions.

8. That we arraign the radical party for its profligacy, corruption, and extravagance in public expenditures; for its tyranny, extortion, and disfranchisement; for its contempt of constitutional obligations; for placing the city of Washington in the hands of semi-civilized Africans; and we particularly condemn the appointment of healthy and able-bodied negroes to office while the land is filled with capable white citizens who are suffering for the common necessaries of life.

9. That we heartily endorse and approve of the manner in which the democracy have administered the state government, and point with pride to the acts to protect the wages of labor, to lessen public and official expenses, and to the fact that during the present state administration the state debt has been reduced nearly $1,000,000, and taxation reduced from $1.13 on $100 to 97 cents.

C. T. Ryland introduced the following which were also adopted:

10. That the so-called Alabama treaty having been rejected by the treaty-making power of the government, the democratic party, true to its record as the only political party which on such issues has uniformaly proved itself faithful to our own country, will now, as heretofore, be found ready to sustain all measures demanded by the honest dignity and rights of the republic in its relations with all foreign powers.

11. That all voters in California who are opposed to the radical measures of congress, including the proposed fifteenth amendment to the constitution of the United States, and who are opposed to the appointment of negroes to office, be invited to unite with the democracy in the coming contest.

J. B. Crockett was nominated for justice of the supreme court, to fill the vacancy occasioned by the resignation of O. L. Shafter; and, in like manner, William T. Wallace was nominated for justice of the supreme court, to succeed Lorenzo Sawyer. Samuel Bell McKee was placed in nomination against Wallace, but his name was withdrawn. A committee of nine, consisting of J. R. McConnell, C. T. Ryland, T. R. Wise, T. A. Coldwell, J. H. Hardy, E. T. Hogan, J. H. Budd, J. C. Burch, and D. W. Gelwicks, was appointed to draft an address to the people upon the Chinese question. (On

August 4th, the report of the committee was published, and it occupied six columns in the newspapers.) The convention appointed a state central committee, composed of Harry Linden, J. W. Mandeville, D. W. Gelwicks, J. W. Coffroth, R. C. Haile, P. H. Ryan, J. K. Luttrell, John Boggs, Wm. Watt, R. O. Cravens, J. W. Freeman, J. G. Downey, J. P. Hoge, James H. Hardy, J. H. Baird, Joseph Naphtaly, J. C. Maynard, and Thomas N. Cazneau.

W. W. Pendegast offered the following resolution, which was adopted :

That the Western Union Telegraph Company, which controls all the wires connecting the Atlantic with the Pacific, has, in instituting a tariff designed to give a virtual monopoly of eastern news to a few newspapers of one political party in this state, been guilty of a great public wrong, has betrayed the trust confided to it, and effectually restricted the liberties of the press, and that its action in this regard calls loudly for such legislative interference as shall prohibit discriminations, prevent the use of the telegraph as a political engine, and make it, like the mails, free to all.

The republican state central committee met at San Francisco, April 29th, and appointed a state convention to be held at Sacramento on July 21st. A resolution was adopted requesting the convention to take into consideration the expediency of adopting the "Crawford county" plan in nominations to be thereafter made by the party—that is, permitting each voter at a primary election of the party to vote directly for the persons whom he desires to have nominated for the various offices. In 1869, the republican primaries in the counties of Sierra, Santa Cruz, Trinity, Nevada, and Napa were conducted upon that plan, and it was very generally in favor. Pursuant to the call of the state committee, the republican convention met at the Fourth-street Baptist church, at Sacramento, on Wednesday, July 21st. It was called to order by Richard Chenery; T. B. McFarland, and C. A. Tuttle were placed in nomination for temporary chairman. During the balloting, Walter Van Dyke received nine votes from Alameda. The chair announced the vote to be 136 for McFarland and 143 for Tuttle, when it was announced that the Alameda votes would be changed from Van Dyke to McFarland. The point of order was raised that that vote could not be changed after it had been announced by the chair. After some little debate, the election of McFarland was made unanimous, and immediately afterward a motion was carried that the temporary officers be permanently elected. The committee on resolutions consisted of John P. Stearns, John Dick, W. Van Dyke, John F. Miller, N. M. Orr, George Cadwalader, George Oulton, C. A. Garter, W. C. Belcher, F. M. Pixley, G. W. Schell, A. C. Niles, M. C. Briggs, D. B. Hoffman, and others. They presented the following resolutions, which were unanimously adopted :

1. That the republican party of California gives its earnest support to the administration of President Grant, and hereby endorses the acts and policy of the administration. We recognize the earnest effort of the government to secure an economical administration of its affairs, to reduce expenses, to honestly pay the national debt, to prevent speculation and fraud upon the treasury, to enforce the collection of the revenue, and to cause the speedy restoration of public confidence in our financial strength and integrity.

2. That the negro question has ceased to be an element in American politics, and that the ratification of the fifteenth amendment to the constitution ought to be followed by an act of universal amnesty and enfranchisement of the southern people.

3. That we regard with pride and satisfaction the evidences of an increasing immigration to this state of industrious and intelligent people from the Atlantic states and Europe, with whom we are anxious to share the benefits of a fruitful soil, a genial climate and an advancing civilization; but while giving preference to the immigration of people of our own race, we hold that unoffending immigrants from China to this state are entitled to full protection for their lives, liberty, and property, and due process of law to enforce the same, but we are opposed to Chinese suffrage in any form, and to any change in the naturalization laws of the United States.

4. That we recognize the power of the general government to restrict or prevent Chinese immigration, whenever the welfare of the nation demands such a measure, by terminating our commercial relations with China; but it should be considered that the adoption of a non-intercourse policy in respect to China surrenders to Europe the commerce of the empires of Asia. We believe that the general prosperity will be greatly enhanced by fostering commercial intercourse with Asia, and that the closing of our ports at this time against Chinese would be most injurious to the material interests of this coast, a reproach upon the intelligence of the American people, and contrary to the spirit of the age.

5. That the republican party having ever had in its especial

keeping the rights of labor and of the laborer, and removed therefrom the blighting curse of slavery and inaugurated a new era, in which the wages of labor have greatly advanced, while the hours therefor have been correspondingly diminished, claim to have originated in this state, and steadily supported what is known as the "Eight-hour law," the sound policy of which has been proclaimed by a republican congress, and by proclamation of a republican president made applicable to the public works of the United States.

6. That we endorse the action of the senate of the United States in rejecting the so-called "Alabama treaty," and consider it the duty of the general government to demand full reparation for the injuries inflicted by the British government and her people upon our commerce during the late rebellion.

7. That we are in favor of imposing upon all kinds and classes of taxable property in the state an equal share of the burdens of taxation, and to that end favor the organization of a state board of equalization or review, that the inequalities now existing under the present system of assessment and collection of the state revenues may be avoided.

8. That we are opposed to grants of state aid to railroads, and are in favor of limiting taxation to the amount of revenues absolutely requisite to pay the actual expenses of the state government, and to maintain the financial credit of the state.

9. That we hail with joy the return of peace, and the promising signs of an increasing development of the country and the permanent prosperity of the whole people. We earnestly invite the co-operation at the ballot-box of all who agree to the foregoing declarations, regardless of old party ties or previous differences of opinion upon the now settled questions of slavery, rebellion, reconstruction, and negro suffrage.

Lorenzo Sawyer was unaminously renominated for justice of the supreme court (full term).

O. C. Pratt, Nathaniel Bennett, and G. N. Swezy were placed in nomination for justice of the supreme court to fill the vacancy caused by the resignation of Shafter, and on the first ballot, Pratt received the nomination, by a vote of 181, to 88 for Bennett, and 20 for Swezy.

A state central committee was appointed, consisting of C. E. Huse, S. J. Clarke, W. Van Dyke, J. Stratman, N. M. Orr, W. C. Crossette, L. H. Murch, N. D. Rideout, A. Deering, J. H. Neff,

D. B. Hoffman, E. L. Sullivan, A. Barstow, H. S. Sargent, S. O. Houghton, H. W. Bragg, and O. M. Gorham.

The election of the county officers and members of the legislature was held September 1st, and resulted generally in a democratic success. The judicial election was held October 20th, when Wallace received 36,705 votes; Sawyer, 30,936; Crockett, 38,997; and Pratt, 28,705.

CHAPTER XXII.

1871. Letter of Governor Haight—Divisions among Democrats— Democratic State Convention—Divisions among Republicans— Republican State Convention—"Brick" Pomeroy—Tape Worm Ballots.

Early in 1871, the matter of the selection of a candidate for governor from the democratic side was actively agitated. James A. Johnson, Frank McCoppin, and Thomas Findley were prominently mentioned in connection with the nomination, and each had his quota of warm and active supporters. It had been understood that Governor Haight was not an aspirant for a second term, but in Jannary, a letter was addressed to him by Senator Minis, dated on the 10th, asking if the report was true that he was not disposed to enter into the contest. The governor replied on the 12th, and said:

It was my desire and design to release myself from office at the end of my present term, and devote some attention to my private affairs. This resolution was a fixed one, and I did not suppose any influence or arguments would avail to change it. The reasons for this purpose were, in brief, the serious pecuniary sacrifice involved in a continuance in office, a desire for rest from burdensome responsibilities, repugnance to the calumny and misconstruction to which public officers are commonly subjected, with considerations of health and other plans for the future not entirely compatible with public life. * * * The determination thus formed has been reluctantly abandoned, because of the conviction which seemed to prevail, that persistence in it would be a virtual surrender of the principles for which we have contended, and which we believe to be inseparably connected with public welfare. I am not willing to make such a surrender, nor to be justly chargeable with aiding, by my default, in the success of the measures which, for the benefit of the favored few, will load with grievous burdens a people already taxed to the limit of endurance, and which seek to appropriate the property and earnings of the whole mass of taxpayers to enrich private corporations. To such a system as this, which is neither democratic, just, nor salutary, I am opposed, now and henceforth, at all times and under all circumstances, against all combinations and compromises. Opposition to such a system results logically from, and is inseparably blended with, the time honored doctrines advocated by Jefferson, and which lie at the basis of the democratic organization, to-wit: The largest liberty to the individual, and the least possible interference by government with his person or his property, and then, the least possible delegation of power to a central and, to some extent, irresponsible control, and the most careful reservation of it to local authorities. Allied to these are opposition to the exercise of doubtful powers, strict construction of those delegated, and a careful limitation of them in the interest of the people; acting upon the maxim that, while the government was made for the people, the less there is of it, after affording that security which is its primary object, the better it is for them. Hence our opposition to special legislation, to protective tariff, to profligate grants of the public domain to corporations, regardless of the rights of settlers, to military interference with elections, and to all the abuses practiced heretofore. These principles will be at issue in 1872. That contest will be between the corporations on one side and the people on the other; not that we desire to deny to corporations anything which a liberal policy would fairly suggest, but we do desire to see the governments, state and federal, administered for the benefit of the whole people and not for the benefit of a privileged few. In this way only can our system fully accomplish the beneficent ends had in view by its founders. With these views and in this spirit, if our convention should think proper to present my name for re-election, their expressed will would control my action, and be accepted as another proof of that confidence so generously accorded to me heretofore by the democracy, notwithstanding any errors of judgment which I may have committed through inexperience of public affairs.

Governor Haight met with active opposition from a considerable element of his party, based—as it was charged—upon the position he had taken on the question of granting aid to railroad corporations; and one of the leading organs of the party, a paper which derived its principal support from the patronage resulting from the passage of the state paper and litigant printing bills, openly and vigorously opposed his renomination. But he was supported by the anti-subsidy element, and it was soon apparent that his nomination was almost inavertable. The primaries began to be held early in May, and from most of the interior counties Haight delegations were returned. On May 26th, the democratic county committee of San Francisco resolved not to call a primary election, and took upon itself the appointment of the delegates to the state and local conventions—the majority of the delegates to the state convention so selected being against Haight. This action of the committee produced great dissatisfaction, and on June 1st a call was circulated, at the instance of prominent members of the party, for a primary election and convention to select the delegates, independent of the committee, but the primary was not held, as by the 15th, Haight had secured a sufficient number of pledged delegates from the interior counties to insure him the nomination. The feud created in the party in San Francisco by this action of the committee was kept up after the meeting of the state convention and centered upon the local nominations. Efforts to conciliate through committees of conference failed, and the breach widened. Finally, three wings of the party developed, whose respective figure-heads were Isaac Friedlander, Eugene Casserly, and Frank McCoppin, and by the day of election it was difficult to determine which of the several local tickets represented the Simon-pure democracy. On June 26th, the democratic committee of Sacramento county passed a resolution repudiating the Sacramento *Reporter*—the official state paper—as a democratic organ, and recommending that the patronage of the party be withdrawn from it. It had been charged by the press that the majority of the stock in the paper had been secured by the managers of the Central Pacific Railroad Company, and that its expressions were controlled by their dictation.

On May 12th, the democratic state central committee met in San Francisco and called a state convention, to meet at Sacramento on June 20th. The apportionment was fixed at 319 members, and the test at the primaries included all who were opposed to the radical measures of congress, and who would pledge themselves to support the ticket, Pursuant to this call, the convention met in the assembly chamber, in the capitol, at 12 M. on Tuesday, June

20th. It was called to order by J. P. Hoge, chairman of the state committee, and James W. Coffroth was unaminously elected temporary chairman. On permanent organization, Coffroth was president; John G. Downey, M. L. McDonald, William Minis, and W. A. Eakin, vice-presidents; and Henry George, secretary. The committee on resolutions was composed of Russell Heath, P. O. Hundley, W. Z. Angney, S. Heydenfeldt, J. W. Mandeville, A. A. Bennett, John C. Burch, James T. Ryan, William Irwin, J. T. Farley, J. P. Hoge, P. D. Wigginton, James K. Byrne, A. H. Rose, W. A. Conn, and others.

On the 21st, the committee on resolutions reported the following, which were unaminously adopted :

1. That waiving all differences of opinion as to the extraordinary means by which they were brought about, we accept the natural and legitimate results of the war, so far as waged for the ostensible purpose to maintain the union and the constitutional rights and powers of the federal government.

2. That we regard the three several amendments to the constitution, recently adopted, as a settlement in fact of all the issues of the war, and that the same are no longer issues before the country.

3. That we demand that the rule of strict construction, as proclaimed by the democratic fathers, and embodied in the tenth amendment to the federal constitution, be applied to the constitution as it is, including the three recent amendments to that instrument; that the absolute equality of each state within the union is a fundamental principle of the federal government; that we shall always cherish and uphold the American system of state and local government for state and local purposes, and of the general government for general purposes only, as essential to the maintenance of civil liberty; and are unalterably opposed to all attempts at centralization or consolidation of power in the hands of the federal government.

4. That we demand of congress universal amnesty for all political offences.

5. That while we condemn all riotous and unlawful combinations to disturb the peace or infringe the rights of any citizens, we denounce the act commonly called the "bayonet bill," passed by congress, and the more recent act, commonly called the "Ku-Klux bill," as enacted for no other purpose than to complete the work of centralization, and by establishing a military despotism to perpetuate the present administration without regard to the will of the

people; that these measures are not only inconsistent with the whole theory and character of the federal government, and revolutionary and dangerous in their tendency, but are in direct conflict with the spirit and letter of the constitution, including amendments which they pretend to enforce.

6. That we are in favor of a tariff for revenue only, and we denounce the system commonly called the protective system, as unjust, oppressive, prolific of corruption, and injurious to the best interests of the country; that the tariff legislation of the republican party during the past ten years has destroyed our shipping, paralyzed industry, and plundered the mass of the people for the benefit of capitalists and monopolists.

7. That the profligate grants of vast tracts of the public domain made by the radical majority in congress, to railroad corporations, regardless of the rights of settlers, and without any proper conditions or restrictions, are a fraud upon the people of the country.

8. That the failure of congress to repeal the odious income tax, the maintenance of a vast army of tax gatherers, to harass the people and eat out their substance, and the failure to restrict the importation of Chinese coolies, whose competition tends directly to cheapen and degrade white labor, constitute a catalogue of grievances for which a radical congress will be held justly accountable.

9. That we are uncompromisingly opposed to subsidizing railway or other private corporations out of the public treasury, to the overwhelming increase of debt and taxation; that laws which impose taxes upon the mass of citizens in aid of such corporations, whether in the form of donations, loans, or subscriptions, are an invasion of the rights of private property and a departure from sound maxims of government, and result in the bankruptcy of towns and counties; that they lead to gross abuses, are a prolific source of corruption, and violate the cardinal principle of democracy, to-wit: That government is instituted for the welfare and security of the mass of the people, and not for aggrandizement of a favored few; and that the law upon the statute book known as the five per cent. law, ought to be immediately repealed.

10. That we are in favor of amending the state constitution so as to provide additional safeguards against the taxation of private property in aid of private corporations or individuals, and against improvident legislation, and of securing needed constitutional reforms.

11. That the democratic party, deriving its strength from the

working classes,. is the natural enemy of monopolies, and has always been and always will be ready to support and urge such measures for the elevation of the laboring population and the amelioration of their condition as an enlightened policy may suggest; that we point to the legislation of the past three years, reducing the hours of labor, requiring public work to be done by the day, and seeking to restrict Chinese immigration, as evidence of the sympathy of the democracy with the wishes and interests of the laboring classes.

12. That we believe that the labor of white people should not be brought into competition with the labor of a class of inferior people, whose living costs comparatively nothing, and who care and know little about our churches, schools, societies, and social and political institutions, and that we are, therefore, opposed to Chinese immigration; that congress, by its legislation, having sought to foster such immigration and to prevent our local authorities from interfering with it, and by its attempted abrogation of the foreign miners' license, deserves our severest condemnation, and has given us another illustration of its intention to concentrate all power in the hands of the general government.

13. That the public lands yet left to the United States and the state of California should be disposed of only to actual settlers in limited quantities, and on the most favorable terms; and the laws, both state and federal, should be so framed as to insure this result, so vital to a free people.

14. That the interference by the president of the United States with the military power of the union, in elections, to overawe the people and control the right of suffrage, is treason to the constitution.

15. That we are compelled, by profound convictions of their injustice and impolicy, to record our solemn protest against the leading measures of the national administration, and we pledge all the power with which we may be intrusted to earnest efforts to lessen the expenditures of the government, to reduce and equalize taxation, to hasten the extinction of the public debt, and by honest legislation to protect the public domain against the rapacity of speculators and robbers, and restore early and cordial union and fraternity to the states and the people of the republic.   ·

16. That by thorough organization and concerted action, another victory is within the reach of the democratic party of this state, and this convention pledges itself to effect such organization and action,

and to secure, by all honorable means, the election of the candidates this day nominated.

17. And whereas, since the advent of the democratic party to power in 1867, the rate of taxation for state purposes has been reduced from $1.13 to 86 cents on each $100 of property, and the state debt reduced more than $1,000,000, at the same time that the school fund has been increased, and large sums of money have been judiciously expended upon public buildings, a state university organized and put in operation, the tide lands of the state rescued from the grasp of speculators, and sold for the public benefit, special franchise legislation successfully checked for the first time by executive veto, laws enacted for the revision of our civil and criminal codes, the equalization of assessments and the refunding of the state debt, and a successful opposition inaugurated to any taxation of the people for the benefit of railway or other private corporations, besides other useful reforms; therefore, resolved, that we heartily endorse the democratic state administration, and declare it eminently entitled to the confidence and approval of the whole people.

The following nominations were then made:

Henry H. Haight, for governor, without opposition.

E. J. Lewis, for lieutenant-governor, on the first ballot, having received 195 votes, to 8 for William Holden, and 124 for Charles Gildea.

Jackson Temple, for justice of the supreme court, to fill the Sanderson vacancy, without opposition.

For justice of the supreme court to succeed Rhodes, Peter Van Clief, S. Bell McKee, Creed Haymond, John W. Armstrong, W. C. Wallace, Delos Lake, and Selden S. Wright were submitted; Armstrong, Van Clief, and Lake were withdrawn, and on the first ballot, McKee had 146 votes; Haymond, 47; Wallace, 53; Lake, 9, and Wright, 90. On the second ballot, McKee had 134; Wright, 136; Haymond, 45; and Wallace, 3. Haymond and Wallace were then withdrawn, and on the third ballot, Wright was nominated, by a vote of 180 to 139 for McKee.

For secretary of state, H. L. Nichols, L. B. Harris, Presley Dunlap, H. C. Clarkson, Charles L. Weller, and W. B. C. Brown were named. On the first ballot, Nichols had 100; Harris, 39; Dunlap, 6; Weller, 32; and Brown, 137. On the next ballot, Brown was nominated by a vote of 198 to 101 for Nichols, 3 for Harris, 1 for Dunlap, and 8 for Weller.

For controller, James S. Mooney, Marion Biggs, Michael Gray, C. Cappleman, Joseph Roberts, Jr., John C. Origler, and R. O. DeWitt were presented. First ballot—Roberts, 57; Origler, 46; Mooney, 15; Gray, 41; Cappleman, 35; Biggs, 40; and DeWitt, 80. Second ballot—DeWitt, 93; Roberts, 66; Gray, 44; Crigler, 37; Biggs, 36; Cappleman, 29; and Mooney, 11. Biggs withdrew. Third ballot—DeWitt, 137; Roberts, 75; Gray, 48; Crigler, 23; Cappleman, 22; and Mooney, 10. Origler, Mooney, Cappleman, and Gray withdrew. On the fourth ballot, DeWitt was nominated, by a vote of 227 to 91 for Roberts.

On the 22d, the convention met again. Joseph Walkup offered the following resolution, which was referred to the committee on platform :

That it is the duty of the legislature to reduce, equalize, and regulate the rates of freight and fare on all the railroads in the state, and to enact such penalties as will enforce such legislation.

The following additional nominations were made :

For treasurer, Antonio F. Coronel was nominated on the first ballot, by a vote of 200 to 31 for Jose Ramon Pico, and 88 for Juan B. Castro; L. B. Engelberg withdrawing.

Jo Hamilton, for attorney-general, without opposition.

John W. Bost, for surveyor-general, without opposition.

For printer, Walter Turnbull, J. F. Linthicum, Robert Ferral, John T. Barry, M. D. Carr, and W. A. January were named. Ferral withdrew. First ballot—Turnbull, 19; Linthicum, 49; Barry, 137; Jannary, 87; Carr, 27. Linthicum, Carr, and Turnbull withdrew. On the second ballot, Barry was nominated by a vote of 164 to 155 for Jannary.

For superintendent of public instruction, O. P. Fitzgerald, by acclamation.

For clerk of the supreme court, T. J. Shackleford, Newton Benedict, Thomas Laspeyre, George Seckel, and J. F. Wilcoxson were presented. First ballot—Seckel, 30; Shackleford, 106; Benedict, 53; Laspeyre, 65; Wilcoxson, 61. Seckel withdrew. Second ballot—Shackelford, 124; Benedict 55; Wilcoxen, 57; Laspeyre, 78. Wilcoxson and Benedict withdrew. · On the third ballot, Laspeyre was nominated by a vote of 174 to 141 for Shackleford.

For harbor commissioner, J. C. Pennie, Henry Seals, William F. White, C. Kopf, Isaac Friedlander, and F. S. Malone were named, but Kopf withdrew. First ballot—Friedlander, 120; Pennie, 90;

White, 27; Seals, 42; Malone, 37. White withdrew. On the next ballot, Friedlander was nominated by a vote of 198, to 96 for Pennie, 17 for Malone, and 7 for Seals.

A state central committee was selected, consisting of W. J. Graves, W. P. Tilden, J. C. Pennie, J. W. Mandeville, J. W. Coffroth, William McPherson, T. M. Brown, John Boggs, I. N. Walker, Joseph Walkup, W. A. Conn, James A. Johnson, William Watt, Frank McCoppin, J. P. Hoge, D. J. Oullahan, A. A. Bennett, James H. Budd, Thomas Findley, Paul Shirley, and others.

On June 23d, Friedlander declined the nomination for harbor commissioner, and on July 8th, the state committee nominated John Rosenfeld for that office.

The democratic congressional convention for the first district met at San Francisco, on June 23d. The candidates for congressmen were Lawrence Archer, W. D. Sawyer, T. N. Wand, S. B. Axtell, King of Los Angeles, and James H. Lawrence. A number of ballots were taken, the highest vote received by each candidate being: Archer, 30; Sawyer, 13; King, 28; Wand, 26; Lawrence, 16; and Axtell, 26. At the evening session, Archer received the nomination.

The second district democratic convention met at Sacramento, on June 22d, and James W. Coffroth was unanimously nominated for congressman.

The third district democratic convention met at Sacramento, on June 23d. The candidates for congressman were George Pearce, J. B. Lamar, and N. E. Whiteside. On the first ballot, Pearce had 41 votes; Lamar, 32; and Whiteside, 9. A dozen ballots were taken without much change. Finally, Lamar and Whiteside were withdrawn, and Pearce was unanimously nominated.

Early in 1871, Newton Booth was suggested as an appropriate person as the republican candidate for governor, and his claims for the nomination were endorsed and advocated by the Sacramento *Union* and the other republican organs that had taken a stand against the granting of subsidies to railroad corporations. The subsidy question was made the principal issue of the campaign. Charles A. Washburn was also named as a suitable candidate, but he developed no strength, and did not long remain in the field. In February, Thomas H. Selby was brought out as a candidate, but it was charged that he had not long been a member of the party, and that he was the candidate for the railroad corporations. The contest was soon resolved to between Booth and Selby, and the latter was urged to declare himself upon the leading issue before the public, which he did on June 24th, in the following card :

To the public.—Being a candidate, not by my own seeking, for the gubernatorial nomination, at the hands of the republican convention about to assemble, and my political status having been frequently called in question and my views on the leading topics variously stated, I deem it due to you and myself to say: First— That I voted for presidents Lincoln and Grant, and gave both administrations my most hearty support. Second—In regard to state, county, or municipal aid or subsidies to railroads, my views are in harmony with those of leading republicans with whom I have conversed; gentlemen whose opinions are likely to give shape to the platform that will be adopted by the republican convention at Sacramento. To avoid misapprehension, I am opposed to granting subsidies to railroads by the state, counties, cities or towns of California. I am in favor of the repeal of what is commonly called the five per cent. law.

On May 24th, the republican county committee of San Francisco adopted a resolution asking the chairman to appoint a committee of three to suggest the best mode of selecting delegates to the state convention. The committee so appointed declared against the primary election plan, because it was liable to corrupt influences, and against the "club" plan as being obnoxious for the same objection. They recommended that the delegates be selected by the county committee, and they presented the names of 62 delegates to the state convention. The county committee ratified this action, and when the proceeding was made public much indignation was manifested. The following evening, the executive committee of the young men's republican club of that city held a meeting, and adopted the following protest :

WHEREAS, The union republican state central committee, on the 18th day of May, called upon the union republican voters of the state of California to choose delegates to a state convention, to be held June 8th; and whereas, the city and county of San Francisco is apportioned 62 delegates, and the county committee of San Francisco, unsolicited by the union republican voters of this city, have assumed to themselves the authority of appointing all the delegates from this city and county to said convention, thereby expressly declaring that they alone are vested with the power of designating exponents to express the wishes and political views of *all* the union republican voters of the city and county; and whereas, in the struggle for party supremacy about to be inaugurated, fair dealing to the whole of our party, unity of action, and the imperative and immediate denunciation of any action on the part of a minority tending to disregard the wishes or rights of the majority, are abso- lutely necessary to our success in the coming campaign ; now, there- fore, be it resolved that we, the executive committee of the young men's republican club, do most earnestly and sincerely condemn the action of the republican county committee, and enter our protest against it.

Like protests were adopted by the other local clubs, and on the 26th the county committee rescinded the action complained of, and called a primary election for June 24th, to select the delegates. At the primary election, Selby delegates were elected. A disagreement subsequently arose in regard to local matters, and two republican tickets were run in the city. Booth succeeded, however, in securing pledged delegates from most of the other counties, and his nomina- tion was assured some time before the meeting of the state conven- tion.

On May 4th, the republican state central committee met at San Francisco and apportioned the representation in the state conven- tion, but referred the matter of fixing the time and place for holding the convention to its executive committee. On the 18th, the execu- tive committee directed that the convention be held at Sacramento on June 28th. Accordingly, at 1 o'clock on the day fixed, the con- vention met in the assembly chamber, in the state capitol. It was called to order by Walter Van Dyke, chairman of the state com- mittee, and C. E. Filkins was elected temporary chairman, without opposition. A committee on resolutions was appointed, composed of Henry Edgerton, George C. Perkins, A. W. Poole, M. Ashbury, Stephen Wing, W. S. Wells, L. H. Murch, E. Wadsworth, L. E. Crane, H. F. Page, E. L. Bradley, H. C. Rolfe, and others. While the convention was awaiting the report of the committees, it was addressed by the Hon. John A. Bingham, of Ohio. The committee on credentials accompanied their report by a resolution that the practice of county committees selecting delegates to conventions by themselves, instead of calling primaries, should be utterly condemned, and the resolution was adopted. On permanent organization, Filkins was president, and Col. J. D. Stevenson, Stephen Wing, and George C. Perkins, vice-presidents. The committee on resolutions reported the following, which were unaminously adopted:

1. That the republicans of California, by their representatives in state convention assembled, avow their determination to maintain and perpetuate the principles of the national republican party. That we recur with pride and satisfaction to the many practical and substantial triumphs of those principles achieved during the past ten years, in the coercion by force of the rebellious states into obedience of the federal constitution and laws; in maintaining through a long, severe, and bloody struggle the authority of the general government against powerful armies in front, English and French interference on the flank, and the democratic party in the rear; in rooting out the democratic institution of slavery, and banishing it forever from the jurisdiction of the United States; in prohibiting any state from abridging the privileges of any citizen of the republic; in providing irrepealable guarantees for the payment of the public debt incurred in suppressing the late rebellion, and securing the people of all the states against being taxed for the payment of the debt of the late rebel confederacy; in declaring the civil and political equality of every citizen, and in establishing all these principles in the federal constitution, by amendments thereto, as the permanent law.

2. That in Ulysses S. Grant we recognize a large measure of the patriotism, ability, and honesty which distinguished the presidential career of Abraham Lincoln, and we feel assured that the storm of falsehood and petty slander directed against him by the malice of defeated enemies will no more prevail in depreciating his character in the minds of the people than when the same means were employed by the same agencies to destroy his great co-laborer and predecessor; that his services, both military and civil, entitle him to the confidence and regard of the whole American people, and give assurance that the wisdom, perseverance, and capacity which commanded success at the head of great armies will, in the civil affairs of the government, accomplish results equally important and valuable.

3. That the present national administration, inaugurated amid political, civil, and social disorders incident to civil war, and confronted by complications, foreign and domestic, unparalleled in their

difficulty and extent, has thus far achieved a most gratifying success,. and given universal assurances of the stability and power of popular government. That by its judicious conduct of our foreign relations, its firm and impartial attitude toward the great powers of Europe recently involved in a desolating and destructive war, its prompt and rigid enforcement of the laws of neutrality, its successful solution of grave and threatening issues long pending between our own country and Great Britain, its wise and economical management of the national finances, its correction of frauds in the revenue and efficient collection of the same, its retrenchment of expense in all the departments of government, its reducing of the public debt by more than two hundred millions of dollars, its diminution of taxation eighty millions of dollars per annum, and its establishment of the public credit upon a secure basis, commands universal respect at home and abroad, and deserves the continued confidence and support of the American people.

4. That the concentration of the landed property of the country in the possession and ownership of a few, to the exclusion of the many, is in contravention of the theory of American government, subversive of the rights, liberties, and happiness of the masses of the people, and, if permitted, would inevitably terminate in the speedy establishment of an aristocracy upon the ruins of our free institutions; and we are in favor of such legislation, both by the nation and the state, as shall secure a just and equal distribution of the public lands remaining to them respectively, to actual settlers and proprietors in small quantities, at the lowest reasonable prices, and for homestead purposes only.

5. That the safety and perpetuity of republican institutions depend mainly upon popular education and intelligence. We therefore approve and recommend a common school system that shall not only extend its benefits to all, but which shall be compulsory upon all—and we are inflexibly opposed to any application of the public school moneys with any reference to distinction in religious creeds.

6. That religious liberty in its broadest sense is a fundamental principle of American government; and legislative enactments having in view the establishment of creeds, the regulation of modes of worship, or the enforcement of religious observances of any kind, are inconsistent therewith, and invasions of the rights of the citizen.

7. That the presence in our midst of a large number of Chinese, who are incapable of assimilation with our own race, ignorant of the nature and forms of our government, and who manifest no disposi-

. tion to acquire a knowledge of the same, or to conform to our own manners, habits, and customs, is a serious and continuing injury to the best interests of the state; that their employment, under the plea of cheap wages, is offensive to the exalted American idea of the dignity of labor, detrimental to the prosperity and happiness of our laboring classes, and an evil that ought to be abated; that while we unsparingly reprobate and denounce all acts of violence wheresoever and by whomsoever committed upon them, we are inflexibly opposed to their admission to citizenship, and demand of the federal government the adoption of such treaty regulations and legislation as shall discourage their further immigration to our shores.

8. That the subsidizing of railroads, or other private corporations, by grants of public lands, or by taxation of private property in any form, is contrary to sound maxims of government, productive of gross corruption and abuse, and a plain invasion of the rights of the citizen. And we hereby pledge the republican party to an uncompromising opposition to any and all legislation for such purpose; and whereas, the supreme court has decided that such legislation is not in conflict with the constitution; therefore, resolved, that we are in favor of an amendment to that instrument prohibiting the enactment of any law granting such subsidies.

9. That we demand an immediate repeal of the act of the last legislature commonly known as the "five per cent. subsidy law."

10. That the scandalous abuse of power exhibited by a democratic legislature in the creation of useless offices, boards, and commissions, and the exorbitant increase of salaries and fees, for partisan purposes; its palpable and wanton violation of a plain provision of the constitution by the infamous enactment commonly known as the "lottery bill;" its measureless subserviency to a corrupt lobby, evinced by numerous profligate grants of subsidies to railway companies; official sanction of most of these pernicious measures, including the aforesaid "lottery bill," by the present democratic state executive, and, in addition thereto, his official approval of a series of legislative enactments, whereby railway corporations have been subsidized to the extent of $4,000,000, afford convincing proof of the apostacy of a democratic administration to all the pledges upon the faith of which it was elevated to power; and that the affairs of the state cannot with safety be recommitted to its control.

11. That we extend to our newly enfranchised citizens a cordial welcome to the rights of citizenship now permanently secured to them after a hard-fought struggle with their old oppressors; that

they do not underestimate the responsibility which rests upon them as freemen we fully believe; and as they advance in the path of freedom and intelligence, none will regret the act of justice by which the republican party gave to them by constitutional guarantees civil and political equality.

Newton Booth was nominated for governor without opposition, Thomas H. Selby withdrawing.

On the 29th, the following additional nominations were made:

Romualdo Pacheco, for lieutenant-governor, on the first ballot, by a vote of 196 to 131 for Thomas B. Shannon.

For secretary of state, N. M. Orr, John Yule, L. H. Murch, and Drury Melone were named. First ballot—Orr, 86; Yule, 39; Murch, 40; Melone, 157. All of the candidates withdrew except Melone, who was nominated by acclamation.

Addison C. Niles, for supreme judge, short term, on the first ballot, by a vote of 217 to 110 for J. B. Southard.

A. L. Rhodes for supreme judge, full term, without opposition.

James J. Green for controller, on the first ballot, by a vote of 169 to 54 for Walter B. Lyon, 40 for H. O. Weller, and 73 for P. W. Bennett.

Ferdinand Baehr for treasurer, without opposition.

For surveyor-general, A. S. Easton, Sherman Day, Charles G. Bockius, and Robert Gardner, were presented. First ballot—Easton, 53; Day, 109; Rockins, 55; Gardner, 107. Rockius withdrew, and on the second ballot Gardner was nominated.

For attorney-general, Walter Van Dyke, John Lord Love, J. G. Eastman, Lewis Shearer, and L. B. Mizner were named. During the first ballot Van Dyke and Shearer withdrew, and Love received 173 votes, and was declared the nominee.

For clerk of the supreme court, Charles Grunsky, Frank J. French, Henry McCrea, Grant I. Taggart, and J. G. Moore were placed before the convention. First ballot—Grunsky, 108; French, 13; McCrea, 9; Taggart, 153; Moore, 45. French and Moore withdrew. On the second ballot Taggart was nominated by a vote of 176 to 152 for Grunsky.

H. N. Bolander, for superintendent of public instruction, without opposition.

Thomas A. Springer, for printer, on the first ballot, by a vote of 175 to 146 for John G. Howell.

For harbor commissioner, S. S. Tilton, John A. McGlynn, A. J.

Bryant, Charles B. Porter, and B. N. Bugbey were named. Tilton withdrew. First ballot—Bryant, 55; Porter, 61; Bugbey, 86; McGlynn, 124. Bryant withdrew. On the second ballot McGlynn was nominated by a vote of 207 to 38 for Porter, and 82 for Bugbey.

A state central committee was selected, consisting of Walter Murray, I. A. Am##erman, H. S. Sargent, A. J. Rhoads, H. F. Page, J. P. Ames, J. E. Hale, E. L. Sullivan, M. M. Estee, W. W. Dodge, W. W. Crane, Jr., and others.

On June 30th, the republican first district convention met at San Francisco. Thomas H. Selby was unanimously nominated for congressman, and a committee was appointed to wait on him and tender him the nomination. Selby positively declined to accept. S. O. Houghton, R. G. McClellan, and W. H. Sears were then proposed. McClellan withdrew, and Houghton was nominated on the first ballot, by a vote of 86 to 39 for Sears.

The second district convention met at Sacramento on June 29th, and Aaron A. Sargent was unanimously nominated for congressman.

On June 21st, the third district convention met at Marysville. John M. Coghlan, Charles F. Reed, Jesse O. Goodwin, and C. B. Denio were placed in nomination for member of congress. First ballot—Coghlan, 39; Reed, 27; Goodwin, 24; Denio, 6. On the third ballot Coghlan was nominated by a vote of 62, to 27 for Reed and 13 for Goodwin.

During the campaign, clubs composed of colored men were organized in the larger cities, and addresses were issued urging every colored citizen to support the republican ticket; and the advice was generally followed. This element manifested a disposition to demand the rights which had ever been denied them, and in January, at an emancipation celebration meeting in San Francisco, the following resolutions were adopted:

1. That we must make our future political watchword admission to our public schools for every child in the state, without regard to color.

2. That we will vote for no man, for any position, who is opposed to that means of justice.

During the campaign, Mark M. Pomeroy ("Brick") delivered several speeches in the interest of the democratic ticket, and a report that he had announced his intention to deliver a lecture at Oakland, showing the necessity for the assassination of President Lincoln, greatly excited the citizens of that place, and threats were freely made that he would be prevented from delivering his lecture. The democrats denied that Pomeroy had expressed such an intention. On August 22d a republican club of that city resolved:

1. That the city of Oakland is not the locality where an applauding crowd of rebels and their sympathizers may be entertained with the glorification of assassins hired by the late so-called confederate government.

2. That the members of this club hereby pledge their honor that no such an address as the one above indicated shall be delivered in Oakland.

3. That instead of adjourning *sine die* after the election this club holds itself in readiness to assemble at the call of the president, which call shall be issued as soon as published notice is given of the intention to deliver said lecture.

4. That a copy of these resolutions be forwarded to M. M. Pomeroy, through the democratic central committee.

Pomeroy made no attempt to deliver the lecture.

The general election was held on Wednesday, September 6th, and the official canvass of the votes that had been polled developed the following results: For governor—Booth, 62,581; Haight, 57,520. Lieutenant-governor—Pacheco, 62,555; Lewis, 57,397. Secretary of state—Melone, 61,750; Brown, 57,907. Controller—Green, 62,-708; DeWitt, 57,181. Treasurer—Baehr, 62,467; Coronel, 57,515. Surveyor-general—Gardner, 61,967; Bost, 57,866. Attorney-general—Love, 61,726; Hamilton, 58,161. Clerk of the supreme court —Taggart, 62,422; Laspeyre, 57,469. Printer—Springer, 62,650; Barry, 57,043. Harbor commissioner—McGlynn, 58,626; Rosenfeld, 60,353. Members of congress: First district—Houghton, 25,-971; Archer, 24,374. Second district—Sargent, 18,065; Coffroth, 15,382. Third district—Coghlan, 18,503; Pearce, 17,309. All of the nominees of the republican party were elected except McGlynn. The judicial and school election was held on Wednesday, October 18, and resulted as follows, all of the republican nominees being successful: For justice of the supreme court (full term)—Rhodes, 46,-829; Wright, 36,606. Justice of the supreme court (to fill the Sanderson vacancy)—Niles, 47,373; Temple, 36,500. Superintendent of public instruction—Bolander, 48,860; Fitzgerald, 34,212.

It had been the custom in the state for the various political parties to print their tickets in a manner to make it inconvenient, if not impossible, to change them in any particular, and to print conspicuous figures or marks upon the backs by which their character could be ascertained as voters handed them to the officers of election. Tickets were printed without margins, on so poor a quality of paper that "scratches" could not be written upon them, and in other instances the names of the candidates and designation of offices were printed in curved lines to prevent "pasters" from being used. The republican tickets used at the September election at Vallejo and Mare Island went to a greater extremity than had before been practiced. They were used principally among the men employed at the United States navy yard; the tickets were rather more than half an inch in width by five and one-half inches in length. They were printed without margins, in the very finest type set solid, the lines running lengthwise, and on thin cardboard. A colored figure was printed on the back. There was no opportunity afforded to change a ballot either by writing or pasting. Ballots narrower, but in all other respects similar, were used at the judicial election. The use of these ballots excited discussion as to the propriety of a uniform ballot law, to prevent the abuses to which the use of the prevalent styles of tickets had subjected voters.

CHAPTER XXIII.

1872. Republican Convention, April 25th—Democratic Convention— Republican Convention, August 1st—Liberal Republican Movement —Straight-out Democrats.

The republican state central committee met at San Francisco on March 4th and issued a call for a state convention of 325 members, to be held at Sacramento on April 25th, to select delegates to attend the national convention to meet at Philadelphia on June 5th. At 1 o'clock on the day mentioned the convention assembled in the assembly chamber in the state capitol, and it was called to order by E. L. Sullivan, chairman of the state committee. Charles

E. Filkins was unanimously elected president, and Claus Spreckles, W. H. Sears, A. G. Abell, Samuel Myers, Joseph Phelps, C. L. F. Brown, J. O. Goodwin, M. J. C. Calvin, J. F. Tobin, S. G. George, W. H. Mace, and W. M. Williamson, vice-presidents. The committee on resolutions consisted of J. M. Cavis, James A. Duffy, J. H. McNabb, C. F. Reed, Cyrus Palmer, and others, and they reported the following:

1. That we have a firm and abiding faith in the principles of the republican party, and point with pride to its achievements, believing that the party which brought order out of chaos, saved and preserved the nation, is alone worthy of administering its affairs in the future.

2. That we fully and heartily indorse the wise, patriotic, just and economical administration of U. S. Grant as president of the United States, and that our delegates to the national convention are hereby instructed to use all honorable means to secure his renomination, he being the unanimous choice of the republican party of California.

3. That the delegates from this state to the national republican convention are hereby instructed in the selection of a candidate for the vice-presidency to vote as a unit for the best interests of the republican party; and that upon all questions arising in said convention they are hereby instructed to cast the vote of the state in such a manner as the majority of the delegates may determine.

M. S. Deal moved to strike out so much of the last resolution as related to matters other than the selection of a candidate for the vice-presidency. Henry Edgerton moved the following as a substitute for the entire resolution:

3. That the delegates from California to the national convention at Philadelphia be instructed to vote as a unit for the candidate for vice-president.

Sears moved to strike out the portion of the resolution relating to the candidates for vice-president, but the motion was lost, and the Edgerton substitute was adopted. Sears offered the following, which was adopted:

That Governor Newton Booth, by the prudence and wisdom with which he has conducted the state administration, and by his watchful regard for public interests, has vindicated the choice of the people in the last election and deserves the confidence and thanks of every citizen.

The resolutions were then adopted as a whole, without opposition.

The following were unanimously selected as delegates to the national convention : First district—Eugene L. Sullivan, James H. Withington, and James Otis. Second district—F. K. Shattuck, J. W. B. Dickson, and H. S. Sargent. Third district—E. Wads-worth, A. D. Starr, and O. M. Patterson. Fourth district—O. S. Abbott, Thomas Fallon, and A. Bronson.

A state central committee was appointed, consisting of Walter Murray, Walter VanDyke, M. O. Conroy, John Sedgwick, Charles F. Reed, David E. Gordon, L. B. Ayer, Charles Marsh, Cyrus Coleman, Frank Eastman, Josiah Belden, Alvinza Hayward, F. D. Atherton, Paul Newman, C. N. Felton, John F. Miller, William Sherman, E. B. Mott, Jr., and others.

The caucus of the second district members was held during a recess of the convention, for the purpose of agreeing on three dele-gates to be presented from the district. The names of F. K. Shattuck, James A. Duffy, J. W. B. Dickson, Charles Kent, H. S. Sargent, and A. J. Rhoads were proposed. Duffy withdrew, and on the first ballot Shattuck received 87 votes; Dickson, 73; Sargent, 73; Rhoads, 16; Kent, 21, and Duffy, 6. The first three were therefore elected.

On May 23d, the democratic state central committee met at San Francisco. James W. Coffroth moved that the committee appoint the delegates to attend the national convention to meet at Baltimore; Frank McCoppin moved as an amendment that a state convention be called, and the latter motion carried. A resolution was then adopted calling a state convention of 339 members, to meet at San Francisco on June 19th, to select 12 delegates to attend the national convention, and to nominate an electoral ticket. In pursuance of this call, the convention met at 12 o'clock on the day named, and was called to order by James W. Mandeville, chairman of the state com-mittee. J. T. Farley and J. W. Coffroth were nominated for tem-porary chairman. Coffroth withdrew, and Farley was unanimously elected. Farley then declined, when Coffroth was chosen. On per-manent organization, Coffroth was president; and Frank McCoppin, W. Neely Johnson, William McP. Hill, John Daggett, John G. Downey, Peter Donahue, O. T. Ryland, John O. Hays, Thomas Hope, J. D. Carrington, William Irwin, and others, vice-presidents. The committee on resolutions consisted of O. H. Johnson, J. O. Martin, William Van Voorhies, J. H. Budd, J. W. Coffroth, J. B.

Lamar, John Daggett, A. M. Rosborough, P. W. Keyser, George E. Williams, F. McCoppin, William Watt, P. Reddy, J. G. Downey, O. T. Ryland, and others. A resolution was adopted to refer all resolutions to this committee without debate. The committee on order of business recommended the selection of 12 delegates to the national convention—two from each congressional district and four at large; and that the state central committee be authorized to nominate candidates for presidential electors. The following resolutions were reported by the committee and adopted by the convention :

1. That the best interests of the nation require a change in the administration of the government, and all good citizens should disregard the prejudices and differences of the past, and unite in one grand effort to restore the government to its original purity.

2. That we earnestly condemn and protest against the machinations, tyranny, extravagance, and corruptions of the administration of U. S. Grant, which, for lobbying schemes and building up monopolies, has no parallel in the history of our country.

3. That we fully recognize the patriotism and pure motives of the liberal republicans, and trust that such action may be taken at the Baltimore convention as will result in the hearty co-operation of all parties opposed to the present administration, and that we recommend to the consideration of the national democratic convention the principles enunciated in the platform of the Cincinnati convention.

4. That having an abiding confidence in the wisdom and patriotism of the democratic national convention soon to be assembled at Baltimore, we pledge ourselves to give the nominees of that convention a hearty support.

5. That we leave our delegates to the national convention free and untrammelled, believing that wise counsels and devoted patriotism will govern their action.

The following resolutions were presented by Menzies, but they were sent to the committee on resolutions, without reading, and were not reported to the convention :

1. That we are in favor of a tariff for revenue only and pronounce the protective system as unjust, oppressive, prolific of corruption, and injurious to the best interests of the country. That the tariff regulations of the republican party have destroyed our shipping,

paralyzed industry and plundered the people for the benefit of monopolists.

2. That we are uncompromisingly opposed to the granting of Goat island to the Central Pacific Railroad, or any other railroad, for railroad purposes, under any circumstances whatever. The preservation of our noble harbor, in the interests of commerce and the property interests in this great city, demands this public declaration from the democratic state convention, and we pledge our candidates in good faith to oppose any act which would grant Goat island for railroad purposes.

On the 20th, the convention elected a state central committee, consisting of P. W. Murphy, P. O. Hundley, R. Beverly Cole, Tyler Curtis, E. R. Galvin, J. W. Coffroth, John Daggett, Dr. J. E. Pelham, C. E. Wilcoxson, J. T. Farley, Wm. Hayes, J. B. Sensabaugh, Jo Hamilton, Paul Shirley, Thomas Laspeyre, J. P. Hoge, R. Watt, E. J. Lewis, Michael Hayes, W. F. White, and others.

George Pearce offered the following resolution, but no action was taken on it:

That the democracy of California recognize the right of a democratic convention, state or federal, to meet and adjourn either with or without designating or naming a partisan candidate of the democracy, but utterly deny the authority of such a convention to nominate other than a democratic partisan as their candidate for any elective office in their gift.

The following were selected as delegates to the national convention: First district, C. T. Ryland and McD. R. Venable; second district, Robert O. Cravens and George D. Roberts; third district, Joseph C. Wolfskill and W. F. Goad; fourth district, Frank McCoppin and Henry George—all of whom were elected by acclamation. James H. Hardy, J. G. Downey, William M. Gwin, Samuel Butterworth, James H. Lawrence, Eugene Casserly, Charles L. Weller, Martin Tarpey, J. D. Cochrane, T. G. Cockrill, H. C. Patrick, and Thomas Hope were placed in nomination for delegates at large. Lawrence and Weller withdrew, and on the first ballot, Downey, Hardy, Gwin, and Casserly were selected, the vote being: Downey, 239; Hardy, 244; Casserly, 185; Gwin, 170; Patrick, 117; Butterworth, 90; Tarpey, 82; Cochrane, 89; Cockrill, 48, and Hope, 16.

U. S. Grant and Henry Wilson were nominated respectively for president and vice-president of the United States on the 6th day of June, and the republican state central committee immediately met and called a state convention of 325 delegates, to meet at Sacramento on August 1st, for the purpose of nominating an electoral ticket. At 11:30 o'clock on the day named the convention met in the assembly chamber and was called to order by John F. Miller, a member of the state committee. J. G. Eastman was elected temporary chairman without opposition. The committee on resolutions consisted of W. E. Lovett, P. J. Hopper, M. S. Deal, Walter Van Dyke, Henry Bahr, J. H. McNabb, W. N. DeHaven, O. A. Purington, and J. E. Wyman. On permanent organization, Eastman was president, and T. B. McFarland, George C. Perkins, J. W. North, and Joseph Lipman, vice-presidents.

The following resolutions were reported and unanimously adopted:

1. That the republican party of California, in convention assembled, heartily indorse the declaration of principles embodied in the platform of the national convention of the republican party, adopted at Philadelphia, and pledge themselves to the cordial support of the standard bearers there selected for president and vice-president of the United States.

2. That in U. S. Grant we recognize the patriot and statesman under whose leadership the union was preserved, and whose record as a soldier is fully equalled by his wise and prudent administration of national affairs, by which peace has been restored and the union cemented, debt and taxation greatly reduced, and the national flag respected throughout the world.

3. That in Henry Wilson we hail the true friend of labor, whose whole career has illustrated that the republic recognizes true merit in her sons, who, by their ability, honesty, and worth, commend themselves to the confidence of the people.

4. That General U. S. Grant and Henry Wilson, by their course in civil life, and by their public and official acts, have proved themselves to be the true, fast and firm friends of labor and labor reform.

5. That the party claiming to be followers of Jefferson and Jackson, that originated and enunciated the doctrine of "principles, not men," having by indorsement of Greeley and the Cincinnati platform, made an unconditional surrender of all that was left of its political principles, it only remains for the national republican party,

by its votes on November 6, 1872, to consign it with its unholy coalition, to political oblivion forever.

6. That republicans need no "new departure," and have no faith in that so-called liberal reform which involves desertion of true and tried leaders, or abandonment of the principles of republican government and the rights of man.

7. That we fully concur in the opinion of Horace Greeley, that General Grant never has been beaten and never will be, and we propose to fight it out on this line until November, when said prediction will be fully realized by the verdict of the American people.

The following were nominated for presidential electors, without opposition: First district, Claus Spreckles; second district, James E. Hale; third district, Jesse O. Goodwin; fourth district, T. H. Rose; at large, John B. Felton and John F. Miller.

In like manner the following were nominated for alternate electors: First district, A. R. Baldwin; second district, S. W. Sperry; third district, Isaac G. Wickersham; fourth district, W. Canfield; at large, F. E. Spencer and Benjamin Shurtleff.

The first district republican convention met at San Francisco on August 15th, and adopted resolutions endorsing the national ticket and platform, and opposing the granting of Goat island to any corporation. The names of Henry Baker, Charles Clayton, J. C. Merrill, A. D. Splivalo and Cornelius Cole were presented as candidates for the congressional nomination. All were withdrawn except Clayton, but some of his opponents insisted upon a ballot being taken. Clayton was nominated upon the first ballot, by a vote of 55, to 5 for Cole. The second district convention met at Sacramento on August 1st. H. F. Page, Charles A. Tuttle, Nathan Porter, and J. M. Cavis were placed in nomination. On the first ballot Page had 43 votes; Tuttle, 7; Porter, 27, and Cavis, 15. The result was the same on the second ballot, except that Page drew one vote from Porter and one from Tuttle. On the third ballot Page drew two more votes from Tuttle, when the entire Sacramento delegation voted for him, and he was nominated.

The third district convention met at Washington, Yolo county, on August 2d, and renominated John M. Coghlan, without opposition.

The fourth district convention met at Sacramento on August 1st, and renominated S. O. Houghton, by acclamation.

On May 3d, Horace Greeley was nominated for president of the United States by a convention at Cincinnati, which adopted the name of "Liberal Republican" for a new political party, which was designed to occupy the middle ground between the then existing national parties. On the 22d, a meeting was held at San Francisco for the purpose of organizing the party in the state. F. M. Pixley stated the object of the meeting, and J. F. Chellis was made chairman. A committee was appointed to correspond with the friends of the movement in the various counties and to appoint a state central committee, consisting of A. J. Bryant, S. S. Tilton, George Barstow, Thomas Gray, F. M. Pixley, J. P. H. Wentworth, J. A. McGlynn, and others. This committee appointed a state committee, consisting of George Barstow, George D. Nagle, Seth Wetherbee, S. S. Tilton, F. B. Taylor, M. Fennell, E. L. Beard, J. H. Keyes, J. Winchester, J. W. Snowball, C. G. Bockius, William Sexton, A. J. Snyder, and others.

On August 3d, the state central committees of the democratic and liberal republican parties met jointly at San Francisco and nominated the following Greeley and Brown electoral ticket: F. M. Pixley, J. C. Shorb, F. H. Rosenbaum, Jo Hamilton, John Yule, and Peter Donahue. The following were nominated for alternate electors: Albert Hagan, Austin Sperry, Juan B. Castro, Robert McGarvey, John Daggett, and A. J. Spencer. A state executive committee was appointed, consisting of the following: Democrats—Michael Hayes, William Hayes, J. W. Coffroth, Robert Watt, Tyler Curtis, R. Beverly Cole, J. P. Hoge, Frank Lawton. Liberals—E. W. Corbett, Seth H. Wetherbee, S. S. Tilton, W. C. Schmidt, S. E. Hartwell, F. B. Taylor, William Sexton, A. J. Snyder.

The first district liberal and democratic congressional convention met at San Francisco on July 25th, and passed resolutions endorsing the amendments to the federal constitution, the national liberal candidates, pledging the nominee to oppose the granting of Goat island to any railroad, and in favor of building another railroad line to the east below the snow belt. The candidates before the convention were W. A. Piper, Thomas N. Wand, Frank M. Pixley, R. Beverly Cole, and Leander Quint. On the first ballot Piper had 43 votes; Wand, 8; Pixley, 2; Cole, 1, and Quint, 1, and Piper was declared to be the nominee.

The second district democratic and liberal conventions met separately, at Sacramento on September 4th, but coalesced, and nominated Paschal Coggins on the first ballot, over Henry Larkin, and G. J. Carpenter. The ballot stood : Democratic delegates— Coggins, 33; Carpenter, 28; Larkin, 24. Liberal delegates— Coggins, 43. A series of anti-monopoly resolutions were adopted.

The third district joint convention was held at Marysville on August 22d. J. B. Lamar, George Pearce, L. A. Norton, and J. K. Luttrell were placed in nomination. All withdrew except Luttrell, who was nominated by acclamation.

The fourth district democratic convention met at San Francisco on June 20th, and on the first ballot nominated E. J. C. Kewen, by a vote of 51, to 32 for Lawrence Archer. The liberals acquiesced in the nomination.

On October 14th, a meeting was held at San Francisco of democrats who favored the maintaining of their party organization, and opposed the liberal movement. A committee of five was appointed to prepare an address to the people, and to nominate an electoral ticket in the interest of Charles O'Conor and John Quincy Adams, who had been nominated, respectively, for president and vice-president by the national democratic convention. This committee made the following nominations : For presidential electors—J. Mora Moss, Jackson Temple, Zach. Montgomery, William J. Graves, M. R. C. Pulliam, and A. J. King. For alternate electors—G. W Hunter, E. F. McCarthy, Daniel Taylor, A. P. Bernard, E. N. Foote, and Charles E. Beau. A state central committee was selected, consisting of John Nugent, Charles T. Botts, Thomas Golden, W. D. Sawyer, James C. Goods, N. P. Jones, E. A. Rockwell, James Van Ness, George Seckel, Jacob R. Snyder, and others. On the 18th, Temple declined the nomination for elector, and John Nugent was placed on the ticket in his stead. On the 29th, the state central committee made the following nominations for congressmen : First district, W. D. Sawyer; second district, G. W. Hunter; third district, J. N. Bailhache; fourth district, James Van Ness. Hunter, on November 1st, declined to run.

During the campaign the principal speakers were: Republican— John F. Swift, H. F. Page, J. M. Coghlan, J. G. Eastman, John F. Miller, J. M. Cavis, George C. Gorham, S. J. Finney, O. H. La Grange, S. O. Houghton, Henry Edgerton, John B. Felton, John L. Love, George M. Pinney, H. G. Rollins, and Warner Oliver.

Liberal—M. M. Estee, P. Coggins, J. K. Luttrell, Jo Hamilton, James T. Farley, N. Greene Curtis, Henry Larkin, G. J. Carpenter, W. B. C. Brown, W. W. Pendegast, F. M. Pixley, P. F. Walsh, Creed Haymond, Stuart M. Taylor, Eugene Casserly, J. C. Shorb, J. B. Frisbie, E. J. C. Kewen, William Irwin, J. R. Sharpstein, and J. F. Cowdery.

The election was held on Tuesday, November 5th, and the official canvass exhibited the following result: Republican electors—Felton, 54,007; Spreckles, 54,044; Goodwin, 54,020; Miller, 54,013; Hale, 54,020; Rose, 53,998. Liberal electors—Shorb, 40,718; Pixley, 40,703; Hamilton, 40,749; Rosenbaum, 40,674; Donahue, 40,-718; Yule, 40,717. Democratic electors—Moss, 1,068; Nugent, 1,035; Montgomery, 1,064; Graves, 1,051; Pulliam, 1,028; King, 1,053. Members of congress: First district—Clayton, 11,938; Piper, 10,882. Second district—Page, 13,803; Coggins, 12,819. Third district—Coghlan, 13,105; Luttrell, 14,033. Fourth district—Houghton, 10,391; Kewen, 9,012. The republican electors were therefore elected, and Clayton, Page, Luttrell, and Houghton were elected to congress, to take office March 4, 1873.

The republican presidential electors met at the state capitol on December 4, and cast the six votes of the state for Grant and Wilson. James E. Hale was appointed messenger to convey the returns to Washington.

CHAPTER XXIV.

1873. Independent Movement—San Francisco Politics—Republican
State Convention — Democratic State Convention — Independent
Party Organized—Independent State Convention.

Early in 1873, the organization of farmers' clubs was very general in the state. The clubs held weekly meetings at which subjects of interest to agriculturists were discussed in open session, but soon the club system was abandoned and a secret order styled Patrons of Husbandry, or grangers, absorbed the membership of the clubs, and by the close of the year most of the clubs had ceased to exist. These organizations exerted considerable influence in the politics of the state, as the questions of railroad transportation rates, reduction of public expenditures, etc., were debated at the meetings and acted upon by resolution. On April 26th, the Vacaville grange, one of the first organized in the state, adopted and published the fol·lowing resolutions, which are similar to those afterward adopted by other granges and clubs:

1. That we will support no men for law makers, or for adminis-trators of our laws, or for any position of public trust, no matter to what party they may belong, whose character for integrity and hon-esty of purpose, and whose fidelity to the true interests of the farmer (which are the true interests of the country) are not beyond a doubt.

2. That we wage no war against railroads and other modes of transportation, or upon grain buyers, or commission merchants, only so far as their treatment of the farming interest is manifestly unjust and oppressive. So far as they are governed by honesty and fair dealing, our aims and interests are identical, and we wish to co-op-erate with them harmoniously. But when they form "rings" or odi-ous combinations to oppress the farming interests and cripple and crush out the vitality of this great paramount industry of the coun-try, then we may be compelled to beat our plowshares into swords and our pruning hooks into spears, and go after the common enemy.

The third resolution directed that a copy be sent to each grange in the state "asking their co-operation in carrying out the princi-ples and measures proposed, so far as they accord with their ideas and views of the necessity of the case and the exigencies of the times."

On September 24, 1872, delegates from a number of farmers' clubs met at Sacramento and effected the organization of the State Farm-ers' Union, the design of which was to promote the agricultural and industrial interests of the state. John Bidwell was elected presi-dent; J. R. Snyder, Dr. E. S. Holden, T. Hart Hyatt, W. S. Man-love and others, vice-presidents, and I. N. Hoag, secretary. A called meeting of the union was held at San Francisco on April 9th, which was attended by delegates from about twenty different counties. On the 10th the following resolutions were adopted:

1. That the rates charged for freights over the railroads in this state are ruinous to our agricultural interests.

2. That in our opinion the corporations operating these roads, being the creations of law, are, and should be, under control of our·

statutes, and that the maximum rates of freights should be so fixed by statute as to prevent extortion, and leave the producer a margin of profit on his productions, and that way freights be charged only in proportion to the distance the freight is sent with the charges for through freight.

3. That if we find it impracticable under present management of such roads to obtain a fair reduction on such freights, we will agitate the subject, and insist that the railroads built by money of the government shall be operated by the government in the interest of the people, rather than by private persons for personal aggrandizement.

4. That as these matters are political, we will so far make this a political body as to cast our votes and use our influence for such men for our state legislature as will carry our views into effect.

The fifth, sixth and seventh resolutions directed the executive committee to consider the propriety of utilizing the state prison labor in the production of grain sacks sufficient for home consumption, to be sold to farmers at cost. The eighth, ninth and tenth resolutions directed the committee to prepare plans for a co-operative bank; for a co-operative system for selling agricultural supplies; and to provide storage for grain with the intention of retaining it until it should bring the highest price.

The resolutions were adopted, the fourth, by a vote of 38 to 20.

The railroad question absorbed the entire interest of the campaign of 1873 for the election of the county officers and members of the legislature. A strong anti-railroad party had grown up under the leadership of Governor Booth, and with the support of the Sacramento *Union* and other prominent journals, although it had no organization. Within the republican party Booth had a numerous and active following to second his aspirations for the United States senatorship, to succeed Casserly, and some of the republican county conventions pledged their candidates for the legislature to support Booth for senator. It was urged by the Booth republicans that the organization of the party in the state was in the hands of men under the railroad influence, and that the party managers frequently misused their power. The first open bolt occurred in Sacramento county. The republican committee of that county, on May 28th, issued a call for a Crawford primary, to be held on June 7th, to select delegates to the county convention. On the 29th, a meeting of the Booth republicans was held and a resolution was passed objecting to the call, because the time was too short for the voters to prepare for the election; because a democratic primary was to be held on the same day, "giving color to the belief that the same voters, in the interest of the same parties, were intended to be used to carry both elections; because the appointment of delegates and the election of officers of the primary was unfair." A committee was appointed to wait on the county committee and to request a postponement of the primary for one week, and a representation on the boards of election. On June 2d, this committee reported that the central committee had refused to make any change in the call. The Booth meeting then appointed a committee of thirteen to arrange for an independent primary and convention. This committee adopted the name "Independent Taxpayers' Party," and called a primary for June 21st, at which all were invited to vote who had not voted at any previous primary, and who would support the ticket to be nominated by the convention. On the 4th, the committee issued a call to the people, defining the object of the movement to be to elect members to the legislature who would command the confidence of the whole people, and who would be free from the control of rings and corrupt combinations. They also declared that they would act independent of party. The convention met on the 26th, and nominated Henry Edgerton for state senator, and a complete legislative and county ticket. The party was christened by its opponents the "Dolly Varden" party. A similar movement was inaugurated soon afterward in most of the counties, resulting in placing three tickets in the field. At the September election the "dolly vardens" were generally successful.

In San Francisco the following tickets were presented for the September election, each containing a full list of legislative and municipal nominations, but the nominees for mayor and state senators alone are here given: Citizens' Independent—Mayor, James M. McDonald; senators, Philip A. Roach and Washington Bartlett. Democratic—Mayor, McDonald; senators, Frank McCoppin and Roach. Liberal Reform—Mayor, McDonald; senators, McCoppin and Roach. Citizens' Union—Mayor, James Otis; senators, W. H. Sears and Irving M. Scott. People's Union—Mayor, Otis; senators, A. S. Hallidie and Bartlett. Anti-sectarian—Senators, Hallidie and Scott. Republican—Senators, Sears and Scott. Taxpayers' and People's—Mayor, Otis. At the election on

September 3d, Otis was elected Mayor, by a vote of 13,648, to 12,406 for McDonald. Roach and Bartlett were elected senators, Sears receiving 9,869 votes; Scott, 6,956; Hallidie, 9,869; Bartlett, 9,551; McCoppin, 8,512, and Roach, 10,134.

On January 6th, a suit was instituted in the district court at San Francisco, by L. E. Crane, an expert who had been appointed by the governor to investigate the affairs of the state board of harbor commissioners, to oust John J. Marks and Jasper O'Farrell from their positions as members of the board, because of fraud alleged to have been discovered. Marks was also indicted by the grand jury for fraud. Pending the civil suit, on February 21st, Marks resigned, and Governor Booth appointed Lewis Cunningham to the position. O'Farrell resigned later, and Samuel Soule was appointed in his place. John Rosenfeld, the remaining member of the board, and who had held the office but a very short time, also resigned, and T. D. Mathewson was appointed to fill the vacancy.

On August 29th, the republican state central committee nominated Paul Newman for harbor commissioner from the state at large; and on the same day, the democratic committee named John W. Bost for the office. Bost was endorsed by the independents generally. At the September election, Newman was elected, by a vote of 31,696, to 30,867 for Bost.

In San Francisco, Charles L. Taylor was nominated for harbor commissioner by the citizen's union, people's union and taxpayers' conventions, and Thomas E. Farish by the democratic, citizens', independent, and liberal reform conventions. Taylor was elected. Commissions were issued to Newman and Taylor by Governor Booth on November 12th.

On July 23d, the republican state central committee met at San Francisco, and called a state judicial convention of 362 delegates, to meet at Sacramento on August 20th. On August 16th, another meeting of the committee was held at San Francisco, when a resolution was unanimously adopted postponing the meeting of the convention to September 16th, because no proclamation had been issued by the governor calling the state judicial election, and a doubt existed whether one or two judges of the supreme court were to be elected. Pursuant to this amended call, the convention met at Sacramento, on September 16th, and was called to order by Walter

Van Dyke, the acting chairman of the state committee. .William H. Sears was elected chairman, without opposition. On motion of H. F. Page, the convention decided to refer all resolutions to the committee on resolutions, without debate. A committee on resolutions was appointed, consisting of H. F. Page, E. P. Lovejoy, W. E. Lovett, G. M. Pinney, M. C. Andross, T. B. McFarland, and W. R. Wheaton. The committee reported that in their opinion, as the convention was purely judicial, it would be improper to adopt a platform, and they submitted a resolution that the convention would not entertain any resolution relating to political subjects, and the resolution was adopted. John B. Felton announced that I. S. Belcher would not be a candidate for justice of the supreme court.

Samuel H. Dwinelle was nominated for judge of the supreme court, to serve out the term made vacant by the death of Judge Sprague, without opposition.

Ansen Bronson was unanimously nominated for judge of the supreme court, to succeed Justice Crockett.

On August 26th, the democratic state central committee met in San Francisco and ordered a state judicial convention to be held at Sacramento, on September 17th. The primary test included all democrats and all persons who were opposed to the national administration. At 12 o'clock on the day named, the convention met and was called to order by J. P. Hoge, the committee chairman. James T. Farley was elected chairman. After a lengthy discussion, the convention decided to have a committee on resolutions appointed, and W. W. Pendegast, William Watt, Delos Lake, W. F. White, G. J. Carpenter, Thomas P. Bond, and John G. Downey were selected. The committee reported the following resolutions, which were adopted :

Notwithstanding the fact that this is a judicial convention, convened mainly for the purpose of selecting candidates for judicial positions, we nevertheless deem it a proper occasion to solemnly declare our views and principles; therefore, the democracy of California, in state convention assembled, do adopt the following resolutions as a statement of the principles which they believe should be carried into effect.

1. That we demand the utmost economy in the management of public affairs, and to that end recommend the incoming state legislature to largely reduce the fees and salaries of all public servants,.

commencing the reform in the office of the chief executive of the state, and prosecuting the same through all departments of the government.

2. That we unqualifiedly condemn the action of the United States congress in enacting the law commonly known as the "back-pay salary steal," as well as the action of the president of the United States in approving the bill, whose sole recommendation was that it made him richer in dollars.

3. That we point to the history of the state and nation as demonstrating the fact that the democratic party has always been the friend of the people, the advocate of every needed reform, the staunch defender of the rights of the laborer, and the uncompromising foe of all monopolies, railroad corporations, or others, and we congratulate ourselves and the people of California that every candidate at the late election was forced to plant himself squarely on the good old democratic anti-monopoly platform, whether he solicited votes under the republican or democratic standards, or the flag of an independent organization.

4. That we make no war upon railroads as such, but we protest against their being managed in the interests of any ring or clique, or political man or party, and believing it to be a proper subject of state legislation, we demand that such action be taken by the incoming legislature as will properly adjust the vexed question of railroad fares and freights so as to enable the railroad companies to earn a fair profit upon their investment, and at the same time remove all onerous charges from the people, and prevent any unjust discrimination for or against any section of the state.

5. That we regard the presence of the Chinese in our midst as an unmixed evil, ruinous alike to the people and the state, while the prospect of an increase of their numbers is appalling to the hearts of all; and we demand that the incoming legislature, through its own enactments and its urgent appeals to congress, take steps not merely to prevent the further influx of the mongolian horde upon us, but to secure the speedy exodus of those already here; and to this end we urge that measures be at once instituted to decrease the subsidy to the Pacific Mail Steamship Company, and to abrogate the so-called Burlingame treaty.

6. That we hail with pleasure the action of the farmers in this and other states in the formation of granges and societies for the protection and advancement of their own interests. We are proud to observe this class of our people, hitherto quiet, has of late

asserted its rights, and is beginning to demonstrate its power; that we now pledge ourselves that our candidates for all offices, legislative, executive or judicial, shall be in full sympathy with all these farmers in all just and honest demands; and that in event of their failure to do so, they shall never receive our support in the future.

The convention selected a state central committee, consisting of P. O. Hundley, R. B. Cole, W. H. Cronise, Caleb Dorsey, Harrison Guinn, R. A. Thompson, Thomas Rector, John McMurray, N. E. Whiteside, R. H. Ward, William Watt, Paul Shirley, Thomas Laspeyre, Franklin Lawton, W. B. C. Brown, Grove L. Johnson, Thomas N. Wand, J. C. Pennie, A. H. Rose, James T. Farley, J. P. Hoge, and others.

Samuel Bell McKee was nominated for justice of the supreme court, to fill the vacancy caused by the death of Judge Sprague, on the first ballot, by a vote of 161, to 121 for William C. Wallace.

A. B. Dibble moved to nominate Niles Searls for justice of the supreme court to fill the vacancy should the term of Judge Crockett be declared expired, but after discussion the motion was withdrawn, and it was agreed that the central committee should place the name of a candidate upon the ticket if they should deem it necessary.

Immediately when the result of the September election became known the suggestion was thrown out by the portion of the press that had assisted in the election of the independent legislative and county tickets, that the advantage be followed up by organizing an independent party in the state, with the view of nominating a candidate for justice of the supreme court, to be voted for at the October election, and of presenting tickets at the subsequent state elections. About the middle of September, the independent county committee of Sacramento county called a meeting for the 18th, and invited the members of the independent taxpayers' and people's union committees from the other counties to attend, the object of the meeting being to take steps leading to a state organization. A. P. Catlin called the meeting to order, and Edward Gibbons was elected chairman, on motion of John F. Swift. Catlin offered the following resolution :

That in the opinion of this meeting, the people of this state demand, and, therefore, it is expedient, that a state organization of an independent people's party be immediately formed; and to that end that a state central committee be formed, and that steps be at once taken to put before the people nominations for justices of the supreme court, and to call a state convention.

A division of the question was ordered on the resolution and the first branch was unanimously adopted. The last branch was then withdrawn. On motion of Samuel T. Leet, a committee of seven was appointed, consisting of Leet, Catlin, Swift, F. T. Baldwin, J. G. Howell, B. F. Myers and P. Van Clief, to prepare a plan for a state organization. The committee recommended the calling of a state convention, to meet at Sacramento on September 25th. The call recited:

The representatives of the several county independent organizations, believing it expedient for the public good to form a state organization opposed to monopolies, and to all forms of partial and special legislation, and in favor of consolidating and organizing into actual and effective form the sentiment of the people of California upon all questions of reform in legislation, especially with respect to securing the rights of the people in the contest now being waged between them and the railroad power of the state and nation, and other monopolies, and having in view the approaching judicial election, as well as political movements of a like character in other states, request that delegates be sent to a state convention to be held in Sacramento on September 25th, from every county in the state, to perfect a state organization, to nominate one or more justices of the supreme court, to appoint a state central committee, and transact such other business as may come before it. In counties where independent movements are already established, the delegates to be selected by or under the central committees of such independent organizations. In counties where such movements have not yet been made, the delegates to be selected by patrons of husbandry, or other associations or persons in sympathy with our movement.

The report was unanimously adopted. About sixty persons took part in the meeting.

The people's independent judicial state convention met at Sacramento on September 25th, and was called to order by Edward Gibbons, who announced that the object of the convention was to organize the independent party, and to consider the propriety of nominating candidates for justices of the supreme court. Jonas Spect was unanimously elected temporary chairman, P. Van Clief withdrawing. A motion by J. W. Dwinelle that all resolutions offered before the convention be referred to the committee on resolutions without debate, was discussed by Dwinelle, W. C. Norton, James Johnson, William Jones, C. C. Terrill, A. Maurice, jr., and Alexander Campbell, jr., and finally withdrawn. A committee on resolutions was appointed consisting of Alexander Campbell, jr., J. W. Dwinelle, A. P. Catlin, G. T. Elliott, W. S. Buckley, W. C. Norton, W. Jeff. Gatewood, M. C. Winchester, J. R. Sharpstein, C. C. Terrill, and I. N. Randolph. On permanent organization, P. Van Clief was president. The following preamble and resolutions were unanimously adopted:

This convention, representing what it believes to be the honest sentiment of the people of this state, and encouraged by the splendid success achieved in the recent state election, wherein the people, almost without organization, met and overthrew the combined power of the incorporated monopolists and the corrupt political and financial rings, does hereby resolve to organize into a party all good citizens who desire to join in the work of reform and political regeneration throughout the state, the better to enable them to move forward upon the enemy, to rout such corporations from their stronghold as rulers and practically as law makers, and, finally, to rescue the government from the clutches of the corporationists who have so long held it in subjection; therefore, be it resolved,

1. That the opponents of incorporated greed and organized corruption do form themselves into a political body, to be known as the people's independent party.

2. That one of the most serious obstacles in the way of political and governmental reform lies in the doctrine of so-called "party fealty," that tyranical rule which degrades the citizen and sinks him to the servile partisan, rendering him the helpless tool of selfish wire pullers and caucus manipulators. In view of this long-standing evil, the people's independent party now, in its very inception, once for all, lays down its fundamental principle that parties are mere instrumentalities to be employed only in the furtherance of good government; that they should be followed no longer than while they act in the interest of the entire people, of which fact each individual must judge for himself; and that it is the duty of the citizen to abandon instantly any party which swerves from the path of right or passes into the control of unscrupulous leaders, and finally it utterly spurns and repudiates the doctrine that any citizen owes

allegiance to any political organization, or that a pure and upright man in public life can or ought to be under special obligation to any source short of the people for office or position.

3. That one of the great evils which earnestly demands correction is the tyranny of party discipline, which, as maintained through the system of primaries and caucuses by professional politicians aided by governmental patronage and moneyed power, and has become a despotic rule of the few over the many, and that we hold and affirm that any citizen has the right to take part in good faith in the actions and deliberations of any political organization, caucus, or convention without being bound thereby except so far as his own judgment and conscience may approve, and that the obligations of the citizen and patriot are a paramount to those of the partisan before and after party nominations are made.

4. That we are determined to use all lawful efforts to drive out the corrupt political rings that control the action of the national government, wielding its power and dispensing its patronage with the sole end of benefiting themselves and their hangers-on, and of perpetuating their vicious rule; and to that end we hereby and for all time instruct all representatives of the people elected under the auspices of the people's independent party to urge and enforce a strict examination into the affairs and management of the great railroad corporations of the country as well as of their auxiliaries, the credit mobilier and contract and finance companies, and their several dealings with the various departments of the government, executive, legislative, and judicial, in order that their past corrupt practices may be exposed, the rights and property of the people recovered, the guilty punished, and purity and economy in administration and legislation be restored throughout the land.

5. That the abominable and infamous practice of securing election to office by the corrupt use of money at the polls, and in bribing members of legislative bodies, which has become so prevalent in late years, is an evil which strikes at the very foundation of free government, and that no man guilty of the atrocious crime of obtaining or attempting to obtain office by such means can ever merit the confidence of the people.

6. That affirming and asserting the absolute and final sovereignty of the people, we claim and will ever assert the right and authority of the people's representatives to control and regulate all such corporations as exercise any franchise or special privilege obtained by legislative enactment, and especially the incorporated common car-

riers of the country, and that such right of control and regulation is an undeniable prerogative of the state and nation; and, further, that we will use all lawful means to bring said corporations within a just and reasonable control, to reduce their rates of freight, fare, and charges to an equable and uniform standard, prohibiting all unjust discriminations and oppressive regulations leveled at localities or individuals, to overthrow their political power, and finally to reduce them to the legitimate purposes for which they were created and endowed, as the servants and beneficial aids and not the masters of the people. We further denounce the acceptance of free passes by public officers, and believe that it should be prohibited by law.

\ 7. That we are pledged to a thorough reform of the civil service of the country, to the end that capacity, honesty, and fitness, and not political zeal and partisanship, shall be the only indispensible qualifications for place. And especially we utterly oppose the pernicious custom now so common and so productive of evil of the interference of federal officials with state and local politics. And we denounce the law passed at the last session of congress, known as the "back pay steal," as a shame and disgrace to American legislation.

8. That we take ground absolutely against the system of land distribution now in vogue, whereby the public domain is granted away in vast tracts to railroad and other corporations or to private individuals, through the means or scrip and warrants issued under various pretenses, or by private entry on the part of non-resident speculators; that the true policy of the nation is to retain its public lands for the benefit of actual occupants upon the sole condition of residence thereon, in order to secure to each family a home.

9. That we are opposed to granting aid in subsidies of money, lands, bonds, or interest on bonds, to any railroad or other corporation, either by the federal, state, county, or municipal governments, and to all laws designed to procure any such subsidies under the specious plea of submitting to a vote of the people the question as to whether or not a particular subsidy shall be granted.

10. That we take ground against the present tariff, believing that it is the result of a dishonest and corrupt system of bargaining in congress, whereby each interest seeking protection conspires with all other interests to support them in their claim, to the great injury of the cause of good government and to the loss of the people, who are taxed thereby.

11. That in view of the climate of California, wherein rain falls only during a portion of the year, rendering irrigation an absolute necessity for the perfect development of the agricultural capabilities of our soil, we hold it to be the duty of the legislature to retain control of all rivers, lakes and other bodies of water, to prevent their appropriation and monopoly by speculators, and to form and perfect a system whereby they can be turned upon the land at the expense of the district benefited thereby, and for the use of the people residing on said land.

12. That the surest safeguard for the perpetuity of this government and the rights of the people must always be found in the education of the masses, therefore we will stand by the common school system, to maintain it in its integrity, as well as to urge and support all improvements in popular education that the most advanced spirit of the age may suggest or discover.

13. That we regard the primary election system, as now conducted, especially in the larger cities, as being practically a device which deprives the honest citizen of his political influence and clothes the demagogue with power; it has driven statesmen from our halls of legislation, and made political economy subservient to personal aggrandizement; it has subverted the design of our government by depriving the people of their constituent power to correct abuses, and rendered the ballot a snare to the unwary and a mockery of the elective franchise.

14. That all property, including solvent debts, as well as railroads and railroad property, should be taxed in proportion to its actual cash value, but taxation of solvent debts should be so regulated by law as to obviate all objection on the score of double taxation; and if this cannot be obtained by legislation under the constitution as it is, the fundamental law should be amended so as to accomplish such result.

15. That the legislatures of the state and nation should use all constitutional methods to facilitate commerce between the interior portions of the country and the sea; to cheapen freights and fares, as well as to increase the means of conveyance, in order that the produce of our farmers and products of our manufactures may be transported to market at the smallest possible cost.

16. That it is the duty of congress, as well as the state legislatures, to institute and enforce the strictest inquiry into the affairs and management of the railroad companies, and other corporations exercising franchises of a public nature, and to root out and put

down the pernicious practice of watering stock, whereby the people are oppressed by extortionate rates and charges in order to pay dividends upon capital which does not exist, and which only stands upon the books of the companies by fraud and false pretense.

17. That we are opposed to the election of a president of the United States for more than one term of four years, and we will support no man for congress who is not in favor of amending the constitution to accomplish that object.

18. That we are in favor of all reasonable measures of labor reform, and of maintaining and enforcing the eight-hour law in regard to manufacturing and mechanical pursuits, and upon all public works. .

19. That we are opposed to further influx of the mongolian race; to the further subsidizing of steamship lines for the purpose of enabling them to bring in this degraded class at mere nominal rates; and to this end we demand that the treaty with China, known as the Burlingame treaty, be abrogated, or modified to one for commercial purposes only; and that the whole moral and legal force of the state should be bent to this purpose, as the Chinese are a standing menace to the moral, physical, and pecuniary welfare of the people of this state.

20. That the manly and noble stand taken by Governor Newton Booth in behalf of the popular rights and against the encroachments of unscrupulous politicians and railroad corporations on the rights of the masses, has justly endeared him to the people of California, and that his official conduct and conscientious performance of his duty commend him to our grateful approval.

Elisha W. McKinstry was unanimously nominated for justice of the supreme court, to fill the unexpired term of Judge Sprague.

The following were selected to constitute a state central committee: John Bidwell, G. W. Bowie, A. S. Hallidie, T. A. Talbert, James Burney, C. E. Greene, James Johnson, D. W. Welty, J. G. Howell, E. Steele, C. P. Berry, William Jones, A. K. Dudley, W. C. Norton, G. W. Applegate, A. Delano, J. H. Carothers, J. F. Cowdery, D. B. Hoffman, Edgar Briggs, F. P. Dann, A. W. Poole, C. T. Ryland, and others. An executive committee was chosen, consisting of M. J. O'Conner, M. M. Estee, A. Helbing, A. J. Gunnison, M. C. Conroy, J. R. Sharpstein, Thomas Tobin, W. W. Dodge, James H. Hardy, C. C. Terrill, E. B. Mott, jr., A. P. Catlin, W. S. Manlove, and others.

The judicial election was held on Wednesday, October 15th, when McKinstry was elected justice of the supreme court, by a vote of 25,609, to 14,380 for Dwinelle, and 19,962 for McKee. Bronson received 11,446 votes for the supposed Crockett vacancy.

CHAPTER XXV.

1875. Republican Convention—Independent Convention—Democratic Convention—Prohibition Convention.

The republican state convention met at Sacramento on June 10th, and was called to order by Walter Van Dyke, the chairman of the state committee. A. A. Sargent was elected temporary chairman, by a vote of 238, to 111 for H. O. Beatty. The committee on resolutions consisted of George C. Gorham, W. H. Sears, Philip Teare, H. T. Dorrance, and others. In the evening a permanent organization was effected, by the selection of Sargent as president; and H. O. Beatty, H. S. Sargent, Solomon Jewett, A. G. Abell, and others as vice-presidents. The committee reported the following platform :

The republican party of California, in state convention assembled, reaffirming the state platform of 1871 and the national platform of 1872, makes the following additional declaration of principles :

1. That we have an undiminished confidence in the patriotism, wisdom, and integrity of the present chief magistrate of the United States, Ulysses S. Grant, and join our political brethren throughout the nation in cordial and earnest support to his administration, in fullest recognition of his illustrious career in the military and civil service, and in condemnation of that rancorous party spirit which prompts his and our enemies to the unconsidered and unjust attacks upon him as those to which his great predecessors, Washington, Jackson, and Lincoln were subjected during their administrations.

2. That the letter addressed by the president to the chairman of the Pennsylvania republican state convention upon the subject of the succession is a full and complete refutation of the slanders of those who charged him with intriguing for a re-election, and that we accept it as an explicit and final settlement of the third-term agitation created by the enemy solely to arouse jealousies and dissensions in the republican party.

3. That the thirteenth, fourteenth, and fifteenth amendments to the constitution of the United States, added to that instrument by the votes of the requisite three-fourths of the states of this union, are as sacred and binding as are any of its provisions, and that they are to be maintained by the enforcement of all proper congressional enactments, notwithstanding the opposition, secret or avowed, of the democratic party, or of hostile white leagues in the southern states.

4. That the conduct of that portion of the people in the south, who defy the fifteenth amendment, and seek by intimidation or force to prevent the lawful exercise of the elective franchise by the great body of colored citizens resident therein, is a rebellious defiance of the national authority. An attempt to prevent the election of the next president by the people is calculated to arouse the worst passions of men, and to disturb the peace of the nation, and should be met by all law-abiding citizens, both north and south, as an effort to revive the flames of civil war. While admitting that honest differences of opinion exist as to the extent of this conspiracy against the fair and constitutional election of a president in 1876, we deem it well to caution the people against slumbering in the face of danger.

5. That with all our countrymen, of whatever section, who yield obedience to the constitution and the laws, and who do not defend or justify those who disobey them, we desire to cultivate fraternal relations, without regard to mere party differences, and we will at all times unite with them to promote justice, order, and public tranquility.

6. That the cost of the state and several county governments can, and ought to be, reduced one-half, and to that work the next legislature should address itself. This can be done by a comprehensive re-adjustment of the public business, a curtailment, of the large list of officers and their employes; such a reduction of salaries and fees as will place public servants on a footing, as to compensation, with persons in private business, and incidentally abate the almost universal preference for public over private employment; honesty and economy in the maintenance of the various institutions of the state; a total abandonment of the practice of voting the people's money to institutions which were called into existence without state action; and by additional checks and safeguards to render official peculation difficult of concealment, and surer of punishment when discovered.

7. That the burden of taxation should not only be reduced, but

the laws concerning assessment and equalization should be so revised and amended as to better insure a just division of that burden among those who enjoy the benfits of government; and that in aid of the law a wholesome public opinion should be cultivated against all who seek to evade their just proportion of taxation, and in favor of swift and certain punishment alike of citizens and officials who by fraudulent and corrupt practices may offend against the law.

8. That the republican party will aid the development of the resources of the state by all legitimate means, and as it is apparent that the agricultural capabilities of large sections cannot be fully shown unless some practical system of irrigation is adopted, the republican party demands of the legislature that it assume control of the waters of the various lakes and rivers, subject only to mining and mechanical rights, and provide for its distribution over the largest possible area of irrigable land, by the adoption of a comprohensive system that shall make the canals and irrigation works to be constructed for this purpose a part and portion of the realty of the various districts, to be wholly subject to the control and management of the owners of the irrigable land therein.

9. That the freedom of the state from ecclesiastical control is of equal importance with the maintenance of religious freedom from state control; that the common school system is an institution of the state, established as a preventive of the crime and poverty which attend ignorance, and we will tolerate no interference with it from any quarter; and that any effort to divide the school fund for the purpose of supporting sectarian schools with a portion thereof, shall be met with all the resistance in our power.

10. (*a*) That the Central Pacific railroad company is a state corporation, and as such is amenable to the laws of the state concerning corporations. (*b*) That the relations of that company to the nation are simply those of agent and principal, and debtor and creditor, so far as their property within this state is concerned. (*c*) That the power of the state over the said corporation, so far from having been surrendered by the act of the legislature of April 4, 1864, as claimed by that company, was rather affirmed thereby, in these words: "Said company to be subject to all the laws of this state concerning railroad and telegraph lines." (*d*) That the right to regulate fares and freights, whenever it exists, is a condition annexed to the franchise, and is necessarily vested in the government by which the franchise has been granted. The right to collect

22

tolls is one of the essential franchises of railroad corporations, and
the power to regulate them is simply a power to regulate the franchise under which they are collected, and the power must be exercised by the authority creating the corporation.   (e) That the existence of the Central Pacific railroad corporation, and its right to
operate its roads in California, rests exclusively upon the authority of
state law, and that its national-character is limited to certain functions, which it derived, by the state's consent, from congress—such
as the right to operate its road outside of the state, and to create
liens upon its entire line in favor of the national government and
other creditors.   (f) That as a necessary result of the foregoing,
while. congress has the right to regulate tolls over the road, on
through and inter-state traffic, the state legislature has absolute and
exclusive power to regulate the rates of freights and fares between
all points within the state.   (g) That experience has shown that
railroad companies, when left uncontrolled, naturally look exclusively to their own interests, and often disregard the interests and
convenience of the public they were created to serve, whereby
unreasonable rates of fares and freights have been, and are still
imposed, unjust discrimination made against communities and
classes of merchandise; and many settlements and towns incon-
venienced, and even severely injured, for the building up of the
localities in which members of the companies are interested.   (h)
That we recommend that the people should exact in advance from
candidates for the legislature unequivocal pledges.   First, that they
will, if elected, vote for such a reduction of freights and fares as
will leave to the railroad companies a fair income upon the actual
cost of constructing the roads, and allow for maintaining and operating the same, and enable them to meet their just obligations;
second, that they will, to that end, institute a thorough investigation into the affairs of the corporations, as they have ample power
to do, in order to ascertain the real cost of the construction of the
roads and the annual outlays for maintaining and operating the
same; third, that they will, in adjusting a tariff of freights and
fares, abolish all unfair discrimination between the same classes of
merchandise, and equalize the rates between different localities,
having due regard for grade and curves.   (i) That while the
republican party disclaims any sympathy with indiscriminate war
upon associated capital, with a blind disregard of its rights, it is
entirely independent of all corporate power; it is opposed to all
schemes in state, county or city, whereby, under the pretext of pro-

viding gas and water to communities, or irrigation for farming, a few men seek to enrich themselves by imposing heavy burdens upon the people; it repels all attempts of corporations to force into office, through republican conventions, men who will guard their interests rather than those of the public, and expects to be judged by its acts, and the character of its candidates, rather than by the false accusations of its enemies, who, after having had the executive power of the state for the past eight years equally divided between them, can present no better claim for the public confidence than loud and empty professions of horror at alleged corruptions and profligacy in public affairs, which they themselves have managed and controlled.

11. That we earnestly invite the co-operation of the great farming interests of the state in the reduction of the cost of transportation, the reduction and equalization of taxes, and the inauguration of a plan for irrigation, by representatives of their own selection in the legislature.

12. That, confident of the substantial agreement on national and state questions of all who sustained the nation during the great civil war, regretting the alienations among republicans, which have been too apparent during the past few years, desirous of making all becoming concessions to secure harmony, we cordially invite all who are opposed to the restoration to power of the democratic party, to forget the strifes of faction, to disregard the counsels of those who seek to continue unseemly and unnecessary division, and, keeping in view the overwhelming importance of the approaching presidential election, aid in reuniting the republican party of the state, and securing a victory for the cause of republicanism and real reform.

The resolutions were taken up *seriatim.* The first resolution was adopted without opposition. The following was offered as a substitute for the second

That it has become a part of the unwritten law of the land, that no man should be elected for more than two terms to the office of president of the United States.

The substitute was lost by a pronounced vote, and the original resolution adopted. The following was added to the ninth: "That all citizens, without distinction of race or color, are entitled to equal advantages of public school education."

The following was offered as a substitute for the tenth resolution:

That with respect to railroad companies and other corporations, we reassert the resolution passed by the republican state convention in 1871, viz.: That we are opposed to any further subsidies in land or money to such corporations; that corporations are creatures of legislation, and are entitled only to those rights guaranteed them by the constitution and the laws; that while they should be protected in those rights, they should not be allowed to trespass beyond their chartered privileges upon the rights of the people; that it is the duty of the legislature to enforce a fair and reasonable exercise of corporate privileges; but that it is not wise or politic to force corporations into politics by resolutions pointedly hostile to them and their just interests.

The substitute was lost, 113 to 250, and the resolutions as reported were adopted. The following additional resolution was also adopted :

That the republican party of California is opposed to double taxation in every shape, and we favor such reform measures as will remedy the evil, believing that every person should only be taxed on what he owns, and not on what he owes.

The following ticket was nominated :

Timothy G. Phelps, for governor, without opposition, Romualdo Pacheco withdrawing.

Joseph M. Cavis, for lieutenant-governor, without opposition.

Edward Hallett, for secretary of state, without opposition, Drury Melone withdrawing.

James J. Green, for Controller, without opposition.

Robert Gardner, for surveyor-general, on the first ballot, over William H. Norway.

William Beckman, for treasurer, on the first ballot, over Jonas Marcuse.

E. D. Sawyer, for attorney-general, without opposition, L. B. Mizner withdrawing.

Grant I. Taggart, for clerk of the supreme court, without opposition.

Ezra S. Carr, for school superintendent, without opposition,

A state committee was selected, consisting of Jarrett R. Richards, William Sharkey, F. K. Shattuck, James A. Duffy, W. S. Wells, William Jennings, M. C. Andross, James E. Hale, A. D. Splivalo, S. E. Jewett, M. D. Boruck, A. G. Abell, Louis Sloss, A. Briggs, O. N. Fox, and others.

The first district convention met at San Francisco on August 9th, and on the first ballot nominated Ira P. Rankin for congressman, by a vote of 59, to 4 for Frank Soule.

The second district convention met at Sacramento on June 9th, and nominated H. F. Page for congressman, without opposition. The following resolutions were there adopted :

That the republicans of the second congressional district recognize in the brief congressional record of the Hon. H. F. Page a series of acts, important alike to the people of the district, state and nation; reflecting distinguished honor upon himself, and the party who confided to his care the high trust of representative. That his successful exertions in obtaining the restoration of government lands upon the Folsom and Placerville and the Stockton and Copperopolis railroads (the former alone estimated to be of the value of three million dollars), the passage of an act for the relief of settlers within the limits of forfeited railroad grants, obtaining appropriations for the improvement of Oakland harbor, the act to prevent the immigration of Chinese coolies into the country, to prevent Chinese naturalization, to prevent straw bids for United States mail contracts (thereby saving to the government, according to the last report of the postmaster-general, about three million dollars for the period of four years), his votes for the reduction of salaries, the repeal of the mileage law, his vote upon the bill which provided for the regulation of the price of transportation upon interstate railroads, and his votes against subsidies of every kind, form a record of honesty, ability and usefulness, which commends him to the fullest confidence of the people of the district and state. That we recognize his votes on the civil rights, force and bounty bills as being in harmony with the principles of the republican party, as enunciated in the state platform of 1871.

The third district convention met at Washington, Yolo county, on June 9th, and C. B. Denio was nominated for congressman, without opposition, Jesse O. Goodwin and J. A. Hutton withdrawing.

The fourth district convention met at San Jose, on June 14th, and Sherman O. Houghton was nominated for congressman, without opposition.

The independent state convention met at Sacramento, on June 22d, and was called to order by W. W. Dodge, chairman of the state committee. C. T. Hopkins was elected temporary chairman.

A committee on resolutions was selected, consisting of John F. Swift, W. C. Bartlett, J. S. Thompson, T. J. Sherwood, W. S. Montgomery, John Bidwell, F. S. Freeman, Noble Martin, and others. On permanent organization, Henry Edgerton was president; and D. B. Hoffman, Samuel Soule, Seneca Ewer, William Johnston, T. M. Ames, and others, vice-presidents. The committee on resolutions made the following report :

Whereas, The bitter dissensions that have divided the citizens of California into opposite parties, upon purely national questions, for so many years, having passed away with the civil war and the reconstruction measures growing out of the war, it has become obvious that serious local evils are weighing heavily upon the people of this state, requiring our earnest and thoughtful attention, lest they become, through our indifference, perpetual ; and whereas, the so-called national parties in California have fallen into the control, in a large measure, of the more worthless elements of society, managed in the interest of certain powerful corporations and associations of individuals, who systematically seek to accumulate wealth at the public expense, through and by means of the machinery of government, until affairs have reached a point where the people can no longer safely trust the political control of the state to either of them; therefore, resolved :

1. That the people's independent party seeks to unite together the honest and law-abiding citizens of all portions of California, irrespective of class, local, or business distinctions, and regardless of religious or previous political opinions, for the purpose of bringing about a thorough system of reform in state, county, and municipal governments generally, and especially with the view of securing retrenchment in public expenditures and consequent reduction in taxation ; the regulation and control of all corporations exercising franchises of a public nature, the reduction to reasonable rates of fares and freights on railroads, as well as steamboats operated in conjunction with railroads; and the prevention and punishment of unjust discriminations by railroad and other corporations against localities and against individuals; the securing from the power or possibility of monopoly the natural waters of the rivers, streams, and lakes of the state, and revesting them once more in the people; the rescue of the inhabitants of our cities and towns from the oppressive power of water and gas companies, and other kindred monopolies; the purification of the administration of justice throughout

the state, by reforming the grand jury system so that powerful crim. inals may be punished as well as weak, and generally to secure such improved legislation in the interest of good government as wisdom and an honest purpose of reform may suggest.

2. That for the more perfect accomplishment of the foregoing ends, this convention, composed of delegates representing all parts of California, pledges the "people's independent party," and its nom. inees for office throughout the state, to support and carry out by all lawful and proper means, the policy and purposes of the party as set forth in this platform.

3. That to this end the agricultural and mining counties of the interior hereby enter into a solemn league and covenant to and with the cities, and the cities pledge themselves as solemnly to the counties of the interior, that all officers, executive, legislative, and judi. cial, elected by this party, in any part of California, shall in good faith endeavor, in their official capacity, lawfully to remedy the grievances of the people, not only such as are peculiar to their own special constituencies or locality, but of all other portions of the state as well.

4. That we repeat and reaffirm the principles of the party, as laid down and resolved upon by the judicial convention of the people's independent party, held at Sacramento, in September, A. D. 1873, and make them a portion of this platform as fully as if herein set forth at large.

Whereas, Through improvident and inconsiderate legislation, the funds generously appropriated by the nation, and materially increased by our state, its cities and counties, to aid in constructing the Pacific railroad, have been so employed that a small number of individuals, acting in corporate capacity, now own and control the only transcontinental railroad in the country, together with almost the entire railroad system of the state, as well as the river steamers and ferry boats plying upon our interior waters, thereby practically monopolizing not only the entire overland traffic, but likewise the general carrying trade of the state and coast; and, whereas, the corporations controlling these railroads and steamboats possess and exercise the power to arbitrarily make, levy, and collect their rates of freights and passenger fare, and to exact and enforce rules and regulations at their own pleasure; and, whereas, it is apparent that there can be no final relief from the excessive charges and unjust discriminations of the railroad corporations through competition, because of their vast wealth and power, which are invariably used to break down all rival enterprises, and to ruin the projectors, and failing in that, then to combine with them against the people ; and, whereas, in order to retain this power to fix rates, and to discriminate at pleasure, and to prevent any legislative relief from being extended to the people, the railroad corporations have, in the past, systematically intermeddled with and corrupted the politics of the state, using their wealth and influence to elevate scheming men, and in many instances their interested partisans, and to place them in the legislature and other stations of trust where they could vote away the people's rights, until the domination of the railroad and other corporations in our politics and government has become an intolerable evil ; therefore, resolved :

5. That there is and can be no safety to good government, to capital, or to production, so long as the corporations engaged in transportation by railroad and steamboat in this state possess the power, independently of the law, to make their own rules and regulations, or to establish and collect tolls and rates of freight and fare at their own unrestricted will and pleasure.

6. That the rates of freight and fare charged and collected upon the railroads of California, and upon the steamboats owned and operated in connection with them, in most places where there is no competition, are unjust, unequal, and excessively high. And that the power now exercised by the railroad corporations in making their rules and regulations, as well as their said rates, is exercised in an unjust and oppressive manner, to the injury of individuals and localities, as well as the general productive interests of the state.

7. That the people's independent party hereby pledges its nominees for office throughout the state, to reduce said rates of freight and fare, by law, to a just and fair standard, based upon the actual cost of the road and the expenses of operation; and also to the enactment of laws to prevent and punish all manner of unjust discriminations against individuals or localities, and generally to reduce the railroad corporations to the supervision and control of the laws of the land.

8. That while we seek by all lawful means to drive the railroad corporations out of politics, and to protect the people by wise and calmly considered laws from extortion and unjust discrimination at their hands, yet we fully acknowledge the great value to the community of a properly constructed and justly managed system of rail-

roads, and will ever stand ready to accord due appreciation and generous treatment to those who so construct and manage them.

9. That we favor the construction of all independent lines of competing railroads, to connect the Atlantic states with California, provided they be built and operated in the interest of the people, and not solely in that of the monopolists, as is the case with the railroads now existing in this state.

Whereas, In certain parts of the state irrigation of the soil is absolutely essential to the proper development of our agricultural interests; therefore, resolved:

10. That to this end the waters of the lakes and rivers of the state should be and remain forever in the ownership and control of the public, and never allowed upon any pretence to become the subject of private monopoly.

11. That the separation of the proprietorship of the land from that of the water necessary for its irrigation, is fraught with danger, not only to the agriculturists, but to the entire commonwealth, and should be discouraged by law.

12. That the legislature should speedily enact proper laws to encourage and favor irrigation in the agricultural districts of the state wherever needed, and to prevent the monopoly by speculators of the natural waters necessary thereto, at the same time having due regard for the wants of the mining localities, and fostering and protecting the just rights of those engaged in mining pursuits.

Whereas, The Spring Valley water company is a corporation which has been permitted by the legislature to obtain a practical monopoly of the fresh water within and adjacent to the city and county of San Francisco, so that it now claims control of all the sources of water supply within an area of 180 miles of the chief city of the state; and, whereas, said corporation was allowed to obtain said monopoly upon the express condition specified in the law authorizing its existence, that it would supply the inhabitants of said city and county with pure, fresh water for domestic uses, at reasonable rates, and likewise, that it would furnish the municipal government thereof with water in case of fire, or other great necessity, free of charge; and, whereas, said Spring Valley water company has willfully violated the conditions set forth in its said charter, amongst other things, by extorting from the inhabitants of said city and county excessive and enormous rates for water for domestic uses, so that in said city and county it has come to pass that the

∖ water necessary for a family costs more than their bread, while the rates charged for manufacturing purposes make it so expensive as to be a grievous burden upon productive industry; therefore, resolved:

13. That this convention pledges the people's independent party and its nominees throughout the state, if elected, to join with the representatives from the city and county of San Francisco, in their efforts to place said corporation, and all other water companies in the state, under just control of the law, to reduce and fix its rates so that they shall be reasonable to the inhabitants of the said city and county, and so that in no event shall said corporation levy or collect any rate for water beyond what shall be necessary to pay interest upon the actual capital invested in the construction of said works and the purchase of land, disregarding all watered stock or sham and pretended outlays of money.

Whereas, The greatest obstacle to the construction of a proper system of water-works for our cities and towns, and especially for the city and county of San Francisco, is to be found in the bands of organized schemers and corruptionists who infest the state, and who, through the vicious laws now upon our statute books providing for the appropriation of lakes and water courses, by corporations for speculative purposes, seize upon or make claim to all the waters within convenient distance of any town or city, and then by fraud and corruption induce the municipal authorities to buy them out at enormous and exaggerated prices; nor is this the sole and only danger: The speculators do not hesitate to influence the elections, and to corrupt the politics of the state, so as to secure the election of officers favorable to their purposes, sheltering themselves and their schemes under the false pretense of supposed benefits to the public, which they are only seeking to despoil; therefore, resolved:

14. That this party and its nominees throughout the state are pledged to oppose all attempts on the part of any water company, corporation and individual, to sell any water-works scheme or pretended water rights to the city of San Francisco, or to any town or city of this state, at a price in excess of the money or capital actually expended by such company or individual in land and works, exclusive of the supposed value of any water right, disconnected from the ownership in fee simple of land; it being a cardinal principle with the people's independent party that the fresh water in the rivers and lakes of this state, as well as the rains that descend from the clouds, belongs of right to the whole people, and that any ownership

or monopoly of it by any corporation or person, beyond what they shall put to some beneficial use, is a wrong to the entire community.

Whereas, The city of San Francisco has been for years suffering from the exactions of the San Francisco gas company, a corporation which, by issuing bonds or stock from time to time to buy off opposition and to prevent competition, as well as by watering its stock many times over in order to conceal its enormous earnings, has increased its capital to a sum vastly beyond the real value of its works, but yet, nevertheless, continues to charge excessive prices for gas, and to pay dividends upon this pretended capital, greatly to the injury of the inhabitants of said city and county; therefore, resolved :

15. That the people's independent party and its nominees are pledged to the enactment of laws regulating the quality and illuminating power of gas furnished by said company, and by all gas companies in this state, as well as the price thereof, so that gas shall be furnished at such a rate as shall afford a fair profit upon the cost of production and distribution of the same, and no more.

Whereas, The expenses of the government of the state of California, its cities, counties, and towns, have been allowed to greatly exceed the expenses of other states, cities, counties, and towns in this union, by reason of the payment of salaries in excess of the earnings of citizens engaged in private business pursuits, as well as by the prevalence of a spirit of improvidence, and even jobbery, in many of the departments, until the weight of taxation rests heavily upon the masses of the people; therefore, resolved:

16. That this party is pledged to a general retrenchment in public expenditures, and a reduction of official salaries throughout the state, and in the cities and counties.

17. That the people's independent party pledges its nominees to endeavor to secure a repeal of all laws permitting public officers, upon any pretence whatever, to collect fees for their own use or benefit; and further, to require their payment, in all cases where collected, into the public treasury.

18. That the people's independent party stands by the constitution of the state, which provides that taxation shall be equal and uniform, and that all property should be taxed once, and no more; and that any law which taxes the same capital in any form more than once, is a law of discrimination, and should be repealed.

Whereas, It is of paramount importance that each and every citizen, whether rich or poor, shall be made to bear his just share of taxation to support the government under which he lives, and in proportion to his wealth and no more; and, whereas, it has been found in practice that assessors have in some instances arbitrarily decreased the assessments of favored individuals at the expense of the general community, thereby inflicting an injury striking at the very foundation of our system of government ; therefore, resolved :

19. That this party is pledged to use all lawful means, by the enactment of proper statutes and otherwise, to eradicate and put an end to this vicious practice.

20. That this party is pledged to a thorough and careful revision of the laws regulating the qualifications of grand and petit juries, and to a reform in the method of drawing the same, to the end that powerful criminals, and especially corrupt public officers and those tampering with them, may be punished, and confidence in the administration of public justice maintained.

21. That the people's independent party re-affirms with increased emphasis the principle that individual conscience, and not party discipline, is the only guide to the voter who in good faith seeks reform in government; and further, that we ask no one to vote for any candidate upon the people's ticket upon the sole ground that such candidate is the party nominee, but, on the contrary, assert it as the paramount duty of all citizens to scrutinize the work of this and all other conventions with care, and to repudiate and vote against any candidate whose past life or character justify them in believing he will be false to the people and the principles of good government.

22. That the sole purpose of the people's independent party in placing candidates before the people of California for election this year is that of securing needed reforms in this state, and that the objects of said party sought to be obtained in the movement for better local government are in no wise dependent upon the question whether there will or will not be an independent national party or an independent nomination for president in 1876; and that the vote of any citizen for the nominees of the people's independent party of California in 1875 does not foreshadow or have any manner of significance or bearing upon the question of national politics or the contest for president, but that each citizen will be free to vote and act when that time shall arrive as his conscience may dictate.

A motion was lost to strike out that portion relative to the gas and water rates of San Francisco, as was also a motion to strike out the last resolution.

The following was introduced and lost:

That no man should be removed from appointed office for political opinion's sake, and that the political dogma, that to the victors belong the spoils, is demoralizing and pernicious.

The following resolution was offered and withdrawn, after debate:

That the public school system is worthy of the commendation and support of every American citizen, and should be maintained on the basis of free unsectarian schools and an undivided fund.

The platform as reported was adopted.

The following nominations were made on the 23d:

For governor, John Bidwell, M. M. Estee, and A. P. Catlin were named. On the first ballot, Bidwell had 106; Catlin, 86; and Estee, 92. Estee then withdrew. On the third ballot, Bidwell was nominated, by a vote of 197, to 79 for Catlin.

Romualdo Pacheco, for lieutenant-governor, without opposition.

For secretary of state, the candidates were James O. Carey and William Roush. After the first ballot, Carey was declared to be the nominee, but it was afterward ascertained that there had been a miscount of the votes, and on motion of Carey, the nomination was given to Rousch.

Lauren E. Crane, for controller, without opposition.

Ferdinand Baehr, for treasurer, without opposition.

Peter Van Clief, for attorney-general, on the first ballot, over John Lord Love.

Edward Twitchell, for surveyor-general, on the second ballot, over John F. Wade and A. S. Easton.

Paul Morrill, for clerk of the supreme court, without opposition.

J. M. Guinn, for school superintendent, without opposition; Ezra S. Carr, James O. Carey, G. R. Kelley, Joseph LeConte, and John Swett being withdrawn.

A state committee was selected, consisting of A. S. Hallidie, Peter Dean, J. F. Linthicum, E. B. Mott, jr., J. K. Doak, A. Maurice, S. M. Buck, T. J. Sherwood, D. B. Hoffman, J. F. Cowdery, and others.

The first district convention met at San Francisco on July 1st, and nominated John F. Swift for congressman, without opposition.

The second district convention met at Sacramento on June 23d, and nominated Charles A. Tuttle for congressman, without opposition.

\ The third district convention met at Sacramento on June 23d, and nominated Charles F. Reed for congressman, without opposition. The name of Luttrell was proposed in the convention, but it was not considered, as a telegram was read from him stating that he would abide by the democratic convention for his endorsement.

The fourth district convention met at Santa Barbara on July 14th, and J. S. Thompson was nominated for congressman, without opposition.

The democratic state convention met at San Francisco on June 29th. It was called to order by J. P. Hoge, chairman of the state committee. John G. Downey was elected temporary chairman on the first ballot, by a vote of 175, to 147 for Leander Quint. · The committee on platform consisted of E. J. Lewis, J. R. Jarboe, Niles Searls, James T. Farley, G. J. Carpenter, Eugene Casserly,. and Frank McCoppin. On the 30th, a permanent organization was effected by the election of Downey as president; and L. Archer, J. T. Farley, E. J. Lewis, A. F. Coronel, A. M. Rosborough, C. H. Mitchell, George W. Henley, and others, vice-presidents. The committee reported the following resolutions, which were unanimously adopted :

The democratic party of California, in state convention assembled, in compliance with usage, do assert the following principles as the basis of their political action, and pledge the candidates about to be nominated to their hearty support. We declare :

1. That we are opposed to the unconstitutional interference of the federal administration in the domestic affairs of the states, by which one portion of the union is ground with taxation to keep another portion of the union in a state of bankruptcy and servitude.

2. We condemn the republican party, not only for its contempt of constitutional obligations, but for its extravagant, partisan, and corrupt administration of the federal government; for the perversion of the functions of the latter to enrich great corporations at the expense of the public; for the jobbery and frauds which have brought re-

proach upon democratic institutions; for the Sanborn and Jayne frauds; for the infamous Washington ring; for the back-pay steal; the iniquities of the protective system; the curse of inconvertible paper money; the nepotism of the president; for its disgraceful diplomatic service, and unfit appointments; for its attempts to pass an unconstitutional force bill, which were fortunately frustrated by the determined front of the democratic minority in both houses of congress; and for a catalogue of other enormities which have rendered that organization offensive even to the mass of those who were once its supporters.

3. That now, as at all periods, we are in favor of a strict construction of the constitution, and against the exercise of doubtful powers; in favor of limiting the powers of legislative bodies; in favor of a tariff for revenue only, and a currency convertible into gold and silver at the will of the holder; against the profligate and wasteful system of local improvements by the federal government, and in favor of reducing the expenditures of the state government, and of the counties and towns, and the salaries of officials, which have been largely increased since the state election of 1871.

4. That the school system and fund of this state are under the guarantee of the constitution inviolable, and we are opposed to any diversion of the fund to any purposes except those ordained by the constitution.

5. We assert the traditional policy of the democratic party, in declaring that it is the right and duty of the legislature to regulate corporations, whether railway, gas, telegraph, water, or otherwise; to limit their charges in the interest of the public, and to compel them to serve all citizens without discrimination, and at reasonable rates; and that when they refuse to do so, we recognize the right and declare the intention of making them do so; and we further assert it to be the duty of the government to preserve the waters of the state for irrigation and other public uses, instead of permitting them to be made the means of extortion and monopoly.

6. That the democratic party has no occasion to make any new departure or declaration of opposition to the system of subsidies, when we recall the fact that it is to a democratic state administration that this state owes its deliverance from this oppressive, unjust, and corrupting system.

7. That we are in favor of calling a convention of delegates elected by the people, to amend the constitution of the state, as the only mode of creating a system of government at once harmonious and

efficient, and are therefore opposed to the amendments to the constitution proposed.

8. That the time-honored democratic doctrine of local self-government is sufficient when properly administered to afford an efficient remedy for the evils now caused by Chinese labor, and the presence among us of an inferior race, detrimental to our moral and physical health; that in the interest of all classes in California, especially that of the white working people, we demand such amendment to the Burlingame treaty as shall reduce it to a mere commercial convention.

9. That we condemn the doctrine whereby the power of the state to prevent the importation to our shores of degraded persons for immoral purposes has been denied.

10. That we favor the speedy completion of a trans-continental railway on the thirty-second parallel, subject to such limitations by the federal and state governments as shall protect the rights of the people.

11. That we are in favor of equal taxation, and any departure from this principle, or any system of taxation which imposes a double tax upon the same object, is in violation of the spirit of the constitution and unjust to the best interests of the state.

12. That all legislation intended to regulate the social habits and customs of the people, so long as those habits and customs do not interfere with the welfare of society at large, and all legislation of the character known by the general name of prohibitory laws, is opposed to the principles of the democratic party, and is calculated to promote a pretense of social morality rather than a well-founded system of public order and decency.

13. That we invite the hearty co-operation of all persons, whatever may have been their past political affinities, to unite with us in carrying out the principles herein enunciated.

14. That we condemn, as subversive of the rights of the people, and ruinous to the best interests of the state, the policy of permitting the lands of the state to become a monopoly in the hands of the few at the expense of the many, and we hereby pledge the democratic party to the correction of this giant evil.

For governor, Thomas Findley, James A. Johnson, William Irwin, C. T. Ryland, and Philip A Roach were named. Irwin was nominated on the seventh ballot. On the first ballot, four votes were cast for John S. Hager. The ballots were as follows:

	1	2	3	4	5	6	7
Findley	87	90	91	94	92	92	75
Johnson	53	54	61	59	54	43	19
Irwin................................	104	109	117	119	128	141	193
Ryland	63	70	76	73	71	67	58
Roach	34	22	Withdrawn.				

For lieutenant-governor, James A. Johnson, R. O. Haile, George Pearce, Frank McCoppin, Marion Biggs (declined), and A. C. Bradford were named. First ballot—Johnson, 119; Pearce, 44; McCoppin, 92; Bradford, 50; Haile, 37. During the second ballot Haile and Pearce withdrew, and Johnson was nominated by a vote of 194, to 143 for McCoppin, and 6 for Bradford.

The following additional nominations were made:

Thomas Beck for secretary of state, on the first ballot, by a vote of 182, to 157 for W. B. C. Brown.

J. W. Mandeville for controller, on the first ballot, by a vote of 214, to 37 for O. C. Coleman, 64 for Joseph Roberts, and 11 for R. Gibbons.

J. G. Estudillo for treasurer, on the first ballot, by a vote of 175, to 18 for J. M. Estudillo, of Alameda, 40 for Juan B. Castro, 8 for Otto Kloppenburg, and 103 for A. G. Escandon.

Jo Hamilton for attorney-general, on the first ballot, by a vote of 180, to 165 for Thomas P. Ryan.

William Minis for surveyor-general, on the first ballot, over T. J. Shackleford, G. W. Smith, W. Neely Johnson, G. Howard Thompson, and William A. Ord.

On July 1st, the following additional nominations were made:

D. Barney Woolf for clerk of the supreme court, on the first ballot, over L. C. Branch, W. R. Hinkson, and Sands W. Forman.

O. P. Fitzgerald for school superintendent, without opposition.

A state committee was selected, consisting of E. J. Lewis, Joseph F. Black, Caleb Dorsey, W. B. C. Brown, J. B. Lamar, P. H. Ryan, H. J. Glenn, W. M. Gwin, jr., Peter Donahue, J. B. Campbell, C. H. Mitchell, Paul Shirley, J. W. Satterwhite, C. T. Ryland, Thomas Findley, Eugene Casserly, L. Quint, P. A. Roach, R. A. Thompson, A. H. Rose, D. S. Terry, J. P. Hoge, and others.

The first district democratic convention met at San Francisco, on

July 6th, J. O. Shorb, Mark L. McDonald, Robert Ferral, and W. A. Piper were named for congressman. Ferral withdrew, and Piper was nominated on the first ballot, by a vote of ·35, to 9 for McDonald, and 10 for Shorb.

The second district convention met at San Francisco, on June 30th, and Henry Larkin was nominated for congressman, on the first ballot, by a vote of 47, to 41 for A. W. Roysdon.

The third district convention met at San Francisco, on June 29th, and J. K. Luttrell was nominated for congressman, without opposition.

The fourth district convention met at San Francisco, on July 2d, and P. D. Wigginton was nominated for congressman, on the first ballot, by a vote of 47, to 24 for B. D. Wilson, and 16 for Charles H. Johnson.

The state convention of the temperance reform party met at San Francisco, on June 30th. The body embraced about one hundred delegates, representing nearly every county in the state. A number of the delegates were ladies. The convention was called to order by W. E. Lovett, chairman of the state committee. Joel Russell was elected president. Resolutions were adopted favoring economy in the administration of the government; remonstrating against the monopoly of lands by speculators; favoring the increase of railroad facilities, but opposing subsidies; demanding for the whole country a real, changeable currency, and the enforcement of all laws tending to the recognition of equal rights of all citizens. The platform also set forth the evils of intemperance; demanded a license tax of at least $30 per month; opposed the sale of liquors in groceries; favored a mingling of physical labor with school studies; demanded the establishment of mechanical and agricultural colleges in connection with the university; favored an eight hour law, and all societies formed by the masses; demanded congressional interference to prevent Chinese labor; claimed that mechanics and laboring men should be represented in congress by their own class; asserted that taxes should be paid upon luxuries, and that the revenue should be drawn from accumulated capital rather than from the current products of labor; opposed legislation restricting commerce; demanded that cities be vested with the right to control their own affairs; favored a transfer of the city front to the municipality; deprecated the abuse of capital; demanded a sailors' home, and opposed convict labor.

For governor, the names of John Bidwell and W. E. Lovett were presented. A dispatch was read from Bidwell, in answer to one asking him to accept the nomination, in which he said: "I stand upon the people's independent platform. Believe firmly in temperance. Will accept no further nomination." Lovett was nominated by a vote of 63, to 34 for Bidwell.

The following additional nominations were made, without opposition:

J. V. Goodrich, for lieutenant-governor.

W. H. Baxter, for secretary of state.

Joel Russell, for controller.

George B. Katzenstein, for surveyor-general.

C. P. Thompson, for treasurer.

G. W. Anthony, for clerk of the supreme court.

Ezra S. Carr, for school superintendent.

R. E. Thompson, for attorney-general.

No nominations were made for congressmen.

On July 16th, Goodrich, Baxter, and Anthony declined their nominations, and on the 22d, the state committee nominated W. D. Hobson for lieutenant-governor, E. H. Hallett for secretary of state, and Grant I. Taggart for clerk of the supreme court.

The general state election was held on September 1st, and the result was as follows:

For Governor—Phelps, 31,322; Irwin, 61,509; Bidwell, 29,752; Lovett, 356.

Lieutenant-Governor—Oavis, 30,932; Johnson, 58,424; Pacheco, 33,335; Hobson, 242.

Secretary of State—Hallett, 34,174; Beck, 59,746; Roush, 28,772.

Controller—Green, 36,901; Mandeville, 57,064; Orane, 28,535; Russell, 262.

Treasurer—Beckman, 34,222; Estudillo, 59,090; Baehr, 29,042; Thompson, 258.

Attorney-General—Sawyer, 34,002; Hamilton, 60,915; Van Clief, 27,769.

Surveyor-General—Gardner, 35,098; Minis, 59,677; Twitchell, 27,816.

Clerk of the Supreme Court—Taggart, 34,642; Woolf, 59,723; Morrill, 28,569.

Congressmen: First district—Piper, 12,417; Rankin, 6,791; Swift, 6,103.

Second district—Page, 13,624; Larkin, 12,154; Tuttle, 5,589.

Third district—Luttrell, 18,468; Denio, 14,284; Reed, 6,770.

Fourth district—Wigginton, 15,649; Thompson, 5,343; Houghton, 11,090.

At the judicial election held on October 20th, Carr was elected school superintendent, by a vote of 45,257 to 39,630 for Fitzgerald.

CHAPTER XXVI.

1876. Republican Convention, April 26th—Democratic Convention, May 24th—Democratic Convention, July 26th—Republican Convention, August 9th.

The republican state committee met at San Francisco, on March 19th, and called a state convention to meet at Sacramento on April 26th, to select twelve delegates to attend the national convention, to meet at Cincinnati on June 14th. The following test was adopted : "Opposition to the restoration to power of the democratic party, and an intention to act in good faith with the republican party."

At the time and place indicated, the republican state convention met, and was called to order by A. G. Abell, chairman of the state committee. W. C. Norton, L. E. Pratt, and L. B. Mizner were nominated for temporary chairman. Mizner withdrew, and Norton was selected, by a vote of 246 to 116 for Pratt. The committee on resolutions consisted of George G. Blanchard, P. H. McGowan, E. W. Roberts, Charles F. Reed, and J. V. Kelly. On permanent organization, Norton was president, and Mizner and Pratt, vice-presidents.

The following resolutions were reported :

1. That we have undiminished faith in the integrity of the republican party of the nation; that in its principles is the only security of national existence, prosperity, and honor. .

2. That in suppressing the great rebellion, begun and prosecuted by one wing of the democratic party, and countenanced and aided by the other, and in destroying slavery and preserving the nation,

the republican party justly earned the gratitude of the lovers of liberty and good government everywhere; yet as a political party it cannot long endure and receive popular support solely on renown already achieved, however brilliant, but must go forward and courage- ously deal with other questions now demanding consideration; and that among such questions there is none more pressing or important than reform in the civil service of the government, and the complete extirpation of the *spoils system*, inaugurated by the democratic party.

3. That we both admire and approve the action of those who have been, and are still, engaged in the prosecution and punishment of official dishonesty. That we are in favor of an economical adminis- tration of the government by honest, faithful, and capable officers.

4. That the republican party of California deprecates now, as it has done at all times in the past, the presence among us of hordes of servile Chinese, inimical to our advancement as a nation. That, while the democratic party has repeatedly resolved against the intro- duction of these people, it has never taken action to prevent it. That we fully endorse the course of our representatives, to whom is due the credit of the only laws of reform upon this subject. That we are in favor of such a modification of the existing treaty with China as will effectually prevent any further influx of these people into our state.

5. That we favor a return to metallic currency, and the restoration of the silver coin of the United States to its constitutional equality with gold as a legal tender.

6. That the funded debt of the nation, the principal and interest of which was by law made payable in gold, should be so paid, and that any and every scheme of repudiation, direct or indirect, meets the hearty condemnation of the republicans of California.

7. That the democracy of this state is not to be trusted as a na- tional party with the possession of the presidential office or of congress, because of its purpose to add hundreds of millions to the national debt, for pensions to confederate soldiers, claims for cotton legally and justly confiscated, and in the end, over a thousand millions as compensation for the loss of slaves of the south, the allowance of which would most surely result in another war, since loyal union men will never peacefully consent to be taxed to pay treason for its losses.

An amendment was offered and withdrawn, expressing the opinion that no person should be elected president for a third term. The resolutions as reported were unanimously adopted. The following were elected delegates to the national convention :

First congressional district—John Martin and Isaac. Hecht.

Second congressional district—L. H. Foote and E. H. Dyer.

Third congressional district—N. D. Rideout and A. P. Whitney.

Fourth congressional district—Josiah Belden and M. E. Gonzales.

For delegates at large, A. G. Abell, George S. Evans, Drury Melone, Charles F. Reed, Eugene L. Sullivan, and J. M. Pierce were nominated. On the first ballot, Abell had 349 votes ; Evans, 317 ; Melone, 127 ; Pierce, 285 ; Reed, 327, and Sullivan, 119. Abell, Evans, Pierce, and Reed were therefore elected.

J. M. Fulweiler moved that the convention express itself in favor of James G. Blaine for president, and Ira P. Rankin offered the following :

That while the republican party contains many men who, by their recognized ability and devotion to the principles of the party, have proved themselves worthy of public support and confidence, and capable of filling honorably the highest office in the gift of the people, the republican party of California especially recognizes in the Hon. James G. Blaine an eminently able and tried exponent of the principles of the party, of large experience in public life, of the purest public and private character, and possessing in a marked degree those personal qualities which would do honor to the office of president of the United States.

That while thus expressing our preference for the Hon. James G. Blaine, yet having confidence in the intelligence and patriotism of our delegates to the national convention, we leave them unembarrassed by instructions, and free to exercise their own deliberate choice in the convention as the interests of the country may in their judgment seem to demand.

The resolution was adopted.

The democratic state committee met at San Francisco on April 12th, and called a state convention to meet at that city on May 24th, to select twelve delegates to attend the national convention to assemble at St. Louis on June 27th, and to nominate presidential electors. The state convention was to be composed of 355 delegates. The test included "all persons who intended to vote for the nominees of the democratic party at the ensuing election."

On the day named the state convention convened at San Francisco, and was called to order by John C. Maynard, secretary of the state committee. C. T. Ryland was elected temporary chairman, without opposition. The committee on resolutions consisted of J. S. Hager, Senator Howe, J. T. Farley, Jo Hamilton, J. C. Burch, W. J. Tinnin, and others. Considerable difficulty was experienced in settling contests for seats. In the evening a permanent organization was effected by the election of Ryland as president, and A. J. Bryant, R. J. Tobin, F. M. Warmcastle, T. F. Bagge, M. Biggs, and others, vice-presidents. The committee on order of business reported in favor of electing three delegates from each congressional district, but the convention, by a vote of 196 to 151, decided to elect two from each district, and four at large. The committee also reported that in regard to nominating presidential electors at that convention, they were equally divided, and they referred the matter to the convention. After debate, it was decided, by a vote of 227 to 117, to postpone the nominations until after the adjournment of the national convention. On the 25th, a state committee was selected, consisting of M. R. C. Pulliam, Jos. F. Black, R. J. Tobin, J. D. Spencer, W. B. C. Brown, J. C. Wolfskill, P. H. Ryan, W. J. Tinnin, John Boggs, J. C. Maynard, A. B. Dibble, A. H. Glasscock, Paul Shirley, J. W. Freeman, A. P. Overton, A. Newman, Peter Donahue, J. H. Baird, H. F. Williams, S. A. Sharp, T. M. O'Connor, and others. The committee on resolutions reported the following :

The democracy of California, in convention assembled, adopt and promulgate the following declaration of principles:

1. Fidelity to all the provisions of the constitution of the United States.

2. A perpetual union of the states, with local self-government in every section.

3. Civil service reform. A restitution of the traits of honesty, fidelity, and capacity in the selection and qualifications of public officers.

4. Retrenchment and economy in federal, state, and municipal administration; reducing the burdens on labor by the reduction of offices and taxation.

5. Exposure and speedy punishment, by penal laws, of corruption and peculation in the administration of public affairs.

6. The private use and appropriation of public funds by official

custodians, means embezzlement and robbery. Official accountability exacted and enforced by the better administration of civil and criminal laws.

7. State corporations supervisable by and subordinate to state legislation, in the interests of the people.

8. Free schools, exempt from all sectarian control. A free press, accountable for abuses to civil and criminal laws. ·

. 9. Preservation of public faith and credit, and the honest payment of the public debt.

10. The money of the constitution, gold and silver, the only legal tender.

11. A tariff for purposes of revenue only.

12. No Chinese immigration. It is so thoroughly obnoxious to our people and institutions, that its prohibition is imperatively demanded, and all the powers of the government should be exerted to that end.

The committee also recommended the adoption of the following:

That the majority of our delegation to the national convention cast the vote of this state as a unit.

E. J. Lewis offered the following amendment to the committee report :

Whereas, The Hon. Samuel J. Tilden, governor of New York, by his manly defense of the people against the corrupt schemes of political tricksters, has pointed him out as the true reformer and fit champion of the people in the conflict with official corruption, and by his bold advocacy of hard money as the circulating medium of our country, has made himself an unobjectionable leader of the democratic party; therefore, resolved, that his nomination for president of the United States, by the national democratic convention would be acceptable to the democratic party of California, and a glorious victory in the cause of honest government.

After a discussion, the report of the committee was unanimously adopted, so far as the platform was concerned. The resolution to instruct the delegation to vote as a unit was then carried by a vote of 257 to 96. The Lewis resolution was adopted without opposition. Delegates to the national convention were then selected as follows :

First congressional district—William Dunphy and George H. Rogers.

Second congressional district—John C. Hays and F. T. Baldwin. Third congressional district—Armand Bay and George N. Cornwell.

Fourth congressional district—J. F. Moultrie and T. D. Mott.

For delegates at large, John S. Hager, Joseph P. Hoge, J. W. Taylor, John G. Downey, James L. English, and Eugene Casserly were named. On the first ballot, Hager had 250 votes; Taylor, 257; Hoge, 282; Downey, 139; English, 267; and Casserly, 239. Hager, Hoge, English, and Taylor were therefore elected.

The convention then adjourned to meet on the last Wednesday in July.

Pursuant to adjournment, the democratic convention met at San Francisco on July 26th. The committee on resolutions reported the following, which were unanimously adopted :

1. That the democracy of California accept and endorse the democratic declaration of principles, adopted at their recent national democratic convention assembled at St. Louis, as a true and faithful exposition of democratic sentiments upon the political issues of the day.

2. That the Chinese plank of our national platform is in strict conformity with our resolutions adopted at our late session, and is so bold and unequivocal a stand on this important question, so vital to our prosperity as a state, that we congratulate the people of the Pacific slope on the prospect thus afforded of speedy relief.

3. That the thanks of this convention are hereby tendered to our national delegates for their faithful and efficient representation of the democracy of this state in the national councils of our party.

4. That we hail with pleasure the names presented for the presidency and vice-presidency, the model governors of the union, Samuel J. Tilden, of New York, and Thomas A. Hendricks, of Indiana, and unqualifiedly ratify their nominations.

5. That the great issue of local self-government and reform against centralization and official corruption is now fairly before the people of the union, and we as patriots dare not anticipate defeat.

6. That one mission above all others in the war we are now waging against the present administration and its allies, is the enforcement of that God given command, "Thou shalt not steal."

The following nominations were made for presidential electors :

First district, Stuart M. Taylor ; second district, Joseph H. Budd;

third district, Barclay Henley; fourth district, Frank Ganahl; at large, J. Campbell Shorb and John S. Hager.

For alternate electors, the following were named :

First district, John Mullan; second district, Theodore F. Bagge; third district, Marion Biggs; fourth district, Juan B. Castro. At large, Joseph Naphtaly and Cameron H. King were nominated, over M. G. Vallejo and O. M. Wozencraft.

A motion was made and lost to nominate a candidate for state controller, to fill the vacancy caused by the death of J. W. Mandeville.

The first district convention met at San Francisco on May 25th, and nominated William A. Piper for congressman, without opposition.

The second district convention met at Sacramento on September 20th, and nominated G. J. Carpenter for congressman, without opposition.

The third district convention met at San Francisco on July 26th, and nominated J. K. Luttrell for congressman, without opposition; Barclay Henley withdrawing.

The fourth district convention met at San Francisco on May 25th, and nominated P. D. Wigginton for congressman, without opposition.

The second republican state convention met at San Francisco on August 9th, and was called to order by A. G. Abell, the chairman of the state committee. W. C. Norton was elected temporary chairman, without opposition. The committee on resolutions consisted of G. G. Blanchard, E. W. Roberts, Calvin Edgerton, James E. Hale, R. Burnell, S. F. Gilcrest, and E. S. Salomon. On permanent organization, Norton was president; and W. H. Sears, L. H. Foote, H. W. Briggs, and R. Burnell were vice-presidents. The convention determined to nominate a candidate for state controller. An adjournment was then taken until evening.

During the recess, the delegates from the first congressional district met and nominated D. A. McKinley for elector, on the first ballot, over Paul Neuman, George F. Baker, Louis R. Lull, Dr. H. Cox, and J. McM. Shafter. O. F. Von Rhein was nominated for alternate elector, without opposition.

The second district delegates nominated John B. Felton for elector, without opposition; L. H. Foote withdrawing. George G. Blanchard was nominated for alternate.

The third district delegates nominated John H. Jewett for elector, without opposition. For alternate, Jerome Banks, A. P. Whitney, H. W. Byington, and L. W. Watkins were named, and Banks was nominated, on the first ballot.

The fourth district delegates nominated H. J. Ostrander for elector, on the first ballot, over Thomas Fallon and W. E. Lovett. G. O. Reed was nominated for alternate, on the first ballot, over J. F. Richards and C. S. Abbott.

In the evening, the state convention met. D. M. Kenfield was nominated for controller, without opposition; Bernard Lande withdrawing. The nominations which had been made by the district conventions for electors and alternates were ratified.

John F. Miller and Morris M. Estee were nominated for electors at large, without opposition; and Paul Neuman and J. McM. Shafter were nominated for alternate electors at large.

A state committee was selected, consisting of J. T. Richards, William Sharkey, N. W. Spaulding, H. T. Dorrance, A. Briggs, R. Burnell, E. A. Davis, J. Buhlert, C. Rowell, J. H. Neff, Sol. Jewett, J. R. Brierly, M. D. Boruck, Thomas Fallon, J. G. Wickersham, R. Chute, C. Clayton, A. G. Abell, W. W. Dodge, E. B. Mott, jr., L. Sloss, W. F. Whittier, O. N. Felton, F. K. Shattuck, S. O. Houghton, and others.

The committee on resolutions reported the following:

1. That the delegates of the republican party of California, in state convention assembled, do reaffirm and endorse the platform of the national republican convention held at Cincinnati, and adopt the same as the chart of our political principles.

2. That we heartily endorse the action of that convention in nominating Rutherford B. Hayes as our candidate for president and William A. Wheeler, vice-president, and recognize in them champions of honest and stable government—the true representatives of popular reform and popular liberty.

3. That we do reaffirm and endorse the announcement of principles contained in the letters of acceptance of those of our national candidates, that "office should be conferred only on the basis of high character and particular fitness, and should be administered only as public trusts and not for private advantage."

4. That as a great national party, devoted to the interests of the laboring masses, we are opposed to the further immigration of the Chinese, and we demand, and will use all the means in our power

o procure, a modification of the present treaty between the government of the United States and the Chinese empire, so as to entirely prevent the further immigration of a people among us, who, by reason of their uniform, ingrained character and national antecedents are equally incapacitated from becoming American citizens, or of becoming desirable members of our American communities, and whose presence and further introduction is prejudicial to the industrial interests of the nation.

5. That the interests of California and the welfare of the country demand resumption of specie payment at the earliest practicable moment, and the maintenance of all laws and statutes providing for resumption.

The resolutions were adopted, without opposition.

The first district convention met at San Francisco on August 10th, and nominated Horace Davis for congressman, without opposition.

The second district convention met at San Francisco on August 10th, and nominated H. F. Page for congressman, without opposition.

The third district convention met at San Francisco on August 9th, and nominated Joseph McKenna for congressman, without · opposition.

The fourth district convention met at San Francisco on August 10th, and nominated R. Pacheco for congressman, without opposition.

The election was held on Tuesday, November 7th, and the official canvass developed the following result:

Democratic Electors— Shorb, 76,460; Hager, 76,464; Taylor, 76,461; Budd, 76,451; Henley, 76,458; Ganahl, 76,460.

Republican Electors—Miller, 79,258; Estee, 79,259; McKinley, 79,254; Felton, 78,264; Jewett, 79,260; Ostrander, 79,255.

Greenback Electors—B. K. Lowe, S. H. Herring, J. H. Redstone, J. Condia, A. Cridge, and C. B. Smith, 47 each.

Congressmen — First District — Piper, 19,363; Davis, 22,134. *Second District—*Carpenter, 15,916; Page, 20,815. *Third District—*Luttrell, 19,846; McKenna, 18,990. *Fourth District—*Wigginton, 19,103; Pacheco, 19,104.

*Controller—*W. B. C. Brown, 75,567; Kenfield, 78,529.

On December 6th, the republican electors met in the office of the secretary of state, in the state capitol, and cast the vote of California for Hayes and Wheeler for president and vice-president. John F. Miller was selected messenger to convey the returns to Washington.

After the official canvass, Kenfield filed his oath of office and bond as controller, but Governor Irwin refused to deliver to him a com- ✝ mission for the office. Kenfield instituted an action in the district court for a writ of mandate, to be directed to the governor, to compel him to issue the commission. The district court sustained a demurrer to the petition, and the supreme court, at its April term, 1877, affirmed the judgment of the court below. Brown therefore held over during the entire term.

The secretary of state refused to issue a certificate of election to Pacheco as a member of congress, and at the January term, 1877, the supreme court of the state directed that a peremptory writ of mandate issue to the secretary of state, commanding him to canvass the vote as it had been transmitted to him by the county clerks, and to issue a certificate of election to the person having the highest number of votes. In accordance with this decision, the certificate of election was issued to Pacheco, and he proceeded to Washington, and was sworn in as congressman on December 3d, 1877. Wigginton instituted a contest for the seat. A minority of the committee on elections of the house of representatives reported in favor of admitting Pacheco, but the majority sustained Wigginton. The majority report was adopted on February 7th, 1878, by a vote of 126 to 137, and Wigginton took the oath of office on that day and served out the remainder of the term.

CHAPTER XXVII.

1877. Workingmen's Movement and the Kearney Excitement.

On the evening of September 21st, a meeting of unemployed workingmen was held at San Francisco, attended by about 2,000 persons. Philip A. Roach was the first speaker. Dennis Kearney addressed the meeting afterward. He said that as the question of labor then stood, every workingman should add a musket to his household property. He predicted that within one year there would be at least 20,000 laborers in San Francisco, well armed, well organized, and well able to demand and take what they will, despite the military, the police, and the "safety committee." He said that a little judicious hanging about that time would be the best course to pursue with the capitalists and stock sharps who were robbing the people. It was resolved that a headquarters be established, and that the unemployed workingmen should sign their names as members of a self-protective organization.

On the afternoon of September 23d (Sunday), an open-air meeting of unemployed workingmen was held on the vacant lot in front of the new city hall in San Francisco, and was attended by about seven hundred persons. This was the first of a series of meetings that were held at the same place, the design of which was to secure the co-operation of the working element. On account of the place where the meetings were held, they were called "sand lot gatherings." At this meeting J. G. Day was elected president of the organization, and Kearney treasurer. One week later, on the 30th, another meeting was held, at which very intemperate language was indulged in, and a division occurred in the ranks of the new party. One branch adjourned to meet on the following Friday evening, and the other on the following Sunday afternoon. On October 5th a meeting was held, which was attended by about one hundred and fifty persons. Kearney was elected president of the organization; Day, vice-president, and H. L. Knight, secretary. A committee of five was appointed to prepare a set of principles, and they reported as follows :

The object of this association is to unite all poor and working men and their friends into one political party, for the purpose of defending themselves against the dangerous encroachments of capital on the happiness of our people and the liberties of our country.

We propose to wrest the government from the hands of the rich and place it in those of the people, where it properly belongs.

We propose to rid the country of cheap Chinese labor as soon as possible, and by all the means in our power, because it tends still more to degrade labor and aggrandize capital.

We propose to destroy land monopoly in our state by such laws as will make it impossible.

We propose to destroy the great money power of the rich by a system of taxation that will make great wealth impossible in the future.

We propose to provide decently for the poor and unfortunate, the weak, the helpless, and especially the young, because the country is rich enough to do so, and religion, humanity and patriotism demand that we should do so.

We propose to elect none but competent workingmen and their friends to any office whatever. The rich have ruled us until they have ruined us. We will now take our own affairs into our own hands. The republic must and shall be preserved, and only workingmen will do it. Our shoddy aristocrats want an emperor and a standing army to shoot down the people.

For these purposes we propose to organize ourselves into the workingmen's party of California, and to pledge and enroll therein all who are willing to join us in accomplishing these ends.

When we have 10,000 members we shall have the sympathy and support of 20,000 other workingmen.

The party will then wait upon all who employ Chinese and ask for their discharge, and it will mark as public enemies, those who refuse to comply with their request.

This party will exhaust all peaceable means of attaining its ends; but it will not be denied justice, when it has the power to enforce it. It will encourage no riot or outrage, but it will not volunteer to repress, or put down, or arrest, or prosecute the hungry and impatient, who manifest their hatred of the Chinamen by a crusade against "John," or those who employ him. Let those who raise the storm by their selfishness, suppress it themselves. If they dare raise the devil, let them meet him face to face. We will not help them.

The other faction of the party was headed by a man named Bates. On October 7th the two factions met at the sand lots, and in the course of his remarks, Kearney referred to the rival faction in this language: "You will have to mob these white Sioux and white pigtail men first. You will have to shoot them down on the streets, before you begin on the Chinese." At this point, the crowd began to follow out the instructions of the speaker by overturning the stand from which one of the rival orators was addressing the people. The stand was righted, and again overturned, and the speaker was chased back to his own crowd, who occupied a different portion of the lot. On October 8th, notwithstanding the inclemency of the weather, about twelve hundred workingmen of the Kearney faction held a meeting on the steps of the United States mint, and a club was organized in the tenth ward. On that day the board of supervisors of San Francisco considered the subject of providing for the unemployed, and the finance committee reported that the board had no power to appropriate money from the public treasury to meet the emergency. Mr. Wise offered the following resolution, which was laid over:

That the finance committee be and are hereby authorized to confer with such of the influential citizens of this city and county as in their judgment they may think proper, to the end that they may, together with his honor, the mayor, devise such ways and means as they may think most expedient to provide employment, and relieve the distress at present existing among a large class of the inhabitants of this city.

After that, meetings were held nightly at different points in San Francisco to organize ward clubs. On October 11th, about eight hundred persons met at the corner of Fifth and Folsom streets, and after the adjournment, an attack was made on a Chinese washhouse, the windows of which were broken. On the following Sunday, at the sand-lot meeting, Kearney stated that the attack on the washhouse had been made by a vicious boy, and that the object of the organization was not to sack individual washhouses, but to strike a blow that would break up the entire Chinese institution. On October 16th, a manifesto, signed by Kearney, as president of the workingmen's party of California, and Knight, as secretary, appeared in the San Francisco *Chronicle*, to the editor of which paper it was addressed. The document recited:

We have made no secret of our intentions. We make none. Before you and before the world we declare that the Chinaman must leave our shores. We declare that white men, and women, and boys, and girls, cannot live as the people of the great republic should and compete with the single Chinese coolie in the labor market. We declare that we cannot hope to drive the Chinaman away by working cheaper than he does. None but an enemy would expect it of us; none but an idiot could hope for success; none but a degraded coward and slave would make the effort. To an American, death is preferable to life on a par with the Chinaman. What then is left to us? Our votes! We can organize. We can vote our friends into all the offices of the state. We can send our representatives to Washington. We can use all legitimate means to convince our countrymen of our misfortunes and ask them to vote the moon-eyed nuisance out of the country. But this may fail. Congress, as you have seen, has often been manipulated by thieves, peculators, land grabbers, bloated bondholders, railroad magnates, and shoddy aristo-crats—a golden lobby dictating its proceedings. Our own legisla-ture is little better. The rich rule them by bribes. The rich rule the country by fraud and cunning; and we say that fraud and cun-ning shall not rule us. We call upon our fellow workingmen to show their hands, to cast their ballots aright and to elect the men of their choice. We declare to them that when they have shown their will that "John" should leave our shores, and that will shall be thwarted by fraud or cash, by bribery and corruption, it will be right for them to take their own affairs into their own hands and meet fraud with force. Is this treason? Then make the most of it. Treason is better than to labor beside a Chinese slave. Your cor-respondent " Citizen" thinks these expressions dangerous to the pub-lic peace, and calls upon the officers of the law to prosecute us. He makes the old plea of oppressors everywhere, that such teachings tend to disturb the public tranquillity. MacMahon says this of the speeches of Gambetta. Every tyrant has said the same. King George spoke thus of the utterances of Patrick Henry. Who is this "Citizen" who dares not write his name? this coward, who would have somebody else shoot down his own race to make room for the moon-eyed Mongolian? Let him know that the workingmen know their rights, and know, also, how to maintain them, and mean to do it. The reign of bloated knaves is over. The people are about to take their own affairs into their own hands, and they will not be stayed either by "Citizen," vigilantes, state militia, nor United States troops. The people make these things, and can set them aside. The American citizen has a right to express himself as he pleases, as he thinks, and to arm himself as he will, and when organized and strong enough, who shall make him afraid? There is none.

On October 29th, about three thousand persons held a meeting on the summit of "Nob Hill," in San Francisco, in the vicinity of the residences of the directors of the Central Pacific railroad company, and speeches of a very inflammatory nature were made. The public excitement which was engendered by these frequent meetings be-came great, and on November 1st the city authorities of San Fran-cisco held a consultation with Kearney and the other leading agita-tors, but no understanding was arrived at.

On November 3d, a meeting was held at the corner of Washing-ton and Kearny streets, and while Kearney was addressing the crowd, a number of policemen ran up stairs into a room which opened on the balcony where the speaker was, and arrested him. This created an intense excitement in the audience, but Kearney motioned the crowd back and was taken to the city prison. The following resolutions were then adopted by the meeting:

That as workingmen of this city and representatives of the industrial interests of California, we hold that the system of strict party caucusing for the nomination of candidates by the legislature does not best tend to secure the rights and interests of all classes alike.

That we earnestly request our legislature either to dispense with the usual party caucusing in the nomination of United States senator, or that, if strict party caucuses are held, a conservative caucus also be held to nominate such a man for the position as will be the true friend of the industrial classes and not the mere slave of capital or party.

Two complaints were lodged against Kearney for misdemeanor. One charged him with having uttered language tending to incite the assemblage of persons on " Nob Hill," whom he addressed, to deeds of violence, and the following is the language credited to him :

The Central Pacific men are thieves, and will soon feel the power of the workingmen. When I have thoroughly organized my party we will march through the city and compel the thieves to give up their plunder. I will lead you to the city hall, clear out the police force, hang the prosecuting attorney, burn every book that has a particle of law in it, and then enact new laws for the workingmen. I will give the Central Pacific just three months to discharge their Chinamen, and if that is not done Stanford and his crowd will have to take the consequences. I will give Crocker until November 29th to take down the fence around Yung's house, and if he does not do it, I will lead the workingmen up there and tear it down, and give Crocker the worst beating with the sticks that a man ever got.

The other charge was for the following language, which was alleged to have been used in a speech delivered at the Irish-American hall :

I want to make a motion. The man who claims to be a leader— the first man who flags interest in this movement—I want to make a motion that he be hung up to a lamp post. By the eternal, we will take them by the throat and choke them until their life's blood ceases to beat and then run them into the sea. A fine young man

asked me : "What position are you going to give me ?" His name
is Lynch. I said: "I will make you chief judge." His name is
Lynch, recollect—Judge Lynch—and that is the judge that the
workingmen will want in California if the condition of things is not
ameliorated. I advise everyone within the sound of my voice, if he is
able, to own a musket and a hundred rounds of ammunition.

On the night of Kearney's arrest, it was apprehended that an
attempt would be made to rescue him by force, and the military of
San Francisco were called out and remained in their armories in
anticipation of trouble. The Chinese became fearful that an attack
would be made on their quarters, and on November 3d, the following
appeal, signed by the presidents of the Chinese six companies, was
received by the mayor of San Francisco :

We, the undersigned, presidents of the Chinese six companies of
this city and state, desire to call your immediate attention to a state
of things which seems to us to threaten the lives and property of the
Chinese residents, as well as the peace and good name of this municipality.

In the multitude of responsibilities which tax your time and
strength, it may possibly have escaped your notice that large
gatherings of the idle and irresponsible element of the population of
this city are nightly addressed in the open streets by speakers who
use the most violent, inflammatory, and incendiary language, threatening in plainest terms to burn and pillage the Chinese quarter and
kill our people unless, at their bidding, we leave this "free republic."
The continuance of these things for many days with increasing fury,
without any check or hinderance by the authorities, is causing the
Chinese people great anxiety, and in the immediate danger which
seems again to threaten us as well as to threaten the peace and
good name of the city, we (as on a former occasion) appeal to you,
the mayor and chief magistrate of this municipality, to protect us to
the full extent of your power in all our peaceful, constitutional and
treaty rights against all unlawful violence and all riotous proceedings now threatening us. We would deprecate the results of mob
violence, for we not only value our property and cherish our lives,
which now seem in jeopardy, but we should also regret to have the
good name of this christian civilization tarnished by the riotous proceedings of its own citizens against the "Chinese heathen." As a
rule, our countrymen are better acquainted with peaceful vocations than with scenes of strife, yet we are not ignorant that self-

defense is the common right of all men ; and should a riotous attack be made upon the Chinese quarter, we should have neither the power nor disposition to restrain our countrymen from defending themselves to the last extremity and selling their lives as dearly as possible.

But we trust and believe that it is entirely within the scope of your honor's power and in accordance with your high sense of justice, to prevent these threatened evils. That we may do all in our power as good citizens to preserve the peace and avert a riot, we most respectfully submit these statements and make this earnest appeal to your honor.

On the 4th, a large meeting of the workingmen was held and intense excitement pervaded the entire city of San Francisco. J. G. Day, Wm. Kennedy, H. L. Knight, James Willey, C. C. O'Donnell, and Charles E. Pickett, who had been prominent as speakers at the meetings, were placed under arrest. On the 7th, the executive committee of the workingmen's party issued an address to the members of the party, which was signed by A. A. Stout and Wm. Wellock.

The address was as follows :

Our leaders having been arrested and incarcerated in the city prison for having dared to exercise the right of free speech—a right guaranteed by the constitution of our government, the first impulse, no doubt, that filled your breasts, was to liberate them by force— the expression of which you gave utterance to when the arrests were made—but better counsels prevailed, and the officers were allowed to carry them off, contrary to what we consider to be lawful. Very well. Now we, as the only remaining officers of the workingmen's party of California, out of jail, wish to give you sound words of advice. Do not commit any deeds of violence; do not in any way harass the officers of the law. Await a full and impartial expression of the law. It is the wish of the imprisoned; it is the programme of the workingmen's party of California that they be arrested, tried, and if not convicted, then you will know that it is lawful for a speaker to express his opinion in this boasted free country. If the law says they are not guilty, then, having committed no offense against the law, they are entitled to speak and be protected, forcibly if necessary, in that right. But until the law passes on that right, you have no right to object, in any way, to the arrest of any of us.

Have patience in this hour of trouble, and you will all see that this martyrdom of our leaders will in the end redound to their glory, and the liberation of the workingmen of California from the thralldom of capital and the incubus of the Chinese.

In the meantime, organize. Join the roll in your respective wards. "Truth crushed to earth will rise again." If our cause is just, we can stand temporary delay; if not, it deserves to fall.

Our lawyers assure us that the complaint will "not stick." Have patience and all will be well.

On the 15th, Kearney and Knight were released on bail, and on the 21st the cases were tried in the city criminal court and dismissed by the judge. On the 29th—Thanksgiving day—the workingmen held a grand demonstration in San Francisco. About ten thousand men were in line, and addresses were delivered by Kearney, Wellock, and O'Donnell. At the meeting the following resolutions were adopted:

We, the workingmen of California, in mass meeting assembled in San Francisco, November 29, 1877, do hereby resolve that we are opposed to any further grant by congress of lands, money, or bonds in aid of any corporation or railroad monopoly, of whatever pretension, whereby the people are impoverished and robbed of their heritage. Therefore we are opposed to the passage of the Texas Pacific railroad bill. And whereas, the Union and Central Pacific railroad companies have defrauded the people of millions of dollars' worth of property and bonds, therefore we favor the passage of the Chaffee bill, now pending in congress, for the government to declare the charter of the Union Pacific railroad forfeited for willful violation of the law, and to take possession of the road, unless legal impediment exists to prevent immediate action; and, whereas, the national currency banking system of the United States gives double interest to the capitalist, fosters monopoly, and centralizes the money of the republic into the hands of the few; therefore we further resolve that we favor the passage of the resolution of Townsend, of Illinois, in congress, authorizing the winding up of the national banks, withdrawing their circulation, and substituting greenbacks or other similar currency in its stead.

CHAPTER XXVIII.

1878. The Workingmen's Excitement Growing in Intensity—Success of the Movement at the Polls—Workingmen's State Convention—A Joint Meeting of the Republican and Democratic State Central Committees—Delegates to Constitutional Convention—Division of Workingmen's Party—The Greenback Party.

On January 3d, about four hundred unemployed workingmen met on O'Farrell street and resolved to fall into line and march to the city hall, where a committee, headed by Kearney, was selected to interview the mayor. The crowd increased to about fifteen hundred when the city hall was reached. The committee demanded of the mayor that the workingmen be provided with work, bread, or a place in the county jail. Kearney stated that he could not keep them in check any longer if one of three things was not provided, and he did not want to be responsible for what might happen if they were not provided for. The mayor then addressed the meeting and stated that the city authorities had no power to provide them with work, and if they were set to work for the city, there was not money enough in the treasury to pay them. The crowd then met at the sand lot and speeches were delivered. So demonstrative was the meeting that several of the city officers, becoming apprehensive that a raid would be made on the city hall, put the moneys of their departments in their safes and vacated their offices.

Early in January, a committee of safety was organized by the leading citizens of San Francisco, to take action on what they considered was an alarming state of public excitement. Secret meetings were held, and it was understood they had provided themselves with arms, and that a perfect system had been adopted so that at a given signal they could meet for defence, if necessary. On January 5th, the grand jury of San Francisco found several indictments against Kearney, Wellock, O'Donnell, Knight, Helm, and Pickett, and they were arrested, but released on bail. The indictments charged them with conspiracy and riot, in endeavoring to drive the Chinese and the railroad managers from the state. Within the next ten days Kearney was arrested several times for the utterance of incendiary language. One of the complaints charged him with the utterance of the following:

We are not to be intimidated by anybody. It would take 50,000 men in California to intimidate the workingmen that are now ready, and if we can get through this without the shedding of blood, so much the better for ourselves. I do not care about dying just now, but if it comes to that, I am ready. To carry my point I do not care who suffers, or who sacrifices his life in the attempt. We are going to carry this thing to either death or victory, recollect.

One of the indictments was tried in the criminal court, and on the 22d, Kearney and Wellock were acquitted by the jury. The remaining charges were not pressed.

On January 6th, Nathan Porter, state senator from Alameda county, died, and a special election was called for the 22d, to elect a person to fill the vacancy. J. W. Bones was nominated by the workingmen, and elected by a large majority, over W. W. Crane jr., republican, and J. B. Lamar, democrat. On February 19th, a special election was held in Santa Clara county for a senator and assemblyman, to fill vacancies caused by deaths, and S. W. Boring, the people's candidate, was elected senator, and J. E. Clark, the nominee of the workingmen, was elected assemblyman.

In March, at the city elections in Sacramento and Oakland, the workingmen elected their candidates for mayor, and several other offices. These successes had the effect of giving considerable political importance to the movement, and steps were actively taken to perfect the organization, and make it a factor in state politics. In January, military companies were organized in San Francisco by the workingmen, to offset the organization of the committee of safety. At a meeting held on January 15th, in San Francisco, the workingmen speakers defied the authorities, and boldly announced that they were purchasing rifles, forming military companies, and maturing plans for blowing up Chinatown. They also intimated that they intended to blow the steamships of the Pacific Mail company out of the water. A rope with a hangman's noose tied in it was suspended from a gas jet on the stand. The next day, the press of the city admonished the workingmen that they were going too far, and expressed grave apprehension of violence.

The legislature passed an act in January authorizing the board of supervisors of San Francisco to employ a number of men to work on the streets, with the hope of affording some relief. Another act was passed authorizing the supervisors to increase the police force of that city to four hundred. At a special meeting of the board of supervisors of San Francisco, held on January 16th, the district attorney submitted an amendment to the penal code, in relation to riots, and a committee of seven was appointed to proceed to Sacramento and urge its passage by the legislature. After lengthy debates, the bill was passed and approved. It provided that any person, who in the presence or hearing of twenty-five or more persons, should utter any language, with intent either to incite a riot at the present or in the future, or any act or acts of criminal violence against person or property; or who should suggest, advise, or encourage any acts of criminal violence against person or property; or should advise or encourage forcible resistance to any state law, should be deemed guilty of felony, and on conviction, imprisoned not exceeding two years, or fined not exceeding five thousand dollars, or by both. On January 17th, Mayor Bryant, of San Francisco, issued the following proclamation.

Whereas, Persons assemble in this city and county, and threaten to commit offenses against the property and lives of the inhabitants, and such assemblies are not held for any lawful purpose, but to create disturbances, in which public offenses may be committed; now, therefore, by virtue of the authority vested in me by law, as mayor of this city and county, I do hereby declare that such assemblies are unlawful, and will not be permitted, but will be dispersed, and all persons composing them and taking part in their proceedings will be arrested. And I advise all persons to stay away from such meetings, and not be present as spectators, from curiosity or any other idle motive, for such attendance encourages those engaged in promoting disturbances, interferes with the operations of those who seek to keep the peace, and may result in harm to the innocent as well as the guilty. I trust that the men who guide these assemblies will not compel the use of force in securing obedience to law. But I shall not shirk from using all the power at my command to preserve the peace of the city and county. Such assemblies, wherever held, in halls, upon the streets, or on sand lots, will be suppressed, and the supremacy of law and order resolutely maintained.

On the 17th, Kearney and Wellock, who were in the city prison, issued the following address:

Workingmen, be calm! be peaceful! Show your discipline! Do not distrust the law. We will come out all right. If you come to the courts, when we come on the streets, do not crowd the officers. Do not run after us. Our cause shall yet be won. You show your power best when you show your prudence. We are confident and happy. There is no misery where there is a good conscience. We must bide our time. We never can be defeated.

On the evening of the 17th, the workingmen attempted several times to hold meetings in San Francisco, but they were dispersed by the police. On the 18th, Charles Crocker offered to give employment to one thousand men at $1 a day, to fill in certain portions of Mission creek, and on the morning of the 21st, two hundred and fifty men went to work, and the force was increased daily.

The first state convention of the workingmen's party was held at San Francisco on the evening of January 21st. Advertisements appeared in the papers announcing that the convention would be held at several different places, and these conflicting announcements were intended to throw the police off the scent, as it was expected that they would, by the instruction of the mayor, disperse the meeting. The delegates had been informed of the place of the meeting, and they entered the hall in small groups, through an adjoining saloon. The main entrance to the hall was closed, and from the outside everything looked dark. The police did not discover the place of meeting until about midnight, and when they entered they found that the proceedings were conducted in an orderly manner. The convention was called to order by President Rodney, of the eighth ward club, who was chosen temporary chairman. About one hundred and forty delegates were present. A motion was carried to employ counsel to have the mayor brought into court on a writ of mandate, to show cause why he broke up the workingmen's meeting. An adjournment was then had until the following evening. The next day the mayor announced that he would not interfere with the convention so long as they did not violate the law. At the meeting on the 22d, no particular business was transacted. On the 23d, J. P. Dunn was chosen secretary, and a committee on platform was chosen, consisting of Kearney, Rodney, Knight, Wellock, and others. On permanent organization, Kearney was elected president; D. F. Manning, of Mono, and Wellock, vice-presidents, and Knight and Dunn, secretaries. On the 24th, the committee on platform reported the following, which was adopted:

That the time has come for the formation of a party of labor, to embrace within its ranks all those engaged in productive industry and its distribution. Upon signing the roll of membership, each person will publicly and solemnly pledge himself henceforth to sever all connection with the republican and democratic parties, and shall abide by the result of the majority in all cases duly expressed; and, furthermore, shall at all times aid in the selection of the most competent person from our ranks to serve us in an official capacity.

A vote of thanks to the fifteen members of the legislature who opposed the passage of the incendiary bill was passed. The following resolutions were also adopted :

Whereas, In the state there is almost a total disregard by employers of labor of adequate protection of the life and limb of the employes ; therefore, resolved, that we request of the present legislature, suitable laws for the protection of life and limb of employes in factories, the erection of buildings, and all other occupations involving risk of life and limb. That a committee of three be appointed to draft a bill for presentation to the legislature, affording the desired protection.

Whereas, The workingmen's party of San Francisco recognize in Dennis Kearney their president, and view with abhorrence his persecution and imprisonment by the city authorities; therefore, resolved, that we extend to President Kearney and his coadjutors, Wellock, Knight, and others, our sympathy and support in their laudable efforts to wrest this city and the great state of California from control of professed politicians, whose only desire is to plunder our people and thereby enrich themselves.

That we behold in the infamous gag laws recently enacted by our board of supervisors and our state legislature, an abrogation of the fundamental principles of the constitution of the United States and the inauguration of anarchy.

That we hold Mayor Bryant strictly accountable for his heartless betrayal of the men who elected him to office, and believe that his unwarrantable attack upon our president and officers was to divert public attention from his alleged complicity in the escape of Duncan, the villain and forger.

That we will use all legal measures to bring to justice official disturbers of the peace, and venal officers of every grade.

Resolutions were adopted prescribing an oath for the members of the party, by which they should bind themselves to oppose, by all lawful measures, the introduction and maintenance of coolie laborers in the United States, and that they should not employ or sell to or buy from them; and urging that a reasonable compensation be paid to the delegates of the proposed constitutional convention, so that poor men could afford to attend it.

The committee on platform made the following report :

Whereas, The government of the United States has fallen into the hands of capitalists and their willing instruments; the rights of the people, their comfort and happiness are wholly ignored, and the vested rights of capital are alone considered and regarded, both in the states and the nation; the land is fast passing into the hands of the rich few; great money monopolies control congress, purchase the state legislatures, rule the courts, influence all public officers, and have perverted the great republic of our fathers into a den of dishonest manipulators. This concentration and control of wealth has impoverished the people, producing crime and discontent, and retarded the settlement and civilization of the country. In California, a slave labor has been introduced, to still further aggrandize the rich and degrade the poor, and the whole tendency of this class of legislation is to undermine the foundation of the republic and pave the way to anarchy and misrule; and this convention therefore declares, as follows :

Section 1. The workingmen of California. desire to unite with those of other states in effecting such reforms in our general government as may be necessary to secure the rights of the people as against those of capital, to maintain life, liberty, and happiness against land and money monopoly. Only in the people, the honest workingman can hope to find a remedy.

Sec. 2. Chinese cheap labor is a curse to our land, a menace to our liberties and the institutions of our country, and should, therefore, be restricted and forever abolished.

Sec. 3. The land is the heritage of the people, and its appropriation by the government for the furtherance of the schemes of individuals and corporations is a robbery; and all land so held should revert to its lawful possession, to be held for actual settlement and cultivation, and individuals holding by purchase or imperfect title land in excess of one square mile shall be restricted to the use of that amount only for cultivation and pasturage; and all lands of equal and productive nature shall be subject to equal taxation. Our previous legislatures have abused the trust confidingly reposed in them by a misguided people, by allowing a corrupt ring of land monopolies to exist who have appropriated vast tracts of the fairest land on earth to themselves; we, therefore, in the name of humanity,.

consider a resurvey of the state necessary in order to ascertain as far as possible the extent to which the law in this instance has been violated. As the land is the natural heritage of the children of men, we deem, in the laws of equity and justice, that one section of six hundred and forty acres is a sufficiency for any one man to own or transmit to his offspring. All import duties on raw material not produced in the United States should be abolished.

Sec. 4. The industries of the country are depressed or improved by the fluctuation in our financial system; and we therefore insist that the national government shall give to the people a system of finance consistent with the agricultural, manufacturing, and mercantile industries and requirements of the country, uncontrolled by rings, brokers, and bankers.

Sec. 5. The pardoning power conferred on the president of the United States, and the governors of the several states, should be abolished, and the same be vested in commissions.

Sec. 6. Malfeasance in public office should be punishable by imprisonment in the state prison for life, without intervention of the pardoning power.

Sec. 7. We demand the abrogation of the contract system in our state prisons and reformatory institutions. They should be managed in the interests of the people, and the goods therein manufactured should not be sold at less than current market rates for the product of free labor.

Sec. 8. All labor on public works, whether state or municipal, should be performed by the day, at current rates of wages.

Sec. 9. Eight hours is a sufficient day's work for any man, and the law should make it so.

Sec. 10. All public officers should receive a fixed salary, and the fees should be accounted for as public moneys.

Sec. 11. Millionaires and money monopolists are destructive to the happiness and dangerous to the liberty of the people, and we demand that they be made impossible by a proper system of taxation.

To section 6 an amendment was offered that the attention of congress be drawn to the fact that abuses exist in the custom house, internal revenue, and land office departments of California, that should not be tolerated under any civilized government; but the amendment was lost. Section 11 was stricken out and the following adopted in its place:

We demand that the constitution of the United States be amended to the effect that the president and vice-president of the United States, and senators of the several states, shall be elected by the direct vote of the people.

The following resolution was opposed by Kearney, and laid on the table:

That all speakers of this party engaged in organizing or advocating the interests of the party, shall be subject to the supervision of the various county committees, and all language of a violent character must be repressed by the party at all times.

A state committee was selected, consisting of Kearney, Knight, Wellock, and others. On the 25th the following resolutions were adopted:

That we regard the present common school system of the United States as the foundation of our civilization, and it will be forever cherished and supported by the workingmen's party.

That a system of compulsory education should be provided for the children of our country, so comprehensive in its details as to enable the attendance of such poor children as would otherwise be unable to attend. For this end a special fund for the assistance of such indigent children should be maintained, under proper safeguards; such education to be entirely secular; that there should be instituted in all our public schools lectures at stated intervals, whose primary aim should be to uphold the dignity of labor and mechanical vocations as paramount to all other walks in life.

A resolution was also adopted to the effect that all unoccupied lands in the United States should be declared open to settlement by all citizens, and when a citizen had taken possession of a piece of land of 640 acres, he should be protected in such location, no matter who held the title, and the holder of the title should be remunerated by the government.

On April 24th, the state committees of the republican and democratic parties met in different rooms in the Palace hotel, in San Francisco. The object of the meeting was to endeavor to effect a fusion of the parties in view of the election of delegates to the constitutional convention. The republican committee agreed that joint tickets should be nominated and a committee was sent to the democrats inviting them to co-operate, but the latter committee had no quorum present.   On the 25th, meetings were again held but no conclusion was arrived at.   Subsequently the democratic committee adopted the following resolutions :

1. That the people, having recognized the necessity for certain important and necessary changes in our organic law, we heartily approve of the call for a constitutional convention, so imperatively demanded and provided for by the vote of the people.

2. That we deem it above and beyond any partisan association of any character whatever to control so important a body, or any member thereof, selected for the formation of the constitution of our state.

3. That, as the representatives of the democratic party, we do hereby solemnly declare it to be our desire, in the approaching election for members of the state constitutional convention, that all past party issues should be discarded, and that none should be selected for membership in that body but the fittest, without regard to previous political affiliations; therefore, we recommend that the people of the several counties and senatorial districts, irrespective of parties, choose two delegates for each member of the senate and assembly, to which each county and senatorial district is entitled, to meet in the city of Sacramento, on Wednesday, the 22d of May, to nominate eight delegates from each of the four congressional districts of the state, to be voted for by the people of the state at large; and we further recommend, that the people of the several counties and senatorial districts, in selecting their local candidates for the other delegates to the constitutional convention, apportioned to said counties and senatorial districts, ignore party politics entirely, and select the very best men.

When the resolutions were received by the republicans, considerable indignation was manifested, and it was charged that the democrats had acted in bad faith.   The republican committee then unanimously adopted the following:

Whereas, At the commencement of this session of the republican state central committee it was unanimously resolved that it is inexpedient to make party nominations for delegates to the constitutional convention of this state; and, whereas, said resolution was transmitted to the democratic state central committee, then in session, with the expectation that some joint action might be had with that committee, for the nomination of delegates at large to the state convention; and whereas, this expectation has been disappointed by the refusal or neglect of said committee to co-operate with us in that respect, and by their independent adoption of certain resolutions; now, therefore, it is

Resolved, That the republican state central committee, in accordance with the spirit of the resolution sent to the democratic state central committee, as above set forth, recommend to the republicans of California, that they unite with their fellow citizens in the selection of the ablest, fittest, and best known gentlemen, to represent them in the convention which has been called for the purpose of preparing a new constitution for this state, and that for the nomination of such candidates, meetings be held in the several counties, and senatorial and congressional districts, at such times and places as they and their fellow citizens shall determine to be most suitable and convenient.

On May 4th, a very extensive petition was published in San Francisco, requesting certain prominent gentlemen of that city, who were designated regardless of party, to meet and nominate the delegates to be voted for in the first congressional district and in the city of San Francisco. On the 10th the gentlemen designated met and nominated a non-partisan ticket. This course was also adopted in other portions of the state.

On April 27th, at a meeting of the workingmen's state committee, a misunderstanding occurred, which resulted on May 2d in the expulsion of Kearney from the committee, and on the 6th he was removed from his position of president of the party by the committee. He was charged with being corrupt and with using the organization to advance his private ends. On the 12th the presidents of the various ward clubs favorable to Kearney, met and issued a lengthy address to the members of the party. Two state conventions of workingmen were called to meet in different halls, in San Francisco, on the 16th.

The Kearney convention met at Charter Oak hall and was called to order by Kearney. There were but 57 delegates present. The country delegates held a separate meeting and deliberated for a long time as to which convention they would join. About 5 o'clock the delegates from Alameda, Marin, Monterey, Sonoma, Santa Clara, Santa Cruz, and San Joaquin came in. Among those who participated in the proceedings were J. P. Dunn, C. C. Conger, Elihu

Anthony, W. F. White, D. J. Oullahan, and J. H. Budd. A resolution was adopted to recognize Kearney as an organizer worthy to
rank among the great organizers of history, and worthy of the support and confidence of the people. On permanent organization
Kearney was elected president. At the meeting of the country delegates, 20 voted to join the Kearney convention. 9 to join the anti-
Kearney convention, and 8 were in favor of joining neither. On
the 17th, the Kearney convention held another meeting. The committee on resolutions submitted the following:

Whereas, The duty of making the laws of our country has hitherto been confined to the non-producing element of society, who
have failed to secure us in our inalienable rights, utterly ignoring
the welfare of the producers, upon whose labors individual and national prosperity depends; reducing our farmers and wage-laborers
to a state of dependence, compelling them to compete with a degraded class of Mongolian laborers imported from abroad, and whose
presence is demoralizing as well as dangerous to the preservation of
our liberties; and, whereas, our legislative halls, national, state, and
municipal, have become infested by thieves who do not scruple to
take bribes, until our national forum has become a by-word and reproach among the nations; and, whereas, our courts have become
corrupt, the equal rights of the people violated until the administration of justice has become a mockery and farce; therefore, resolved:

1. That we recognize the constitution of the United States as the
great charter of our liberties and the paramount law of the land,
and the system of government thereby inaugurated by its framers
as the only truly wise, free, just, and equal government that has
ever existed; the last, best, and only hope of man for self-government.

2. That the public lands are the heritage of the people, and
should be open to actual settlers in limited quantities.

The next resolution denounced all communism and all subsidies
by the government.

4. Land grabbing must be stopped.

5. Vested rights in property must be respected, but land monopoly must be restricted, and in the future prohibited.

6. Money, mortgages, and bonds must be taxed.

7. The dignity of labor must be upheld, and the labor of women,

when of equal value to that of men, should receive an equal compensation.

8. The legislator who violates his pledges given to secure his election, should be punished as a felon.

9. The pardoning power now vested in the national and state executives should be abolished.

10. The contract system of the labor of criminals should be abolished, and that labor should be so managed as not to conflict with free labor.

11. All public officers should receive a fixed salary, and fees accounted for as public money.

12. All labor on public works should be done by the day, at the current rate of wages, and eight hours is a sufficient day's work.

13. A system of compulsory education for children under 14 years of age should be established.

14. Education in our public schools should be free, and the books provided at the expense of the state government.

15. The president and vice-president of the United States, and United States senators, should be elected by the direct vote of the people.

16. Malfeasance in public office should be punished as a felony.

17. All criminals should be punished by imprisonment, and punishment by money fine should be abolished.

18. All money made a legal tender for private debts should be received in payment of taxes, and for all public dues.

19. The Chinese laborer is a curse to our land, is degrading to our morals, is a menace to our liberties, and should be restricted and forever abolished, and "the Chinese must go."

20. The employment of Chinese laborers by corporations formed under the laws of this state should be prohibited by law.

21. Interest exceeding 7 per centum per annum for the use of money should be prohibited by law.

22. Contracts by the debtor for the payment of the fees of the attorney of the creditor should be prohibited.

23. No person should be taxed for that which he does not own; in other words, debts due by the person assessed should be deducted from the assessable value of his property and should be assessed against the person to whom they are payable.

24. The property of every person to an amount not exceeding $500 should be exempt from taxation.

25

25. All farming lands of equal productive value should be equally taxed, without reference to the improvements.

26. Growing crops should not be taxed.

27. The property of the deaf, dumb, and blind should be exempt from taxation.

28. There should be no special legislation by the state legislature, and no state legislature should meet oftener than once in every four years.

The following was added to the fourteenth resolution :

That the principal of every public school should, at least once every school week, deliver to the school a lecture on manual labor, showing that its importance is paramount to that of any other kind.

An addition was adopted to the twenty-eighth resolution : that all laws passed by the legislature should be ratified by the people before becoming laws. The following was also adopted :

That all lakes exceeding one mile in area shall be declared public property, excepting artificial reservoirs; and all rivers shall be declared public property.

The platform was then adopted as a whole. Kearney was elected president of the party; Wellock, vice-president, and H. M. Moore, secretary.

The following were nominated for delegates-at-large to the constitutional convention : First congressional district—Paul Bonnett, Anthony Fischer, J. W. Jamison, James Kidney, J. R. Pico, John R. Sharpstein, Charles Tillson, John A. Whelan. Second district—P. S. Dorney, J. B. Kelly, H. P. Williams, H. L. McKelvey, John Greenwell, L. J. Morrow, George Thom, J. M. Todd. Third district—W. F. Stone, W. H. Northcutt, D. M. Gloster, John C. Crigler, J. C. Garber, H. A. Boyle, Jonas Spect, W. M. Thorp. Fourth district—Isaac Bicknell, D. A. Dryden, William Vinter, B. Pilkington, J. F. Breen, Isaac Kinley, R. D. Pitt, and O. T. Chubb. After adopting the following constitution, the convention adjourned *sine die:*

Section 1. This organization shall be known as the workingmen's party of California, having for its object the redemption of the state and nation from the hands of political tricksters, thieving officials, and all corruption; the substitution of honest men in all offices; the abolition of all special legislation, and the restoration to the people of all power not delegated to their servants, and for all just purposes.

It shall be composed of all engaged in productive and distributive industry, and who honestly desire the establishment of the principles of the platform of the workingmen's party. Each person, on becoming a member of a club, shall be required to take the following pledge: "I, ——, do solemnly pledge myself that from henceforth 1 will dissolve all affiliation with all other political parties; that I will work faithfully for the establishment and maintenance of good government, through the workingmen's party of California, and place in power only those pledged to its support; that I will discourage all office seeking; that I will not employ, in any manner, any Chinese labor, and will discourage such employment by others, and that I will work and vote for the election to office of all persons of known honesty and integrity, nominated by the workingmen's party."

Sec. 2. Members of the party, in good standing, may form clubs in any election precinct in this state, but such clubs shall not be branches of the party until they are recognized as such by the executive committee of the county in which they are formed.

Sec. 3. The presidents of the recognized clubs in each county shall constitute the executive committee of the party in such county.

Sec. 4. The executive department of the party shall be composed of a president, vice-president, treasurer and grand secretary, who shall reside in San Francisco, who shall be elected by the state convention, and shall hold office until the meeting of the next state convention held after their election, at which state convention, their successors in office shall be elected.

Sec. 5. There shall be a state executive committee, composed of the president, vice-president, general secretary and treasurer, and of one president of a club in the city of San Francisco, to be elected by the presidents of the recognized clubs in that city, and of one president of a club in each county in the state, to be elected by the executive committee of such county. Eight members of the state executive committee shall constitute a quorum for the transaction of business. Any member of the state executive committee may be recalled at any time by the powers which elected him, and another qualified person elected in his place. The president, or in case of his absence or inability to act, the vice-president, shall be the chairman of the state executive committee, and the general secretary shall be the secretary thereof.

Sec. 6. All candidates of the party shall be temperate, of good character, and they shall pledge themselves to the principles of the party, and to integrity and economy in the public service. They shall be elected by the party, without cost to themselves; and no money shall be used by this party for or at any election, except for ballots, and to procure speakers and documents to instruct the people.

Sec. 7. Every person nominated for office by the workingmen's party of California shall, upon acceptance of his nomination, take and sign the following pledge: "I, ——, do hereby pledge my sacred honor that I will support the platform and declared principles of the workingmen's party of California, and in every instance use my best efforts to secure their adoption, and that, if elected, will, in every instance, conform to the wishes of my constituents, and if requested by them to resign, I will at once comply, under the penalty of ever thereafter being considered a man without honor or principle, and a person unworthy ever afterward to be a candidate for any office of trust in the nation."

Sec. 8. There shall be a state convention at such times as may be deemed necessary by the state executive committee.

Sec. 9. There shall be district and county conventions whenever the county committees deem it necessary for election purposes, or to promote the interests of the party.

Sec. 10. From and after the general election in 1879, all representation in the party shall be based upon the vote cast at the preceding election.

Sec. 11 All primary clubs of branches of this party shall make their own by-laws, not inconsistent with this constitution.

Sec. 12. No person shall be a member of two clubs at the same time; each member on joining a club shall present a proper transfer from the club of which he was previously a member, in order to prevent such membership representation.

Sec. 13. Every candidate taking office from the workingmen's party of California shall resign such office when demanded by a convention called for that purpose by his constituents.

Sec. 14. The state executive committee shall, as soon as practicable, establish a bureau of labor statistics in this state, with the head at the city of San Francisco, and branches in each county.

The anti-Kearney convention met at Tittle's Hall, in San Francisco, on May 16th. Frank Roney was elected chairman. The convention was but slimly attended. A platform was adopted, and delegates were nominated only to represent the first congressional district in the constitutional convention.

In most of the counties, the democrats and republicans made joint nominations for delegates to the constitutional convention. In each of the congressional districts conventions were held without regard to politics, and delegates at large were nominated.

The non-partisan candidates at large were as follows :

First congressional district—M. M. Estee, W. H. L. Barnes, Joseph W. Winans, John F. Miller, Eugene Casserly, Joseph P. Hoge, John S. Hager, and Samuel M. Wilson.

Second district—Henry H. Haight, Walter Van Dyke, Henry Edgerton, Hugh M. La Rue, J. B. Hall, Rufus Shoemaker, James E. Hale, and J. M. Porter.

Third district—Isaac S. Belcher, Marion Biggs, W. J. Tinnin, W. F. Heustis, J. McM. Shafter, John M. Kelley, A. P. Overton, and Benjamin Shurtleff.

Fourth district—John Mansfield, P. B. Tully, George W. Schell, Edward Martin, W. J. Graves, J. J. Ayers, Byron Waters, and George Venable Smith.

The following were nominated for delegates at large on a regular democratic ticket :

First congressional district—J. C. Shorb, John J. Williams, J. W. Harding, J. L. Ord, Charles A. Sumner, Cameron H. King, Edward C. Marshall, and H. P. Irving.

Second district—Joseph F. Montgomery, W. A. Selkirk, S. A. Nott, George W. Terrill, Theodore F. Bagge, John Anderson, R. B. Thompson, and John Nugent.

Third district—C. W. Lightner, M. G. Vallejo, R. C. Haile, A. D. Bell, George H. Crossette, John Boggs, Clay W. Taylor, and John S. Sanders.

Fourth district—Byron Waters, Brice Grimes, J. O. Lovejoy, C. G. Sayles, Lawrence Archer, J. M. Montgomery, J. W. Freeman, and J. R. McConnell.

The regular republicans nominated the following ticket for delegates at large : Frederick Fillmore, Henry Horstman, S. W. Holliday, James A. Waymire, Christopher Green, Walter Van Dyke, E. B. Mott, jr., H. T. Dorrance, Joseph McKenna, Benj. Shurtleff,

I. S. Belcher, N. W. Scudder, S. O. Houghton, David Fessenheld, John Mansfield, Edward Martin, L. Huerate, O. W. Dannals, Samuel Soule, J. G. Severance, J. M. Porter, James E. Hale, E. W. Roberts, John A. Eagon, William F. Heustis, J. M. McBrown, Charles A. Garter, D. M. Burns, Paris Kilburn, Robert Widney, George W. Schell, and G. V. Smith.

The election for delegates to the constitutional convention was held on Wednesday, June 19th. The non-partisan ticket for delegates at large was elected. The following table exhibits a list of the delegates who served :

List of Delegates to Second Constitutional Convention.

NAME AND PARTY ELECTING.	COUNTY.	FORMER POL.	OCCUPATION.
W. H. L. Barnes _____Non-partisan	At large _____	Republican___	Lawyer.
Eugene Casserly_____Non-partisan	At large _____	Democrat_____	Lawyer.
Morris M. Estee_____Non-partisan	At large _____	Republican___	Lawyer.
John S. Hager _____Non-partisan	At large _____	Democrat_____	Lawyer.
Joseph P. Hoge _____Non-partisan	At large _____	Democrat_____	Lawyer.
John F. Miller _____Non-partisan	At large _____	Republican___	
Samuel M. Wilson _____Non-partisan	At large _____	Democrat_____	Lawyer.
Joseph W. Winans . _____Non-partisan	At large _____	Republican___	Lawyer.
Henry Edgerton_____Non-partisan	At large _____	Republican___	Lawyer.
*J. West Martin_____Convention	At large _____	Democrat_____	Banker.
James E. Hale _____Non-partisan	At large _____	Republican___	Lawyer.
J. B. Hall _____Non-partisan	At large _____	Democrat_____	Lawyer.
Hugh M. La Rue_____Non-partisan	At large _____	Democrat_____	Farmer.
J. M. Porter_____Non-partisan	At large _____	Republican___	Lawyer.
Rufus Shoemaker_____Non-partisan	At large _____	Democrat_____	Journalist.
Walter Van Dyke_____Non-partisan	At large _____	Republican___	Lawyer.
Isaac S. Belcher _____Non-partisan	At large _____	Republican___	Lawyer.
Marion Biggs _____Non-partisan	At large _____	Democrat_____	Farmer.
W. F. Heustis_____Non-partisan	At large _____	Republican___	Clerk.
John M. Kelley_____Non-partisan	At large _____	Democrat_____	Farmer.
A. P. Overton _____Non-partisan	At large _____	Democrat_____	Lawyer.
James McM. Shafter_____Non-partisan	At large _____	Republican___	Lawyer.
Benjamin Shurtleff_____Non-partisan	At large _____	Republican___	Physician.
W. J. Tinnin_____Non-partisan	At large _____	Democrat_____	Merchant.
James J. Ayers_____Non-partisan	At large _____	Democrat_____	Editor.
William J. Graves_____Non-partisan	At large _____	Democrat_____	Lawyer.
John Mansfield _____Non-partisan	At large _____	Republican___	Lawyer.
Ed. Martin_____Non-partisan	At large _____	Republican___	Merchant.
George W. Schell _____Non-partisan	At large _____	Republican___	Lawyer.
George V. Smith_____Non partisan	At large _____	Republican___	Lawyer.
P. B. Tully_____Non-partisan	At large _____	Democrat_____	Lawyer.
Byron Waters_____Non-partisan	At large _____	Democrat_____	Lawyer.
A. Campbell, jr. _____Non-partisan	Alameda _____	Republican___	Lawyer.
Daniel Inman _____Non-partisan	Alameda _____	Ind. Dem. ___	Farmer.
John G. McCallum_____Non-partisan	Alameda _____	Ind. Repub. __	Lawyer.
Wm. Van Voorhies_____Non-partisan	Alameda _____	Democrat_____	Lawyer.
Jonathan V. Webster_____Non-partisan	Alameda _____	Ind. Dem. ___	Farmer.
John A. Eagon_____Non-partisan	Amador_____	Republican___	Lawyer.
Wm. H. Prouty_____Non-partisan	Amador_____	Democrat_____	Farmer.
Josiah Boucher _____Non-partisan	Butte _____	Republican___	Farmer.
Mark R. C. Pulliam_____Non-partisan	Butte _____	Democrat_____	Miner.
J. B. Garvey _____Democrat	Calaveras_____	Democrat_____	Dep. Sheriff.
B. B. Glascock _____Non-partisan	Colusa _____	Democrat_____	Farmer.
Hiram Mills_____Republican	Contra Costa____	Republican___	Lawyer.
James E. Murphy_____Non-partisan	Del Norte_____	Democrat_____	Lawyer.
Henry Larkin _____Workingmen	El Dorado_____	Democrat_____	Farmer.
Samuel A. Holmes_____Democrat	Fresno _____	Democrat_____	Farmer.
W. J. Sweasey _____Workingmen	Humboldt _____	Independent_	Merchant.
V. A. Gregg _____Republican	Kern_____	Republican___	Lawyer.

NAME AND PARTY ELECTING.	COUNTY.	FORMER POL.	OCCUPATION.
Alonzo E. Noel_____Independent	Lake_____	Democrat_____	Lawyer.
Edward Evey, Farmer and Workingmen	Los Angeles ____	Democrat_____	Farmer.
Volney E. Howard_____Democrat	Los Angeles·____	Democrat_____	Lawyer.
John P. West, Farmer and Workingmen	Los Angeles ____	Republican___	Farmer.
Hugh Walker_____Workingmen	Marin_____	Republican___	Cooper.
F. O. Townsend _____Democrat	Mendocino ____	Democrat_____	Farmer.
N. G. Wyatt_____Workingmen	Monterey _____	Democrat_____	Lawyer.
Robert Crouch _____Republican	Napa _____	Republican___	Lawyer.
C. W. Cross_____Workingmen	Nevada_____	Republican___	Lawyer.
Hamlet Davis_____Workingmen	Nevada _____	Democrat_____	Merchant.
John McCoy _____Workingmen	Nevada _____	Republican___	Miner.
John T. Wickes_____Workingmen	Nevada _____	Democrat_____	Sch'l teach'r
Samuel B. Burt _____Non-partisan	Placer _____	Republican___	Miner.
J. A. Filcher _____Non-partisan	Placer _____	Democrat_____	Journalist.
James Caples _____Non-partisan	Sacramento_____	Democrat_____	Farmer.
Presley Dunlap _____Non-partisan	Sacramento_____	Democrat_____	Lawyer.
Abraham C. Freeman_____Non-partisan	Sacramento_____	Republican___	Lawyer.
Thomas McConnell_____Non-partisan	Sacramento_____	Republican___	Farmer.
Thomas B. McFarland____Non-partisan	Sacramento_____	Republican___	Lawyer.
Edmund Nason _____Independent	San Benito _____	Republican___	Dairyman.
Randolph S. Swing_____Democrat	San Bernardino	Democrat_____	Lawyer.
Eli T. Blackmer_____Republican	San Diego _____	Republican___	Music teach.
Clitus Barbour_____Workingmen	San Francisco __	Republican___	Lawyer.
Charles J. Beerstecher____Workingmen	San Francisco__	Republican___	Lawyer.
Peter Bell_____Workingmen	San Francisco __	Democrat_____	Painter.
John D. Condon _____Workingmen	San Francisco __	Democrat_____	Cabinetm'kr
Patrick T. Dowling_____Workingmen	San Francisco	Democrat_____	Miner.
Luke D. Doyle_____Workingmen	San Francisco __	Democrat_____	Gardener.
Simon J. Farrell _____Workingmen	San Francisco __	Democrat_____	Gasfitter.
Jacob R. Freud _____Workingmen	San Francisco __	_____	Merchant.
Joseph C. Gorman_____Workingmen	San Francisco __	Republican___	Tinner.
William P. Grace _____Workingmen	San Francisco __	Republican___	Carpenter.
Thomas Harrison _____Workingmen	San Francisco __	Democrat_____	Rigger.
Conrad Herold_____Workingmen	San Francisco __	Democrat_____	Grocer.
William P. Hughey_____Workingmen	San Francisco __	Democrat_____	Sign painter.
Peter J. Joyce_____Workingmen	San Francisco __	Independent	Furn. dealer
Bernard F. Kenny_____Workingmen	San Francisco __	Democrat_____	Tel. operator
†John J. Kenny _____Convention	San Francisco __	Democrat_____	Merchant.
Charles R. Klein_____Workingmen	San Francisco __	Republican___	Bootmaker.
Raymond Lavigne_____Workingmen	San Francisco __	Democrat_____	Lithograph'r
John F. Lindow _____Workingmen	San Francisco __	Republican___	Tailor.
‡S. B. Thompson _____Convention	San Francisco __	Republican___	Carpenter.
Thorwald K. Nelson_____Workingmen	San Francisco __	Republican___	Turner.
Henry Neunaber_____Workingmen	San Francisco __	Republican___	Merchant.
Charles C. O'Donnell_____Workingmen	San Francisco __	Independent	Physician.
James O'Sullivan _____Workingmen	San Francisco __	Democrat_____	Printer.
James S. Reynolds_____Workingmen	San Francisco __	Republican___	Lawyer.
Charles S. Ringgold _____ Workingmen	San Francisco __	Democrat_____	Clerk.
Henry W. Smith_____Workingmen	San Francisco __	Republican___	Plumber.
John C. Stedman _____Workingmen	San Francisco __	Republican___	Bookkeeper.
Charles Swenson _____Workingmen	San Francisco __	Republican___	Restaurant.
Alphonse P. Vacquerel __Workingmen	San Francisco __	Republican___	Cook.
Patrick M. Wellin _____Workingmen	San Francisco __	Independent	Carpenter.
John R. W. Hitchcock____Non-partisan	San Joaquin____	Democrat_____	Farmer.
David Lewis _____Non-partisan	San Joaquin____	Republican___	Farmer.
Justus Schomp_____Non-partisan	San Joaquin____	Republican___	Farmer.
David S. Terry _____Non-partisan	San Joaquin____	Democrat_____	Lawyer.
George Steele _____Non-partisan	San Luis Obispo	Republican___	Farmer.
William S. Moffat_____Workingmen	San Mateo _____	Democrat_____	Farmer.
Eugene Fawcett _____Non-partisan	Santa Barbara__	Republican___	Dist. Judge.
Dennis W. Herrington____Workingmen	Santa Clara_____	Republican___	Lawyer.
Thomas H. Laine_____Non-partisan	Santa Clara_____	Democrat_____	Lawyer.
Rush McComas _____Non-partisan	Santa Clara_____	Republican___	Farmer.
E. O. Smith _____Non-partisan	Santa Clara_____	Democrat_____	Farmer.
Joseph R. Weller _____Non-partisan	Santa Clara_____	Republican___	Farmer.
Daniel Tuttle_____Workingmen	Santa Cruz_____	Republican___	Farmer.
Henry K. Turner _____Non-partisan	Sierra _____	Republican___	Farmer.
Jonathan M. Dudley _____Republican	Solano _____	Republican___	Farmer.
Joel A. Harvey_____Republican	Solano _____	Republican___	Lawyer.
S. G. Hilborn_____Republican	Solano _____	Republican___	Lawyer.
J. M. Charles_____Non-partisan	Sonoma_____	Republican___	Farmer.
G. A. Johnson_____Non partisan	Sonoma_____	Democrat_____	Lawyer.
W. W. Moreland _____Non-partisan	Sonoma_____	Democrat_____	Lawyer.
C. V. Stuart _____Non-partisan	Sonoma_____	Republican___	Farmer.
Tyler Davis Heiskell _____Democrat	Stanislaus _____	Democrat_____	Farmer.

NAME AND PARTY ELECTING.	COUNTY.	FORMER POL.	OCCUPATION.
George Ohleyer _____Non-partisan	Sutter_____	Democrat_____	Farmer.
H. C. Wilson_____Democrat	Tehama _____	Democrat_____	Farmer.
Joseph C. Brown _____Democrat	Tulare _____	Democrat_____	Farmer.
John Walker _____Democrat	Tuolumne _____	Democrat_____	Physician.
Charles G. Finney, jr. ____Workingmen	Ventura _____	Republican___	Lawyer.
John M. Rhodes_____Republican-	Yolo _____	Republican___	Miller.
D. H. Cowden_____Non-partisan	Yuba _____	Republican___	Lawyer.
John F. McNutt_____Non-partisan	Yuba _____	Democrat_____	Carpenter.
Augustus H. Chapman_____Non-partisan	Butte, Plumas and Lassen_____	Republican___	Lumb'r de'lr
Thomas H. Estey_____Non-partisan	Contra Costa and Marin_____	Republican___	Farmer.
J. E. Dean _____Workingmen	} El Dorado {	Republican___	Justice Pe'ce
G. W. Hunter _____Workingmen	and Alpine {	Democrat_____	Merchant.
‖J. M. Strong_____Convention	} Mariposa {	Democrat_____	Planter.
¶William J. Howard_____Convention	and Merced {	Democrat_____	Lawyer.
L. F. Jones_____Non-partisan	Mariposa, M'rc'd and Stanislaus	Democrat_____	Lawyer.
James N. Barton_____Workingmen	Mn'cino, Hmblt. and Del Norte_	Democrat_____	Farmer.
Patrick Reddy_____Non-partisan	Mono and Inyo_	Democrat_____	Lawyer.
H. C. Boggs_____Non-partisan	Napa, L'ke, Son.	Democrat_____	Farmer.
Edmund Barry_____Workingmen	Nevada, Sierra__	Republican___	Lawyer.
Ezra P. Soule _____Workingmen	Plumas, Lassen_	Republican___	Carpenter.
Horace C. Rolfe _____Republican	San Diego and San Bernardino	Republican___	Lawyer.
Lucius D. Morse _____Workingmen	San Francisco and San Mateo_	Republican___	Physician.
W. L. Dudley _____Non-partisan	San Joaquin and Amador___	Republican___	Lawyer.
William F. White_____Workingmen	St. Cruz, Mont'ry and San Benito	Democrat_____	Farmer.
J. Berry_____Democrat	Siskiyou, Modoc	Democrat_____	Lawyer.
David C. Stevenson_____Non-partisan	Siskiyou, Modoc, Trinity, Shasta	Republican___	Merchant.
Chas. F. Reed _____Republican	Solano, Yolo____	Republican___	Farmer.
A. R. Andrews_____Non-partisan	Trinity, Shasta__	Democrat_____	Lawyer.
R. M. Lampson_____Non-partisan	Tuol'ne, Cal'v'as	Republican___	Physician.
James H. Keyes _____Republican	Yuba and Sutter	Republican___	Farmer.

* H. H. Haight was elected a delegate on the non-partisan ticket, but died before the convention met, and J. West Martin was elected by the convention to fill vacancy.
† Bernard F. Kenny died during the session of the convention, and John J. Kenny was elected by the convention to fill vacancy.
‡ S. B. Thompson was chosen by the convention in place of Thomas Morris, who was disqualified, not being a citizen.
¶ George M. Hardwick died before the convention met. The convention elected J. M. Strong to fill vacancy, who served a short time, when he also died; the convention then elected William J. Howard.

In the month of September, the state central committee of the national greenback party met at San Francisco, and adopted the following :

Whereas, The demand for the "greenback," perfected and made a full legal tender as the money of the nation, is the fundamental principle of the national greenback labor party; and, whereas, in nearly all the states the name "national greenback labor party" has been adopted as the party name; therefore, resolved :

That the party shall hereafter be known in this state as the "national greenback labor party," until otherwise ordered by a national convention.

Whereas, The national greenback labor party was organized for the very best interests of the workingmen of America, and is to-day the only party whose principles, if carried out, will alleviate their present condition; and, whereas, the workingmen and women of this country are being falsely led by an unprincipled, ignorant, and designing demagogue; therefore, be it resolved:

That we do not indorse nor will we in any way affiliate with Dennis Kearney, and we do most earnestly deprecate the action of the eastern clubs of this party in their reception of the blatant, profane, and low humbug, as he does not in any way represent the sentiment of the workingmen of California.

CHAPTER XXIX.

1879. Adoption of the New Constitution—Formation of the New Constitution Party—Workingmen's Convention—Republican Convention—Convention of New Constitution Party—Democratic Convention—Prohibition Convention.

The second constitutional convention met at Sacramento on September 28th, 1878, and adjourned on March 3d, 1879. The new constitution was submitted to the people for ratification at an election held on May 7th, 1879, and it was adopted by a vote of 77,959 in its favor, to 67,134 against it. Most of the newspapers of the state were bitterly opposed to its adoption, the San Francisco *Chronicle* being the only leading newspaper that favored it. Immediately after the election, the *Chronicle* urged the formation of a new political party, to be composed of the supporters of the constitution, with the view of electing the first state officers of persons who were friendly to it and would in good faith endeavor to carry its provisions into effect. On May 10th a mass meeting of the friends of the constitution was held at Stockton, with a view of taking the preliminary steps toward the formation of the new party. Similar meetings were held soon after in the other counties.

On the 17th, a conference of the leading advocates of the new movement was held in San Francisco. John H. Burke called the meeting to order, and Cornelius Cole was elected chairman. Among those present were John C. Burch, A. C. Bradford, Clitus Barbour, W. T. Baggett, C. J. Beerstecher, Nathaniel Bennett, Alex. Campbell, John P. Dunn, Caleb Dorsey, J. R. Freud, Volney E. Howard, S. T. Leet, H. M. La Rue, John L. Love, J. G. McCallum, Thomas McConnell, James V. Coffey, John H. McKune, W. B. Norman, H. C. Patrick, George H. Rogers, George V. Smith, J. B. Southard, J. C. Stebbins, David S. Terry, T. A. Talbert, J. V. Webster, William F. White, J. A. Waymire, O. M. Wozencraft, Coleman Younger. Among those who had received invitations and were unable to attend, but who sent letters of regret, were Marion Biggs, Calvin Edgerton, James Johnson, Henry Larkin, Benj. Shurtleff, John R. Sharpstein, E. O. Tully, W. J. Tinnin, J. P. West, T. J. Sherwood, J. J. Ayers, J. W. Satterwhite, O. C. Pratt, John G. Downey, P. H. Ryan, and Warren Chase. A committee was appointed on resolutions, and they reported the following:

Whereas, The new constitution has been adopted by the people of California, without regard to past political affiliations, by over 11,000 majority—a majority more than three times as great as the republicans had in the last presidential campaign, when California polled its very largest vote; and, whereas, it is apparent that the victory has been achieved by the united efforts of men of integrity and patriotism in the three existing parties of the state, the democratic party, the republican party, and the workingmen's party; and, whereas, we believe that the wealth producers of California have made it possible to inaugurate reforms and provide a government that will dispense equal and exact justice to all, and are furthermore convinced that this result can only be accomplished through the prompt and united action of those who supported and advocated the adoption of the new constitution, leaving national questions to be decided at the presidential election; and, whereas, the new fundamental law must be put in operation by the legislative, executive, and judicial officers of the state government who are to be chosen in September next; and, whereas, if the duty of construing and putting in force the new constitution be handed over to the persons and the corporations opposed to its adoption, instead of relieving the state and the citizens of the burdens which now overwhelm them in the shape of monopoly power, greed, fraud, and dishonest government, and unjust and unequal taxation, it will be turned into an engine of oppression, and all our efforts be rendered futile and of no avail; now, therefore, be it resolved:

1. That for the good of the state we will here and now sink all past political differences, and maintain that position until California

is firmly and securely planted upon the foundation of the new constitution.

2. That there being now no vital national questions before the people for discussion or decision, the paramount duty of the hour is to devote all our energies to the work of electing such state officers as will enforce the new organic law in the spirit of fairness intended by its framers, and promote peace and prosperity where heretofore injustice and discontent have prevailed.

3. That we will retain and perfect our present organization throughout the state; and to this end we call upon and invite all good citizens to meet and assemble in every election precinct in this state on Saturday, the 24th day of May, and that they then and there form "new constitution clubs," to carry on the campaign.

4. That the chairman appoint an executive committee, to consist of twenty-three members—one from each judicial district and five at large—with full power to call a state convention, to fix the apportionment of delegates, and take charge of the organization, with whom all who are in harmony with the cause are requested to correspond.

5. That we will never falter in this work or in our purpose hereby enunciated until we have driven every vestige of monopoly oppression, corporate misrule, and political corruption from the government of this commonwealth.

6. That we will persevere in our good work until we make the state of California a government of the people, by the people, for the people, and until there shall be no man or corporation so great as to be above the law, and no one so lowly as to be beneath it.

7. That this organization shall be known as "the new constitution party," and that this shall be our shibboleth.

8. That we know no national issues or national politics in this campaign; that we rise above all parties, at the same time leaving every voter hereafter to act for himself in matters appertaining to old party lines, as he shall be advised.

The resolutions were adopted without opposition. The members of the workingmen's party spoke against the movement, declared that the workingmen would not abandon their organization, and declined to participate further in the meeting. A state executive committee was appointed, consisting of La Rue, Downey, Terry, Campbell, Younger, McConnell, Walter Van Dyke, Charles A. Tuttle, Burke, Shurtleff, George Steele, C. Grattan, Julius Chester, H. K. S. O'Melveny, James H. Keyes, Calvin Edgerton, G. W.

Hunter, P. H. Ryan, G. W. Hancock, Tipton Lindsey, E. T. Blackmer, J. A. Filcher, W. W. Moreland, Biggs, Cyrus Jones, H. C. Wilson, Leet, Bradford, Burch, Love, and Waymire. On May 11th, at a meeting of workingmen held at San Francisco, it was resolved not to affiliate with the new constitution party.

The workingmen's state convention met at San Francisco on June 3d, and was called to order by Kearney. Among the delegates were John P. Dunn, T. K. Nelson, Pierce H. Ryan, S. M. Buck, and John P. West. On permanent organization, Kearney was president, and J. J. Flynn secretary. On the 4th, the committee on resolutions reported the following:

The workingmen of California, in convention assembled, do adopt and proclaim the following as their platform and declaration of principles:

1. That we recognize the constitution of the United States of America and the constitution of the state of California as the great charters of our liberties, and the paramount law of the land, and California as an inseparable part of the American union, and the system of government thereby inaugurated as the only wise, free, just and equal government that has ever existed—the last, best, and only hope of man for self-government.

2. The letter and spirit of the new constitution must be enforced.

3. We utterly repudiate all spirit of communism or aggrarianism.

4. No land or other subsidies shall ever be granted to corporations.

5. Vested rights in property must be respected, but land monopoly must be prohibited.

6. Money, mortgages, and bonds must be taxed.

7. The dignity of labor must be upheld, and labor of male and female, when of equal value, must be equally compensated.

8. Any official who shall violate the pledges given to secure his election should be punished as a felon.

9. The contract system of labor of criminals should be abolished, and criminal labor so regulated as not to conflict with free labor throughout the United States.

10. All public officers shall receive fixed salaries, and all fees must be accounted for as public money.

11. That the honors and legal pay of all officials should be considered equivalent for the best services they can render the state, while official jobbery, bribery, or corruption, must be visited by sure and severe punishment.

12. All labor on public works shall be performed by the day, at ruling rates, and eight hours must constitute a day's work.

13. A system of compulsory education for children between the ages of eight and fourteen years, must be adopted; education free in public schools, and all books paid for by the state. That the state should acquire a copyright for school text-books, which must be the property of the state forever, and the state print the same at the state printing office.

14. We pledge this party to maintain in its purity the public school system authorized by the constitution, and will, when in our power, establish in connection therewith, departments for industrial education.

15. Article XI of the constitution must not be construed in favor of the appointment of public officials, whenever their election by the people direct is at all practicable.

16. Lobbying having been declared a felony in the new constitution, we demand that the legislature shall enforce said provision of the fundamental law by the most stringent enactment.

17. Foreigners ineligible to citizenship, shall not be licensed to peddle goods or commodities of any character throughout the state of California.

18. Land monopoly being contrary to the spirit of republican institutions and detrimental to the progress of society, and conducive to the creation of a wealthy class of landholders side by side with a landless multitude; therefore, we hereby declare ourselves in favor of adopting every legitimate means to prevent the monopoly of the soil in a few hands.

19. Malfeasance in public office must be punished as a felony.

20. That the laws now existing for the punishment of buying and selling votes are insufficient, in that both the buyer and seller being equally guilty, neither can be obliged to give evidence of the guilt of the other. We therefore favor the enactment of laws by which the person bribing or attempting to bribe an elector shall alone be punished.

21. We demand that the fullest investigation be had, under the authority of the ensuing legislature, into the alleged scandalous character of the opposition to the adoption of the new constitution; and if the charges prove true, that condign punishment be visited upon the guilty ones.

22. The legislature should cause to be examined and prosecuted, land frauds in California.

23. The same value should not be taxed twice the same year under the same system of taxation.

24. Interest on money should not exceed 6 per cent. per annum.

25. We demand the immediate restoration to pre-emption and sale of all forfeited railroad lands, and that no further extension be granted.

26. We condemn the action of our senators and representatives in congress, in depriving this state of representation for one year, while her most important interests are at stake, as an unwarrantable perversion of their official duties, made under a false pretense of economy, but really in the hope to gain a political advantage over the workingmen's party of California.

27. That we condemn the inaction of our senators and representatives in congress, in not attempting to have the withdrawal from pre-emption and sale of lands illegally claimed by the defunct Atlantic and Pacific railroad company removed, and said lands restored to the people, and re-opened to pre-emption and sale.

28. We condemn the "desert land bill," and all other land grabs, under whatever name or on whatever pretense.

29. Contracts by debtors for the payment of fees of the attorneys of creditors, should be prohibited.

30. Laws should be passed providing for the deduction of debts due *bona fide* residents from unsecured credits in matters of taxation.

31. That notaries public should be elected by the people, one from each county. That the best protection of our frontier will be a population of settlers owning their own lands, and that it will be the part of wisdom for the government to expend the money now squandered for such protection, by settling the people on the unoccupied land.

32. Whereas, Great apprehension exists in the mining counties that some legislation under the new constitution might be unfavorable to mining interests, we declare that under the protection of our party their vested rights shall be respected.

33. That the president and vice-president of the United States, and United States senators, shall be elected by the direct vote of the people, and no man should be elected to the office of president or vice-president of the United States for two consecutive terms.

34. We are tired of the dreary discussion of dead issues in our national congress, while great, living issues are confronting the country. The people want bread and not stones. We hail the awakening

of the oppressed workingmen and impoverished farmers, to the east of us, to a sense of their power and the cause of their sufferings, as a harbinger of a new revolution in behalf of human rights, against vicious systems and dishonest politicians.

35. That the national bank law should be repealed, and all moneys issued by the United States be a full legal tender for all debts, public and private.

36. Congress ought to pass fares and freights bills, and bills to prohibit unjust discrimination and other abuses in the management of overland routes.

37. That the government of the United States should establish throughout the states, a system of postal savings banks.

38. Charges for freights and fares on railroads, and for the use of water, gas, etc., must be so regulated that there shall be no discrimination between persons and places, and that capital actually invested in railroad, water, and gas rights should yield no greater net income than capital invested in farming and other productive industries. The legislature must pass laws to carry into effect the police power of the state, in order to prevent the importation of Chinese, and congress should abrogate all treaties that come in conflict with the nineteenth article of the new constitution.

39. We hold that the state and county tickets formed under the auspices of the workingmen's party of California must be made up of friends of the new constitution, irrespective of party predilections. To further secure the efficiency of the new organic law, we will attack its opponents with the most effective weapons; but among ourselves, in difference of opinion, we will allow liberal discussion, give considerate attention, and exercise the largest charity. To these ends we invite the co-operation of all the friends of the new constitution. We must do all in our power as a party to prevent any conflict between the interests of mining and agriculture, by just laws, engineering skill, and public aid.

40. That the cardinal principle of true reform in politics is, that the office shall seek the man, and not the man the office; and that honesty, capability, and faithfulness to our republican system of government, are the main requirements in the selection of candidates for office. That the democratic and republican parties have signally failed to apply these principles, inasmuch as both have been completely controlled by "rings," seeking office only to betray the people. That we denounce and condemn the efforts of both old political par-

ties to create a solid north or a solid south, and thereby sectionize the country; that in the organization of our party we know no north, no south, no east, no west. That we are determined the government of our country shall be so administered as to secure equal rights to all our people, be they high or low, rich or poor, black or white; and that by so doing the union can and will be perpetuated forever.

Signed by M. F. Quinn, chairman ; W. W. Broughton, secretary; D. A. Leonard, F. F. O'Leary, P. F. Warde, Anson Clark, John Allyn, H. M. Moore, James O'Sullivan, John Knotwell, John T. Wickes, and W. J. Sweasey.

Kearney moved to strike out the third section, but after a discussion he withdrew the motion, finding that the sentiment of the convention was against him. A motion that the candidates for judicial offices be excused from taking the oath required by the constitution of the party was lost. On the 5th, the following was added to the platform :

Water for the use of any city, town, or county in this state, or the inhabitants thereof, can only be appropriated by the lawfully constituted authorities of such city and county, or city or town. Any appropriation of water heretofore made by any person, association, or corporation for supplying any city and county, or city or town, or the inhabitants thereof, not carried into actual operation by the construction of water works and the furnishing of water, shall be declared void.

Gambling devices have always victimized productive industry, and they must be vigorously suppressed. Stock gambling must be prohibited, and stock stealing must be regulated.

Corporations must discharge their Chinese employes, or go out of business. Laws must be passed to purge the communities of the state of the presence of Chinese, and to prevent their acquiring any further foothold among us.

The man who owns the labor must be given as perfect a lien on the thing produced or improved thereby as the man who owns the capital is given on his investment.

Justice is too dear. The courts are inaccessible to poor men and men of limited means by reason of the cost bills exacted from them. We demand a reduction of these expenses.

The following nominations were then made :

William F. White, for governor, on the first ballot, by a vote of 110, to 20 for Henry Larkin, and 22 for John O. Origler. J. V. Webster was named for the office, but withdrew, and John G. Downey sent a telegram declining to be a candidate.

W. R. Andrus, for lieutenant-governor, on the first ballot, over Charles Krug; Henry Larkin withdrawing.

A. A. Smith for secretary of state, without opposition.

Charles Krug for treasurer, on the first ballot, over L. B. Clarke. Krug declined the nomination, and Clarke was nominated.

Hugh L. Jones for controller, without opposition.

C. W. Cross for attorney-general, without opposition.

H. J. Stevenson for surveyor-general, on the first ballot.

D. H. Trout for school superintendent, over A. L. Mann. Trout declined on the 13th, and the state committee nominated S. N. Burch.

R. F. Morrison for chief justice of the supreme court, without opposition.

S. B. McKee, J. R. Sharpstein, Charles A. Tuttle, George A. Johnson, J. H. Budd, and W. T. McNealy, for associate justices, over E. W. McKinstry, John H. McKune, A. L. Rhodes, E. D. Sawyer, and S. M. Buck. Tuttle, Johnson, McNealy, and Budd declined the nominations, and J. D. Thornton, Buck, McKinstry, and E. M. Ross were nominated in their stead.

O. F. Thornton for clerk of the supreme court, without opposition.

Henry Larkin from the first district, C. J. Beerstecher from the second district, and George Stoneman from the third district, for railroad commissioners.

The first district convention met on June 7th, and nominated Clitus Barbour for congressman, without opposition; Robert Ferral withdrawing. Wm. C. Hoagland was nominated for member of the state board of equalization.

The second district convention met at San Francisco on June 5th, and nominated Peter J. Hopper for congressman, and George Thom for member of the board of equalization. Both of these candidates withdrew the next day, and H. B. Williams was nominated for congressman, over J. C. Martin, Thom, John Greenwall, and B. K. Low; and W. B. G. Keller was nominated, without opposition, for member of the board of equalization. Williams withdrew on August 19th in favor of the democratic candidate.

26

The third district convention met on the 6th at San Francisco, and nominated C. P. Berry for congressman, over Benjamin Shurtleff and J. T. Rogers. J. P. Cavanaugh was nominated for member of the board of equalization. On July 10th, Berry declined to take the pledge, and G. T. Elliott was nominated, but he declined on the 21st, and the name of Berry was again placed on the ticket.

The fourth district convention met at San Francisco on the 5th, and nominated James J. Ayers for congressman, over Charles McDougall; and O. T. Chubb for member of the board of equalization.

The republican state committee met at San Francisco on March 5th, and called a state convention to meet at Sacramento on June 17th. On May 22d, another meeting of the committee was held, and it was resolved not to postpone the convention. The following address was issued by the committee to the voters of the party:

The republican state central committee desires to urge upon you the necessity of organizing promptly for an earnest and vigorous campaign. You are called upon this year to perform a double duty : to assist in securing a faithful and effective administration of the new constitution, and to support the time-honored principles of your party. The contest, which has just resulted in the adoption of that change in our organic law, was waged without reference to national party lines, and had but one issue : whether the new con-constitution should be ratified.

The republican party accepts the result as an absolute finality, and pledges itself to a faithful interpretation and administration of its provisions in all honesty and sincerity. That party is pre-eminently the representative of loyalty, of respect for law, of faithful adherence to compacts. The principles on and by which it stands are inseparable from these characteristics; its members have ever been noted for their insistence upon strict regard for constitutional requirements; and, in urging the republicans of the state to rally round their party banners, we are only giving the best assurance conceivable that the candidates whom they will put forward may be trusted to administer the new constitution fairly and fully, and in all sincerity and good faith.

It is the more necessary to stand by the party organization to-day, because great and momentous national issues are in controversy. In addition to four congressmen, California elects a state senate, whose members will vote on the election of a United States senator. These considerations alone point to the absolute necessity of a vigorous party campaign. But these are not the only incentives to energetic action. In 1880, the presidential campaign opens, and the republicans of California cannot afford to be negligent in the preparation for a struggle which may involve the whole future of the republic. The issues now presented are inferior in gravity to none which the party has been called to confront since its defense of a threatened union.

Advancing with ever-growing audacity, the democratic leaders have conspired to paralyze the federal government, and to revive the obsolete and heretical doctrine of state's rights, with extravagance. To compass their purpose they have undertaken to intimidate the executive, by threatening to withhold supplies; and, further to embarrass the administration, they have resorted to the device of appending political measures to appropriation bills, and causing it to be inferred that they will bring the government to a standstill if their demands are not conceded. It is against the dangers which this condition of national politics involves, that the republican party must prepare to contend with all its energies. We have exaggerated nothing in ascribing to the situation a gravity only second to that which confronted the nation in 1861. The occasion calls for all the loyalty and resolution which the memories of a glorious past can inspire and evoke. Though almost a generation has elapsed, the patriots who fought to preserve the union are not yet dead. The policy which periled their lives, their fortunes, and their sacred honor to uphold and defend, is not yet abandoned by its friends; and it is to that spirit of patriotism, to that stern resolve, to that noble liberalism, that we confidently appeal to-day.

The mission of the republican party is not ended while the enfranchisement of the negro continues to be a sham and a pretense; while republican government in ten states is a mockery; while the men who fought to destroy the union stand triumphantly upon the steps of the national capitol, and plot the reversal of the judgment which the swords of our patriots recorded. That party stands pledged to preserve the faith of the government in all its promises to its creditors; to provide, as a circulating medium for the use of the people, a currency which shall be of uniform value, whether gold, silver, or paper; and to make a dollar, whatever its form, absolutely worth a dollar.

To disband, to falter, to fail now in recognizing the duty and need of action, would be to surrender the purposes of a lifetime, to satisfy the teachings of a generation, to renounce the approval of cotemporaries and the gratitude of posterity.   It is not from the republican party that such weakness, such apathy, is to be expected. That party is to-day, as ever, the responsible depository of whatever high and holy aspirations the people of these United States cherish. It stands for ordered liberty, equal justice, enlightened education, constitutional government, and equitable legislation.   It is the exponent and guardian of that liberty which rests upon understanding, and of that freedom which is distinguished from license.   It stands to-day, as ever, for the poor as for the rich, for the passionless administration of a justice which knows no respect of persons, and for all that can enfranchise, elevate, and ennoble mankind.   And because it stands for these, it is the natural and implacable foe of that party which aims at anarchy, sanctions license, and seeks to tamper with justice, under the plea of a more perfect democracy; and which shelters and sanctions corruption, under the pretext of a magnanimous catholicity.

Against the doctrines which assault the freedom, purity, and republicanism of our institutions, it is the duty of all republicans to oppose to their utmost efforts; and to such a contest you are now invited, in the full and abiding confidence that you will respond with characteristic enthusiasm to the summons, and that you will not cease until your efforts shall be crowned by a glorious success.

The convention met at the time and place agreed upon and was called to order by A. G. Abell, the chairman of the state committee. Obed Harvey, Frank M. Pixley, and George L. Woods were nominated for temporary chairman.   On the first ballot Harvey had 188 votes, to 140 for Woods, and 74 for Pixley.   On the third ballot Pixley was elected by a vote of 206, to 186 for Harvey.   The committee on platform consisted of G. G. Blanchard, C. B. Porter, E. W. Roberts, George C. Gorham, George L. Woods, John H. Jewett, and O. Sanders.   On the 18th a permanent organization was effected and Pixley was elected president, and R. Burnell, G. L. Woods, O. Harvey, and W. B. May, vice-presidents.   The majority of the committee on resolutions reported the following :

1. That we reaffirm our allegiance to the principles of the grand national party of free soil, free labor, equal rights of the people, honest money, good public faith, and the integrity of the national

union—the party whose record furnishes some of the grandest and most illustrious chapters of our nationalhistory.

2. That the attempts by the democratic majority in congress to repeal the laws for the preservation of the purity of the ballot-box at elections for members of congress, is in keeping with the history of the party whose crimes against the ballot in New York city under the Tweed dynasty in 1868, led to the enactment of those laws; that the method by which they seek to accomplish this result —by withholding appropriations for the courts of the United States unless the president will join them in their conspiracy, is revolutionary; and that the denial of the power of congress to make regulations for the conduct of congressional elections—a power specifically granted in the constitution of the United States—is a palpable attempt to revive the baneful doctrine of state supremacy, which was the cause of the great rebellion.

3. That the firm and united opposition of the republican party in congress, and of the president, to this new revolt against the nation, should be sustained by all patriotic and law-abiding people throughout the land.

4. That the new constitution is the organic law of the state, adopted by the people in accordance with our republican form of government. It must and will be sustained by the republican party in loyalty. It must and will receive honest legislation. It must and will receive a just and generous judicial interpretation. It must and will be enforced by an honest executive administration; and we condemn any effort to evade its provisions as unwise and treasonable to the popular will legally expressed.

5. That an independent and intelligent agricultural population is' the chief element of a nation's strength and prosperity, and it should be the policy of state and general government to encourage the acquisition of lands in small holdings for actual use, and to discourage the monopoly by individuals or corporations of large bodies.

6. The Chinese question is one of national importance, demanding the consideration of the national congress. Unrestricted Chinese immigration imperils the best interests of our coast, and ultimately that of the whole country. It menaces the labor class with unequal competition and is dangerous to our civilization. Not unmindful of its history and our own part therein, regarding the rights of present immigrants acquired, we demand of the general government such legislation as shall restrict or control Chinese immigration in

the future, and the repeal or modification of so much of the Burlingame treaty as interferes with the accomplishment of that object. We will spare no effort within our own state to secure by legislative enactment a judicial enforcement of the same results. Chinese immigration must be restricted and controlled.

7. That it is a paramount duty and interest of the state to provide ample educational opportunities for its youth, and to permit none to be deprived of their enjoyment, and that so far as the provisions of the new organic law will permit, legislation should facilitate and encourage the adoption of a uniform standard of qualifications for teaching, courses of study, and text books for the public schools.

8. That the republican party—always the true friend of labor, in all its varied forms—pledges itself to secure the passage of such laws under the new constitution as will foster, protect and promote the development and growth of all the industries of the state.

9. That the republican party, as a just arbiter of the people, pledges itself to insist upon the passage of such laws as will prevent any conflict between the mining and certain portions of the agricultural districts and interests of the state—and we declare that vested rights of all parties shall be scrupulously respected and protected.

10. The republican party, claiming to represent the principles of justice, honesty, and moral sentiment, declares its fidelity to the law and its unalterable opposition to any attempt on the part of any class to disturb the ownership of property; and while it would disfavor the accumulation of great landed estates in the possession of individuals or corporations, it would as firmly protect all the rights of all persons to all the wealth that they may legally and honestly acquire.

Whereas, The regulation of fares and freights upon all inter-state railroad travel and traffic is subject to the action of the congress of the United States, and the regulation of fares and freights within a state is subject to local legislative jurisdiction and control, resolved,

11. As the opinion of this convention, that the railroad commissioners who shall be nominated by the district conventions should make such reductions in the rates of fares and freights upon all local travel and traffic carried over railroads which have received national or state aid, operated within this state, as will reduce the same by a certain specified percentage upon the rates declared, collected, or charged by published rate bill in force upon any such road on the

first day of June, 1879, and that such commissioners shall hereafter make such further reductions as may seem to them just and demanded by the interests of the people, but shall in no case authorize or per. mit any increase thereafter upon such rates so ordered.

Gorham moved that the report be adopted except that portion which related to railroad matters, and the motion was carried. He then read the minority report of the committee, as follows :

Whereas, The railroad company has received $132,000,000 from freight and passengers, and the transportation cost $58,000,000 upon property derived through legislation, and valued by the president of the company at $100,000,000 over all liabilities; whereas, notwith. standing the depressed condition of other business during six years, the people have paid to the company over $15,000,000 per annum; whereas, the expenses of the company were but $6,000,000; and, whereas, the company has exacted in six years over $8,000,000 net earnings; and, whereas, the producing and commercial interests will be ruined unless relief is afforded; and, whereas, the new constitution was adopted mainly because of the railroad section; and, whereas, tolls within the state can be reduced one-fourth; therefore, resolved,

That a remedy does not lie in any indefinite advocacy of reduced rates, as the will of the people, expressed at the polls, has been repeatedly defeated in the legislature by a system of parliamentary legerdemain; that relief lies in requiring candidates for governor, lieutenant-governor, the legislature, and any railroad commissioner, to take a pledge; that the true and needed reform is to fix rates between points in the state on railroads which have received national or state aid, less than rates actually charged June 1, 1879; that for each dollar usually and actually demanded and received by the company a reduction of twenty-five cents should be made; that the question should be settled in advance of all other questions; that a pledge after election cannot be broken without endangering the peace of society, and revolution will probably follow; that all candidates for governor, lieutenant-governor, state senator, or assemblyman, or railroad commissioner, shall take the following pledge : .

"Pledge for the railroad commissioner:

I do solemnly pledge my sacred honor that I will, if elected a railroad commissioner, faithfully support, without any modification or change, the following order : Ordered that the rates of fares and freights on all railroads between all points within this state which have received national or state aid, shall, from and after the 1st day of February, 1880, be fixed at three-fourths the usual rates demanded and received on the 1st day of June, 1879, or at any time during the six months prior thereto; and the words 'usual rates,' above used, shall be deemed to mean the rates actually and usually charged in each case, whether the same be nominally fixed or special rates; and . it is further ordered that no change shall be made in the mode of computing charges, or in the weight or measurement of freight, or in the classification of service which shall affect the substantial rights of parties under this order—the true object being to reduce all charges for services rendered by railroads between points within the state over roads which have received national or state aid, one-fourth below the present rates; and I further solemnly pledge myself that, during my term of office, I will never vote for any increased rate of charge for any railroad service, but that any charge voted for by me after February 1st, 1880, shall be a reduction.

"*Pledges for governor, lieutenant-governor, assemblymen, and rail-road commissioners:*

"I do solemnly pledge myself to the earnest and faithful support of the new constitution, and that I will exert all the influence I possess to aid in the election of the railroad commissioners pledged to a reduction of one-fourth on all railroad fares and freights on roads which have received national or state aid; and if elected I pledge myself, in the performance of my official duties, to act in accordance with this pledge."

S. O. Houghton offered the following, as a substitute for both reports:

That in the opinion of this convention justice demands that the present rate of freights and fares upon all lines of railroads in this state, that have received state or national aid, ought to be reduced at least 25 per cent.

After a lengthy debate the Houghton substitute was adopted.

The following nominations were made on the 18th and 19th:

George C. Perkins, for governor, on the first ballot, by a vote of 215, to 53 for Horace Davis, 106 for George S. Evans, and 31 for John F. Swift.

John Mansfield, for lieutenant-governor, without opposition.

Daniel M. Burns, for secretary of state, on the first ballot, by a vote of 269, to 51 for Edward Martin, and 71 for Drury Melone.

D. M. Kenfield, for controller, without opposition.

John Weil, for treasurer, on the first ballot, by a vote of 221, to 122 for Adam Wasson, and 70 for W. E. McArthur.

Augustus L. Hart, for attorney-general, on the first ballot, by a vote of 217, to 190 for George W. Schell.

James W. Shanklin, for surveyor-general, on the first ballot, by a vote of 239, to 161 for W. H. Crane ; John A. Eagan withdrawing.

Frank W. Gross, for clerk of the supreme court, over Grant I. Taggart, Alexander Campbell, jr., and H. H. Russell.

F. M. Campbell, for school superintendent, over J. H. C. Bonte.

A. L. Rhodes, for chief justice, without opposition.

A. P. Catlin, Isaac S. Belcher, M. H. Myrick, James E. Hale, E. D. Wheeler, and J. T. Richards, for associate justices, on the first ballot, which resulted as follows: John W. Dwinelle, 105; John W. North, 63; Hale, 357; Catlin, 371; Wheeler, 251; Belcher, 362; John Reynolds, 122; Myrick, 269; L. D. Latimer, 241; Robert Harrison, 22; and Richards, 245. A state committee was selected composed of Max Brooks, A. J. Rhoads, S. G. Hilborn, W. H. Parks, G. G. Blanchard, E. F. Spence, M. D. Boruck, S. O. Houghton, H. W. Byington, P. B. Cornwall, and others.

The first district republican convention, for the nomination of a candidate for railroad commissioner, met at Sacramento on June 19th, and nominated Joseph S. Cone, on the first ballot, by a vote of 121, to 21 for Christopher Green, and 32 for H. Cummings—Charles F. Reed and William Jennings withdrawing.

The second district convention met at San Francisco on June 24th. Gorham offered a series of resolutions similar to the minority report of the committee of resolutions of the state convention. At an adjourned meeting of the district convention, held on July 1st, the resolutions were tabled, by a vote of 52 to 27. T. G. Phelps was nominated for commissioner, on the first ballot, by a vote of 50, to 22 for George A. Fisher, 8 for D. W. Grant, and 3 for J. G. Jackson ; John McComb and L. W. Walker withdrawing.

The third district convention met at Sacramento, on June 19th, and nominated C. H. Phillips, on the first ballot, by a vote of 92, to 22 for C. S. Abbott, 15 for H. K. W. Brent, 7 for H. J. Ostrander, and 3 for L. U. Shippee; George W. Tyler withdrawing.

The first district republican equalization convention met at San Francisco on June 23d, and nominated James L. King for member

of the state board of equalization, without opposition, C. S. Capp withdrawing.

The second district convention met at Sacramento on June 19th, and nominated M. M. Drew on the first ballot, by a vote of 70, to 46 for L. C. Morehouse.

The third district convention met at Sacramento on June 19th, and nominated Warren Dutton, without opposition; Charles F. Reed declining.

The fourth district convention met at Sacramento on the same day, and nominated James A. Clayton, over John Baker and P. Y. Baker.

The first district republican congressional convention met at San Francisco on June 23d, and nominated Horace Davis, without opposition.

The second district convention met at Sacramento on June 17th, and nominated Horace F. Page on the first ballot, by a vote of 85, to 25 for Stephen G. Nye.

The third district convention met at Sacramento on June 19th, and nominated Joseph McKenna on the first ballot, by a vote of 92, to 37 for Jerome Banks.

The fourth district convention met at Sacramento on the same day, and nominated Romualdo Pacheco, without opposition; S. O. Houghton declining.

The executive committee of the new constitution party met at San Francisco on May 22d, and called a state convention to meet at Sacramento on June 25th. The convention was called to order by Marion Biggs, the chairman of the committee, and he was chosen temporary chairman. The committee on resolutions consisted of Cornelius Cole, H. P. Irving, L. Hamilton, D. S. Terry, J. I. Caldwell, A. Campbell, Dr. A. W. Thompson, E. Comstock, Volney E. Howard, and others. On the 27th, a permanent organization was effected by the election of Biggs as president; and Cornelius Cole, Dr. C. Grattan, J. W. Snowball, and D. C. Reed, as vice-presidents. The committee on platform reported the following, which were adopted:

Whereas, In the recent election on the adoption of the new constitution the voters of this state, without regard to party lines, obtained a glorious victory over the combined power of the moneyed rings, banks, and corporations, and have thus shown to all the world that they have sufficient intelligence, honor, and patriotism to preserve, guard, and protect the liberty bequeathed to them by the illustrious fathers of the republic; and, whereas, the banded cohorts of capital are now endeavoring by their usual corrupt means to wrest the fruits of the recent victory of the people of this state from them, by electing to office those who are inimical to the new constitution, for the purpose of construing and administering the same in behalf of the moneyed power, and against the rights of the laboring and producing classes; and, whereas, the opposition to the new law was unequalled in violence, and the efforts to defeat it were characterized by bribery and coercion theretofore unparalleled ; and, whereas, a constitution cannot execute itself, but must be vitalized by appropriate legislation, and be enforced by just interpretation and friendly construction; and, whereas, a single transportation company is collecting from the people an annual revenue so enormous as to cripple all the industries of the state ; and, whereas, from the commencement of its existence that company has been operating upon capital furnished entirely by the people of the state and nation ; and, whereas, the democratic and republican party organizations which, openly professing to ignore the subject of the adoption of the new constitution, did in fact use the machinery of those parties in the interests of the enemies of the new constitution in order to defeat it; and, whereas, the people adopted the new constitution without the aid of either the democratic or republican party organizations ; and, whereas, the presence of the Chinese in California is an unmitigated evil and an intolerable nuisance; therefore, be it resolved :

1. That the new constitution embodies principles just to all, oppressive to none, dear to ourselves, and of untold benefits to posterity.

2. That the people of California would prove recreant to their own interests, false to their professions of friendship to the new constitution, and deficient in a proper spirit of manhood, if they were to submit that instrument to the hands of its enemies, and thus permit it to be strangled in its infancy.

3. That the new constitution party, organized for the purpose of releasing the people from the oppressions and thralldom of capital in California, cannot have, and is not intended to have, any influence whatever on the national politics of any individual.

4. That in a republic, where the people are the source of all political power, and where the avenues to promotion and wealth are open

and free to all alike, there is not and cannot be any room for agrarianism, socialism, or communism.

5. That the new constitution party will protect the liberty, labor, and property of every citizen, and that therefore it commends itself to the support of all.

6. That the first legislature elected under the new constitution shall put into immediate effect the stringent clauses of that instrument against the Chinese, and that everything that can be done shall be done to make the Chinese cease coming, and to cause those now here to speedily depart.

7. That, in accordance with a joint resolution passed by the last legislature, the governor be urged to submit to the people of the state, at the general election in September next, the question of Chinese immigration to this state, and that whether such question be submitted officially or not, we hereby recommend that every ticket of the new constitution party have printed immediately following the names of the candidates, the words, "Against Chinese immigration."

8. That our principles are embodied in the new constitution; that while we believe in the doctrine that principles and not men should be subserved by party action, we cannot safely submit the execution of the instrument that embodies our principles to men who were but yesterday violently opposed to them, and who have shown no better evidence of conversion than a desire to hold office.

9. That the rates of freights and fares of those railroad companies in California which have received government aid, should be reduced at least one-third, and that each person receiving a nomination from the new constitution party for an office, in the exercise of which and whose duty it shall be to establish rates of charges for the transportation of passengers and freights, shall be deemed and held to be pledged to carry out in good faith the policy enunciated in this resolution, and as far as possible relieve the people of California from the extortion and oppression by those great corporations.

10. That laws shall be passed to carry into effect the provisions of the new constitution, that all property shall be taxed according to its value, once in each year; strictly avoiding all species of double taxation.

11. That it is the duty of the legislature to provide for the election by the people, of all state and county officers under the constitution, except in cases where their appointment is specially provided for in the new constitution.

The following additional resolution was adopted :

For many years after California became a state, mining for gold was the leading industry—even now, it is the second; many of our most enterprising citizens, as individuals and as associations under incorporation laws, have invested millions of dollars in developing placers and constructing ditches to enable the miners to work the same; and with the foregoing facts in view, resolved:

That the new constitution party pledges itself that it will stand firm as the miners' friend, and in case any attempt shall be made at any time to pass unfriendly legislation, the new constitution party will openly and boldly oppose any and all attempts to impinge upon the vested rights of the miners and ditch owners. .

The following nominations were made:

Hugh J. Glenn, for governor, on the first ballot, by a vote of 128, to 115 for J. V. Webster ; Volney E. Howard, John G. Downey, and Hugh M. LaRue declining.

John P. West, for lieutenant-governor, without opposition; J. V. Webster, Thomas McConnell, Marion Biggs, O. Wolcott, W. S. Manlove, C. Cole, and James A. Waymire declining. West declined the nomination, and on the 27th D. C. Reed was nominated in his place, without opposition; Charles Kent, G. W. Hancock, C. R. Weller, and Milton Wasson declining.

Lauren E. Crane, for secretary of state, on the first ballot, over George W. Wedekind, W. D. Lawton, and H. M. LaRue.

Hugh M. LaRue, for controller, without opposition.

Cyrus Jones, for treasurer, on the first ballot, over Charles Kent and H. Holmes.

Charles W. Cross, for attorney-general, without opposition. He declined on August 19th, and David S. Terry was nominated by the committee.

F. J. Clark, for surveyor-general, without opposition.

Edwin F. Smith, for clerk of the supreme court, on the first ballot, over L. J. Mowry.

A. L. Mann, for school superintendent, on the first ballot, over J. R. Kelso and L. D. Morse.

Nathaniel Bennett, for chief justice, without opposition ; O. C. Pratt and David S. Terry declining.

Alexander Campbell, jr., Calhoun Benham, Charles A. Tuttle, John H. McKune, Caleb Dorsey, and John C. Burch, for associate justices, on the first ballot, over E. W. McKinstry, E. B. Spencer,

A. C. Freeman, J. R. Sharpstein, H. P. Irving, J. H. Budd, A. W. Thompson, George A. Johnson, O. C. Pratt, C. Cole, James E. Hale, and John L. Love.

A state committee was selected, consisting of L. C. Granger, Charles F. Lott, M. Biggs, jr., Dr. Grattan, Charles Krug, Jonas Spect, W. B. Norman, J. I. Caldwell, D. C. Reed, C. L. Weller, William Holden, J. L. Love, J. H. Burke, H. J. Dam, G. H. Rogers, J. A. Filcher, J. V. Webster, C. Younger, G. W. Hancock, J. W. Snowball, B. Langford, Charles Kent, B. Shurtleff, M. Biggs, and others.

The first district new constitution convention, for the nomination of a candidate for railroad commissioner, met at Sacramento on June 27th, and nominated Henry Larkin, on the seventh ballot, over J. N. Blood, George W. Hancock, William Holden, and W. B. Norman.

The second district convention met on the same day, and nominated Samuel Soule, without opposition; W. H. Mills, C. A. Stombs, and George W. Thomas withdrawing.

The third district convention met at Sacramento on June 26th and nominated George Stoneman on the first ballot, by a vote of 71, to 12 for George W. Smith.

The first district equalization convention met at Sacramento on June 27th and nominated A. C. Bradford, without opposition.

The second district convention met at the same time and place, and nominated W. M. Crutcher on the first ballot, over L. Brusie, Joel Russell, and W. B. G. Keller. Crutcher declined on July 22d, and Keller was nominated by the committee on August 19th.

The third district convention met at Sacramento on the 27th, and nominated John M. Kelley on the first ballot, over J. M. Charles.

The fourth district convention met at the same place and nominated T. D. Heiskell on the first ballot, over C. Younger.

The democratic state committee held a meeting at San Francisco, at which many of the leading members of the party were called in to consider the matter of the advisability of calling a state convention. W. J. Tinnin moved that a state convention be called to meet at Sacramento on May 27th, to nominate a state ticket. J. D. Spencer moved to substitute San Francisco as the place for holding the convention. The amendment was rejected, and the original resolution carried. It was resolved as a sense of the conference that the state committee should issue an address to the members of the party. The committee met immediately afterward, and endorsed the action of the conference in reference to calling the convention, but after a long discussion, failed to endorse the resolution to issue thè address. On May 14th, the executive committee of the state committee held a meeting at San Francisco, at the suggestion of leading democrats who were in favor of postponing the state convention, and a call was issued for a meeting of the state committee on the 20th. At that meeting, the state convention was postponed to July 1st. On the last named day, the convention met at Sacramento, and was called to order by J. O. Maynard, the secretary of the state committee. J. O. Shorb was elected temporary chairman without opposition. The committee on resolutions consisted of James O'Meara, S. M. Taylor, A. J. Bryant, Thomas J. Clunie, W. A. Selkirk, A. B. Dibble, Jo Hamilton, W. J. Tinnin, G. H. Crossette, J. W. Satterwhite, L. Archer, J. D. Spencer, and J. O. Shorb. On permanent organization, Shorb was president, and S. M. Taylor, John O. Hays, G. H. Crossette, and O. T. Ryland, vice-presidents. The committee reported the following resolutions:

1. That the democratic party is the only party which has always observed, obeyed, and maintained the federal constitution, and is, therefore, the only political party which the people can safely trust to administer the organic law of the state.

2. The democratic sentiment is an indissoluble union of indestructible states, under the paramount authority of the federal constitution, in all powers which have not been reserved by the states.

3. That as suffrage is a privilege conferred exclusively by the states, each state for itself, agreeably to the constitutionally expressed will of the people thereof, any attempt of the general government to interfere with the elections in the states, or in any of them, is dangerous to the liberties of the people and destructive of the sacredness of the elective franchise; and therefore we condemn as unconstitutional and subversive of the freedom of the ballot the odious laws, of republican origin and adoption, by which federal supervisors of elections and deputy marshals are empowered to interfere with the registration of voters at the polls, and United States troops are stationed at polling places to intimidate or disfranchise citizens, native or naturalized.

4. That in unison with their party brethren throughout the republic, the democrats of California denounce the repeated abuses of

the vetoes by Rutherford B. Hayes, sitting as the executive officer of the government, in defeating the will of the people as expressed by congress, in his rejection of the bills passed by that body to repeal obnoxious and unconstitutional laws during the present special session.

5. That the democracy of California earnestly approve the conduct of the democrats in both houses of congress for their firm adherence to the just determination to repeal the laws by which the rights of voters are interfered with, at the instance and under the authority of the republican administration, to the extremity of depriving citizens of suffrage for the purpose of carrying elections by force and fraud.

6. That the democracy of California are united and devoted in support of, and obedience to the new constitution, and maintain it as a sacred duty to administer the state government in strict and unqualified accordance with the spirit and letter of that instrument.

7. That the democratic party is pledged by its principles and immemorial usages to reform, retrenchment, and the utmost economy compatible with good government, in the administration of public affairs ; that it adheres to the cardinal doctrines of its founders, that taxation and representation should go together ; that the lowest practicable tax-rate commensurate with the expenses of state, should be levied, and taxation should be equally and justly imposed on all property, to the end that one class shall not be burdened with the taxes fairly due from another, and that no exemption of tax should be allowed to capital which is withheld from other species of property.

8. That the democrats of California were the first in the early establishment of the state government to proclaim antagonism to Chinese immigration and coolie cheap labor ; that it was under a republican administration the Burlingame treaty was made, by which Chinese were admitted to the rights and privileges accorded to immigrants from Europe ; that it was a republican occupant of the presidential chair who vetoed the bill passed by a democratic congress to prohibit the further immigration of Mongolians, and that the republican minority in congress prevented the passage of the bill over the veto ; and that, therefore, it is only to the democratic party the people can confidently look to secure legislation that shall abate and abolish the evil and curse of coolie importation, which cripples trade and palsies the arm of white labor.

9. That the democrats of California approve the action of the democrats in congress who secured the passage of the Thurman bill, by which the Pacific railroads are compelled to pay to the government the just share of interest annually due from them upon the bonds, agreeably to the terms of the charters granted to the respective companies.

10. That the railroad and other transportation corporations in California should be subject to state regulation of rates for passengers and freight in order that a material reduction should be made; that unjust and discriminating rates shall not be imposed or extorted, and that the enforcement of the reduction should particularly apply to the railroads which have been subsidized.

11. That mining, as the original and still a very important interest of California, is entitled to the fostering care, and should be fostered and receive the fullest protection from the state government, and the property and possessions of all engaged in mining enterprises should be guarded by the legislative, judicial and executive departments of the state and federal governments.

12. That the large reduction of expenditures in the public service in the administration of the state government during the past four years under democratic management, at this time of general depression in trade and labor, especially commend to the people of this commonwealth the election of the candidates of the democratic party at the coming election to administer the state government for the ensuing constitutional term.

The resolutions were adopted without opposition. On the 2d, a motion was made by W. M. Cutter to reconsider the vote by which the platform had been adopted, in order to strike out the eleventh resolution, but it was lost. Mr. Pearce offered the following:

That no candidate shall be deemed eligible to the nomination of this convention who is now affiliating with any political organization in opposition or antagonistic to the democratic party.

This resolution created considerable excitement, and was finally lost by a vote of 290 to 67. A state committee was selected, consisting of W. D. English, John H. Wise, Frank P. Baldwin, R. D. Stephens, C. W. Taylor, W. S. Green, A. B. Dibble, Warren B. English, Christopher Buckley, T. L. Thompson, Philip A. Roach, A. J. Bryant, J. P. Hoge, W. T. Coleman and others.

27

The committee on resolutions reported the following as a substitute for the eleventh resolution, and it was adopted :

That mining and agriculture, as the foreshadowing interests of California, should equally receive the fullest protection from the state government, and the property and possessions of all engaged in either pursuit should be carefully guarded by the legislative, judicial and executive departments of both the state and federal governments.

The following nominations were made:

Hugh J. Glenn for governor, without opposition.

Levi Chase for lieutenant-governor, on the first ballot, by a vote of 181 to 173 for J. D. Lynch ; A. B. Dibble and J. W. Satterwhite declining.

W. J. Tinnin for secretary of state, without opposition; Thomas Beck and W. B. C. Brown withdrawing.

G. T. Pauli for treasurer, without opposition ; J. G. Estudillo, George Pearce and Thomas Fowler withdrawing.   Pauli afterward declined, and on August 13th the state committee nominated A. G. Escandon.

W. B. C. Brown for controller, without opposition,

William Minis for surveyor-general, without opposition.

Jo Hamilton for attorney-general, without opposition.

H. C. Gesford for school superintendent, without opposition; W. M. Cutter and A. L. Mann withdrawing.

D. B. Woolf for clerk of the supreme court, without opposition.

Robert F. Morrison for chief justice, without opposition.

S. B. McKee, E. M. Ross, E. W. McKinstry, T. B. Reardan, Thomas P. Stoney and J. D. Thornton for justices of the supreme court, on the first ballot, over Joseph A. Moultrie, S. Heydenfeldt, Jr., J. B. Campbell and J. R. Sharpstein.   Reardan afterward declined, and on August 13th the state committee nominated Sharpstein in his place.

Immediately after the nomination of Glenn, Cutter offered the following, which created a wild excitement, but was finally adopted by a vote of 198 to 148 :

That no candidate, except for a judicial office, shall hereafter receive a nomination at the hands of this convention who has accepted a nomination from any other state convention.

The first district democratic convention met at Sacramento on July 3d, and nominated G. J. Carpenter for railroad commissioner, on the first ballot, over Henry Wilson, John T. Dare, and A. L. Nott.

The second district convention met at San Francisco on July 14th, and nominated George W. Thomas, on the first ballot, over Frank G. Edwards and William Corcoran.

The third district convention met at Sacramento on July 2d, and nominated George Stoneman, without opposition.

The first district democratic convention met at San Francisco on August 5th, and nominated A. C. Bradford for member of the board of equalization, without opposition.

The second district convention met at Sacramento on July 2d, and nominated Charles H. Randall, without opposition.

The third district convention met at Sacramento on July 2d, and nominated C. E. Wilcoxen, without opposition; T. B. Bond and W. H. DeJarnett withdrawing.

The fourth district convention met on the same day, and nominated T. D. Heiskell, on the first ballot, over Brice Grimes and T. D. Harp.

The first district democratic congressional convention met at San Francisco on August 5th, and nominated Robert Ferral, without opposition. He declined, and on the 19th the convention again met and in like manner nominated Charles A. Sumner.

The second district convention met at Sacramento on July 2d, and nominated Thomas J. Clunie, on the first ballot, by a vote of 45, to 31 for Charles H. Randall.

The third district convention met on the same day, and on the first ballot, nominated C. P. Berry, by a vote of 52, to 37 for Barclay Henley, and 14 for J. K. Luttrell.

The fourth district convention met on the same day, and nominated Wallace Leach, without opposition.

On May 28th, a meeting was held at Sacramento, and a call was issued for a prohibition convention to meet at San Francisco on July 16th. The convention was called to order by M. C. Winchester, who was elected president.

The following nominations were made:

A. G. Clark, for governor.
George Bramall, for lieutenant-governor.

A. A. Smith, for secretary of state.

M. C. Winchester, for controller.

W. O. Clark, for treasurer.

Charles W. Cross, for attorney-general.

J. W. Shanklin, for surveyor-general.

S. N. Burch, for school superintendent.

D. B. Woolf, for clerk of the supreme court.

A. L. Rhodes, for chief justice.

J. D. Thornton, S. B. McKee, M. H. Myrick, J. H. McKune, Thomas P. Stoney, and Charles A. Tuttle, for associate justices. Afterward, McKune declined, and James E. Hale was nominated in his stead.

For members of the board of equalization, A. C. Bradford was nominated in the first district; W. M. Crutcher, in the second; John M. Kelley, in the third; and James A. Clayton, in the fourth.

For railroad commissioners, G. J. Carpenter, in the first; T. G. Phelps, in the second; and George Stoneman, in the third.

On August 30th, the central committee of the prohibition party withdrew the ticket from the field.

In July, meetings were held in San Francisco of the state central committees of the new constitution and democratic parties with a view of attempting to consolidate their state tickets, and on the 15th, the democratic committee determined to make no change. About that time, the new constitution committee considered the question of the advisability of taking Glenn from their ticket, but they decided to let him remain. The next day the democratic committee considered the same proposition, and Glenn was called before them. He stated that he had been nominated by the new constitution party first, and that in justice he was compelled to support that ticket and the platform of that party. The democratic committee, by a vote of 16 to 10, determined not to take his name from the ticket.

On June 18th, Rev. I. S. Kalloch was nominated by the workingmen for the office of mayor of San Francisco. During the campaign, he was attacked by the San Francisco *Chronicle*, and the affair grew into a personal discussion of the characters of himself and the proprietors of the paper. On August 23d, Charles DeYoung, one of the owners of the paper, shot and seriously wounded Kalloch in front of the Metropolitan Temple. The assault created intense excitement, and it was feared that mob action would be taken by the workingmen. Kallock was elected by a large majority. The feeling between the parties remained, however, and on April 23, 1880, Charles De Young was shot and killed in his own office by I. M. Kallock, the son of the mayor. Young Kallock was afterward tried for murder and acquitted.

The election was held in September, 1879, and the official canvass developed the following result: For governor, Perkins received 67,-965 votes; Glenn, 47,647; White, 44,482; Clark, 119. For lieutenant-governor, Mansfield, 67,284; Andrus, 42,405; Chase, 31,226; Reed, 19,933; Bramall, 78. For secretary of state, Burns, 67,666; Smith, 41,045; Tinnin, 32,128; Crane, 19,926. For controller, Kenfield, 67,390; Jones, 40,837; Brown, 32,193; LaRue, 21,030; Winchester, 86. For treasurer, Weil, 67,791; L. B. Clark, 40,905; Escandon, 30,193; Jones, 20,034; Pauli, 1,009; W. O. Clark, 66; E. W. Maslin, 23. For attorney-general, Hart, 66,937; Cross, 40,-628; Hamilton, 28,904; Terry, 23,079. For surveyor-general, Shanklin, 67,166; Stevenson, 41,226; Minis, 32,291; Clark, 20,-080. For school superintendent, Campbell, 67,293; Burch, 40,798; Gesford, 31,627; Mann, 20,997. For supreme court clerk, Gross, 64,632; Thornton, 40,744; Woolf, 35,221; Smith, 20,363. For chief justice, Morrison, 72,588; Rhodes, 68,226; Bennett, 19,906. For associate justices, McKinstry, 79,987; Thornton, 78,229; McKee, 75,879; Ross, 72,372; Sharpstein, 70,115; Myrick, 68,234; Belcher 67,592; Catlin, 66,397; Hale, 66,210; Wheeler, 65,367; Richards, 60,556; Buck, 41,894; Stoney, 31,660; Dorsey, 20,888; Campbell, 20,784; Tuttle, 20,216; Benham, 20,192; McKune, 20,-114; Burch, 20,076; C. Williams, 1,191. For members of the board of equalization—First district, King, 18,996; Hoagland, 18,-442; Bradford, 3,947. Second district, Drew, 18,343; Keller, 13,-843; Randall, 6,290. Third district, Dutton, 16,023; Wilcoxson, 12,318; Kelley, 7,369; Cavanaugh, 5,370. Fourth district, Heiskell, 16,716; Clayton, 13,507; Chubb, 8,485. For railroad commissioners—First district, Cone, 22,829; Larkin, 22,374; Carpenter, 14,526. Second district, Beerstecher, 20,207; Phelps, 18,033; Soule, 3,519; Thomas, 2,523. Third district, Stoneman, 35,518; Phillips, 19,410. For congressmen—First district, Davis, 20,074; Barbour, 18,449; Sumner, 2,940. · Second district, Page, 19,386; Clunie, 12,847; Williams, 5,139. Third district, Berry, 20,019; McKenna, 19,830; Elliott, 121. Fourth district, Pacheco, 15,385; Leach, 12,109 ; Ayers, 10,528.

CHAPTER XXX.

1880—Democratic Convention—Workingmen's Convention—Republican Convention, April 29th—Prohibition Convention—Greenback Convention—Republican Convention, August 11th.

The democratic state committee met at San Francisco, on April 14th, and called a state convention, to meet in Oakland, on May 19th, to select twelve delegates to the national convention to meet at Cincinnati on June 22d. When the convention met it was called to order by A. J. Bryant, chairman of the state committee. Samuel M. Wilson and W. J. Tinnin were nominated for temporary chairman, and Wilson was elected by a vote of 212½ to 123½ for Tinnin. On permanent organization, Wilson was president, and Tinnin vice-president. The committee on resolutions consisted of Geo. Pearce, J. A. Filcher, James O'Meara, J. W. Gally, S. M. White, Wallace Leach, F. T. Baldwin, and others. On the 20th, a state central committee was selected, consisting of John H. Wise, Robt. Tobin, F. G. Newlands, Gus Reis, Peter Hopkins. Niles Searls, Paul Shirley, W. A. Selkirk, W. D. English, Clay W. Taylor, J. K. Dollison, Dennis Spencer, J. D. Spencer, Philip A. Roach, Stuart M. Taylor, William Blanding, J. C. Wolfskill, and others. The roll was called to ascertain the preference of the convention for the presidential candidate, and Thurman received 133 votes; Tilden, 97; Seymour, 95; Field, 2; Hancock, 2; and Hendricks, 1. Thurman was therefore declared to be the choice of the convention. On the 21st, the following were selected as delegates to the national convention: First district, W. P. Frost, John Foley, and J. B. Metcalfe. Second district, J. E. McElrath, G. H. Cassell, and R. D. Stephens. Third district, Thomas L. Thompson, Andrew Stevenson, and W. C. Hendricks. Fourth district, C. H. Maddox, Jesse D. Carr, and Wallace Woodworth. For presidential electors at large, William T. Wallace and David S. Terry were nominated without opposition; and J. Campbell Shorb from the first district, W. B. C. Brown from the second district, Barclay Henley from the third district, and R. F. Del Valle from the fourth district, were also nominated without opposition. For alternate electors at large Thomas B. Bishop and P. F. Walsh were nominated without opposition, Charles A. Sumner and S. M. White declining. Cameron H. King from the first district, A. Caminetti from the second district, J. H. Seawell from the third district and R. H. Ward from the fourth district were also nominated without opposition. The committee on resolutions reported the following, which were adopted :

1. We affirm our fidelity to the principles enunciated by the democratic convention of St. Louis in 1876,

2. We denounce the fraud by which R. B. Hayes and W. A. Wheeler were declared president and vice-president of the United States, and the fairly elected candidates, Samuel J. Tilden and Thomas A. Hendricks counted out.

3. We declare that among the leading issues of the campaign are the vindication of the right of the people to self-government; the condemnation of the crime against the ballot committed four years ago; resistance to imperialism, the maintaining of the reserved rights of the states, and opposition to Chinese immigration.

4. That the drift of the republican party toward empire, through the oppressive concentration of capital, is a fraud upon the voting masses and an insult to the men who carry the guns in defense of our liberties.

5. We affirm our devotion to the union, deprecate all sectionalism, hold the republican party responsible for the agitation of dead issues, and regard the preservation of local self-government as necessary to the perpetuation of the republic.

6. That we favor continual lawful agitation of the subject of Mongolian immigration to this country until the federal government is moved to so modify our treaties with the Chinese empire as to prohibit it, and thus save those of our fellow-citizens who depend upon labor for support from unjust and degrading competition. We condemn and denounce the veto of R. B. Hayes of the bill limiting Chinese immigration to the United States, and declare that there is no relief from the scourge except through a democratic administration.

7. That we regard with alarm the doctrine of centralization recently announced by the republican majority of the supreme court of the United States as having been made in the interest of party and intended to blot out the last vestige of state rights and change the federal union to an empire.

8. That the labor of the country is its capital, and deserves the protection and guardianship of our governments—state and federal.

9. We impose no instructions upon our delegates to the convention to meet at Cincinnati, save and except to vote for the retention

of the so-called "two-thirds rule" in nominating candidates for president and vice-president, and to vote as a unit in accordance with the will of the majority of the delegation from this state; and confident in the collective wisdom of the democratic national convention, we pledge in advance to their nominees the electoral vote of California in November, 1880.

The first district convention met at San Francisco on September 20th. Wm. S. Rosecrans, Charles A. Sumner, Robt. Ferral and John S. Enos were named for congressman. Fifteen ballots were taken without result, and an adjournment was had to the 27th, when Rosecrans was nominated on the first ballot.

The second district convention met at Sacramento on August 21st, and nominated John R. Glascock, on the first ballot, over Charles W. Cross; Thos. J. Clunie withdrawing.

The third district convention met at Sacramento on May 20th, and nominated C. P. Berry, without opposition.

The fourth district convention met at Los Angeles on August 4th, and nominated Wallace Leach, on the first ballot, over L. J. Rose, J. W. Satterwhite, and P. B. Tully.

On May 2d, the ward presidents of the workingmen's party met at San Francisco and called a state convention, to meet in that city on the 17th, to choose delegates to attend the national greenback convention, which was to meet in Chicago on June 9th. The convention was called to order by H. W. Smith, the vice-president of the party, and 143 delegates were present. B. Pilkington was elected chairman. On the 18th, the committee on platform submitted a lengthy report of resolutions similar to those which had been adopted by prior state conventions of the party. A resolution was carried by a vote of 60 to 41 in favor of Thurman as the presidential candidate. On the 19th, the convention split, and each branch selected a set of delegates to attend the national convention.

The first republican state convention met at Sacramento on April 29th, and was called to order by W. W. Morrow, the chairman of the state committee. George F. Baker was elected temporary chairman, without opposition, and was afterward chosen president. The committee on resolutions consisted of Grove L. Johnson, John W. Cherry, George Barstow, W. A. Stuart, B. J. Watson, John A. Eagon, Wm. Sharkey, C. W. Craig, W. A. Cheney, C. Rowell, B. C. Whiting, and others. They reported the following:

The republicans of California, in state convention assembled, as expressive of their views, do hereby resolve :

1. That they reaffirm their adherence to the republican national platform of 1876, and the California republican state platform of 1879.

2. That the policy of resumption which has made the greenback of war days equal to gold in days of peace should be maintained.

3. That the amendments to the federal constitution, and all laws passed in pursuance thereof, should be sacredly and jealously maintained and enforced, so that every citizen of the United States, regardless of color or condition, shall be protected in all his rights, and a full, free, and fair election be held in all the states of the union.

4. That the free public schools should be guarded and fostered by all the appliances within reach of the state and national governments, to the end that the children of all may be educated to know, and thereby to enjoy and perform, their full duties and privileges as American citizens.

5. That all peaceful measures should be used to prevent the further immigration of Chinese into the United States, and to rid the country of those now here.

6. That we will cordially support the nominees of the republican national convention, whoever they may be; but we know that the six electoral votes of our state are certain to be given for the republican ticket if James G. Blaine be nominated, wherefore we do hereby instruct our delegates to the republican national convention to vote as a unit—first, last, and all the time—for James G. Blaine, and to use all honorable means to secure his nomination for president of the United States.

A motion was made to amend the sixth resolution by adding, "until his name is withdrawn from the convention, when the delegates from California shall vote as a unit for the candidate of the majority of the delegation." The amendment was lost, by a vote of 122 to 124, and the resolutions as reported were adopted. Resolutions were also adopted that all candidates for delegates or alternates be pledged to carry out the sixth resolution; instructing the delegates to urge the insertion of a plank in the national platform pledging the party to opposition to Chinese immigration; and that no proxies from the state be allowed in the national convention, and that the delegation cast the vote of any absentee.

The following were selected as delegates to attend the national convention : First district—J. C. Wilmerding, Samuel Mosgrove, and Alexander D. Sharon. Second district—Creed Haymond, S. Huff, and J. K. Doak. Third district—H. T. Fairbanks, Joseph Russ, and E. A. Davis. Fourth district—John Mansfield, D. S. Payne, and F. M. Pixley. The following were selected as alternate delegates : First district—C. Mason Kinne, George A. Fisher, and F. J. French. Second district—J. R. Johns, James Foster, and J. A. Benton. Third district—John V. Scott, Frank A. Leach, and S. G. Hilborn. Fourth district—William M. Smith, Charles Sherman, and J. P. Stearns. A resolution was adopted favoring Newton Booth as the nominee for vice-president.

The state central committee of the prohibition party met at Oakland on July 17th, and nominated for presidential electors : J. W. Webb and George Bramall at-large, G. W. Coldwell from the first district, W. O. Clark from the second, M. C. Winchester from the third, and Jesse Yarnell from the fourth. Yarnell afterward withdrew, and John Woods was nominated in his place. For congressmen, F. A. Sawyer was nominated for the second district, A. G. Clark for the third, and W. H. Wheeler for the fourth.

The state convention of the national greenback labor party met at San Francisco July 21st, to nominate electors and congressmen, and to perfect the organization of the party. As a precaution against the admission of obnoxious characters, cards of admission were issued to the delegates, two of whom were women. Silas Selleck called the convention to order, and L. M. Manzer was chosen president. The following platform was adopted :

1. That this convention cordially indorses the platform and resolutions of the Chicago convention, and the nomination of James B. Weaver, of Iowa, as president, and Benjamin J. Chambers, of Texas, as vice-president.

2. That congress has no constitutional right to grant the public lands to corporations.

3. We declare that land, light, air, and water are the free gifts of nature to all mankind ; and any law or custom of society that allows any person to monopolize more of these gifts than he has a right to, to the detriment of the rights of others, we earnestly condemn and seek to abolish.

4. In all cases where either the congress of the United States or the legislatures of the several states have made grants to corporations or private persons, predicated on contingences to happen, by reason of something to be done by the beneficiary under the grant, and the beneficiary has neglected to comply with the conditions thus imposed, the grants themselves should be declared forfeited by the powers making them.

In the opinion of this convention, the grants made to the Southern Pacific railroad, and the Atlantic Pacific railroad have been disregarded by the beneficiaries thereunder, and should be declared forfeited at the next congress, and the land thrown open for preemption and actual settlement.

5. That in our legislative bodies all political opinions should be represented in proportion to the number of those who hold them, regardless of district or ward lines, thus avoiding party mechanisms, which not only do not express, but in effect nullify the will of the people. That as our law-making bodies do not in fact represent any considerable number of their nominal constituents, but merely a few politicians and their monopolistic ring masters, the laws which they enact, when unjust, are not morally binding, because, "governments derive all their just power from the consent of the governed" and not from their mere acquiescence.

6. That suffrage is a right inherent in citizenship and not a mere privilege to be granted or withheld at the pleasure of the party in power.

7. That the possession and control of the public highways by private individuals or corporations is contrary to democratic principles, and inimical to national prosperity.

8. That the state has a right to so control its educational system as to insure and compel the efficient education of all children in the branches of learning and industrial pursuits. All children must be educated alike, and all the expense must be borne by the state.

9. We demand a national paper money, a full legal tender for all money payments.

10. The prohibition of banks of issue, and the abolishment of the national banking system.

11. The payment of the bonded debt of the United States, and that no further refunding of the same be authorized or permitted.

12. That no discrimination be made between gold and silver in the freedom and facilities afforded for coinage.

13. That Chinese immigration be prohibited by law, and that those who are already here shall not be admitted to citizenship. That if any commercial treaty is maintained with China, it shall provide that the number of Chinese, of any given occupation residing in the United States, shall at no time exceed the number of our citizens of the same occupation residing in China. That in the absence of such enactments, the laws and courts of and in this state should not be used to force Asiatic barbarism, with all its attending horrors, on the people of this state, in defiance of their nearly unanimous vote.

14. That the "specific contract laws" of this state be repealed, and that all contracts or obligations for the payment of "dollars" be solvable in any lawful money of the United States.

15. That the federal government issue a loan, by way of direct loans on landed surety, a volume of money at three per cent. per annum, one per cent. of which shall be paid into the county treasury of the county where the land is situated, one per cent. into the sinking fund of the state, and one per cent. into the sinking fund of the federal government.

16. That the government shall issue money to the people, on good security, at a rate of interest that shall not exceed the cost of the issuance thereof.

17. That the government furnish the means for indigent families to go upon the public lands and build houses and stock and cultivate their farms, and also furnish the means to laboring operatives to establish co-operative industrial enterprises.

For presidential electors, F. P. Dann and J. E. Clark were nominated at large. L. M. Manzer from the first district, J. H. Redstone from the second, George T. Elliott from the third, and T. J.. McQuiddy from the fourth. James Kidney was nominated for alternate from the first district, B. K. Low from the second, W. Ayres from the third, and W. Jackson from the fourth.

For congressmen, Stephen Maybell was nominated from the first district, Benjamin Todd from the second, A. Mussleman from the third, and J. F. Godfrey from the fourth. Todd died October 29, 1880.

The second republican state convention met at Sacramento on August 11th, and was called to order by W. W. Morrow. Charles N. Fox was elected president, without opposition. The committee on resolutions consisted of T. B. McFarland, L. B. Mizner, George F. Baker, John H. Dickinson, M. D. Boruck, H. T. Dorrance, E. W. Roberts, A. P. Whitney, F. M. Pixley, Calvin Edgerton, G. G. Blanchard, G. W. Tyler, O. W. Hollenbeck, and David McClure. They submitted the following, which were adopted :

1. That we adopt and affirm the principles so clearly set forth in the platform adopted by the national republican convention recently assembled at Chicago.

2. That we recognize in James A. Garfield and Chester A. Arthur honest and representative citizens of our nation, able and intelligent exponents of the principles of the republican party, and that their election will be a triumph of those principles upon which our national existence and industrial prosperity depends.

3. That in the most emphatic manner we declare that the presence of Chinese laborers upon this continent is detrimental to the best interests of the American people. That their immigration should be prohibited, and to that end that the Burlingame treaty should be abrogated, and that congress should pass such laws as will prevent the further immigration of Chinese to this coast. We indorse and approve the act of President Hayes in the appointment of a commission to the government of China for the purpose of modifying the Burlingame treaty. We especially indorse and approve that part of the national republican platform that opposes Chinese immigration, and thus declares the question to be one of national importance. That we indorse and approve the declarations of General Garfield in his letter of acceptance, in which he says: " We cannot consent to allow any form of servile labor to be introduced among us under the guise of immigration," and that "it will be the duty of congress to mitigate the evils already felt, and prevent their increase by such restriction as without violence or injustice will place upon a sure foundation the peace of our communities and the freedom and dignity of labor." We call attention to the significance of General Hancock's silence upon this Chinese question in his letter of acceptance, and accept it as proof conclusive that the democratic party under the influence of a solid south, cannot be trusted to legislate upon this question of Chinese immigration.

4. That we recognize as a fundamental principle of American liberty " that it is only by a full vote, a free ballot and a fair count that the people can rule," but that throughout the solid south, as ruled by the democratic party, neither a full vote, nor a free ballot

now exist, nor can a fair count be had except through the complete victory of the republican party and the triumph of its principles.

The following were nominated for presidential electors: John F. Miller and Henry Edgerton, at large; Claus Spreckels from the first district, Charles N. Fox from the second district, W. W. McKaig from the third district, and T. R. Bard from the fourth district. Early in September Spreckles declined to run, and the state central committee nominated John A. Bauer in his stead. The following were nominated for alternate electors: Henry Cowell and W. T. Garratt, at large; Charles Kohler from the first district, James A. Louttit from the second district, Samuel Cassidy from the third district, and Walter S. Moore from the fourth district.

A state committee was selected, consisting of William Jennings, J. B. Reddick, George Hagar, W. H. Brown, A. R. Conklin, W. H. Sears, H. J. Ostrander, Joseph Wasson, Paris Kilburn, E. W. Roberts, O. W. Hollenbeck, A. J. Rhoads, Obed Harvey, J. K. Doak, S. O. Houghton J. O. Zuck, H. W. Wallis, George W. Schell, C. A. Garter, C. W. Craig, C. H. Garoutte, J. H. Jewett, M. C. Conroy, J. W. Shaffer, J. P. H. Wentworth, W. B. May, David McClure, J. J. Green, P. B. Cornwall, S. G. Hilborn, H. W. Byington, W. W. Morrow, D. B. Jackson, M. D. Boruck, W. F. Whittier, David Bush, A. P. Williams, Richard Chute, W. M. Bunker, J. R. Hardenbergh, J. P. Ames, and others.

The first congressional district republican convention nominated Horace Davis, without opposition.

The second district convention nominated H. F. Page, without opposition; John A. Eagon withdrawing.

The third district convention nominated George A. Knight, without opposition; W. A. Cheney withdrawing.

The fourth district convention nominated R. Pacheco, on the first ballot, by a vote of 70, to 27 for F. Adams, and 1 for George F. Baker.

The election was held on November 2d, and resulted as follows: For presidential electors—Republicans, Miller, 80,282; Edgerton, 80,348; Bauer, 80,281; Fox, 80,229; McKaig, 80,242; Bard, 80,253. Democrats, Wallace, 80,426; Terry, 79,858; Shorb, 80,430; Brown, 80,413; Henley, 80,428; Del Valle, 80,442. Greenback, Dann, 3,381; Clark, 3,394; James Kidney, 3,378; Redstone, 2,531; Elliott, 3,369; McQuiddy, 3,365; B. K. Low, 830. Prohibition,

Bramall, 54; Webb, 49; Coldwell, 56; Clark, 56; Winchester, 61; Woods, 56. About six votes were cast for electors on the anti-masonic ticket. For congressmen—First district, Davis, 19,496; Rosecrans, 21,005; Maybell and others, 688. Second district, Page, 22,036; Glascock, 18,859; Todd and others, 296. Third district, Knight, 20,494; Berry, 21,743; Musselman and others, 274. Fourth district, Pacheco, 17,768; Leach, 17,577; Godfrey and others, 3,461. All of the democratic electors except Terry were elected, he being beaten by Edgerton. Rosecrans, Page, Berry, and Pacheco were elected congressmen.

On December 1st the presidential electors met in the governor's office. All were present except Shorb, and L. C. Branch was elected to fill the vacancy. Five votes were cast for Hancock and English, and one vote—that of Edgerton—for Garfield and Arthur. Stephen Cooper was selected messenger to convey the returns to Washington.

CHAPTER XXXI.

1882—Democratic Convention—Republican Convention—Prohibition Convention—Greenback Convention—Grangers' Convention.

On March 15th, the democratic state committee met at San Francisco, and called a state convention to meet at San Jose, on June 20th, and to consist of 457 delegates. The test prescribed for the primaries was "that the person offering to vote shall have voted for Hancock and English electors in 1880, or would have so voted had he been present and qualified." The convention met in the theater in San Jose, and was called to order by W. D. English, chairman of the state committee. John Boggs was elected temporary chairman, on the first ballot, by a vote of 264, to 193 for J. C. Martin. The committee on resolutions consisted of George Flournoy, Joseph Naphtaly, A. B. Dibble, J. C. Martin, George Ohleyer, Robert McGarvey, J. T. White, Thomas Harding, and David S. Terry. On the 21st, on permanent organization, Boggs was elected president, and J. C. Martin, Niles Searls, J. H. Budd, J. DeBarth Shorb, and T. B. Bishop, vice-presidents. The following resolutions were reported by the committee:

The democracy of the State of California, as represented in convention, hereby declare that with unshaken faith in the soundness of the constitutional principles and traditions of the democratic party, as illustrated by the teachings and examples of a long line of democratic statesmen and patriots, and expressed in the platform of the last presidential convention of the party, we pledge ourselves to maintain these principles, and to labor to make them paramount in the administration of the state and the general governments :

1. That the democratic party of California tender its thanks to the democracy of the union for a long, earnest and partially successful struggle, through the democratic congressmen, with a hostile republican administration, against Chinese immigration, and in behalf of the highest interests of the people of this coast. Such action again illustrates the fidelity of the party to its pledges given to the people in the platforms of successive presidential conventions; again recognizes that the people of each locality are the best judges of their own wants and necessities, and again declares the great doctrine that it is the duty of the general government to heed their complaints and to extend its strong arm for their protection.

2. That the democratic party of California recognizes with the highest appreciation the prompt and determined movement in their behalf made by the workingmen of the eastern states, and notably of Pennsylvania, in presenting the menace of a free people as an irresistible power against the combined efforts of vast moneyed corporations and the monopolists of the Chinese trade, who, in the name of the brotherhood of man, and under the cloak of universal charity, were endeavoring to thwart every effort made in behalf of the permanent existence of the white man in California; and we recognize the interests of white labor everywhere as in full alignment with the advancing movement of the democracy of the union in its purpose to preserve the heritage we have a right to enjoy from the merciless ravages of the Asiatic hosts, who have already captured many of our best industries, impoverished thousands of our people, driven large numbers into debauchery and crime, and almost excluded eastern and European immigration.

3. That the Chinese now in California are an unmixed curse to this people, their presence an ever-increasing evil, reaching out to blast every avenue of labor and every branch of trade; that they are, and so long as they remain will continue to be, an unsurmountable barrier in the pathway of California toward the high destiny for which nature has so amply equipped her; that in view of this condition we confidently appeal to the democrats of the union for our

deliverance, and claim, as one of the first duties of the party, that the next presidential convention of the democracy shall declare the doctrine of self-preservation as the highest law of nature and of nations upon this subject, as upon all others, and the government of the United States, when placed under a democratic administration, will indicate its just appreciation of the imperative necessities of the people of California by providing such certain and speedy means as may be deemed most just and proper for the removal of every Mongolian from this country; and to the accomplishment of this end we hereby pledge to the people our earnest and persistent efforts, inviting every citizen of this state, who has the common weal at heart, whatever his present or previous political affiliation, to lend us the aid of his personal support, as a freeman, toward strengthening the right arm of the democratic party of the union, whose fidelity has been proven, for the early and perfect accomplishment of this great work.

4. That the constant pretense of the republican party organs, and of the republican leaders in California and in the eastern states, that the ten-year law has taken the Chinese question from the arena of politics, and that it is no longer a political issue, is deceptive in purpose, and will ever be false in fact, so long as the Chinese remain in this country.

5. That the democratic party, inheriting the doctrines of Jefferson and Jackson, hereby declares its unqualified enmity to all sumptuary legislation, regarding all such exercise of the law-making power as against the just objects of free government, and that all laws intended to restrain or direct a free and full exercise by any citizen of his own religious and political opinion, so long as he leaves others to enjoy their rights unmolested, are anti-democratic and hostile to the principles and traditions of the party, create unnecessary antagonism, cannot be enforced, and are a violation of the spirit of republican government; and we will oppose the enactment of all such laws, and demand the repeal of all those now existing.

6. That railroad fares and freights should be materially reduced; discriminations in favor of localities or persons should be prohibited, and we condemn the majority of the railroad commissioners of this state for their faithlessness in the discharge of their official duties. The nominees of the democratic party will, if elected, carry out, in letter and spirit, the declarations of this resolution, and relieve the

28

people to the extent of their jurisdiction from the exactions and injustice now practiced with impunity by the railroad corporations.

7. That most speedy and effective measures should be taken to
compel the railroad corporations of California to pay their taxes.
No compromises should be made. The property of every corporation, as well as of every individual, should be assessed at its true
value, and the payment of the resulting tax strictly and impartially
enforced.

8. That all railroad land grants, forfeited by reason of the non-
fulfillment of contracts, should be immediately revoked by the government, and that hereafter the domain should be reserved exclusively as homes for actual settlers.

9. That the rivers and harbors of this state belong to all the people, and that it is the duty of the federal government to protect
them from destruction, and so improve them from time to time as
to keep them forever open as channels of commerce.

10. That the democratic party declares its unalterable purpose to
restrain all private and public corporations within the exact letter
of their lawful powers, and to prevent any and all imposition upon
individuals or the public, whether attempted under the pretense of
lawful right or in the arrogance of accumulated money power, and
favors the offering and enactment of all needed legislation toward
this end.

11. Recognizing the fact that much of the corruption in politics
results from the enormous patronage in the hands of the president
of the United States, and its unscrupulous use in carrying elections
and maintaining the party in power, and that so long as the tempta-
tion exists this patronage will be so used, thereby degrading party
contests to the debasing level of a mere scramble for the petty
offices in the gift of the executive department, the democratic party
of California announces itself as in favor of a reform of the civil
service of the country, upon principles similar to those proposed in
the bill introduced in the senate of the United States by Senator
Pendleton, of Ohio.

12. That the democratic party of California denounces the efforts
made by the republican state executive, contrary to the constitution
and laws of this state, to manage the state university of California
in the interests of the republican party.

Martin and White, the minority of the committee submitted the
following resolution as an addition to the majority report :

That the present schedule rates of railroad fares and freights, as fixed by the railroad commissioners within the state of California, are excessive and oppressive, and that a reduction of at least fifteen per cent. upon all rates of companies operating more than one hundred miles of road, should be at once made, and that the several district conventions of the democratic party, whose duty it is to nominate railroad commissioners, be requested to require each candidate nominated for the office of railroad commissioner to pledge himself that if elected he will, within sixty days after the organization of the board of railroad commissioners, vote to reduce such rates at least fifteen per cent., and place the same in immediate operation.

Thomas Fowler offered the following as a substitute for the resolution reported by the minority of the committee, but it was rejected by a vote of 195 to 221, and the minority resolution was adopted :

Whereas, The Central and Southern Pacific railroads were granted by the federal government a subsidy of money, bonds and lands in sufficient value to build and equip three or four lines of railroad ; and, whereas, the official returns of the gross and net receipts of those corporations show that their clear income exceeds $10,000,000 per year, an amount grossly beyond that of all enterprises carried on by those owning in their own right the money invested ; therefore, be it

Resolved by the state convention of the democratic party, That the nominees put forward by our party for the office of railroad commissioners be, and they are hereby instructed and directed, as their first official act, to reduce the present schedule of fares and freights of those corporations, so that their receipts shall be reduced at least twenty per cent., and that this reduction shall not be rescinded during their term of office, and to make such other and further reductions as careful investigation show to be just to the people and not unjust to the railroads.

The resolutions were considered seriatim, and sections 1, 2, 3, and 4 were adopted, without opposition. A motion to strike out the latter part of the fifth section, which demanded a repeal of the then existing Sunday law, was lost—166 to 280—and the original resolution was adopted. The remainder of the majority report, together with the resolution of the minority, were then adopted. A state committee was selected, composed of W. H. Conklin, J. D. Spencer, M. C. Haley, H. T. Hammond, William P. Frost, P. Connolly, Lewis McLane, R. O. Cravens, J. C. Ball, O. P. Richardson, C. H.

Mitchell, B. W. Howser, John McMurray, Peter Hopkins, John H. Wise, W. D. English, John Foley, J. C. Wolfskill, Wallace Leach, and others.

For governor—Clay W. Taylor, Campbell P. Berry, James A. Johnson, George Hearst, George Stoneman, and Lawrence Archer were placed in nomination. Seven ballots were taken on the 22d and seven more on the 23d, with the following result:

BALLOTS.	Hearst......	Stoneman......	Taylor......	Johnson......	Berry......	Archer......	B. D. Murphy
First Ballot......................	126	117	60	67	65	20	.....
Second Ballot...................	128	117	61	65	66	17	1
Third Ballot	129	123	62	63	66	12	.....
Fourth Ballot....................	134	120	72	62	15	8	1
Fifth Ballot.....................	143	122	91	55	37	9	.....
Sixth Ballot.....................	146	130	96	52	23	8	.....
Seventh Ballot	151	136	92	52	17	4	.....
Eighth Ballot....................	159	132	84	54	25	1	1
Ninth Ballot.............. ...	166	133	91	44	19	1	1
Tenth Ballot.....................	169	147	93	32	11	1	1
Eleventh Ballot	170	166	92	23	1	1	1
Twelfth Ballot	174	189	75	13	.....	.....	.....
Thirteenth Ballot....	170	204	65	16	.....	.....	.....
Fourteenth Ballot...............	170	243	32	1	.....	.....	.....

Stoneman was declared the nominee on the fourteenth ballot.

On the 22d, the following resolution was read while the balloting was in progress, and it was referred to the committee:

That the correct principle which should govern the railroad commissioners elected under the constitution of this state, in fixing the rates of fares and freights to be collected by the railroads of this state, is, first, to ascertain the value in cash of the franchise, rolling stock and road bed and appurtenances, and upon such valuation to fix the rate of fares and freights so as, after paying the running expenses of the road, to pay to the shareholders 6 per cent. per annum on the valuation made as aforesaid.

The closing paragraph pledged the nominees for railroad commissioners to this plan. On the 24th, the following additional nominations were made:

John Daggett for lieutenant-governor, without opposition.

Erskine M. Ross for associate justice, on the third ballot, by a vote of 233, to 211 for James R Sharpstein, 124 for Jackson Temple, 104 for I. Sepulveda, 98 for John W. Armstrong, and 88 for O. P. Evans. The first ballot stood—Sharpstein, 154; Ross, 154; Armstrong, 114; Sepulveda, 125; Temple, 114; Evans, 113; Philip W. Keyser, 53; W. C. Wallace, 65; T. J. Bowers, 13.

J. R. Sharpstein for associate justice, on the first ballot, by a vote of 247, to 73 for Temple, 49 for Armstrong, 35 for Evans, and 29 for Sepulveda.

John R. Glascock and Charles A. Sumner for congressmen at large, on the first ballot. Glascock received 318 votes; Sumner, 231; J. E. Murphy, 20; and W. T. Wallace, 155.

Thos. L. Thompson for secretary of state, on the second ballot, by a vote of 229, to 68 for W. J. Tinnin, 125 for Thomas Beck, and 20 for Wm. H. Coombs. The first ballot stood—Thompson, 154; Beck, 120; Tinnin, 75; Coombs, 41; Thomas H. Carr, 28; W. W. Kellogg, 19; W. M. Donahue, 16.

John P. Dunn for controller, on the first ballot, by a vote of 209, to 154 for E. W. Maslin, and 93 for Russell D. Stephens.

Wm. A. January for treasurer, on the third ballot, by a vote of 228, to 223 for Paul Shirley, and 3 for Otto Kloppenberg. On the first ballot, Shirley had 161; January, 158; David L. Poole, 90; Kloppenberg, 37; and A. C. Busch, 4.

Edward C. Marshall for attorney general, on the second ballot, by a vote of 242, to 203 for Fred Baldwin. On the first ballot, Baldwin had 175; Marshall, 144; John C. Burch, 65, and E. J. Edwards, 54. W. D. Grady withdrew during the first ballot.

H. I. Willey for surveyor-general, without opposition; E. Rosseau, Wm. Minis, and Alexander Dunn withdrawing.

Wm. T. Welcker for school superintendent, on the first ballot, by a vote of 293, to 76 for J. H. Kennedy, 51 for Jesse Wood, and 28 for J. W. Johnson.

John W. McCarthy for clerk of the supreme court, on the first ballot, by a vote of 250, to 95 for J. B. Stevenson, and 110 for Cameron; D. B. Woolf withdrawing.

The first district democratic congressional convention met at San Jose on June 24th, and nominated Wm. S. Rosecrans, on the first ballot, by a vote of 75, to 23 for Wm. P. Frost; Robert Ferral withdrew.

The second district convention met at the same place on the 23d, and nominated James H. Budd, without opposition.

The third district convention met at the same place on the 23d, and nominated Barclay Henley, on the first ballot, by a vote of 86, to 40 for L. D. Freer.

The fourth district convention met at the same place on the 23d, and nominated P. B. Tully, without opposition.

The first district democratic convention for the nomination of railroad commissioner met at San Jose on June 22d. The candidates were G. J. Carpenter, W. S. Green, Wm. M. Crutcher, and H. M. LaRue. The convention adjourned without choice, the last ballot standing—Carpenter, 66; Green, 30; LaRue, 70. Crutcher withdrew after the fourth ballot. On the 23d, on the seventh ballot, Carpenter was nominated, by a vote of $91\frac{1}{2}$, to $61\frac{1}{2}$ for Green, and 21 for LaRue.

The second district convention met at the same place on the 24th, and nominated William P. Humphreys, on the first ballot, by a vote of 69, to 39 for Philip A. Roach.

The third district convention met at the same place on the 23d, and nominated W. W. Foote, by a vote of 81, to 61 for John H. Moore, and 7 for Thomas Fowler.

On the 24th, Charles Gildea was nominated for member of the state board of equalization, from the first district, Wm. M. Crutcher from the second district, O. E. Wilcoxon from the third district, and John Markley from the fourth district.

A meeting of the republican state central committee was held at San Francisco in April, and the state convention was called to meet at Sacramento on August 30th. On June 29th another meeting was held, and the proposition to have the convention meet on August 15th was voted down. The convention therefore met at the time originally set, and was called to order by W. W. Morrow, chairman of the state committee. Newton Booth was chosen temporary chairman, without opposition. The committee on resolutions consisted of L. D. Latimer, S. B. Lieb, J. H. Neff, John F. Swift, Horace Davis, John H. Jewett, E. W. Roberts, S. Meyers, B. G. Hurlburt, John Yule, F. Adams, J. W. North, and others. A delegation from the prohibition party waited on the committee on resolutions and asked them to embody in the platform a local option plank in the following form, and stated that nothing else would be acceptable:

That the legal control, regulation and restriction of the sale of intoxicating liquors should be fostered by such legislation as will carry into effect the provisions of section 11, of article XI, of the state constitution, which declares that any county, city, town, or township, may make and enforce within its limits all such local, police, sanitary, and other regulations, as are not in conflict with general laws.

On the 31st, Booth was elected president; Horace Davis, J. R. Hardenbergh, Wm. H. Sears, and A. E. Wagstaff, vice-presidents. The committee on resolutions reported the following:

The republicans of California, in state convention assembled, do announce and declare:

1. We reaffirm our adherence to the principles of the republican party as embodied in its history.

2. We lament the death of our late president, James A. Garfield. His lofty patriotism and heroic character endeared him to the people. His memory will be fondly and forever cherished by his countrymen.

3. We reaffirm the platform of the national republican party as declared in Chicago in 1880. We have faith in the wisdom of the present administration, and confidence that it will result in honor and additional laurels to our party and its cause.

4. We point with pride to the financial policy of republican administrations, which has with unexampled rapidity .reduced the national debt while improving the national credit, lessened taxes while increasing revenues, and lowered the rate of interest on the national bonds while adding to their value in the markets of the world.

5. History and experience unite to prove the necessity of preserving one day in seven as a day of rest from labor. Without legislation on this subject, the laboring classes might be compelled to continue in unceasing toil. Therefore, we are in favor of observing Sunday as a day of rest and recreation; and while we expressly disavow the right or the wish to force any class of our citizens to spend that day in any particular manner, we do favor the maintenance of the present Sunday laws, or similar laws, providing for the suspension of all unnecessary business on that day.

6. Corporations are creatures of law and subject to law, and all legal means should be taken to render it impossible for aggregations of capital to become oppressive.

7. While we recognize the fact that the building of railroads has proved one of the most potent agencies in the development and progress of the country, we at the same time remember that the great power which authorized such roads to be built, including the sovereign right of eminent domain, was granted to the railroad companies by the people, for the people, and on the sole ground that the building of railroads is a public use and such roads public highways. [The convention changed the last portion of this paragraph to read: "And on the sole ground that the construction and working of railroads constitute a public use," etc.] We declare that railroad companies, the same as individuals, should be dealt with in fairness and without injustice; but, by reason of their relation to the people, they must be kept subordinate to the interests of the people, and within governmental control. The people should be protected by law from any abuse or unjust exactions. Unjust discriminations against individuals or localities should be prohibited. Equal service upon equal terms to all persons should be enforced. Charges for transporting persons and property should be limited to what is required to pay the legitimate expenses of operating such railroads, their maintenance in good repair, and a fair interest on their actual value. Such value shall bear the same relation to its assessed value that the value of other property does to its assessed value. Charges in excess of this are in violation of the fundamental law of public use which allows railroads to be built; and we hereby pledge our nominees for railroad commissioners to the enforcement of these principles by such a material and substantial reduction of the rates of fares and freights as will secure that result—the basis being cost of service, with reasonable allowance for interest and repairs, as above indicated, instead of the mercenary exaction of "all the traffic will bear."

8. That the proper public authorities should not refuse to act in regulating freights and fares by reason of lack of exact information in any particular, if such information could be given but is refused by the railroad corporation; but in such cases these authorities should act as near correctly as possible, taking care however that the public interest should not suffer, and holding themselves in readiness to correct any error, if error there should be, upon the corporation giving the necessary information to enable such error to be corrected.

9. We denounce the railroad contract system as a deliberate attempt to enslave the commerce and trade of the whole Pacific coast, and subjugate them to the control and caprice of the railroad com_

panies. It is against public policy, because it seeks to make use of the national bounty to break down that healthful competition which it is the policy of the nation to encourage. It is unjust and oppress-ive, because it discriminates in favor of the strong at the expense of the weak, and offers bribes to the rich which it collects back from the poor. It is arbitrary and tyrannical, because it arrogantly inter-feres with the freedom of trade, and proposes to prohibit those who make use of its transportation facilities from doing business with any one who refuses to submit to its dictation. Its existence is a threat and its abolition a necessity. The republican party pledges itself to prohibit the making of such contracts by proper legislation, to the extent, if necessary, of making the same a public offense.

10. We demand of congress legislation governing the carrying trade between the states, or states and territories. The rates of freights and fares of all railroads engaged in such trade should be justly regulated and restricted, and any unjust discrimination be-tween persons or places should be absolutely prohibited.

11. That we are opposed to granting any further subsidies to companies or corporations, and are in favor of the immediate revoca-tion of all land grants and subsidies forfeited by non-fulfillment of the conditions of such grants, and the restoration of such lands to the public domain, to be held exclusively for actual settlers.

12. All property should pay its just share of taxation. The prop-erty of corporations, like other property, should be assessed at its actual cash value, and the corporations and individuals alike should be compelled to pay their just taxes without abatement, diminution, or compromise.

13. The republican party has always advocated liberal appropria-tions for the improvement of rivers and harbors; and we declare it to be the duty of the federal government to maintain the natural channels of internal commerce in their highest standard of useful-ness, as a trust committed to it by the constitution of the United States, and as a constant check upon the exorbitant exactions of artificial highways.

14. We believe in exact justice being done on the merits of the contest between the conflicting mining and agricultural interests, and to that end we resolve that in all cases where it is claimed that a nuisance is being threatened or committed, and that more than one person or corporation is making such threat or contributing to main-tain such nuisance, a joint action should be allowed against such

persons or corporations to obtain redress, and the laws of this state should be speedily amended to that end.

15. That the republican party, ever alive to the interest of the laboring classes, is in favor of the establishment of a bureau of statistics of labor, for the purpose of inquiring into the condition of the laboring classes, their wages, lack of employment, and chances of obtaining the same.

16. The republican party is unalterably opposed to Chinese immigration. It is a cause for congratulation that this question, which has heretofore engaged the earnest attention of both political parties, has at length been settled by prohibiting further immigration, the treaty having been framed by republican commissioners and ratified and approved by a republican administration. We offer our thanks to our senators and representatives in congress for the legislation procured by them on this subject.

17. The same principles which guide the administration of well-ordered private affairs should prevail in the selection of public officers. Honesty, efficiency, and fidelity should be the essential qualifications for public position, and such rules should be established to regulate appointments to the public service as will insure fitness, to be ascertained by practical tests, and promotion should follow faithful service. The republican party of California demands a thorough, radical, and complete reform in the modes of appointment to subordinate executive offices, founded upon the principle that public office is a public trust, admission to which should depend upon proved fitness, to be ascertained by methods open to all applicants and regulated by law.

18. Finally, we insist upon economy in the administration of the government, integrity in office, and honesty and efficiency in every branch of the public service.

W. H. L. Barnes offered the following additional resolution, which was adopted:

The republican party demands that the public schools shall receive generous support, as the policy of free government; that education from the primary school to the state university shall be free and within the reach of the children of every citizen; that in furtherance of this principle we recommend to the legislature the establishment of some system by which the state shall print and provide the principal reading and other text-books used in the public schools, supplying the same to pupils at actual cost.

The report of the committee was then considered seriatim. A motion to strike out the fifth resolution was lost; and a motion to strike out the sixth, seventh, eighth, ninth and tenth was lost by nearly a unanimous vote. J. M. Walling offered the following as a substitute for the fourteenth resolution:

That all questions of injury arising between the agriculturist and the miner should be left to the adjudication of the courts.

After a discussion, a motion to strike out all reference to the subject was carried by a vote of 333 to 116. The word "suspending" was substituted for "prohibiting" in the sixteenth resolution. The following additional resolution was adopted:

That the republican party points to the conduct of the affairs of the state under its present faithful executive with genuine pride, and as the best hostage it can give the people for the future. While it came into power under the burden of a deficiency exceeding $220,000, and by legislative acts extraordinary expenditures have been necessarily made for the improvement of the labor resources of the state prison, for the rebuilding of the state normal school and the deaf and dumb asylum, exceeding in all $750,000, it nevertheless retires from its post of duty leaving behind it no deficiency to be provided for, and the taxes imposed for all state purposes have been reduced not less than ten per cent.

With the changes indicated, the platform was adopted as a whole. The following nominations were then made:

Morris M. Estee for governor, on the first ballot, by a vote of 238 to 202 for M. C. Blake, 11 for J. McM. Shafter, and 2 for Joseph Russ. Before the changes, the roll had stood, Estee 218, Blake 203, Russ 18, and Shafter 17. The candidates had been named in the evening, and the ballot was taken on the morning after, September 1st.

Alvah R. Conklin for lieutenant-governor, on the first ballot, by a vote of 225, to 132 for J. C. Tucker, and 89 for John P. Stearns.

John Hunt and Samuel C. Denson for justices of the supreme court, on the third ballot, over Anson Brunson, Theodore H. Hittell, John Reynolds, A. P. Catlin, Walter Van Dyke, C. W. C. Rowell, and I. S. Belcher.

Henry Edgerton and Wm. W. Morrow for congressmen at large, without opposition.

Frank A. Pedlar for secretary of state, on the first ballot, by a vote of 254, to 174 for Chas. A. Sherman, and 26 for George W. Gallagher.

Wm. A. Davies for controller, on the first ballot, over D. M. Kenfield and E. F. White.

On the 2d, the committee on resolutions reported the following substitute for the fifteenth resolution, and it was adopted:

We are in favor of establishing a bureau of statistics of labor, for the purpose of collecting and publishing such statistics and other information in regard to labor and wages as may be useful to the laboring classes.

Frank M. Pixley offered a resolution with a preamble, which recited the evils of undesirable immigration of objectionable classes, and resolving that the national legislators be advised to so amend the immigration laws, that such undesirable immigrants shall be denied the privilege of the elective franchise. The resolution also recited:

The temperance movement now inaugurated and active in all of our eastern states is entitled to the moral recognition of the members of this convention. The triumph of temperance principles, so decisive in the states of Kansas and Iowa as to have become a part of their organic law, indicates that the temperance question has become a national one, worthy of consideration by this convention, and demanding the attention of all tax-payers as one of political economy, and of all good citizens as one involving the highest interest of social order, good morals, and good government. That as a first step in the direction of temperance and reform, our legislature should be asked to consider how far local option can be enforced to regulate or prohibit the traffic in alcoholic drinks.

The resolution was ruled out of order.

The following additional nominations were then made:

John Weil for treasurer, on the first ballot, over H. D. Fairbanks.

Augustus L. Hart for attorney-general, without opposition; Hugh K. McJunkin withdrawing.

Wm. Minto for surveyor-general, on the first ballot, over J. W. Shanklin.

S. D. Waterman for school superintendent, on the first ballot, over Fred. M. Campbell.

Frank W. Gross for clerk of the supreme court, without opposition.

A state committee was selected, consisting of Wm. Jennings, George Hagar, W. H. Brown, J. F. Crank, W. H. Sears, T. L. Carothers, J. H. Neff, J. A. Orr, A. J. Rhoads, C. Green, M. C. Briggs, Horace Davis, P. B. Cornwall, J. T. Dare, S. K. Thornton, S. G. Hilborn, G. W. Schell, P. Y. Baker, Jerome Banks, C. E. Street, C. H. Garoutte, W. H. Parks, and others.

The first congressional district republican convention met at Sacramento on September 2d, and nominated Paul Neuman, without opposition.

The second district convention met at the same place on the 1st, and nominated H. F. Page, without opposition.

The third district convention met at the same time and place, and nominated J. J. DeHaven, without opposition.

The fourth district convention met at the same place on the 2d, and nominated George L. Woods, on the second ballot, over W. J. Hill and Oregon Sanders.

The first district republican convention for the nomination of rail-road commissioner met at Sacramento on September 2d, and nominated Chas. F. Reed, on the first ballot, by a vote of 125 to 48 for F. S. Freeman, and 8 for S. B. Burt.

The second district convention met at the same time and place, and nominated Chas. Clayton, without opposition; E. D. Sawyer, Geo. A. Fisher, and Samuel Mosgrove withdrawing.

The third district convention met at the same time and place, and nominated E. M. Gibson, on the fourth ballot, over John Mansfield, Chester A. Rowell, J. G. McCallum, and Edward Martin.

The first equalization district republican convention met at Sacramento on September 2d, and adjourned to San Francisco, where, on the 6th, R. P. Johnson was nominated, on the first ballot, over E. Burke and F. C. Mossback.

The second district convention met at Sacramento on the 1st, and nominated L. C. Morehouse on the first ballot, over William Johnston and James Foster.

The third district convention met at the same time and place, and nominated G. G. Kimball on the first ballot, over Warren Dutton and P. R. Klein.

The fourth district convention met on the 2d, and nominated C. W. Dana, without opposition.

A state convention of the prohibition reform party was held in San Francisco on July 11th, which was attended by about 150 delegates. M. C. Winchester was president, John Woods vice-president, and Rev. George Morris secretary. A committee on resolutions was selected, consisting of Rev. M. C. Briggs, A. D. Wood, and others.

They presented the following report, which was adopted:

1. That no exigencies of the political campaign can release a citizen from the obligations of truth, honor, loyalty, and public decency.

2. That we hold the supremacy of law and the preservation of the laborers' rest day as paramount to party fealty and the hope of political victory or the fear of defeat; and no partisan consideration whatever shall induce us to cast our ballots for a party or a platform which ignores religious rights, fawns on conspirators, or proposes to rob laboring men of a law which protects them, one day in seven, against the oppressions of power and the exactions of greed; nor will we support any nominee of any party who is disqualified by a debasing appetite for alcoholic drinks.

3. That we will vigilantly await the platforms and nominations of existing parties, in the hope that we may find ourselves able to vote like honest and loyal men, without the necessity of separating ourselves from the parties that now divide the state; but should no party take the proper steps to protect an efficient Sunday law, and favor the plan of enforcing the question of license to sell intoxicants to the people, then we will meet and take such steps as shall give the voters of our state an opportunity to express their views on these two important questions.

4. That we hail with gratitude the triumph of local option in Arkansas, and of constitutional prohibition in Kansas, and more recently and gloriously in Iowa, as a presage and prophecy of victory over the impoverishing and demoralizing liquor business, destined ere long to be achieved in every state in the union, the actual results of these beneficent measures having refuted the calumnies of their adversaries and reassured the faith of their friends, all of which encourages us to believe that public sentiment is now ready for prohibitory legislation in this state; and we shall consider that no party or candidate on any ticket that is opposed to prohibiting people to vote upon the question of the discontinuance of this traffic is entitled to our support.

The debate on the resolutions took a wide range, and considerable disgust was manifested at the action of the democratic convention in relation to the repeal of the Sunday law. The convention then adjourned to await the action of the republican convention.

On September 28th, another session of the prohibition reform convention was held at San Francisco. It was called by the executive committee appointed by the July convention, and was largely attended. It was called to order by Winchester and was opened with prayer. On the 30th, the following resolutions were adopted:

The prohibition home protection party of California, now in state convention assembled, declares itself in alliance with the great national organization, having temperance for its first organic law and governing motive, and is in sympathetic co-operation with all reforms calculated to advance the moral and material welfare of the whole American people:

1. We declare that our object, aim, and purpose is to build up a political organization that may safely be intrusted with the conduct of national affairs, and to which may be confided, in all the states and territories of the American union, the political control of all questions involving the moral and material interests of the people.

2. We invite to this work the intelligent, law-respecting, and order-loving men and women of this state; those who own its property, pay its taxes, are interested in the protection and education of its youth, in elevating its moral standards, preserving the union of states, and in developing and perpetuating Christian civilization throughout the world.

3. We declare that the manufacture, sale, and use of alcoholic drinks is the greatest evil of the country and the age. That the traffic enslaves women and degrades children; debases youth and wrecks manhood; corrupts ballots and injures public service; peoples prisons and fills insane asylums; breeds paupers and criminals; imposes enormous burdens of taxation; destroys capital and ruins labor; degrades, impoverishes, and destroys our homes, and now threatens, through organized and criminal conspiracies, to subvert law and order. So believing, we declare the cardinal principles of our party to be prohibition, by constitutional amendment, of the manufacture of all alcoholic liquors not demanded for medicinal, mechanical, or scientific use, and the regulation by law, under severe

penalities, of the sale of alcoholic liquors for such use, and the absolute and total prohibition of the sale for any other purpose.

4. The defiant resistance to law by the liquor dealers of this state
and their associates; their attempted aggressions for the destruction
of our most sacred laws and highest interests, together with the subserviency of the democratic and republican parties to these law-
breakers and law-defiers, have forced upon us an issue of the greatest
importance to the state, which should and must be met with determined courage and intense devotion to the best and highest interests
of the people. This we are now determined fully and energetically
to do. In this we most earnestly invite the co-operation and assistance of every one who desires the best interests of this state and
people.

5. We declare that Sunday is an institution so interwoven into
our laws, our customs, our civilization, and the very structure of our
government; so intricately and beneficently connected with our
social, business, and moral life, that we cannot dispense with it
without sacrificing the very best interests of the country and the
highest welfare of the whole people. And so believing, we demand
the enactment and enforcement of an intelligent and rational Sunday
law, and especially do we demand that all saloons or places of business where intoxicating drinks are now licensed to be sold or permitted to be sold on secular days, shall be absolutely closed on
Sunday.

6. We emphatically protest against all state subsidies or other
countenance to encourage the business of making intoxicating
drinks from grapes, and against appropriating public funds for horse-
racing at our state and district fairs.

7. We are in favor of the universal and enforced education of the
youth of our state, including instruction in regard to the effects of
alcohol upon the human system, with ample provision for the support of an adequate and efficient system of free public schools, and
that the state shall furnish pupils in our public schools text-books,
free of price to such as are unable to buy them, and to all others at
the cost price of their production; and that we are opposed to sectarian education in our free schools, and the appropriation to
denominational schools of the public school moneys.

8. We believe that railroad corporations and companies are
subject to the control of general laws, and to such enactments and
regulations as may be rightfully demanded by reason of their peculiar relations to the general public. We would compel it and its

owners to bear its and their just proportion of the burdens of government. We would compel them to pay taxes upon their property at the same relative valuation that is placed upon all other property, and, in all respects, we would treat railroad owners and railroads with impartiality and justice. We are opposed to all unjust discrimination in fares and freights.

9. The hydraulic miner has no right, in the pursuit of his important and legitimate industry, to injure the property of his agricultural neighbor, or to deposit his detritus in such places that by operation of natural causes it may then, or at some future time, be carried where it will injure land, fill navigable streams, or interfere with the bays and harbors of our coast. It is the duty of the miner engaged in gravel sluicing to so impound his debris—hold it in arrest—that such injuries may not occur, and to this end we insist that proper legislation should be had and the decisions of our courts enforced.

10. We believe that the state should assume control of the water supply for irrigating purposes, and provide at once by suitable legislation for the equitable distribution of the same.

11. We recognize the noble services of woman in the temperance reform, and in every elevating, purifying, beneficent work affecting the interest of our race; and we believe that enlightened patriotism and manly courage demand the assertion at this time that woman is entitled of right to the privileges of the elective franchise; and so believing, in the interest of the temperance cause, in the interest of our common humanity, for the safety of our homes, and the protection of our free institutions now threatened, we shall insist upon such amendments to existing laws as shall fully and forever enfranchise the women of our country.

The following resolution, which was adopted, brought on a warm debate :

We hail with pleasure the cultivation of the grape in this state, as offering our people a most pleasant, healthful, and remunerative occupation, and an incalculable and inexhaustible mine of wealth for many centuries to come. An unlimited market will always be found for all the raisins, syrups, canned fruit, and fresh grapes that the state can produce. We are assured from our own experience so far, and from the past history and the present condition of the people who have prostituted the luscious grape to the vile use of

29

drunkenness, that the wine and brandy manufacture is the most degrading, demoralizing, depraving, and pauperizing business which has ever cursed the world. We point for the truth of this to the utter ignorance, poverty, drunkenness, and moral ruin which has enshrouded Spain, Portugal, Italy, Sicily, Greece, Hungary, and the wine districts of Switzerland; to the vice, turbulence, drunkenness, insanity, and suicides of France, and to the rapid degeneration of its people. We point to the fact that only one half of the young men of France are physically fit for military duty when they arrive at the legal age. We denounce the promises of wealth from the production of wine as entirely baseless and false.

The following were also adopted :

That while by the enactment of a prohibitory law we will deprive the state of the revenue derived from the production and sale of liquors, we guarantee the diminution of expense for punishment of crime arising from the production and sale of liquor will more than compensate for the loss of revenue and licenses.

That the prohibition home protection party of this state, pledges itself and its candidates to an immediate and material reduction in the rates and amounts annually levied for state taxation; that we favor the abolishment of the numerous sinecure offices now drawing large amounts from the state treasury for salaries, and which have been maintained by both the democratic and republican state administrations; that we believe the high valuation of property and the excessive rates so levied have tended and continue to tend to retard the development, growth, and prosperity of the state. We regard it as disgraceful that it should cost annually over three millions of dollars, wrung by taxation from 160,000 voters of the state, to maintain the state government.

That the state central committee urgently recommend the holding of prohibitory conventions, wherever practicable, in all the counties of this state, for the purpose of a thorough organization, to carry into effect the objects of this convention, to also secure the election of members to both houses of the legislature, and to fill their various county offices.

That the state central committee of the prohibition home protection party shall have no power to fill any vacancy occurring in the ticket presented and nominated by this convention, by reason of the declination of the proposed candidate or otherwise, by selecting or substituting the name of any person now a candidate for office on the ticket of either the republican, democratic, or any other party.

The following ticket was nominated, without opposition :

For governor, Dr. R. H. McDonald, of San Francisco.

For lieutenant-governor, William Sims, of Yolo county.

For secretary of state, M. C. Winchester, of Sutter county.

For state controller, Rev. O. A. Bateman.

For state treasurer, Adam Bayne.

For attorney-general, Will D. Gould, of Los Angeles.

For surveyor-general, E. K. Hill, of Marysville.

For superintendent of public instruction, R. A. Grant, of Woodland.

For clerk of supreme court, William Crowhurst, of San Francisco.

For justices of the supreme court, H. A. Mayhew and Robert Thompson.

For members of congress—At large, A. J. Gregg, Jesse Yarnell. First district, James McM. Shafter ; second district, J. L. Coles; third district, H. S. Graves; fourth district, A. B. Hotchkiss.

For members of state board of equalization, H. H. Luse, F. McD. Green, Charles E. Green, D. M. Pyle.

For railroad commissioners, Howard Andrews, Hiram Cummings, A. D. Boren.

Bateman declined the nomination for controller, and the convention nominated John M. Rhodes, of Woodland. He also declined, and the convention named D. K. Zumwalt. He afterward declined, and the state committee named Harvey W. Rice. Bayne declined the nomination for treasurer, and J. B. Mullen was nominated. Mayhew and Thompson declined, and afterward Anson Brunson and Jackson Temple were nominated for supreme justices. Gregg declined, and A. B. Hotchkiss was nominated for congressman at large, and M. V. Wright was nominated for congress from the fourth district. On October 3d, Pyle declined, and the vacancy was not filled.

The greenback labor convention met at San Francisco on September 6th. E. J. Shellhouse was elected temporary president. The proceedings were very stormy throughout. The committee on platform consisted of F. Woodward, Mrs. T. J. McQuiddy, Mrs. Marian Todd, and others. Their report adopted and incorporated the platform of the national greenback party, and contained in addition the following :

1. We demand, as due to the laws of nature, that the present Sunday law be sustained, and so amended as to make it effective and equal and just to all persons.

2. We demand the prohibition of the manufacture, importation and sale of all intoxicating liquors, except for medicinal and scientific purposes, and demand legislative provision for the submission of this and all other important questions upon which there is or may become any considerable difference of opinion, to a direct vote of the people.

Another resolution called for a reduction of 25 per cent. on the rates of freights and fares; another insisted that the lands granted to railroads under conditions which had not been complied with, and not taken up by actual settlers, should revert to the public domain. The platform was adopted after a warm debate.

The following nominations were made: Thomas J. McQuiddy, for governor; W. J. Sweasy, for lieutenant-governor; Mrs. Marian Todd, for attorney-general; Stephen Maybell and Warren Chase, for congressmen at large; Robert Summers, for secretary of state; M. E. Morse, for controller; L. Keating, for treasurer; W. J. Cuthbertson, for surveyor-general; E. J. Shellhouse, for school superintendent; W. C. Stratton and John Clark, for justices of the supreme court; J. F. O'Toole, for clerk of the supreme court; G. T. Elliott, J. H. Redstone, and J. H. Holloway, for railroad commissioners; H. S. Fitch, congressman from the first district; F. Woodward, from the second; W. O. Howe, from the third, and Isaac Kinley, from the fourth; L. W. Kidd, for member of the state board of equalization from the first district; Thomas McConnell, from the second; T. J. Goin, from the third; and J. S. Loveland, from the fourth.

A grangers' state convention met at Stockton on October 7th, and was presided over by J. V. Webster. A lengthy platform was adopted, and the following nominations were made:

For railroad commissioners, Charles F. Reed from the first district, John T. Doyle from the second district, and W. W. Foote from the third district.

For members of the board of equalization, James A. Withington from the first district, L. C. Morehouse from the second, C. E. Wilcoxon from the third, and O. W. Dana from the fourth.

For state controller, John P. Dunn.

It was decided to make no nominations for the other state offices.

The election was held on November 7th, and the official returns developed the following result : For governor, Estee, 67,175; Stoneman, 90,694 ; McDonald, 5,772 ; McQuiddy, 1,020. For lieutenant-governor, Conklin, 71,640 ; Daggett, 87,944 ; Sims, 3,783 ; Sweasy, 1,138. For justices of the supreme court Hunt, 73,259 ; Denson, 69,769 ; Sharpstein, 88,527; Ross, 89,363 ; Brunson, 2,860 ; Temple, 2,402 ; Stratton, 1,096 ; Clark, 718. For secretary of state, Pedlar, 73,471 ; Thompson, 87,170 ; Winchester, 2,893 ; Summers, 1,176. For controller, Davies, 74,152 ; Dunn, 86,031 ; Rice, 2,435 ; Morse, 1,085 ; D. K. Zumwalt, 183. For treasurer, Weil, 74,096 ; January, 86,591 ; Mullen, 2,971 ; Keating, 1,052. For attorney-general, Hart, 72,955 ; Marshall, 87,174 ; Gould, 2,897; Todd, 1,109. For surveyor-general, Minto, 73,599 ; Willey, 86,836 ; Hill, 3,116 ; Cuthbertson, 1,111. For clerk of the supreme court, Gross, 74,351 ; McCarthy, 86,158 ; Crowhurst, 3,176 ; O'Toole, 1,104. For superintendent of public instruction, Waterman, 73,906 ; Welcker, 86,896; Grant, 2,854 ; Shellhouse, 1,101. For railroad commissioners: First district—Reed, 29,125 ; Carpenter, 31,481 ; Andrews, 1,370; Elliott, 705. Second district—Clayton, 14,219; Humphreys, 21,601 ; Cummings, 226 ; Redstone, 71 ; Doyle, 5,455. Third district—Gibson, 26,815 ; Foote, 31,694 ; Boren, 955 ; Holloway, 163. For state board of equalization: First district—Johnson, 16,226 ; Gildea, 22,- 192 ; Luse, 270 ; Kidd, 95. Second district—Morehouse, 20,326 ; Crutcher, 19,332 ; Green, 605 ; McConnell, 103. Third district— Kimball, 17,731 ; Wilcoxon, 22,291 ; Green, 130 ; Goin, 912. Fourth district—Dana, 19,184 ; Markley, 22,602 ; Loveland, 336. For congressmen at large, Morrow, 73,747; Edgerton, 73,454 ; Sumner, 87,233 ; Glascock, 87,259 ; Hotchkiss, 2,786 ; Yarnell, 2,722 ; Chase, 1,139 ; Maybell, 1,090. First district—Neuman, 14,847; Rosecrans, 22,733 ; Shafter, 580 ; Fitch, 67. Second district— Page, 19,246 ; Budd, 20,229; Coles, 478 ; Woodward, 78. Third district—DeHaven, 19,473 ; Henley, 21,807; Graves, 862 ; Howe, 404. Fourth district—Woods, 18,387; Tully, 23,105; Wright, 650 ; Kinley, 355.

' CHAPTER XXXII.

1884. Republican Convention, April 30th—Democratic Convention—Prohibition Convention—People's Convention—Republican Convention, July 23d—Irrigation Convention, May 14th—Irrigation Convention, December 3d.

The republican state committee met at San Francisco on March 4th and called a state convention to meet at Oakland on April 30th, to select 16 delegates to attend the national convention to be held in Chicago on June 3d. The state convention selected E. A. Davis for chairman, and the committee on resolutions consisted of G. G. Blanchard, M. M. Estee, S. C. Denson, C. C. Bush, Charles F. Reed, J. K. Doak, William H. Parks, D. McPherson, Walter Van Dyke, W. G. Long, W. H. Cheney, and others. The committee reported the following, which were unanimously adopted:

1. That the republicans of California endorse the national administration, and hereby renew their allegiance to the principles of the party as illustrated and made conspicuous in the twenty-eight years of its existence.

2. That we are in favor of protecting home industry and enterprise, and such legislation as will tend to maintain and support our own people. We are, therefore, in favor of a tariff for protection, adjusted by a wise discrimination to the wants of the government in the matter of revenue, so as to secure the best results for the greatest number.

3. That we are in favor of such amendments to the Chinese exclusion act as will effectively prevent any evasion of its letter or spirit, and will secure to our people absolute protection against any and all forms of Chinese immigration; and we further declare that the act so amended should be made perpetual.

4. That it is to the republican party that the nation must look to repel the spirit of communism and agrarianism, and for the establishment and protection of the freedmen and rights of the citizen.

5. That the delegates elected to the national republican convention be and they are hereby instructed to vote for and use all honorable means for the nomination of James G. Blaine for president of the United States so long as he remains a candidate before said convention.

6. That the commissioner of agriculture should be made a cabinet officer, and our delegates are instructed to urge a plank in the national platform favoring this idea.

7. That the consideration of all matters affecting state policy be deferred until the meeting of our next state convention.

8. That the services of Senator John F. Miller are deserving of public approbation. His appointment to the chairmanship of the committee on foreign relations in the senate was a just recognition of eminent ability. His able advocacy of the prohibition of servile Chinese immigration has met with a responsive favor from all classes of citizens and has materially strengthened the cause of the republican party.

Wm. W. Morrow, George A. Knight, Thomas R. Bard, and Horace Davis were elected delegates at large, over Horace F. Page, R. W. Simpson, Creed Haymond, Frank M. Pixley, James McM. Shafter, and R. O. Gaskill. Page, Pixley, Gaskill, and Shafter were selected alternates at large. The following were selected from the districts:

First district—C. C. Bush and Byron O. Carr for delegates, over R. K. Nichols, H. W. Byington, and J. D. Byers. Byington and Byers were elected alternates.

Second district—Wm. H. Parks and George W. Schell for delegates, over S. W. Sperry. David E. Knight and Timothy H. Barnard were selected as alternates.

Third district—Wm. Johnston and Eli S. Denison for delegates, over T. H. Thompson, Wallace R. Pond, and Henry P. Wood. Thompson and Pond were selected alternates.

Fourth district—David McClure and Charles F. Crocker for delegates, and Frank French and Wm. B. May for alternates.

Fifth district—Adolph B. Spreckles and Maurice O. Blake for delegates, over J. W. Rea and Sargent S. Morton. Rea and Morton were elected alternates.

Sixth district—David C. Reed and Oregon Sanders for delegates, over W. S. Beebe, W. H. Norway, and Thomas Flint. Edwin W. Crooks and Thomas Flint were elected alternates.

The democratic state committee met at San Francisco on March 11th and called a state convention to meet at Stockton on June 10th, to nominate delegates to the national convention to be held in Chicago on July 8th, and also the presidential electors. The state convention was called to order by John H. Wise, the chairman of the state committee. Stephen M. White was chosen temporary chairman, without opposition; H. M. LaRue declining. The committee on resolutions consisted of D. M. Delmas, Fisher Ames, W. J. Tinnin, M. E. C. Munday, Marion Biggs, Niles Searls, M. F. Tarpey, E. E. Leake, C. P. Berry, Byron Waters, and others. On the 11th, a permanent organization was effected by the selection of White as president; and W. J. Tinnin, Jo Hamilton, Peter Hopkins, and others, vice-presidents. The committee on resolutions reported the following :

The democracy of California, in convention' assembled, hereby announce the following principles :

1. That we do now reaffirm our unwavering fealty and adherence to the anti-monopoly principles which have ever been the doctrine of democrats, not only in this state, but throughout the union, and proclaim our unshaken, faith in the principles set forth in the San Jose platform of 1882.   •

2. That we hold the calling of the extra session of the legislature to have been a wise, politic and patriotic act on the part of Governor Stoneman, warranted by the embarrassment of the finances of the state, caused by the contumacious refusal of the railroad corporations to pay their taxes, and the condition of public affairs engendered by their open defiance of the laws, and their pernicious influence in preventing the regulation of freights and fares and the suppression of abuses in transportation.

3. That the late extra session of the legislature marks an epoch in the contest between the people and the monopolies, and is an event which sets forth in a clear and unmistakable light before the people the baneful arts and corrupt practices by which the railroad monopoly, in furtherance of its own selfish and grasping policy, either controls legislation or defeats measures calculated for the public good.

4. That, as all legislation at the late extra session calculated to relieve the people of the state from the insolent and oppressive rule of railroad corporations was frustrated by the republican party— seven-eighths of whose members in the senate, and three-fourths of whose assemblymen in the house voted solidly and persistently against such legislation; and as the conduct of these republican representatives not only was not rebuked, but was tacitly approved by the late republican convention in Oakland, and as that convention openly condemned as agrarian and communistic all attempts at anti-monopoly legislation, and emphasized its hostile attitude by sending as its chosen delegates to Chicago men who were openly

interested in railroad and other monopolies, or who were notoriously and avowedly the pliant tools of such monopolists; therefore, we denounce the republican party of California as untrue to the people, leagued with the enemies of the state, and subservient to the dictation of wealth and power, against the interest of the people.

5. That we are not unmindful of the conduct of certain democratic officers and legislators, who co-operated with the republicans at the late extra session in frustrating the will of the people and antagonizing the true interests of the state. That while no amount of care can at all times prevent the intrusion into parties of faithless men, who enter with a false pledge upon their lips merely to ruin and betray—yet the party becomes responsible for the conduct of such recreant members only when, having discovered them, it fails to condemn their course; that it is the duty of a party, if it is true to itself and to the people, to expel from its ranks and denounce as unworthy of public trust and lost to all sense of honor, traitors and pledge-breakers. Therefore, we do now denounce railroad commissioners Carpenter and Humphreys, who have broken their pledges with reference to freight and fare reductions; Lieutenant-governor John Daggett, whose casting vote was ever thrown into the scale to turn the balance against the people; Attorney-general Marshall, who violated his solemn pledge, taken at San Jose, that in the collection of revenues from railroads there should be no compromises; and those democratic senators and assemblymen who at the late session of the legislature proved faithless to their pledges and betrayed the cause of the people—men whose recreant conduct has since met with such emphatic denunciation and rebuke at the hands of their own local constituencies.

6. That under the great law of equality of rights and equality of burdens, which is the fundamental principle of all free republics, and the corner-stone of democracy, we favor the passage of revenue laws which shall compel corporations to pay their taxes as individuals pay theirs.

7. That we proclaim our unshaken confidence in the ability of the people to govern themselves and to enforce obedience to their laws, even from overgrown corporations and gigantic monopolies. We denounce as degrading to the dignity of the state and fatal to its sovereignty all compromises in the enforcement of laws, and maintain that the people owe it to themselves not to remit to rich and powerful corporations penalties for violated laws which, under similar circumstances, they exact from individuals.

8. That we reaffirm our adherence to the doctrine laid down in the San Jose platform of 1882, that the democratic party is opposed to all legislation of a sumptuary character and all laws intended to restrain a free and full exercise by any citizen of his own religious and political opinions, so long as he leaves others to enjoy their rights unmolested. That the present system of imposing an excessive license tax upon certain classes of business is contrary to the spirit of democracy.

9. That the interference of the federal judiciary under existing laws in restraining the collection of our state taxes on the property of railroad corporations and in interfering with the enforcement of our state revenue laws has greatly embarrassed the administration of our state government and justly meets with general condemnation; therefore, we invoke congress for such remedial legislation as may protect us in the exercise of this important incident of sovereignty.

10. That while we recognize the importance of encouraging the building and operation of railroads in this state and the advantages which ought to accrue to the people from the facilities which railroad transportation would afford, if fully and impartially given to all, we view with alarm the power of the railroad monopoly as manifested in its pernicious and corrupting interference in politics and in its control of officials elected by the people.

11. That we are opposed to all prohibitory tariffs intended to create or foster monopolies or exclusive privileges. We favor the raising of sufficient revenues for the necessary support of the government and the gradual discharge of all its obligations, and for this purpose we are in favor of a tariff so adjusted as to give incidental protection to home labor and home industries, placing the burdens, as far as possible, on the luxuries and exempting the necessaries of life. The details of this adjustment we submit to the judgment of a democratic congress.

12. That the ownership of large tracts of land by non-resident aliens is an evil not to be tolerated in the United States.

13. That we demand that all grants of public lands heretofore made for the benefit of corporations which have not complied with the conditions of the grant be immediately declared forfeited and the lands restored to the public domain, to be disposed of as all other public lands are now disposed of, in reasonable quantities, and to none but citizens of the United States, or persons who have declared their intention to become such, who are actual settlers thereon.

14. That our delegates to the convention in Chicago be instructed

to use their best efforts to have a plank inserted in the national platform declaring against national banks, believing that all paper money necessary to be used as currency should be issued directly by the national government and not through the instrumentality of national banks—collecting, as they do, a premium on the issuance of public money resting upon a public debt and with no real responsibility on the part of stockholders to their depositors.

15. That we condemn the employment of Chinese or convict labor in competition with the laboring classes of this state; and that the interests of American civilization demand that the gates shall be sealed forever against the immigration or importation of Asiatic coolies under any pretense whatever.

16. That we, condemn the practice of selection by county committees of delegates to conventions, as contrary to the principles of democracy.

17. That we demand of the state board of railroad commissioners the early formulation and passage of a schedule of freights from the interior to tide-water which will secure to the farmers a material reduction on the transportation of the crop of 1884.

18. That, recognizing the transcendent importance of agriculture and the fact that its success is indispensable to the prosperity of our country, we believe it should have a voice in the cabinet councils of the nation; and that our delegates to the Chicago convention be and they are hereby instructed to use their best efforts to procure the insertion of a clause in the platform pledging the party to create the office of secretary of agriculture, the incumbent of which shall be a practical agriculturist and a member of the president's cabinet.

19. That we favor the adoption of the proposed amendment to the state constitution, providing for the publication of text-books for the public schools of the state.

20. That we adhere to the democratic doctrine that it is the imperative duty of the government of the United States to protect alike the native-born and the naturalized citizens, and that the whole force of the government should be exerted in behalf of a naturalized citizen should he be conscripted in a foreign army.

21. That the choice of the democracy of California for president and vice-president is Samuel J. Tilden and Thomas A. Hendricks; not only because they are living representatives of the traditional principles of the democratic party, but also because their nomination and election is a necessity of retributive justice.

22. That in case any unforeseen cause should prevent the accept-

ance of the presidential nomination by Samuel J. Tilden, our second choice is Allen G. Thurman.

23. That the democracy of California unanimously repudiates the presidential aspirations of Stephen J. Field, and that we hereby pledge ourselves to vote for no man as delegate to the national convention of July 8, 1884, who will not before this convention pledge himself to use his earnest endeavors to defeat these aspirations.

A motion to strike out the 23d resolution was lengthily debated, and lost by a vote of 19 to 453. A motion to strike out the censure of Attorney-general Marshall was also lost by a vote of 229 to 242. The resolutions as reported by the committee were then adopted. The following resolution was also adopted:

That it is the sense of this convention that a constitutional amendment, proposing the election of three railroad commissioners, should be presented by the next legislature to the people, to be voted on within 90 days, the election to be at large, and at the same time as the general election of 1886, and the term to be four years. On the adoption of the amendment by the people, the governor to appoint three commissioners, to take the place of the three removed by the adoption of the amendment.

A state central committee was selected, consisting of W. D. English, Robt. Tobin, Archibald Yell, Thomas F. Barry, W. A. Selkirk, R. O. Cravens, George T. Marye, Patrick Reddy, J. D. Goodwin, J. T. Harrington, D. N. Hershey, J. W. Oates, J. G. Wolfskill, D. A. Ostrom, E. G. Blessing, John Foley, A. M. Burns, J. J. Flynn, Peter Hopkins, D. J. Oullahan, J. D. Spencer, Wallace Leach, and others.

The following were elected delegates to the national convention:

At large—William Dunphy, of San Francisco; C. F. Foster, of Tehama; Thomas J. Clunie; Hugh M. La Rue, of Sacramento. T. H. Williams, T. G. Hill, W. W. Lyman, Hugh J. Mohan, alternates.

First district—H. C. Wilson, of Tehama; Dennis Spencer, of Napa. W. E. McConnell, of Sonoma; Archibald Yell, of Mendocino, alternates.

Second district—J. W. Breckinridge, of Merced; Niles Searls, of Nevada. W. E. Eichelroth, R. B. Hugg, alternates.

Third district—W. B. English, of Contra Costa; M. F. Tarpey, of Alameda. Dr. Dobbins, of Vacaville; H. H. Reid, of Alameda, alternates.

Fourth district—J. A. Wright, of San Francisco; Louis Holtz, of San Francisco. Abe Neuman, A. M. Burns, alternates.

Fifth district—Maurice Schmidt, of San Francisco; Lawrence Archer, of Santa Clara. J. W. McDonald, Jesse Cook, alternates.

Sixth district—L. J. Rose, of Los Angeles; A. B. Butler, of Fresno. T. J. Arnold, of San Diego; J. W. Ferguson, of Fresno, alternates.

The following were nominated for presidential electors and alternates:

At large—Charles Kohler, of San Francisco; C. P. Berry, of Sutter. J. C. Shorb, of San Francisco; J. T. Harrington, of Colusa, alternates.

First district—W. J. Tinnin, of Trinity. Richard Bayne, of Colusa, alternate.

Second district—G. G. Goucher, of Mariposa. F. D. Nicol, of Tuolumne, alternate.

Third district—J. C. Martin, of Alameda. Nathaniel Jones, of Contra Costa, alternate.

Fourth district—George T. Marye. J. M. Eaton, alternate.

Fifth district—James T. Murphy, of Santa Clara. Edward White, of Santa Cruz, alternate.

Sixth district—W. H. Webb, of Monterey. A. J. Atwell, of Tulare, alternate.

On June 17th, Shorb, a nominee for alternate elector at large, published the following declination:

Anticipating a speedy and entire restoration to health, and desiring, in the coming presidential campaign, to speak, and with authority, in behalf of those principles which the democratic party has always illustrated and maintained as vital and essential to the perpetuity of our form of government, and indispensable to the preservation of the liberty, prosperity, and happiness of the people, I allowed my name to be presented as an alternate elector before the Stockton convention. To this position I was elected, I believe, by acclamation. I wish now to resign this position.

The convention at Stockton was called for the purpose of selecting delegates to the national convention, and electors on the national ticket. It was not called to pass resolutions of eulogy on the wisdom of calling the extra session of the legislature, or to relate the reasons of its ignominious—indeed, its absolute failure. It was not called to pass resolutions of repudiation of any aspirant to the presidency, here or elsewhere, or to rehearse the alleged or suspected infamy and treason of certain democratic officers of the state government, or members of the legislature in the upper and lower house. It was not called to signalize the ambition of some men, or to vent the spite and disappointment of others. Finally, it was not called to invade, even by resolution, vested rights, to terrorize corporations, or put on exhibition the purity of one newspaper, and its devotion to the interests of the people, or crystallize the claims of certain men for future preferment in the party.

Reading over the platform of this convention, an outsider would be led to regard the selection of national delegates and presidential electors as entirely secondary to the manifestations of demagogism, communism, persecution, injustice, spite, and tyranny that pervade the platform and resolutions from beginning to end. If I went before the people they would understand I indorsed the spirit and letter of this platform. This, I cannot in conscience do, for I am a democrat, and democracy means freedom in its largest and holiest aspect. It means equal rights to all; the right to worship God according to our own light; the right to act and vote in harmony with our own ideas and convictions of principle and utility. The attempt, unparalleled in the history of all conventions, democratic and republican, to force men to think and act with us under any and all circumstances, and meeting disaster and failure as it ought; the attempt, I repeat, by resolution, to expel them from the party for such reason, is tyranny and insolence, and not democracy. Finally, it is a movement which, I believe, will not be indorsed by men of intelligence, honesty and patriotism in the democratic party throughout the state of California, for it is in deadly antagonism to the spirit and performance of those pure civic virtues which should fill and animate the breast of every good citizen—virtues without whose cohesive force parties themselves must fall into decay and ruin at last.

On the 19th, Charles Kohler, a nominee for elector at large, addressed the following to the state committee:

The democratic convention that recently met at Stockton adopted a platform, condemned several gentlemen for their official conduct, and gratuitously assailed a distinguished citizen of California, whose name will be presented to the democratic national convention for the highest office in the gift of the American people.

The state convention placed my name on the electoral ticket, and if I remain silent I shall be regarded as approving all the doctrines enunciated in the Stockton platform. There are principles embodied in that declaration which I do not approve; and I most emphatically dissent from each and every expression condemnatory of Judge Field. Entertaining such views, I deem it my duty to the democratic party to state them thus publicly.

It is my purpose to give my cordial support to the ticket that shall be nominated at Chicago in July, and notwithstanding what was said and done at Stockton, I sincerely hope that Judge Field will be nominated at Chicago. If the committee over which you preside is not satisfied with my attitude as herein stated, it is at liberty to substitute another name for mine as an elector.

Kohler afterward withdrew his resignation. On July 26th, the state committee met at San Francisco for the purpose of filling the vacancies caused by resignations. Thomas H. Laine was nominated for alternate elector at large in place of Shorb; Edwin Swinford was substituted in place of Bayne, as alternate from the first district, and John A. Stanly for elector from the third district in place of Martin. Afterward Goucher declined, and on August 26th, the second district convention nominated Marion Biggs for elector.

The various district conventions met at Stockton on June 10th, and nominated the following for congressmen.

Barclay Henley from the first district, without opposition.
James H. Budd from the second district, without opposition.
John R. Glascock from the third district, without opposition.
R. P. Hastings from the fourth district, on the first ballot, by a vote of 56, to 9 for Charles A. Sumner; W. S. Rosecrans declining.
Frank J. Sullivan from the fifth district, without opposition.
R. F. Del Valle from the sixth district, without opposition.
Budd afterward declined to be a candidate, and on August 26th, the second district convention again met at Stockton and nominated Charles A. Sumner, without opposition.

The prohibition state convention met at San Francisco on June 17th, and was called to order by George Babcock, the chairman of the state committee. About 200 delegates were present. Babcock was elected temporary chairman, and on permanent organization, Joel Russell was president.

R. H. McDonald, J. L. Coles, J. A. Fairbanks, and T. M. Wills were elected delegates at large to attend the national convention to be held at Pittsburg on July 23d, and the following were chosen from the districts.

First district—H. A. Mayhew, W. G. Swan, and J. N. Lining.

Second district—W. M. Tharp, O. A. Bateman, and F. McD. Green.

Third district—H. J. Becker, O. N. Goulding, and H. L. Ross.

Fourth district—Captain A. D. Wood, Colonel George Babcock, and S. F. Dutton.

Fifth district—Mrs. E. P. Stevens, E. B. Fowler, and Mrs. A. P. Ellis.

Sixth district—Judge George Steele, Will D. Gould, and Samuel Fowler.

The committee on platform and resolutions submitted the following report, which was adopted :

The prohibition home protection party, now in state convention assembled, reaffirms and pledges itself anew to the following declarations :

1. We declare that our object, aim and purpose is to build up a political organization that may be safely intrusted with the conduct of national affairs, and to which may be confided, in all the states and territories of the American union, the political control of all such questions, involving the moral and material interests of the people, as are proper subjects of legislation.

2. We invite to this work the intelligent, law-respecting, and order-loving men and women of this state; those who own its property, pay its taxes, are interested in the protection and education of its youth, in elevating its moral standards, preserving the union of states, and developing and perpetuating Christian civilization throughout the land.

3. We declare that the manufacture, sale and use of alcoholic drinks is the greatest evil of the country and the age. That the traffic enslaves women and degrades children ; debases youth and wrecks manhood ; corrupts the ballot and injures the public service ; peoples prisons and fills insane asylums ; breeds paupers and criminals, and thereby imposes enormous burdens of taxation; destroys capital and ruins labor; degrades, impoverishes, and destroys our homes, and threatens, through organized and criminal conspiracies, to subvert law and order. So believing, we declare the cardinal principles of our party to be the prohibition, by national and state constitutional amendments, of the manufacture and importation of

all alcoholic, vinous, and malt liquors not demanded for medicinal, mechanical, or scientific use, and the regulation by law, under severe penalties, of the sale of such liquors for such use, and the absolute and total prohibition of the sale for any other purpose.

4. We deprecate all attempts to substitute any system of high-license, so-called, in place of prohibition of the liquor traffic; and while the traffic continues, we also oppose any reduction of the burdens or restrictions now imposed upon it. We are in favor of the rigid and impartial enforcement of all laws tending to restrict the sale of intoxicating liquors, and demand of our executive authorities the arrest and punishment of all persons engaged in criminal combination to obstruct or prevent the enforcement of laws intended for the protection of society against the wrongs, injuries and crimes growing out of the saloon business.

5. That while we regard prohibition of the liquor traffic as the most important political question before the American people, we are not unmindful that there are other issues seriously, if not vitally, affecting the general welfare; but these issues we refer to the action of the national prohibition convention to meet July 22d, assured that it will properly represent the sentiment of our state and the nation.

On motion of Colonel Babcock, it was ordered that the delegates to the national convention be authorized to cast the twenty-three votes to which the state is entitled, and also that the delegates be instructed to present and urge the name of Dr. R. H McDonald upon the convention for the nomination for president of the United States.

The following congressional nominations, made by the district delegations during the recess, were reported and ratified by the convention: First district, Rev. C. O. Bateman, of Tehama; second district, Joshua V. Webster, of Stockton; third district, Josiah B. Wills, of Contra Costa; fourth district, Colonel George Babcock, of San Francisco; fifth district, Rev. A. P. Morrison, of San Jose; sixth district, Will D. Gould, of Los Angeles.

For electors, the following were chosen: First district, J. W. Tharp, of Sonoma; second district, H. S. Graves, of Sutter; third district, Joel Russell, of Alameda; fourth district, Stephen H. Varney, of San Francisco; fifth district, J. D. Wood, of Santa Clara; sixth district, George Steele, of San Luis Obispo; at large, M. O. Winchester, of Sutter, and Dr. A. B. Nixon, of Sacramento.

30

Afterward, Jesse Yarnell was substituted for Nixon, as candidate for elector at large; D. E. Bushnell for Wood, as candidate for elector in the fifth district; A. D. Boren for Steele, as candidate for elector in the sixth district, and William Crowhurst for Morrison, as candidate for congressman in the fifth district.

Pursuant to a call issued on May 23d, by the executive committee of the California branch of the national anti-monopoly party, a state convention to nominate presidential electors, convened at San Francisco on July 16th, the delegates to which were chosen from the national anti-monopoly greenback, labor, and national union parties. Dr. George Hewston called the convention to order, and was chosen temporary chairman. The committee on resolutions consisted of P. J. Merwin, J. M. Kinley, George T. Elliott, L. F. Moulton, and others. On permanent organization, A. E. Redstone, was president. The following resolutions were adopted :

Whereas, Through the neglect of government to enforce the constitution and laws in the spirit of republican equality, corporate, moneyed, and property interests have become paramount to the interests of humanity. Home and foreign capital, through corrupt legislation, have monopolized the land of the nation and fastened its grasp on all industries, thereby forcing land and labor to pay tribute to corporate and individual rapacity. The improved materials and forces of modern civilization, which are essential to the uses of life, liberty, and the pursuit of happiness, are so monopolized that the industrial classes are forced into destructive competition, one with another; and through this means, and by party intrigue, their political liberties have been rendered little better than a dead letter. The government, by delegating the exercise of its functions to others, through subsidy grants and united action with corporations and favored individuals, has placed itself in a position to be fairly charged with collusion with capital and conspiracy against labor. And the continuance of conditions such as are in operation at present must eventually lead to the extinction of republican institutions, to be followed by a state of anarchy or despotism. Resolved,

That we, the national anti-monopoly, the national greenback, and the national union parties, in joint convention assembled, in the name of the national party, declare as our platform of principles the following:

1. We hold that the late decision of the supreme court on the

legal tender question, to be a full vindication of the right and authority of congress over the issue of legal-tender notes, and we hereby pledge ourselves to uphold said decision, and defend the constitution and laws against alterations and amendment thereof.

2. We demand the payment of the public debt as it falls due, in the spirit of its original contraction; the free coinage of gold and silver, and the issuance of sufficient treasury and fractional currency to meet the requirements of our industrial and commercial interests, to be kept in circulation under a uniform system.

3. We condemn the granting of special privileges, or the use of the public domain by a few persons or corporations to the detriment of the individual rights of any and every citizen.

4. We declare directors of corporations and individuals who refuse to pay their taxes, or otherwise refuse to contribute to the support of the government which protects them, in open rebellion, and they should be dealt with as other criminals who defy the law.

5. The public lands being the natural inheritance of the people, we denounce that policy which has granted to corporations vast tracts of land; and we demand that immediate and vigorous measures be taken to reclaim from such corporations all such land grants as have been forfeited by reason of non-fulfillment of contract, or that may have been wrongfully acquired by corrupt legislation; and that such reclaimed lands and other public domain be henceforth held as a sacred trust, to be used only by actual settlers in limited quantities; and that any citizen of the United States may initiate legal proceedings in any court to invalidate such grants, in the name of the United States when public lands, and the state when state lands, without the consent of the United States attorney-general or attorney-general of the state, on defraying the expenses thereof. We demand that alien ownership of land, individual or corporate, shall be prohibited.

6. We demand an amelioration of the condition of labor by enforcing sanitary laws in industrial establishments, by abolition of the contract convict-labor system, by rigid inspection of mines and factories, by fostering non-sectarian educational institutions, and by abolishing child labor.

7. We advocate reduction of the hours of labor, and demand that importation of Chinese, servile, pauper, and contract labor shall cease.

8. We demand congressional regulation of inter-state commerce; we denounce "pooling," stock-watering, and discrimination in rates and charges, and demand that congressional and state legislation

shall correct these abuses, even, if necessary, by the construction of national railroads; and that a postal telegraph system shall be established by the government.

9. All private property, all forms of money, and obligations to pay money, shall bear their just proportion of public taxes.

10. We demand a protective tariff system by which the importation of luxuries shall be heavily taxed, and the necessaries of life for common use, not competitive, be admitted free; and a graduated tax of other imports be adopted, whereby those most needed shall bear the lowest duty, and those less needed the highest duty; and that all competitive raw materials be excluded.

11. We demand that the property either of corporations or private persons, whether consisting of franchises or other values, on a just remuneration, be subject to appropriation for public use under the law governing eminent domain.

12. We demand the submission to the people of the United States of amendments to the constitution, granting the right to legislate in favor of female suffrage and prohibition of the liquor traffic.

13. We demand a change in our Indian policy, whereby each reservation, or so much thereof as may be required, be appropriated and used as agricultural farms, and the Indians kept thereon and disciplined by being compelled to perform manual labor enough for their own support.

14. We demand the abrogation of the Clayton-Bulwer treaty.

15. We endorse the nomination of Benjamin F. Butler, of Massachusetts, and A. M. West, of Mississippi, respectively, for president and vice-president of the United States.

The following were nominated for presidential electors: P. J. Merwin, W. J. Sweasy, L. F. Moulton, George H. Stebbins, R. Butterfield, H. D. Barbour, H. M. Couch, and S. A. Waldron. Afterward Sweasy, Stebbins, and Barbour declined, and N. Curry, A. D. Nelson, and A. T. Dewey were nominated in their stead.

The following were nominated for alternate electors: T. J. McQuiddy, W. H. Moody, W. J. Sweasy, H. D. Barbour, Thomas Graham, and E. J. Shellhouse.

The nomination of congressmen was left to the state committee, and on the 17th the following nominations were announced:

First district, L. F. Moulton; second district, E. J. McIntosh; third district, A. B. Burns; fourth district, Henry S. Fitch; fifth district, J. M. Kinley; sixth district, Isaac Kinley. Afterward W. O. Howe was substituted for Moulton, Charles A. Sumner for McIntosh, and Frank J. Sullivan for J. M. Kinley.

The republican state committee met at San Francisco on June 23d, and called a state convention, to meet at Sacramento on July 23d, to nominate presidential electors and alternates. At the time and place named the convention met, and was called to order by P. B. Cornwall, the chairman of the state committee. M. M. Estee was chosen temporary chairman and afterward president, without opposition. The committee on resolutions consisted of F. Adams, W. H. Brown, Chester Rowell, David McClure, A. L. Chandler, J. H. Neff, W. H. Parks, D. McPherson, W. A. Cheney, D. N. Sherbourne, W. E. Dargie, and others.

The following nominations were made for presidential electors: At large, A. R. Conklin, Henry Edgerton; first district, Benjamin Shurtleff; second district, J. B. Reddick; third district, Henry Vrooman; fourth district, James Simpson; fifth district, Marcus H. Hecht; sixth district, Chester Rowell; Simpson resigned and Horace Davis was nominated in his stead. Shurtleff afterward declined, and J. D. Byers was nominated in his stead. On September 1st Vrooman resigned his place on the ticket, for the reason that the question had been raised that he was not eligible to serve as an elector, from the fact that he was holding the office of state senator, and Charles F. Reed was nominated in his place.

The convention nominated the following for alternate electors: At large, Ira P. Rankin and R. W. Waterman; first district, J. D. Byers; second district, L. T. Crane; third district, Charles F. Reed; fourth district, A. G. Booth; fifth district, Robert Effey; sixth district, Paris Kilburn.

The committee on resolutions reported the following, which were unanimously adopted:

1. That the republicans of California, in convention assembled, endorse and reaffirm the national platform of the republican party, adopted at its convention, recently held in Chicago, and we congratulate the country upon the nomination of Blaine and Logan, the true representatives of the American policy of progress and unity.

2. That we declare that the welfare of California demands, and that the property of labor and the interests of capital require, the

maintenance by the national government of the American system of tariff for protection. Under this policy which has been consistently supported by the republican party since its foundation, our varied industries have been fostered and extended, our laboring classes have enjoyed better wages than in any other part of the world, and the whole country has achieved unparalleled prosperity. We denounce the free trade policy, which the democratic party has advocated since 1840, as dangerous to the material interests of the country and to the well-being of American labor. We arraign the democratic party of California for supporting the national democratic party, which stands upon a platform that declares, in effect, for the free-trade doctrine of tariff for revenue only, as admitted by prominent members of the committee that framed the plank. We insist that the success of the British policy would destroy the growing industries of our commonwealth, especially the grape, raisin, wool, and manufacturing interests, and would reduce the wages of our workingmen to the starvation point.

3. That we ask and demand that the industry of the manufacture of the raisin shall be protected by a protective duty, and resolved, that we demand the restoration of the tariff on wool as fixed by the law of 1867.

4. That we are in favor of the adoption of the proposed amendment to section seven of article nine of the constitution of this state, authorizing the furnishing of free text-books for use in the common schools throughout the state.

5. That the republican party of California has a consistent record in its unswerving devotion to the interests of the people in opposition to all monopolies. First—We declare that railroad corporations, being organized for a public use, all unjust discrimination as between persons and places is in direct violation of the constitution of this state, and should be prohibited. Second—We declare that charges for freight by all transportation companies should only be what the service is reasonably worth. Third—It is the duty of the railroad commission to regulate freights and fares justly in the interest of the people. We call attention to the section of the platform of the national republican party which favors congressional legislation to carry out the constitutional power of congress to regulate interstate commerce, and especially to the language declaring that "the principle of the public regulation of railroad corporations is a wise and salutary one for the protection of all classes of the people, and we favor legislation that shall prevent unjust discrimination and excessive charges

for transportation, and that shall secure to the people and to the railways alike fair and equal protection of the laws." We endorse this declaration. We charge that the platform of the national democratic party evades this great issue. We arraign the democratic party of California for supporting a candidate for president whose public record identifies him as as a friend of monopoly and an enemy to the rights and the interests of the people. We particularly denounce the doctrine advanced by the nominee of the democratic party for president in his veto in the New York legislature of the bill reducing fares on the elevated railroads, in which he declared that there was no constitutional power in our legislature to regulate and abridge privileges granted by a former legislature to a public agency. This extreme monopolistic view had been condemned by the higher courts of the land, is wrong and dangerous, and marks him as unfit to hold the high office of chief magistrate of the republic.

6. That the commissioner of agriculture be constituted a cabinet officer of the nation as and under the title of "Secretary of Agriculture."

7. That, recognizing the claims of our soldiers, and the especial obligations of California to those through whose faithful services our territory was acquired, we favor the payment of pensions to all surviving veterans of the Mexican war.

8. That all property should bear its equal share of taxation. That all property, whether owned by individuals or corporations, should be assessed at its actual cash value, and be compelled to pay its just taxes.

9. That we commend our representatives in congress for their efforts in behalf of restrictive Chinese legislation, thus redeeming the pledges of the party made for them, and renew our determination to make such restriction effective, and in every way prevent the competition of Chinese with American labor. We thank the republican national convention for its emphatic declaration upon this subject; refer with pride to the attitude of James G. Blaine in congress when the subject first became a national one, and have implicit faith that the republican party of the nation will protect us in all our interests as against Chinese.

10. That we invite and welcome to our state the people of all countries which belong to our division of the human family, whose moral, physical and intellectual qualifications entitle them to the rights and privileges of American citizenship.

A state committee was selected, consisting of Aaron Bell, James A. Orr, H. W. Byington, W. H. Parks, E. W. Roberts, J. H. Neff, W. H. Brown, Richard Chute, C. H. Garoutte, A. J. Rhoads, Christopher Green, Obed Harvey, S. G. Hilborn, Eli S. Denison, W. W. Camron, F. K. Shattuck, Henry Vrooman, E. D. Wheeler, J. P. H. Wentworth, M. C. Briggs, A. W. Poole, A. R. Conklin, J. F. Crank, and others, and the executive committee was appointed afterward by the chairman.

The first congressional district convention met at Sacramento on July 23d, and nominated Thomas L. Carothers for congressman, without opposition.

The second district convention met at Sacramento on July 24th, and nominated James A. Louttit for congressman, on the second ballot, over Charles A. Tuttle and John A. Eagon.

The third district convention met at Benicia on July 14th, and nominated Joseph McKenna for congressman, on the twelfth ballot, over W. W. Camron, Carroll Cook, George W. Tyler, and Henry Edgerton.

The fourth district convention met at Sacramento on July 23d, and nominated Wm. W. Morrow for congressman, without opposition.

The fifth district convention met at Sacramento on July 23d, and nominated Charles N. Felton for congressman, without opposition.

The sixth district convention met at Sacramento on July 23d, and nominated H. H. Markham for congressman, without opposition.

The election was held on November 4th, and the official canvass developed this result: Blaine electors—Edgerton, 102,369; Byers, 102,397; Reed, 102,411; Hecht, 102,223; Conklin, 102,378; Reddick, 102,416; Davis, 102,306; Rowell, 102,391. Cleveland electors—Kohler, 89,288; Tinnin, 89,200; Stanly, 89,221; Murphy, 89,235; Berry, 89,214; Biggs, 89,204; Marye, 89,229; Webb, 89,-201. Butler electors—Curry, 2,037; Merwin, 1,722; Moulton, 2,019; Nelson, 2,021; Butterfield, 2,012; Dewey, 2,009; Couch, 2,005; Waldron, 1,974. St. John electors—Winchester, 2,963; Boren, 2,345; Yarnell, 2,501; Tharp, 2,932; Graves, 2,961; Russell, 2,962; Varney, 2,952; Bushnell, 2,360. For congressmen: First district—Carothers, 16,316; Henley, 16,461; Bateman, 321. Second district—Louttit, 18,327, Sumner, 18,208; Webster, 558.

Third district—McKenna, 17,435; Glascock, 13,197; Burns, 273; Wells, 322. Fourth district—Morrow, 15,083; Hastings, 10,422; Babcock, 6; Fitch, 123. Fifth district—Felton, 17,014; Sullivan, 15,676; Crowhurst, 232. Sixth district—Markham, 17,397; Del Valle, 16,990; Gould, 821; Kinley, 237.

The republican electors met at the state capitol in Sacramento, on December 3d. All were present except Reddick and Byers. Those present chose A. P. Catlin to act for Reddick, and Robert T. Devlin to serve for Byers. The eight votes of the state were recorded for Blaine and Logan, and Henry Edgerton was chosen messenger to convey the returns to Washington.

The state irrigation convention assembled at Riverside, May 14th, and was called to order by A. P. Johnson, temporary chairman elected at the original convention that assembled March 12th, and adjourned on account of the storm. By the adoption of the report of the committee on permanent organization, J. W. North was made president and L. M. Holt, secretary of the convention. The session continued for three days, most of the time being consumed in discussion of the subject of the use of water for irrigation, and cognate topics. A committee on resolutions was appointed, consisting of George Rice, L. M. Holt, and O. H. Congar. The following were adopted:

1. That a cordial invitation is hereby extended to all parties interested—those interested in existing canal companies, and those owning lands under the same, and all land owners requiring irrigation—to be present by representation at the next irrigation convention.

2. The California state irrigation convention recommend to the irrigators of the Pacific states and to all persons interested in the measurement of water, the cubic foot of water per second as the unit of measure of water, fifty inches of water under a four-inch pressure being equal to one cubic foot of water per second.

3. That it is the duty of the legislature of this state to repeal section fourteen hundred and twenty-two of our civil code in order that there may be upon our statute books no seeming recognition of the English common law of riparian rights, which has not, and never had, an existence in this state. That the present law giving the absolute power to fix water rates to supervisors and governing

bodies of municipal corporations, is in the interest of justice, is the only protection of water buyers against extortionate demands, and that any amendment of it would be a calamity to irrigators. That the state owes it to the irrigators to interfere promptly and to adjust speedily differences arising between them and water corporations, and that it should be within the power of irrigators to compel the bringing of suits, in the name of the state, to settle such differences.

4. That the political parties of the state, during the coming campaign, should, in the construction of their platforms and the selection of candidates for the legislature, keep in view the interests of the irrigators of this state, as expressed in this convention.

5. That the thanks of this convention are due Hon. Wm. Ham. Hall, state engineer, for his attendance at this convention, and his able paper presented on the irrigation question; that we recognize in Mr. Hall an able head to the irrigation system of this state, and we trust the state legislature will give him the necessary assistance and endorsement to enable him to carry to completion the work he has so efficiently commenced.

6. That the thanks of the delegates to this convention from abroad are due, and they are hereby tendered, to the citizens of Riverside for the cordial manner in which they have been received and entertained.

7. That it is the sense of this convention that thanks are due to Judge J. W. North for the able manner in which he has presided over the deliberations of this convention, also to those gentlemen who have favored us with able papers on subjects of such vital interest to the irrigators of the state, and especially to our secretary, L. M. Holt, who originated the call for this convention, and who has labored so earnestly and successfully to make this convention the success that it is.

8. That the thanks of this convention are due to Dr. S. F. Chapin, of San Jose, state inspector of fruit pests, for the interest he has taken in promoting the interests of this convention.

The following resolutions were also reported by the committee on resolutions, and referred to the committee on legislation:

1. That it is the judgment of this convention, in order to facilitate the development of California, that the water and land should be sold and held together; that by or under laws to be procured, there be formed irrigation districts with power, where more than

half the owners in number and value desire it, to bond the whole land to improve the whole property, with proper safeguards as to amount or proportion of value to be raised, time of payment, etc., and that a committee be made to take charge of and conduct the passage of such a law, or laws, through the legislature.

2. That congress is hereby memorialized to withdraw from sale all timber lands located on the head of irrigating streams, or mountain timber lands, as the removal of such forests by fire and the ax are having a seriously detrimental effect on our water sources, and that if longer continued, such denudation of forests will seriously affect the agricultural and horticultural interests of the state.

3. That congress be memorialized to make sufficient appropriation of money at its next session to project a system of deep artesian wells in those sections of the state not otherwise sufficiently supplied with irrigable water

4. That in the sense of this convention the English common law rule of riparian rights does not exist, nor has it, practically, ever existed in this state.

5. That this convention endorse a certain declaratory act and preamble reported by the majority of the assembly committee on irrigation, at the session of 1883, which said preamble and act ran as follows: "Whereas, the state of California was acquired from the republic of Mexico, and prior to such acquisition, and from its first settlement, the laws of that republic, and the usages and customs of the people, recognized no right upon the owners of the land bordering upon streams to the water flowing in such streams, superior to the right of any other person, who, by enterprise and diligence, diverted such water and applied it to useful purposes, and especially to the purposes of irrigation; and, whereas, from the acquisition of this state by the government of the United States, down to a very recent period, the aforesaid usages and customs have prevailed in and been recognized in said state, without question; and, whereas, it is now asserted that such usages and customs are violative of the common law of England, and riparian owners have the right to the full flow of such water, undiminished in quantity, and unimpaired in quality; and, whereas, none of the conditions exist in this state which admit of the application of the rule claimed, but, on the contrary, the enforcement of such a rule in a country like this, which can only be peopled and cultivated by a system of irrigation, and without which system a great portion of this state must ever remain a desert, would be destructive; and, whereas, it is claimed and as-

serted that section 1422 of the civil code is a recognition of the unwholesome rule; and, whereas, it never was the intention of the framers of the code, nor of the legislature which adopted it, that such a construction should be placed upon it, now, therefore,

"The people of the state of California, represented in senate and assembly, do enact as follows:

"Sec. 1. That section 1422 of the civil code of California is hereby repealed.

"Sec. 2. That in all actions relative to water rights, the courts shall take judicial notice of the usages and customs in the preamble to this act set out, and of the condition and nature of the country which do not, and never did, admit of the application of the rule of the English common law relative to riparian rights."

6. That it is not the sense of this convention that the doctrine of appropriation be carried so far as to deprive the riparian owner of sufficient water for such domestic, or other purposes for which he may have actually utilized it, nor to such an extent as to interfere with the use for commercial purposes of any of the navigable waters of this state.

. 7. That in the opinion of this convention the legislature of this state properly may and should pass a law relative to the administration and settlement of irrigation claims, similar to that now in successful operation in the state of Colorado.

8. That this whole matter be submitted, for their earnest consideration, to the committee on legislation appointed by this convention, with the hope that their deliberations may result in the proposal of practical and wholesome measures that, approved by the people and legislature of this state, will result in the increased prosperity of the former.

9. That we earnestly commend the consideration of these questions to the irrigators and miners of this state, and urge upon them the importance of electing as their nominees for legislative and judicial positions, such men as may be depended upon to give their interests due study and justice.

The committee on legislation, above referred to, was composed of J. DeBarth Shorb, John G. North, J. A. Wilcox, Will S. Green, J. W. North, and F. H. Wales. On May 16th, the convention adjourned to meet at Fresno, December 3, 1884. At the Fresno convention, in December, to these were added the names of L. M. Holt, J. F. Wharton, and L. B. Ruggles.

The convention assembled at Fresno, December 3d. It was called to order by J. W. North. J. DeBarth Shorb was elected permanent chairman, and J. F. Wharton, Secretary. The membership was not confined to delegations from counties, but included interested per. sons who subscribed their names on the roll of the convention. The sessions continued until December 6th, on which date it adjourned *sine die*. Much of the time was consumed in hearing addresses on the subject of irrigation. The committee on legislation submitted a report, but the preparation of matter for legislative action was placed in the hands of an executive committee, which met after the adjournment of the convention. The following resolutions were adopted :

1. That Dewey & Co. be employed to print 1,000 copies of the proceedings of this convention, in pamphlet form, for the sum of $100, to be delivered in two weeks.

2. That a finance committee of seven be appointed to raise funds to meet expenses incident to this convention, and for all other necessary expenses.

3. That Will S. Green be appointed a committee of one, with authority to expend a sum not to exceed $150 for the printing and circulation of a newspaper supplement containing the address of George E. Church and the reports of the joint committee as adopted by this convention.

4. That the sincere thanks of the members of this convention, who have come from a distance, are due and are most cordially tendered to the citizens of Fresno for many courtesies extended and the attention shown to visiting members.

5. That the secretary of this convention prepare a petition to the state legislature, setting forth the principles adopted by this convention, in guiding its legislative committee in the drafting of proposed legislative enactments, and asking the legislature to favorably consider the same, and that these be circulated through the state with a view to securing the largest possible number of names to the same.

6. That this committee would earnestly request that all friends of irrigation, now members of this convention, will in their individual capacity visit Sacramento during the session of the legislature, to aid and assist the executive legislative committee to secure such legislation now demanded by not only every irrigator, but also by every true citizen and lover of his state.

7. That any member of the executive committee who may not be able to attend the meetings of such executive committee may appoint another member of the committee on legislation to represent him at such meetings.

8. That the members of this committee are authorized and requested to use all proper influence in obtaining the indorsement of all public bodies in this state on the action of this convention.

9. That the chair appoint a committee of three to proceed to San Francisco and attend the meeting soon to occur of the board of trade and board of irrigation of that city, there to represent our interests and to obtain their aid and indorsement, and that the chairman of the convention be made the chairman of the committee.

10. That it is the sense of this committee that an effort should be made to have repealed section 1422 of the civil code, and that a law be passed to the effect that the common law of England relative to riparian right to water shall not apply to this state.

11. That we recommend that the office of state engineer be continned, and that the necessary appropriations be made by the next legislature to complete the work already laid out, and such further work as may be necessary in connection with the duties of said office.

12. That the thanks of the convention, and we believe we hazard nothing in saying the thanks of every one connected with the subject of irrigation, are most heartily tendered to the present incumbents, for the very able effort and thorough manner in which the work has been conducted so far, and we believe it was a wise and fortunate selection when the duties of the office were committed to the care of that very efficient officer, William Ham. Hall.

13. That the chairman of this convention appoint a committee of three, who shall examine the reporter's transcript, arrange the proceedings of this body in proper order, make all necessary corrections, and turn same over to the publisher.

14. That whereas the supreme court has ordered a rehearing of the water case recently decided, in order to give an opportunity for others than the parties to the suit to intervene and be heard before a final decision of the case; and whereas, other appropriators are preparing to represent their interests before that court; and, whereas, the number of irrigators is as a hundred to one when compared with the appropriators :

15. That this convention recommends to the small irrigators of the state, whose places must become desolate if riparian rights pre

vail, to take measures to be properly represented before that court, that they make a final appeal for a fair consideration of their rights before their ruin becomes final.

CHAPTER XXXIII.

1886. Anti-Chinese Conventions—Memorial to Congress—Prohibition Convention — Irrigation Convention — Republican Convention — Democratic Convention—Farmers' Convention—United Labor Party —Organization of the American Party.

A convention of anti-Chinese leagues met in San Jose on February 4th, and remained in session for two days. One hundred delegates, representing nine counties were in attendance. Robert Summers was elected temporary chairman. On permanently organizing, C. F. McGlashan was elected president ; Robert Summers and A. M. Church, vice-presidents, and W. H. Holmes, secretary. It was resolved that the name of the organization be the non-partisan anti-Chinese association. Other resolutions were adopted, and a state central committee appointed. The convention adjourned to meet at Sacramento on the 10th of March, following. On this date, the convention assembled pursuant to adjournment, with C. F. McGlashan in the chair. After appointing a committee to confer with the citizens' anti-Chinese convention then in session in the assembly chamber with regard to coalition, and adopting the following resolutions reported by the committee, the convention was merged with that of the citizens. The coalition resolutions were :

1. That we favor the passage of a bill introduced into congress by United States Senator Mitchell, having for its object the abrogation of all treaties with China permitting the immigration into the United States of any Chinese.

2. That if the passage of the bill cannot at present be secured, then we favor the passage of either of the bills introduced into congress by Morrow, Felton or Henley, restricting Chinese immigration.

3. That we favor the adoption and use of all peaceable and legal means needed to rid the state of the Chinese now here and to prevent the coming into the state of any more Chinese, but we are opposed to any unlawful means to that end.

4. That the two conventions meet in joint session, every member of each convention being entitled to a seat in the joint convention, and that the joint convention proceed to elect officers and to formulate a platform and to adopt measures best calculated to carry into effect the above resolution.

5. That C. F. McGlashan and George B. Katzenstein act jointly as chairmen of this joint convention until it is permanently organized, and that said joint convention meet in the assembly chamber.

The citizens' anti-Chinese state convention assembled in Sacramento, March 10th, under a call issued by the citizens' anti-Chinese association of Sacramento. This call said: The convention shall be composed of the officers and members of the executive committee and various sub-committees of the citizens' anti-Chinese association of Sacramento, and delegates from all the counties in the state, to be selected by the supervisors thereof. The supervisors of each county are requested to appoint the number of delegates hereafter apportioned to each county, to furnish them with proper credentials, and to notify Robert T. Devlin, of Sacramento, secretary of the committee on branch organization, of the names of the delegates immediately after their appointment. This convention will represent all branches of business and labor, and must result in great good.

The convention was called to order by George B. Katzenstein. Before proceeding to permanently organize, a committee was appointed to confer with the San Jose convention. This committee made a majority report of the coalition resolutions above quoted, which was adopted. The two conventions then united. The number of delegates to the Sacramento convention was reported to be 415, and to the San Jose convention 198, or 613 in the joint convention.

The committee on permanent organization recommended Leon D. Freer, for president; C. F. McGlashan and George B. Katzenstein, for vice-presidents; and G. W. Peckham, for secretary. A motion was made to substitute the name of McGlashan for that of Freer, but was lost by a vote of 261 to 259.

On the following day, March 11th, a committee on resolutions was appointed, composed of three members from each of the six congressional districts. It consisted of E. F. Dinsmore, A. M. McCoy, P. E. Davis, C. F. McGlashan, U. S. Gregory, G. H. Crossette, E. Frisbie, Joseph Steffens, J. E. McElrath, W. B. May, N. C:

Cornwall. P. J. Mervin, M. D. Boruck, D. McPherson, Horace Davis, M. R. Merritt, J. M. Garretson, and S. E. Crowe.

John F. Swift, A. A. Sargent, H. V. Morehouse, E. A. Davis, and Elihu Anthony were appointed a committee to prepare a memorial to congress. They presented the following report, which was adopted:

To the president and the senate and house of representatives of the United States: The anti-Chinese convention of the state of California, assembled at Sacramento, called for the purpose of proposing relief for the Pacific coast from the Chinese evil, submit the following memorial:

Speaking for the entire people of this state, your memorialists represent that for thirty-six years we have been settled upon the shores of the Pacific, and thus brought face to face with the great Mongolian hive, with its 450,000,000 of hungry and adventurous inhabitants; that for thirty-six years we have watched the operation of the industrial and social system that has resulted from it, and weighed the advantages and disadvantages as they have developed.

Under these circumstances we feel that we understand better than any others can, the necessity of resisting the tide of emigration setting out from China, which has already done so much mischief to nations bordering upon that country, and which threatens so much more. We feel that our fellow-countrymen east of the mountains have been too much in the habit of forming their judgment upon the Chinese question from its material aspect, and as a mere question of industrial development and progress and the creation of wealth, wholly overlooking and ignoring its social, moral and political sides.

We do not deny that the people of the Pacific coast are influenced by material considerations, and that each of us is trying, by all legitimate means, to better his condition.

But we say that, regarded from the standpoint of immediate material results, and considered as the coldest question of dollars and cents, and putting aside all considerations of government, social and moral order, and even patriotism, there is no advantage or profit in the mixed race system now being forced upon this coast, or in any mixed race system whatever.

That there is more mere money profit in dollars in a homogeneous population than in one of mixed races, while the moral and political objections are unanswerable.

31

For while the Chinaman works industriously enough, he consumes very little, either of his own production or of ours.

That he imports from China much that he eats, and much that he wears, while a vast catalogue of articles consumed by our own people, the production and sale of which makes our commerce and our life what it is, the Chinaman does not use at all.

Indeed, so far as he is concerned, hundreds of useful occupations essential to our system of civilization might as well, and if they depended on him would have to be, abandoned altogether.

That he underbids all white labor and ruthlessly takes its place, and will go on doing so till the white laborer comes down to the scanty food and half-civilized habits of the Chinaman, while the net results of his earnings are sent regularly out of the country and lost to the community where they are created.

And while this depleting process is going on the laboring white man, to whom the nation must in the long run look for the reproduction of the race, and the bringing up and educating of citizens to take the place of the current generation as it passes away, and above all to defend the country in time of war, is injured in his comfort, reduced in his scale and standard of life, necessarily carrying down with it his moral and physical tone and stamina.

But what is even more immediately damaging to the state, is the fact that he is kept in perpetual state of anger, exasperation, and discontent, always bordering on sedition, thus jeopardizing the general peace, and creating a state of chronic uneasiness, distrust, and apprehension throughout the entire community.

That this alarms capital, and forces it into concealment or out of the state in search of better security, checks enterprises, increases the cost of government, especially for police purposes, while decreasing the sources of revenue from which taxes can be raised.

And that whether the producing classes are right or wrong in their opinions, is practically immaterial, for experience has shown that the opinions and the results from them are permanent and ineradicable.

If there were no other and higher reasons for getting rid of the Chinese, these facts alone would be sufficient to convince the practical statesman of the necessity of doing so as speedily as possible to do it lawfully.

Any other notion, it would seem, can exist only in the mind of the merest doctrinaire, who, without experience or the capacity of profiting by experience, imagines that the world can be governed by some fixed rule of thumb contained in his own narrow brain.

But there are other and higher considerations involved in the Chinese question than that of mere industrial progress or material development, and to these we invite the attention of every American citizen who places his country and its permanent good above immediate money profit.

We assure our fellow countrymen east, that the dominance, if not the existence, of the European race in this part of the world is in jeopardy.

We call their attention to the fact that the Malayan peninsula, as well as other countries bordering upon China and the China seas, have already been overrun by the Chinese, and that the Malayan, one of the great races or types of the human species, is being rapidly annihilated to make place for them.

That the islands of the Pacific are undergoing the same process, and that this coast is now attacked, and in the end must inevitably succumb unless speedily relieved by rescue. That on the entire Pacific coast there are at this time less than 1,000,000 people, of all races, inhabiting a territorial area designed by nature to accommodate a population of at least 50,000,000, of which 30,000,000 will be here in a period of time so brief that it is but a passing moment in the lifetime of a nation.

Now, and while this territory is still practically unoccupied, and within the lifetime of the present generation, the type of human species that is to occupy this side of the American continent is to be determined for all time.

Whether the Pacific states are to be the home of 30,000,000 free citizens of the race that produced Columbus and Washington, Lafayette and Montgomery, Von Steuben and Andrew Jackson, or of 30,000,000 of Mongolians from eastern Asia, or, perhaps, even worse, of 30,000,000 mixed and mongrel half-breeds, possessing none of the virtues of either and all the vices of both, is to be settled finally and irrevocably.

That in the life and death struggle now going on for the possession of the western shores of the American continent the Chinese have advantages that must secure to them, if not a complete victory, at least a drawn battle in a division of occupancy with us.

To begin with, they have a hive of 450,000,000 to draw from, with only one ocean to cross, which dividing water modern science and Caucasian ingenuity has reduced to the dimensions of the merest ferry, and they have behind them an impulsive force of hunger unknown to any European people.

But this is by no means the most important advantage they have. They have an important ally in the cupidity of our own people, who too often think that cheap labor and the money profit to be gained by it is of more value than the happiness and permanence of their own country and kindred.

For, let men say what they please about the "inherent and inalienable right of expatriation and immigration," about "America being the refuge of the oppressed of all nations," at the bottom of it all will be found "old Mammon" anxious to sell a nation's birthright for money profit in some form.

The people of the Pacific make no pretense to an exceptionally high standard of public virtue; but they are not willing to admit that the accumulation of wealth, public or private, is the chief end and purpose of organized society. The leading purpose of the first colonists from Europe was not the acquisition of wealth, and if we cannot equal them in unselfishness we can at least honor their memory by making an effort to preserve that which we have received from them.

Among our other duties as American citizens we hold ourselves to be the trustees of posterity. We are keeping the soil of this fair land for the 30,000,000 Americans of our own race and kindred who are to come after us. To barter away their places while they are yet unborn is a gross violation of duty. To do so under the pretense of humanity, morality, or national generosity, is to add the sin of hypocrisy to that which, without it, would be a great public crime.

Our common ancestors came to the American continent to found a state. The greatness of a nation does not lie in its money or in its material prosperity, but in its men and women; and not in their number, but in their quality, in their virtue, honor, integrity, truth, and, above all things, in their courage and manhood.

To a nation that is to remain free the capacity to fight is indispensable. It is not enough that it be able to trade and barter, or to work and produce; it must be able to fight and defend what it has.

The nation that cannot defend itself against all comers will find that its days are numbered; and this is as true in the nineteenth century as in any other age of the world.

The strong nations of the earth are now, as they always have been, the most thoroughly homogeneous nations, that is to say, the most nearly of one race, language and manners.

And when they are of one race, it is not so material what race, as that they be of a pure race. The purest-blooded man of any race is the strongest man of that race.

The largest body of men of a single pure race on the earth to-day, is in China. There are 450,000,000 of them, as like as one barley-corn is like another. All the white men on the globe, whenever so carefully counted, scarcely amount to so much, and they are divided into a score or more of independent sovereignties, ten times as many languages, and as for religious sects, the boldest statistician has not the courage to attempt their enumeration.

While we of the European race are divided into fifty hostile camps, and fight each other like so many savage Apaches, China is one and indivisible. They are as united and homogeneous as France.

And though the Chinese are as timid as a flock of sheep, know nothing of physical science and its resources, and have none of the arts of attack and defense, yet the very inertia of that huge mass of crystallized homogeneity has thus far withstood the plundering instincts of the western powers, and China remains unconquered.

There they stand, one full third of the human race, a great, invincible, concrete, ethnological fact, commanding respect, and requiring mankind to pause and consider whether the Chinese may not yet, without discharging a gun or drawing a sword, gently elbow the rest of the human family off the planet.

And if they have such force unarmed, what will they do when they learn, as they will sometime, the art of war?

There is no such complete and unanswerable demonstration of the power of race homogeneity on the globe, as the example of China.

All political history shows homogeneity to be a vast power in a state, and that heterogeneity is a corresponding source of weakness.

The great states of Europe—England, France, Germany and Russia—those powers that dominate the world, are so entirely of one race, that the presence of a black, or red, or yellow man, in any of those countries outside the great cities, is a subject of wonder and astonishment.

And race prejudice or antagonism, that unfailing concomitant of race contact and friction, is scarcely known there.

No state where the great distinct types of the human species have been mixed together on the same territory, has ever held power for any considerable time. And no race of mongrels, if such a thing is possible, has ever held empire, or even kept its own independence.

In the very dawn of history, the Carthaginians—the dominant class of which were white men from Syria, while the masses were Africans of various types—encountered the pure blooded natives of Italy, and went down before them.

It is said they succumbed to the Roman sword. They were conquered by pure Roman courage and Roman muscle, cemented into singleness of purpose by race homogeneity.

When later on, through conquest, the Roman empire had come to consist of the mixed races of western Asia, she transferred her capital to the shores of the Bosphorus, and was in turn overthrown by the Turks, a race of pure, flat-faced Mongolians from east of the Caspian sea.

The once master race of Turks, having become mixed and hybridized with all the mongrels of Africa and the east, now in the nine teenth century find themselves about to be expelled from Europe, lacking strength to hold the place their pure-blooded ancestors conquered for them.

The inhabitants of Egypt have always been a mixed and particolored people, and have always been in slavery to some pure-blooded power. Alexander, at the head of his Macedonian Greeks, seized them and founded a dynasty, which settled down and hybridized with the natives, with a similar result. Their next masters were the Turks, and the English now hold them in subjection.

By the last census, 266,000,000 of human beings inhabit the peninsula of Hindoostan, the most productive spot on the globe. The soil produces three good crops a year. They possess everything to make a happy people, if soil and climate would do it. In the words of Bishop Heber, "Every prospect pleases, and only man is vile." For they are cursed with the evil of heterogeneity in everything.

In the Indian village, the inhabitants are often of several different races, or subdivisions of three or four races, differing both in color and physical type, while their antagonism is so intense that, though born in the same village, they cannot sleep in the same camp, or eat of the same food, or drink at the same fountain, lest they be defiled and cast out as unclean by their own people.

As a consequence of these facts, and as a direct and natural result of them, this fair land of India, with its 266,000,000 of mixed and mingled races, its mongrels and half-breeds, is a great slave pen to Great Britain.

One hundred thousand blue-eyed, pure-blooded, Anglo-Saxons tell this mighty throng of parti-colored humanity to go, and they go, to come, and they come. The English take advantage of Indian heterogeneity to subjugate the land.

They arm and drill the Mahrattas and set them over the Bengalese. The Rohillas are held in check by the Seikhs, while the flat-faced, almond-eyed Ghoorkas, of Nepaul, terrorize both Mussulman and Hindoo, with knife at throat.

Each one of these sees in the other a born enemy, more hateful if possible, than the Englishman, and at the word of command kills him with unmixed delight.

This could not be done with any homogeneous nation. China would be a richer prize to England than two Indias. And what England wants she takes, if force will take it. But the Chinamen are all of one kind, one family, one race, one language and literature, and one religion, and can no more be set to kill each other than could the same number of white sheep. The Englishman may kill the Chinaman, but he can't give him a gun and make him kill his brother, nor his neighbor, nor his countryman, and so China remains free.

The Chinese, weak and timid as they are, are still the strong people of Asia. No intelligent man can visit the far east without being impressed strongly with respect for that nation, both in its collective character as a state, and its individual people, when compared with the other Asiatics.

It is one of the great strong powers of the earth, and it is on the earth to stay.

It is true St. Paul said in his sermon at Athens : "God hath made of one blood all nations of men," but he added in the same sentence "He hath fixed the bounds of their habitations."

The Chinaman has his habitation ; let him stay in it, as God has fixed it.

But our eastern fellow-citizens ask us : "What are we going to do with our grand American principles of the sacred rights of expatriation and of free immigration ?" Has not a man in the pursuit of happiness the right to go anywhere he may choose to go ? Is not expatriation a natural and inalienable human right ? We say no. There is no such thing as an absolute right, either of expatriation or emigration.

A man has the right to enter and inhabit any country that will consent to it ; in a word, that will allow him to come, and there his right as a right ceases, and passes into the domain of necessity and force.

In one sense, any man or body of men, driven from their own country by necessity, have the right as a matter of self-preservation to enter another country by force, but it is justified as the struggle for existence is justified, and comes to be the right of the strongest, like the struggle over a plank in a shipwreck.

The children of Israel emigrated from Egypt because they were badly situated. When they came to the land of promise, after having satisfied themselves that it was a land to their minds and flowing with milk and honey, they drew their swords, entered and took it. It is true the Lord had given it to them, but it was their swords and spears that availed to put them in possession.

We do not hear that either party talked about the sacred right of emigration or expatriation.

No law-writer of any reputation has ever maintained to the contrary.

M. Vattel is a high authority upon public and international law. This is what he says :

"The country which a nation inhabits, whether that nation has emigrated thither in a body or the different families of which it consists were scattered over the country, and then uniting formed themselves into a political society, that country I say, is the settlement of the nation, and it has a peculiar and exclusive right to it." Vattel, book 1, chap. xviii., sec. 203.

"The whole of the country possessed by a nation and subject to its laws forms its territory, and is the common country of all the individuals of the nation." Ibid.

He goes on : "As the society cannot exist and perpetuate itself otherwise than by the children of the citizens, these children naturally follow the conditions of their fathers and succeed to all their rights." Vattel, book 1, chap. xix., sec. 212.

"The sovereign may forbid the entrance to his territory either to foreigners in general or in particular cases, or to certain persons or for particular purposes, according as he may think it advantageous to his state."

"Formerly the Chinese fearing least the intercourse with strangers should corrupt the manners of the nation and impair the maxims of a wise but singular government, forbid all people entering the empire—a prohibition that was not at all inconsistent with justice. It was salutary to the nation without violating the rights of any individual, or even the duties of humanity, which permits us in case of competition to prefer ourselves to others."—Ibid, book 2, chap. vii., sec. 94.

Many rulers have in the world's history invited immigration to to their country. Sometimes it has been beneficial; sometimes the reverse. The Emperors Probus and Valeus, being too weak or cowardly to resist, permitted the Gepidae, as well as the Goths and Vandals, to cross the frontier and settle in the empire, greatly to the public injury, for they contributed materally to the final destruction of the Roman power.

Bands of armed emigrants from Denmark and north Germany poured in upon the British islands in the early centuries of the Christian era, and the Normans overran central and southern Europe. In both instances, they were resisted in the same way they came, with force and arms. There was then no thought of the rights of men to emigrate in pursuit of happiness.

The emperors of Russia at various periods in the history of that country, and especially toward the close of the last century, invited German immigration, and there is no doubt that the result in that case proved the wisdom of the policy; but it was a people of her own race and religion, and who assimilated with the natives of the country in a single generation.

Our country has without doubt been benefited by the coming hither of emigrants from Europe of our own race and religion, some speaking our own language and all speaking closely allied languages, and with similar manners and customs—people who have become identical with ourselves in a short time.

How long now this character of immigration will continue to be beneficial is problematical.

It therefore appears that immigration, even of people of the same race and general type of the human family, of people capable of rapid assimilation with the possessors of the country, is sometimes beneficial and sometimes mischievous, depending upon circumstances that are liable to change.

But we assert that the immigration, whether voluntary or forced, into a country of non-assimilative races, is always an unmixed evil and a public calamity.

The same spirit of greed and avarice which is at the bottom of the coolie immigration of this age, lay at the bottom, and was the impelling motive, for the forced immigration of African slaves into the country all through the eighteenth century.

No doubt the slave-traders and slave-purchasers of that day tried to make the world believe that they were doing good, and that their motives were noble and patriotic. Men are fond of giving themselves credit for lofty motives in all they do.

No doubt they talked loudly about developing the resources of the country, and about christianizing the poor African. But at the bottom was the old Mammon of cheap labor, and the money to be gotten out of it. The world has not changed much.

The selfishness of those men has already borne much bitter fruit; through it the curse of race heterogeneity has taken deep root in the soil of our common country. Out of that evil we have had one bloody war for which the nation has not yet thrown off its mourning. But the war was nothing to what it left behind. It is true that it has settled the slave question. But the negro question, the question of the relations between the white man and the black man, and the relations of each to the state, has only just begun. Twenty generations of men will not see it ended.

And our fellow-countrymen at the south, who are compelled to carry on a government under such conditions, to preserve order and maintain law and civilized society, are entitled to the sympathy of all thoughtful people; they have à task the difficulties of which are not appreciated.

But for the effort to get cheap labor a hundred years ago all the states of the union, from the lakes to the gulf, would to-day have the same people, the same prosperity, and the same political system, the same schools and academies, that now exist in Pennsylvania, Ohio, and Illinois.

The only difference, if any, would be that the territory south of the Ohio, having the mildest climate and the richest soil, would now have the densest population and most rapid progress and development, and the greatest accumulation of wealth and enlightenment.

Is there any man, east or west, north or south, white or colored, who, after reflection, will not admit that it would be better if the colored man had been left in Africa, and the southern states were without race friction and race antagonism?

But for the mixed population of the south those states would never have gone to war; there would have been no rebellion. And had they gone to war, having 12,000,000 white men united in sentiment, as the white men were, instead of 8,000,000 white and

4,000,000 colored, and fighting as they did a defensive war on interior lines, they could not have been conquered.

Their weakness, which, like blind Sampson, they saw not, lay in the 4,000,000 men of another race planted there in the heart of their country, carrying information, aid, and comfort to the enemy, always requiring to be watched, and whom they did not dare to trust with arms.

It will be said that this was because they were slaves. It is doubtful if they would be more dangerous and a greater source of weakness free than as slaves. If the south should have another war, they would find this to be the case.

And if ever this country is invaded by a foreign foe, it is in South Carolina, and in Louisiana and in Florida the enemy will attempt a lodgment. Not because of the disloyalty of the white population, but the indifference, the discontent, the disaffection of the colored. And as for the difficulties of governing such a society, even in time of peace, it is only infatuation or ignorance that does not see it now, from day to day. As it now is, it will always be, while race heterogeneity exists there.

We doubt if a genuine republican government—as we Americans understand the term, meaning a government in which all the people govern, participate equally—under the conditions existing in the south, namely, with one-third of the population of one race and two-thirds of another, is a practical possibility. One race will always dominate the other, and no power can prevent it, except by destroying the liberties of both. They can only be equal in a common servitude, that overwhelms both.

We do not undertake to say which race will rule the other; that will vary with circumstances depending upon their relative numbers and strength. In the south, just now, it is the white race that dominates; in San Domingo, it is the black.

We do not put these race antagonisms and the fruit of them upon supposed superiority of one race over the other. These are terms the thoughtful man will be very cautious about employing.

One race may be the superior for one place, and not for another. We only say they cannot live well or happily together, and ought not to be made to do it.

The statesmen who look for a change that is to harmonize the south, so that both races shall stand equal and be equal, have never lived in any mixed community, and know nothing about it. They know nothing of the hereditary and instinctive race antagonism,

always latent in every individual human breast, and always spring-
ing into active vitality on bringing together two different races
or types of men into the occupancy of the same territorial habitation.

Such statesmen overlook an unfailing human quality or instinct,
and one too universal not to have a profound purpose in the general
economy of nature.

The efforts that have been made in the past by nations to rid
themselves of the evils of mixed races, and even of mixed tribes,
tongues, and religions, and to reach homogeneity, and the repose,
strength, and security it affords, are well worthy of consideration in
examining the Chinese problem in this country.

It is much the fashion of history to condemn such policy, but the
thoughtful man will be slow in putting his own judgment against
that of the statesmen and people living at the time on the spot, and
who necessarily understood every side of the question.

For eight hundred years the Moors carried on a struggle for
possession of the Spanish peninsula. It was eight centuries of perpetual warfare, in which the soil was drenched with human gore.
At last Ferdinand and Isabella, of Castile and Aragon, gained a
decisive victory, and without waiting for the enemy to recuperate
and renew the struggle, deported the entire mass of the Moorish
people.

It was for a time money out of pocket, for the Moors were skill-
ful artisans, and very industrious.

The cheap labor and material prosperity advocates think it was a
mistake, and books have been written to show the unwisdom of it.

But was that a mistake which made Spain homogeneous; which
gave her that which she had not had for eight hundred years—peace
at home, and security abroad?

Was that a mistake which saved Spain from being to-day what
Bulgaria and Roumelia are, and what all European Turkey is? We
cannot think it was.

And in support of this theory, within a century of the expulsion
of the Moors, there rose up the Spanish empire of Charles V. and
Phillip II., the first powers of the globe, and which dominated both
hemispheres. We admit that historians condemned the policy of
sending away the Moors, putting it chiefly on industrial grounds
and the loss of wealth.

They may have lost with the Moors the art of making Cordovan
leather, but they retained that of making good steel. Within fifty

years after the Moors had gone, the Toledo sword had carried the name and power of Spain from Seville to Sacramento, where we now stand.

But for the expulsion of the Moors, it is possible that Cortez, instead of carrying the Spanish banner to the Gulf of California, might have spent his valor and his life fighting that people for his own home in Andalusia, as his own people had been doing for eight centuries.

Toward the end of the seventeenth century there occurred what has been called the expulsion of the Huguenots from France, by Louis XIV.

That people, from religious persecution, or what goes in our histories by that name, took refuge in England. But it should not be forgotten that where church and state are one, and especially in a religious age, politics and religion are so merged as to be practically identical.

In the case of the Huguenots, like that of the Moors, historians generally agree in condemning the injustice and folly of the act which led to that emigration.

As to the injustice of forcing the consciences of men in matters of faith, it will not, in this day and age, be questioned. But as to the supposed folly of France losing the Huguenot, there are plainly two sides to the question.

The Huguenots, while in many respects excellent people, and in all respects as good as the rest of the people of their time, were religious fanatics of the most exasperating type, in an age of extreme religious fanaticism. They were always ready to persecute or be persecuted, to suffer or inflict martyrdom, as the wheel of fortune should give to or take from them the power.

They were disaffected and seditious to a degree that made them always an element of danger to the general peace and safety. They were constantly corresponding, and intriguing, and plotting with every public enemy, and especially with England, the most dangerous of them all.

The position of France, then as now surrounded by powerful and aggressive states, was one of great peril, and the Huguenots contributed at all times to materially increase this danger, by their disaffection and disloyal machinations; in this respect, at least, their departure was a distinct benefit to France.

No doubt they were a considerable advantage to England, and that she was the gainer in every respect by their coming. They were in·accord with the English on the very point of their disagreement with the French people—that of religion—and they carried over with them well-established habits of industry and thrift, considerable skill in the arts, and more or less money.

But France was not the loser, nor in the long run were the Huguenots. They found a country where the people agreed with them, while France obtained homogeneity and peace, which she sorely needed; and as for the arts, she has ever since held and still holds the first place.

One hundred years after the departure of the Huguenots, when France was making that supreme effort against despotism that has made the age memorable, and when the allied monarchs of Europe, with great armies, were at her frontiers, France, now become the most homogeneous people on the globe—as homogeneous as China— rose up as one man, confronted coalesced tyranny, erect and defiant, and "hurled at its feet, as gage of battle, the head of a king," and drove them back.

No heterogeneous population, no nation of mongrels that ever existed, could have stood in the place of France in 1792, and survived as an independent power.

Had the Huguenots remained in France without materially changing their manners, they must have been an element of weakness and might have ruined the country.

One of the first living statesmen of our time, Prince Bismarck, is just at this time favoring for Germany something of the same kind which the statesmen of this country are very ready to condemn, but which European thinkers are at least willing to admit that he on the spot may possibly understand better than they do, and so are silent. Bismarck supports a measure for expelling from Germany a disaffected and discontented colony of Poles—a most excellent and intelligent people, a people of the same general ethnological type as the Germans and with what ought to be considered the same religion; in short, a case where invariance and heterogeneity is almost a minimum; and he is doing it on the sole ground that their presence in Germany is a constant peril to the public safety. " We must show," says the German chancellor, " that we stand not upon feet of clay, but of iron."

The abstract justice of this proceeding we do not discuss; and as for the policy, we do not understand enough of the facts to have an opinion, but, considering the dangers that beset the German nation on every side, it is a question that must be left to the German people alone. It is not for us to decide it for them. If it is necessary for the safety of the state, it is just. On that ground, the Germans can safely take their stand.

We do not refer to the efforts of these people for homogenity and that rest and peace which at times it alone can bring, either to justify or condemn the act in any particular instance.

Nor are we by any means willing to place the desire of our people to rid themselves of a class of adult male Chinese, living among us in the abnormal and corrupting condition of separation from their families, in the same category with the Huguenots in their native land, or with the Moors, who with their wives and children were living in what might after eight hundred years be fairly considered their native land, or with the Poles, men, women, and children, in east Germany.

To even send away these Chinese by act of law, if such a law could be obtained from congress, would be only to send them back to their wives and homes and children, where in the interest of morality and decency they ought to be.

The weakness of states with mixed and homogeneous populations, has had a striking illustration in our time and at our very door.

Mexico, a country with 10,000,000 people, part European, part Indian, part African, with a considerable part mongrel, was seized by an expedition from France so contemptible in numbers that had it been sent against a country with 10,000,000 Caucasians of Europe or America, it would have run great risk of being expelled by the women with their brooms.

But being Mexico and Mexican people, such as they are, it marched in triumph to the capital, set up an imperial state with an Austrian prince on the throne, which for anything the Mexicans could have done to prevent, would have been as permanent as the holy Roman empire.

But in a twelve month from the fall of Richmond, the Mexican throne was in the dust, and the emperor shot to death at Queretaro.

But will any man say that result was produced by the power of the mongrels and half-breeds called the Mexican people ? No, for history tells a different story.

The forces of France were ordered out of Mexico by the diplomatic representative of a nation that itself had an organized army of 250,-000 homogeneous white soldiers, with a pure blooded white general, without a cross in his Caucasian pedigree in a hundred generations. His name was Grant.

And we warn our countrymen on both sides of the continent, that if we go on mixing and mongrelizing the people of this nation, as we have been doing, and as sentimentalists would have us continue to do, a time will come when a foreign expeditionary force will put a European emperor in the white house and keep him there. We are willing to pass into history with that prediction charged to our account.

We do not believe in the cessation of wars, or the final triumph of peace congresses and arbitration of international disputes.

Man is a fighting animal, and wars will not cease while he is what he is. Let it once be seen that we are unable to defend ourselves, and England will have an army in the country within a year, fighting for a market of English goods.

Our Chauvinists are fond of boasting of our population and its wonderful increase, of our fifty or sixty millions of people—words which we keep rolling off our tongue as if in love with the sound.

But what avail all our millions of people for defense if they are not of the right quality and stamina? And even they have courage and can fight, what avails it if they are inharmonious, burning with race antagonism, so that the cunning enemy can set one race cutting the throats of the other? The people of India are numerous enough if numbers go for anything.

We can hardly expect to outnumber them with their 266,000,000.

But England dresses one-half of them in uniforms, with feathers in their hats, and red stripes down their legs, and sets them to shooting the other half.

For the last two years Great Britain has been carrying on a war in the Soudan and upper Egypt, as usual for the extension of trade and a market. The population of the country consists of Arabs mixed with various types of blacks from the Guinea negro down. In a late number of the London *Times* is the following news dispatch which will show how England conquers such populations and brings them to commercial relations with her. The incident occurred only three weeks ago, in fact, since this convention was called. The article in the *Times* reads as follows:

CAIRO, February 14, 1886.

"Osman Digna, for the past three days, has been harrassing our patrol. Sir Charles Warren yesterday armed 200 'friendlies' and started them off on their own account. In the afternoon they returned with 306 camels and 31 cattle. Sir Charles Warren gave them this spoil as a present."

That telegram tells its own story, and requires no comment. No "friendlies" could be found in France to aid an invading foe, nor in Germany, nor in Old England, nor in New England, nor in New Jersey. They could not be found in China. Are you quite certain there could not be found in South Carolina, or in Florida, or in western Texas, about the mouth of the Rio Grande—friendlies to go off on their own account to drive in stock, if they knew it would be given to them as a present on their return?

Such a thing is only possible where there exists some prejudice or antagonism that divides the people of the country against each other, to a degree that will cause them to prefer the rule of the stranger and the foreigner to that of their countrymen, against whom the prejudice is held. There are various causes of antagonism that will produce this effect, but race friction is the most unfailing. It always disintegrates and destroys the very bond and fiber of a nation.

To give another example of the strength of homogeneity, we point to Chile, which country within the last two or three years has conquered both Bolivia and Peru. Any one might have foretold in advance what would have been the outcome of a war between those countries. Chile is the nearest to a pure-blooded people of all the nations of South America. Peru is another Mexico, if not even more mixed and mongrelized than Mexico. What possible sympathy could the Indians and half-breeds of Peru have with the pure Spaniards of that country, to give them any heart in a war of defense? What do they care who shall be their masters?

While that war was going on, we here on the Pacific had reason to fear a complication might arise in which we would be attacked by Chile, and we were not free from uneasiness. We telegraphed east for more cannon for our forts. But what good are cannon with no men behind them? Fifty per cent. of the able-bodied males on this coast of the age for bearing arms are alien Chinese. Do you imagine they would care very much whether the Chileans or the Americans are masters of California, or would burn much gunpowder to prevent a change of rulers! Is that a condition of things for a true American to be proud of?

The growth and development of the sham sentimentality about the right of free immigration to this country has always had Mammon as its chief underlying motive. The money-seeking sentimentalist has recognized the obvious fact that the increase of population has

32

increased the value of property, and made business lively, and there he has seen his profit.

If it were once demonstrated that the coming hither of any number of the best people in the world—English, Irish, Scotch, or German—reduced the market value of property 10 per centum, or regularly made business dull, that very day the last whisper about the inherent and inalienable right of immigration, and about this country being the home of liberty and the refuge of the oppressed of all nations, would be hushed forever, and in a week the country would be in arms to keep the intruders out.

Mammon, masquerading in the disguise of humanity, patriotism, and national generosity, worked its way into our diplomatic service and gave us the Burlingame treaty.

We charge that Anson Burlingame deliberately sold his country's birthright for Chinese money; and if ever the true history of that document is written, the facts will be found as we have stated them. We will give you our understanding of how it was brought about:

Burlingame was American minister at Peking. While there he found out what is well known to everybody familiar with China, that the Chinese have always been angry and dissatisfied with the concessions extorted from them by England, and particularly by the opium traffic and the extra territorial rights, by which foreigners are exempt from the jurisdiction of the Chinese courts, and other concessions, all odious and rasping almost beyond endurance to the Chinese. With the instinct of the pettifogger Burlingame saw here a chance to make some money, and he seized it. He convinced Tsung-li-Yamen that if they would make him Chinese embassador, with a general roving commission, he could get the United States to back him up with moral, and, if necessary, with physical force, and that thus he could frighten and bully Great Britain into surrendering those concessions so galling to China.

He got a contract to get rid of the opium traffic, and the extra territorialities, by a diplomatic negotiation with England. For this service he was to have a large sum of money—report says a hundred thousand taels cash in hand, and a large additional sum, contingent upon success. It is a shameful and humiliating fact to confess that the minister of no other power on the globe would have dared to cast off his connection with his own country, and thus taken foreign service. Any European power would have treated him as a disgraced man for doing it. China would have cut off his head. With a numerous suite of Chinese officials Mr. Burlingame started for Europe in 1868, by the way of Washington. London, the real objective point of his diplomatic expedition, was purposely and cunningly left till the last. He knew well enough that the English foreign office would detect the Yankee renegade under the disguise of the Chinese mandarin, and that he might have difficulty in getting in at the front door, much less to be received as representing China in any diplomatic capacity.

He went to Washington, not because it was necessary to make a treaty with the United States, for there was not the slightest necessity either for China or for us that such a thing should be done. We were not forcing opium upon China. We had not extorted the extra territorial rights from her. We had never so much as pointed a gun at her. It was not necessary, so far as immigration was concerned, for the law permitted them to come at will. Burlingame went to Washington to get recognition and prestige for European uses. He felt it would be a great card if he could show in Europe that he had been received as Chinese embassador by the government of the United States.

To have negotiated and signed a treaty with them, would seem to make him solid everywhere. So he set about that at once. He began, as might be expected from a man capable of such a career, with a misstatement. He assured the state department that he had been sent on a special mission connected with the opening up of China to railroad building, of which he hoped in time to give our people a monopoly. He knew us to be the children of Mammon, and took advantage of his knowledge.

. Just who suggested those clauses of the Burlingame treaty about the inherent right of immigration, we do not know, but considering the state of mind prevailing about the state department at that time it is probable it came from our side.

But it did not make any difference to Burlingame what the treaty contained so long as it did not disgrace him with China. What he wanted was a treaty. So he lobbied at Washington waiting to get the prestige of American recognition to take with him to England.

At last he worked the instrument through, which goes into history with his name. Then he went away to Europe, but never got across the threshold of any court or foreign office to say good morning

For the purpose of obtaining prestige, with which he might work upon Great Britain in the interest of China and earn his fee, Mr. Burlingame induced his own country to yield up a sovereign attribute, never before surrendered by any free people, a right infinitely more valuable than all the opium privileges and extra territorialities and trading concessions extorted from China by English arms in a hundred years' war.

Among them they bartered away, as far as it can be bartered away, the right to determine who shall come and who shall not come to this new and growing country of ours, live on its soil, enjoy its privileges, and mingle freely with its people.

All that the early colonists had earned by their toil and suffering, all our revolutionary heroes had purchased with their blood, the land that has been wrested from savage nature and savage men by the courage of our race, was thrown open to four hundred and fifty million Chinese to run over it, to take it, to enjoy it as freely as we, in order that Mr. Burlingame could earn a hundred thousand taels in Chinese silver.

He did not even reserve the right for the cheated Americans, when squeezed out of their own country, to seek refuge in China, for our residence there remains strictly limited to some fifteen or twenty seaports, named long before in older treaties. In the history of the world no such fraud was ever perpetrated upon a free and sovereign people.

For all this the only equivalent we are supposed to get back occurs in article eight in the treaty. It provides in substance that whenever China shall build railroads the United States shall furnish the engineers and China will pay them their salaries.

Whether these engineers are to drive the locomotives or do the surveying does not seem absolutely clear. But let it be what it may, China has within the last year deliberately violated and broken this treaty by making a new one with France, in which it is agreed that not Americans, but Frenchmen, are to not only engineer the railroads in China, but to construct and operate them as well.

That treaty, cheating us out of the mess of pottage we were to have for our birthright, was concluded in Peking some time in May, and ratified in Paris on the 28th of November, 1885; and now all that is left to us under the treaty is an unlimited and inexhaustible supply of coolies.

This is the true history and inwardness of the Burlingame treaty. It was conceived in fraud and chicane. It was negotiated at a time when no treaty was wanted by either country, and not for the purpose named in the treaty. It lays that down to be a public and natural law which never was, and never in the nature of things can be such.

It is an international lie, patent on its face. It never ought to have been entered into. It has been deliberately and solemnly abrogated in its spirit, if not in the letter, by the Chinese, in giving away to the French the railroad privileges guaranteed to us. For these reasons it ought to be abrogated and got out of the way by our own government. We do not believe it is kept in force by the wish of China, or that they would make any serious objections to our bringing it to an end. The objection to terminating the Burlingame treaty has its stronghold in America, with the cheap labor interests alone. The people of this coast are willing to accept cheap labor when it comes naturally by excessive population, as in the growth and development it will come in time. We object to nothing that is natural and inevitable. Labor will be cheap when the country is full of people, and the conditions of life hard. Doubling in population as we do once in twenty-five years, God knows it will come soon enough. But we are against hastening it at the expense of the quality, fiber and stamina of the nation.

Again we say what we said in the beginning, a nation's wealth is not in its money, but in its men and women. When they deteriorate the country sinks down with them.

The people of the Pacific states are holding the gates against a system that will, if persisted in, bring the country of Washington to the condition of Mexico, if not to that of Panama or Jamaica. This may not be true of every part of the country, but it is certainly true of portions of it, and those portions having the richest soil and the mildest and most agreeable climate.

We would only be following the common instincts of human nature in preferring our own race to that of the alien Chinaman, even were it less worthy than his, and for no higher reason than because it is our own. But when we remember that ours was the race which was first to seize upon nature's forces and harness them to the car of progress that has smoothed the earth's surface and made it more fit for man's habitation, we think he has earned the right, even if he had it not before, to hold any place he has once secured, to the exclusion of all comers; and we will make an effort to hold this place as our home and settlement. The noblest impulse of human nature is that which prompts men to secure a habitation and place of abode for their families and those who are to come after them, and by all lawful means we will try to maintain this land on the shores of the Pacific ocean for ourselves.

The people of California are a loyal people to the American

nation, of which they are proud to be an integral part. As such they appeal to the legislature of the union to grant them speedy relief from a situation that has become practically insupportable.

The committee on resolutions, of which Horace Davis was chairman, reported the following:

Whereas, The people of the State of California are, with an unanimity of sentiment unparalleled in history, opposed to the presence of Chinese in their midst, and are likewise opposed to the further immigration of that race into the United States; and whereas, this opposition is not of sudden growth, but is the result of more than thirty years' experience; and whereas, the history of all countries where the Chinese have been permitted to reside among other races, is a precise counterpart of our own; and whereas, the evils arising from the presence of the Chinese are:

1. Their coming is an invasion, not an immigration.

2. They have no families or homes among us.

3. Their domestic relations and mode of life are such as forever preclude their assimilation with our people.

4. By education and customs they are antagonistic to a republican form of government.

5. They maintain in our midst secret tribunals in defiance of our laws.

6. The presence of so many adult males owing allegiance to a foreign government is dangerous.

7. They deter laboring men from coming to California.

8. The contract system by which they come to this country is virtually a system of peonage, hostile to American institutions.

9. Their presence deters the growth of a reliable labor element among our boys and girls.

10. After subsisting on the lowest possible portion of their earnings they remit the residue, amounting to many millions annually, to China, while the substitution of American labor would retain this vast sum of money in our own country.

For these and other reasons they are a constant and growing source of irritation and danger to our State, and it is necessary that their immigration be immediately stopped, and every lawful measure be adopted to remove those now among us. Therefore, be it resolved,

1. That we demand that the government of the United States take immediate steps to prohibit absolutely this Chinese invasion.

2. That to encourage the early removal of the Chinese we accept the suggestion of the constitution of California, which says that no Chinese shall ever be employed upon any public work of the state, except in punishment for crime.

3. That the interests of the people of the state of California demand, in harmony with the organic law of the State, that the presence of Chinese should be discouraged in every particular, and that in every instance preference should be given to white labor; and we earnestly appeal to the people to do their utmost to supplant the Chinese with such labor. We are not in favor of any unlawful methods, but so firmly are we impressed with the great importance of discouraging the employment of the Chinese, that we recommend that they be not patronized in any way, and we are in favor at the earliest moment of boycotting any person who employs Chinamen directly or indirectly, or who purchases the products of Chinese labor. The date at which the boycott commences in different localities shall in all cases be left to the local leagues.

4. That a permanent state organization be perfected by this state convention, to be known as the "California Anti-Chinese Nonpartisan Association."

5. That an executive committee be selected by the chairman of the convention, consisting of three from San Francisco, and one from each other county of the state, who shall be fully empowered to have control of the state work, fill vacancies in their own body, call state conventions at such times and places as they may deem proper, and devise ways and means for advancing the cause.

6. That we recommend that a state organizer be selected by the convention, whose compensation shall be fixed by the executive committee.

7. That the state executive committee be requested to solicit subscriptions, in order that the work of excluding the Chinese may not be crippled from lack of funds, and we recommend that printed copies of all subscriptions received, and of all expenditures made by the committee, be sent to every newspaper in the state, with a request for publication.

8. That these resolutions be printed, and that copies thereof be mailed to the president of the United States, the justices of the supreme court of the United States, to the members of the cabinet, to the California delegates in congress, to the members of the senate and house of representatives from the other states and territories,

to the governors of the several states and territories, and to each newspaper in California.

On motion of John Bidwell, the resolutions were considered *seriatim.* They were unanimously concurred in until the third, relative to boycotting, was reached. The adoption of this resolution was opposed by John Bidwell, F. M. Pixley, F. G. Newlands, A. A. Sargent, and M. H. Hecht, while speeches in favor of it were made by F. W. Hunt, Henry Wilson, A. Sbarboro, N. F. Rawlin, James H. Barry, Patrick Reddy, W. H. Sears, M. M. Estee, and H. Weinstock. The previous question was moved by O. F. Mc-Glashan. The motion was put and declared carried by a *vive voce* vote. A demand for a call of the roll from Sargent and others was denied on the ground that it came after the result had been declared. Sargent and Bidwell retired from the convention.

The remaining resolutions were adopted as reported, with the exception of the fifth, which was amended by striking out the words "fill vacancies in their own bodies," and adding the provision "that all vacancies in said executive committee shall be filled by election of the clubs and leagues of the county in which the vacancy occurs, and that in case any county is not represented in this convention, then that the committeeman from that county be filled by the election of clubs and leagues of that county."

The question of the adoption of the resolutions as a whole was put, and carried with only two or three dissenting votes.

N. F. Rawlin was elected state organizer, by acclamation.

On Friday afternoon, March 12th, the convention adjourned *sine die.*

The state executive committee of the prohibition party met at San Francisco, March 8th, and issued a call for a state convention to meet at Sacramento, May 12th. The convention met on the latter date. It was called to order by J. A. Fairbanks, chairman of the executive committee. George B. Katzenstein was elected temporary chairman, and subsequently was made permanent chairman. Two hundred and forty-five delegates, representing thirty counties, were reported by the committee on credentials as being entitled to seats.

The committee on platform and resolutions, composed of M. C. Winchester, W. H. Martin, and C. Henderson, reported the following:

Relying upon the favor of Almighty God and the justice of our cause, we, the prohibition party of California, through the representatives thereof in convention assembled, do announce the following as our political faith:

1. While we are unalterably opposed to the enactment of all sumptuary laws, properly so named, we believe it not only a constitutional right, but the bounden duty of the state, to prohibit the manufacture, sale, and importation of all alcoholic beverages.

2. The combined testimony of philanthropists, statesmen, and jurists for the past two hundred and fifty years declares that the use of intoxicating drinks tends directly and inevitably to the propagation of disease, the suppression of industry, the promotion of vice and crime, and the destruction of mankind; and believing that so far-reaching an evil can only be remedied by legal means, we demand the enactment of constitutional and statutory laws for the state and nation that shall forever prohibit the manufacture, sale, and importation of alcoholic beverages, and we solemnly pledge ourselves to vote for no one for office who will not pledge himself to use his influence and vote to secure the enactment of such laws.

3. That the old parties are the servile supporters of the liquor power is evidenced by the open and shameless espousals of the saloons by the one and the contemptuous refusal of the other to legislate to protect the home from the giant curse of intemperance, though repeatedly petitioned to do so. Therefore, we declare that those parties who thus pander to the vicious elements of society to maintain political power, merit and should receive the condemnation of all good citizens, and are unworthy the countenance and support of christians and patriots, and are totally unfit to govern a free people.

4. Inasmuch as a day of rest is absolutely necessary to the physical and mental well-being of man, especially that of the laboring classes, as well as for the purpose of moral and spiritual culture, therefore, we demand the enactment of a Sunday law, whereby all places of business, whose keeping open that day is not absolutely necessary to the public welfare, shall be closed on the first day of the week.

5. We are in favor of the largest personal liberty consistent with orderly civil government, and would gladly welcome to our free country all those who come with the intention of enjoying our institutions as they find them, but we demand the exclusion of those whose purpose in coming here is to overthrow our government and destroy our liberties. We demand further that the right of fran-

chise be withheld from all foreigners till they shall have lived in this. country for a period sufficiently long to enable them to become· familiar with our institutions and politics, and to demonstrate their· disposition to live in conformity therewith.

A motion to insert a resolution in favor of woman suffrage was·· lost, and the platform was adopted as reported. The vote by which it was adopted was subsequently reconsidered and the fourth and fifth resolutions, relative to the Sunday law and foreign voters were· stricken out.

The following nominations were made :

For governor, Joel Russell, by acclamation.

For justices of supreme court, William G. Murphy and Robert· Thompson (resigned).

For secretary of state, Frank E. Kellogg.

For controller, J. A. Fairbanks.

For treasurer, H. S. Graves.

For attorney general, George Babcock.

For surveyor-general, George B. Tolman.

For superintendent of public instruction, D. A. Mobley.

For clerk of supreme court, Julius Lyons.

For members of state board of equalization, J. S. Reynolds, A. J. Gregg, Charles E. Green (J. L. Mansfield afterward substituted), and L. B. Hogue.

For railroad commissioners, W. C. Damon, E. O. Tade, and S. M. McLean.

For members of congress, first district, L. W. Simmons ; second' district, W. O. Clark ; third district, W. W. Smith ; fourth district,. R. Thompson ; fifth district, O. Henderson ; sixth district, Will A. Harris.

The following, resolution, introduced by George Babcock, was adopted, without opposition :

Whereas, This convention has excluded from its platform a declaration in favor of woman suffrage, and it appearing that such exclusion may lead to misapprehension in regard to the opinions of· the members of the convention ; therefore, be it resolved,

That we most emphatically declare it to be our opinion that the· immediate and unconditional enfranchisement of woman would surely tend to the highest interest of the whole people, and forever· put an end to the traffic in intoxicating liquors ; and that for these· reasons, as individuals, we will at all times use every lawful and·

proper means to secure an amendment to the constitution of the state conferring upon women the right to vote.

The officers of the state central committee were announced to be as follows : J. A. Fairbanks, president; Joel Russell, vice-president; George Morris, secretary; R. H. McDonald, treasurer. These, with M F. Clayton, E. B. Fowler, and O. Henderson, were to compose the executive committee. The convention adjourned *sine die* at 12 M. on May 13th.

The state irrigation convention met at the Grand Opera House, San Francisco, May 20th. It was composed of delegates from some fifty irrigation clubs, and other persons who became entitled to seats by signing the following :

Articles of Association of the Anti-riparian Irrigation Organization of the State of California :

Whereas, The necessities of the people of this state, growing out of our peculiar climatic and physical conditions, require that all the waters of the state should be applied to beneficial uses, and especially to irrigation; and whereas, it has been the well-established custom and usage of the inhabitants of the state ever since the territory was acquired from Mexico, and long prior thereto, to enjoy and permit the free appropriation and diversion of water to all who would apply it to a beneficial use; and whereas, by virtue of such usage and custom, capital and labor have created out of deserts and rivers enormous wealth to the state, and the irrigation interests have assumed gigantic proportions; and whereas, several hundred thousand people are now dependent upon and directly or indirectly supported by means of irrigation; and whereas, attempts are now being made to resurrect the English common law doctrine of riparian rights from the grave to which the will of the people long since consigned it, and to impress it upon the jurisprudence of the state; and whereas, such attempt, if successful, means the desolation of thousands of homes; means that the desert shall invade vineyard, orchard, and field; that the grape shall parch upon the vine, the fruit wither on the tree, and the meadow be cursed with drought; means that silence shall fall upon our busy colonies, and their people shall flee from the thirsty and unwatered lands; means that the cities built upon the commerce irrigation has created shall decay, and that in all this region the pillars of civilization shall fall, and unprofitable flocks and herds shall graze the scant herbage where once there was a land of corn and wine, flowing with milk and honey; and whereas, if this attempt to forbid the useful appropriation of water is defeated by a righteous public opinion crystallized into law, the homes now planted in the midst of fruitful acres will remain the shelter of a happy people, enriched by the productive soil, and irrigation will advance the frontier of verdure and flowers and fruit, until the desert is conquered and has exchanged its hot sands for happy garlands, its vagrant herds for valiant people, and the bleak plains grow purple with the vintage and golden with the harvest, and the pleasures and profits, the peace and plenty that come out of the useful rivers will make this land the promised land to millions of free people; and whereas, we have, then, on the one hand the certainties of agriculture and horticulture, of profitable immigration, of surplus production for export of articles universally desirable and necessary, and always in demand; the growth of our cities and the greatness of our state; on the other hand are thirst and famine, ruin and decay, farms dismantled, colonies abandoned, cities subjected to dry rot, and the state denied her career by denying to her people their birthright; and whereas, the court of highest resort of the state, whose final determination is conclusive of law, is divided upon the question, and the right of appropriation and irrigation now stands upon uncertain ground; and whereas, the legislature has failed to take measures for the protection of irrigation; and whereas, there are 40,000 voters in this state ready and anxious to fight and vote as a unit for irrigation; and whereas, the safe and sure road to a successful issue in the courts and in the legislature is to organize, and by united and harmonious action control the result of the coming election; resolved,

That we, the undersigned, associate ourselves together under the name of the "Anti-riparian Irrigation Organization of the State of California," and pledge ourselves to use all honorable means to carry out the purposes of our organization, as follows:

1. To maintain that the right of appropriation of water for beneficial purposes, is and always has been paramount to any alleged rights of riparian owners, in this state.

2. To secure the adoption of an amendment to the state constitution, and amendments to the laws declaring that the common law of England is not and should not be the rule of property, or the rule of decision in the courts of this state, in controversies concerning the right to appropriate, divert and use water, nor in actions by or against actual appropriators of water for beneficial purposes; and

that priority of appropriation for a beneficial purpose determines the right without regard to the ownership of the banks of a water-course.

3. To maintain both as a physical and legal proposition that the conditions and necessities of the people of this state, and the climatic and physical characteristics of the state are, and ever have been, such as to render the common law doctrine of riparian rights inapplicable here.

4. To secure the passage of any and all other amendments to the constitution or laws which will contribute to establish the rights of irrigation against the riparian doctrine.

5. To procure the election of members of the legislature who openly and without qualification favor and will act upon the foregoing principles, regardless of political affiliations.

6. To oppose through the ballot box and by every other legitimate means the election of any person to office, executive, legislative or judicial, who is not known to be in full and active accord with every proposition contained in these articles of association.

7. To obtain confirmation by the courts and the legislature as the law and the fact, that the use of the waters of streams for the purpose of irrigation, is a natural want in this state, and to be preferred to all other uses.

The convention was called to order by J. De Barth Shorb, chairman of the executive committee. A committee on credentials, with L. M. Holt as chairman, and a committee on organization, with J. F. Wharton as chairman, were appointed, as was also a committee on resolutions, composed of W. S. Green, John P. Irish, Charles Mulholland, S. Jewett, and M. E. C. Munday.

On permanently organizing, J. De Barth Shorb was elected president, and J. F. Wharton, W. S. Green, R. Hudnut, L. B. Ruggles, E. H. Tucker, D. K. Zumwalt, L. M. Holt, William T. Coleman, N. D. Rideout, John P. Irish, and William B. Carr, vice-presidents.

The following platform was reported by the committee on resolutions, and finally adopted :

· 1. That the cubic foot per second be adopted as the unit of measurement throughout the state.

2. A declaration by the legislature that all the unnavigable waters of the state, in natural streams and lakes not rising or wholly included in lands under private ownership, belong to the people thereof, and are subject to appropriation by the people for irriga-

tion, mining, manufacturing, and other useful purposes, and that the customary law of appropriation of water for these purposes, as it has grown up in this state, should receive the formal sanction of that body, as follows:

3. That there is no individual or corporate ownership of water, except that which rises upon land under such individual or corporate ownership, this ownership continuing so long only as it remains upon the premises, or so long after it leaves them, as they may control it in pipes, ditches, or any other means of conveyance, and apply it to useful, beneficial, and necessary purposes.

4. That the appropriation of water from all public sources does not imply individual or corporate ownership, but that it is taken for the time and to the extent only that it is applied to a useful and necessary purpose, after which it is free to other or subsequent appropriators under the same conditions.

5. That the appropriation of water and its conveyance through canals and ditches for sale, rental, or distribution is a useful, necessary, and beneficial purpose, sale or rental not implying ownership of the element, but just remuneration for the use of the franchise and the plant employed in its conveyance.

6. That a system of law should be adopted providing for the control, management, and just distribution of the waters of the state, in accordance with the foregoing principles.

7. To so extend the law of eminent domain as to allow an irrigation district, when formed, corporation or individual, to condemn and pay for rights of way, lands, canals, ditches and water claims, and rights of whatever nature held by any person or corporation, or any other private rights of property, however existing or acquired, or by whatever name designated, which may be necessary for the appropriation or use of water; provided, that in condemning water used at the time of the commencement of an action for the same a manifestly greater public advantage and use can be shown.

8. That section 4468 of the political code should be amended to read as follows: "The common law of England, in so far as not repugnant to or inconsistent with the constitution of the United States or the constitution and laws of this state, except as it applies to streams and watercourses, is the rule of decision in all the courts of this state."

9. That section 1422 of the civil code, which declares that the rights of riparian proprietors are not affected by the preceding sec-

·tions of the code providing for rights to water by appropriation, ·should be repealed.

The committee on resolutions made a further report, which was ·also adopted. It was as follows:

We respectfully submit the accompanying measures, which are proposed for adoption by the legislature and as a pledge to be re- ·quired of candidates, as hereinafter set forth. These measures con- ·sist, first, in a proposed constitutional amendment to fix and deter- ·mine the nature of water rights; second, a proposed constitutional ·amendment to regulate the use of water appropriated for irrigation; third, a proposed act of the legislature concerning the right to ac- ·quire the use of water by appropriation; fourth, the repeal of sec- ·tion 1422 of the civil code. These proposed measures were prepared by the state executive committee after careful consideration, and after taking the best advice in the state we believe that these meas- ·ures are absolutely necessary to secure a permanent irrigation policy. We therefore propose the following resolutions:

1. That the accompanying bills and amendments be adopted as ·expressing in part the legislative policy of this convention.

2. That the friends of irrigation should exact a full and unquali- fied indorsement of these measures from all candidates who can ·promote or affect the interests of irrigation.

3. That we ask the irrigation clubs to remain organized and con- ·tinue organizing from now until irrigation shall become the perma- nent law and practice of the state, and that the members of such ·clubs and all in agreement and alliance with us so use their votes as to promote the political success of such candidates only as accept ·these measures without amendment.

W. S. GREEN, Chairman.

An act to amend the constitution of the state of California:

The legislature of the state of California, at its session commenc- ·ing on the —— day of ———, 188–, two thirds of all the members ·elected to each of the two houses of the said legislature voting in favor . thereof, hereby propose that article XIV of the constitution of the state of California be amended by adding the following new sections ·at the end thereof:

Sec. 3. The water of every natural stream, not heretofore appro⁻ priated, within the state of California, is hereby declared to be the ¡property of the public, and the same is dedicated to the use of the people of the state, subject to appropriation as hereinafter provided.

Sec. 4. The right to divert unappropriated waters of any natural' stream to beneficial uses shall never be denied. Prior appropriation to any such use, whether heretofore or hereafter made, shall give the better right, and the right of appropriation shall be ever exercised under such regulations as the legislature has heretofore prescribed or may hereafter prescribe, and the English common law of riparian rights, so far as it conflicts with this or the preceding section, shall not be recognized as a rule of decision or rule of property in any of the courts of this state.

Number two is a proposed constitutional amendment:

Section 1. The use of all water now appropriated or that may hereafter be appropriated for irrigation, sale, rental, or distribution, is hereby declared to be a public use, and subject to the control and regulation of the state, in a manner to be prescribed by law, provided that the rates of compensation to be collected by any person, company, corporation, or irrigation district in this state for the use of water supplied to any city and county, or city, town, or irrigation district, or the inhabitants thereof, shall be fixed every three years by the supervisors, or city and county, or city, or town council, or other governing body of such city and county, or city, or town, or irrigation district, and shall continue in force for three years, and until new rates are established; but in establishing such rates they shall take in consideration the cost of construction and maintenance of the works by which the water is supplied, and the rates so established shall be such as will yield to the person, company, or corporation so supplying water a net return of at least 7 per cent per annum upon the amount invested in the construction and maintenance of such works. Such rates shall be fixed in the month of February and take effect on the first day of July thereafter. Any board or body failing to fix the water rates where necessary within such time, shall be subject to peremptory process to compel action at the suit of any party interested, and shall be liable to such further process and penalties as the legislature may prescribe. Any person, company, or corporation collecting water rates otherwise than as so established shall forfeit the franchise of such person, company, or corporation, to the city and county, or city, town, or irrigation district from which the same are collected, for the public use.

An act concerning the ownership of water in natural streams and providing for the acquisition thereof by appropriation :

Section 1. The water of every natural stream, not heretofore ap. propriated, within the state of California, is hereby declared to be the property of the public, and the same is dedicated to the use of the people of the state, subject to appropriation as hereinafter pro. vided.

Sec. 2. The right to divert unappropriated waters of any natural stream to beneficial uses shall never be denied. Prior appropria. tion, whether heretofore or hereafter made, to any such use shall give the better right, and the right of appropriation shall be exercised under such regulations as the legislature has heretofore provided or may hereafter prescribe, and the English common law of riparian rights, so far as it conflicts with this or the preceding section, shall not be recognized as a rule of decision or rule of property in any court of this state.

Sec. 3. All acts and parts of acts which conflict in any way with the provisions of this act are hereby repealed.

The convention adjourned *sine die*, on the conclusion of its business, May 22d.

The republican state committee met in San Francisco, April 27th, and issued a call for the state convention to meet at Los Angeles, August 25th, to consist of 458 delegates, the test of voters at primaries being: "Did you vote for James G. Blaine, or would you have done so if you had the chance? Will you vote the republican ticket at the next election?" On the appointed day, the convention assembled at Armory Hall, Los Angeles. It was called to order by A. P. Williams, chairman of the state central committee. W. H. L. Barnes was unanimously elected temporary chairman, and was made permanent chairman on final organization.

The committee on platform and resolutions consisted of G. G. Blanchard, J. H. G. Weaver, E. A. Davis, Obed Harvey, R. O. Gaskill, L. B. Mizner, J. H. Dickinson, Henry Edgerton, J. H. Barber, Robert Effey, H. V. Morehouse, H. A. Barclay, A. Bell, J. E. Hale, and C. F. McGlashan. The following platform, reported by the committee on the 26th, was unanimously adopted :

The republican party of California, in convention assembled, re-affirms its devotion to the great purposes for which it was organized

33

and for which it has been maintained. It has preserved free government and secured to all the inhabitants of these United States the great rights which lie at the foundation of all just government—the right to life, property, and the pursuit of happiness—and its mission will not be fully accomplished until the laws are so construed and administered that an invasion of these inalienable rights, even against the humblest person, shall become impossible. It points with pride to the fact that it has engrafted these principles upon the national constitution, thereby giving to every one the protection which the power of 60,000,000 of freemen affords. Guided by a firm faith in these great principles, it has during its long and eventful history, done nothing for which it has to apologize. When it took the government from the democratic party it found a country disturbed by dissensions ; states seceding and threatening secession ; the treasury empty and the public credit impaired ; the arsenals plundered and fortresses invested ; a hostile government, whose foundation was human slavery fully armed in our midst ; with open foes at the south and secret enemies at the north. When called upon to surrender its great trust, it delivered to its successors a united country, a free people, an overflowing treasury, public credit higher than that of any other nation on earth, arsenals and the government works intact, the flag of the union floating in peace over a great, prosperous, happy nation, commanding the admiration and respect of mankind. Reaffirming the principles enunciated in the national platform adopted at Chicago in 1884, and the state platform adopted at Sacramento in the same year, in so far as now applicable, the republican party of California makes the following additional declaration of principles :

1. Labor is honorable, and the labor in every walk of life should be honored. Upon free, intelligent labor and its wise direction depends the prosperity of the nation. Everything which is useful and valuable to man is the result of labor in some form, and its careful protection should be the first consideration of the statesman. The value of labor must depend on its producing capacity, and this must be measured by the intelligence of the laborer. The liberal education of the laborer, therefore, is the first step toward the greatest, the wisest and the most profitable development of the resources of the country and the elevation of its workmen. To accomplish this the public school system should be preserved, protected and extended, until its ennobling influence penetrates to every hearthstone and increases the usefulness of every person. The

republican party declares its firm belief that co-operation among laborers is for the best interest of society; that while capital is entitled to all safeguards necessary to induce its generous investment, and while assaults upon social order proceeding from persons falsely representing themselves as friends of labor must be sternly repressed, the republican party will never sanction any legislation which will restrict wage-earners from co-operating and organizing for their general protection and advancement, but, on the contrary, will enact liberal laws fostering and encouraging co-operation.

2. Mining is one of the material interests of this state and coast, and one of the most valuable productions is silver. This industry, not alone because of the worth of its production, but also because of the fact that it affords employment to many thousands of people, and because of the fact that over sixty per cent of the value of the product represents the wages of labor, should be protected and encouraged. To this end we are in favor of free coinage of silver, the product of our mines, and of the issuance by the government of silver certificates. We denounce the policy of the democratic national administration, which, in the interest of the few, would deprive the people of silver as a circulating medium.

3. The Chinese cannot and will not assimilate with our own race. Their peculiar characteristics are utterly incompatible with those of our own people. So long as they are here they must be among us, yet apart from us. Such a population is most undesirable. The republican party therefore declares that their coming here must be stopped, while those who are here under treaty stipulation must be treated humanely and receive the protection of law. It points with just pride to the fact that the republican senate of the United States, by unanimous vote, has passed a bill for the restriction of Chinese immigration, and denounces the action of the democratic house of representatives for refusing its concurrence in a measure universally demanded by the people of this coast, and which is necessary for the protection and elevation of free labor.

4. The supreme court of the United States having failed to determine whether or not the method of taxing railroad corporations as declared by our state constitution is in conflict with the constitution of the United States, we are without an authoritative rule which might otherwise relieve the question of its present embarrassing complications, and this subject requires of our legislature and executive most careful and deliberate action. There is to be submitted to the people at the ensuing election the "Heath amendment," so-called,

relating to railroad taxation. Without making this a party question, or assuming a position for or against this amendment, yet some remedy for existing defects in the law must be provided at the earliest moment possible. The gravity of this matter puts it on a plane above the range of party politics, and demands the serious attention of the best thinking people of the state. In this respect, and in all others, we favor equal and just taxation for the maintenance of the government, and affirm that all should pay a full share of the public taxes fairly due and in accordance with the broad principles of equity.

5. One of the most important questions soon to be considered by the people of California is the proper utilization of its water courses for the purpose of irrigation, and when this great work is accomplished our state will support per acre a greater population than any other state in the union, and fertilize and fill with prosperity vast domains otherwise dedicated to perpetual barrenness. The republican party approaches this great question with a careful deliberation, not less grave than that with which it has debated and happily determined other momentous subjects, in the confident expectation that, if entrusted with the power so to do, it will enact such laws as will secure and receive the approval of the people ; and it here affirms as follows : First—It is in favor of the immediate passage of a law declaring that henceforth no rights to water shall be acquired by appropriation which will in any manner obstruct the state in the control thereof, whenever it shall see proper to exercise such control. Second—It is in favor of the passage of laws which will prevent the monopolizing of the waters of the state and promote the utilization to the greatest extent possible. Third—In the passage of any laws upon this subject individual rights must be protected ; but if those rights are found to interfere with effectuating a just distribution of water and its utilization by the people upon equal terms, then such rights should be condemned and taken for public use, under the same principles upon which all private property is condemned and taken for public use, upon compensation being made therefor.

6. We denounce the present state administration as most wasteful and incompetent. Its weakness, extravagance, and vacillating policy has brought reproach upon the fair fame of California.

7. We recognize the great truth that no government can be republican in form unless the three departments—legislative, judicial, and executive—are separate and independent, the one from the other. We declare that the calling of an extra session of the legislature for

the purpose of reversing a decision of the supreme court of the state has no parallel in the history of this country; that the policy which dictated it was un-American and revolutionary, and that no words of censure can adequately characterize this attempt to destroy the independence of a co-ordinate branch of the government.

8. The republican party submits its platform and its candidates to the intelligence and the patriotism of the people, and invokes to their support all, without regard to past affiliation, who desire just laws, good government, peace, and security. True to its mission, it will bring to the solution of the important subjects involved, broad, statesmanlike, and equitable methods. Born to protect human rights, it never can be brought, by any argument or by any pressure, to deprive anyone of a right, however small, without awarding just compensation. Upon this platform of principles and upon its past record it appeals with confidence to the candid judgment of an intelligent people, and as to the consequences, is willing to take its chances and abide its destiny.

On the 26th the making of nominations was commenced. For justices of the supreme court, long term, A. Van R. Paterson, Anson Brunson, L. D. Latimer, T. B. McFarland and Noble Hamilton were placed in nomination. Paterson was nominated on the first ballot, receiving 318 votes; McFarland, 227; Brunson, 194; Hamilton, 167; Latimer, 8. On the second ballot McFarland was chosen the other nominee by 286 votes to 102 for Brunson and 65 for Hamilton. For justice for the short term, Noble Hamilton, Anson Brunson, George A. Nourse and J. B. Southard were placed in nomination. Hamilton was nominated on the first ballot, receiving 249 votes to 172 for Brunson, 24 for Nourse, and 11 for Southard.

For governor, John F. Swift, Chancellor Hartson, William H. Dimond, and Charles F. Reed were placed in nomination. On the first ballot Swift received 108; Dimond, 153; Reed, 84, and Hartson, 108; necessary to a choice, 229. After taking six ballots without making a choice, the convention adjourned until the next day. The balloting was continued on the 27th, and on the eighth ballot Swift was nominated. The vote stood: Swift, 325 ; Dimond, 74; Reed, 20; Hartson, 36. The other nominations were :

R. W. Waterman, for lieutenant governor, by $239\frac{1}{2}$ votes to $131\frac{1}{2}$ for William Johnston, 84 for John P. Stearns, and 1 for George E. Whitney.

Walter S. Moore, for secretary of state, by 239 votes to 91 for James A. Orr, and 126 for O. W. Craig.

J. E. Denny, for controller, by 268 votes to 181 for H. L. Weston.

Jacob H. Neff, for treasurer, by 304 votes to 80 for John Weil, 38 for William Jackson and 33 for Charles M. Levy.

W. H. H. Hart, for attorney-general, by acclamation, the other candidates withdrawing before the completion of the roll-call on the first ballot.

Theodore Reichert, for surveyor-general, by 252 votes to 90 for William Minto, 35 for Robert Gardner, and 52 for C. E. Grunsky.

Ira G. Hoitt, for superintendent of public instruction, by 263 votes to 187 for S. D. Waterman.

James A. Orr, for clerk of the supreme court, by acclamation,

The convention adjourned *sine die* at midnight on the 27th.

The following nominations were made by the district conventions :

For representative in congress, first district, Charles A. Garter ; second district, J. C. Campbell ; third district, Joseph McKenna ; fourth district, W. W. Morrow ; fifth district, Charles N. Felton ; sixth district, W. Vandever.

For member of state board of equalization, first district, A. C. Dithmar ; second district, L. C. Morehouse ; third district, John Beattie, Jr. ; fourth district, Mark D. Hamilton.

For railroad commissioner, first district, A. Abbott ; second district, J. M. Litchfield ; third district, James W. Rea.

The democratic state central committee met May 11th and issued the call for the convention to meet in San Francisco, August 31st. The convention met at the appointed time in Odd Fellows' hall. It was called to order by W. D. English, chairman of the state central committee. N. Greene Curtis and Stephen M. White were nominated for the position of temporary chairman. White was elected on the first ballot by 260 votes to 224 for Curtis.

The following were appointed on the committee on platform and resolutions : Barclay Henley, Dennis Spencer, R. F. Del Valle, N. Greene Curtis, M. E. C. Munday, A. H. Rose, Henry Mahler, N. Martin, J. E. McElrath, E. McGettigan, A. T. Spotts, Frank Mc-Coppin, Thomas J. Clunie, N. Bowden, A. Kearney, and B. Grimes.

On permanently organizing, White was elected chairman. The following platform was adopted September 2d :

1. That with becoming pride we cordially endorse the administra. tion of President Grover Cleveland for the honesty, frugality, and success with which it is conducting the affairs of government, carry. ing out the principles of democracy in administering public trusts and keeping faith with the people. A respect for constitutional law, the protection of the rights of our fellow citizens at home and abroad, a desire to reform the unjust inequalities of customs, to reduce tax. ation to limit the expenditures, to actual necessities, the revival of trade, the increase of commerce, the restoration of the unearned public lands to the people's heritage, the peace that happily extends throughout our whole land, and the extinction of sectional animosities, are the salient marks which signalize the restoration of the democratic party to power and the response it has given to the trust reposed in it. We commend the discrimination which the president has made in favor of the honest soldier, and call attention to the fact, that while he has vetoed spurious and unworthy claims, he has signed more pension bills than any of his predecessors.

2. This convention proudly invites attention to the fact that the last democratic house of representatives passed bills forfeiting and restoring to the public domain railway land grants amounting to over 75,000,000 of acres, and also the further fact that in the forty-eighth congress the democratic lower house passed the Regan inter-state commerce bill, which failed of passage in the republican senate; also, that in the last session of congress the Regan bill was again passed by the democratic lower house.

3. That this convention recommends the passage of an act of congress providing for the free coinage of both gold and silver, by the terms of which act all gold and silver bullion offered at the several mints of the United States shall be received in exchange for money on gold or silver certificates at the rate now fixed by law for standard dollars of gold or silver, which certificates shall be receivable for all public purposes and interchangeable for gold or silver, as the case may be.

4. That the present tariff on wool, prepared by a republican com-mission, appointed by a republican president, is an unjust discrimination against a great industry, and we denounce the same and demand the restoration of the tariff of 1867. That in view of the brilliant future that awaits California in the development of its wine interests, we most heartily favor the bills now pending in congress for the release from taxation of spirits used in the fortification of sweet wines and the protection of our wine industries from the in-

jurious effects of fraud and the unrestricted sale of spurious wines. And we also favor legislation providing for the protection of the raisin industry.

5. We are in favor of liberal wages and free labor. All associations formed for the purpose of developing intelligence, promoting the welfare and protecting the interests of the laborer and mechanic, and to enable them successfully to contend for and maintain their rights by peaceful and efficient means against powerful and oppressive combinations, should be encouraged and expressly sanctioned by law. We regard the contract convict labor system as detrimental to the interests of free labor and ruinous to certain lines of legitimate business with which it comes in conflict. We commend the present state administration for its late efforts to abolish this system, and pledge our candidates, if elected, to do all within their power to carry out the spirit of the constitution upon this question. But in no way shall this be construed to prohibit the manufacture of grain bags and jute goods within the walls of the state prison.

6. We are unalterably opposed to Chinese immigration, and demand the abrogation of the Burlingame-Swift treaty—a treaty through whose loopholes slave labor creeps upon our shores. We pledge the best efforts of the democratic party of this state to the enforcement of laws which shall permanently prohibit and prevent such immigration. We regard Chinese labor as an unmixed evil. Therefore, we favor legislation providing for the deportation of the Chinese from this country, and their exclusion forever. In the meantime, and pending proper legislation upon this subject, the democratic party of this state, as a friend of free labor, and in the interest of the people, recognizes the legal right of any citizen to employ whom he pleases, yet we hold that it is the right and duty of the people of this state to withhold their patronage from the Chinese, and that such labor should not be resorted to when any other character of labor is available.

7. That we reaffirm the principle contained in the national democratic platform, declaring that the democratic party is unalterably opposed to all sumptuary legislation.

8. We condemn the great railroad companies of this state for their defiance of the state power, their corrupt practices and their persistent refusal to contribute their just and lawful proportion of the revenue. The contempt and disgrace they thus throw upon free government is a first and long step to encourage communism and anarchy. If the rich may with impunity defy the law, upon what

principle, in a government which is based upon the corner stone of equality, shall the poor be compelled to yield obedience? All law abiding citizens should unite with the democracy in their efforts to exact from these powerful corporations observance of the law and an honest and faithful discharge of their obligations to the state and its inhabitants.

9. We are opposed to the adoption of the proposed amendment to the constitution of this state commonly known as the "Heath amendment." Its approval by the people would be in accord with the wishes of the non-taxpaying monopolists of California. Our present system of railroad taxation should not be abandoned unless the supreme court of the United States should hold it to be invalid. If the "Heath amendment" is adopted, the railroad corporations will be their own assessors, and will contribute toward the support of government such sums only as, according to their own chosen phrase, "they are minded to pay." An examination and comparison of the official returns made for the year 1885, by the railroad corporations to the state board of equalization, demonstrate the fact that under the operation of the "Heath amendment" the state and counties would lose yearly the sum of $478,067.32. The county committees of the counties of this state are requested to print their tickets against said amendment.

10. No free people, who are unable to defend, can long maintain their freedom. We therefore advocate the proper protection of our coasts against invasion, and the creation of a navy and forts to replace decayed and worthless remnants of forts and ships left to the country by the republican administration. We deem a good national guard necessary to the safety of our country and institutions. We therefore favor a liberal treatment of our citizen soldiers and advocate measures to increase the efficiency of their organization.

11. We extend our sympathy to all people struggling to engraft upon their political system the principles of individual liberty and self government, and with special emphasis do we extend that sympathy to the present heroic efforts of the Irish people.

12. That the democratic party recognizes the importance of the water question and the absolute necessity for its speedy settlement, and the party can and will settle it on a basis of equal and exact justice to all interests involved. Navigation shall not be impaired under any pretext. No class of individuals shall take, injure, or destroy the property or rights of any other class except under the operations of the law of eminent domain. These rights being

guarded and protected, the waters of the state are the property of the people of the state, to be used for irrigation, mining, manufacturing, and other useful purposes. Appropriation of water, whether heretofore or hereafter made, should give no right to more water than is absolutely used in an economical manner for a beneficial purpose. To guard against a monopoly of water for irrigation, irrigation districts should have the right to acquire by purchase or condemnation the means necessary in conducting the water to the lands comprising such irrigation districts. The English law of riparian rights is inapplicable to the circumstances and conditions of California. The state may at any time assume control of the diversion, use and distribution of water under general laws enacted for that purpose; provided, the state shall in no event be called upon by taxation, or otherwise, to construct irrigation works.   .

13. Believing in the fullest representation by the people in all political assemblies, we ask this convention to declare for the primary system of selecting delegates to all conventions of the democratic party in this state, and against the practice of county committees naming representatives thereto; and, further, that it is the duty of every county committee to carry out the work and policy of the convention which creates it; that the functions of every such committee should, therefore, be limited to such work, and that its tenure of office should expire at the moment every new county convention assembles.

14. That our public schools will always have the fostering care of the democratic party of California. We demand for them the utmost efficiency, and a liberal expenditure, with no limit so long as honesty, economy, and business method cover all their works. The education of the children is the best guarantee of republican liberty.

15. That mining is one of the great and beneficial industries of this state; therefore, it is the duty of the government to devise some way for mining to be continued without injury to any other industry.

The fifth resolution in its original form occasioned considerable discussion, and it was amended by adding the words "But in no way shall this be construed to prohibit the manufacture of grain bags and jute goods within the walls of the state prison." The platform adopted was as reported by the committee, with the exception of the preceding sentences, and the fourteenth and fifteenth resolutions, which were added in convention.

The following resolution was offered by D. S. Terry, on September 4th, and adopted:

That we demand the enactment of a law whereby supplies furnished to all asylums, prisons, hospitals, almshouses, and other institutions under the control of the state, or of counties, cities, and towns of the state, shall be the product of white labor only; and we pledge that the same shall be made the law of the state when the democracy shall have control of the legislature.

The following, offered by G. W. Jeffries, was also adopted:

That the democratic party of the state of California demands the removal of every republican now in office by appointment, except those holding under civil service rules, and that democrats be appointed to their places.

On September 1st, nominations were made for the office of justice of the supreme court. Jackson Temple was nominated by acclamation for the short term, to succeed Judge Ross. For the long term, J. F. Sullivan, Byron Waters, Niles Searls, J. M. Corcoran, and J. W. Armstrong were placed in nomination. Before votes were changed, the roll-call on the first ballot showed 250 for Sullivan, 50 for Waters, 53 for Searls, 28 for Corcoran and 100 for Armstrong. Sullivan was therefore declared nominated. S. B. McKee was then also placed in nomination and a ballot taken for the second nominee for the long term. On this second ballot McKee received 116 votes, Searls 100, Armstrong 105, Waters 127, and Corcoran 34. There was no choice and an adjournment was taken until the following day. On the first ballot taken September 2nd, Waters was nominated by 279 votes, to 107 for McKee and 106 for Searls, Armstrong and Corcoran having been withdrawn.

For governor, A. J. Bryant, Patrick Reddy, Washington Bartlett, C. P. Berry, and M. F. Tarpey were placed in nomination. Bryant and Reddy were withdrawn after the first ballot, and on the second ballot Bartlett was nominated, receiving 315 votes, to 135 for Berry and 46 for Tarpey.

The other nominations were:

M. F. Tarpey, for lieutenant governor, without opposition, his opponent, C. P. Berry withdrawing before the completion of the first roll-call.

Adam Herold for treasurer, over D. J. Oullahan and Jefferson G. James.

W. C. Hendricks for secretary of state, by acclamation, his opponent, G. W. Peckham, being withdrawn.

John P. Dunn for controller, without opposition.

G. A. Johnson for attorney-general, over John T. Carey, W. D.
Grady, and Edward Swinford.

A. J. Moulder for superintendent of public instruction, by acclamation.

E. O. Miller for surveyor-general, over Franklin P. McCray.

J. D. Spencer for clerk of the supreme court, by acclamation.

The following nominations were made by the district conventions:
Members of board of equalization: First district, Gordon E.
Sloss; second district, C. H. Randall; third district, C. E. Wil-
coxon; fourth district, John T. Gaffey.

Railroad commissioners: First district, Joseph A. Filcher; second
district, Patrick J. White; third district, William W. Foote.

For congress: First district, Thomas L. Thompson; second district, Marion Biggs; third district, Henry C. McPike; fourth district; Frank McCoppin; fifth district, Frank J. Sullivan; sixth district, Joseph D. Lynch.

After selecting a state central committee, the convention adjourned
sine die, Saturday, September 4th.

A call for a conference of farmers was issued by Eden Grange,
March 27th. It was proposed to consider the best means to remedy
the grievances of agricultural and other industrial classes, and
to arrange for placing a ticket before the people for congressional,
legislative, and county officers. The conference was held in Granger's hall, Sacramento, April 8th and 9th. Fifty-one delegates,
from some eleven counties were reported entitled to seats. W. C.
Blackwood was elected temporary, and later, permanent chairman.
It was resolved to organize, if necessary, an independent farmers'
and producers' political party. A committee was appointed to prepare an address to the farmers and manufacturers of the state. The
address which was reported and adopted urged the taxpayers to take
an active part in the precinct primaries in order to secure the
nomination of candidates who would use their best endeavors to reduce public expenditures, and thereby reduce taxation. The following resolution, offered by C. A. Hull, was adopted:

That it is the desire of this conference that the different granges
of the state of California invite the farmers of their respective
localities to assemble in mass meeting at their different halls, on the

last Saturday in June, to then and there determine if they shall in-- struct the committee here appointed by this conference to call a convention; and it is further the sense of this conference that if they determine to call a convention, that it be called before any of the party conventions.

The conference adjourned April 9th. On September 15th, in re- sponse to a call from Eden and Temescal granges some seventy-five delegates, representing sixteen granges assembled at Granger's hall, Sacramento, many of the delegates being the same that were in at- tendance at the conference held in April. W. C. Blackwood was elected chairman. A committee on resolutions was appointed and it submitted the following, which were adopted:

1. We favor an amendment of the constitution providing for the election of United States senators by a direct vote of the people.

2. We favor the free coinage of gold and silver, the abolition of national banks, the issuance by the government of its own money, which shall be legal tender for all debts. That the bonds of the government be paid as fast as under the law may be possible, and that the government issue no more bonds.

3. We recognize the vast importance of a system of irrigation for the state of California, and that the ownership of water shall be inalienably vested in the state, and shall be administered and distrib- uted by the state, dividing the state into districts by natural water sheds or catchments, the expense to be borne by the districts irrigated.

4. We are in favor of a stringent law to punish adulterations of food, drinks, and medicines, and the use of short weights and measures.

5. We are opposed to the "Heath amendment," which will appear on our ballots as "against constitutional amendment No. 1."

6. We are opposed to any increase of our standing army in time of peace.

7. We denounce any movement looking toward any increase of appropriation of state money for maintaining a state militia.

8. We favor the abrogation of the Burlingame treaty and the ex- clusion of Chinese by all lawful means.

9. In furtherance of these ends, we ask the co-operation of all fair-minded people. We wage no war against classes, but only against vicious institutions. We are not content to endure further discipline of our present rulers, who, having dominion over money, over transportation, over the press and the machinery of the

government, wield unwarranted power over our free institutions, and our lives, liberty, and property.

10. The transportation question being of the greatest importance to the farmers and manufacturers, and especially in our low-priced staple, wheat, we are in favor of the Eads ship railway.

11. That the fees, salaries, and emoluments of county officers should be reduced commensurately with the salaries paid for like services in private business.

12. That woman shall be placed on an equality with man in clerical employment in official positions.

Joel Russell was nominated for governor; J. V. Webster for lieutenant-governor; A. L. Hart for attorney-general; Jackson Temple and Jeremiah F. Sullivan for justices of the supreme court; H. S. Graves for state treasurer; Ira G. Hoitt for superintendent of public instruction; John P. Dunn for controller; J. D. Spencer for clerk of the supreme court. For congress, George Ohleyer was nominated from the second district, and W. W. Smith from the third. O. E. Wilcoxon was nominated for member of the state board of equalization; and W. W. Foote and J. A. Filcher for railroad commissioners.

The remaining positions on the state ticket were to be filled by the state central committee, which was then appointed. This committee organized by electing W. C. Blackwood, chairman; S. T. Sanders, secretary; and A. T. Dewey, treasurer. It was decided to call the meeting the "farmers' convention." It adjourned *sine die*, September 16th.

The united labor party convention met in San Francisco, September 24–28th. A. E. Redstone presided, and John O. Green acted as secretary. A platform was adopted urging united action on the part of the knights of labor, farmers, trades' unions, greenbackers, and all friends of united labor; recommending government ownership of railway, telegraph, and telephone lines; limitation by taxation on the accumulation of wealth; election of United States senators by the people; free coinage of gold and silver; abolition of national banks, etc. A state ticket was nominated, headed by C. F. McGlashan for governor, and Horace Bell for lieutenant-governor.

The state convention of the American party met at Fresno, September 28th, in response to the following call:

Believing that the time has come when it is necessary that the people of these United States of America should take full charge and control of their government, to the exclusion of the restless revolutionary horde of foreigners who are now seeking our shores from every part of the world; and recognizing that the first and most important duty of an American is to perpetuate this government in all attainable purity and strength; we, citizens of these United States, do make the following declaration:

1. That all law-abiding citizens of these United States, be they native or foreign born, are political equals, and all citizens are equally entitled to the protection of our laws.

2. That the naturalization laws of the United States should be unconditionally repealed.

3. That the soil of America should belong to Americans, and that no alien, resident or non-resident, should ever be permitted to own real estate.

4. That no person, not in sympathy with our government and the principles upon which it is founded, should ever be permitted to immigrate to these United States.

Whereas, The above declaration of principles was adopted by the mass of citizens assembled at a meeting called for that purpose, and held at Fresno city, Cal., May 27th; and whereas, at that meeting the two great parties of the country were urged and requested to incorporate said principles and doctrines into their respective platforms; and whereas, said parties have, in convention assembled, ignored said principles and doctrines, and have refused to incorporate them into their, or either of their platforms, thereby repudiating the best interests, wishes and rights of the American voter and property-owner; now, then, be it resolved,

1. That a state convention of the American party assemble at Fresno city, on Tuesday, September 28th, at two o'clock P. M., for the purpose of adopting a platform and nominating a full ticket to contest the right, at the coming election, of holding the various state and federal offices for the next ensuing term.

2. All persons from all parts of the state who endorse the above principles and doctrines are cordially and earnestly requested to attend said convention and participate in its labors.

By order of the executive committee.

THOMAS E. HUGHES, President.

E. F. SELLBECK, Secretary.

Delegates representing eight counties were present. The follow-. ing resolutions were adopted, which later were embodied in a plat. form adopted by the state central committee :

1. We reiterate the doctrine promulgated by the executive com-. mittee of the American party.

2. Believing that Americans should rule America, we favor the education of American youths, boys and girls, as artisans and mechanics, to fill the places of foreigners, who now have nearly the exclusive control of all the great industries of our country, save agriculture alone.

3. Bossism in politics is the outgrowth of foreign influence. We condemn it and declare that the American party has not and shall not have bosses.

4. The waters of the state belong to the lands they will irrigate, and we favor a broad and comprehensive system of irrigation that looks to the benefit of the irrigator to the exclusion of so-called rights of riparian and appropriator; a system controlled by the government, free to all, under the control of no class of persons, and established and maintained by a revenue derived from those only whom the system will benefit.

5. We believe in equal taxation, and to accomplish that desirable reform we favor the reduction of taxes on the real estate of the cultivator of the soil and the laying of additional burdens on the luxuries.

6. We would foster and encourage American industries and to that end would protect home productions and manufactures and inaugur-- ate and maintain a system that would not only exclude the cheap-labor productions of other countries but would also exclude the cheap laborers of all other countries and prevent their coming here to compete with Americans.

7. We believe that American free schools are indispensable supports to liberty; that reason and experience both teach us that national existence depends on the influence of liberal and refined education.

The platform as adopted by the state central committee was as follows:

Believing that the time has arrived when a due regard for the present and future prosperity of our country makes it imperative that the people of the United States of America should take full and entire control of their government, to the exclusion of the revolutionary and incendiary horde of foreigners now seeking our shores from every quarter of the world ; and recognizing that the first and most important duty of an American citizen is to maintain this government in all attainable purity and strength, we, as such citi. zens, do make the following declaration of principles:

1. That all law-abiding citizens of these United States, whether native or foreign-born, are political equals, and all citizens are enti. tled to and should receive the full protection of the laws.

2. That the naturalization laws of the United States should be unconditionally repealed.

3. That the soil of America should belong to Americans; that no alien non-resident should be permitted to own real estate in the United States, and that the real estate possessions of the resident alien shall be limited in value and area.

4. That all persons not in sympathy with our government should be prohibited from immigrating to these United States.

5. That we unqualifiedly favor, and we ask all who believe that Americans should rule America to assist in educating the boys and girls of American citizens as mechanics and artisans, thus fitting them to fill the places now filled by´foreigners, who supply the skilled labor and thereby almost entirely control all the great industries of our country, save, perhaps, that of agriculture alone.

6. That we believe bossism in politics to be an outgrowth of foreign influence. We condemn it as un-American and tending to a corruption of the ballot-box. We declare that the American party has not and shall not have bosses.

7. That the waters of the state belong to the lands they will irrigate, and we favor and will aid in maintaining a broad and comprehensive system of irrigation that looks to the benefit of the irrigator as primary to the assumed rights of the riparian and the appropriator; a system controlled by the government, free to all, under the control of no class of persons, and established and maintained by a revenue derived from those whom the system will benefit. We believe the water is the property of the people, and that it should be so used as to secure the greatest good to the greatest number.

8. That we believe in equal and just taxation, and to accomplish this necessary reform we favor a uniform reduction of taxes on the real estate of the cultivator of the soil, and the imposing of advanced rates on property coming under the head of luxuries.

9. That we are in favor of fostering and encouraging American

34

industries of every class and kind, and to that end would protect our home productions and manufactures, and inaugurate and maintain a system that will not only exclude the cheap labor productions of other countries, but will also exclude the cheap laborers of all other countries, and prevent their coming here to compete with American workingmen.

10. That we believe the American free school system the guarantee of human liberty, and that the teachings of reason and the lessons of experience lead to the conviction that national existence depends on the influence of universal education.

The convention nominated an incomplete ticket and appointed a committee of seven, with authority to increase its members to twenty-five, to manage the affairs of the party.

John F. Swift, the republican candidate, was nominated for governor, but he declined the nomination in the following letter :

FRANK M. PIXLEY, ESQ., Editor *Argonaut:*

DEAR SIR : I observed in this morning's issue of the *Argonaut* that twelve gentlemen, whose names are not given, have done me the honor to nominate me for governor upon what is printed in the paper as an "American ticket," with my name at the head. The supposed views of the twelve gentlemen are set forth in the same issue of your journal, and coincide substantially with the opinions which have been urged by the *Argonaut* for some years past. I do not agree with those views. I can easily understand how you, in your kind feeling toward me personally, based upon our long-standing friendly relations, should be willing to vote for me, even though conscious, as I know you to be, that I do not agree with the *Argonaut* in its attitude toward Roman Catholics and foreign-born citizens.

But I can not so easily understand why the twelve gentlemen you refer to should also desire to confer this unsolicited and undesired honor upon me. But I am not sorry they have done so, for it gives me an opportunity of expressing my opinions upon the questions raised by your article.

I have never in my life, either in public or private, expressed or entertained any such views as are contained in the article suggesting my name, and which the twelve gentlemen are understood to agree with.

I have never made or felt any distinction between men of our race, citizens or not citizens, on account of their nationality or religion, and I never shall.

I believe that the policy adopted in the early days of the republic, of extending the right of .citizenship to all Europeans, in order to encourage their coming hither, was a wise policy, and I would not change it if I had the power. And I think, further, that even if the policy as an original question was of doubtful advantage, it is in my opinion in the highest degree unjust, and unwise because unjust, to agitate the matter over again after millions of good men and excellent citizens have accepted the invitation and acted upon it.

I believe that Roman Catholics are as loyal to republican institutions and to the United States as protestant christians or people of anỹ other faith. And I believe that they, whether born in the United States or in foreign lands, if citizens, ought to enjoy precisely the same right as to holding office, and all other rights of citizenship under the constitution and laws, with myself or any other native-born citizen.

Such being my views, as you know—I may say almost better than anybody, for I have so often told you so—I take it for granted the twelve gentlemen will not want me longer at the head of their ticket, but will promptly take me down.

But whatever may be their wishes on that subject, I beg that you will see that my name is taken down, and not again printed in that connection.

I am, dear sir, very truly and sincerely, your friend,

JOHN F. SWIFT.

824 Valencia street, San Francisco, September 18, 1886.

The name of Swift was accordingly withdrawn, and the nomination given to P. D. Wigginton.

The other nominations were as follows: Frank M. Pixley for lieutenant-governor; C. N. Wilson for secretary of state; J. E. Denny for controller; George T. White for treasurer; Alfred A. Daggett for attorney-general; Ira G. Hoitt for superintendent of public instruction; Theodore Reichert for surveyor-general; Samuel Frew for clerk of supreme court. F. M. Pixley declined, and R. W. Waterman was substituted as the nominee for lieutenant-governor. The completed ticket as prepared by the state central committee, included the foregoing and Jackson Temple, A. Van R. Paterson, and Thomas B. McFarland for justices of the supreme court; for railroad commissioners, Henry Wilson from first district, J. M. Litchfield from second district, and James W. Rea from third district; for congress, Charles A. Garter from first district, W. O. Clark from second district, H. C. McPike from third district, W. W. Morrow from fourth district, Charles N. Felton from fifth district, and William Vandever from sixth district; for members of the state board of equalization, J. S. Reynolds from first district, C. H. Randall from second district, Thomas Bair, from third district and John T. Gaffey from fourth district.

The state central committee was composed of F. G. Berry, W. L. Dickinson, S. Hannon, George M. McLane, J. R. White, E. B. Churchill, N. M. Orr, W. J. Hunt, P. E. Platt, James McNeal, John F. Taylor, J. M. Bassett, Jubal Clark, W. A. Caswell, Moses Rogers, F. M. Pixley, George W. Grayson, E. M. Freeman, Wm. Irelan, Sr., Robert Ash, J. F. Chapman, C. W. Weston, O. B. Culver, P. Veasey, W. B. Collier, J. B. Whitney, James Durham, W. M. Hanks, and James B. Havner.

The state election was held November 2d, and resulted in the election of the democratic candidates for governor, secretary of state, controller, treasurer, attorney-general, clerk of the supreme court, associate justice for the unexpired term, a railroad commissioner, three members of the state board of equalization, and two congressmen; while on the republican ticket were elected the candidates for lieutenant-governor, surveyor-general, superintendent of public instruction, two associate justices, two railroad commissioners, one member of the state board of equalization and four congressmen. By the death of Bartlett, September 12th, 1887, Lieutenant-governor Waterman became governor. The official returns were as follows:

For governor—Washington Bartlett, 84,970; John F. Swift, 84,-316; Joel Russell, 6,432; P. D. Wigginton, 7,347; C. C. O'Donnell, 12,227.

For lieutenant-governor—R. W. Waterman, 94,969; M. F. Tarpey, 92,476; A. D. Boren, 5,836; Horace Bell, 1,658.

For secretary of state—William C. Hendricks, 93,481; Walter S. Moore, 87,647; Frank E. Kellogg, 4,498; C. N. Wilson, 5,940.

For controller—John P. Dunn, 95,469; J. E. Denny, 94,833; J. A. Fairbanks, 4,921.

For treasurer—Adam Herold, 91,572; J. H. Neff, 90,963; H. S. Graves, 5,822; George T. White, 5,717.

For attorney-general—George A. Johnson, 93,102; W. H. H. Hart, 91,716; George Babcock, 5,146; Alfred Daggett, 5,533.

For surveyor-general—Theodore Reichert, 98,240; E. O. Miller, 91,398; George B. Tolman, 5,976.

For clerk of the supreme court—J. D. Spencer, 92,589; James A. Orr, 90,705; Julius Lyons, 5,258; Samuel Frew, 3,554; Samuel True (wrongly printed), 1,594.

For superintendent of public instruction—Ira G. Hoitt, 94,448; Andrew J. Moulder, 94,250; D. A. Mobley, 3,868.

For associate justices of supreme court, full term—A. Van R. Paterson, 101,685; T. B. McFarland, 96,884; Jeremiah F. Sullivan, 92,741; Byron Waters, 90,853; Wm. C. Murphy, 5,292. Unexpired term—Jackson Temple, 108,645; Noble Hamilton, 83,837.

For railroad commissioner, first district—A. Abbott, 35,069; J. A. Filcher, 33,804; Henry Wilson, 520; W. C. Damon, 155; C. Bateman, 588. Second district—P. J. White, 23,120; J. M. Litchfield, 22,858; John C. Green, 2,496. Third district—James W. Rea, 36,466; W. W. Foote, 36,283; S. M. McLean, 3,174.

Member of state board of equalization, first district—Gordon E. Sloss, 22,161; A. C. Dithmar, 20,663; Waldron Shear, 2,207; J. S. Reynolds, 283. Second district—L. C. Morehouse, 22,760; Charles H. Randall, 20,688; A. J. Gregg, 1,048. Third district—C. E. Wilcoxon, 24,338; John Beattie, Jr., 23,627; J. L. Mansfield, 919; Thomas Bair, 600. Fourth district—John T. Gaffey, 27,222; M. D. Hamilton, 24,458; L. B. Hogue, 2,587.

For representatives in congress, first district—Thomas L. Thompson, 16,499; Charles A. Garter, 15,526; L. W. Simmons, 849. Second district—Marion Biggs, 17,667; J. C. Campbell, 16,594; W. O. Clark, 1,076. Third district—H. C. McPike, 13,277; Joseph McKenna, 15,801; W. W. Smith, 707. Fourth district—W. W. Morrow, 11,413: Frank McCoppin, 9,854; Chas. A. Sumner, 2,104; Robert Thompson, 84. Fifth district—Charles N. Felton, 16,328; F. J. Sullivan, 16,209; A. E. Redstone, 470; C. Henderson, 460. Sixth district—W. Vandever, 18,259; Joseph D. Lynch, 18,204; W. A. Harris, 2,159.

CHAPTER XXXIV.

1888. Prohibition Convention.—Republican Convention, May 1st.—Democratic Convention.—American Party Convention.—Republican Convention, July 31st.

The executive committee of the prohibition party ·met at San Francisco, January 24th, and arranged for the holding of a convention in the same city on the fourth of April following. On that date the convention assembled at Metropolitan hall. John Bidwell was elected temporary chairman, and permanent chairman on the subsequent organization of the convention. The committee on credentials reported two hundred and seventy-seven delegates entitled to seats.

The following platform was adopted :

1. The prohibition party of California declares itself in alliance with the great national organization, having prohibition for its first organic law and governing motive, and is in sympathetic co-operation with all reforms calculated to advance the moral and material welfare of the whole American people. Whereas, the legalized and tolerated liquor traffic is a legalized infamous crime which is visited with a corresponding curse upon our country and people, and is a war against American civilization and liberty, and is subversive of all things which good men and women love and value, we earnestly invite all good citizens, without distinction of sex, race, sect, or party, to unite with us to stamp out this death-dealing plague. We demand the extinction of the manufacture, import, export, transport and sale of all intoxicating beverages by law enforced by effective preventive penalties. And we pledge ourselves to give our vote and influence only for persons or parties committed and pledged to use all proper means to this end,––fidelity to this plank being our only test of party fealty.

2. We invite to this work the intelligent, law-respecting, and order-loving men and women of this state; those who are interested in the protection and education of its youth, in elevating its moral standards, preserving the union of states, and in developing and perpetuating christian civilization throughout the world.

3. We declare that the manufacture, sale, and use of alcoholic drinks is the greatest evil of the country and the age; that the traffic enslaves women and degrades children, debases youth and wrecks manhood, corrupts ballots and injures public service, peoples prisons and fills insane asylums, breeds paupers and criminals, imposes .enormous burdens of taxation, destroys capital and ruins labor; degrades, impoverishes, and destroys our homes, and, through organized and criminal conspiracies, subverts law and order. So believing, we declare the cardinal principles of our party to be prohibition, by constitutional amendment, of the manufacture of all alcoholic liquors not demanded for medicinal, mechanical, or scientific use; and the regulation by law, under severe penalties, of the sale of

alcoholic liquors for such use, and the absolute and total prohibition of the sale for any other purpose.

4. We believe that voting for men or parties that license the dramshop is an active participation in all the guilt of the dramseller and his license.

5. We hail with pleasure the cultivation of the grape in this state, as offering our people a most pleasant, healthful, and remunerative occupation, and an incalculable and inexhaustible mine of wealth for many centuries to come. An unlimited market will always be found for all the raisins, syrups, canned fruit, and fresh grapes that the state can produce. We denounce the prostitution of the grape industry to the manufacture of wine, brandy or other intoxicating liquors.

6. We emphatically protest against all state aid for the encouragement of the business of making intoxicating drinks.

7. We declare that Sunday is an institution so interwoven into our laws, our customs, our civilization, and the very structure of our government, so intricately and beneficently connected with our social, business, and moral life, that we cannot dispense with it without sacrificing the very best interests of the country and the highest welfare of the whole people. And so believing, we demand the enactment and enforcement of an intelligent and rational Sunday law.

8. We are in favor of the universal and enforced education of the youth of our state, including instruction in regard to the effects of alcohol upon the human system, with ample provision for the support of an adequate system of free public schools.

9. We recognize the noble services of woman in the temperance reform, and in every elevating, purifying, beneficent work affecting the interest of our race, and we believe that enlightened patriotism and manly courage demand the assertion at this time that woman is entitled of right to the privileges of the elective franchise.

10. We gratefully recognize the heroic and successful work of the Woman's Christian Temperance Union—national, state, and local—and welcome our sisters as the strong right arm of the prohibition reform and of our party, and we lament the injustice and misfortune that deprive our cause of the help of their ballots.

11. That we sympathize with every proper effort to improve th moral, social, and financial condition of the laborer and the wage-earner, and urge this question as a proper subject of legislative enactment. But we declare that total abstinence for the individua

and the prohibition of the liquor traffic by the state lie at the threshhold of labor reform.

12. That the sectional feeling between the north and south should be obliterated. Let us therefore know no north, south, east or west, but combine in a fraternal union to free the nation from the blighting curse of rum.

13. We demand that the inheritance of the children of America in this country shall be preserved, and that the immigration of criminal and dangerous classes be positively prohibited; and to that end we demand a reformation of our naturalization laws.

14. We favor the government ownership and control of railroads and telegraphs, seeing that otherwise they will soon own and control the government.

15. We commend a complete reform in the civil service, and the application of sound business principles to the selection of officers for the public service.

16. We favor the election of United States senators by a direct vote of the people.

Delegates to the national convention were elected as follows:

At large—Mrs. Joel Russell, Samuel Fowler, John H. Hector, Jesse Yarnell, John Bidwell, and R. H. McDonald.

Provisional delegates—W. W. Smith, C. J. Covillaud, L. J. Becket, Mrs. Whitmore, John Dewey, and W. H. Somers.

First district—L. Ewing, J. Robinson. Alternates—L. B. Scranton, Mrs. F. A. Lake.

Second district—W. O. Clark, S. M. McLean. Alternate—L. W. Elliott.

Third district—C. H. Dunn, J. Wells. Alternates—W. W. Smith, S. P. Meads.

Fourth district—R. H. McDonald, Mrs. Skelton.

Fifth district—L. W. Kimball, T. B. Stewart. Alternate—L. J. Becket.

Sixth district—H. C. Witner, W. R. Goodwin.

The following were chosen presidential electors: Jesse F. Wilson, W. H. Briggs, A. J. Gregg, H. H. Luse, Charles W. Pedlar, A. D. Boren.

Robert Thompson was nominated for chief justice of the supreme court.

The republican state central committee met at San Francisco, March 14th, and issued a call for a convention to meet at Sacramento on May 1st following, to elect delegates to the national republican convention. The convention met in the assembly chamber, and was called to order by A. P. Williams, chairman of the state central committee. M. M. Estee was elected temporary, and later, permanent chairman. The committee on platform and resolutions was composed of Grove L. Johnson, J. A. Barham, S. D. Woods, John A. Eagon, L. B. Mizner, W. H. Dimond, A. P. Williams, John F. Swift, T. G. Phelps, H. V. Morehouse, R. B. Carpenter, R. C. Gaskill, F. S. Sprague, W. S. Woods, George A. Knight, and N. P. Chipman. The following was submitted as a majority report:

1. We heartily indorse the administration of Governor Waterman as able, honest, and economical, giving good promise for the future, and as demonstrating most conclusively that the affairs of the state of California can be conducted upon business principles, with honor to the officer, satisfaction to the people and credit to the state.

2. We commend the republican members of the house of representatives from California, Messrs. McKenna, Felton, Morrow and Vandever, for their fidelity to the interests of their constituents, and for the ability with which they have discharged the duties of their high and responsible positions. One and all they deserve well of the people.

3. For more than the third of a century the senior senator from California has lived amongst us. He was our war governor, and in the hour of the nation's supreme peril he rendered most important and illustrious services to his country. The executive skill displayed by him in private and in public life, his commanding business ability, his intimate and thorough acquaintance with public affairs, the clean record made by him in all official positions, as well as in the business world, his loyalty ever manifested to California, his broad and unparalleled philanthropy, which has dedicated a princely fortune to the erection and maintenance of an institution where the advantages of the highest education will be open, without cost, to the child of the poorest laborer, as well as the scion of the millionaire, his entire freedom from factional feeling or strife in the party, added to his purity of character and lifelong devotion to the principles of the republican party, justly entitle Leland Stanford to the confidence of the people of California.

4. We hail with pleasure the action of the republican United States senate in its amendment to the so-called bond purchase bill, made in the interest of silver coinage; and we denounce the conduct of the democratic house of representatives in smothering the bill and amendment in committee, at the reprehensible dictation of the president, as bad policy, conducive only to the benefit of the speculators in gold. We demand the remonetization of silver and its free coinage, believing that its rehabilitation as lawful money equal to gold will be of great advantage to the people, particularly the poorer classes of our citizens. We favor the issue by the national government of certificates for every dollar of silver bullion deposited in its vaults, for by so doing the country will be furnished with a safe currency adapted to the wants of the people and increasing in amount with the wealth and population of our nation.

5 We view with alarm the increase of immigration into the United States of anarchists, nihilists, and socialists and other undesirable persons who have no just appreciation of political liberty or understanding of the duties or dignities of American citizens; and we favor such legislation as will prevent the coming of such persons into our country. We demand the rigid enforcement of the law which provides for the exclusion of European or other laborers under contract from our shores. We demand the strictest and most rigid enforcement, in their true spirit as well as their letter, of the naturalization laws by the various courts of the state.

6. The republican party, from its birth, has always been the special friend of the free public schools of the country. We are now, as ever, in favor of the most watchful care over such schools, to the end that they may be kept forever free from sectarian or political influences. The education of the children of the land is the sacred duty of the citizens thereof. That duty can only be properly performed by strict attention to the details of their management, as well as to the funds so lavishly provided by the people for their support. The end of popular government in America will quickly and surely follow the disintegration of the schools or the school fund, hence all attacks made thereon, whether open or covert, in the name of politics or religion, must be sternly discountenanced and promptly defeated. The republican party calls attention, with pardonable pride to its labors in the past for our free public schools as a boundless guaranty for its conduct in the future.

7. We arraign the present democratic administration of the coun-

try as having been false at once to its pledges and the interests of the nation confided to its care. Its foreign policy has been characterized by cowardly stupidity and the absence of any true American spirit. The dominion of Canada, not even an independent power, destroys our fishing fleet, maltreats its owners, and ruins our fishermen, without any effort at redress being made by the government. Weak and distracted Mexico, that exists as a nation merely by sufferance, imprisons and judicially murders our citizens, without even a protest from Washington authorities. The barbarians of Morocco, once soundly whipped by American sailors, now insult the United States consul, while confiscating the property and scourging the bodies of United States citizens, with no reproof or punishment. The empire of Germany forces naturalized citizens into its army, despite their pleas as Americans for protection and exemption, and no demand for their release is made or insisted upon. Its home policy has been one unbroken series of assaults upon the faith of the nation and abject subserviency to the south and its sectional demands. Maimed veterans of the war that saved the union are displaced from office to make room for unrepentant rebels. The civil service rules are flagrantly disregarded in all the large cities of the nation, that the thugs of Baltimore, the heelers of Philadelphia and the "b'hoys" of New York may receive reward for their fraudulent election services. The cry for aid from the suffering and dependent poor of that grand army of soldiers and sailors who followed Grant and Porter, Sherman and Farragut, to victory, is contemptuously disregarded and the pension law bill for them is vetoed, while every bill for the payment of claims from southern brigadiers for losses in the war is promptly signed.

8. The interests of the navy have been shamefully neglected and our flag permitted to be discredited by reason of the inability of our ships of war to sail the ocean, or to resist a collision in peaceful waters with an ordinary yacht. The whole seaboard coast of the country has been left unprotected, and not a dollar has been expended in its defense, until to-day our great cities are at the mercy of the ironclads of blustering tenth-rate powers, while our forts in San Francisco harbor are destitute of powder enough even to fire a salute of welcome to visiting men-of-war of friendly nations; and at the same time the vast surplus accumulated by economical republican administrations has been allowed to remain unused in the treasury vaults, a standing invitation to corrupt schemes of bounty legislation.

9. And, finally, the magnificent manufacturing and industrial

interests of the whole people, so long the boast of every true citizen, have been and are now threatened with total destruction by the free-trade fallacies, born of a belief in the principles of the beaten southern confederacy, and given power in the halls of congress by a solid south, led by the same forces and filled with the same spirit that made secession possible and the civil war a necessity.

10. We regard the presence of the Chinese in our midst as an evil fraught with the most dangerous consequences to the people and country alike. We rejoice that our eastern brethren have at last awakened to the curses inevitably attendant upon the admixture of Chinese with Anglo-Saxon or English-speaking population, and we beg them to heed our warning, ere it becomes too late to save the republic from the myriad hordes of Asiatic barbarians that threaten to overwhelm us with their numbers and customs. We demand the unconditional repeal and abrogation of all laws or treaties that permit these Mongolian locusts to land upon our shores, and the enactment of such laws as will speedily rid us of those now here. We denounce the treaties suggested by the president and his secretary of state as mere trifling with a great question and unworthy the support of any good citizen.

11. The theory upon which this nation was founded is that the majority shall govern. To ascertain the will of that majority elections are held, at which, in theory, the people express their sentiments, and their ballots when counted decide the results. Practically, however, such is not the case in some of the states of this union dominated by the democratic party and officered by the chiefs of the late southern confederacy. The perpetuity of our free government depends upon the fact that there shall be a fair ballot and an honest count in every precinct of every county of every state in the federal union. Up to the present time, such is not the case in a number of states of this union, but, on the contrary, the will of the majority therein is stifled by fraud and violence, and the republican majorities which would be given in six of the southern states are suppressed by the bowie-knife and the shotgun. We demand of the national administration that it secure to republicans and democrats alike this inestimable blessing of a free citizen, that his vote shall be freely given and honestly counted, whether it is cast in the state of Louisiana or Massachusetts, in Mississippi or California; and until the time comes when every citizen of whatever color shall be permitted openly to express his sentiments in all parts of the union, and his vote shall be freely given and honestly counted, the day of

reconstruction, made necessary by the blackness of an unholy rebellion, is not yet ended. We pledge the entire energies of the
republican party to securing the desired result of a free ballot and
an honest count in every state.

12. We proclaim anew our allegiance to the doctrine that protection to our home industries is the fundamental law of our nation's
career. The republican party for a quarter of a century has been
the defender of that principle, and has maintained it in full force in
national affairs, and to-day appeals to the people to support that
doctrine, because of the glorious results that have followed its enforcement. Under its beneficent influence, the industrial, mechanical, and manufacturing industries of the United States have developed with marvelous rapidity, filling the whole land with the
healthful music of loom and forge, of shop and factory, and enabling
by their productive and enlarging capacity the country to absorb,
without financial or social disturbance, a million soldiers into peaceful pursuits ; to bear with ease an unprecedented national debt,
frequently to reduce the interest, and regularly each month the
principal of that debt; to give remunerative employment to the
labor and capital of American citizens and to make the credit of our
country so good that its bonds sell at a premium equal to one-fourth
of their par value. We denounce the effort now being made to alter
the American protective system as an attempt by foreign capitalists,
northern theorists, and southern schemers to place the underpaid and
poorly-fed labor of the old world into unfair competition with the
full-paid and full-fed labor of our country, and thus to degrade the
American workingman to a level with the paupers of Europe. We
believe in judicious and enlightened tariff reform, but demand that
such reform be initiated by the friends, not the enemies of the
American protective system, and that it be carefully timed, so as to
give all our varied industries an equal chance in the commerce of
the nation and the world.

13. The republicans of this state four years ago instructed their
delegates to the national republican convention to vote for James G.
Blaine, and we regret his refusal to allow his name to be used as a
candidate at the coming national convention. The republicans of
the state of California, through this convention, now reiterate their
confidence in the integrity, patriotism and eminent ability, as well
as their admiration for the conspicuous public services of James G.
Blaine, and we are proud of his career as an American statesman.

George A. Knight presented the following as a minority report: That while the republican party contains many men who, by their recognized ability and devotion to the principles of the party, have proved themselves worthy of public support and confidence and capability of filling honorably the highest gift of the people, the republican party recognizes in the Hon. James G. Blaine an eminently able and tried exponent of the principles of protection of home industries, of large experience in public life, of the purest public and private character, and possessing in a marked degree those personal qualities which would do honor to the office of president of the United States, but leave our delegates unpledged and unembarrassed by instructions, and free to act for the best interests of the country.

The minority report was rejected, and the majority report adopted.

John F. Swift, Creed Haymond, Henry T. Gage, and M. M. Estee were elected delegates at large to the national convention, with N. W. Spaulding, E. P. Danforth, Richard Gird, and J. A. Clayton as their respective alternates. Delegates from the congressional districts were elected as follows: First district, H. W. Byington and J. F. Ellison; alternates, W. H. Pratt and M. C. Been. Second district, D. E. Knight and A. M. Simpson; alternates, W. A. Long and W. G. Long. Third district, R. D. Robbins and Eli S. Denison; alternates, M. P. Ivory and W. C. Van Fleet. Fourth district, W. H. Dimond and C. F. Crocker; alternates, John T. Cutting and David McClure. Fifth district, M. H. De Young and F. C. Franck; alternates, P. Beamish and Duncan McPherson. Sixth district, H. L. Osborne and Paris Kilburn; alternates, J. M. Martin and F. H. Heald.

The convention adjourned *sine die* on May 1st, having finished its work in one day.

The democratic state central committee met at San Francisco, April 2d, and issued a call for a convention to be held at Los Angeles, on May 15th. On that day the convention met and was called to order by W. D. English, chairman of the state central committee. R. F. Del Valle was elected temporary chairman, and permanent chairman on final organization. The committee on platform and resolutions consisted of Stephen M. White, J. A. Hill, E. S. Lippitt, D. A. Ostrom, A. C. Paulsell, W. S. Manlove, W. W. Foote, P. J. Murphy, P. F. Dunne, N. Bowden, John Foley, W. H. Hamᵣmond, J. P. Haynes, E. W. Townsend, U. S. Gregory, Russell Heath, and J. W. Levison.

The committee made the following report, which was unani‑ ᵤmously adopted :

We indorse the administration of Grover Cleveland. His earnest and intelligent efforts in the interests of the people have justly won the plaudits of all patriotic citizens. When he was elected to per‑ form the duties of the high office the functions of which he has so ably discharged, our political opponents confidently avowed that his incumbency would result in disaster and ruin. The prosperity which ᵣhas accompanied his administration, the unflagging zeal which he has manifested in promoting the welfare of all, the unsullied char‑ acter of the public servants of his selection by whom he is sur‑ rounded have demonstrated that the people were right in demanding a change of administration, and that the permanency of our insti‑ tutions and the maintenance of our proud position as a people de‑ pend upon democratic ascendency. The democracy, under the leadership of Grover Cleveland, seeks to deal at once with the issues of the day and to utilize governmental authority to improve the condition of the governed. The republican organization, controlled as it is by persons whose transgressions have driven them from place, seeks restoration to power by appealing to issues buried in the ob‑ livion of a quarter of a century. Its aspiration, as contained in the declarations of its leaders, is to revive dissensions and discord, which have long since been forgotten by all right-thinking men.

The democracy is pledged to an equitable revision of the tariff. The republican party, while admitting the inequality and injustice of the revenue laws enacted under the excitement and necessities of a great war, persistently fails to suggest any reform, and obsti‑ nately seeks to defeat all efforts directed at the adoption of a just and comprehensive measure. We believe in fostering American industry, but we oppose the subsidizing of great monopolies and the centralization of money in the hands of a few autocrats whose aims and wishes are wholly at variance with the welfare of the toilers of the land. We heartily indorse that progressive measure, commen‑ surate with and made necessary by the growth and needs of our country, the message of the president urging a reform in our tariff which will lessen the exactions now practiced upon our people.

1. That this convention recommend the passage of an act of con‑ gress providing for the free coinage of both gold and silver, by the

terms of which act all gold and silver bullion offered at the several' mints of the United States shall be received in exchange for money, or gold or silver certificates, at the rate now fixed by law for stand- ard dollars of gold and silver, which certificates shall be receivable for public purposes and interchangeable for gold and silver, as the case may be.

2. We are, as ever, absolutely opposed to Chinese immigration. We congratulate the people upon the success which has attended the efforts of the democratic administration in so amending our treaty with the Chinese empire as to practically exclude the Mongol- ian from our shores. Long years of republican control failed to accomplish this result, and it was left for the administration of Grover Cleveland to formulate successfully a treaty which settles a question with which republicans have been incompetent to deal. By this treaty all prior-residence pleas are rendered ineffectual, and all return certificates now extant absolutely invalidated. We pledge our representatives in congress to procure the enactment of such legislation as will render it impossible for republican federal judges to defeat its purposes or nullify the provisions of a treaty which has for the first time rendered absolute exclusion possible.

3. The public lands of the United States should be disposed of to actual settlers only. During republican dominancy, immense bodies of the national domain passed into the hands of corporate and for- eign syndicates formed for the creation of individual fortunes. The terms of these grants were persistently violated by the beneficiaries, and these violations passed unheeded until a democratic administra- tion, in obedience to the platform of its principles and the last na- tional convention, declared them forfeited, thus tendering to those seeking homes in good faith more than forty millions of acres which had been withheld from the people under republican rule for the benefit of the selfish few. We commend the policy of Grover Cleveland in this regard, and congratulate our chief executive upon the success which has attended the administration of the affairs of the United States land and survey offices within the state of Cali- fornia.

4. We are in favor of the election of United States senators by direct vote of the people of the several states, and earnestly urge the adoption of such an amendment to the constitution of the United States as will accomplish that result.

5. That the democracy of this state hereby proclaims itself in favor of the establishment of a postal telegraph law, whereby the

general government shall combine with its present cheap postal system a system of cheap postal telegraphy.

6. We endorse the action and policy of our democratic senator and representatives in congress, and are confident that the welfare of our state is safe in their keeping.

7. That we favor the enactment of such measures as shall place our various industries on an equality before the law in the use and distribution of the waters of the streams of this state for irrigation, mining, milling, and other beneficial purposes.

8. We commend the action of our democratic state officials in pressing the California tax cases toward ultimate decisions, and hope this most important issue will not be permitted to rest without final adjudication upon its merits. We once more condemn the acts of those corporations which have persistently refused to pay their lawful portion of the public revenue. This failure to respond to a just demand has seriously contracted the public school fund and must render our educational system less effective until collection is enforced or the honest taxpayer is compelled to contribute beyond his proportionate share. The republican party, ever sincere in its professions, has finally disavowed all intention to resist the demands of its corporate masters. It refuses to stigmatize their encroachments or to question their misconduct, but on the contrary, as the action of its late state convention demonstrates, yields ready compliance to their dictation. While fully appreciating the benefits of organized capital, we declare that the protection of those privileges which our constitution declares are the common heritage, is paramount to the increase of individual wealth.

9. We believe that the public should be protected from the great non-taxpaying trusts and corporations which now challenge the authority of the government. The democratic party was founded to maintain the interests and liberties of the people; it alone is competent to resist those encroachments which imperil the safety of the state. The republican party, while professing to be the friend of labor, has demonstrated by its uniform action that its tendencies are toward the creation of monopolies and trusts through whose instrumentality alone it hopes to perpetuate its existence. The democratic party emanated from the people. Its aim has always been to care for the weak and to be just to the strong. While it is ever ready to promote the industries and to stimulate enterprise, it will never permit wealth to shirk its rightful obligations or to impose

35

upon poverty the expenses of a government formed for the benefit of all.

10. That in the death of our late governor, Washington Bartlett, the state of California lost an upright citizen and an honorable and conscientious executive. As county clerk and mayor of San Fran-·cisco, and as senator from that city, he gave unmistakable proof of his capability and integrity. Elevated to the high office of governor of the state, he had but just begun to give the people the benefits of his great experience when he was summoned to his lasting rest. Appreciating the lofty qualities which made him the favorite of the people, we join in the universal sorrow which has followed his untimely demise. His life furnishes an example which may be well imitated. His faithful discharge of public duties demonstrated the sincerity of his democracy.

11. As Grover Cleveland possesses the great qualities essential to a chief magistrate of this great republic, and satisfied that the most· sacred interests of the people have never been committed to purer or abler keeping, we express the earnest hope that he will for a second time be selected as the standard-bearer of the democratic party.

Nominations were made as follows:

For electors-at-large: B. D. Murphy and C. P. Berry, they receiving 366 and 479 votes respectively, to 185 for John P. Irish. R. B. Mitchell and H. J. Corcoran were elected alternates.

Niles Searls for chief justice, on the second ballot, by 284 votes to 179 for J. F. Sullivan, and 47 for J. W. Armstrong.

J. F. Sullivan for associate justice.

For representatives in congress: first district, Thomas L. Thompson; second district, Marion Biggs; third district, Ben Morgan; Fourth district, Robert Ferral; fifth district, Thomas J. Clunie; sixth district, R. B. Terry.

For presidential electors: First district, F. Beringer; alternate, E. S. Lippitt. Second district, A. Caminetti; alternate, A. T. Vogelsang. Third district, Charles A. Jenkins; alternate, E.. E. Leake. Fourth district, P. J. Murphy; alternate, P. F. Dunne. Fifth district, N. Bowden; alternate, Joseph Napthaly. Sixth district, Byron Waters; alternate, B. S. Hayne.

For delegates to national democratic convention: At large, M. F. Tarpey, Stephen M. White, Clay W. Taylor, and W. D. English; alternates, R. M. Fitzgerald, Victor Montgomery, M. T. Dooling, and E. H. Bryant; first district, James E. Murphy and Robert Cosner; alternates, F. E. Johnston and W. P. Mathews; second dis. trict, J. A. Filcher and George H. Castle; alternates, J. D. Young and L. Burwell; third district, J. J. White and E. G. Blessing; alternates, E. McGettigan and L. B. Adams; fourth district, Joseph Clark and Edward Curtis; alternates, Samuel Newman and S. Braunhart; fifth district, C. T. Ryland and Maurice Schmidt; alter. nates, J. S. Potts and C. P. Stone; sixth district, William Graves and V. D. Knupp; alternates, B. Cohn and W. D. Grady.

The convention adjourned *sine die*, May 17th.

Pursuant to a resolution adopted by the state central committee of the American party, May 16th, the convention assembled in Pioneer hall, San Francisco, July 4th. Two hundred and seventeen delegates were present, representing more than half the counties of the State. L. A. Garnett was elected temporary chairman. P. D. Wigginton, S. S. Holl, A. A. Daggett, B. C. Cuvillier, V. J. Robertson, W. L. Peet, Chapman, Norton, and Wilson were appointed members of the committee on platform and resolutions. On permanently organizing, P. D. Wigginton was elected chairman without opposition, and A. A. Daggett and S. S. Holl, vice-chairmen.

The following platform was adopted:

Whereas, Believing that the time has arrived when a due regard for the present and future prosperity of our country makes it imperative that the people of the United States of America should take full and entire control of their government to the exclusion of the revolutionary and incendiary horde of foreigners now seeking our shores from every quarter of the world; and recognizing that the first and most important duty of an American citizen is to maintain this government in all attainable purity and strength, we make the following declaration of principles:

1. That all law-abiding citizens of the United States of America, whether native or foreign born, are political equals, and all are entitled to and should receive the full protection of the laws.

Whereas, There are seventeen states in this union wherein persons are allowed to vote at all elections, without being citizens of the United States; and whereas, such a system tends to place the management of the government in the hands of those who owe no allegiance to our political institutions, therefore, be it resolved,

2. That the federal constitution should be so amended that the federal and state governments shall be forbidden and prevented from

conferring upon any person the right to vote, unless such person be a citizen of the United States.

3. That the naturalization laws of the United States should be unconditionally repealed.

4. That the soil of America should belong to Americans; that no alien non-resident should be permitted to own real estate in the United States, and that the real possessions of the resident alien should be limited in value and area.

5. That all persons not in sympathy with our government should be prohibited from immigrating to the United States of America for the purpose of business or the intention of permanent residence;

6. That we favor educating the boys and girls of American citizens as mechanics and artisans, thus fitting them to fill the places now filled by foreigners, who supply the greater part of our skilled labor and thereby almost entirely control all the great industries of our country, save, perhaps, that of agriculture alone. And, in order to accomplish the object here stated, we demand that the states establish free technical schools, wherein American boys and girls may be taught trades and thereby become skilled artisans and mechanics.

7. That we believe "bossism" in politics to be an outgrowth of foreign influence. We condemn it as un-American and tending to a corruption of the ballot-box. We declare that the American party shall not have bosses.

8. That we believe in equal and just taxation, and to accomplish this necessary reform we favor a uniform reduction of taxes on the real estate of the cultivator of the soil, and the imposing of advanced rates on property coming under the head of luxuries.

9. That we are in favor of fostering and encouraging American industries of every class and kind, and to that end would protect our home productions and manufactures, and inaugurate and maintain a system that will not only exclude the competitive cheap labor productions of other countries, but will also exclude the cheap laborers of other countries and prevent them coming here to compete with American workingmen; and,

Whereas, One of the greatest evils of unrestricted foreign immigration is the reduction of the wages of the American working-man and woman to the level of the underfed and underpaid labor of foreign countries,

10. Therefore, we demand that congress pass an immigration law whereby a per capita tax shall be levied upon and collected from all

immigrants coming to the United States; and that such tax be made large enough to restrain further immigration from all foreign coun-·tries.

11. That universal education is a necessity of our government, and that our American free-school system should be maintained and preserved as the safeguard of American liberty; that in our free common schools there shall be no language taught except the English language.

12. That under no circumstances should any of the public funds be diverted to or used for the benefit of any sectarian or ecclesiastical school or institution whatever.

13. That in view of the neglected and defenseless condition of our harbors and sea coast, a liberal expenditure of the surplus which accumulates from our system of taxation should be devoted to erecting fortifications for the defense of our harbors and sea-coast and for the creation and support of an efficient navy; and that such expenditures should be made in the employment of American citizens only.

14. That the American party recognizes in the saloon the great agency by which corruption in politics is fostered and the power of the bosses maintained; and hereby pledges itself honestly and earnestly to work for the restriction of the evil to the narrowest possible limit.

The following were elected delegates to the national convention of the American party, to be held at Washington: F. M. Pixley, V. J. Robertson, P. D. Wigginton, and A. A. Daggett, delegates at large; E. E. Hall and Wilfred Page, from first congressional district; N. M. Orr and J. F. McSwain, from second; J. M. Bassett and G. W. Grayson, from third; N. S. Keith and L. A. Garnett, from fourth; N. P. Cole and N. F. Spear, from fifth, and C. N. Wilson and L. S. Rogers, from the sixth congressional district. This list of delegates was increased by the addition of the names of M. J. Donahoe, Charles Riggs, N. George, and G. C. Jennings.

Presidential electors were nominated as follows:

P. D. Wigginton, F. M. Pixley, A. A. Daggett, J. West Martin, and Drury Melone were nominated for electors at large. On a ballot being taken, Wigginton and Pixley receiving 81 and 70 votes respectively, were declared the nominees over Daggett 69, Martin 7, and Melone 5. Alexander Duncan was named for elector for the first congressional district, N. M. Orr for the second, J· West

Martin for the third, L. A. Garnett for the fourth, D. Lambert for the fifth, and C. N. Wilson for the sixth. J. West Martin afterward resigned, and Daniel Inman was substituted by the state central committee. J L. Lyon was substituted for P. D. Wigginton, who was afterward nominated for the office of vice-president.

The nomination of a candidate for the office of chief justice was referred to the state central committee, as was also the selection of alternates for the national delegates and presidential electors. The convention adjourned *sine die* on July 5th.

The state central committee nominated W. H. Beatty for chief justice and J. D. Works for associate justice. The following were nominated for congress: W. D. Reynolds, from first district; J. F. McSwain, from second district; S. Solon Holl, from third district; Frank M. Pixley, from fourth district; Frank M. Stone, from fifth district, and A. A. Daggett from sixth district.

The republican state central committee met at San Francisco, May 4th, and issued a call for a convention to be held in San Francisco, July 31st. Nominations were to be made for the offices of presidential electors, congressmen, chief justice, and associate justice of the supreme court. The delegates assembled at the appointed time and were called to order by W. H. Dimond, chairman of the state central committee. George G. Blanchard was elected temporary, and later, permanent chairman. The committee on platform and resolutions was appointed, to consist of David McClure, Pratt of Humboldt; C. A. Garter, J. C. Campbell, J. M. Fulweiler, C. T. Jones, J. P. Abbott; Bayless of San Francisco, John T. Dare, Cooper of Santa Cruz, A. R. Conklin, J. G. North, W. H. Dimond, R. B. Carpenter, L. B. Mizner, G. W. Francis, and W. S. Wood.

The committee made the following report, which was unanimously adopted:

1. That the republicans of the state of California, in convention assembled, indorse and re-affirm the national platform of the republican party adopted at its convention recently held in Chicago, and we congratulate the country upon the nomination of Harrison and Morton, the true representatives of the American policy of protection to American industries and American labor.

2. That we declare the welfare of California demands and the dignity of labor and the interests of capital require the maintenance

by the national government of the American system of a tariff protection. Under this policy, which has been constantly supported by
the republican party since its foundation, our varied industries have
been fostered and extended, our laboring classes have enjoyed better
wages than in any other part of the world, and the whole country
has achieved unparalleled prosperity. We denounce the free-trade
policy which the democratic party has advocated since 1840 as dangerous to the national interests of the country and to the welfare of
American labor. We arraign the democratic party of California
for supporting the national democratic party, which stands upon a
platform that declared for British free trade, as promulgated by the
Mills bill, and view with alarm this assault upon our American
labor. We insist that the success of this British policy would destroy
the growing industries of our commonwealth, especially the grape,
raisin, nut, wool, lumber, borax, lead, quicksilver, sugar-beet, and
cereal industries, and also our manufacturing industries, and would
reduce the wages of our workingmen.

3. That we pledge to the American people, and especially the
people of California, that our candidates for congress, if elected, will
sustain the protection policy of the republican party and will oppose
the British and solid south policy of the democratic party; that our
American industries shall be protected for the benefit of the American people, and that American labor shall be fostered and protected
as against the competition of foreign cheap labor. We denounce
as un-American and contrary to the best interests of the republic
the cheap-labor policy of the democratic solid south of to-day as we
did the slave-policy of the democratic solid south of 1861, and we
declare that the one was and the other, if permitted to continue,
will be destructive of the best interests of the laboring classes of this
republic.

4. That the purity of the ballot is the pillar of the state, and the
denial of a free ballot to the humblest American citizen, whatever
his color or race, imperils the liberties of the people. We, therefore,
denounce as dangerous to our country the democratic policy of the
solid south in depriving the colored people living there of their right
to vote. A government based upon frauds committed against the
elective franchise cannot long survive.

5. That a financial policy, whereby both gold and silver shall
form the basis of circulation, whether the money used by the people
be coin, or certificates redeemable in coin, or both, as convenience
may require, is imperatively demanded.

6. That we commend the republican members of congress from California for their fidelity to the interests of their constituents, and for the ability with which they have discharged the duties of their high and responsible positions.

7. That we commend our representatives in congress for their efforts in behalf of restrictive Chinese legislation, thus redeeming the pledges of the party made for them, and renew our determination to make such restriction effective and in every way to prevent the competition of Chinese with American labor. We thank the republican national convention for its emphatic declaration on the subject, and we have implicit faith that the republican party of the nation will protect us in all our industries against the Chinese.

Nominations were made as follows:

William H. Beatty for chief justice, by 312 votes, to 123 for W. E. Greene, and 23 for G. G. Clough.

J. D. Works for associate justice, by acclamation.

W. H. L. Barnes and John F. Swift for electors at large, by acclamation, with G. G. Blanchard and C. T. Jones as alternates.

The following were nominated by the respective district conventions:

For representatives in congress: first district, J. J. DeHaven; second district, John A. Eagon; third district, Joseph McKenna; fourth district, W. W. Morrow; fifth district, T. G. Phelps; sixth district, William Vandever.

For presidential electors: first district, T. L. Carothers; alternate, C. C. Bush. Second district, G. W. Schell; alternate, F. W. Street. Third district, L. B. Mizner; alternate, J. P. Abbott. Fourth district, Samuel M. Shortridge; alternate, C. Dunker. Fifth district, George A. Knight; alternate, James R. Lowe. Sixth district, H. M. Streeter; alternate, H. V. Morehouse.

The convention adjourned *sine die* on the same day.

At the election held in November all of the candidates on the republican ticket were elected, with the exception of two of the six congressmen. The official returns were as follows:

For presidential electors: Republican—Swift, 124,754; Barnes, 124,754; Schell, 124,751; Carothers, 124,789; Knight, 124,816; Streeter, 124,809; Shortridge, 124,781; Mizner, 124,802. Democratic—Berry, 117,698; B. D. Murphy, 117,676; Beringer, 117,697; Caminetti, 117,729; Jenkins, 117,626; P. J. Murphy, 117,634;

Bowden, 117,640; Waters, 117,675. American—Lyon, 1,340; Inman, 1,545; Garnett, 1,555; Wilson, 696; Duncan, 1,545; Pixley, 1,591; Lambert, 1,544; Orr, 1,539. Prohibition—Bidwell, 5,761; McDonald, 5,760; Luse, 5,744; Wilson, 5,748; Briggs, 5,745; Gregg, 5,737; Pedlar, 5,746; Boren, 5,736.

For chief justice, unexpired term—W. H. Beatty, 124,617; Niles Searls, 119,901; Robert Thompson, 5,261.

For associate justice, unexpired term—J. D. Works, 123,477; J. F. Sullivan, 122,974.

For representatives in congress: First district—J. J. De Haven, 19.345; T. L. Thompson, 19,019; W. D. Reynolds, 428. Second district—Marion Biggs, 19,064; John A. Eagon, 17,541; S. M. McLean, 913; J. F. McSwain, 138. Third district—Joseph McKenna, 19,912; Ben Morgan, 14,633; W. W. Smith, 657; S. Solon Holl, 338. Fourth district—W. W. Morrow, 14,217; Robert Ferral, 13,624; Frank M. Pixley, 173. Fifth district—T. J. Clunie, 20,276; T. G. Phelps, 20,225. Sixth district—W. Vandever, 35,406; R. B. Terry, 29,453; J. G. Miller, 2,375; A. Daggett, 150.

The presidential electors, Barnes, Mizner, Knight, Shortridge, Streeter, Swift, Carothers, and Schell, met at Sacramento, January 14th, 1889, and cast their votes for Benjamin Harrison and Levi P. Morton for president and vice president, respectively, of the United States. Mizner was selected to convey the returns to Washington.

CHAPTER XXXV.

1890. Prohibition Convention.—American Party Convention.—Republican Convention.—Democratic Convention.

The state convention of the prohibition party convened at Pioneer hall, San Francisco, April 9th. It was called to order by George Morris, chairman of the executive committee. John Bidwell was elected temporary chairman. M. C. Winchester, George T. Elliott, D. C. Taylor, C. H. Dunn, and others were appointed a committee on platform and resolutions. On permanently organizing, L. W. Elliot was made chairman.

The following platform was reported by the committee, and after much discussion was adopted:

1. That the national prohibition platform meets our unqualified approval and endorsement.

2. That the liquor traffic has become an evil of such vast magnitude, boldly and insolently violating and defying the laws that have been made to control it, endangering the stability and perpetuity of free government, debauching and dominating the political parties that foster and protect it, wasting the wealth of the state and nation, driving out the sunshine of peace and happiness from the homes of the people, making them wretched and desolate; breeding immorality, vice, and crime; filling our jails, penitentiaries, and insane asylums with its wretched and ruined victims, the best interests of society and good government demand the total suppression of the liquor traffic by both state and national constitutional amendments, and that we will continue to make this the cardinal principle of the prohibition party.

3. That the attitude of the old political parties toward the temperance question is such as to destroy all confidence in their promises to suppress or control the liquor traffic, and that, therefore, the prohibition party, as a political organization, is an imperative necessity, and will make no compromise with those parties on high license, or other compromise measures, whose only object is to secure the liquor vote.

4. That we enter our emphatic protest against the appropriation of money from the state treasury to advance the wine interests, and for other pernicious and immoral purposes, and denounce it as an outrage upon the tax-payers of the state, and will not vote or give our influence to any candidate for office who is not opposed to such appropriations.

5. That we affirm the dignity of labor, and are in hearty sympathy with all just and enlightened movements for the elevation of the laboring classes and the harmonious co-operation of labor and capital, and to this end, we are in favor of the closing of our shops and factories on Saturday afternoon when practicable.

6. That we most kindly and cordially invite to our ranks the fathers and mothers whose homes are endangered, the artisan in his shop, the mechanic at his bench, the toiler in the field, every wage earner of whatever profession or occupation, and every organization that has for its purpose the betterment of their fellow man, for the overthrow of this gigantic evil.

7. That the combination of trusts and monopolies to subsidize the public press, corrupt legislation and courts of justice, increase the

price of commodities, and oppress the wage-worker, is a gigantic usurpation of the people's rights, and that we favor the entire over-throw of such monopolies and trusts in the state and nation.

8. That we view with alarm the wholesale corruption, bribery, and political bossism that has obtained in the state elections, and demand such a revision of our laws in the system of voting as shall secure to citizens of every class equal rights, and most effectually prevent the abuses now existing, and to that end we favor the Aus-tralian ballot system.

9. That we recognize a common bond of sympathy between the prohibition party of California and the farmers' alliance, an organi-zation recently formed by the union of the grangers and the knights of labor, and inasmuch as the farmers' alliance has come out squarely for prohibition, we extend to them the right hand of fellowship, and invite them to make common cause with us in the coming cam-paign.

10. That we favor the enactment and rigid enforcement of what are known as civil service reform laws, and their extension to all clerical positions and the postoffice system.

11. That we favor the changing of the tax system of the state so as to secure the payment of taxes in equal amounts half yearly.

12. That we are in favor of government ownership and control of the railroads and telegraph lines, and the management of the same for the public good. And that we favor the establishment of postal savings banks.

13. That we favor the election of United States senators by the direct vote of the people.

14. That we favor a modification of the naturalization laws of the United States so as to require a longer residence than now required, and so as to guard more carefully against the naturalization of ignorant, vicious, and criminal persons.

15. That we favor a law requiring an educational test for the right of suffrage, and that we favor extending the right of suffrage to all persons otherwise qualified, without regard to sex.

16. That we recognize the Woman's Christian Temperance Union as one of the most successful of all the allies of the temperance cause, and especially of the prohibition work, and that we ask their con-tinued co-operation in our work.

17. That we favor the enactment of a law requiring one day in seven as a day of rest as a civil institution, but providing that when any individual habitually rests from labor upon a certain day of the

week, such person shall not be required to rest upon any other day; and providing further that in no case shall intoxicating liquors be sold upon such rest day.

Nominations were made as follows:

For governor, John Bidwell; for lieutenant-governor, A. M. Hough; for secretary of state, F. E. Kellogg; for treasurer, Henry French; for controller, M. C. Winchester; for attorney-general, Chauncey H. Dunn; for superintendent of public instruction, Miss S. M. Severance; for surveyor-general, E. M. Chase; for clerk of supreme court, J. T. Price; for members of congress, first district, L. B. Scranton; second district, J. S. Witherell; third district, O. O. Felkner; fourth district, J. Rowell; fifth district, E. F. Howe; sixth district, O. R. Dougherty. For railroad commissioners: first district, R. G. Hart; second district, H. H. Luse; third district, J. G. Miller. For members of state board of equalization: first district, H. B. Burlingame; second district, D. C. Taylor; third district, E. C. Gilbert; fourth district, S. Fowler.

The convention adjourned *sine die* on April 10th.

By a resolution of the state central committee of the American party the convention was called to meet in San Francisco, July 4th, but at a subsequent meeting of the committee held June 12th, the date was changed to August 4th. On the latter date the convention met at Pioneer hall, San Francisco. It was called to order by F. W. Eaton, chairman of the state central committee, and A. A. Daggett was elected temporary chairman. The committee on platform and resolutions was composed of J. M. Bassett, William Winnie, E. C. Williams, Clark Blethen, W. Mayerhofer, S. Solon Holl, I. N. Wright, H. C. Goodyear, and W. D. J. Hambly. On permanently organizing, A. A. Daggett was continued as chairman. The committee presented the following resolutions, which were adopted:

Whereas, Believing that the time has arrived when a due regard for the present and future prosperity of our country makes it imperative that the people of the United States of America should take full and entire control of their government to the exclusion of the revolutionary and incendiary horde of foreigners now seeking our shores from every quarter of the world, and recognizing that the first and most important duty of an American citizen is to maintain this government in all attainable purity and strength, we make the following declaration of principles:

1. That all law-abiding citizens of the United States of America, whether native or foreign born, are political equals and are entitled to and should receive the full protection of the laws.

Whereas, there are at least seventeen states in this union wherein persons are allowed to vote at all elections, without being citizens of the United States; and whereas such a system tends to place the management of the government in the hands of those who owe no allegiance to our political institutions; therefore, be it resolved,

2. That the federal constitution should be so amended that the federal and state governments shall be forbidden and prevented from conferring upon any person the right to vote, unless such person be a citizen of the United States.

3. That the naturalization laws of the United States should be unconditionally repealed.

4. That the soil of America should belong to Americans ; that no alien non-resident should hereafter be permitted to acquire real estate in the United States.

And whereas, tracts of millions of acres of land have heretofore been acquired and are now owned by subjects of foreign governments, which under existing laws may be transmitted, intact, from generation to generation, thus enabling foreigners to build up and maintain immense landed estates in this country ; therefore, resolved,

5. That we favor an amendment to the constitution of the United States prohibiting non-resident aliens from transmitting real property by will; and render for ever incompetent all persons whomsoever from taking real property from non-resident aliens by devise or descent.

And whereas, by reason of the lax condition of the state and national land laws, in reference to the disposition of the public land, aliens, resident and non-resident, have been enabled to acquire and have acquired vast tracts of the public lands, and have thereby deprived American citizens of their birthright; now, therefore, in order to prevent the continuance of this great evil, be it resolved,

6. That we demand that the national and state land laws be so amended that no persons except native born citizens shall be permitted to enter or purchase any public land from the state or national governments.

7. That the ownership of land by resident aliens should be limited in area and value.

8. That we favor educating the boys and girls of American citi-

zens as mechanics and artisans, thus fitting them to fill the places now filled by foreigners, who supply the greater part of our skilled labor and thereby almost entirely control all the great industries of our country, save, perhaps, that of agriculture alone, and, in order to accomplish the object here stated, we demand that the state establish free technical schools wherein American boys and girls may be taught trades and thereby become skilled artisans and mechanics.

9. That we believe in equal and just taxation, and to accomplish this necessary reform we favor a uniform reduction of taxes on the real estate of the cultivator of the soil, and the imposing of advanced rates on property coming under the head of luxuries.

10. That we are in favor of fostering and encouraging American industries of every class and kind, and to that end would protect our home productions and manufactures, and inaugurate and maintain a system that will not only exclude the competitive cheap labor productions of other countries, but will also exclude the cheap laborers of other countries and prevent them coming here to compete with American workingmen; but we denounce the so-called issue of protection versus free trade, as used by the democratic and republican parties, as a fraud and a snare, and we charge that the consideration which these parties manifest for the rights of American labor is a sham and a pretense. The best "protection" is that which protects the labor and life blood of the republic from the degrading competition with and contamination by imported foreigners; and the most dangerous "free trade" is that in paupers, criminals, communists, and anarchists, in which the balance has always been against the United States.

Whereas, One of the greatest evils of unrestricted foreign immigration is the reduction of the wages of the American workingman and woman to the level of the underfed and underpaid labor of foreign countries,

11. Therefore, we demand that congress pass immigration laws whereby a per capita tax shall be levied upon and collected from all immigrants coming to the United States, and that such tax be made large enough to restrain further immigration from all foreign countries; and that all persons not in sympathy with our government should be prohibited from immigrating to these United States.

12. We regard the American common school system as one of the chief factors in the formation and one of the principal powers for the perpetuation of our republican form of government. In a

government "of the people, by the people and for the people" intelligence is one of the principal elements of safety, and a common
school education should be made compulsory by law. Education is
a sacred debt which the present generation owes to the future.
The common schools must continue to be the nurseries of citizenship,
where our youths shall be taught the common branches, the history,
the principles, and the spirit of American institutions, and where
the highest standard of excellence as regards moral, mental, and industrial education shall be maintained, and from which shall be
rigidly excluded all sectarian and denominational teaching, in order
that children of all nationalities molded by them shall become
Americans. The common schools must be protected from all assaults, native or foreign, sectarian or ecclesiastical; and all private
schools must be under state inspection, and teach the English language as a preparation for intelligent citizenship. The American
flag ought to float over every school building in the land as an object
lesson in patriotism for childhood, and as a symbol to the world
that we consider these buildings the arsenals of our strength. As
an important step in defense of the common school system of education and the perpetuation of the separation of church and state we
join with other citizens in seeking to incorporate in the constitution
of the United States a sixteenth amendment embodying the following prohibitions: "No state shall pass any law respecting an
establishment of religion or prohibiting the free exercise thereof, or
use its property or credit, or any money raised by taxation, or
authorize either to be used for the purpose of founding, maintaining, or aiding by appropriation, payment for services, expenses, or
otherwise, any church, religious denomination, or religious society,
or any institution, society, or undertaking which is wholly or in part
under sectarian, or ecclesiastical control."

13. That after the year 1898, no person shall be allowed to exercise the right of suffrage unless he can speak, read, and write the
English language intelligently.

14. That the American party recognizes in the saloon the great
agency by which corruption in politics is fostered, and the power of
the bosses maintained; and hereby pledges itself to work honestly
and earnestly for the restriction of the evil to the narrowest possible limit.

15. That the American party believes in and will do its utmost
toward maintaining a pure ballot-box, and to that end we are in

favor of an election law which embodies the features and principles of the Australian ballot system.

16. That the American party believes in a free and full expression of the people upon all questions of public interest, and for the better attainment of this end we favor the enactment of a law by which any question of general import, upon the petition to the governor of three per cent of the total vote cast at the last previous election, shall be submitted to the electors at the next general election for their approval or rejection. Believing that the industries of America demand an increase of circulating medium, the American party hereby declares itself in favor of the free coinage of silver.

17. That we are heartily in favor of the bill introduced in the senate of the United States by the Hon. Leland Stanford, providing for loaning the money of the government to agriculturists at low rates of interest, taking as security therefor the land of the borrower; and we earnestly urge upon congress the passage of this bill.

A motion to strike out the last resolution was lost by a vote of 24 to 72.

Nominations for state officers were made on Tuesday, August 5th. For governor, John Bidwell received 71 votes on the first ballot, against 53 for Ben Morgan, and 7 for N. P. Chipman. The other nominations made were: For lieutenant-governor, Ben Morgan; for secretary of state, William S. Lyon; for state treasurer, Guy E. Grosse; for controller, M. C. Winchester; for attorney general, Chauncey H. Dunn; for surveyor-general, William L. Dixon; for superintendent of public instruction, D. Lambert; for clerk of supreme court, W. A. Beatty. Nominations for justice of supreme court were referred to the state central committee, and for congressmen, railroad commissioners, and members of board of equalization, to the delegates of the several districts. The name of J. D. Spencer was afterwards substituted for that of W. A. Beatty as nominee for clerk of supreme court. The ticket as finally completed, comprised, in addition to the foregoing, the names of W. H. Beatty for chief justice of the supreme court; Charles H. Garoutte, Ralph C. Harrison, and John J. De Haven, for associate justices; Thomas J. Geary, John P. Irish, T. V. Cator, and O. R. Dougherty, for congress from the first, third, fourth, and sixth districts, respectively; J. S. Swan, J. L. Lyon, R. H. Beamer, and H. A. Blodgett, for members of the state board of equalization, and William Beckman, J. M. Litchfield, and J. W. Rea, for railroad commisioners.

The republican state committee met in San Francisco, April 23d, and issued a call for a convention to be composed of 677 delegates, to meet at Sacramento, August 12th, for the purpose of nominating state officers, and by the delegates sitting in district conventions, to nomi. nate congressmen, members of the state board of equalization, and railroad commissioners. The convention met as appointed. It was called to order by W. H. Dimond, chairman of the state central committee.· J. C. Campbell was elected temporary chairman, and continued as permanent chairman by the adoption of the report of the committee on permanent organization.

The committee on platform and resolutions was composed of G. G. Blanchard, W. H. Dimond, Henry C. Dibble, W. S. Wood, R. H. Lloyd, Drury Melone, R. B. Carpenter, A. R. Conklin, John F. Ellison, A. L. Hart, F. P. Tuttle, C. M. Shortridge, Frank McGowan, F. H. Short, T. L. Carothers, D. E. Knight, E. C. Voorhies, G. M. Francis, V. H. Metcalf, and J. P. Abbott. The following report was presented by the committee and adopted :

The republicans of California, by their delegates in convention assembled, appealing to the intelligence and patriotism of the people confidently submit this their declaration of principles :

1. We believe that the paramount object of government should be to secure to the individual the highest possible measure of civil and political liberty. The republican party came into existence thirty-four years ago, insisting that the primary object and ulterior design of the federal government was to secure "the inalienable rights of life, liberty and the pursuit of happiness" to all persons. It has always maintained that as the constitution of the United States was adopted "in order to form a more perfect union, establish justice, insure domestic tranquillity, provide for the common defense, promote the general welfare, and secure the blessings of liberty to ourselves and our posterity," that constitution should be liberally construed to accomplish those ends. In pursuance of this broad policy and these high aims, it has, in the face of the most persistent and unscrupulous opposition, successfully conducted the government of the nation for nearly thirty years, performing deeds of statesmanship and military achievement worthy to live forever upon the brightest pages of history. It has contributed to our country statesmen such as Lincoln, Seward, Chase, Sumner, Garfield, Logan, Conkling, and Blaine; and such soldiers as Grant, Sherman, Sheridan, and Thomas—names whose fame will live in the world's

galaxy of heroes so long as the love of liberty survives in the human heart. It has preserved the union of the states against the attack of a million of men in armed rebellion. It found the nation without credit at home or abroad, and it organized a financial system under which we have steadily advanced until our country has become the most powerful of all the nations on earth. Better than all, it has not only been true to its original purpose of preventing the establishment of slavery in any of the territories of the United States, but it has also destroyed slavery in all the states of this union wherever it existed, and by the force of example has led all other civilized nations to abolish that curse so long cherished and maintained by the democratic party of this country. Thus has the party demonstrated its ability to govern, its fidelity to the principles of human liberty and equality, and its desire always to secure the greatest good to the greatest number.

2. "The. right to the free ballot is the right preservative of all rights ; and must and shall be maintained in every part of the United States." We cordially endorse this declaration of the democratic national platform of 1880, but we denounce the shameful manner in which that party has violated this pledge in many of the states of the union, and we insist that henceforth it shall be observed, so far as it is within the power of the federal government to effect that object.

3. We reaffirm the principles announced in the republican national platform adopted in 1888.

4. As shown by its opposition to slavery and in the enactment of the homestead and other similar laws, the republican party has always been watchful of the interests of those who depend upon their daily labor for their support, and in pursuance of the same policy we favor legislation by which some satisfactory plan may be devised for the arbitration of disputes and controversies relative to wages and hours of labor between those who labor and those who employ labor.

5. We renew our former declarations in favor of the most rigid exclusion of Chinese from the country, and we urge that such restriction be made permanent.

6. The Sacramento and San Joaquin rivers, which are navigable for hundreds of miles through the most fertile portions of the state, are the natural and cheap highways for one-half the transportation of the state. It is, therefore, the duty of the federal government, by

adequate appropriation, to straighten and deepen the channels of said rivers so as to make them and keep them available for commerce.

7. We approve the legislation already enacted for the reclamation and irrigation of our arid and other lands, and recommend such further legislation as may be necessary to fully accomplish that pur. pose, and reaffirm the resolution contained in the republican plat. form of 1886 on the subject of irrigation, and commend the legisla. tion already adopted in accord therewith.

8. We declare an unchanging belief in free public schools as a necessity to free government.

9. That we indorse the course pursued by Speaker Reed and the members of the republican party in the present session of congress, whereby the rules of proceeding have been so amended that the public business is now being conducted in the orderly way designed for its conduct by the framers of this government. We wholly repudiate the claim of the right of any number of the members of congress to interrupt and delay its business by refusing to vote when required, and we rejoice that the speaker and other members of the republican side of the house have been able to destroy the pretense that members can be present and absent at the same time.

10. That we affirm and commend the administration of President Harrison and the course pursued in the general legislation of the country by the republican members of congress.

11. That we desire to especially commend and mark with approval the manner in which the administration of President Harrison, through Secretary Blaine, has managed the Bering sea difficulty with England. And we have every confidence that the result will be adjusted honorably to this country and in full recognition of its rights.

12. That we are in favor of all the laws recognizing the claims of the soldiers of the late war and the war with Mexico, and recommend that they ever be considered the wards of the nation.

13. That the nominees of this convention are pledged to give their support to the enforcement of the law which provides that eight hours shall constitute a legal day's work for all state and municipal employes.

14. Whereas, the last legislature under the control of the democratic party, appropriated $12,534,000—and for the purpose of raising that sum the rate of taxation was increased to the unprecedented rate of 72 cents on each $100 of assessable property—therefore, resolved, that we arraign the democratic party of this state for

the waste and extravagance shown by the last legislature in the appropriation of public money, and we .promise the people that in the hands of the republican party the state finances shall be handled with honest and rigid economy, and with a view to administer the affairs of the state in a business-like and economical manner ; and we do further declare that in the judgment of this convention, considering the past experience of the state, an annual tax of 50 cents on each $100 of assessable property ought to, and will raise a revenue sufficient for all the wants of the state. And we pledge the nominees of this convention to an observance of this rule. And we declare to the people of this state that the success of the republican party means the establishment of a state limit of taxation as in this resolution declared. And we call upon all republican county conventions to pledge their candidates for the senate and assembly to the same limit.

15. That in the interest of the agricultural and other industries of the country we endorse the action of the republican members of congress in the passage of what is known as the silver bill, and that we favor a proper increase of the currency of the country to the extent demanded by its business interests.

16. That we favor the enactment of stringent laws against trusts, pools, combines, and monopolies whereby legitimate competition is destroyed and the necessities, comforts, and luxuries of life are enhanced in prices.

The following nominations were made : Henry H. Markham, for governor. On the first ballot, the roll-call showed 299 votes for Markham, 281 for W. W. Morrow, 61 for N. P. Chipman, and 30 for L. U. Shippee, but before the result was announced, many votes were changed to Markham, until finally a motion was carried to make his nomination unanimous.

John B. Reddick, for lieutenant-governor, by acclamation, the name of William H. Jordan, which was also before the convention, being withdrawn before the completion of the first ballot.

William H. Beatty, for chief justice of the supreme court, by acclamation.

Ralph C. Harrison and Charles H. Garoutte, for associate justices of the supreme court, by 381 and 546 votes, respectively, over Charles N. Fox, who received 212, and C. W. C. Rowell, who received 215 votes.

John J. De Haven, for associate justice, unexpired term, by

acclamation, the name of George A. Nourse being withdrawn before the completion of the first ballot.

Edward G. Waite, for secretary of state, by acclamation.

Edward P. Colgan, for controller, by acclamation, the names of S. L. Hanscom and J. B. Fuller, being withdrawn during the second ballot.

James R. McDonald, for treasurer, by 343 votes, against 333 for L. Rackliffe.

William H. H. Hart, for attorney-general, by 351 votes, against 264 for E. C. Hart, and 61 for George D. Collins.

Theodore Reichert, for surveyor-general, by acclamation, the name of James M. Gleaves being withdrawn before the completion of the roll-call on the first ballot.

Lewis H. Brown, for clerk of the supreme court, over Charles B. Overacker, A. J. Raisch, and E. J. Wolf.

James W. Anderson, for superintendent of public instruction, by acclamation, the name of Ira G. Hoitt, also before the convention, being withdrawn.

Anticipating an increase in the state's representation in congress as a result of the increased population which would be shown by the United States census of 1890, the state central committee had called for the nomination of two congressmen at large. The convention accordingly nominated W. W. Morrow and J. C. Campbell. This action was premature, as the new congressional apportionment was not made until after the election.

The convention completed its labors and adjourned *sine die*, August 14, 1890.

The following were nominated by the district conventions: For representatives in congress: First district, J. A. Barham; second district, G. G. Blanchard; third district, Joseph McKenna; fourth district, John T. Cutting; fifth district, E. F. Loud; sixth district, W. W. Bowers. For members of state board of equalization: First district, J S. Swan; second district, L. C. Morehouse; third district, D. T. Cole; fourth district, J. R. Hebbron. For railroad commissioners: First district, William Beckman; second district J. M. Litchfield; third district, James W. Rea.

The democratic state central committee met at San Francisco, May 20th, and issued a call for a convention, to meet at San Jose, August 19th. The convention met at the stated time and place, and was called to order by John Daggett, vice-chairman of the state central committee. Byron Waters was elected temporary chairman, and was continued as the permanent chairman on final organization. The committee on platform and resolutions was composed of R. B. Terry, A. B. Ware, H. J. Corcoran, M. H. Mead, W. J. Hancock, John McGonigle, Russell J. Wilson, Joseph Napthaly, H. G. Platt, D. A. Ostrom, Clay W. Taylor, J. F. Thompson, J. De Barth Shorb, J. H. Lawrence, and John Boggs. On the following day, the 20th, the committee submitted the following report:

1. The democratic party of the state of California, in convention assembled, renews the pledges of its fidelity to the democratic faith, and reaffirms the doctrines of the national platform of 1888, adopted at St. Louis, Missouri.

2. A depleted treasury, the imposition of unequal and oppressive taxes, the effort to enact coercive legislation, the arbitrary disregard by the speaker of the house of representatives of all parliamentary rules, and the shameless servility displayed by the majority in the house of representatives in yielding ready obedience to his tyrannical mandates, their refusal to join the democracy in its efforts to procure the passage of a measure permitting the free coinage of silver, the neglect of the present administration in a manner to modify an admitted erroneous tariff, suggest with more emphasis than words that the reins of government should be placed in safer hands.

3. We denounce and condemn the republican majority in the national house of representatives for the passage of the infamous Lodge election bill, by which that majority seeks, masquerading under the guise of "a free ballot and a fair count," to perpetuate itself in power by insidiously destroying the liberties of American citizens, usurping the functions of state government, and bringing the federal election machinery into interminable conflict and collision with the statutory efforts of the people of the various commonwealths of our union to institute a genuine, practical, and permanent reform. We hold that this species of federal interference with the people in the registration of their sovereign will is despotic and centralizing in its tendencies, dangerous to the liberty, peace, and prosperity of the people, revolutionary in its nature and purpose, and in direct contravention of the principles of free government as bequeathed to us by the framers of our constitution.

4. We denounce the McKinley bill as being opposed to the best interests of the producing and consuming classes of the country.

5. The democratic party is now, as it has ever been, unalterably

opposed to Chinese immigration. The Chinese restriction act, adopted as the result of democratic effort, is about to expire, and it is the duty of congress to enact a law perpetually excluding all Chinese from the United States.

6. We favor the free coinage of silver, and demand that it be made an unlimited legal tender for all purposes, public and private.

7. We favor the enactment of stringent laws against trusts, pools, combines, and monopolies, whereby legitimate competition is destroyed and the necessities and comforts of life are enhanced in price.

8. We are in favor of the election of United States senators by a direct vote of the people, and earnestly urge the adoption of such an amendment to the constitution of the United States as will accomplish that result.

9. We indorse the course of the democratic senator and represen. tatives in congress, and commend them for their vigorous defense of the public interests and their zeal in behalf of the welfare of our state.

10. We call attention to the hypocrisy of the late republican state convention in attempting to place upon the slender democratic majority in the legislature the entire responsibility of the appropriations made during the last session. The republican members of the legislature voted in favor of the appropriations which were made the subject of criticism, and in every instance the appropriations so made were approved by a republican executive who had not the manliness to indorse nor the courage to condemn.

11. We declare that a state rate of taxation not exceeding 45 cents on each $100 of assessable property (according to the assessed valuation of 1889), being a reduction of 27 cents and 2 mills, is sufficient to raise ample revenue to meet the annual expenses of the state government; and we pledge our nominees to a strict and faithful adherence to the above, and we do demand that the different county conventions pledge their legislative candidates to the same limit.

12. The democracy of California pledges its nominees to the legislature to use all lawful means to secure the enactment of a law embodying the Australian ballot system substantially as that now existing in the state of Massachusetts.

13. We favor the election by the people of the superintendent of state printing.

14. We pledge our senators and representatives in congress to use

all honorable means to secure liberal appropriations from the general government for the purpose of making those great national commercial highways, the Sacramento and San Joaquin rivers and their tributaries, and all other navigable waterways, freely navigable at all seasons of the year.

15. The democratic party of California reaffirms its resolution of 1886 on the water question, reiterating its assertion that "the English law of riparian rights is inapplicable to the circumstances and conditions of California"; reaffirming the doctrine that the waters of the state belong to the people of the state, to be used for irrigation, mining, manufacturing, and other useful purposes, and that they should never be subject to private ownership or monopoly ; reaffirms the policy of the district system, and pledges itself to foster, amend, and perfect the system inaugurated under and by virtue of the resolution of 1886.

16. We believe in a liberal support of our citizen soldiers and national guard. It is an integral and necessary part of our state government and should be fostered and encouraged.

17. We are opposed to all forms of sumptuary legislation and to all unjust discrimination against any business or industry.

18. We believe that the wine-growing industry of this state should be fostered, nourished, and encouraged by suitable legislation, both state and national.

19. We believe that eight hours should constitute a legal day's work, and that the present law to that end should be rigidly enforced.

20. We condemn as extravagant, wasteful, and wrong, the administration of the affairs of the state prison at San Quentin under the republican management.

21. The democratic party of California declares itself unalterably opposed to all schemes having for their object the division of the state of California, and pledges itself to maintain this great commonwealth, brought into the American union by democratic statesmanship, undivided in its greatness.

After some discussion on the fifteenth section, relative to water, the report was adopted without amendment.

On the 20th, the names of E. B. Pond, James V. Coleman, W. D. English, and A. C. Paulsell were placed in nomination for the office of governor, and two ballots taken without making a choice. On the fourth ballot, taken on the following day, E. B. Pond was nominated, receiving 430 votes, to 138 for Coleman, 66 for English, and 5 for Paulsell.

The other nominees were as follows:

R. F. Del Valle, for lieutenant-governor, by acclamation.

John A. Stanly, for chief justice, by 339 votes, over William T. Wallace, who received 282.

Jackson Hatch, for associate justice, unexpired term, over J. W. Hughes and R. Y. Hayne. The nomination was made unanimous before the completion of the second ballot.

James V. Coffey and George H. Smith, for associate justices, full term, over John G. Presley, John D. Goodwin, J. W. Armstrong, James E. Murphy, and George A. Johnson.

W. C. Hendricks, for secretary of state, by 341 votes, to 203 for C. F. Singletary, and 86 for George W. Peckham.

John P. Dunn, for controller, by 365 votes, against 270 for R. D. Stephens, and 1 for F. A. Merriman.

Adam Herold, for treasurer, by acclamation.

Walker C. Graves, for attorney-general, by 369 votes, to 265 for J. R. Kittrell.

Stanley C. Boom, for surveyor-general, by 362 votes, to 271 for H. W. Patton, and 5 for Preston R. Davis.

H. C. Hall, for superintendent of public instruction, by 440 votes, on the second ballot, to 101 for W. T. Welcker, 47 for D. C. Clark, 46 for C. S. Smyth, and 34 for W. A. C. Smith.

J. D. Spencer, for clerk of the supreme court, by 406 votes, to 228 for W. L. Ashe.

Nominations were made by the respective district conventions as follows:

For representatives in congress: First district, T. J. Geary, on the twenty-first ballot, over T. W. H. Shanahan, A. P. Haines, and Rodney Hudson; second district, A. Caminetti, by acclamation; third district, John P. Irish, by acclamation; fourth district, Robert Ferral; fifth district, T. J. Clunie, by acclamation; sixth district, W. J. Curtis.

For railroad commissioners: First district, Archibald Yell; second district, C. H. Haswell; third district, L. Archer.

For members of the state board of equalization: First district, Gordon E. Sloss; second district, Henry Dusterberry (substituted for James Brady); third district, R. H. Beamer; fourth district, John T. Gaffey.

The making of nominations was completed August 22d, when the convention adjourned *sine die.*

The state election was held November 4th, 1890. All of the candidates on the republican ticket were elected, with the exception of one member of the board of equalization and two congressmen. The results, according to the official returns, were as follows :

For governor, H. H. Markham, 125,129 ; E. B. Pond, 117,184 ; John Bidwell, 10,073.

For lieutenant-governor, J. B. Reddick, 126,244 ; R. F. Del Valle, 115,783 ; A. M. Hough, 6,878 ; Ben Morgan, 3,342.

For secretary of state, E. G. Waite, 129,900 ; W. C. Hendricks, 114,216 ; F. E. Kellogg, 6,466 ; W. S. Lyon, 1,948.

For surveyor-general, Theodore Reichert, 131,172 ; Stanley C. Boom, 112,765 ; E. M. Chase, 6,476 ; W. L. Dixon, 2,049.

For clerk of the supreme court, L. H. Brown, 130,036; J. D. Spencer, 115,719 ; J. T. Price, 6,455.

For superintendent of public instruction, J. W. Anderson, 130,594 ; H. C. Hall, 112,717 ; Miss S. M. Severance, 6,478.

For controller, E. P. Colgan, 128,042 ; J. P. Dunn, 116,036 ; M. C. Winchester, 8,405.

For treasurer, J. R. McDonald, 128,926 ; Adam Herold, 115,041; Henry French, 6,563 ; G. E. Grosse, 1,997.

For attorney-general, W. H. H. Hart, 130,520 ; W. C. Graves, 113,381 ; C. H. Dunn, 8,603.

For chief justice, W. H. Beatty, 133,095 ; J. A. Stanly, 113,018 ; Robert Thompson, 5,645.

For associate justices: Full term, C. H. Garoutte, 130,719; J. V. Coffey, 111,361 ; R. C. Harrison, 129,509; C. H. Smith, 113,101. Unexpired term, J. J. DeHaven, 131,625 ; Jackson Hatch, 106,435 ; S. C. Brown, 4,011.

For members of state board of equalization : First district, J. S. Swan, 27,942 ; G. E. Sloss, 27,246 ; H. B. Burlingame, 168. Second district, L. C. Morehouse, 28,417; H. Dusterberry, 16,288 ; D. C. Taylor, 1,181 ; James Brady, 5,751 ; J. L. Lyon, 622. Third district, R. H. Beamer, 28,329 ; D. T. Cole, 28,154 ; E. C. Gilbert, 1,096. Fourth district, J. R. Hebbron, 42,235 ; J. T. Gaffey, 40,-791 ; S. Fowler, 3,654.

For railroad commissioners: First district, William Beckman, 41,-274 ; Archibald Yell, 37,327 ; R. G. Hart, 1,611. Second district,

´ J. M. Litchfield, 31,478 ; C. H. Haswell, 27,619; H. H. Luse, 173.
Third district, J. W. Rea, 57,312 ; L. Archer, 50,508 ; J. G. Miller,
4,416.

For representatives in congress: First district, T. J. Geary, 19,-
334 ; J. A. Barham, 19,153 ; L. B. Scranton, 759. Second district,.
A. Caminetti, 18,644 ; G. G. Blanchard, 18,485 ; J. S. Witherell,
912. Third district, Joseph McKenna, 20,834 ; John P. Irish, 15,-
997; O. O. Felkner, 774. Fourth district, John T. Cutting, 13,196;
Robert Ferral, 12,091 ; Thomas V. Cator, 1,492 ; Joseph Rowell,
50. Fifth district, E. F. Loud, 22,871 ; T. J. Clunie, 19,899; E. F.
Howe, 574. Sixth district, W. W. Bowers, 33,522 ; W. J. Curtis,.
28,904 ; O. R. Dougherty, 3,130.

CHAPTER XXXVI.

1892. Republican Convention, May 3d—Democratic Convention—
Prohibition Convention—Organization of the People's Party—
People's Party Nominating Convention—Republican Convention,
July 26th.

The republican state committee met in San Francisco, March 14th,
and issued a call for a convention to be composed of 552 delegates,
to meet at Stockton, May 3d, for the purpose of electing delegates.
and alternates to the republican national convention. The test
adopted for voters at primaries was: "Will you pledge yourself to
support the nominees of the republican national convention at the
coming election ?" The convention met as called. J. H. Neff was
elected temporary chairman by acclamation, and was continued as
permanent chairman by the adoption of the report of the committee
on permanent organization. The following were named as the committee on platform and resolutions : Grove L. Johnson, T. M. Sel-
vage, A. B. Lemon, A. L. Levinsky, John F. Davis, J. A. Waymire,
H. A. McCraney, W. H. L. Barnes, E. S. Pillsbury, M. Cooney,
H. V. Morehouse, E. H. Heacock, H. Z. Osborne, George Fuller,
and Richard Gird.

The committee made the following report, which was adopted :

1. The administration of national affairs by a republican president has been such that to it we give our unqualified indorsement.
The prudent business manner in which the finances of the nation
have been managed, so that while no niggard hand has been shown

in disbursements, yet the expenses have been kept within bounds and the national debt greatly reduced; the carrying into full practical effect of the American doctrine of protection to American manufactures under that wise and beneficent law known as the McKinley bill; the courageous putting into operation of the reciprocity clauses of that law against clamor without and concealed antagonism within the party; the adjustment in a masterly and dignified manner of the unforeseen and peculiar differences with our old friend Italy, by which the friendship between the two countries has been restored on terms satisfactory to each; the firm and successful management of the controversy with Chile, whereby the honor of the nation was guarded, its flag made powerful to guard alike our sailors and citizens, as well as political refugees seeking shelter, and yet the self-respect of Chile was observed with scrupulous care; the carefully prepared and determined stand taken in the Bering sea dispute with Great Britain, whereby the so-called mistress of the seas was taught that the American banner must be respected, whether it waved over land or ocean, over man or seal, and by which a glorious diplomatic triumph was won; these and other achievements stamp the administration of President Harrison as wise, patriotic, and useful, and endear him to the hearts of all true Americans, while giving just pride to every republican. We feel that the republican party needs no better leader in the battle of 1892 than the man who led us to victory in 1888.

2. We indorse the administration of Governor Markham as wise and efficient, and most heartily commend the care with which he is endeavoring to economize and improve the management of our state institutions.

3. We reaffirm our belief in and adherence to the republican national platform of 1888. Upon the doctrine there enunciated of protection to American industries and American labor we won the contest, and all subsequent experience has but strengthened our confidence in that system of governmental policy of which our party is the exponent, and we confidently ask the closest scrutiny of its working under the present tariff as the strongest argument for its maintenance.

4. The policy of our government has always been to welcome to our shores all good people from all parts of the world, but we recognize the fact that our hospitality has been abused, that thousands of undesirable immigrants have been imposed upon us, or have voluntarily come to us, and we deem that the time has arrived

for a reform in our laws that shall protect the United States from the socialist, the criminal, the pauper, the anarchist, and the nihilist, and shall place stronger guards around the sacred privileges of becoming an American citizen, so that no man shall be given that inestimable right unless he be unmistakably entitled thereto.

5. We hail with glad hearts the cessation of legal warfare between the miners and the agriculturists of California, and the blending together of the two great interests of our commonwealth into one harmonious effort to advance the common good without injury to either. We indorse the efforts that have been made to bring farmer and miner into a union, and call upon congress to enact immediately into laws such measures as will enable the hydraulic miner again to pour into the pathway of commerce his millions of treasure from the streams of the Sierra Nevada without damage to the valleys, or waters, or agricultural interests of the state, so that the busy hum of labor and the music of the school shall be heard in the now deserted mining camps of California as in the days of old.

6. The Sacramento and San Joaquin rivers and their tributaries are the natural highways of commerce within the state, and we are in favor of so improving their channels and constructing navigable canals through the valleys of said rivers, connecting them with the tide water, as to secure forever to the people of the state cheap transportation for the products of our soil and our factories.

7. The Nicaragua canal, by means of which the distance between the Atlantic and Pacific seaports of our country will be shortened by 10,000 miles, thus affording a highway for quick and cheap transportation without limit, is an enterprise which, if properly guarded, can never be monopolized by any private interest. And because of its vast importance to the commercial world, especially to the states and territories contiguous to our sea coast, we urge upon congress to take such action as will insure the early completion of said canal, and at the same time secure the control of the canal to the government of the United States, and we heartily indorse the views expressed on this subject by President Harrison in his message to congress thereon.

8. We believe that the wool-growing interests of the country are entitled to and should receive as full and adequate protection under the tariff laws as that granted any other industry.

9. We believe silver, equally with gold, to be the money of the people, and in behalf of the farmer, the laborer, and the mechanic of the nation, for whom the republican party has

always labored, we demand the passage of such laws as will provide for the free and unlimited coinage of the silver product of the mines of the United States, as soon as the same can be done without injury to the business interests of the nation.

10. The republican party has ever been the friend and protector of the laborer of the country, and in line with the legislation which our party has given them we favor the passage of such laws by congress as will protect American labor against the importation of the products of pauper labor, as well as against the importation of contract or pauper laborers, believing that by so doing only can we adequately secure to the American laborer the full reward of his exertions; and we demand the rigid enforcement of the law limiting the hours of labor on public works to eight hours per day; and we also demand such legislation as shall utterly prohibit all Chinese immigration into the United States.

11. We favor an amendment to the constitution of the United States, providing for the election of United States senators by direct vote of the people.

12. While we abate nothing of our words of praise regarding the chief magistrate of the nation, we must express our profound conviction that in the whole foreign policy of the administration we see the traces of a master hand so long and lovingly known by all our party; we recognize again and again that man who stands in the very foremost rank of living statesmen, whose fame is world-wide, whose name is a household word in every American home, and who is the "favorite son" of every republican in every state of the American union, James G. Blaine.

The following resolutions were also adopted:

13. That the principles of civil service reform inaugurated by the late lamented, the Honorable James A. Garfield, would, if carried out in their strict and true sense, redound to the credit of the administration and serve as a safeguard to the rank and file of the republican party, therefore, be it further resolved,

14. That this convention indorse and recommend the carrying out in their fullest extent the principles of civil service reform.

For delegates at large to the national convention, the names of W. H. L. Barnes, M. M. Estee, E. F. Spence, N. D. Rideout, C. N. Felton, and M. H. DeYoung were placed in nomination. On the first ballot Spence received 459; Rideout, 421; DeYoung, 369; Felton, 347; Estee, 326, and Barnes, 281 votes. The four first named were declared elected. Isaac Trumbo, Philo G. Hersey, H. G. Otis, and J. R. Carrick were elected alternate delegates at large by acclamation.

Delegates were elected by the district conventions as follows: First district, D. T. Cole and E. V. Spencer; alternates, S. I. Mathews and J. T. Matlock. Second district, J. F. Kidder, A. J. Rhoads; alternates, E. C. Voorhies and N. Sposati. Third district, Eli Denison and R. D. Robbins; alternates, H. A. McCraney and R. F. Crist. Fourth district, E. S. Pillsbury and J. S. Spear; alternates, Reuben H. Lloyd and D. S. Dorn. Fifth district, O. A. Hale and George A. Knight; alternates, John T. Dare and Mitchell Phillips. Sixth district, E. P. Johnson and R. E. Jack; alternates, J. Frankenfield and J. T. Porter. Seventh district, P. Y. Baker and R. W. Button; alternates, W. H. Scribner and A. S. Emery.

The convention adjourned *sine die*, May 4th, 1892.

The democratic state central committee met at San Francisco, April 6th, and issued a call for a convention, to be composed of 643 delegates, and to be held at Fresno, May, 17, 1892. The test adopted for primaries was: "Did you support and vote for E. B. Pond for governor in 1890, or would you have done so had you cast a vote? Will you support the nominees of the national democratic convention at Chicago, and the democratic ticket nominated in May, 1892, by the Fresno convention?" The convention was to select delegates to the national convention, and by district conventions, to nominate congressmen, and electors and alternates for president and vice-president of the United States.

The convention met at the appointed time and place, and was called to order by R. P. Hammond, vice-chairman of the state central committee. B. D. Murphy was elected temporary chairman by 343 votes, over D. A. Ostrom, who received 286. The committee on platform and resolutions was appointed to consist of R. F. Del Valle, Henry Hogan, John Markley, George E. Williams, D. A. Ostrom, M. F. Tarpey, R. A. Long, J. F. Sullivan, S. Braunhart, Jackson Hatch, Barry Baldwin, Stephen M. White, J. D. Harvey, Oscar A. Trippit, and M. T. Dooling.

By the report of the committee on permanent organization, which was adopted, the temporary officers of the convention were made permanent, and Ostrom was made vice-chairman.

The majority of the committee on platform and resolutions submitted the following report:

We pledge anew our fealty to the principles first declared by the illustrious men who founded our free institutions and established the democratic party to protect and preserve them.

1. That the paramount reform now demanded of the federal legislature is the reform of the tariff laws upon the basis of the democratic platform of 1888, to the end that no money shall be needlessly exacted from the industries and necessities of the people, and that our industrial interests shall not be prejudiced by excessive taxation, false systems of finance or extravagant cost of production. To this end the McKinley tariff bill should be repealed, the essential raw material of American manufactures should be put upon the free list and a revised tariff should be adopted, with due regard for the rights of American labor and the preservation of our manufactures. That consistently with that issue and with this demand the sentiment of the California democracy is overwhelmingly for the renomination to the presidency of the man who gave to his party intellectual and political leadership and to the country a pure and elevated administration. We declare our conviction that the best interests of the party and of the country demand the nomination of Grover Cleveland for president. He is the choice of this convention for that exalted station, and we are confident that under his leadership the principles of democracy will win a glorious victory; and to the end that the vote and influence of California may be most effectively heard and felt the delegates this day chosen are directed to act as a unit in all matters intrusted to their charge, said action to be determined by the vote of the majority of the delegates.

2. That we congratulate the democratic party and the people of the state of California upon the successful efforts of our two democratic congressmen in behalf of the best interests of the state, and we confidently contrast their earnest labors with the inactivity and apathy of their republican colleagues in the house and senate. The whole state owes a debt of gratitude to Hon. A. Caminetti and Hon. T. J. Geary; to the one for salutary and wise legislation introduced by him for the relief of our suffering mining industries without interfering with agriculture, and the preservation of our waterways; to the other for the splendid anti-Chinese legislation wrung by his tireless advocacy of California's welfare from a reluctant republican senate.

3. That the construction of the Nicaragua maritime canal is of the greatest political and commercial importance to our country,

and especially to the Pacific states, and that we respectfully urge the democratic national convention to pronounce distinctly in favor of congress taking such action as may facilitate its construction, but we are opposed to a subsidy being granted to any corporation for such purpose.

4. That we ask that the constitution of the United States be so amended as to provide for the election of United States senators directly by the people, avoiding so far as possible the scandals that regularly attend the election to this important office and bringing its incumbent nearer to the people of the state whose representative he is.

5. That we demand the rigid enforcement of the law limiting the hours of labor on public works to eight hours per day. We reaffirm our opposition to the immigration of Chinese and other pauper labor.

6. That we denounce the acts of the republican party against silver, particularly the act demonetizing it, and we believe that there should be kept in constant circulation a full and sufficient volume of money consisting of gold, silver, and legal-tender paper currency at par with each other.

7. That we denounce the legislative and congressional apportionments made by the late republican legislature as unfair and partisan in the extreme. For the purpose of increasing republican representation, districts were formed without reference to the just demands of localities affected, and without reference to public convenience. The provision of our constitution requiring that legislative districts shall be as nearly equal in population as may be, was deliberately and shamelessly violated.

8. That we demand the enactment of stringent laws which will protect the people from the adulteration of food products, which results in the destruction of many of our industries and is highly injurious to the health of the people.

9. That the waterways of the state, being the natural distributing arteries of commerce as well as the means of irrigating our arid lands and increasing our productive capacities, are of the first importance to the citizen; and we demand of congress a fulfillment of the obligations to the state to maintain our navigable waters which come under their direct control in the best navigable condition; and of the state the preservation of its waters for the use and benefit of our citizens.

10. That we heartily approve of the resumption within our state of hydraulic mining under such conditions as shall be just and equit-

37

able to both miner and farmer, and we pledge our best efforts to aid in the adjustment of that most important question. We most respectfully petition congress for immediate assistance and pledge our congressional nominees to the hearty advocacy and support of such measures as may be necessary to practically solve that problem. The suppression of hydraulic mining in California has congested the circulating medium not only at home, where the results are most acutely and infamously felt, but throughout the commercial world, and we look forward to an era of great prosperity upon its resumption.

11. That we deem it the duty of congress to make ample appropriations for the rectification and restoration of the navigable rivers of this state; that such appropriations should be expended in the improvement of the channels and in the construction of restraining and impounding dams; that such dams should be erected at such places and of such dimensions and capacity as will restrain the debris now in the channels and also the amount that will hereafter be deposited in the tributaries of said rivers by natural or mining washings, thereby preserving the navigability of the rectified rivers, and also restoring the great industry of hydraulic mining; that we deem the passage of the mining bill introduced in the house of representatives of the United States by Hon. A. Caminetti to be of vital importance to the people of the state; that in view of such fact we urgently request the delegation in congress from this state to co-operate in securing the passage of said act at this session, in order that hydraulic mining may be speedily resumed.

12. That in 1890 congress restored to the public domain in this state a vast territory covered by forfeited railroad land grants. The interior department, acting in compliance with the wishes of the corporations affected, has wilfully neglected to place this great domain at the disposal of the people. The land thus withheld should be immediately thrown open for actual settlement and occupancy.

13. We denounce the use of money in elections as subversive of good government, and we are in favor of the Australian ballot system, and all other legislation tending to prevent such evil.

14. That we are unalterably opposed to any extension of time for fifty years, or for any other time, for the payment of the indebtedness of the Pacific railroads to the general government.

Whereas, The Central and Southern Pacific railroad companies and their branches owe to the state and several counties the sum of $2,547,000 for taxes; therefore, be it resolved,

15. That we demand of the senatorial and assembly district conventions that they pledge their nominees to vote for a law providing for the reassessment of the property of said companies for the years they have escaped taxation.

16. That we believe that the public should be protected from the great non-taxpaying trusts and corporations which now challenge the authority of the government. The democratic party was founded to maintain the interests and liberties of the people. It alone is competent to resist those encroachments which imperil the safety of the state. The republican party, while professing to be the friend of labor, has demonstrated by its uniform action that its tendencies are toward the creation of monopolies and trusts, through whose instrumentality alone it hopes to perpetuate its existence. The democratic party emanates from the people; its aim has always been to care for the weak and to be just to the strong. While it is ever ready to promote industries and to stimulate enterprises it will never permit wealth to shirk its rightful obligations or to impose upon poverty the expenses of a government formed for the benefit of all.

17. That we advocate the continuance of the democratic policy inaugurated during the presidency of Grover Cleveland providing for the construction of a thoroughly efficient navy, and we favor the establishment of adequate coast and harbor defenses and the construction of a national gun foundry upon this coast.

18. That we deem a well equipped national guard promotive of public safety, and we therefore favor liberal treatment of our citizen soldiery.

19. That the democratic party of the state of California resents the interference in the politics of this state of the Southern Pacific Company of Kentucky; that we denounce the system of boss politics largely created and fostered by that corporation which has corrupted public men and public life, and under which few but those who find favor in the eyes of the corporation and stand ready to do its bidding have held office. Under this influence our youths have been taught and trained to believe that political principle and political duty may be justly traded off for personal gain and preferment at the hands of the boss to the almost entire destruction of that healthy public spirit without which no government of the people can hope to continue in existence.

20. That we heartily indorse the bill introduced by Congressman Caminetti to admit jute bags free of duty, and we call upon our congressional delegation to use their utmost endeavor to accomplish the passage of that measure.

21. That we favor the strict enforcement of the civil service laws.

22. That we are opposed to the payment of any subsidy to any company for carrying the United States mails when such company is directly or indirectly subsidized by any railroad or other private corporation.

23. That the democratic party denounces the inaction of the board of railroad commissioners of the state and earnestly sympathizes and commends the effort of the Traffic Association of California to compel them to perform their constitutional duty and accomplish a much needed reduction in railroad rates in California.

24. That it is absolutely essential to the promotion of the commercial interests of California that a competing railroad be introduced within her borders.

25 That democratic ascendancy is dependent upon the intelligence and education of the people. We favor liberal appropriations for the maintenance and perfection of our public school system, and pledge our legislative nominees to the exercise of a liberal discretion in providing for its maintenance and thorough equipment.

26. That the democratic party is now, as ever, unalterably opposed to all sumptuary legislation.

27. That we denounce the billion-dollar congress and the legislature of a thousand scandals.

28. That the success of the democratic party offers to a suffering people the only escape from a recurrence of corrupt and extravagant rule.

29. That it is the sense of this convention that the next legislature of this state submit to the people for adoption a constitutional amendment providing for a maximum tariff and classification, and abolishing the board of railroad commissioners; and the democratic party demands that all candidates for the assembly and senate at the coming election be pledged to said action.

White submitted a minority report offering as substitutes for the twenty-third and twenty-ninth sections, respectively, the following:

23. That the democratic party denounces the inaction of the board of railroad commissioners of this state and earnestly sympathizes with and commends all efforts to compel them to perform their

constitutional duty by accomplishing a much needed reduction in railroad rates in this state.

29. That it is the sense of this convention that the next legisla-ture of this state. provide for a maximum railroad freight and fare tariff.

A second minority report was submitted, signed by Harvey, White, Dooling, and Braunhart, offering the following substitute for the sixth section:

6. That this convention denounces the act of the republican con-gress in demonetizing silver. We are in favor of the double stand-ard and of the enactment of such laws as will result in the free coinage of silver.

White's report was rejected, by a vote of 355 to 255; the second minority report was then withdrawn, and the majority report adopted without amendment.

The following resolution, introduced by I. Gutte, was adopted by acclamation :

That whereas, the prosperity of the state of California is, in a great measure, dependent upon an increased population, we recom-mend such measures as will tend to encourage the immigration of orderly and decent people, to the exclusion of the members of the criminal and pauper classes and refuse of other nations, and that in heartily favoring the immigration of decent and orderly members of the Caucasian race, it should always be remembered that American citizenship is a boon to be conferred only upon such persons as are in accord with our system of constitutional government.

W. W. Foote, Stephen M. White, A. B. Butler, and J. V. Cole-man were elected delegates at large to the national democratic con-vention by acclamation, while as alternates, Lawrence Archer, John Bryson, Sr., Louis Metzger, and R. H. Beamer were also elected by acclamation. For presidential electors at large, J. F. Thompson and Joseph D. Lynch were chosen by acclamation, and in the same man-ner E. B. Price and P. H. Griffin were chosen alternates.

The convention adjourned *sine die*, May 18th. During intervals in its sessions the delegates assembled in district conventions for the purpose of nominating congressmen, presidential electors and dele-gates to the national convention.

First congressional district: The convention for this district nominated Thomas J. Geary for representative in congress, by acclamation. Thomas L. Thompson and Clay W. Taylor were elected delegates to the national convention, with John D. Goodwin and H. H. Harris, as alternates. R. P. Hammond was chosen presidential elector, and Henry Hogan, alternate. The following resolutions were adopted :

Whereas, After many years passed in a minority, and after the experiments with expediency which are common to minorities, the democratic party in 1876, under the leadership of Tilden, planted itself firmly upon affirmative principles and won a victory; and whereas, this affirmation was rendered, vitalized, and reasserted by Grover Cleveland, with the result of so educating the country that the republican party was nearly expelled from representation in the popular branch of congress; therefore be it resolved by this first district convention of the democracy of California,

That we charge our delegates to the national convention to keep in issue the principles that will live forever in the masterly statement made by Mr. Cleveland, and to recognize and obey the wish of the party that the coming fight be made under the leadership and candidacy of Grover Cleveland, of whom it may be truthfully said that he never dodged an issue nor evaded a responsibility; who destroyed sectionalism, defied the protected monopolies, and brightened with hope the face of the toiler and taxpayer; who sprung from the people himself, overcame the disinheritance of fortune by his own exertions, reaching the highest honors by deserving them, and received the greatest earthly trust by reason of confidence that his honor was equally great. Resolved,

That under his leadership we expect victory by deserving it, and in the affections of the people which run to him in every state we recognize a foundation for success which no artifice nor expenditure can displace. First amongst Americans, foremost in courage and patriotism, we hereby record our pride in him as our countryman, our confidence in him as a statesman, and our perfect trust in him as a party leader; and we commit this estimate of him to our national delegates, charging them to faithfully reflect our impression in the national convention, and by vote and action to conform their conduct thereto.

Second congressional district: This convention nominated A. Caminetti for representative in congress ; J. A. Filcher for elector, and Charles Mitchell for alternate; and elected R. D. Stephens and W. J. McGee delegates to the national convention, with A. F.

Jones and E. Armstrong for alternates. The following resolutions, introduced by W. S. Leake, were adopted without opposition :

Whereas, We believe that Grover Cleveland is the first choice and favorite of the democracy of California and of the United States, as a candidate for the presidency; therefore be it resolved,

That it is the wish of the delegates of this district, representing the will of the people, that our delegates to the national convention reflect this first choice and preference of the party in their action and votes at Chicago. Resolved,

That the foregoing expression is our emphatic counsel and charge to our representatives, in whom we expect fidelity and force in this expression of our will. Resolved,

That we think it neither wise nor safe to change materially the plan under which the battle of 1888 was fought. We are confident we were right then, and the right is always the same. We have implicit confidence in the mind that conceived and the hands that executed the details of that noted contest. We also believe in the wisdom, and honesty, and heroic courage of him who has led us in that assault, and now, refreshed, revived, united, and fearless in our faith, we demand to be led against an enemy fortified by the spoils of an oppressive tariff levied upon the suggestion of private greed to promote monopoly and extortion, to build up the fortunes of a few beneficiaries and favored classes at the expense of the general welfare, under the same great general, Grover Cleveland.

Third congressional district : The convention of this district deferred the nomination of a congressman until a later date. R. A. Long was nominated for presidential elector and C. Y. Brown, alternate. Frank J. Moffitt and L. W. Buck were elected delegates, with Paul Shirley and M. J. Laymance as alternates. At an adjourned meeting of the convention, held in Oakland, September 24th, Warren B. English received the nomination for congressman, by a vote of 51, to 17 for H. C. McPike.

Fourth congressional district : By this convention James G. Maguire was nominated for representative in congress; Marcus Rosenthal for presidential elector and P. F. Dundon for alternate. Jeremiah F. Sullivan and Joseph Clark were elected delegates, and A. Andrews and R. P. Doolan, alternates.

Fifth congressional district: J. W. Ryland was nominated for representative in congress; Jackson Hatch for elector and J. C. Ruddock for alternate. L. A. Whitehurst and Thomas F. Barry were elected delegates, with L. G. Flannigan and ·F. M. Mills as alternates. A resolution was passed indorsing Cleveland and instructing the delegates to support him while he remained a candidate.

Sixth congressional district: The nomination of a congressman was postponed. Thomas Renison was nominated for elector and N. A. Covarrubias for alternate. George S. Patton and Jesse D. Carr were elected delegates and J. H. Russell and J. C. Kays, alternates. At an adjourned meeting of the convention, held at Los Angeles, September 10th, Marion Cannon, the nominee of the people's party was nominated for congressman, and William Graves for elector, vice Renison, resigned.

Seventh congressional district: W. L. Silman was chosen for presidential elector and Charles F. Hume for alternate. Henry W. Patton and W. W. Phillips were elected delegates to the national convention, with M. T. Dooling and E. E. Young as alternates. A resolution was unanimously adopted instructing the delegates to use all honorable means to secure the nomination of Cleveland for president. The nomination of congressman was postponed until August 30th when, at a convention assembled at Santa Ana, Olin Wellborn was nominated by acclamation, John R. Kittrell withdrawing.

The prohibition convention met at Fresno, May 25th, with more than 300 delegates in attendance. It was called to order by Henry French of the state central committee. M. C. Winchester was elected temporary chairman. The report of the committee on permanent organization, which was adopted, named P. T. Durfy as chairman. The committee on platform and resolutions consisted of C. H. Dunn, C. E. Rich, A. J. Gregg, L. W. Elliott, Robert Thompson, Mrs. Ada Van Pelt, R. Summers, R. H. McDonald, George Thresher, F. M. Porter, James Hopkins, Jr., H. C. Waddell, Garrison Turner, F. M. Willis, O. R. Dougherty, and Mrs. L. H. Addington. The report of the committee was considered *seriatim* and amended in some particulars. As adopted it was as follows:

1. We hereby reaffirm our allegiance to the platform of the national prohibition party of the United States.

2. We declare for the suppression of the manufacture, importation, transportation, exportation, and sale of all intoxicating liquors by both state and nation, except for medicinal and mechanical purposes.

3. We declare in favor of a suffrage based upon an educational qualification without regard to sex; and in this connection we declare on the question to be submitted to the voters of this state at the next election, of requiring an educational qualification of voters, that every voter be required to be able to write his own name, and to read any section of the constitution in the English language.

4. We are in favor of the government ownership and control of the railroads, the telegraph and the telephone lines, and the management of the same for the public good.

5. The combination of trusts and monopolies to subsidize the press, corrupt legislation, and courts of justice, increase the price of commodities, and oppress the wageworker is a usurpation of the people's rights, and that we are opposed to such monopolies and trusts in both state and nation.

6. We favor a currency, issued by the government alone, sufficient in amount to transact the business of the country, not exceeding $50 per capita, of gold and silver coin, and treasury notes, the same to be a full legal tender for all debts.

7. Our immigration laws should be so revised and enforced, as to exclude pauper, vicious, criminal, and other undesirable immigrants; to extend the time of residence required before naturalization; to require that no immigrant be naturalized until able to read English, nor be permitted to vote until fully naturalized.

8. We favor the election of United States senators by a direct vote of the people.

9. In consideration of the great value of the proposed Nicaragua canal to the commerce of the nation, we favor the construction of the same, and that it be owned and controlled by the general government in the interest of the people.

10. We declare for the preservation of one day in seven, as a day of rest as a civic institution, without oppressing or interfering with any who observe any other day of the week as such day of rest.

The following minority report was read to the convention:

11. We sympathize with those who toil for the support of themselves and families, and we heartily agree to assist them, through their labor unions and otherwise, in all lawful means, to secure from corporations and other employers shorter hours of labor, and we reaffirm our former resolutions to give to employes a Saturday half-holiday.

The nominations made by the convention were as follows: For presidential electors: At large, R. H. McDonald and F. M. Porter; first district, Archibald McArthur; second district, William P. Miller; third district, T. L. Hierlihy; fourth district, H. H. Luse; fifth district, F. E. Caton; sixth district, F. E. Kellogg; seventh district, Samuel Fowler.

For representatives in congress: First district, W. P. Stafford; second district, Chauncey H. Dunn; third district, L. B. Scranton; fourth district, Henry Collins; fifth district, William Kelly; sixth district, O. R. Dougherty; seventh district, M. B. Harris.

For delegates to national convention: At large, Mrs. E. P. Stevens, B. H. Hoag, F. J. Tuttle, Robert Thompson, J. M. Hall, Mrs. L. H. Mills, George B. McIntosh, John Bidwell, M. C. Winchester, and S. N. Marsh. First district, J. R. Nichol and Charles T. Clark. Second district, J. E. Barnes and James A. Anderson; alternates, W. H. Barron and M. A. Thompson. Third district, M. D. Edholm and D. C. Taylor. Fourth district, R. H. McDonald and Mrs. M. F. Gray; alternates, T. S. Harrison and J. S. Clark. Fifth district, T. B. Stewart and C. B. Williams. Sixth district, L. B. Palmer and Daniel Tuttle. Seventh district, J. N. Crawford and A. H. Seccombe; alternates, D. K. Zumwalt and J. S. Edwards.

The convention adjourned *sine die*, May 26th.

The organization of the people's party in California was effected at Los Angeles, October 22, 1891, when delegates representing the farmers' alliance, patrons of husbandry, and other agricultural, labor, and reform organizations, assembled for the purpose of forming a people's party in the state, to adopt a platform, to appoint a state central committee, and to organize district and county committees. The convention included about 600 delegates. It was called to order by M. Cannon. H. F. Gardner was unanimously elected temporary chairman, and afterward permanent chairman. The committee on platform and resolutions consisted of J. W. Hines, H. C. Dillon, William Ayers, William P. Rogers, Mrs. A. F. Smith, John S. Dore, C. W. Pedlar, George Thresher, J. C. Williams, Frank Kelsey, J. F. Greenough, A. P. Merritt, James Morgan, David Reed, and J. M. Sharp. The platform, as adopted, was as follows:

"We, the representatives of the industrial and reform organizations of the state of California, in convention assembled at the city of Los

Angeles, October 22, 1891, firmly convinced that our cause is just, and that the time has come for independent political action, do hereby submit to the candid judgment of all men the following declaration of our principles and purposes :

' That we forever renounce and abjure all former allegiance held or claimed by us in either the republican, democratic, or other political party, and severing our connection therewith, do hereby form and organize in the state of California the people's party of the United States, and pledge to the support of its principles our lives, our fortunes, and our sacred honor.

That we approve the action of the convention of the people's party held at Cincinnati on the 19th of May last, and further demand':

1. The right to make and issue money is a sovereign power to be maintained by the people for the common benefit ; hence, we demand the abolition of the national banks as banks of issue, and as a substitute for national bank notes, we demand that legal tender treasury notes to be issued in sufficient volume to transact the business of the country on a cash basis without damage or especial advantage to any class or calling, such notes to be a legal tender in payment of all debts, public and private, and such notes, when demanded by the people, shall be loaned to them at not more than two per cent per annum upon non-perishable products, as indicated in the sub-treasury plan, and also upon real estate, with proper limitation upon the quantity of land and amount of money.

2. We demand the free and unlimited coinage of silver.

3. We demand the passage of laws prohibiting alien ownership of land, and that congress take prompt action to devise some plan to obtain all lands now owned by alien and foreign syndicates, and that all lands held by railroads and other corporations, in excess of such as is actually used and needed by them, be reclaimed by the government and held for actual settlers only.

4. Believing in the doctrine of equal rights to all and special privileges to none, we demand that all taxation—national, state, and municipal—shall not be used to build up one interest or class at the expense of another.

5. We demand that revenues—national, state, or county—shall be limited to the necessary expenses of the government, economically and honestly administered.

6. We demand the government ownership of all the means and agencies of public transportation and communication, and that they be operated in the interest of the people at actual cost.

7. We demand the election of president, vice-president, and United States senators by a direct vote of the people.

8. We are opposed to the saloon and liquor business in all its forms.

9. We demand that all government and all public work shall be done by the day, under proper superintendents elected by the people; that eight hours only should be a day's work on the same, and strictly enforced; that only American citizens, or those who have declared their intention to become citizens, should be employed on any public work, and that all manufacturers should put their names on all their goods.

10. We hold that no citizen of the United States should be deprived of the electoral franchise on account of sex.

11. Whereas, we believe the strong arm of the government, through its military and police force, affords sufficient protection to life and property; therefore, be it resolved, that we demand the abolition of all private armed bodies of men, such as the Pinkerton police force, and that no person or persons shall act as militiaman, policeman, or marshal unless duly appointed and commissioned by the government, state, or municipality in which they reside.

12. We demand that the pay of the honorably discharged union soldiers which was given to them in depreciated currency, worth only fifty cents on the dollar, shall now be made equal to the gold paid the bondholder.

A state central committee was appointed, composed of one representative from each county and several from industrial organizations. E. M. Wardall was elected chairman of the committee. The convention concluded its labors and adjourned October 22d.

The second convention of the people's party was held at Stockton, June 1st, 1892. It was composed largely of representatives of the farmers' alliance, although other labor organizations were represented. More than 175 delegates were present from thirty-three counties. The convention was called to order by E. M. Wardall of the state executive committee of the party, and John G. Dawes was elected temporary chairman. The committee on permanent organization recommended William Boyne for chairman, and the report was adopted. The committee on platform and resolutions consisted of M. Cannon, J. A. Johnson, A. L. Warner, S. D. Wheeler, W. A. Vann, J. B. McCormick, D. C. Feely, Stephen Bowers, and J. S.

Dore. The committee reported the following, known as the "St. Louis platform:"

1. We demand a national currency, safe, sound and flexible, issued by the general government only, a full legal tender for all debts, public and private; and that without the use of banking corporations, a just, equitable and efficient means of distribution direct to the people at a tax not to exceed two per cent be provided, as set forth in the sub-treasury plan of the farmers' alliance, or some better system ; also, by payments in discharge of its obligations for public improvements. (*a*) We demand free and unlimited coinage of silver. (*b*) We demand that the amount of circulating medium be speedily increased to not less than fifty dollars per capita. (*c*) We demand a graduated income tax. (*d*) We believe that the money of the country should be kept as much as possible in the hands of the people, and hence we demand all national and state revenue shall be limited to the necessary expenses of the government economically and honestly administered. (*e*) We demand that postal savings banks be established by the government for the safe deposit of the earnings of the people and to facilitate exchange.

2. The land, including all the natural resources of wealth, is the heritage of all the people and should not be monopolized for speculative purposes, and alien ownership of land should be prohibited. All land now held by railroads and other corporations in excess of their actual needs, and all lands now held by aliens, should be reclaimed by the government and held for actual settlers only.

3. Transportation being a means of exchange and a public necessity, the government should own and operate the railroads in the interest of the people. The telegraph and telephone, like the post-office system, being a necessity for the transmission of news, should be owned and operated by the government in the interest of the people.

And also the following resolutions :

4. That the people's party denounce the present board of railroad commissioners for refusing to reduce the rates of fares and freights on the railroads of this state, and that when traitors and boodlers get into office the remedy is not the abolition of the office but that of the officers.

5. That the Traffic Association has our sympathy and support in its efforts to compel the railroad commissioners to do their duty in regulating the fares and freights upon the railroads of this state.

6. That we are in favor of the free and unlimited coinage of silver, and we denounce the republican party for demonetizing it in 1873, and the democratic party for not remonetizing it in 1892; and we also denounce the scheme of both old parties for calling a council of foreign aristocrats to sit in judgment upon the monetary affairs of this nation.

7. That we are in favor of the speedy construction of the Nicaragua canal, and to that end we demand treaty rights with the government of Nicaragua before we invest $100,000,000 in the enterprise, and that the government of the United States should own and operate the canal when completed, in the interests of the commerce of the United States and the world.

8. That we denounce the attempt now being made to transfer the government lands known as arid lands to states and territories as a measure in the interest of capital and monopoly, which must result in defrauding honest settlers from acquiring and occupying such lands.

9. That we have read the resolutions adopted at the labor convention held in San Francisco, May 24th, 1892, and we extend to the organizations represented in said convention our cordial co-operation in their efforts to secure the enactment of just laws for the protection of their rights and to secure justice to the toilers in the shops and factories of the cities, and we invite their hearty union with us in the same great cause.

The report was adopted. The platform adopted at Los Angeles, October, 1891, was reaffirmed.

The following were chosen as presidential electors : At large, J. S. Dore and Stephen Bowers. First district, A. L. Warner; second district, J. N. Barton; third district, L. F. Moulton; fourth district, Thomas V. Cator; fifth district, William McCormick; sixth district, W. C. Bowman; seventh district, D. T. Fowler.

The following were elected delegates to the national convention : First district—H. J. Ring, L. Leighton, E. G. Furber, and Carl Browne. Second district—C. A. Jeukins, J. E. Camp, J. M. Benson, and J. W. Schofield. Third district—H. R. Shaw, J. L. Lyon, A. H. Rose, and J. R. Garner. Fourth district—J. A. Williams, J. C. Gore, C. H. Johnson, and T. V. Cator. Fifth district—A. W. Thompson, E. M. Piercy, D. C. Vestal, and C. W. Pedlar. Sixth district—J. S. Loveland, E. M. Hamilton, J. C. Drew, and A. R. Hathaway. Seventh district—C. F. Bennett, G. Burns, W. Penn

Rogers, and B. F. Dixon. At large—Jesse Poundstone, J. S. Dore, J. E. Manlove, G. B. Johnson, Marion Cannon, Mrs. Nettie B. Snow, Mrs. T. V. Cator, and E. M. Wardall.

For representatives in congress, the following were nominated : First district, C. C. Swafford in place of A. J. Bledsoe, declined ; second district, H. B. Riggins; third district, J. L. Lyon ; fourth district, Edgar P. Burman ; fifth district, Jonas J. Morrison ; sixth district, M. Cannon ; seventh district, Hiram Hamilton.

The convention adjourned *sine die* on June 2d.

The republican state central committee met at San Francisco, June 20th, and issued a call for a state convention to be held in Sacramento, July 26th, for the purpose of nominating presidential electors and alternates and representatives in congress. The convention was held in the assembly chamber of the capitol at the appointed time and was composed of 552 delegates. It was called to order by F. H. Meyers, chairman of the state committee. N. P Chipman was chosen temporary chairman by acclamation, and on final organization was made permanent chairman. The committee on platform and resolutions was composed of R. B. Carpenter, George Fuller, George H. Crafts, George A. Nourse, C. M. Shortridge, J. A. Louttit, Obed Harvey, Frank J. Murphy, C. F. Roberts, D. T. Cole, T. W. Harris, A. Hockheimer, W. H. Dimond, Drury Melone, and F. S. Chadbourne. The committee reported the following resolutions, which were unanimously adopted :

1. We reaffirm the principles enunciated in the platform and resolutions of the republican state convention, adopted at Stockton, May 4, 1892.

2. We adopt the platform and resolutions of the national republican convention at Minneapolis, June 9, 1892.

3. We hereby pledge the earnest, cordial, and united support of the republican party to the nominees of the Minneapolis convention, Harrison and Reid.

4. That in the organization of the National League of the United States and in the American Republican College League, we recognize able and efficient auxiliaries, and welcome them to the ranks of the republican party and to active participation in the affairs of state.

5. That the republican party of California has always stood for the material development of the state ; and, believing that increased facilities of transportation, both by water and rail, will conduce to

that end, it demands from the general government the early completion, under government control, of the Nicaragua canal, and the liberal expenditure of money to improve our harbors and internal, waterways; and it invites capital to build into the state other and competing transcontinental lines of railway, pledging protection and support to all instrumentalities existing and to exist that may promote the general welfare and give to the people the benefit of the law of competition.

6. That the secretary of this convention be instructed to telegraph our representatives in the senate of the United States, urging the immediate passage of the mining bill, now pending in that body.

Thomas R. Bard and J. C. Campbell were nominated for electors at large by acclamation, and their alternates, George B. Cook and A. S. Hallidie, were also nominated in the same manner.

The delegates, sitting in district conventions, made the following nominations for electors from their respective districts :

First district—William Carson, elector, and Henry W. Walbridge, alternate ; both by acclamation.

Second district—George B. Sperry for .elector, and M. L. Mery, alternate. Sperry afterwards resigned, and M. L. Mery was substituted by the state committee.

Third district—James A. Waymire for elector, and W. P. Harrington for alternate.

Fourth district—I. Hecht for elector, and J. B. Stetson for alternate.

Fifth district—H. V. Morehouse for elector, and E. F. Donnelly for alternate.

Sixth district—John T. Porter for elector, and E. L. Williams, alternate. Porter resigned, and J. R. Willoughby was substituted by the state committee.

Seventh district—S. L. Hanscom for elector, and L. V. Olcese, alternate.

For representatives in congress the following were nominated by the district conventions :

First district—E. W. Davis, over J. T. Matlock.

Second district—John F. Davis, over Grove L. Johnson.

Third district—S. G. Hilborn, by acclamation. He was nominated also for the short term, occasioned by the resignation of Joseph McKenna.

Fourth district—Charles O. Alexander, by acclamation.

Fifth district—Eugene F. Loud, by acclamation.

Sixth district—At an adjourned meeting of this convention, held at Santa Cruz, July 29th, Hervey Lindley was nominated by 66 votes, to 16 for H. W. Magee.

Seventh district—The delegates of this district assembled at Merced, July 25th, and nominated W. W. Bowers, by acclamation.

The state convention completed its work and adjourned, July 26th.

The election was held throughout the state on November 8th, with the exception of one precinct in Inyo county, where none was held, owing to the loss of the official ballots. Governor Markham issued the following proclamation for an election to be held in this precinct on December 13th:

STATE OF CALIFORNIA,
 EXECUTIVE DEPARTMENT. }

Whereas, a general election, as required by law, was held in the state of California on Tuesday, the 8th day of November, A. D. 1892; and whereas, the board of supervisors of the county of Inyo, by order, duly established an election precinct within said Inyo county, known and designated as Cerro Gordo Election Precinct, No. 13, and appointed John Thomas inspector of elections for said precinct; and whereas, John N. Yandell was duly nominated for the office of county clerk, recorder and auditor of said Inyo county, in accordance with the provisions of sections 1186 and 1187 of the Political Code; and whereas, John Thomas, inspector as aforesaid, has made affidavit that an election was prevented in said Cerro Gordo Precinct, No. 13, Inyo county, by the loss or destruction of the ballots intended for that precinct, and has transmitted the same to me, in accordance with the provisions of section 1201 of the Political Code; and whereas, the said John N. Yandell, candidate for county clerk, recorder and auditor as aforesaid, in accordance with the provisions of said section 1201, has made application to me for an order for a new election in said precinct; and whereas, the requirements of the statutes in such cases made and provided have in all respects been complied with, and it being my duty by law to order a new election in said precinct;

Now therefore, I, H. H. Markham, governor of the state of California, do hereby give notice that an election will be held in said Cerro Gordo Precinct, No. 13, Inyo county, state of California, on

38

the thirteenth day of December, A. D. 1892, for all the officers who were to be voted for at said general election on said 8th day of November, A. D. 1892, in said Cerro Gordo Precinct, No. 13, Inyo county, and whose names were printed upon the general ticket intended for said precinct at said general election.

And I do hereby offer a reward of one hundred dollars for the arrest and conviction of any and every person violating any of the provisions of title 4, part 1 of the Penal Code, said rewards to be paid until the total to be hereafter expended for the purpose reaches the sum of ten thousand dollars.

In witness whereof I have hereunto set my hand and caused the great seal of state to be affixed at Sacramento, this twenty-sixth day of November, A. D. 1892.

H. H. MARKHAM.

. Attest: E. G. WAITE, Secretary of State.

The returns showed that of the presidential electors chosen eight were democratic and one republican. Of the congressmen three were republicans, three democrats and one people's party, indorsed by the democrats. The official returns were as follows :

For presidential electors : Democratic—Filcher, 118,151; Graves, 118,109; Hammond, 118,112; Hatch, 118,096; Long, 118,174; Lynch, 118,029; Rosenthal, 118,008; Silman, 117,962; Thompson, 117,840. Republican—Bard, 118,027; Campbell, 117,743; Carson, 117,747; Mery, 117,670; Waymire, 117,717; Hecht, 117,613; Morehouse, 117,711; Willoughby, 117,605; Hanscom, 117,504. People's party—Bowers, 25,311; Dore, 25,254; Warner, 25,256; Barton, 25,243; Moulton, 25,237; Cator, 25,229; McCormick, 25,217; Bowman, 25,201; Fowler, 25,170. Prohibition—McDonald, 8,096; Porter, 8,028; McArthur, 8,007; Miller, 8,029; Hierlihy, 7,991; Luse, 7,972; Caton, 7,980; Kellogg, 7,995; Fowler, 7,921.

For Congressmen, first district—Geary, 19,308; Davis, 13,123; Swafford, 1,546. Second district—Caminetti, 20,741; Davis, 16,781; Dunn, 1,507; White, 122. Third district (unexpired term)—Hilborn, 16,911; English, 14,493; Lyon, 4,326; Scranton, 34. Full term—Hilborn, 13,163; English, 13,138; Lyon, 3,495; Scranton, 671. Fourth district—Maguire, 14,997; Alexander, 13,226; Burman, 1,980; Collins, 296. Fifth district—Loud, 14,660; Ryland, 13,694; Morrison, 2,484; Kelly, 771. Sixth district—Cannon, 20,676; Lindley, 14,271; Dougherty, 1,805. Seventh district— Bowers, 15,856; Wellborn, 14,869; Hamilton, 5,578; Harris, 1,844.

BIOGRAPHICAL SKETCHES OF GOVERNORS

AND

REGISTER

OF

OFFICERS OF THE STATE OF CALIFORNIA,

1849 — 1892.

Biographical Sketches of Governors.

Peter H. Burnett.

Born in Nashville, Tennessee, November 15, 1807; removed with parents to Howard county, Missouri, in the fall of 1817; removed again in 1822 to Clay county; at the age of eighteen accepted the position of clerk in a hotel in Bolivar, Hardeman county, Tennessee, at a salary of $100 per annum; in the winter of 1827 took charge of a store on Clear Creek, some ten miles from Bolivar, in the employ of Rev. W. Blount Peck; on the 20th of August, 1828, married Miss Harriet Rogers; continued in the mercantile business for several years, studying law meanwhile; in 1839 began the practice of law, and edited a weekly newspaper, *The Far West*, published at Liberty, Missouri; in the same year was appointed district attorney in a new judicial district, composed of the counties of Clinton, Andrew, Buchanan, Holt, and Platte; in 1843, left Missouri with his wife and six children for Oregon; was a member of the "Legislative Committee of Oregon," of 1844, which was composed of nine members and consisted of only one house; on the 18th of August, 1845, was elected by the house of representatives judge of the supreme court of Oregon; in 1848, gold having been discovered in California, he left Oregon with a wagon party for that territory; remained in the mines until December 19, 1848, when he started for Sutter's fort and arrived there on December 21; was employed as attorney and agent for General John A. Sutter; removed to San Francisco in 1849, became a member of the legislative assembly and took an active part in its proceedings; on the 13th of November, 1849, was elected governor of California; resigned on January 8th, 1851; resumed the practice of law, in partnership with C. T. Ryland and William T. Wallace; appointed a justice of the supreme court of California, January 13, 1857, by Governor J. Neely Johnson; in June, 1863, was elected president of the "Pacific Accumulation Loan Society," afterward the Pacific bank of San Francisco; resigned from the presidency of the bank in 1880, and is now living in retirement.

John McDougal.

Born in Russ county, Ohio, in 1818; was bred to mercantile pursuits; removed to Indiana, and at the breaking out of the Mexican war was superintendent of the state prison of that state; was a captain of volunteers during the war; came to California in 1848, and engaged in mining and the transportation of supplies to Sacramento; represented Sacramento district in the constitutional convention of 1849; elected lieutenant-governor November 13, 1849; became governor on the resignation of Governor Burnett, and was inaugurated January 9, 1851; died at San Francisco March 30, 1866, of apoplexy.

John Bigler.

Born near Carlisle, Pennsylvania, January 8, 1806, of German antecedents; educated at Dickinson college; removed to Mercer county with his family; learned the printing business in Pittsburg; in 1827 took charge of the Center

County *Democrat*, and edited and published it until 1832; admitted to the bar in 1840; practiced law for nine years in Pennsylvania and Illinois; came to California in 1849, arriving at Sacramento August 31st; engaged himself as an auctioneer, in wood-cutting, mattress-making, etc.; represented Sacramento county in the assembly in 1850 and 1851; elected speaker February 5, 1850, and served in that capacity during the session of 1851; elected governor September 3, 1851, and re-elected September 7, 1853; defeated for that office in 1855; appointed United States minister to Chili by President Buchanan in 1857, which office he held until 1861; was a democratic nominee for congress in 1863, but was defeated; practiced law at Sacramento; was a delegate to the national democratic conventions of 1864 and 1868; appointed assessor of internal revenue for Sacramento district by President Johnson in 1866, but the appointment was not confirmed; in 1867 was appointed by the President one of the commissioners to pass upon the Central Pacific railroad work; established the *State Capital Reporter* in January, 1868, and was its editor until his death; died at Sacramento, November 29, 1871.

J. Neely Johnson.

Born in Johnson township, Gibson county, Indiana, August 2, 1825; removed to Evansville in 1826; admitted to the bar at Keokuk, Iowa, before he was twenty-one; came to California in 1849, arriving at Sacramento in July; engaged in teaming and mining; opened a law office in a tent at Sacramento; elected city attorney in the spring of 1850; was elected as the agent of the state in the autumn following to go to the aid of suffering immigrants; appointed by President Fillmore special territorial census agent; appointed colonel on the staff of Governor McDougal in the spring of 1851 and sent to the seat of the Mariposa Indian troubles; represented Sacramento county in the assembly in 1853; elected governor September 5, 1855; early in 1860 he removed to Nevada; represented Ormsby county in the constitutional convention of that state in 1863; was president of the second convention in 1864; appointed a justice of the Nevada supreme court in 1867, and was elected to that office at the succeeding general election; resumed the practice of law in January, 1871; was appointed soon after by the president one of the visitors and examiners of the West Point military academy; died at Salt Lake city August 31, 1872, from the effects of sunstroke.

John B. Weller.

Born February 22, 1812, at Montgomery, Hamilton county, Ohio; removed with his parents to Oxford, Butler county, where he was educated at the Miami university; studied law in the office of Jesse Corwin, and was admitted to the bar before he had attained his majority; elected prosecuting attorney of Butler county; elected to congress from the then second district of Ohio in 1838, and was twice re-elected; served in the Mexican war, and rose from the rank of a private to be colonel; ran for governor of Ohio in 1848 on the democratic ticket, but was defeated; appointed by President Polk, in January, 1849, a commissioner, under the treaty of Guadalupe Hidalgo, to run the boundary line between the United States and Mexico; elected United States senator from California, January 30, 1852; elected governor, September 2, 1857; inaugurated January 8, 1858; appointed minister plenipotentiary to Mexico by President Buchanan, but was recalled by President Lincoln; located in New Orleans in 1867, where he died, August 17, 1875.

Milton S. Latham.

Born in Columbus, Ohio, May 23, 1827; graduated at Jefferson college, Pennsylvania, in 1845; removed to Alabama and studied law; appointed clerk of the circuit court for Russell county in 1848; removed to California in the winter of 1849; appointed clerk of the recorder's court of San Francisco in 1850; elected district attorney of Sacramento and El Dorado counties; elected a representative in congress November 2, 1852; appointed collector at San Francisco by President Pierce in 1855, and held office until 1857; elected governor September 7, 1859; resigned January 14, 1860; elected United States senator, January 11, 1860; after the expiration of his term he engaged in business in San Francisco; died at New York, March 4, 1882.

John G. Downey.

Born at Castle Sampson, county of Roscommon, Ireland, June 24, 1827; embarked for America at the age of 14; attended school in Charles county, Maryland; at the age of 16 became an apprentice to a druggist in Washington, D. C.; in 1846, removed to Cincinnati, where he became a partner of John Darling, a leading apothecary of that city; came to California by way of the Isthmus in 1849; obtained employment in the wholesale drug store of Henry Johnson & Co., on Dupont street, San Francisco; in 1850, opened a drug store in Los Angeles in partnership with Dr. McFarland, of Tennessee; elected to the legislature in 1856; elected lieutenant-governor of the state in 1859, and became governor four days after the inauguration, Milton S. Latham resigning.

Leland Stanford.

Born near Albany, New York, March 19, 1824; his father was a strong advocate of the Erie canal, and among the first promoters of the railroad between Albany and Schenectady—the first railroad built on the American continent; studied law but never practiced; came to California in 1852 and engaged in mining and merchandising; candidate for state treasurer on the republican ticket in 1857; republican candidate for governor in 1859; elected governor September 4, 1861; engaged in the work of constructing and was president of the Central Pacific railroad, the last spike of which was driven May 8, 1869; was president of the Southern Pacific Company until April 9, 1890; elected United States senator, January 28, 1885; re-elected January 14, 1891.

Frederick F. Low.

Born in Frankfort, Maine, January 30, 1828; received a thorough English education there; arrived in San Francisco, June 14, 1849; mined a few months; engaged in business in San Francisco; commenced business as a banker at Marysville in 1855; elected to congress September, 1861; appointed collector of the port of San Francisco; elected governor September 2, 1863; appointed envoy extraordinary and minister plenipotentiary to China, to succeed J. Ross Browne, September 28, 1869; engaged in the banking business in San Francisco.

Henry H. Haight.

Born in Rochester, New York, May 20, 1825; graduated from Yale college in 1844; studied law in the office of his father at St. Louis; admitted to the bar in Missouri; practiced his profession there till late in 1849, when he emigrated to California, arriving in San Francisco January 20, 1850; practiced law in that city; removed his residence to Alameda county in 1867; elected governor September 4, 1867; defeated for that office in 1871; elected a member of constitutional convention June 19, 1878; died at San Francisco, September 2, 1878.

Newton Booth.

Born in Washington county, Indiana, December 30, 1825; in 1841 his family removed to Terre Haute; was educated at the Asbury (now De Pauw) university, and graduated in 1846; admitted to the bar in 1849; arrived in California October 18, 1850; resided for a time in Amador county, and located in Sacramento in February, 1851 and engaged in mercantile business; elected senator from Sacramento county in 1862; elected governor September 6, 1871; inaugurated December 8, 1871; resigned February 27, 1875; elected United States senator December 20, 1873, for a term to commence March 4, 1875; died at Sacramento July 14, 1892.

Romualdo Pacheco.

Born at Santa Barbara, California, October 31, 1831; was educated by private tutors; engaged in nautical pursuits, and subsequently in agriculture; was a member of the state house of representatives in 1853; was elected county judge in 1854, serving four years; was a member of the state senate in 1858, and again in 1861; was elected state treasurer in 1863; was elected lieutenant-governor in 1871, and became governor of the state when Governor Booth resigned to become United States senator; was nominated on the republican state ticket for the house of representatives of the forty-fifth congress; he was elected to the forty-sixth, and also to the forty-seventh congress, as a republican; during the war he commanded the fifth brigade of state militia; was appointed minister of the United States for the Central American republics in December, 1890.

William Irwin.

Born in Butler county, Ohio, in 1827; was graduated at Marietta college in 1848, and went to Port Gibson, Mississippi, where he taught school for one year, and then returned to Marietta college where he taught until the fall of 1851; in the spring of 1852 he sailed from New York in the ship "Pioneer" for California; upon arriving here he took a trip to Oregon, returning to San Francisco in 1853, where he established a lumber yard on the corner of Market and Steuart streets; in the fall of 1854 he removed to Siskiyou county, and for a few years engaged in merchandising; later he purchased the Yreka *Union*, which he owned and edited until the spring of 1875; he was elected to the assembly in 1861, and re-elected in 1862; was senator at the sessions of 1869–70 and 1871–2, and was re-elected in 1873; and at the session of 1873–74 was elected president pro tem. of the senate; in 1875, Newton Booth having resigned the office of governor, and Lieutenant-Governor Pacheco assuming the office of governor, by virtue of his office of president pro tem. Irwin became lieutenant-governor and resident director of the state prison at San Quentin; was elected in 1875 upon the democratic ticket as governor, and held office until January, 1880; on March 12, 1883, was commissioned by Governor Stoneman one of the harbor commissioners for the port of San Francisco. Died while commissioner, at San Francisco, on March 15, 1886, and his remains were buried in the state plot at Sacramento city.

George Clement Perkins.

Born in Kennebunkport, Maine, August 23, 1839; at the age of 12 years secreted himself on the vessel "Golden Eagle" about to sail for New Orleans, and after leaving port was accepted by the captain as one of the crew; passed the next four years of his life at sea; worked for several months at placer mining in the northern counties of California; obtained employment as porter in a store at Oroville; was promoted to a clerkship and finally became owner of the establishment; in connection with N. D. Rideout and others established the Bank of Butte County, of which he became a director; elected to the state senate for the senatorial district of Butte county in 1869, and again in 1873 to fill the unexpired term of Senator Boucher, deceased; in 1872 became a partner in the firm of Goodall & Nelson, which was later incorporated as the Pacific Coast Steamship Company; appointed trustee of the Napa state insane asylum by Governor Irwin, in 1876; in 1879 was president of the San Francisco Chamber of Commerce; elected governor September 3, 1879; inaugurated January 8, 1880; appointed in 1888 by Governor Waterman, trustee of the asylum at Berkeley for the deaf, dumb, and blind, and again in 1891 by Governor Markham; appointed trustee of the State Mining Bureau in 1889, by Governor Waterman.   •

George Stoneman.

Born in Busti, Chautauqua county, New York, August 8, 1822; attended the Jamestown academy, and at the age of 20 was named by Hon. Staley N. Clarke, congressman from that district, to go to West Point; graduated with high honors on July 1, 1846, in company with Generals Geo. B. McClellan, I. N. Palmer and others; upon leaving school was promoted in the army to brevet second lieutenant, first dragoons, stationed at Fort Leavenworth, Kansas; during the war with Mexico was ordered to San Diego, California, and was engaged as acting assistant quartermaster of the Mormon battalion; arrived at San Diego mission January 30, 1847, after a long and arduous march which brought the first overland wagon train to this state; in 1848–49 was placed in command of the San Francisco Presidio; served on the Pacific coast until March 3, 1855; appointed captain of the second cavalry and reported at Jefferson Barracks, Missouri, to join his company; thence went to Camp Cooper, Texas, doing ordinary frontier duty for several months; was granted a leave of absence for eighteen months; returned in 1859 and went again into active service, commanding the Pesos expedition along the Mexican frontier; at the beginning of the war of the rebellion figured in the defense of the capital, and was made major of the first cavalry; was afterward chosen a member of General McClellan's staff; on August 13, 1861, was made brigadier-general of the United States volunteers and chief of cavalry of the army of the Potomac; from March to August, 1862, was in the Virginia peninsular campaign and laid siege to Yorktown on April 5th; on November 29, 1862, was made major-general of the volunteer army; from December, 1862, to June, 1863, was occupied with the army of the Potomac in the Rappahannock campaign; during the engagement before Fredericksburg, participated as commander of the third corps; at the conclusion of that contest, was made a brevet colonel of the regular army, his promotion specially stating "for gallant and meritorious service at the battle of Fredericksburg;" from January 28 to April 4, 1864, was in command of the twenty-third infantry corps in east Tennessee, being promoted on March 30th to lieutenant-colonel, third cavalry; on July 31, 1864, was taken prisoner of war at Clinton, while in command on a raid to Macon and Andersonville to release union

troops confined there; was released on October 27, 1864, and transferred to·
the temporary command of the department of Ohio, at Louisville, Kentucky;
during the month of December, 1864, commanded a raid into southwest
Virginia, successfully engaging in affairs at Kingport, Bristol and Marion
within four days, and on the 21st capturing Saltville; from February 14 to
March 20, 1865, commanded the district of East Tennessee, after which he·
had charge of an expedition from Knoxville, Tennessee, to Asheville, North
Carolina, and southwest Virginia; on this march captured Wytheville and
Charlottesville; was promoted to brevet brigadier-general of the United
States army "for gallant and meritorious conduct at the capture of Charlottesville;" was farther promoted on the same day to brevet major-general "for
gallant and meritorious service in the field during the war of the rebellion;"
on April 7, 1865, destroyed the Bristol and Lynchburg railroad to prevent the
withdrawal of the enemy over that route; on April 15th, commanded a·
brigade of cavalry at the capture of Talisbury, North Carolina; on April 20th
captured the garrison at Asheville, North Carolina; from June 7, 1865, to
June 5, 1866, was stationed in command of the department of the Tennessee,
engaged in mustering out troops; from June 9 to August 13, 1866, commanded the department of the Cumberland, and from August 13th to the
31st, the district of the Cumberland; on July 28, 1866, was appointed by
President Johnson colonel of the twenty-first infantry; was mustered out of
the volunteer service September 1, 1866, being one of the last to go; on December 17, 1866, was placed in command of the district of Petersburg,
Virginia; on June 2, 1868, was appointed to the command of the first military district of Virginia, as organized under the reconstruction laws of
congress; was recalled from Virginia by President Grant and sent to
Arizona, being placed in command of the district there; from May 3, 1870,
to June 4, 1871, was in command of the department of Arizona; on August
16, 1871, retired from active service for "disability contracted in the line of
duty;" moved with his family to the San Gabriel valley, Los Angeles
county; appointed by President Hayes a member of the Indian commission;
in 1876, was appointed railroad commissioner by Governor Irwin, serving
until 1879, when he was elected by the people to the same position; elected
governor of California November 7, 1882; inaugurated January 10, 1883.

¡Washington Bartlett.

Born in Savannah, Georgia, February 29, 1824, being the eldest son of
Cosane Emir and Sarah E. (Melhado) Bartlett; he was of English puri-
tan ancestry on the father's side, long domiciled in America; educated
in private schools in Georgia and Florida; he learned the printer's trade
in his father's office in Florida; was elected state printer of Florida in 1846,
and served one term of two years. Arrived in San Francisco, California,
November 17, 1849, having come around Cape Horn in a sailing vessel; immediately opened a job printing office, having shipped from Charleston, S.
C., printing material, which .arrived in advance of him; in January, 1850,
issued the *Daily Journal of Commerce*, which made its appearance simul-
taneously with the *Daily Alta California*, the first daily newspapers published
in California; in 1850, published the first book printed in California; lost
heavily by the destructive fires which visited San Francisco during the years
1850, 1851, and 1853; continued in the printing and newspaper business until
1857, being interested in the publication of the *Evening News* and *True Californian*; appointed deputy county clerk of San Francisco in 1857; elected
county clerk in 1859, and re-elected in 1861; admitted to the bar, and practiced law in partnership with his brother, Columbus Bartlett, from 1864 to

1867, when he was again elected county clerk of San Francisco county and served his term; in 1870 was appointed by Governor Haight, state harbor commissioner, to fill vacancy occasioned by the death of J. H. Cutter; elected state senator in 1873, and served term of four years; went to Europe in 1878, and spent a couple of years abroad and in the Atlantic states; elected mayor of San Francisco in 1882, and re-elected in 1884, serving two full terms; nominated in August, 1886, by the democratic party, for governor, and was elected by a close vote over Hon. John F. Swift, republican, although the republican candidate for lieutenant-governor (R. W. Waterman) and the greater part of the republican ticket were successful; inaugurated governor of California, January 8, 1887, and served until his death, September 12, 1887; in addition to these public stations, Governor Bartlett held many positions of trust and honor, such as president of the Society of California Pioneers, vice-president of the San Francisco Savings Union bank, secretary of the Chamber of Commerce, etc.; Governor Bartlett was never married.

Robert W. Waterman.

Born in Fairfield, Herkimer county, New York, December 15, 1826; when very young moved to Sycamore, Illinois; was clerk in a store until he was 20 years of age, when he engaged in the mercantile business on his own respon-sibility at Belvidere, Illinois; came to California with a party of immigrants in 1850; returned to Illinois in 1852 and published the *Wilmington Independ-ent*; came again to California in 1873; established a home in San Bernardino county, where he resided until 1890, when he moved to San Diego; elected lieutenant-governor, November 2, 1886; became governor on the death of Washington Bartlett, and was inaugurated September 13, 1887; died at San Diego, April 12, 1891.

Henry Harrison Markham.

Born in Wilmington, Essex county, New York on the 16th day of November, 1840, and received his education at the public and private schools of his native town, and at Wheeler's academy, Vermont.; he performed all the manual labor incident to a farm hand of that day, and became proficient in every branch of farming as it was then conducted; he removed to the state of Wisconsin in 1861, and entered the army from that state; was with General Sherman on his famous march to the sea, and was severely wounded at the battle of Whippy Swamp, in South Carolina, on the 3d day of February, 1865, from which wound he never fully recovered; at the close of the war he returned to Wisconsin and studied law with the noted firm of Waldo, Ody, & Van, of Milwaukee; he was admitted to the circuit and supreme courts of that state, to the United States district and circuit courts for the district of Wisconsin, and afterward to the supreme court of the United States; he pursued the practice of his profession in the city of Milwaukee until the fall of 1878, when, owing to the loss of health and continued suffering from his wound, he was compelled to give up his practice; he removed with his family to Pasadena, Los Angeles county, in this state, where he has since continued to reside; he was successfully engaged in quartz mining, of both gold and silver, in California, until the summer of 1884, when he was nominated by the republican party for congress in the sixth congressional district, and elected; he served during the forty-ninth congress, securing the passage of many important measures for the benefit of his district, and especially for Los Angeles county; his health not permitting, he was compelled to refuse a renomination so flatteringly tendered him by his entire constituency, and at the end of his term in congress he retired to private life; he was not permitted, however, to remain in retirement long, as the congress of the United States soon elected him one of the managers of the national soldiers' homes of the United States; in this position he devoted a very large amount of his time to all the homes, but especially to the one at Santa Monica, and although this service was performed without compensation it was a work in which he took a deep and active interest; as a business man he has been successful in all his undertakings, and is now interested in several important business enterprises; he was nominated by his party and elected governor of this State in 1890, which position he now occupies.

*REGISTER OF STATE OFFICERS.

Abbott, Augustus, Railroad Commissioner, First District, 1887–90.
Abbott, C. S., Assemblyman, Monterey, 1875–76, 1877–78.
Abbott, J. P., Senator, Marin and Contra Costa, 1887.
Abell, Alex. G., Senator, San Francisco, 1863. *Died, San Francisco, December 28, 1890.*
Ables, T. J., Assemblyman, Marin, 1867–68, 1873–74.
Adams, A. C., Judge Eleventh Judicial District, appointed 1869, elected 1880.
Adams, Alonzo W., Senator, Butte, Shasta, etc., 1851.
Adams, Amos, Assemblyman, Sacramento, 1861, 1863.
Adams, James, Assemblyman, Sonoma, 1880.
Adams, L. B., Assemblyman, Yolo, 1887, 1889.
Adams, P. R., Assemblyman, Santa Cruz, 1893.
Adams, W. S., Assemblyman, Tulare and Kern, 1877–78.
Adkison, D. O., Assemblyman, Yuba, 1855, 1863. *Died, San Francisco, November 3, 1887.*
Aitkin, John R., Superior Judge, San Diego County, elected 1888.
Aldrich, Lewis, Judge Sixth Judicial District, elected 1851. *Died, San Francisco, May 19, 1885.*
Aldrich, W. A., Assemblyman, San Francisco, 1871–72, 1873–74.
Alexander, Charles O., Assemblyman, Alameda, 1887, 1889; Harbor Commissioner, 1889–
Alexander, J. K., Superior Judge, Monterey County, elected 1879, 1884.
Alexander, J. S., Assemblyman, Stanislaus, 1891.
Alford, W. H., Assemblyman, Tulare, 1893.
Allen, Charles C., Adjutant-General, 1891–
Allen, Charles D., Assemblyman, Marin, 1877–78.
Allen, E. H., Assemblyman, San Joaquin, 1863–64.
Allen, Isaac, Senator, Yuba, 1858, 1859.
Allen, J. M., Superior Judge, San Francisco, elected 1879.
Allen, James, State Printer, 1856–58. *Died, Washoe, Nevada, October 31, 1863.*
Allen, James M., Adjutant-General, 1868–70.
Allen, R. G., Assemblyman, San Bernardino, 1863.
Allen, Samuel I., Assemblyman, Sonoma, 1885.
Alley, S. H., Assemblyman, Sierra, 1863–64.
Almy, Joseph, Assemblyman, Marin, 1885.
Alvarado, Juan B., Governor under Mexican rule, 1836–42. *Died, San Pablo, July 13, 1882.*
Alviso, Valentine, Assemblyman, Alameda, 1881.
Amerige, George, Assemblyman, San Francisco, 1862.
Amerman, I. A., Assemblyman, Alameda, 1873–74. *Died, San Leandro, February 14, 1877.*
Ames, A., Assemblyman, Alameda, 1891.
Ames, J. P., Assemblyman, San Mateo, 1877–78; Warden of State Prison at San Quentin, 1880–83.
Ames, T. M., Assemblyman, Mendocino, 1862, 1863.
Amyx, Fleming, Assemblyman, Tuolumne, 1855, 1861. *Died, Stockton, November 4, 1861.*
Anderson, Alexander, Senator, Tuolumne, 1852; Supreme Justice, 1852.
Anderson, Francis, Assemblyman, Sierra, 1854; Senator, Sierra, 1863.
Anderson, J. W., Superintendent of Public Instruction, 1891–
Anderson, James, Senator, Placer, 1858, 1859, 1860. *Died, Auburn, October 12, 1866.*
Anderson, R. M., Lieutenant-Governor, 1856–58. *Died, Swan Lake, Arkansas, March 24, 1872.*
Anderson, T. H., Assemblyman, Napa, 1857, 1858.
Anderson, W. A., Assemblyman, Sacramento, 1893.

---

*Officials holding by appointment, such as trustees of institutions, commissioners, etc., with few exceptions, are not included in this list.

Anderson, W. F., Assemblyman, San Francisco, 1877-78. *Died, Idaho, July 7, 1883.*

Anderson, W. L, Senator, Napa, Lake, and Sonoma, 1880, 1881.

Andrews, A. B., Assemblyman, Amador, 1863. *Dead.*

Andrews, A. R., Assemblyman, Shasta, 1856, 1869-70, 1871-72; Member Second Constitutional Convention, 1878-79, Trinity and Shasta District.

Andrews, Moses, Assemblyman, Placer, 1855. *Died, Auburn, December 9, 1883.*

Andross, Moses C., Senator, Tuolumne, 1871-72, 1873-74. *Died, San Francisco, June 15, 1881.*

Androus, S. N., Assemblyman, Los Angeles, 1893.

Angelotti, Frank M., Superior Judge, Marin County, elected 1890.

Angney, W. Z., Assemblyman, Santa Clara, 1867-68; Senator, Santa Clara, 1875-76, 1877-78. *Died, Gilroy, January 28, 1878.*

Anthony, Elihu, Assemblyman, Santa Cruz, 1880.

Anthony, William, Assemblyman, Santa Cruz, 1865-66. *Died, Livermore, January, 1890.*

Appling, P. C., Assemblyman, Fresno, 1869-70.

Aram, Joseph, Assemblyman, San Jose District, 1849-50; Member First Constitutional Convention, 1849, San Jose District.

Archer, Lawrence, Assemblyman, Santa Clara, 1875-76.

Arguello, Jose Dario, Governor under Spanish rule, 1814-15. *Died, Guadalajara, 1828.*

Arguello, Louis, Governor under Mexican rule, 1823-25. *Died, San Francisco, March 27, 1830.*

Arick, Rufus E., Assemblyman, Tulare and Kern, 1881; Superior Judge, Kern County, elected 1884, 1890. *Died, Bakersfield, December 31, 1890.*

Arms, Charles S., Assemblyman, San Francisco, 1891; Senator, 1893-

Armstrong, C. B., Superior Judge, Amador County, appointed 1886, elected, 1886, 1890. *Died, Jackson, Amador County, November 9, 1892.*

Armstrong, John W., Trustee of State Library, 1870-82; Superior Judge, Sacramento County, appointed 1883, 1886, elected 1888.

Armstrong, William R., Assemblyman, Nevada, 1859.

Arnot, N. D., Superior Judge, Alpine County, elected 1879, 1884, 1890.

Arrillaga, Jose Joaquin, Governor under Spanish rule, 1792-94, 1800-14. *Died, Soledad, 1857.*

Arrington, J. J., Assemblyman, Klamath, 1855.

Ashe, R. I., Assemblyman, Kern and Ventura, 1885.

Ashley, D. R., Assemblyman, Monterey, 1854, 1855; Senator, Monterey and Santa Cruz, 1856, 1857; President pro tem., 1856; State Treasurer, 1862-63. *Died, San Francisco, July 18, 1873.*

Asmussen, A., Assemblyman, San Francisco, 1877-78.

Atherton, J. W., Assemblyman, Marin, 1887, 1889.

Atwell, A. J., Assemblyman, Tulare and Kern, 1883.

Aud, Francis L., Assemblyman, Yuba, 1858, 1859.

Aull, T. M., Assemblyman, San Joaquin, 1857.

Avery, Benjamin P., State Printer, 1862-63. *Died, Peking, China, November, 8, 1875.*

Avery, John M., Assemblyman, Nevada, 1861, 1862.

Axtell, Samuel B., Representative to Congress, 1867-70: *Died, New Jersey, August 6, 1891.*

Ayer, Isaac, Assemblyman, Calaveras, 1865-66, 1867-68.

Ayers, James J., Member Second Constitutional Convention, 1878-79, Fourth Congressional District; State Printer, 1883-86; Trustee State Library, 1885-86.

Aylett, W. D., Assemblyman, Siskiyou, 1854.

. Babcock, Jasper, Assemblyman, San Francisco, 1860.

Backus, Samuel W., Assemblyman, San Francisco, 1877-78; Adjutant-General, 1880-82.

Bacon, P. B., Assemblyman, Tuolumne, 1871-72.

Badgley, William H., Judge Sixteenth Judicial District, appointed 1862, elected, 1862.

Badlam, Alex., Jr., Assemblyman, Sacramento, 1863-64.

Baechtel, Martin, Assemblyman, Mendocino, 1861.

Baehr, Ferdinand, State Treasurer, 1871-75.

Bagge, T. F., Assemblyman, Alameda, 1875-76. *Died, Oakland, March 26, 1886.*

Bagley, John W., Assemblyman, San Francisco, 1854. *Dead.*

Bailey, D. B., Assemblyman, Santa Clara, 1860. *Died, ' Mountain View, September 9, 1888.*
Bailey, G. W., Assemblyman, Tuolumne, 1860.
Bailey, Hiram, Assemblyman, Alameda, 1887.
Bailey, W. C., Senator, Santa Clara, 1891, 1893.
Baird, Curtis, Assemblyman. San Mateo. 1871–72.
Baird, J. H., Senator, San Francisco, 1853.
Baker, F. E., Assemblyman, Yolo, 1881.
Baker, George F., Senator, Santa Clara, 1880, 1881; President pro tem., 1880. *Died, San Francisco, March 11, 1882.*
Baker, James H., Senator, Placer, 1858, 1859.
Baker, John E., Assemblyman, Sacramento, 1881. *Died, Sacramento, May 2, 1881.*
Baker, Thomas, Assemblyman, Tulare, 1855; Senator, Tuolumne and Fresno, 1862, 1863. *Died, Bakersfield, November 24, 1872.*
Baldwin, D. P., Assemblyman, San Joaquin District, 1849–50; Tuolumne, 1851. *Dead.*
Baldwin, F. T., Senator, San Joaquin, 1883, 1885; Superior Judge, San Joaquin County, appointed 1886.
•Baldwin, Joseph G., Supreme Justice, 1858. *Died, San Francisco, September 29, 1864.*
Ballou, S. A., Assemblyman, El Dorado, 1854, 1858; Senator, Plumas and Butte, 1859, 1860.
Banbury, J., Assemblyman, Los Angeles, 1885.
Bangs, V. E., Assemblyman, Stanislaus, 1889.
Banks, James A., Assemblyman, San Francisco, 1858, 1859, 1861, 1863; Senator, San Francisco, 1862. *Killed by Indians in Nevada, August 1, 1867.*
Banks, W. O., Senator, San Francisco, 1889, 1891.
Banning, Phineas, Senator, Los Angeles, 1865–66, 1867–68. *Died, San Francisco, March 8, 1885.*
Banvard, E. M., Senator, Placer, 1869–70, 1871–72.
Barber, T. H., Assemblyman, San Francisco, 1875–76.
Barbour, Clitus, Member Second Constitutional Convention, 1878–79, San Francisco District.
Barbour, William T., Judge Tenth Judicial District, elected 1851, 1852. *Died, Virginia City, Nev., May 11, 1872.*
Barclay, James, Assemblyman, Calaveras, 1863.
Barclay, William P., Assemblyman. Placer, 1859.
Bard, Thomas R., Presidential Elector, 1893.
Barlow, Chas. A., Assemblyman, San Luis Obispo, 1893.
Barker, S., Assemblyman, Nevada, 1871–72.
Barklage, William, Assemblyman, El Dorado, 1871–72.
Barker, C. O., Assemblyman, San Bernardino, 1893.
Barnard, T. H., Assemblyman, Butte, 1891.
Barnes, B. W., Assemblyman, Plumas and Lassen, 1871–72.
Barnes, D. G., Assemblyman, Solano, 1883, 1885.
Barnes, William H. L., Member Second Constitutional Convention, 1878–79, First Congressional District; Presidential Elector, 1888.
Barnett, A. T., Assemblyman, San Francisco, 1891. .
Barnett, J. D., Assemblyman, Sonoma, 1891.
Barnett, Robert, Assemblyman, Colusa, 1885.
Barrett, H., Assemblyman, Yuba, 1857.
Barri, Felipe de, Governor under Spanish rule, 1771–74.
Barry, Edmund, Member Second Constitutional Convention, 1878–79, Nevada and Sierra District.
Barry, Michael H., Assemblyman, San Francisco, 1887.
Barry, Thomas F., Assemblyman, San Francisco, 1883.
Barstow, George, Assemblyman, San Francisco, 1862, 1863, 1877–78; Speaker of the House, 1862. *Died, San Francisco, September 9, 1883.*
Bartlett, Columbus, Private Secretary to Governor Washington Bartlett.
Bartlett, Washington, County Clerk of San Francisco, 1859–63, 1867–69; Harbor Commissioner, 1870–71; Senator, San Francisco, 1873–74, 1875–76; Mayor of San Francisco, 1883–85; Governor, 1887. *Died, Oakland, September 12, 1887.*
Barton, Benjamin, Assemblyman, San Bernardino, 1862.
Barton, Hiram M., Assemblyman, San Bernardino, 1887.
Barton, W. H., Assemblyman, Sacramento, 1862, 1863.

Barton, James N., Assemblyman, Sacramento, 1873–74; Member Second Constitutional Convention, 1878–79, Mendocino, Humboldt, and Del Norte District.
Bass, J. S. P., Assemblyman, Trinity and Shasta, 1880. *Died, Redding, January 7. 1892.*
Bassham, W. R., Senator, San Jose District, 1849–50.   *
Batchelder, A. J., Assemblyman, Yuba, 1856, 1865–66, 1867–68.
Bateman, E. B., Assemblyman, San Joaquin District, 1849–50.
Bates, Fordyce, Assemblyman, Trinity, 1859.
Bates, Henry, Assemblyman, Shasta, 1855; State Treasurer, 1856–57. *Died,. San Francisco, November 18, 1862.*
Battelle, T. S., Assemblyman, Sierra, 1867–68.
Battles, William W., Assemblyman. San Francisco, 1862.
Baughman, W. E., Assemblyman, El Dorado. 1891.
Bausman, William, Private Secretary to Governor J. Neely Johnson.
Bayley, A. J., Assemblyman, El Dorado and Alpine, 1871–72, 1883.
Beach, D. S., Assemblyman, Placer, 1860.
Beach, Horace, Senator, Yuba and Sutter, 1867–68, 1869–70. *Dead.*
Beaman, J. H., Assemblyman, Yuba, 1863–64.
Beamer. R. H., Member of State Board of Equalization, 1891–
Beard, E. B., Assemblyman, Stanislaus, 1883, 1885.
Beard, J. S., Superior Judge, Siskiyou County, elected 1890.
Beard, Joseph R., Clerk of the Supreme Court, 1855–56. *Died, San Francisco, 1882.*
Beatty, E. T., Assemblyman, Calaveras, 1855, 1856, 1857; Speaker, 1857. *Dead.*
Beatty, William H., Trustee State Library, 1886–87; Chief Justice, 1888–
Beauvais, A. B., Senator, Tuolumne, 1885. *Died, Columbia, June, 1886.*
Beazell, James, Senator, Alameda, 1875–76, 1877–78.
Beck, Thomas, Senator, Santa Cruz and Monterey, 1871–72, 1873–74; Secretary of State, 1876–80.
Beckman, William, Railroad Commissioner, First District, 1891–
Beecher, J. L., Assemblyman, San Joaquin, 1891.
Beerstecher, Charles J., Member Second Constitutional Convention, 1878–79,. San Francisco District; Railroad Commissioner, Second District, 1880–82.
Beeson, J. B., Assemblyman, Sonoma, 1863.
Belcher, Isaac S., Judge Tenth Judicial District, elected 1863; Supreme Justice, 1872–73; Member Second Constitutional Convention, 1878–79, Third Congressional District; Trustee State Library, 1882–90; Supreme Court Commissioner, 1884–
Belcher, W. C., Trustee State Library, 1866–70.
Belden, David, Senator, Nevada, 1865–66, 1867–68; Judge Twentieth Judicial District, appointed 1872, elected 1873; Superior Judge, Santa Clara County, elected, 1879, 1884. *Died, San Jose, May 14, 1888.*
Bell, Aaron, Superior Judge, Shasta County, elected 1879, 1884.
Bell, John C., Assemblyman, El Dorado, 1860. *Shot and stabbed by Dr. W. H. Stone. in the State Capitol, April 11, 1860, and died on the 15th.*
Bell, Peter, Member Second Constitutional Convention, 1878–79, San Francisco District.
Bell, Robert. Assemblyman, Nevada, 1871–72.
Bell, Samuel, Assemblyman, Mariposa, 1853; State Controller, 1854–55.
Bell, Samuel B., Assemblyman, Alameda, 1862; Senator, Santa Clara and Alameda, 1857, 1858.
Bell, Vincent G., Assemblyman, Nevada, 1856. *Died, San Francisco, July 24, 1880.*
Bennett, A., Assemblyman, Solano, 1880.
Bennett, A. G., Assemblyman, Santa Clara, 1893.
Bennett, C. F. Assemblyman, Orange County, 1893.
Bennett, F. C., Assemblyman, San Francisco, 1851.
Bennett, J. W., Assemblyman, Sonoma, 1854.
Bennett, M. P., Superior Judge, El Dorado County, elected, 1890.
Bennett, Nathaniel, Senator, San Francisco District, 1849–50; Supreme Justice, 1849–51. *Died, San Francisco, April 20, 1886.*
Benton. John E., Assemblyman, Sacramento, 1862; Senator, Sacramento, 1863–64, 1865–66. *Died, Oakland, February 18, 1888.*
Berry, Campbell P., Assemblyman, Sutter, 1869–70, 1871–72, 1875–76, 1877–78; Speaker of the House. 1877–78; Representative to Congress, 1879–82.
Berry, George S., Assemblyman, Tulare, 1889; Senator, Inyo, Tulare, and Kern, 1891, 1893.

Berry, J., Senator, Klamath, Siskiyou, etc., 1858, 1859; Member Second Constitutional Convention, 1878-79, Siskiyou and Modoc District.
Bert, Eugene F., Assemblyman, San Francisco, 1891.
Betge, R. J., Senator, San Francisco, 1869-70, 1871-72. *Dead.*
Bever, Tunis S., Assemblyman, Calaveras, 1867-68. *Died, Sacramento, November 27, 1878.*
Bibb, D. H., Assemblyman, San Francisco, 1883.
Bidwell, John, Senator, Sacramento District, 1849-50; Representative to Congress, 1865-67; Trustee State Normal School at Chico, 1887-
Bigelow, Samuel C., Assemblyman, San Francisco, 1862.
Biggs, Marion, Assemblyman, Sacramento, 1867-68, Butte, 1869-70; Member Second Constitutional Convention, 1878-79, Third Congressional District; Commissioner to attend the Centennial Celebration of the Inauguration of George Washington as President of the United States, 1888; Representative to Congress, 1887-91.
Biggs, Marion, Jr., Assemblyman, Sacramento, 1875-76.
Biggy, W. J., Senator, San Francisco, 1893.
Bigler, John, Assemblyman, Sacramento, 1849-50, 1851; Speaker of the House, 1851; Governor, 1852-56; Trustee of State Library, 1870-71. *Died, Sacramento, November 29, 1871.*
Bird, A. B., Assemblyman, El Dorado, 1867-68.
Birdseye, J. C., Senator, Nevada, 1863.
Birney, T. C., Assemblyman, Tuolumne, 1875-76, 1881.
Black, H. M., Assemblyman, San Francisco, 1889.
Black, Joseph F., Assemblyman, Alameda, 1885. *Died, San Francisco, May 9, 1887.*
Blackburn, William, Assemblyman, Santa Clara, 1856. *Died, San Francisco, March 25, 1867.*
Blackmer, Eli T., Member Second Constitutional Convention, 1878-79, San Diego District.
Blackwell, S. L., Assemblyman, Nevada, 1875-76, 1877-78.
Blair, A. W., Assemblyman, Monterey, 1861.
Blake, George H., Assemblyman, San Francisco, 1853. *Died, Waterford, New York, August 27, 1854.*
Blake, M. C., Assemblyman, San Francisco, 1857.
Blake, Seth B., Assemblyman, San Francisco, 1877-78.
Blakeley, F. A., Assemblyman, Tulare, 1893.
Blanchard, D. L., Assemblyman, Tuolumne, 1852.
Blanchard, George A., Superior Judge, Colusa County, appointed 1881.
Blanchard, N. W., Assemblyman, Placer, 1863.
Blankenship, J. A., Assemblyman, Monterey, 1869-70.
Bledsoe, A. C., Assemblyman, Sonoma, 1865-66.
Bledsoe, A. J., Assemblyman, Humboldt, 1891, 1893.
Bliss, Simeon M., Judge Tenth Judicial District, elected 1858. *Died, Marysville, May 25, 1887.*
Blue, Thomas, Assemblyman, Nevada, 1875-76.
Bockius, G. W., Assemblyman, Santa Cruz, 1871-72.
Bodley, Thomas, Assemblyman, Santa Clara, 1851. *Died, San Jose, September 27, 1878.*
Bogardus, Edgar, Assemblyman, El Dorado, 1855. *Dead.*
Bogart, J. C., Senator, San Diego, etc., 1862, 1863. *Died, San Francisco, August 15, 1876.*
Boggs, H. C., Member Second Constitutional Convention, 1878-79, Napa, Lake, and Sonoma District.
Boggs, John, Senator, Colusa, etc., 1871-72, 1873-74, 1887, 1889; Director Napa State Insane Asylum, 1876-80; Member State Board of Agriculture, 1880-84, 1884-88, 1888-92, 1892-; Penology Commissioner, 1885; State Prison Director, 1885-87.
Boggs, L. W., Assemblyman, Sonoma, 1852. *Died, Sonoma, March 11, 1861.*
Bolander, H. N., State Superintendent of Public Instruction, 1871-75.
Boles, John L., Assemblyman, El Dorado, 1855.
Bondurant, James M., Judge Thirteenth Judicial District, elected 1863. *Died, Visalia, November 10, 1865.*
Bones, J. W., Senator, Alameda, 1877-78.
Booker, Samuel A., Judge Fifth Judicial District, elected 1869, 1875. *Died, Stockton, December 15, 1891.*
Boone, John L., Senator, San Francisco, 1885.

39

Booth, Andrew G., Assemblyman, San Francisco, 1883; Trustee of State Library, 1886–90.

Booth, Newton, Senator, Sacramento, 1863; Governor, 1871–75; United States Senator, 1875–81; Commissioner of the Funded Debt Sinking Fund of Sacramento, 1886–92. *Died, Sacramento, July 14, 1892.*

Borica, Diego de, Governor under Spanish rule, 1794–1800. *Died, Durango, July, 1800.*

Boring, Samuel W., Assemblyman, Nevada, 1856; Senator, Santa Clara, 1877–78.

Borland, John, Assemblyman, El Dorado, 1856.

Boruck, Marcus D., Secretary of the Senate Twenty-third and Twenty-fourth Sessions; Director State Board of Agriculture, 1880; Private Secretary to Governor R. W. Waterman.

Bosquit, John, Assemblyman, Placer, 1865–66. *Died, near Lincoln, November 9, 1868.*

Bost, John W., Surveyor-General, 1867–71; Assemblyman, Mariposa and Merced, 1881, 1887.

Bostwick, John H., Assemblyman, Nevada, 1853, 1854.

Botts, Charles T., Member First Constitutional Convention, 1849, Monterey District; Judge Sixth Judicial District. appointed 1857; State Printer, 1860–61. *Died, San Francisco, October 4, 1880.*

Boucher, David, Senator, Plumas, 1871–72. *Died, Dayton, Butte County, September 16, 1872.*

Boucher, Josiah, Member Second Constitutional Convention, 1878–79, Butte District. *Died, Indiana, August 9, 1892.*

Boulware, M., Assemblyman, Sutter, 1863–64.

Bowe, James E., Assemblyman, El Dorado, 1856.

Bowers, S. C., Assemblyman, Marin, 1883.

Bowers, Thomas J., Superior Judge Marin County, elected 1879.

Bowers, W. W., Assemblyman, San Diego, 1873–74; Senator, San Bernardino and San Diego, 1887, 1889; Trustee State Normal School at Los Angeles; Representative to Congress, 1891, 1893.

Bowie, G. W., Assemblyman, Colusa, 1854.

Bowman, James, Assemblyman, San Francisco, 1863–64, 1865–66.

Bowman, John H., Assemblyman, Amador, 1860.

Boyce, W. W., Assemblyman, San Francisco, 1893.

Boyston, John S., Senator, San Francisco, 1877–78. *Died, San Francisco, December 15, 1883.*

Brackett, J. E., Assemblyman, Sonoma District, 1849–50.

Bradford, A. C., Assemblyman, San Joaquin, 1854; Presidential Elector, 1856; Judge Thirteenth Judicial District, elected 1867. Register U. S. Land Office. *Died, Alameda County, February 15, 1891.*

Bradford, John S., Assemblyman, Sonoma District, 1849–50, 1851. *Died, Springfield, Ill., January 28, 1892.*

Bradley, B. T., Senator, Calaveras and Amador, 1859, 1860.

Bradley, E. L., Senator, Placer, 1865–66, 1867–68. *Died, San Jose, July 17, 1880.*

Bradley, J. C., Assemblyman, Yuba, 1871–72, 1873–74, 1875–76.

Bradley, L. R., Assemblyman, San Joaquin, 1861. *Died, Elko, Nev., March 21, 1879.*

Braley, M. A., Assemblyman, San Francisco, 1865–66. *Died, San Francisco, September 7, 1868.*

Branch, L. C., Assemblyman, Stanislaus, 1881.

Brannan, Samuel, Presidential Elector, 1864. *Died, Escondido, San Diego County, May 5, 1889.*

Brannan, T. J., Assemblyman, San Francisco. 1889.

Braunhart, Samuel, Assemblyman, San Francisco, 1880.

Braynard, C. P., Superior Judge, Tehama County, elected 1882, 1884.

Breckinridge, J. W., Assemblyman, Mariposa and Merced, 1883. *Died, Merced, May 9, 1892.*

Breen, James F., Assemblyman, San Benito, 1877–78; Superior Judge, San Benito County, elected 1879, 1884, 1890.

Brent, J. L., Assemblyman, Los Angeles, 1856, 1857.

Bretz, A. Assemblyman, Alameda, 1893.

Brewster, John H., Surveyor-General, 1856–58.

Brewton, J. G., Assemblyman, Sacramento, 1855.

Briceland, J. M., Assemblyman, Shasta and Trinity, 1875–76, 1883; Senator, Trinity, Siskiyou, etc., 1887, 1889.

Brickwedel, H. M., Assemblyman, San Francisco, 1889.
Bridgeford, E. A., Superior Judge, Colusa County, elected 1884, 1890.
Brierly, J. R., Assistant Secretary of Senate, 1880; Journal Clerk of the Senate, 1881; Assemblyman, Los Angeles, 1887, 1889; Speaker pro. tem., 1887. *Died, San Jose, January 6, 1891.*
Briggs, Alfred, Assemblyman, El Dorado, 1854, 1859.
Briggs, H. W., Assemblyman, Santa Clara, 1861.
Briggs, R. M., Assemblyman, Amador; 1858; Superior Judge, Mono County, elected 1879, 1884. *Died, Bridgeport, December 8, 1886.*
Britt, E. W., Assemblyman, Lake, 1885.
Britt, James E., Assemblyman, San Francisco, 1887; Senator, San Francisco, 1889, 1891.
Brocklebank, M. T., Private Secretary to Governor John B. Weller.
Brockway, S. W., Judge Eleventh Judicial District, elected 1863. *Died, San Mateo, March 31, 1869.*
Broderick, David C., Senator, San Francisco, 1849-50, 1851, 1852; President of the Senate, 1851; Lieutenant-Governor, 1851; United States Senator, 1857-59. *Died, San Francisco, September 16, 1859.*
Broderick, John T., Senator, San Francisco, 1891, 1893.
Broderick, William, Assemblyman, San Francisco, 1875-76, 1877-78.
Broderson, B. J., Assemblyman, San Francisco, 1867-68.
Brooks, George J., Assemblyman, San Francisco, 1863-64.
Brooks, J. Marion, Senator, Ventura, etc., 1883; Assemblyman, Kern and Ventura, 1887.
Brooks, Max, Assemblyman, Butte, 1877-78, 1880.
Brooks, Samuel H., State Controller, 1860-61.
Brown, A. C., Assemblyman, Amador and Alpine, 1863-64, 1865-66, 1869-70.
Brown, Alex., Assemblyman, Calaveras, 1891.
Brown, C. L. F., Assemblyman, Calaveras, 1871-72.
Brown, Elam, Member First Constitutional Convention, 1849, San Jose District; Assemblyman, San Jose District, 1849-50; Contra Costa, 1851. *Died, August, 1889.*
Brown, Frank M., Senator, San Joaquin, etc., 1885.
Brown, H. M. C., Assemblyman, Nevada, 1855. *Dead.*
Brown, H. R. K., Assemblyman, Sonoma, 1880.
Brown, J. E., Assemblyman, Yuba, 1869-70.
Brown, J. F., Assemblyman, Solano, 1889.
Brown, J. P., Assemblyman, Yuba, 1880, 1881.
Brown, James B., Assemblyman, San Francisco, 1887.
Brown, John Q., Mayor of Sacramento, elected 1881, 1884; Director of Napa Insane Asylum, appointed 1887. *Died, San Francisco, December 21, 1892.*
Brown, Joseph C., Assemblyman, Tulare and Kern, 1863-64, 1865-66, 1867-68; Member Second Constitutional Convention, 1878-79, Tulare District.
Brown, Joseph E., Assemblyman, Santa Clara, 1862.
Brown, L. H., Clerk of the Supreme Court, 1891-
Brown, R. L. H., Assemblyman, Alameda, 1883.
Brown, Thomas A., Assemblyman, Contra Costa, 1865-66, 1867-68; Superior Judge, Contra Costa County, elected 1879, 1884. *Died, Martinez, August 5, 1889.*
Brown, Warren, Assemblyman, Contra Costa, 1855.
Brown, William A., Assemblyman, San Francisco, 1887.
Brown, William B. C., State Controller, 1876-80; Presidential Elector, 1880. *Died, Sacramento, April 12, 1882.*
Brown, William E., Private Secretary to Governors Leland Stanford and Frederick F. Low.
Brown, William H., Senator, El Dorado and Alpine, 1877-78, 1880-81; Harbor Commissioner, San Francisco, 1889-
Browne, J. Ross, Reporter First Constitutional Convention, 1849. *Died, Oakland, December 8, 1875.*
Brownlie, John, Assemblyman, San Francisco, 1893.
Bruner, Elwood, Assemblyman, Sacramento, 1880, 1891.
Brundage, B., Superior Judge, Kern County, elected 1879.
Brunson, Anson, Superior Judge, Los Angeles County, elected 1884.
Brunton, T. C., Assemblyman, Tuolumne, 1856. *Dead.*
Brush, G. R., Assemblyman, Marin, 1856. *Died, Los Angeles, January 18, 1859.*
Brush, Jesse D., Assemblyman, Tuolumne, 1852, 1853. *Died, New York, January 31, 1871.*

Brusie, Jud. C., Assemblyman, Amador, 1887; Sacramento, 1891.
Brusie, L., Assemblyman, Amador, 1880. *Died, Ione, May 28, 1887.*
Bryan, Charles H., Senator, Yuba and Sutter, 1854; Supreme Justice, 1854–55. *Died, Carson City, Nevada, May 14, 1877.*
Bryan, W. E., Assemblyman, Sacramento, 1873–74.
Bryant, Fred., Assemblyman, Alameda, 1891.
Buck, George H., Superior Judge, San Mateo County, elected 1890.
Buck, L. W., Senator, Solano and Yolo, 1883.
Buck, S. M., Assemblyman, Tuolumne, 1859.
Buckbee, J. R., Assemblyman, Plumas and Lassen, 1867–68. *Died, Stockton, June 28, 1873.*
Buckles, A. J., Superior Judge, Solano County, elected 1884, 1890.
Buckley, John E., Assemblyman, San Francisco, 1893.
Buckley, J. P., Senator, San Francisco, 1863–64. *Died, San Francisco, November 17, 1864.*
Buckley, W. S., Superior Judge, San Joaquin County, elected 1879.
Budd, James H., Representative to Congress, 1883–85.
Budd, Joseph H., Superior Judge, San Joaquin County, elected 1888, 1890.
Buel, David E., Assemblyman, El Dorado, 1858. *Died, St. Louis, March, 1888.*
Buell, W. M., Assemblyman, Klamath, 1861.
Buffam, A. C., Assemblyman, Butte, 1863–64.
Buffum, E. Gould, Assemblyman, San Francisco, 1855. *Died, Paris, December 26, 1867.*
Bugbee, S. C., Assemblyman, San Francisco, 1865–66. *Died, San Francisco, September 1, 1877.*
Buhlert, Julius, Assemblyman, San Francisco, 1885.
Bulla, R. N., Assemblyman, Los Angeles, 1893.
Burbank, Caleb, Assemblyman, San Francisco, 1858; Judge Fourth Judicial District, elected 1858; Senator, San Francisco, 1861. *Died, Stockton, May 5, 1888.*
Burbank, George W., Assemblyman, Marin, 1875–76.
Burch, John C., Assemblyman, Trinity, 1857; Senator, Humboldt and Trinity, 1858, 1859; Representative to Congress, 1859–61; Code Commissioner, appointed 1870. *Died, San Francisco, August 31, 1885.*
Burckhalter, J., Assemblyman, Tulare and Kern, 1871–72. *Died, Santa Rosa, October 28, 1883.*
Burdick, James, Assemblyman, Calaveras, 1859.
Burke, Bart, Senator, San Mateo and Santa Cruz, 1893.
Burke, E., Assemblyman, Mariposa, 1855; Judge Thirteenth Judicial District, elected 1855, 1861. *Died, San Francisco, April 28, 1892.*
Burke, T. W., Assemblyman, San Francisco, 1893.
Burnell, R., Assemblyman (Speaker), Amador, 1861; Senator, Amador, 1862, 1863, 1863–64; President pro tem., 1863–64. *Died, Napa, February 13, 1880.*
Burnett, G. W., Assemblyman, San Francisco, 1889.
Burnett, Joseph, Assemblyman, San Francisco, 1887.
Burnett, Peter H., Governor, 1849–50; Supreme Justice, 1857, 1858.
Burnett, W. C., Senator, Yuba and Sutter, 1856, 1857.
Burnett, William, Senator, Sonoma, 1869–70. *Died, Petaluma, April 6, 1870.*
Burns, Daniel M., Secretary of State, 1880–83; Police Commissioner, San Francisco, 1892–
Burns, John, Assemblyman, San Francisco, 1880, 1881.
Burns, W., Assemblyman, Yuba, 1857.
Burr, James, Assemblyman, El Dorado, 1863.
Burson, L. M., Assemblyman, Humboldt, 1860.
Burt, Samuel B., Assemblyman, Placer, 1873–74; Senator, Placer, 1880, 1881; Member Second Constitutional Convention, 1878–79, Placer District.
Burton, E. F., Assemblyman, Nevada, 1854; Senator, Nevada, 1855, 1856, 1858, 1859; State Controller, 1857–58. *Died, Denver, Colorado, May 12, 1891.*
Burwell, Lewis, Assemblyman, Butte, 1889.
Bush, C. W., Senator, Los Angeles, 1873–74, 1875–76.
Bush, E. R., Superior Judge, Yolo County, elected 1879.
Butler, A. B., Assemblyman, Tulare, 1887.
Butler, T. J., Assemblyman, Colusa and Tehama, 1863.
Byers, James D., Assemblyman, Lassen and Plumas, 1873–74; Presidential Elector, 1884.
Byington, Lewis, Assemblyman, Sierra, 1877–78. *Died, San Francisco, June 30, 1886.*
Bynum, Edward, Assemblyman, Yolo, 1856. *Died, Woodland, October 8, 1881.*

Bynum, Sarshall, Senator, Napa, Solano, and Yolo, 1856, 1857. *Died, Lakeport, November 19, 1876.*

Byrnes, James, Assemblyman, San Mateo, 1873-74; Senator, San Francisco and San Mateo, 1880, 1881, 1887, 1889, 1891.

Cabaniss, T. T., Assemblyman, Shasta, 1853. *Died, San Francisco, July 16, 1887.*

Cahalan, Chris. W., Assemblyman, Nevada, 1859.

Caine, Philip P., Assemblyman, Butte, 1859. *Died, Butte County, January 14, 1864.*

Calderwood, M. H., Assemblyman, Placer, 1869-70.

Caldwell, A. B., Assemblyman, Yolo, 1853.

Caldwell, A. G., Assemblyman, Sutter, 1852.

Caldwell John, Assemblyman, Nevada, 1858, 1859; Superior Judge, Nevada County, elected 1879, 1890.

Caldwell, William, Assemblyman, Sonoma, 1867-68.

Callaghan, J. J., Assemblyman, San Francisco, 1887.

Callahan, James, Assemblyman, San Francisco, 1883.

Callbreath, J. C., Assemblyman, Stanislaus, 1856.

Caminetti, A., Assemblyman, Amador, 1883; Senator, Amador and Calaveras, 1887, 1889; Commissioner Marshall Monument, 1887; Representative to Congress, 1891, 1893–

Cammett, John, Assemblyman, San Francisco, 1855. *Dead.*

Campbell, A., Jr., Member Second Constitutional Convention, 1878-79, Alameda District.

Campbell, A. C., Assemblyman, Santa Clara, 1851.

Campbell, Alexander, Assemblyman, San Francisco, 1861; Judge Twelfth Judicial District, elected 1860. *Died, Oakland, February 16, 1888.*

Campbell, F. M., State Superintendent of Public Instruction, 1880-83.

Campbell, G. J, Senator, Solano, 1889, 1891.

Campbell, J. C., Assemblyman, Colusa, 1889.

Campbell, J. S., Assemblyman, El Dorado, 1863-64, 1865-66.

Campbell, James B., Judge Thirteenth Judicial District, appointed 1875; Superior Judge, Fresno County, elected 1884.

Campbell, John Lloyd, Superior Judge, San Bernardino County, elected 1888.

Campbell, John T., Assemblyman, Sonoma, 1883.

Campbell, R. H., Assemblyman, Del Norte and Siskiyou, 1887; Senator, Trinity, Siskiyou. etc., 1891, 1893.

Campbell, Thomas, Assemblyman, Calaveras, 1862. *Died, San Francisco, December 30, 1862.*

Campbell, Thompson, Assemblyman, San Francisco, 1863-64. *Died, San Francisco, December 7, 1868.*

Campbell, W. L., Assemblyman, San Joaquin, 1860.

Camron, W. W., Assemblyman, Alameda, 1880, 1881.

Canavan, M., Assemblyman, San Francisco, 1867-68.

Canfield, R. B., Superior Judge, Santa Barbara County, appointed 1886.

Canfield, W., Assemblyman, Kern and Tulare, 1873-74.

Cannay, Patrick, Assemblyman, Placer, 1852, 1853; Speaker pro tem. Assembly, 1853. *Died, San Francisco, March 1, 1857.*

Cannon, F. E., Assemblyman, Butte, 1859.

Cannon, Marion, Representative to Congress, Sixth District, 1893–

Caperton, W. W., Assemblyman, Placer, 1857.

Caples, James, Member Second Constitutional Convention, 1878-79, Sacramento District.

Cardoza, J. N., Assemblyman, San Francisco, 1853.

Cardwell, H. C., Assemblyman, Sacramento District, 1849-50. *Died, Los Angeles, July 4, 1859.*

Cargill, C. G., Assemblyman, San Benito, 1891.

Carhart, George, Assemblyman, Colusa, 1853.

Carillo, Joaquin, Judge Second Judicial District, elected 1852, 1858.

Carillo, Jose A., Member First Constitutional Convention, 1849, Los Angeles District. *Died, Santa Barbara, April 25, 1862.*

Carillo, Pedro G., Assemblyman, Santa Barbara, 1854.

Carlock, A. B., Senator, Modoc, Shasta and Trinity, 1880, 1881.

Carlson, W. H., Assemblyman, San Diego, 1893.

Carnes, Henry, Assemblyman, Santa Barbara, 1851; Judge Second Judicial District, appointed 1852.

Carothers, J. H., Assemblyman, Contra Costa, 1869-70.

Carothers, Thomas L., Presidential Elector, 1888; Director Mendocino
  State Insane Asylum, 1889–91, 1891–
Carpenter, G. J., Senator, El Dorado, 1857, 1858; Assemblyman, El Dorado,
  1875–76; Speaker of the House, 1875–76; Supreme Court Reporter, 1878–80;
  Railroad Commissioner, First District, 1883–86.
Carpenter, J., Assemblyman, El Dorado, 1857.
Carpenter, R. B., Senator, Los Angeles and Orange, 1891, 1893.
Carpentier, H. W., Assemblyman, Contra Costa, 1853.
Carr, C. E., Assemblyman, Los Angeles, 1854.
Carr, Ezra S., State Superintendent of Public Instruction, 1875–80.
Carr, Jesse D., Assemblyman, San Francisco, 1851; Member State Board of
  Agriculture, 1889–.
Carr, Seymour, Assemblyman, Sacramento, 1880, 1887.
Carr, T. H., Assemblyman, Yuba, 1880.
Carroll, H. W., Assemblyman, Sacramento, 1887.
Carson, James G., Assemblyman, San Francisco, 1875–76. *Died, San Fran-
  cisco, May 2, 1888.*
Carter, G. W. T., Assemblyman, Contra Costa, 1883, 1885.
Carter, George E., Assemblyman, Contra Costa, 1891.
Carter, H. A., Assemblyman, Amador, 1875–76. *Died, Ione, February 24,
  1886.*
Carter, John, Assemblyman, Yuba, 1873–74.
Carter, R. C., Assemblyman, Solano, 1885.
Cartter, George H., Assemblyman, Sacramento, 1856. *Dead.*
Cary, J. C., Superior Judge, San Francisco, elected 1879.
Cary, L. H., Assemblyman, Alameda, 1883. *Died, Oakland, September 16,
  1888.*
Casserly, Eugene, State Printer, 1851–52; United States Senator, 1869–73;
  Member Second Constitutional Convention, 1878–79, First Congressional
  District. *Died, San Francisco, June 14, 1883.*
Cassin, George, Assemblyman, Nevada, 1857.
Casterline, W. M., Assemblyman, San Diego, 1893.
Castro, Estevan, Assemblyman, Monterey, etc., 1857, 1863–64.
Castro, Jose, Governor under Mexican rule, 1835–36.
Castro, Manuel A., Assemblyman, Monterey, etc., 1856, 1863.
Catlin, A. P., Senator, Sacramento, 1853, 1854; Assemblyman, Sacramento,
  1857; Member of the Board of Equalization, 1872; Superior Judge, Sacra-
  mento County, elected 1890.
Cave, John, Assemblyman, San Joaquin District, 1849–50. *Died, San Jose,
  February 28, 1851.*
Cavis, Joseph M., Senator, Tuolumne and Mono, 1863; Judge Fifth Judicial
  District, elected 1863. *Died, Stockton, January 4, 1892.*
Cazneau, Thomas N., Adjutant-General, 1870–71. *Died, San Francisco, July
  11, 1873.*
Center, Samuel H., Assemblyman, El Dorado, 1871–72.
Chalmers, Robert, Assemblyman, El Dorado, 1871–72.
Chamberlain, C. H., Senator, San Joaquin, 1862, 1863; Assemblyman, San
  Joaquin, 1865–66. *Died, Oakland, July 10, 1890.*
Chamberlain, E. K., Senator, Los Angeles and San Diego, 1849–50; Presi-
  dent pro tem. of the Senate, 1849–50. *Died at Sea, December, 1852.*
Chamberlain, T. L., Assemblyman, Placer, 1880.
Chandler, A. L., Assemblyman, Sutter, 1873–74, 1880, 1881; Senator, Yuba
  and Sutter, 1883, 1885, 1887. *Died, Sutter County, November 5, 1888.*
Chandler, T. J., Assemblyman, Tuolumne, 1861.
Chapman, Augustus H., Member Second Constitutional Convention, 1878–
  79; State Prison Director, 1880–83.
Chapman, J. W. S., Assemblyman, Lassen and Plumas, 1875–76.
Chapman, M. C., Assemblyman, Alameda, 1889.
Chappell, J. N., Assemblyman, Shasta, 1863, 1863–64, 1865–66; Senator,
  Shasta and Trinity, 1867–68, 1869–70. *Died, Redding, May 2, 1885.*
Charles, J. M., Member Second Constitutional Convention, 1878–79, Sonoma
  District.
Chase, E. J., Assemblyman, San Francisco, 1865–66.
Chase, S. H., Senator, Nevada, 1857, 1858, 1860, 1861. *Died, Stockton, Octo-
  ber 28, 1869.*
Chase, Warren S., Senator, Santa Barbara and Ventura, 1880, 1881.
Chauncey, David M., Assemblyman, San Francisco, 1852. *Died, Brooklyn,
  N. Y., July 5, 1881.*

Chellis, J. F., Lieutenant-Governor, 1862–63. *Died, Oregon. September 17, 1883.*
Chenery, Richard, Assemblyman, San Francisco, 1857, *D⁰ḍḍ'*
Cheney, W. A., Senator, Butte, Plumas, and Lassen, 1880, 1881; Superior Judge, Los Angeles County, elected 1884.
Cherry, John W., Assemblyman, San Francisco, 1858, 1859, 1861, 1863–64. *Died, San Francisco, July 25, 1885.*
Chico, Mariano, Governor under Mexican rule, 1836.
Childs, William, Assemblyman, Calaveras, 1861.
Chipman, H. C., Assemblyman, Sacramento, 1893.
Church, A. M., Assemblyman, Alameda, 1867–68. *Died, Oakland, September 1, 1889.*
Claflin, C. L., Superior Judge, Modoc County, elected 1890.
Clark, A. M., Assemblyman, Fresno, 1885.
Clark, J. A., Assemblyman, Sierra, 1858.
Clark, J. B., Assemblyman, Butte, 1873–74.
Clark, J. E., Assemblyman, Santa Clara, 1877–78.
Clark, J. R., Assemblyman, El Dorado, 1863.
Clark, J. W., Senator, San Francisco, 1863.
Clark, Jonathan, Assemblyman, Humboldt, 1875–76.
Clark, L. B., Assemblyman, Yuba, 1867–68. *Died, Marysville, January 15, 1886.*
Clark, R. A., Assemblyman, Plumas, 1863–64.
Clark, Reese, Assemblyman, Yolo, 1891.
Clark, Reuben, Assemblyman, Colusa and Tehama, 1883.
Clark, Robert, Assemblyman, San Francisco, 1861. *Died, Cambridgeport, June 10, 1875.*
Clark, Robert C., Assemblyman, Sacramento, 1857; Senator, Sacramento, 1860, 1861; County Judge, Sacramento, 1878–79; Superior Judge, Sacramento County, elected 1879. *Died, Sacramento, January 27, 1883.*
Clark W. H., Superior Judge, Los Angeles County, appointed 1888, elected 1888, 1890.
Clarke, S. J., Assemblyman, San Francisco, 1849–50.
Clarken, R. M., Assemblyman, San Francisco, 1875–76.
Clayes, O. M., State Printer, 1863–67. *Died, San Francisco, June 23, 1892.*
Clayton, Charles, Assemblyman, San Francisco, 1863–64, 1865–66; Representative to Congress, 1873–75. *Died, Oakland, October 4, 1885.*
Clayton, J. E., Assemblyman, Yuba, 1855.
Cleary, Nicolas, Judge Thirteenth Judicial District, elected 1858.
Clement, W. B., Assemblyman, Alameda, 1883.
Clingan, D., Assemblyman, Marin, 1854.
Clough, F. M., Superior Judge, San Francisco, elected 1882. *Died, Stockton, February 14, 1888.*
Clough, G. G., Judge Twenty-first Judicial District, elected 1877; Superior Judge, Plumas County, elected 1879, 1884, 1890.
Clunie, Thomas J., Assemblyman, Sacramento, 1875–76; Senator, San Francisco, 1887; Representative to Congress, 1889–91.
Coats, T. H., Assemblyman, Klamath, 1852.
Cochran, R. M., Assemblyman, Butte, 1867–68.
Coffey, James V., Assemblyman, San Francisco, 1875–76; Superior Judge, San Francisco, elected 1882, 1888.
Coffey, M. W., Assemblyman, San Francisco, 1891.
Coffman, W. F., Assemblyman, Mariposa and Merced, 1880.
Coffroth, James W., Assemblyman, Tuolumne, 1852; Senator, Tuolumne, 1853, 1854, 1856, 1857; Trustee of State Library, 1870–72. *Died, Sacramento, October 9, 1872.*
Coggins, Paschal, Assemblyman, Sacramento, 1867–68, 1873–74. *Died, San Francisco, November 18, 1883.*
Coghlan, John M., Assemblyman, Napa and Lake, 1865–66; Representative to Congress, 1871–72. *Died, Alameda, March 26, 1879.*
Cohen, Richard, Assemblyman, San Francisco, 1887.
Coil, B. J., Assemblyman, Sierra, 1857. *Died, Laporte, January 29, 1865.*
Colbert, J. H., Assemblyman, San Francisco, 1887. *Died, San Francisco, November 8, 1888.*
Colby, George H., Assemblyman, Placer, 1885.
Colby, Gilbert W., Assemblyman, Sacramento, 1852; Senator, Sacramento, 1854, 1855. *Died, San Francisco, August 20, 1881.*
Cole, Cornelius, Representative to Congress, 1863–65; United States Senator, 1867–73.

Coleman, Cyrus, Assemblyman, Amador, Alpine, etc., 1871–72, 1880, 1881; Alpine, Mono, and Inyo, 1889.
Coleman, E. J., Bank Commissioner, 1878–82.
Coleman, J. V., Assemblyman, San Mateo. 1883, 1885.
·Coleman, John C., Senator, Nevada, 1877–78.
Coleman, William, Assemblyman, El Dorado, 1859, 1861.
Colgan, E. P., State Controller, 1891–
Collier, M. M., Assemblyman, Calaveras, 1865–66.
Collins, J. D., Assemblyman, Fresno, 1875–76.
Collins, James, Assemblyman, Nevada, 1862, 1863. *Died, Nevada City, July 18, 1864.*
Coltrin, C. W., Assemblyman, El Dorado, 1861.
Comte, A., Jr., Assemblyman, Sacramento, 1867–68; Senator, Sacramento, 1869–70, 1871–72.
Condee, George M., Assemblyman, El Dorado, 1859.
Condon, John D., Member Second Constitutional Convention, 1878–79, San Francisco District.
Cone, George, Assemblyman, Sacramento, 1856. *Died, Red Bluff, November 12, 1883.*
Cone, Joseph S., Railroad Commissioner, First District, 1880–82.
Conger, Charles C., Senator, San Francisco, 1880, 188.. *Died, Oakland, June 6, 1888.*
Conklin, Alvah R., Presidential Elector, 1884; Superior Judge, Kern County, appointed 1891.
Conklin, E. B., Senator, Santa Clara, 1887, 1889.
Conly, John, Senator, Butte, Plumas, etc., 1867–68, 1869–70. *Died, San Francisco, September 27, 1883.*
Conn, W. A., Assemblyman, San Bernardino, 1860; Senator, San Diego, etc., 1867–68, 1869–70.
·Conness, John, Assemblyman, El Dorado, 1853, 1854, 1860, 1861; United States Senator, 1863–69.
Connolly, D. W., Assemblyman, San Francisco, 1867–68. *Died, San Francisco, January 21, 1872.*
Connolly, David W., Assemblyman, San Mateo, 1859. *Dead.*
Connolly, James E., Assemblyman, San Francisco, 1877–78.
Connolly, W. C., Assemblyman, Tuolumne, etc., 1871–72.
Conroy, M. C., Assemblyman, San Francisco, 1877–78. *Died, San Francisco, February 4, 1887.*
Conway, Bernard, Assemblyman, San Francisco, 1893.
Cook, J. R., Assemblyman, Siskiyou and Modoc, 1880.
Cook, J. W., Assemblyman, Santa Clara, 1885.
Cook, John, Assemblyman, San Diego, 1851.
·Cook, John, Assemblyman, Stanislaus, 1855.
Cook, John, Assemblyman, Yuba, 1852.
·Cooke, Martin E., Senator, Sonoma, etc., 1851, 1852. *Died, San Francisco, April 14, 1857.*
Cooley, C. H., Assemblyman, Sonoma, 1877–78.
Cooley, F. M., Assemblyman, Alameda, 1887. *Died, San Francisco, November 24, 1890.*
Coombs, Frank Leslie, Assemblyman, Napa, 1887, 1889, 1891; Speaker of the House, 1891; Minister to Japan, appointed March 30, 1892.
Coombs, N. D., Assemblyman, Yuba, 1883. *Died, Marysville, January 17, 1888.*
Coombs, Nathan, Assemblyman, Napa, 1855, 1860. *Died, Napa, December 26, 1877.*
Coombs, Thomas M., Assemblyman, Alameda, 1856. *Drowned in Santa Clara County, December, 1858.*
· Cooper, Joel H., Assemblyman, Santa Barbara, 1871–72.
Cooper, L. F., Assemblyman, Del Norte, 1880.
Cope, Jesse, Assemblyman, Santa Cruz, 1857.
Cope, W. B., Superior Judge, Santa Barbara County, elected 1890.
Cope, W. W., Assemblyman, Amador, 1859; Supreme Justice, 1859–64; Chief Justice, 1863–64; Supreme Court Reporter, 1883–87.
Corcoran, H. J., Assemblyman, San Joaquin, 1880, 1885.
Corcoran, John M., Superior Judge, Mariposa County, elected 1879, 1884, 1890.
Corey, Benjamin, Assemblyman, San Jose District, 1849–50.
Corey, William, Assemblyman, Placer, 1855.

Cornwall, P. B., Assemblyman, Sacramento District, 1849-50.
Cornwell, George N., Assemblyman, Napa, 1854, 1875-76.
Coronel, Antonio F., State Treasurer, 1867-71.
Coronel, M. F., Assemblyman, Los Angeles, 1869-70.
Cory, J. M., Assemblyman, Santa Clara, 1865-66.
Cosby, George B., Journal Clerk of the Senate, 1875-76, 1877-78; Adjutant-General, 1883-87; Recording Clerk in Office of Secretary of State, 1888-90.
Cosby, John D., Senator, Trinity and Klamath, 1856, 1857. *Died, Yreka, May 15, 1861.*
Cott, Juan Y., Assemblyman, Monterey, 1862; Senator, Santa Barbara, etc., 1863-64.
Coulter, John, Senator, Butte and Plumas, 1858.
Councilman, E. W., Assemblyman, Nevada, 1861.
Covarrubias, J. M., Member First Constitutional Convention, 1849, San Luis Obispo District; Assemblyman, Santa Barbara, 1849-50, 1851, 1852, 1853, 1855, 1856, 1857, 1860, 1861. *Died, Santa Barbara, April 1, 1871.*
Covington, J. M., Assemblyman, Mendocino, 1875-76. *Dead.*
Cowden, D. H. Member Second Constitutional Convention, 1878-79, Yuba District.
Cowdery, J. F., Assemblyman, San Francisco, 1873-74, 1880; Speaker of the House, 1880·
Cox, Frederick, Trustee of State Library, 1878-82, Senator, Sacramento, 1883, 1885; Member of State Board of Agriculture, 1887-90, 1890—; elected President of Board, 1891, 1892-
Crabbe, Henry A., Assemblyman, San Joaquin, 1852; Senator, San Joaquin, etc., 1853, 1854. *Killed at Cavorca, Mexico, April 7, 1857.*
Craig, J., Senator, San Francisco, 1875-76, 1877-78.
Cram, E. G., Assemblyman, Alameda, 1891.
Crandall, A. W., Senator, Santa Clara, 1887, 1889, 1891.
Crandall, Dwight, Senator, Calaveras and Amador, 1856, 1857,
Crane, A. M., Senator, Alameda, 1862, 1863, President pro tem., 1863; Superior Judge, Alameda County, elected 1879. *Died, Oakland, October 20, 1887.*
Crane, E. T., Assemblyman, Alameda, 1871-72.
Crane, George W., Assemblyman, Yolo, Colusa, etc., 1851; Monterey, 1858. *Died, Monterey, November, 1868.*
Crane, L. D., Senator, Yuba and Sutter, 1871-72, 1873-74.·
Crane, W. H., Senator, Butte, etc., 1877-78.
Crane, W. W., Jr., Senator, Alameda, 1863-64; Presidential Elector, 1864; Trustee of State Library, 1882-83. *Died, Oakland, July 31, 1883.*
Crank, J. F., Assemblyman, Los Angeles, 1881.
Cravens, Robert O., State Librarian, 1870-82; Assistant Secretary of the Senate, 1883.
Crawford, C. M., Assemblyman, Lake, 1889.
Crawford, J., Assemblyman, Sierra, 1863.
Crawford, R. F., Superior Judge, Sonoma County, elected 1890.
Creaner, Charles M., Assemblyman, San Joaquin District, 1849-50; Judge of Fifth Judicial District, elected by Legislature 1850, elected 1852, 1858. *Died, Stockton, December 7, 1882.*
Creighton, Daniel J., Senator, San Francisco, 1885.
Crenshaw, George H., Assemblyman, Mariposa and Merced, 1859.
Crenshaw, John T., Assemblyman, Nevada, 1853; Senator, Nevada, 1854, 1855. *Killed at the Battle of Vicksburg, 1863.*
Cressler, W. T., Assemblyman, Siskiyou, 1873-74.
Crigler, J. C., Assemblyman, Napa and Lake, 1867-68, 1869-70.
Crimmins, P. J., Senator, San Francisco, 1887.
Crittenden, A. P., Assemblyman, Los Angeles District, 1849-50; Santa Clara, 1852; Supreme Court Reporter, 1870. *Shot by Laura D. Fair, died San Francisco, November 5, 1870.*
Crittenden, R. D., Senator, El Dorado, 1860, 1861.
Crocker, Charles, Assemblyman, Sacramento, 1861. *Died, Monterey, August 14, 1888.*
Crocker, E. B., Supreme Justice, 1863. *Died, Sacramento, June 24, 1875.*
Crockett, J. B., Supreme Justice, 1868-79. *Died, Fruitvale, January 15, 1884.*
Cronan, W., Senator, San Francisco, 1883.
Crosby, E. O., Member First Constitutional Convention, 1849, Sacramento District; Senator, Sacramento District, 1849-50, Yuba and Sutter, 1851.
Cross, C. W., Member Second Constitutional Convention, 1878-79, Nevada District; Senator, Nevada and Sierra, 1883, 1885.

Cross, W. W., Superior Judge, Tulare County, elected 1879, 1884, 1890.
Crouch, Robert, Member Second Constitutional Convention, 1878–79, Napa District; Superior Judge, Napa County, elected 1884.
Crowell, J. M., Assemblyman, Yuba, 1860.
Crump, R. W., Superior Judge, Lake County, elected 1890.
Crumpton, H. J., Assemblyman, Lake, 1881, 1883.
Cruteher, W. M., Assemblyman, Placer, 1875–76.   ·
Culver, C. B., Assemblyman, Yolo, 1885.   Dead.
Culver, E. S., Assemblyman, Alameda, 1889, 1891.
Culver, J. H., Assemblyman, San Francisco, 1883.
Cunnard, J. M., Assemblyman, Butte, 1862.
Cunningham, J. F., Assemblyman, Santa Cruz, 1881.
Cunningham, Lewis, Senator, Yuba, 1863, 1863–64, 1865–66.   Died, San Francisco, October 25, 1879.
Cunningham, N. C., Assemblyman, Sierra, 1855.
Cunningham, W. F., Assemblyman, El Dorado, 1855.
Cunningham, W. S., Assemblyman, Tulare, 1891.
Cureton, W. H., Assemblyman, Mendocino, 1867–68.
Currey, Robert J., Assemblyman, Solano, 1887.
Curry, C. Forest, Assemblyman, San Francisco, 1887.
Curry, John, Supreme Justice, 1864–68; Chief Justice, 1866–68.
Curtis, D. B., Assemblyman, Placer, 1858.
Curtis, E. J., Assemblyman, Siskiyou, 1855, 1856.   Dead.
Curtis, J. M., Assemblyman, San Francisco, 1893.
Curtis, J. S., Assemblyman, Yolo, 1857.   Died, Stockton, November 18, 1872.
Curtis, N. Greene, Assemblyman, Sacramento, 1861; Senator, Sacramento, 1867–68, 1869–70, 1877–78.
Curtis, Samuel T., Assemblyman, Nevada, 1860.
Cusick, T. P., Assemblyman, San Francisco 1893.
Cuthbert, W. W., Assemblyman, San Francisco, 1880.
Cutler, John, Assemblyman, El Dorado, 1852.
Cutler, Nathan, Assemblyman, Solano, 1859.
Cutter, William M., Assemblyman, Yuba, 1883.
Cutting, John T., Representative to Congress, 1891–93,
Da gett, John, Assemblyman, Humboldt and Del Norte, 1859, 1860; Siskiyou gand Modoc, 1881; Lieutenant-Governor, 1883–87; World's Fair Commissioner, 1891–
Daingerfield, W. P., Judge Ninth and Twelfth Judicial Districts, elected 1854, 1858, 1859, 1860, 1875; Superior Judge, San Francisco, elected 1879.   Died, San Francisco, May 5, 1880.
Daly, James H., Assemblyman, San Francisco, 1885, 1891.
Dameron, William B., Assemblyman, Tuolumne, 1852.
Damron, J. M., Assemblyman, Los Angeles, 1889.
Dana, Charles W., Assemblyman, Santa Barbara, etc., 1862.   Dead.
Dana, William A., Assemblyman, San Francisco, 1855.
Dannalls, C. W., Assemblyman, Yuba, 1854.
Dannals, George W., Assemblyman, San Diego, 1871–72.
Dare, John T., Assemblyman, Solano, 1877–78.
Dargie, W. E., Senator, Alameda, 1889, 1891.
Davidson, E. M., Assemblyman, Nevada, 1857.
Davidson, T. R., Assemblyman, Sacramento, 1854.
Davies, William A., Assemblyman, Tuolumne, Mono, etc., 1867–68.
Davis, B. K., Assemblyman, Tuolumne, Mono, etc., 1862.
Davis, Caswell, Assemblyman, Santa Clara, 1856.
Davis, E. L., Assemblyman, Humboldt, 1859.
Davis, Edwin A., Senator, Yuba and Sutter, 1880, 1881; Superior Judge, Sutter and Yuba counties, appointed 1891.
Davis, F. F., Assemblyman, Calaveras, 1863.
Davis, H. B., Assemblyman, Merced and Stanislaus, 1873–74.
Davis, Hamlet, Member Second Constitutional Convention, 1878–79, Nevada District.
Davis, Horace, Representative to Congress, 1877–81; Presidential Elector, 1884; President of State University, 1888–90.
Davis, John, Assemblyman, Placer, 1887, 1889.
Davis, John F., Superior Judge, Amador County, appointed December, 1892.
Davis, N. H., Assemblyman, Solano, 1858.
Davis, Winfield J., Assemblyman, Sacramento, 1885.
Dawley, I. N., Assemblyman, Nevada, 1854.   Dead.

Day, Sherman, Senator, Alameda and Santa Clara, 1855, 1856. *Died, Berkeley, December 14, 1884.*

Days, John M., Assemblyman, Nevada, 1867-68, 1871-72; Senator, San Francisco, 1885.

Deal, W. Grove, Assemblyman, Sacramento District, 1849-50.

Dean, J. E., Member Second Constitutional Convention, 1878-79, El Dorado and Alpine District.

Dean, Peter, Senator, San Francisco, 1877-78.

Dean, Seneca, Assemblyman, El Dorado, 1862.

Deering, Alexander, Judge Thirteenth Judicial District, appointed 1865, elected 1873. *Died, Merced, December 18, 1875.*

Deeth, Jacob, Assemblyman, San Francisco, 1863. *Died, San Rafael, January 16, 1879.*

De Haven, J. J., Assemblyman, Humboldt, 1869-70; Senator, Del Norte, Klamath, etc., 1871-72, 1873-74; Superior Judge, Humboldt County, elected 1884; Representative to Congress, 1889-91; Supreme Justice, 1891-

De Haven, W. N., Assemblyman, Butte, 1871-72.

De la Guerra, Antonio M., Senator, Santa Barbara and San Luis Obispo, 1852. *Died, Santa Barbara, November 28, 1881.*

De la Guerra, Pablo, Member First Constitutional Convention, 1849, Santa Barbara District; Senator, Santa Barbara and San Luis Obispo, 1849-50, 1851, 1853, 1854, 1855, 1856, 1857, 1860, 1861; President of Senate, 1861; Lieutenant-Governor, 1861; Judge First Judicial District, elected 1863, 1869. *Died, Santa Barbara, February 5, 1874.*

Della Torre, Peter, Presidential Elector, 1856. *Died, Brookland, Maryland, October 25, 1864.*

De Long, Charles E., Assemblyman, Yuba, 1858, 1859; Senator, Yuba, 1861, 1862. *Died, Virginia City, October 26, 1876.*

De Long, F. C., Senator, Marin, 1885, 1887, 1889, 1891; Member State Board of Agriculture, 1889-

Del Valle, R. F., Presidential Elector, 1880; Assemblyman, Los Angeles, 1880, 1881; Senator, Los Angeles, 1883, 1885; President pro tem., 1883.

Del Valle, Ygnacio, Assemblyman, Los Angeles, 1852. *Died, Los Angeles, March 30, 1880.*

Denison, Eli S., Senator, Alameda, 1891, 1893; Member Board of Agriculture, District No. 1, San Francisco and Alameda Counties, 1889-

Dennis, John H., Assemblyman, El Dorado, 1862.

Dennis, Thomas W., Assemblyman, San Francisco, 1891.

Denniston, James G., Assemblyman, San Mateo, 1861, 1863. *Died, San Francisco, June 17, 1869.*

Denson, Samuel C., Judge Sixth Judicial District, elected 1875; Superior Judge, Sacramento County, elected 1879.

Dent, George W., Senator, San Joaquin and Contra Costa, 1859, 1860.

Dent, Lewis, Member First Constitutional Convention, 1849, Monterey District. *Died, Washington, District of Columbia, March 22, 1874.*

Denver, A. St. C., Senator, El Dorado, 1859, 1860, 1861, 1862. *Dead.*

Denver, James W., Senator, Trinity and Klamath, 1852, 1853; Secretary of State, 1853-55; Representative to Congress, 1855-57. *Died, Washington, District of Columbia, August 9, 1892.*

Desty, Robert, Senator, San Francisco and San Mateo, 1880.

Deveny, Peter, Assemblyman, San Francisco, 1885.

Devoe, Alfred, Assemblyman, Santa Cruz, 1863-64.

Devoe, James B., State Printer, 1851.

DeWitt, E. L., Assemblyman, Tulare, 1885.

DeWitt, W. M., Assemblyman, Yolo, 1877-78.

Dibble, Henry C., Assemblyman, San Francisco, 1889, 1891.

Dick, John, Assemblyman, Butte, 1856. *Dead.*

Dickenson, W. B., Assemblyman, Sacramento District, 1849-50.

Dickenson, W. L., Assemblyman, Stanislaus and Merced, 1863-64.

Dickinson, John H., Senator, San Francisco, 1880, 1881.

Dickinson, William B., Senator, El Dorado, 1858, 1859, 1860, 1861; President pro tem., 1859.

Dillard, R' M., Superior Judge, Santa Barbara County, elected 1886.

Dimmick, Kimball H., Member First Constitutional Convention, 1849, San Jose District. *Died, Los Angeles, September 11, 1861.*

Dimond, D., Assemblyman, Tuolumne, 1880. *Died, Columbia, January, 1890.*

Dinan, W. E., Assemblyman, San Francisco, 1889.

Dinniene, John H., Assemblyman, San Francisco, 1877–78.
Dixon, James, Assemblyman, Sonoma, 1873–74. *Died,, Oregon, December 15,. 1882.*
Dixon, M. W., Assemblyman, Alameda, 1875–76, 1877–78; Senator, Alameda, 1887, 1889.
Dobbin, H. H., Assemblyman, San Francisco, 1889.
Dodge, C. G., Assemblyman, Alameda, 1893.
Dodge, H. L., Assemblyman, San Francisco, 1863; Senator, San Francisco,. 1863–64, 1865–66.
Dodson, W. B. H., Assemblyman, Napa and Lake, 1863–64.
Doll, J. G., Senator, Colusa and Tehama, 1862, 1863.
Dominguez, Manuel, Member First Constitutional Convention, 1849, Los-Angeles District.
Donovan, M. J., Senator, San Francisco, 1875–76, 1877–78.
Dooling, Maurice T., Assemblyman, San Benito, 1885.
Dore, Benjamin, Assemblyman, San Francisco, 1862, 1863.
Dorn, N. A., Superior Judge, Monterey County, elected 1890.
Dornin, George D., Assemblyman, Nevada, 1865–66, 1867–68.
Dorr, J. C., Assemblyman, Trinity, 1865–66.
Dorsey, Caleb, Assemblyman, Stanislaus, 1877–78. *Died, Sonora, March· 28, 1885.*
Dosh, Samuel H., Senator, Colusa and Shasta, 1856, 1857;, President pro· tem., 1857. *Died, Shasta, June 13, 1861.*
Doss, E. W., Assemblyman, Kern and Tulare, 1869–70.
Doty, Gillis, Assemblyman, Sacramento, 1883, 1891.
Dougherty, J. T., Senator, San Francisco, 1883, 1885.
Dougherty, John, Assemblyman, Sierra, 1861.
Dougherty, S. K., Superior Judge, Sonoma County, elected 1888,.1890.
Doughty, John, Assemblyman, Solano, 1855.
Douglass, Charles D., Assemblyman, San Francisco, 1885.
Douglass, David F., Senator, San Joaquin District, 1849–50; Calaveras,. 1851; Assemblyman, San Joaquin, 1855; Secretary of State, 1856–57.. *Died, San Joaquin County, June 16, 1872.*
Douglass, G. N., Assemblyman, El Dorado, 1859.
Douglass, George A., Assemblyman, El Dorado, 1859. *Died, Austin, Nevada,. August 25, 1881.*
Dow, E. E., Assemblyman, Santa Clara, 1891.
Dow, F. A., Assemblyman, El Dorado, 1863–64.
Dow, J. G., Assemblyman, Sonoma, 1862.
Dow, William, Assemblyman, Tuolumne, 1859.
Dowling, Patrick T., Member Second Constitutional Convention, 1878–79,. San Francisco District.
Downer, J. W., Assemblyman, Sierra, 1867–68.
Downey, John G., Assemblyman, Los Angeles, 1856; Lieutenant-Gover--nor, 1860; Governor, 1860–61.
Downey, P. H., Private Secretary to Governor John G. Downey.
Downing, J. L., Assemblyman, Sonoma, 1865–66.
Downs, R. C., Assemblyman, Amador, 1880.
Doyle, Luke D., Member Second Constitutional Convention, 1878–79, San· Francisco District.
Dray, F. R., Senator, Sacramento, 1887, 1889, 1891.
Drees, E. E., Assemblyman, Sonoma, 1893.
Drew, M. M., Member State Board of Equalization, 1880–82; United States- Marshal, 1882–86.
Drum, Edward F., Senator, San Francisco, 1885.
Dryer, Perry, Assemblyman, Shasta, 1867–68.
Du Brutz, A. B., Assemblyman, Tulare and Kern, 1880.
Duckworth, S., Assemblyman, Monterey, 1893.
Dudley, Charles C., Assemblyman, Placer, 1862, 1863.
Dudley, J. M., Assemblyman, Solano, 1862, 1863; Member Second Consti--tutional Convention, 1878–79, Solano District.
Dudley, W. L., Member Second Constitutional Convention, 1878–79, San Joaquin and Amador District.
Duffy, James A., Assemblyman, Sacramento, 1869–70; Senator, Sacra--mento, 1871–72, 1873–74. *Died, Oakland, September 16, 1889.*
Duffy, Thomas, Assemblyman, Del Norte and Siskiyou, 1893.
Duncombe, Charles, Assemblyman, Sacramento, 1859, 1863. *Died, Hicks--ville, October 1, 1867.*

Dunlap, Elon, Assemblyman, El Dorado, 1860.
Dunlap, H. W., Assemblyman, Colusa and Tehama, 1859.
Dunlap, Presley, Member Second Constitutional Convention, 1878–79, Sacramento District. *Died, Sacramento, September 23, 1883.*
Dunlap, Thomas, Assemblyman, Amador, 1875–76, 1877–78.
Dunn, John P., State Controller, 1888–91.
Dunn, William J., Assemblyman, San Francisco, 1891; Senator, San Francisco, 1893.
Dunne, E. F., Assemblyman, Sonoma, 1863.
Durham, W. W., Assemblyman, Butte, 1880.
Dunsmoor, Charles H., Bank Commissioner, 1890–
Durner, Charles, Assemblyman, Solano, 1891.
Durst, D. P., Assemblyman, Colusa, 1861; Yuba and Sutter, 1893.
Dustin, Daniel, Assemblyman, Nevada, 1856.
Dutton, Henry, Assemblyman, Nevada, 1856.
Dutton, Warren, Member of State Board of Equalization, 1880–82.
Dwinelle, John W., Assemblyman, Alameda, 1867–68. *Drowned at Port Costa, January 28, 1881.*
Dwinelle, Samuel H., Judge Fifteenth Judicial District, appointed 1864, elected 1865, 1871, 1877. *Died, San Francisco, January 12, 1886.*
Dwyer, David, Assemblyman, San Francisco, 1865–66. *Died, San Francisco, September 3, 1869.*
Dyer, Barlow, Assemblyman, Calaveras, 1863–64; Senator, Calaveras, 1871–72, 1873–74.
Eager, Thomas, Assemblyman, Alameda and Santa Cruz, 1862, 1865–66.
Eagon John A., Assemblyman, Amador and Alpine, 1859, 1871–72, Senator, Amador, 1860, 1861; Member Second Constitutional Convention, 1878–79, Amador District. *Died, Jackson, Amador County, October 20, 1892.*
Eakin, W. A., Senator, Tuolumne, Mono, etc., 1873–74, 1875–76.
Eakle, H. P., Assemblyman, Colusa, 1891.
Earl, Guy C., Senator, Alameda, 1893.
Eastman, J. C., Assemblyman, Nevada, 1861.
Echeandia, Jose Maria de, Governor under Mexican rule, 1825–31.
Eddy, William M., Surveyor-General, 1852–53. *Died, San Francisco, March 9, 1854.*
Edgar, William, Assemblyman, Yuba, 1871–72.
Edgerton, Henry, Senator, Napa, Yolo and Solano, 1860, 1861; Sacramento, 1873–74, 1875–76; Presidential Elector, 1880, 1884; Member Second Constitutional Convention, 1878–79, Second Congressional District; Trustee of State Library, 1882–84, 1886–87. *Died, San Francisco, November 4, 1887.* Dead.
Edmonds, M. A., Superior Judge, San Francisco, elected 1879, 1880. Dead.
Edwards, E. E., Assemblyman, Los Angeles, 1885, 1889.
Edwards, L. B., Assemblyman, Alameda, 1881.
Edwards, Philip L., Assemblyman, Sacramento, 1855. *Died, Sacramento, May 1, 1869.*
Edwards, Uriah, Assemblyman, Sonoma, etc., 1857, 1858. *Died, Petaluma, October 5, 1868.*
Eichelroth, W. E., Assemblyman, Tuolumne, Mono, etc., 1869–70.
Eliason, W. A., Assemblyman, Sonoma, 1862.
Ellis, A. J., Member First Constitutional Convention, 1849, San Francisco District; Assemblyman, San Francisco, 1852. *Died, San Francisco, July 27, 1883.*
Ellis, Asa, Assemblyman, Los Angeles, 1867–68, 1871–72, 1877–78. *Died, Fresno, August 20, 1890.*
Ellis, Edward E. W., Assemblyman, Nevada, 1852. *Died, Pittsburg Landing, April 6, 1862.*
Ellis, R. B., Assemblyman, Sacramento, 1859, 1860. *Died, Reno, 1873.*
Ellison, John F., Assemblyman, Tehama, 1885; Superior Judge, Tehama County, elected 1890.
Ellsworth, John, Assemblyman, Alameda, 1887; Superior Judge, Alameda County, elected 1888.
Ely, Benjamin E. S., Assemblyman, Yuba, 1858.
Emeric, H. F., Assemblyman, Contra Costa, 1893.
English, James L., State Treasurer, 1857. *Died, Sacramento, May 29, 1889.*
English, Warren B., Senator, Contra Costa and Marin, 1883.
Enos, John S., Senator, San Francisco, 1880, 1881; Commissioner of Labor Statistics, 1883–86.

Ensworth, A. S., Assemblyman, San Diego, 1859. *Died, Los Angeles, October;_1865.*
Erkson, William, Assemblyman, Santa Clara, 1863–64.
Escandon, A. G., Assemblyman, Santa Barbara, 1869–70, 1873–74.
Estee, Morris M., Assemblyman, Sacramento, 1863; San Francisco, 1873–74; Speaker of the House, 1873–74; Member State Board of Equalization, 1871; Member Second Constitutional Convention, 1878–79, First Con-gressional District; Presidential Elector, 1876, 1888.
Estell, James M., Assemblyman, Marin, 1857; Senator, Napa and Solano, 1852, 1853. *Died, San Francisco, April 26, 1859.*
Estep, J. H., Assemblyman, Sacramento, 1853. *Died, Lakeport, January 11, 1876.*
Estey, C. L., Assemblyman, Marin, 1880, 1881.
Estey, Thomas H., Member Second Constitutional Convention, 1878–79, Contra Costa and Marin District; Assemblyman, Marin, 1891.
Estudillo, Jose G., State Treasurer, 1875–79.
Evans, George S., Secretary of the Senate, 1857; Senator, San Joaquin, 1863–64, 1865–66, 1871–72; Adjutant-General, 1864-65, 1866–68. *Died, San Francisco, September 17, 1883.*
Evans, O. P., Judge Fourth Judicial District, appointed 1879; Superior Judge San Francisco, elected 1879.
Everett, Daniel H., Senator, San Francisco, 1891, 1893–
Everett, Henry, Assemblyman, Nevada, 1871–72.
Evey, Edward, Assemblyman, Napa and Lake, 1862; Member Second Constitutional Convention, 1878–79, Los Angeles District.
Ewalt, John, Assemblyman, San Francisco, 1856.
Ewer, S., Assemblyman, Butte, 1854; Senator, Butte, Plumas, etc., 1865–66, 1867–68.
Ewing, Andrew, Assemblyman, Mariposa and Merced, 1877–78.
Ewing, Luther L., Assemblyman, San Francisco, 1887, 1889.
Ewing, W. P., Assemblyman, Sonoma, 1853.
Fahey, Edward, Assemblyman, Calaveras, 1873–74.
Fair, William D., Senator, San Joaquin District, 1849–50. *Died, San Francisco, December 27, 1861.*
Fairchild, David, Assemblyman, El Dorado, 1860.
Fairchild, John A., Assemblyman, Siskiyou, 1867–68.
Fairfax, Charles S., Assemblyman, Yuba and Sierra, 1853, 1854; Speaker of the House, 1854; Clerk of the Supreme Court, 1857–61. *Died, Baltimore, Maryland, April 6, 1869.*
Fairfield, B. L., Assemblyman, Placer, 1854.
Fajes, Pedro, Governor under Spanish rule, 1782–90.
Fargo, Frank F., Assemblyman, Alameda, 1861; Clerk of the Supreme Court, 1862–63. *Died, New York State, January 12, 1891.*
Farish, T. E., Assemblyman, San Francisco, 1867–68.
Farley, J. W., Assemblyman, San Francisco, 1863. *Dead.*
Farley, James T., Assemblyman, Amador, 1855, 1856; Speaker of the House, 1856; Senator, Amador and Alpine, 1869–70, 1871–72, 1873–74, 1875–76; President pro tem., 1871–72; United States Senator, 1879–85. *Died, Jackson, January 22, 1886.*
Farley, M., Assemblyman, Sierra, 1883.
Farnum, John E., Assemblyman, Alameda, 1877–78; Bank Commissioner, 1882–86.
Farrell, Simon J., Member Second Constitutional Convention, 1878–79, San Francisco District,
Farwell, Seth B., Judge Eleventh Judicial District, appointed 1851, elected 1851. *Died, Carson, Nevada, December 11, 1862.*
Farwell, W. B., Assemblyman, San Francisco, 1855.
Fassett, L. H., Assemblyman, Sacramento, 1889. *Died, Florin, December 16, 1889.*
Faw, Thomas, F., Assemblyman, Monterey, 1883.
Fawcett, Eugene, Judge First Judicial District, appointed 1875, elected 1875; Member Second Constitutional Convention, 1878–79, Santa Barbara District; Judge Santa Barbara County, elected 1879. *Died, Santa Barbara, January 9, 1880.*
Fay, Caleb T., Assemblyman, San Francisco, 1862. *Died, San Francisco, April 20, 1885.*
Fay, John D., Senator, San Francisco, 1893.

Felton, Charles N., Assemblyman, San Mateo, 1880, 1881; Representative in Congress, 1885–93; Commissioner to attend the centennial celebration of the inauguration of George Washington as President of the United States, 1888; United States Senator, 1891–

Felton, John B., Presidential Elector, 1868, 1872, 1876. *Died, Oakland, May 2, 1877.*

Ferguson, John W., Assemblyman, Fresno, 1873–74.

Ferguson, R. D., Assemblyman, Sacramento, 1858, 1863. *Dead.*

Ferguson, W. I., Senator, Saeramento, 1856, 1857, 1858. *Died, San Francisco, September 14, 1858.*

Ferguson, William T., Assemblyman, Sierra, 1855; Senator, Sierra, 1857, 1858. *Died, August 23, 1866.*

Ferral, Robert, Superior Judge, San Francisco, elected 1879.

Ferral, Walter, Assemblyman, Sonoma, 1875–76.

Ferrell, W. C., Assemblyman, San Diego, 1855.

Ferris, L. W., Assemblyman, Sacramento, 1857.

Field, John, Assemblyman, Sonoma, 1883.

Field, Stephen J., Assemblyman, Yuba, 1851; Supreme Justice, 1857–63; Chief Justice, 1859–63; Justice United States Supreme Court, 1863–

Figueroa, Jose, Governor under Mexican rule, 1833–35. *Died, Monterey, September 29, 1835.*

Filcher, J. A., Member Second Constitutional Convention, 1878–79, Placer District; Senator, Placer, 1883, 1885; State Prison Director, 1887–88; Presidential Elector, 1893.

Findley, Thomas, State Treasurer, 1858–62. *Died, Georgetown, El Dorado County, September 19, 1888.*

Finlayson, F. G., Assemblyman, Los Angeles, 1893.

Finlayson, James R., Assemblyma, San Francisco, 1880.

Finn, John F., Superior Judge, San Francisco, elected 1879, 1880, 1886.

Fiuney, Charles G., Jr., Member Second Constitutional Convention, 1878–79, Ventura District.

Finney, Seldon J., Assemblyman, San Mateo, 1869–70; Senator, San Francisco and San Mateo, 1871–72, 1873–74. *Died, San Mateo County, July 27, 1875.*

Firebaugh, H. C., Assemblyman, San Francisco, 1885.

Fiske, Henry M., Senator, El Dorado, 1856, 1857.

Fitch, George K., State Printer, 1852.

Fitch, Thomas, Assemblyman, El Dorado, 1863.

Fitzgerald, O. P., State Superintendent of Public Instruction, 1867–71.

Fitzgerald, W. F., Supreme Court Commissioner, 1890–

Fitzpatrick, E. F., Superior Judge, San Mateo County, appointed 1890.

Flanders, Alvan, Assemblyman, San Francisco, 1861.

Fleming, J. R., Assemblyman, Butte, 1883.

Flemming, Samuel, Assemblyman, Shasta, 1852. *Died, April, 1888.*

Flint, Thomas, Senator, Santa Cruz and Monterey, 1875–76, 1877–78.

Flint, Thomas, Jr., Senator, Monterey and San Benito, 1889, 1891, 1893–

Flint, Wilson, Senator, San Francisco, 1855, 1856. *Died, San Francisco, January 4, 1867.*

Flournoy, T. C., Assemblyman, Mariposa, 1855. *Dead.*

Flower, Samuel, Assemblyman, San Francisco, 1853.

Flynn, James J., Assemblyman, San Francisco, 1883.

Foote, H. S., Supreme Court Commissioner, 1884–

Foote, L. H., Adjutant-General, 1871–75.

Foote, W. W., Railroad Commissioner Third District, 1883–86.

Ford, Charles, Assemblyman, Santa Cruz, 1861.

Ford, Henry L., Assemblyman, Colusa, 1852. *Died at Nome Cult, Mendocino Reservation, July 2, 1860.*

Ford, T. L., Senator, Plumas, Sierra, and Nevada, 1893.

Forman, Ferris, Judge Sixth Judicial District, appointed 1851; Secretary of State, 1858–60.

Forsyth, W. K., Assemblyman, San Francisco, 1877–78.

Fortna, S. R., Assemblyman, Sutter, 1883. *Died, Yuba City, June 27, 1892.*

Fortune, H. W., Assemblyman, San Francisco, 1869–70.

Foster, C. F., Senator, Colusa and Tehama, 1883, 1885.

Foster, Stephen C., Member First Constitutional Convention, 1849, Los Angeles District; Senator, Los Angeles, etc., 1851, 1852, 1853.

Foster, Theron, Assemblyman, El Dorado, 1855, 1861.

Foulke, L. M., Senator, Siskiyou, 1863–64.

Fourgeaud, V. J., Assemblyman, San Francisco, 1857. *Dead.*

Fowler, C. B., Assemblyman, Butte, 1852. *Died, Oakland, October 17, 1866.*
Fowler, Frank L., Assemblyman, Alameda, 1891.
Fowler, Thomas, Senator, Tulare, etc., 1869–70, 1871–72, 1877–78. *Died, Visalia, April 17, 1884.*
Fox, Charles N., Assemblyman, Alameda, 1880; Supreme Justice, 1889–90.
Franck, F. C., Assemblyman, Santa Clara, 1871–72, 1873–74.
Frank, L. J., Assemblyman, San Mateo, 1889.
Franklin, J. J., Senator, Tuolumne, 1860, 1861. *Died, Sonora, May 21, 1875.*
Franklin, Joseph, Assemblyman, San Francisco, 1885.
Franks, L. J., Assemblyman, San Mateo, 1889.
Fraser, Thomas, Assemblyman, El Dorado, 1863–64, 1880, 1881; Senator, El Dorado, 1873–74, 1875–76, 1883, 1889, 1891, President pro tem., 1891.
Frasier, John, Assemblyman, El Dorado, 1862.
Freanor, George, Presidential Elector, 1856. *Died, New York, November 10, 1878.*
Freelon, T. W., Superior Judge, San Francisco, elected 1879. *Died, Oakland, March 30, 1885.*
Freeman, Abraham C., Member Second Constitutional Convention, 1878–79, Sacramento District; Trustee of State Library, 1882–1890.
Freeman, C. J., Assemblyman, San Luis Obispo, 1851.
Freeman, E. A., Assemblyman, Amador, 1891.
Freeman, F. S., Assemblyman, Yolo, 1871–72, 1873–74.
Freeman, I. F., Assemblyman, Sacramento, 1869–70. *Died, Elk Grove, Sacramento County, December 7, 1892.*
Freeman, J. W., Assemblyman, Tulare, etc., 1863; Senator, Fresno, Kern, etc., 1863–64, 1865–66, 1867–68.
Fremont, John C., United States Senator, 1849–51; Major-General U. S. A., 1861; Governor of Arizona, 1878–1881. *Died, New York City, July 13, 1890.*
Freer, Leon D., Assemblyman, Butte, 1881; Superior Judge, Butte County, elected 1884. *Died, San Francisco, September 19, 1888.*
Freidenrich, D., Assemblyman, San Francisco, 1873–74.
French, A., Senator, El Dorado, 1855, 1856. *Dead.*
French, C. G. W., Trustee of State Library, 1866–70; Assemblyman, Sacramento, 1871–72; Chief Justice of Arizona, 1875–84. *Died, San Francisco, August 13, 1891.*
French, Frank, Assemblyman, San Francisco, 1885.
French, Parker H., Assemblyman, San Luis Obispo, 1854. *Dead.*
Freud, Jacob R., Member Second Constitutional Convention, 1878–79, San Francisco District.
Frink, D., Assemblyman, Santa Clara, 1880.
Frink, Miner, Jr., Assemblyman, Amador and Alpine, 1865–66.
Frisbie, John B., Assemblyman, Solano, 1867–68. *Died, Mexico, 1883.*
Frye, Jacob, Senator, Placer, 1852.
Fryer, R. C., Assemblyman, Los Angeles, 1869–70.
Fuller, Mortimer, Assemblyman, Yuba, 1857, 1859.
Gaffey, John T., Member State Board of Equalization, 1887–90.
Gaffey, P. T., Assemblyman, San Francisco, 1880.
Gage, Stephen T., Assemblyman, El Dorado, 1856.
Galbraith, J. D., Assemblyman, El Dorado, 1858.
Galbraith, W. H., Assemblyman, Santa Cruz, 1891.
Gale, John, Superior Judge, Butte County, appointed 1888.
Gallagher, J. G., Assemblyman, San Francisco, 1893.
Gallagher, P. A., Assemblyman, Calaveras, 1860; Senator, Calaveras, 1861, 1862.
Galloway, Joseph W., Assemblyman, Contra Costa, 1871–72.
Galvin, E. R., Assemblyman, Tuolumne, 1855.
Garber, E. R., Superior Judge, San Francisco, elected 1888.
Gardiner, William P., Superior Judge, Los Angeles County, appointed 1887.
Gardner, James H., Assemblyman, Yuba and Sierra, 1852, 1853; Senator, Sierra, 1854.
Gardner, John, Assemblyman, Calaveras, 1889.
Gardner, M., Trustee of State Library, 1889–90; Director Mendocino State Insane Asylum, 1892–
Gardner, Robert, Surveyor-General, 1871–75.
Garfield, S., Assemblyman, El Dorado, 1853. *Dead.*
Garibaldi, S. J., Assemblyman, San Francisco, 1880.
Garoutte, C. H., Superior Judge, Yolo County, elected 1884; Supreme Justice, 1891–

Garratt, W. T., Senator, San Francisco, 1871–72, 1873–74. *Died, San Francisco, January 14, 1890.*

Garretson, John, Assemblyman, San Mateo, 1875–76.

Garrity, P., Assemblyman, San Francisco, 1881.

Garter, E., Senator, Shasta, etc., 1858, 1859; Judge Ninth Judicial District, elected 1863. *Died, Shasta, April 9, 1880.*

Garver, Michael, Assemblyman, Nevada, 1877–78, 1891.

Garvey, J. B., Member Second Constitutional Convention, 1878–79, Calaveras District.

Gaskill, R. C., Senator, Butte, etc., 1862, 1863, 1863–64. *Died, Pittsburg, Pennsylvania, November 2, 1889.*

Gaston, H. A., Assemblyman, Sierra, 1856.

Gately, Wm. H., Assemblyman, San Francisco, 1893.

Gaussail, E., Assemblyman, San Francisco, 1883.

Gaver, E. S., Assemblyman, Yuba, 1855. *Dead.*

Gavigan, W. J., Assemblyman, San Francisco, 1881.

Gay, Milus H., Assemblyman, Santa Clara, 1881.

Gaylord, E. H., Assemblyman, Nevada, 1855. *Dead.*

Geary, Dennis, Assemblyman, San Francisco, 1881.

Geary, T. J., Representative to Congress, 1890, 1891, 1893–.

Geiger, Vincent E., State Printer, 1852–54. *Died, Valparaiso, September 6, 1869,*

Geller, William, Assemblyman, Yuba, 1855. *Dead.*

Gelwicks, Daniel W., State Printer, 1867–71; Assemblyman, Alameda, 1875–76; State Prison Director, 1883–84. *Died, Sacramento, November 24, 1884.*

George, James, Assemblyman, San Francisco, 1856.

George, William, Senator, Nevada and Sierra, 1880, 1881.

Gerberding, A., Bank Commissioner, 1890–.

Gesford, H. C., Senator, Yolo and Napa, 1887; Napa and Lake, 1893–

Gibbons, Edward, Senator, Alameda, 1873–74, 1875–76. *Died, Sonoma County, May 30, 1886.*

Gibson, E. M., Superior Judge, Alameda County, elected 1884.

Gibson, James A., Superior Judge, San Bernardino County, elected 1884; Supreme Court Commissioner, 1888–90.

Gibson, John L., Assemblyman, Calaveras, 1871–72.

Gibson, Joseph H., Assemblyman, Placer, 1852.

Giffen, George W., Assemblyman, Nevada, 1873–74, 1875–76, 1877–78.

Gilbert, Edward, Member First Constitutional Convention, 1849, San Francisco District; Representative to Congress, 1849–51. *Died, near Sacramento, August 2, 1852.*

Gilbert, James A., Assemblyman, San Francisco, 1854.

Gildea, Charles, Assemblyman, El Dorado, 1867–68, 1869–70, San Francisco, 1877–78; Member of State Board of Equalization, 1883–86.

Gill, George M., Superior Judge, Inyo County, elected 1890.

Gillen, James S., State Controller, 1861.

Gillette, M. G., Assemblyman, Tuolumne, 1861.

Gilman, C., Assemblyman, Tuolumne, 1857.

Gilmore, George W., Assemblyman, Calaveras, 1873–74.

Gilmore, J. H., Assemblyman, San Francisco, 1881.

Gilmore, N., Assemblyman, El Dorado, 1873–74.

Giltner, Francis. Assemblyman, Mariposa, 1867–68.

Glascock, B. B., Member Second Constitutional Convention, 1878–79, Colusa District; Senator, Colusa and Tehama, 1880, 1881.

Glascock, John R., Representative to Congress, 1883–84.

Glynn, John P., Assemblyman, San Francisco, 1891.

Gober, W. R., Assemblyman, Santa Clara, 1855.

Godard, H. B., Assemblyman, Tuolumne, 1854.

Godchaux, Edmond, Assemblyman, San Francisco, 1893.

Goodale, David, Senator, Contra Costa, Marin, 1871–72, 1873–74.

Goodall, Charles, Assemblyman, San Francisco, 1871–72.

Goodall, J. E., Assemblyman, Tuolumne and Mono, 1865–66.

Goodman, L. C.. Assemblyman, Sacramento, 1860.

Goods, J. C., Trustee of State Library, 1870–74. *Died, Sacramento, November 23, 1877.*

Goodwin, J. D., Assemblyman, Plumas and Lassen, 1865–66; Judge Twenty-first Judicial District, appointed 1876.

40

Goodwin, Jesse O., Senator, Yuba and Sutter, 1857, 1858, 1877-78; Presidential Elector, 1872. *Died, near Vallejo, July 15, 1879.*
Gordon, Alex., Assemblyman, San Mateo, 1891.
Gordon, Alexander, Assemblyman, Marin, 1862.
Gordon, Martin W., Assemblyman, Calaveras, 1854.
Gordon, S. B., Assemblyman, San Mateo, 1858.
Gordon, Upton M., Assemblyman, Marin, 1861.
Gorley, H. A., Assemblyman, San Francisco, 1880.
Gorman, Joseph C., Member Second Constitutional Convention, 1878-79, San Francisco District; Senator, San Francisco, 1880, 1881.
Gottschalk, C. V., Superior Judge, Calaveras County, elected 1879, 1884, 1890.
Goucher, George G., Assemblyman, Mariposa and Merced, 1885; Senator, Alpine, Mariposa, Fresno, etc., 1887, 1889, 1891, 1893-
Gough, Charles H., Assemblyman, San Francisco, 1877-78.
Gould, A. J., Assemblyman, Alpine, Mono, and Inyo, 1887.
Gould, Frank H., Assemblyman, Merced and Mariposa, 1891; Stanislaus and Merced, 1893.
Gove, A. S., Senator, Sacramento, 1855, 1856. *Dead.*
Grace, William P., Member Second Constitutional Convention, 1878-79, San Francisco District.
Gragg, R. F., Assemblyman, Placer, 1855.
Graham, A. J., Assemblyman, El Dorado, 1858.
Graham, James S., Assemblyman, Solano, 1852.
Granger, L. C., Assemblyman, Butte, 1883, 1887. *Died, Oroville, May 20, 1890.*
Grant, Gilbert A., Senator, San Francisco, 1858, 1859. *Died, San Francisco, December 31, 1860.*
Grant, W. H., Superior Judge, Yolo County, elected 1890.
Graves, William, Presidential Elector, 1893.
Graves, William J., Assemblyman, San Luis Obispo, 1855, 1857; Senator, San Luis Obispo and Santa Barbara, 1873-74, 1875-76; Member Second Constitutional Convention, 1878-79, Fourth Congressional District. *Died, San Luis Obispo, August 2, 1884.*
Gray, Giles H., Assemblyman, San Francisco, 1871-72.
Gray, J. S., Assemblyman, Monterey District, 1849-50.
Gray, John C., Assemblyman, Butte, 1873-74; Superior Judge, Butte County, elected 1890.
Gray, Nathaniel, Assemblyman, San Francisco, 1863-64. *Died, Oakland, April 24, 1889.*
Gray, Thomas, Assemblyman, San Francisco, 1856, 1859.
Gray, Wheaton A., Superior Judge, Tulare County, appointed 1891.
Greeley, F. H., Senator, Yuba and Sutter, 1887, 1889.
Green, A. F., Assemblyman, San Mateo, 1863-64.
Green, Alfred A., Assemblyman, San Francisco, 1854.
Green, E. L., Assemblyman, Calaveras, 1869-70. *Died, San Diego, November 28, 1872.*
Green, James J., Assemblyman, El Dorado, 1861; Senator, Contra Costa and Marin, 1867-68, 1869-70; State Controller, 1871-75; Trustee of State Library, 1874-78.
Green, P. M., Assemblyman, Los Angeles, 1880.
Green, Thomas J., Senator, Sacramento District, 1849-50, 1851. *Died, Warren County, North Carolina, December 13, 1863.*
Green, W. S., Assemblymen, Colusa and Tehama, 1867-68; Trustee of State Library, 1891-
Greene, W. E., Assemblyman, San Joaquin, 1865-66; Superior Judge, Alameda County, elected, 1879, 1890.
Gregg, V. A., Member Second Constitutional Convention, 1878-79, Kern District; Superior Judge, San Luis Obispo County, appointed 1889, elected 1890.
Gregory, Andrew J., Assemblyman, Mariposa and Merced, 1859, 1861.
Gregory, D. S., Senator, Santa Cruz and Monterey, 1859; Superior Judge, San Luis Obispo County, appointed 1883, elected 1884.
Gregory, J. B., Assemblyman, Amador and Alpine, 1867-68.
Gregory, J. M., Superior Judge, Solano County, elected 1879.
Gregory, J. W., Presidential Elector, 1852.
Gregory, U. S., Assemblyman, Amador, 1885.
Grewell, Jacob, Senator, Santa Clara and Contra Costa, 1853, 1854.
Griffeth, A. J., Assemblyman, San Francisco, 1877-78.
Griffeth, E. J., Assemblyman, Fresno, 1881.

Griffith, Humphrey, Assemblyman, Yolo, 1854; Senator, Solano, Yolo, and Napa, 1858, 1859. *Died, San Francisco, March 23, 1863.*

Griffith, S. W., Superior Judge, Amador County, elected 1884. *Died, Jackson, July 31, 1886.*

Griswold, J. W., Assemblyman, Calaveras, 1862.

Griswold, John C., Assemblyman, San Francisco, 1869–70.

Griswold, M., Assemblyman, Inyo and Mono, 1875–76.

Groom, R. W., Assemblyman, San Diego, 1858, 1860.

Gross, Frank W., Clerk of the Supreme Court, 1880–82. *Died, San Francisco, December 4, 1886.*

Gruwell, L. H., Assemblyman, Lake, 1887.

Gunnison, A. J., Assemblyman, San Francisco, 1863.

Gurnett, W. J., Assemblyman, Alameda, 1873–74.

Gutierrez, Nicolas, Governor under Mexican rule, 1836.

Gwin, William McKendree, Member First Constitutional Convention, 1849, San Francisco District; United States Senator, 1849–61. *Died, New York, September 3, 1885.*

Gwin, W. M., Jr., Senator, Calaveras, etc., 1869–70, 1871–72, 1877–78.

Gwinn, Harrison, Assemblyman, Yolo, 1859, 1860. *Died, Knights Landing, July 9, 1881.*

Hagans, W. B., Assemblyman, Humboldt, 1861. *Died, Ukiah, June 18, 1881.*

Hagans, William B., Assemblyman, Sonoma, 1854.

Hager, John S., Senator, San Francisco, 1853, 1854; Judge Fourth Judicial District, appointed 1855, elected 1855; Member Second Constitutional Convention, 1878–79, First Congressional District; Regent University of California; United States Senator, 1873–74; Collector of Port, San Francisco, 1885–89. *Died, San Francisco, March 19, 1890.*

Haight, Henry H., Governor, 1867–71; Member Second Constitutional Convention, 1878–79, Second Congressional District. *Died, San Francisco, September 2, 1878.*

Hail, F. G., Assemblyman, Plumas and Sierra, 1891.

Haile, R. C., Assemblyman, Napa and Solano, 1856, 1869–70, 1877–78. *Died, Vacaville, January 23, 1890.*

Hakes, O. F., Superior Judge, Mono County, appointed 1886, elected 1888.

Haldeman, P. M., Assemblyman, Tuolumne, 1858.

Hale, James E., Senator, Placer, 1863–64, 1865–66; Supreme Court Reporter, 1867–70; Presidential Elector, 1872; Member Second Constitutional Convention, 1878–79, Second Congressional District; Assemblyman, Placer, 1881.

Haliday, Thomas J., Assemblyman, Sierra, 1860.

Hall, A. P., Senator, Placer and El Dorado, 1887.

Hall, Gaven D., Assemblyman, El Dorado, 1851, 1857; Senator, El Dorado, 1854, 1855.

Hall, J. B., Member Second Constitutional Convention, 1878–79, Second Congressional District.

Hall, James A., Assemblyman, Santa Cruz, 1889.

Hall, John T., Senator, Solano and Yolo, 1863–64. *Died, Madison, Cal., January 17, 1884.*

Hall, Sydney, Assemblyman, San Francisco, 1883.

Hall, William Hammond, State Engineer, 1878–89.

Halleck, Henry W., Secretary of State under the Military Governments of General R. B. Mason and General Bennet Riley, 1847–49; Member First Constitutional Convention, 1849, Monterey District; Major-General United States Army, appointed August 19, 1861. *Died, Louisville, Kentucky, January 9, 1872.*

Halley, M. P., Assemblyman, San Joaquin, 1853.

Halsey, C., Superior Judge, San Francisco, elected 1879.

Halstead, James L., Assemblyman, Santa Cruz, 1860.

Ham, E. D., Superior Judge, Napa County, elected 1890.

Hamill, J. E., Senator, San Francisco, 1887, 1889, 1891.

Hamill, John, Assemblyman, San Francisco, 1873–74. *Died, San Francisco, October 7, 1879.*

Hamilton, G. W., Assemblyman, Placer, 1893.

Hamilton, H., Senator, Los Angeles, 1863–64.

Hamilton, Jo, Attorney-General, 1867–71, 1875–79; Trustee of State Library, 1874–82.

Hamilton, Noble, Superior Judge, Alameda County, elected 1882.

Hamilton, W. B., Assemblyman, Del Norte, 1883.

Hamlin, Francis, Assemblyman, Sutter, 1865–66.
Hamlin, Thomas T., Assemblyman, Tuolumne, 1858.
Hamm, S. F., Assemblyman, El Dorado, 1857; Senator, El Dorado, 1858, 1859.
Hammitt, A. W., Assemblyman, Contra Costa, 1873–74.
Hammond, J. B., Assemblyman, Mariposa and Merced, 1860.
Hammond, R. P., Assemblyman (Speaker), San Joaquin, 1852. *Died, San Francisco, November 28, 1891.*
Hammond, R. P., Presidential Elector, 1893.
Hancock, Henry, Assemblyman, Los Angeles, 1858, 1859. *Died, Santa Monica, June 9, 1883.*
Handy, Philo, Assemblyman, Mendocino, 1887.
Hanks, Henry G., State Mineralogist, 1880–86.
Hanks, Julian, Member First Constitutional Convention, 1849, San Jose Distric .
Hanna, William, Assemblyman, Santa Clara, 1877–78.
Hannah, John A., Superior Judge, Inyo County, elected 1879, 1884.
Hansbrow, Thomas, Assemblyman, Sacramento, 1865–66. *Died, Sacramento, August 31, 1868.*
Hanson, James H., Assemblyman, Yuba, 1861.
Haraszthy, Augustus, Assemblyman, San Diego, 1852. *Died, Nicaragua, July 6, 1869.*
Harding, J. W., Assemblyman, San Francisco, 1875–76.
Hardwick, George M., Member Second Constitutional Convention, 1878–79, Mariposa and Merced District. *Died, July 11, 1878.*
Hardy, James H., Judge Sixteenth Judicial District, appointed 1859, elected 1859. *Died, San Francisco, June 11, 1874.*
Hardy, L. J., Jr., Assemblyman, San Francisco, 1880.
Hardy, Thomas, Senator, Calaveras, 1865–66, 1867–68.
Hare, I., Assemblyman, Shasta, 1857. *Died, Shasta County, July 31, 1890.*
Harkness, H. W., Trustee of State Library, 1864–70.
Harlan, J. H., Senator, Solano and Yolo, 1880, 1881.
Harloe, Marcus, Assemblyman, San Luis Obispo, 1891.
Harp, T. D., Senator, Merced, Stanislaus, etc., 1891, 1893.
Harrigan, John, Senator, San Francisco, 1883.
Harriman, W. D., Assemblyman, Placer, 1861; Senator, Placer, 1862, 1863; Clerk of the Supreme Court, 1863–67.
Harrington, D. W., Assemblyman, Santa Clara, 1863.
Harris, G. F., Assemblyman, Siskiyou and Modoc, 1875–76; Superior Judge, Modoc County, elected 1879, 1884.
Harris, J. J., Assemblyman, San Benito, 1880.
Harris, James O., Assemblyman, Sutter, 1858.
Harris, M. K., Superior Judge, Fresno County, appointed 1887, elected 1888.
Harris, P. H., Assemblyman, Butte, 1861.
Harrison, J. W., Assemblyman, Sacramento, 1853.
Harrison, R., Assemblyman, Sonoma and Marin, 1857.
Harrison, Ralph C., Supreme Justice, 1891–
Harrison, Thomas, Member Second Constitutional Convention, 1878–79, San Francisco District.
Harrison, W. J., Assemblyman, Placer, 1861.
Hart, A. S., Senator, Butte and Plumas, 1858, 1859.
Hart, Albert, Private Secretary to Governors Newton Booth and George C. Perkins.
Hart, Augustus L., Attorney-General, 1880–82.
Hart, E. C., Assemblyman, Sacramento, 1889; Senator, Sacramento, 1893–
Hart, Thomas J., Assemblyman, Colusa and Tehama, 1875–76, 1877–78, 1887. *Died, Colusa, September 30, 1891.*
Hart, William H. H., Attorney-General, 1891–
Hartson, Chancellor, Assemblyman, Napa and Lake, 1863, 1880, 1881; Senator, Napa, Lake, etc., 1863–64, 1865–66. *Died, Napa, September 25, 1889.*
Hartsough, J. B., Assemblyman, Yolo, 1863–64.
Harvey, Joel A., Assemblyman, Solano, 1883; Member Second Constitutional Convention, 1878–79, Solano District.
Harvey, Obed, Senator, El Dorado, 1861, 1862, 1863; Assemblyman, Sacramento, 1871–72; Director State Insane Asylum at Stockton, 1891–
Harville, John W., Assemblyman, Placer, 1860.
Haskin, J. W., Senator, Tuolumne and Mono, 1863–64.

Hastings, E. O. F., Assemblyman, Sutter, 1854. *Died, San Francisco, May 1, 1889.*

Hastings, L. W., Member First Constitutional Convention, 1849, Sacramento District. *Dead.*

Hastings, S. C., Chief Justice, 1849-52; Attorney-General, 1852-53.

Haswell, C a S., Assemblyman, Sutter, 1863; Senator, Yuba and Sutter, 1863-64h rles

Hatch, D. P., Superior Judge, Santa Barbara County, elected 1880, 1884.

Hatch, F. L., Superior Judge, Colusa County, elected 1879. *Died, Colusa, October 5, 1881.*

Hatch, F. W., Trustee of State Library, 1874-82. *Died, Sacramento, October 18, 1884.*

Hatch, H. L., Assemblyman, Nevada, 1865-66.

Hatch, Jackson, Presidential Elector, 1893.

Hathaway, B. W., Senator, San Francisco, etc., 1862, 1863. *Died, San Francisco, May 1, 1867.*

Haun, D. L., Assemblyman, Yuba, 1861.

Haun, Heury P., United States Senator, 1859. *Died, Marysville, June 6, 1860.*

Havens, H. W., Assemblyman, Humboldt, 1858.

Hawes, Horace, Assemblyman, San Francisco, 1856; Senator, San Francisco, 1863-64, 1865-66. *Died, San Francisco, March 12, 1871.*

Hawkins, Michael, Assemblyman, San Francisco, 1865-66.

Hawks, W. W., Senator, San Francisco, 1855, 1856. *Died, San Francisco, March 8, 1859.*

Hawley, Asa H., Assemblyman, El Dorado, 1860.

Hawley, B. F., Assemblyman, Nevada, 1869-70.

Hawley, W. A., Assemblyman, Santa Barbara, 1891.

Haworth, James, Assemblyman, San Francisco, 1877-78. *Dead.*

Hawthorne, J. C., Senator, Placer, 1855, 1856. *Died, Portland, Oregon, February 15, 1881.*

Hay, Alexander, Assemblyman, Santa Clara, 1873-74.

Hayes, Benjamin, Assemblyman, San Diego, 1867-68; Judge First Judicial District, elected 1852, 1858. *Died, Los Angeles, August 4, 1877.*

Hayes, George R. B., Assemblyman, San Francisco, 1869-70.

Hayes, H. M., Assemblyman, Monterey, 1871-72.

Hayes, Henry, Assemblyman, Nevada, 1860.

Hayes, John, Assemblyman, San Francisco, 1891.

Hayes, Michael, Assemblyman, San Francisco, 1869-70. *Died, San Francisco, November 8, 1888.*

Haymond, Creed, Senator, Sacramento, 1875-76, 1877-78.

Hayne, Robert Y., Superior Judge, San Francisco, elected 1880; Supreme Court Commissioner, 1887-91.

Hayne, W. A., Assemblyman, Santa Barbara and Ventura, 1875-76.

Haynes, John P., Senator, Humboldt, etc., 1860, 1861, 1887; Judge Eighth Judicial District, elected 1858, appointed 1868, elected 1869, 1875; Superior Judge, Humboldt County, elected 1879,

Hazard, Henry T., Assemblyman, Los Angeles, 1885.

Heacock, E. H., Senator, Sacramento, 1861, 1862, 1863-64, 1867-68; Santa Barbara, 1889, 1891; Superior Judge, Santa Barbara County, appointed 1880.

Head, E. F., Superior Judge, San Mateo County, elected 1879, 1884. *Dead.*

Head, H. W., Assemblyman, Los Angeles, 1883.

Heald, H. G., Assemblyman, Sonoma, 1856.

Heald, J. L., Assemblyman, Solano, 1873-74.

Healy, Thomas, Assemblyman, San Francisco, 1883.

Hearst, George, Assemblyman, San Francisco, 1865-66; Trustee of the State Mining Bureau, 1885-89; United States Senator, 1886, 1887-91. *Died, Washington, D. C., February 28, 1891.*

Heath, Lucien, Assemblyman, Santa Cruz, 1883, 1885. *Died, Santa Cruz, December 19, 1888.*

Heath, R. W., Assemblyman, San Joaquin District, 1849-50.

Heath, Russell, Assemblyman, Santa Barbara, 1858, 1887.

Hebbard, J. C. B., Superior Judge, San Francisco, elected 1890.

Hebbron, J. R., Member of State Board of Equalization, 1891-

Hecht, Marcus H., Presidential Elector, 1884.

Heintzleman, H. P., Senator, Sonoma and Marin, 1855, 1856.

Heiskell, Tyler D., Assemblyman, El Dorado, 1856; Member of Second Constitutional Convention, 1878-79, Stanislaus District; Member of State Board of Equalization, 1880-82.

Hempstead, Charles H., Private Secretary to Governor John Bigler, second term; Secretary of State, 1855–56. *Died, Salt Lake, September 28, 1879.*
Henderson, Robert, Assemblyman, El Dorado, 1861. *Died, Sacramento, July 16, 1864.*
Hendrick, E. W., Assemblyman, San Diego, 1881.
Hendricks, Jas. W., Superior Judge, Lassen County, elected 1879.
Hendricks, William C., Senator, Butte, Plumas, etc., 1873–74, 1875–76; State Prison Director, 1883–87,; Penology Commissioner, 1885; Secretary of State, 1887–91. *Died, Sacramento, January 24, 1892.*
Hendrickson, W., Assemblyman, San Francisco, 1893.
Henley, Barclay, Assemblyman, Sonoma, 1869–70; Presidential Elector, 1880; Representative to Congress, 1883–86.
Henley, G. W., Assemblyman, Mendocino, 1869–70. *Died, Santa Rosa, August 1, 1881.*
Henley, Thomas J., Assemblyman, Sacramento District, 1849–50; Presidential Elector, 1852. *Died, Mendocino County, May 1, 1875.*
Henley, Whit., Assemblyman, Mendocino, 1885.
Henry, A. C., Senator, El Dorado, 1863–64.
Henry, Allen, Assemblyman, Butte, 1885, 1887.
Henry, Brice M., Assemblyman, San Luis Obispo, 1860. *Died, San Francisco, April 8, 1861.*
Henry, J. C., Assemblyman, Mariposa, 1854. *Killed at Cavorca, Mexico, April 7, 1857.*
Henry, J. R., Assemblyman, San Joaquin, 1887.
Henshaw, F. W., Superior Judge, Alameda County, elected 1890.
Herbert, Philip T., Assemblyman, Mariposa,, 1853, 1854; Representative to Congress, 1855–56. *Died, Kingston, Louisiana, July 23, 1864.*
Herold, Adam, State Treasurer, 1887–90.
Herold, Conrad, Member Second Constitutional Convention, 1878–79, San Francisco District.
Herrington, Dennis W., Member Second Constitutional Convention, 1878–79, Santa Clara District.
Hersey, George E., Assemblyman, Santa Clara, 1891.
Hersey, Philo, Assemblyman, Santa Clara, 1889.
Hershey, David N., Assemblyman, Yolo, 1880, 1883.
Hester, C. P., Judge Third Judicial District, appointed 1851, elected 1851, 1852. *Died, February, 1874.*
Heston, Thomas M., Assemblyman, Tulare and Fresno, 1860. *Died, June, 1863.*
Hewell, A., Superior Judge, Stanislaus County, elected 1879.
Heydenfeldt, Elcan, Senator, San Francisco, 1849–50, 1851; President pro tem. of the Senate, 1851; Judge Seventh Judicial District, appointed 1851; Assemblyman, San Francisco, 1853.
Heydenfeldt, Solomon, Supreme Justice, 1852–57; Trustee of State Library, 1861–64. *Died, San Francisco, September 15, 1890.*
Heywood, Walter M., Assemblyman, Alameda, 1885.
Hicks, John A., Assemblyman, San Francisco, 1877–78.
Higbie, A., Assemblyman, Los Angeles, 1873–74.
Higby, William, Senator, Calaveras, 1863; Representative to Congress, 1863–68. *Died, Santa Rosa, November 26, 1887.*
Higgins, F. B., Senator, Placer, 1863.
Higgins, M. R., Private Secretary to Governor H. H. Markham.
Higley, Horace A., Surveyor-General, 1858–61. *Died, San Francisco, November 24, 1873.*
Hihn, F. A., Assemblyman, Santa Cruz, 1869–70.
Hilborn, S. G., Senator, Solano and Yolo, 1875–76, 1877–78; Member Second Constitutional Convention, 1878–79, Solano District; United States District Attorney for California, 1882–86; Representative to Congress, 1892–
Hill, Albert A., Assemblyman, San Francisco, 1859.
Hill, Henry, Member First Constitutional Convention, 1849, San Diego District.
Hill, John H., Senator, Sonoma, Marin, etc., 1861, 1862. *Died, Philadelphia, May 7, 1886.*
Hill, R. D., Assemblyman, Sierra, 1858.
Hill, Ramon J., Assemblyman, San Luis Obispo, 1863, 1863–64, 1865–66.
Hill, Samuel, Assemblyman, El Dorado, 1861.
Hill, W. H., Assemblyman, Nevada, 1873–74.
Hill, W. J., Senator, Monterey, San Benito, etc., 1880, 1881.

Hill, William, Assemblyman, Nevada, 1858. *Dead.*
Hill, William McP., Senator, Sonoma, Napa, and Lake, 1875-76, 1877-78.
Hillyer, E. W., Assemblyman, Placer, 1862. *Died, Carson City, Nevada, May 1st, 1882.*
Hinchman, A. F., Assemblyman, Santa Barbara, 1852.
Hines, Benjamin S., Assemblyman, Contra Costa, 1859.
Hines, J. D., Superior Judge, Ventura County, elected 1879. *Died, Ventura, January 1, 1887.*
Hinshaw, E. C., Assemblyman, Sonoma, 1871-72, 1875-76, 1877-78, 1881; Senator, Sonoma, 1887, 1889.
Hirst, R. P., Assemblyman, Del Norte and Klamath, 1858, 1863-64.
Hitchcock, John R. W., Member Second Constitutional Convention, 1878-79 San Joaquin District.
Hitchens, James, Assemblyman, Butte, 1858.
Hittell, John S., Assemblyman, San Francisco, 1863-64.
Hittell, Theodore H., Senator, San Francisco, 1880, 1881.
Hoag, I. N., Assemblyman, Yolo, 1862.
Hoag, O. H., Assemblyman, Sonoma, 1863-64, 1865-66.
Hobart, J. A., Assemblyman, Alameda, 1858.
Hobson, Joseph, Member First Constitutional Convention, 1849, San Francisco District.
Hocking, Thomas C., Assemblyman, Nevada, 1891.
Hoey, Lawrence, Assemblyman, San Francisco, 1891.
Hoff, John J., Assemblyman, Tuolumne, 1853, 1854.
Hoff, W. C., Assemblyman, San Francisco, 1851.
Hoffman, D. B., Assemblyman, San Diego, 1862; Presidential Elector, 1868. *Died, San Diego, November 20, 1891.*
Hoge, Joseph P., Member Second Constitutional Convention (President), 1878-79, First Congressional District; Superior Judge, San Francisco, elected 1888. *Died, San Francisco, August 14, 1891.*
Hogle, L. I., Assemblyman, Tuolumne and Mono, 1865-66.
Hoitt, Ira G., Assemblyman, San Francisco, 1881; State Superintendent of Public Instruction, 1887-90.
Holden, William, Assemblyman, Mendocino, 1857, 1865-66, 1881; Senator, Tuolumne and Stanislaus, 1858, 1859; Lake, Napa, etc., 1862, 1863; Lieutenant-Governor, 1867-71. *Died, Healdsburg, June 3, 1884.*
Holland, Nathaniel, Assemblyman, San Francisco, 1856.
Holliday, S. W., Assemblyman, San Francisco, 1858.
Hollingsworth, J. McH., Member First Constitutional Convention, 1849, San Joaquin District.
Hollister, Dwight, Assemblyman, Sacramento, 1865-66, 1885.
Hollister, H., Assemblyman, El Dorado, 1854.
Hollister, J. H., Assemblyman, San Luis Obispo, 1883.
Holloway, J. B., Assemblyman, Los Angeles, 1877-78.
Holman, D. B., Assemblyman, Solano, 1861.
Holman, G. C., Assemblyman, San Joaquin, 1858, 1859.
Holmes, E. W., Assemblyman, San Bernardino, 1889.
Holmes, Samuel A., Member Second Constitutional Convention, 1878-79, Fresno District; Superior Judge, Fresno County, elected 1879, 1890.
Hook, G. W., Senator, El Dorado, 1854, 1855, 1856. *Died, San Francisco, November 8, 1868.*
Hook, Henry, Assemblyman, Contra Costa, 1889.
Hoover, A. A., Assemblyman, Sierra, 1856.
Hope, A. W., Senator, Los Angeles and San Diego, 1849-50, 1851. *Died, Los Angeles, June 17, 1856.*
Hopkins, Rienzi, Senator, Calaveras, 1873-74, 1875-76. *Died, San Andreas, January 2, 1879.*
Hopkins, Robert, Judge Seventh Judicial District, elected by Legislature, 1850.
Hopkins, William R., Assemblyman, El Dorado, 1852.
Hoppe, Jacob D., Member First Constitutional Convention, 1849, San Jose District. *Died, San Francisco, April 17, 1853.*
Hopper, Peter J., Assemblyman, Sacramento, 1865-66, 1871-72. *Died, Sacramento, July 22, 1883.*
Horan, M. S., Assemblyman, Sacramento, 1869-70. *Died, San Francisco, December 9, 1892.*
Horr, B. D., Assemblyman, Tuolumne, 1854. *Died, Tuolumne City, February 9, 1869.*

Horrell, T. M., Assemblyman, Amador, 1861.
Hosmer, H. B., Assemblyman, San Francisco, 1855. *Dead.*
Hotchkiss, W. J., Assemblyman, Sonoma, 1887.
Houghtaling, A. J., Assemblyman, Calaveras, 1854.
Houghton, James Franklin, Surveyor-General, 1862–67; Regent State University, 1891–
Houghton, S. O., Representative to Congress, 1871–74.
Houston, J. S., State Controller, 1849–51.
Howard, George H., Assemblyman, San Mateo, 1865–66.
Howard, M. B., Assemblyman, San Francisco, 1881.
Howard, Volney E., Member Second Constitutional Convention, 1878–79, Los Angeles District; Superior Judge, Los Angeles County, elected, 1879.
Howard, W. J., Assemblyman, Mariposa and Merced, 1857; Member Second Constitutional Convention, 1878–79, Mariposa and Merced District.
Howe, A. J., Superior Judge, Sierra County, elected 1879.
Howe, J. F., Private Secretary to Governor John McDougal.
Howe, Robert, Assemblyman, Tuolumne, 1859, 1860; San Francisco, 1873–74; Sonoma, 1889; Speaker, 1889; Senator, San Francisco, 1875–76, 1877–78.
Howell, Charles S., Assemblyman, Sacramento, 1858. *Killed by explosion of steamboat "J. A. McClelland," August 25, 1861.*
Howell, John M., Judge Eleventh Judicial District, elected 1852.
Howell, M. D., Assemblyman, Plumas, 1863.
Hoyt, J. B., Senator, Solano, 1893.
Hoyt, T. J., Assemblyman, Tuolumne, 1854.
Hubbard, J. C., Assemblyman, San Francisco, 1854.
Hubbard, L., Assemblyman, Yuba, 1863–64. *Died, Surprise Valley, Siskiyou County, October 2, 1871.*
Hubbs, Paul K., Senator, Tuolumne, 1852, 1853; State Superintendent of Public Instruction, 1854–56. *Died, Vallejo, November 17, 1874.*
Hubert, N., Assemblyman, San Francisco, 1854.
Hubner, Charles G., Assemblyman, San Joaquin, 1869–70.
Hudson, A. T., Senator, San Joaquin and Amador, 1880, 1881.
Hudson, Rodney J., Superior Judge, Lake County, elected 1879, 1884.
Hudson, T. W., Assemblyman, Sonoma, 1869–70.
Hudspeth, J. M., Assemblyman, Sonoma, 1852; Senator, Sonoma, Marin, etc., 1853, 1854.
Huestis, A. J., Assemblyman, Humboldt, 1865–66.
Huestis, W. F., Member Second Constitutional Convention, 1878–79, Third Congressional District.
Hugg, Benjamin P., Assemblyman, Yuba, 1860, 1877–78.
Hughes, Charles A., Assemblyman, San Francisco, 1883. *Died, Sacramento, March 17, 1883.*
Hughes, J. T., Assemblyman, San Diego District, 1849–50.
Hughey, William P., Member Second Constitutional Convention, 1878–79, San Francisco District.
Hume, John, Assemblyman, El Dorado, 1857. *Died, La Grange County, Indiana, August 27, 1867.*
Humphreys, W. P., Railroad Commissioner, Second District, 1883–86.
Hundley, P. O., Assemblyman, Plumas, 1860; Judge Second Judicial District, appointed 1878; Superior Judge, Butte County, elected 1879, 1888.
Hunewill, F. E., Assemblyman, Alpine, Mono, and Inyo, 1891.
Hunt, A. B., Assemblyman, Santa Clara, 1865–66.
Hunt, J., Assemblyman, Los Angeles, 1853.
Hunt, Jefferson, Assemblyman, San Bernardino, 1854, 1856, 1857. *Dead.*
Hunt, John, Jr., Superior Judge, San Francisco, elected 1879, 1884, 1890.
Hunt, William B., Assemblyman, Sacramento, 1863–64, 1865–66; San Francisco, 1885. *Died, San Francisco, November 13, 1889.*
Hunter, A. B., Assemblyman, Santa Clara, 1883.
Hunter, Alexander, Assemblyman, El Dorado, 1861.
Hunter, E., Assemblyman, Los Angeles, 1854, 1857.
Hunter, G. W., Superior Judge, Humboldt County, appointed 1889, elected 1890.
Hunter, G. W., Assemblyman, San Joaquin, 1856; Senator, El Dorado, 1867–68, 1869–70; Member Second Constitutional Convention, 1878–79, El Dorado and Alpine District. *Dead.*
Hurlburt, B. G., Assemblyman, Humboldt, 1873–74; Senator, Humboldt, 1885.
Hurley, M. J., Assemblyman, San Francisco, 1893.

Huse, C. E., Assemblyman, Santa Barbara, 1853.
Hussey, Frank W., Assemblyman, San Francisco, 1885.
Hutchings, S. C., Senator, Sutter and Yuba, 1869-70, 1871-72.
Hutson, J. L., Assemblyman, San Joaquin, 1893.
Hutton, A. W., Superior Judge, Los Angeles County, appointed 1887.
Hyde, M. D., Assemblyman, Alameda, 1887, 1889.
Hynes, James, Assemblyman, Sonoma, 1880. *Died, Petaluma, March 12, 1882.*
Imas, Hiram A., Assemblyman, Santa Cruz, 1859.
Ingersoll, T. J., Assemblyman, Tuolumne, 1852. *Died, San Jose, April 30, 1880.*
Ingham, G. H., Assemblyman, El Dorado, 1873-74.
Inman, A., Assemblyman, Contra Costa, 1857.
Inman, Daniel, Assemblyman, Alameda, 1869-70; Member Second Constitutional Convention, 1878-79, Alameda District.
Irelan, William, Jr., State Mineralogist, 1886-89, 1889-; ex-officio State Engineer, 1889-91.
Ireland, M. C., Assemblyman, Monterey, 1865-66.
Irwin, Charles F., Assemblyman, El Dorado, 1883.
Irwin, Richard, Assemblyman, Butte, 1853, 1854; Plumas, 1857; Senator, Butte and Plumas, 1861, 1862.
Irwin, William, Assemblyman, Siskiyou, 1862, 1863; Senator, Siskiyou, 1869-70, 1871-72, 1873-74; President pro tem., 1873-74; Lieutenant-Governor, 1875; Governor, 1875-80; Harbor Commissioner, 1883-86. *Died, San Francisco, March 15, 1886.*
Jackson, A. J., Assemblyman, Modoc and Lassen, 1891.
Jackson, A. R., Assemblyman, Sacramento, 1859. *Died, San Francisco, August 30, 1876.*
Jackson, H. J., Assemblyman, San Francisco, 1881.
Jackson, T. O., Assemblyman, Yuba, 1862.
Jacobs, I. W., Assemblyman, Yolo, 1893.
Jacobsen, H. J. T., Assemblyman, Fresno, 1893.
James, D. W., Assemblyman, San Luis Obispo, 1889.
James, J. C., Assemblyman, Sierra, 1854. *Died, Carson, Nevada, January 24, 1874.*
James, John M., Assemblyman, San Bernardino, 1867-68.
James, W. T., Assemblyman, San Francisco, 1871-72.
Jamison, S. I., Assemblyman, Santa Clara, 1875-76.
January, William A., State Treasurer, 1883-84.
Jefferis, E. G., State Printer, 1875. *Died, Sacramento, March 28, 1880.*
Jenkins, T., Assemblyman, San Joaquin, 1857.
Jenkins, T. F., Assemblyman, Mariposa and Merced, 1860.
Jenkins, T. J., Assemblyman, Butte, 1875-76.
Jennison, S., Assemblyman, Colusa and Tehama, 1863-64.
Jessup, Richard M., Assemblyman, San Francisco, 1857. *Died, Panama, February 3, 1865.*
Jewett, John H., Presidential Elector, 1876.
Johnson, A. P., Senator, San Bernardino, 1885.
Johnson, C. H., Assemblyman, San Luis Obispo, 1861.
Johnson, D. J., Assemblyman, Humboldt, 1893.
Johnson, G. A., Assemblyman, San Diego, 1863, 1865-66.
Johnson, George A., Member Second Constitutional Convention, 1878-79, Sonoma District; Senator, Sonoma, 1883, 1885; Attorney-General, 1887-90.
Johnson, Grove L., Assemblyman, Sacramento, 1877-78; Senator, Sacramento, 1880, 1881.
Johnson, H. H., Assemblyman, Santa Clara, 1893.
Johnson, J. C., Assemblyman, El Dorado, 1855.
Johnson, J. K., Assemblyman, Siskiyou and Del Norte, 1885.
Johnson, J. M., Assemblyman, Alpine and Amador, 1869-70.
Johnson, J. Neely, Assemblyman, Sacramento, 1853; Governor, 1856-57. *Died, Salt Lake, Utah, August 31, 1872.*
Johnson, James, Senator, El Dorado, 1865-66, 1867-68. *Died, Oakland, 1888.*
Johnson, James A., Assemblyman, Sierra, 1859, 1860; Representative to Congress, 1867-70; Lieutenant-Governor, 1875-79; Registrar of Voters, San Francisco, 1883-85.
Johnson, Josiah, Senator, Sacramento, 1857, 1858. *Died, Sacramento, December, 10, 1888.*
Johnson, Matthew F., Trustee of State Library, 1883-86; Superior Judge, Sacramento County, 1892-

Johnson, P. C., Assemblyman, Amador, 1860. ' *Died, Jackson, September 8;.*
1861.
Johnson, R. S., Assemblyman, San Joaquin, 1889, 1891.
Johnson, S. M., Senator, El Dorado, 1857, 1858.
Johnson, Sanborn, Assemblyman, Marin, 1863–64.
Johnson, W. Neely, State Librarian, 1870.
Johnston, Alfred J., State Printer, 1891–
Johnston, F. C., Assemblyman, Napa, 1883.
Johnston, George P., Assemblyman, San Francisco, 1855. *Died, San Fran-*
cisco, March 4, 1884.
Johnston, William, Assemblyman, Sacramento, 1871–72; Senator, Sacra-
mento, 1880, 1881; President pro tem., 1881; Member of State Board of
Equalization, 1882.
Jones, Albert F., Senator, Butte, 1887, 1889.
Jones, Charles T., Assemblyman, Sacramento, 1885.
Jones, Cyrus, Assemblyman, Santa Clara, 1875–76.
Jones, F. L., Assemblyman, San Francisco, 1891.
Jones, J. C., Assemblyman, Yuba, 1854. *Died, Carson City, Nevada, January*
24, 1874.
Jones, Joseph P., Assemblyman, Contra Costa, 1881.
Jones, John M., Member First Constitutional Convention, 1849, San Joaquin.
District. *Died, San Jose, December 14, 1851.*
Jones, John P., Senator, Shasta and Trinity, 1863–64, 1865–66.
Jones, Joseph P., Superior Judge, Contra Costa County, elected 1886, 1890.
Jones, L. F., Member Second Constitutional Convention, 1878–79, Mariposa,.
Merced and Stanislaus District. •
Jones, T. E., Assemblyman, Trinity, 1867–68; Superior Judge, Trinity
County, elected 1879, 1884, 1890.
Jones, W. P., Assemblyman, Calaveras, 1852.·
Jones, W. W., Assemblyman, Los Angeles, 1855.
Jordan, William H., Assemblyman, Alameda, 1885, 1887; Speaker of the·
House, 1887.
Josselyn, E. S., Assemblyman, Monterey, 1880.·
Jost, Charles, Assemblyman, San Francisco, 1871–72.
Jourdan, J. W., Assemblyman, San Francisco, 1875–76. · ·
Joyce, Peter J., Member Second Constitutional Convention, 1878–79, San·
Francisco District.
Kabler, Nicolas, Assemblyman, Placer, 1858.
Kahn, Julius, Assemblyman, San Francisco, 1893.
Kalben, E. C., Assemblyman, San Francisco, 1885.
Kane, Thomas, Senator, San Francisco, 1880, 1881.
Keating, Edward, Assemblyman, San Francisco, 1881; Senator, San Fran-
cisco, 1883. *Died, San Francisco, March 11, 1889.*
Keeler, J. M., Assemblyman, Inyo and Mono, 1883.
Keene, B. F., Senator, El Dorado, 1852, 1853, 1854, 1855; President pro tem.,.
of the Senate, 1853, 1854. *Died, Placerville, September 5, 1856.*
Kelley, John M., Assemblyman, Yolo, 1867–68, 1869–70; Member Second Con-
stitutional Convention, 1878–79, Third Congressional District. *Died, Wil-*
lows, May 22, 1881.
Kelley, K. E., Senator, Solano, Yolo, 1883. ·
Kellogg, E. B., Assemblyman, Santa Cruz, 1851.
Kellogg, E. D., Assemblyman, Humboldt, 1891.
Kellogg, H. B., Assemblyman, Yuba, 1854.
Kellogg, W. W., Assemblyman, Plumas and Lassen, 1881; Senator, Butte,.
Plumas, etc., 1883, 1885.
Kelly, M. T., Senator, San Francisco, 1883, 1885.
Kelly, Martin, Senator, San Francisco, 1880, 1881. *Died, Oakland, May 30,.*
1890.
Kelly, R. C., Assemblyman, Plumas, 1856.
Kendall, C. W., Assemblyman, Tuolumne and Mono, 1862.
Kendall, Thomas, Senator, Tuolumne, 1854, 1855.
Kendrick, J. J., Assemblyman, El Dorado, 1851; San Diego, 1856, 1857, 1863–64..
Kenfield, D. M., State Controller, 1880–83. *Died, San Francisco, September 28,.*
1883.
Kennedy, John J., Assemblyman, San Francisco, 1893.
Kennedy, John O'B., Assemblyman, 1875–76.
Kenny, Bernard F., Member Second Constitutional Convention, 1878–79, San·
Francisco District. *Died, San Francisco, November 21, 1878.*

Kenny, John.J., Member Second Constitutional Convention, 1878–79, San Francisco District.

Kent, Charles, Senator, Nevada, 1871–72, 1873–74. *Died, San Francisco, May 21, 1891.*

Kercheval, Reuben, Assemblyman, Sacramento, 1873–74, 1877–78. *Died, on Grand Island, Sacramento County, May 9, 1881.*

Kerns, T. J., Assemblyman, Los Angeles, 1893.

Kerr, George, assigned the contract (George Kerr & Co.) to do the State printing, 1853, law repealed 1854. *Died, Stockton, March 4, 1854.*

Kerrick, J. W., Assemblyman, San Joaquin, 1883.

Ketcham, Lewis Nesbit, Senator, Calaveras and Amador, 1858, 1859. *Died, Yreka, January 17, 1872.*

Kewen, E. J. C., Assemblyman, Los Angeles, 1863, 1863–64; Attorney-General, 1849–50. *Died, Los Angeles, November 25, 1879.*

Keyes, James H., Member Second Constitutional Convention, 1878–79, Yuba and Sutter District. *Died, Cloverdale, August 25, 1880.*

Keys, T. J., Assemblyman, San Joaquin, 1855, 1863; Senator, Mariposa and Stanislaus, 1871–72, 1873–74.

Keyser, Philip W., Senator, Sutter, 1852; Judge Tenth Judicial District, elected 1869, 1875; Superior Judge, Yuba and Sutter Counties, elected 1879, 1884, 1890. *Died, Yuba City, January 15, 1891.*

Kibbe, William C., Adjutant-General, 1852–63.

Kidder, J. F., Assemblyman, El Dorado, 1865–66.

Kiernan, C. H., Assemblyman, San Francisco, 1889. *Died, Oakland, July 16, 1889.*

Kilburn, Paris, Assemblyman, Monterey, 1881.

Kimball, William, Senator, Sierra, 1862.

Kincaid, H., Senator, San Francisco, etc., 1867–68, 1869–70.

Kincaid, J. E., Assemblyman, San Francisco, 1863.

King, A. J, Assemblyman, Los Angeles, 1860.

King, Homer, Assemblyman, Amador, 1858. *Died, Sacramento, February 28, 1876.*

King, James L., Member of State Board of Equalization, 1880–83.

King, W. A., Assemblyman, Nevada, 1869–70.

Kinney, Asa, Assemblyman, Plumas, 1855.

Kip, Alpheas, Assemblyman, Sacramento, 1852.

Kirkpatrick, M., Senator, Sierra, 1859, 1860.

Kittridge, F. M., Assemblyman, Santa Cruz, 1853. *Died, Santa Cruz, February 13, 1879.*

Klein, Charles R., Member Second Constitutional Convention, 1878–79, San Francisco District.

Klotz, Rudolph, Assemblyman, Shasta, 1873–74. *Died, Shasta County, April 7, 1885.*

Knight, Benjamin, Senator, Santa Cruz, etc., 1883, 1885; President pro tem., 1885.

Knight, George A., Insurance Commissioner, 1882–86; Presidential Elector, 1888; Attorney State Board of Health, 1891–

Knight, Samuel, Assemblyman, San Joaquin, 1853. *Died, San Francisco, April 16, 1866.*

Knight, W. H., Bank Commissioner, 1890–

Knox, G. W., Assemblyman, Los Angeles, 1887.

Knox, Martin, Assemblyman, Yuba, 1873–74.

Knox, William J., Assemblyman, Nevada, 1855; Senator, Santa Clara, 1865–66. *Died, San Francisco, November 13, 1867.*

Koll, F. W., Assemblyman, San Francisco, 1854.

Koutz, John, Assemblyman, Sierra, 1869–70, 1875–76.

Kungle, C. H., Assemblyman, Yuba, 1860, 1861.

Kurtz, D. B., Senator, San Diego, 1853, 1854; Assemblyman, San Diego, 1861, 1865–66.

Kutz, Joseph, Senator, Nevada, 1862, 1863, 1863–64, 1865–66. *Dead.*

La Blane, John, Assemblyman, San Francisco, 1887.

Lacey, C. F., Assemblyman, Monterey, 1891.

Lafferty, John, Assemblyman, San Francisco, 1885. *Died, San Francisco, February 24, 1886.*

La Grange, O. H., Presidential Elector, 1868.

La Grave, C. T., Assemblyman, Amador, 1889.

Laine, Thomas H., Senator, Santa Clara, 1873–74, 1875–76; Member Second

Constitutional Convention, 1878–79, Santa Clara District. *Died, Santa Clara, March 15, 1890.*

Lake, Delos, Judge Fourth Judicial District, appointed 1851, elected 1852. *Died, San Francisco, August 8, 1882.*

Lalor, E., Assemblyman, Yuba, 1861.

Lamar, Joseph B., Assemblyman, Sonoma and Mendocino, 1859, 1860. *Died, San Jose, July 27, 1892.*

Lambert, John, Assemblyman, Butte, 1860; Senator, Yolo and Solano, 1877–78. *Died, Woodland, March 20, 1890.*

Lambert, John, Assemblyman, Lassen and Plumas, 1869–70.

Lambourn, Frederick, Assemblyman, Los Angeles, 1875–76.

Lammers, Martin, Assemblyman, San Joaquin, 1875–76.

Lamon, R. B., Assemblyman, Mariposa, 1856.

Lampson, R. M., Senator, Calaveras and Tuolumne, 1880, 1881; Member Second Constitutional Convention, 1878–79, Tuolumne and Calaveras District. *Died, Chinese Camp, March 13, 1885,*

Lane, Michael, Assemblyman, San Francisco, 1880, 1881.

Lane, T. W., Assemblyman, Stanislaus and Merced, 1862.

Langdon, L., Assemblyman, Calaveras, 1863–64.

Langford, B. F., Senator, San Joaquin and Amador, 1880, 1881, 1883, 1885, 1887, 1889, 1891, 1893; Member Board of Agriculture, District No. 2, San Joaquin and Calaveras counties.

Lansing, C. J., Senator, Nevada, 1859, 1860; President pro tem., 1860. *Died, Eureka, Nevada, August 7, 1884.*

Larkin, Henry, Senator, El Dorado, 1869–70, 1871–72; Member Second Constitutional Convention, 1878–79, El Dorado District.

Larkin, Thomas O., Member First Constitutional Convention, 1849, Monterey District. *Died, San Francisco, October 27, 1858.*

La Rue, Hugh M., Member Second Constitutional Convention, 1878–79, Second Congressional District; Assemblyman (Speaker), Sacramento, 1883; Member State Board of Agriculture, 1884–92.

La Rue, J. M., Assemblyman, San Joaquin, 1893.

Larue, James B., Assemblyman, Alameda, 1857. *Died, Brooklyn, California, January 7, 1872.*

Laspeyre, Thomas, Assemblyman, San Joaquin, 1859, 1860, 1861. *Died, Butte City, Montana, September 9, 1883.*

Latham, Milton S., Representative to Congress, 1853–54; Governor, 1860; United States Senator, 1860–63. *Died, New York, March 4, 1882.*

Latimer, L. D., Superior Judge, San Francisco, appointed 1880.

Laughlin, S. N., Assemblyman, Monterey, 1885.

Lavinge, Raymond, Member Second Constitutional Convention, 1878–79, San Francisco District.

Law, J. K., Superior Judge, Merced County, elected 1890.

Law, James L., Assemblyman, Butte, 1852.

Lawler, F. W., Superior Judge, San Francisco, elected 1880, 1886.

Lawrence, A. C., Assemblyman, Trinity, 1860.

Lawrence, A. M., Assemblyman, San Francisco, 1887.

Leach, Frank A., Assemblyman, Solano, 1880, 1881.

Leach, Reuben, Assemblyman, Nevada, 1862, 1865–66.

Leadbetter, W. R., Assemblyman, San Joaquin, 1880.

Leake, Charles A., Assemblyman, Calaveras, 1853; Senator, Calaveras, 1854, 1855. *Died, Pioche, August 12, 1870.*

Leake, E. E., Assemblyman, Solano, 1881; Clerk of the Assembly, 1883, 1889; Member Board of Agriculture, District No. 36, Solano County, 1889–91.

Leary, Daniel J., Assemblyman, San Francisco, 1885.

Lee, Bruce B., Assemblyman, Sacramento, 1867–68; Harbor Commissioner, 1876–80. *Died, Red Bluff, 1890.*

Lee, C. V. R., Assemblyman, Santa Barbara, 1853. *Died, Santa Barbara, January 11, 1863.*

Lee, Harvey, Assemblyman, Amador and Alpine, 1865–66; Supreme Court Reporter, 1856–60; Judge Sixteenth Judicial District, appointed 1866. *Died, Sacramento, August 19, 1866.*

Lee, O. H., Assemblyman, Placer, 1871–72.

Leet, S. T., Senator, Placer, 1860, 1861. *Died, Oakland, December 20, 1890.*

Lefever, Josiah, Assemblyman, Sierra, 1859.

Leihy, George W., Assemblyman, Sacramento, 1856. *Died, Arizona, November 18, 1866.*

Lemon, James M., Assemblyman, Solano, 1865–66.

Lenahan, John, Senator, San Francisco, 1887.
L , W. M., Senator, San Francisco, 1854.
Leonard, W. H., Senator, Calaveras, 1863–64, 1865–66. *Died, Sacramento, September 18, 1875.*
Letcher, William S., Assemblyman, Santa Clara, 1853, 1854.
Levee, J., Assemblyman, Nevada, 1880.
Leverson, M. R., Assemblyman, San Francisco, 1883.
Levy, Walter H., Superior Judge, San Francisco, appointed 1885, elected 1886, 1888.
Lewelling, E. D., Assemblyman, Alameda, 1869–70. *Died, St. Helena, May 1, 1872.*
Lewis, David, Member Second Constitutional Convention, 1878–79, San Joaquin District. *Died, Linden, September, 28, 1883.*
Lewis, E. J., Assemblyman, Colusa, 1856, Tehama and Colusa, 1858; Senator, Colusa and Tehama, 1867–68, 1869–70, 1875–76, 1877–78; President pro. tem., 1869–70, 1877–78; Superior Judge, Tehama County, elected 1879. *Died, Red Bluff, April 20, 1881.*
Lewis, Edwin, Assemblyman, San Francisco, 1887.
Lewis, George E., Assemblyman, San Francisco, 1891.
Lewis, Joseph E. N., Senator, Butte and Shasta, 1852. *Died, Oroville, June 26, 1869.*
Lewis, Oscar, Assemblyman, San Francisco, 1881.
Lewis, Samuel, Assemblyman, Marin, 1860.
Lewis, William T., Senator, Calaveras and Amador, 1858, 1862, 1863. *Died, San Andreas, April 20, 1887.*
Lewison, J. L., Assemblyman, Nevada, 1883.
Lies, Eugene, Assemblyman, Santa Barbara, 1859.
Lightner, C. W., Assemblyman, Calaveras, 1859.
Lincoln, Charles G., Assemblyman, Butte, 1855. *Died, New York, December 18, 1884.*
Lind, John Y., Assemblyman, Calaveras, 1851; Senator, Calaveras and Amador, 1852, 1853.
Lindley, Curtis H., Superior Judge, Amador County, appointed 1884.
Lindow, John F., Member Second Constitutional Convention, 1878–79, San Francisco District.
Lindsey, Tipton, Senator, Fresno, Tulare, and Kern, 1873–74, 1875–76.
Lindsey, William H., Assemblyman, Nevada, 1854.
Lippincott, Benjamin S., Member First Constitutional Convention, 1849, San Joaquin District; Senator, San Joaquin District, 1849–50, 1851; Assemblyman, San Francisco, 1854; Calaveras, 1856. *Died, Red Bank, New Jersey, November 22, 1870.*
Lippincott, Charles E., Senator, Yuba, 1855, 1856.
Lippitt, Francis J., Member First Constitutional Convention, 1849, San Francisco District.
Lisle, D. J., Assemblyman, Sacramento, 1851. *Died, San Francisco, February 8, 1855.*
Litchfield, J. M., Bank Commissioner, 1882–86; Railroad Commisioner, Second District, 1891–
Little, W. A., Assemblyman, Siskiyou, 1871–72.
Littlefield, S. L., Assemblyman, Siskiyou, 1863–64.
Livermore, H. G., Senator, El Dorado, 1854. *Died, Oakland, November 11, 1879.*
Livermore, J., Assemblyman, Amador, 1857.
Loewy, William, Assemblyman, San Francisco, 1862.
Lofton, F. R., Assemblyman, Yuba, 1871–72.
Logan, J., Senator, Colusa, Shasta, etc., 1860, 1861.
Long, Henry, Assemblyman, Placer, 1871–72.
Long, J. D., Assemblyman, San Francisco, 1889.
Long, J. S., Assemblyman, Butte, 1857.
Long, L. F., Assemblyman, Mendocino, 1877–78.
Long, R. A., Presidential Elector, 1893.
Long, W. D., Assemblyman, Nevada, 1881.
Long, W. G., Assemblyman, Tuolumne and Mono, 1873–74, 1885.
Long, William S., Assemblyman, Tehama and Colusa, 1865–66. *Died, Shasta, February 12, 1871.*
Logan, James H., Superior Judge, Santa Cruz County, elected 1879.
Loofborrow, D. T., Assemblyman, El Dorado, 1858.
Lorigan, W. G., Superior Judge, Santa Clara County, elected 1890.

Lott, Charles F., Senator, Butte, 1852, 1853; Judge Second Judicial District, elected 1869.

Loud, Eugene F., Assemblyman, San Francisco, 1885; Representative to Congress, 1891, 1893–

Louttit, James A., Representative to Congress; 1885–86.

Love, David, Assemblyman, Sierra, 1862.

Love, John Lord, Attorney-General, 1871–75.

Lovell, F. M., Assemblyman, San Francisco, 1885.

Lovell, S. W., Assemblyman, Placer, 1860.

Lovett, W. E., Senator, Monterey and Santa Cruz, 1863–64. *Died, Oakland, January, 25, 1883.*

Low, Frederick F., Representative to Congress, 1861–62; Governor, 1863–67; Minister to China, confirmed December 21, 1869.

Lowe, James R., Assemblyman, Santa Clara, 1889, 1891; Senator, Santa Clara, 1885; Trustee Reform School for Juvenile Offenders at Whittier, 1888–92.

Ludgate, Robert, Assemblyman, Amador, 1877–78. *Died, Sacramento, February 15, 1878.*

Ludlow, W. B., Assemblyman, Amador, 1863–64.

Lull, Louis R., Assemblyman, San Francisco, 1859.

Lupton, Samuel L., Assemblyman, San Francisco, 1865–66, 1867–68.

Luttrell, J. K., Assemblyman, Siskiyou, 1865–66, 1871–72; Representative to Congress, 1873–78; State Prison Director, 1887–89.

Luttringer, R. J., Assemblyman, San Francisco, 1893.

Lux, A. L., Assemblyman, San Francisco, 1891.

Lux, Frederick, Assemblyman, Tuolumne and Mono, 1863, 1863–64.

Lynch, J. D., Presidential Elector, 1893.

Lynch, Jeremiah, Senator, San Francisco and San Mateo, 1883, 1885.

Lynch, John, Assemblyman, San Francisco, 1863–64. *Died, Stockton, December 30, 1866.*

Lynch, John C., Assemblyman, San Bernardino, 1891, 1893.

Lynch, Philip, Assemblyman, Placer, 1859. *Died, Gold Hill, February 14, 1872.*

Lyons, Henry A., Chief-Justice, 1852. *Died, San Francisco, July 27, 1872.*

Lyons, William H., Assemblyman, Nevada, 1852; Senator, Nevada, 1853, 1854. *Died, Stockton, June 27, 1885.*

McAllister, A. C., Assemblyman, Marin, 1862.

McAllister, Elliott, Senator, Contra Costa and Marin, 1893.

McBrayer, J. M., Assemblyman, Sacramento, 1854.

McBride, J. W., Assemblyman, Siskiyou, 1873–74.

McCall, J. G., Assemblyman, Alameda, 1891.

McCallion, John J., Assemblyman, San Francisco, 1880, 1881. *Died, San Francisco, June 6, 1883,*

McCallum, D. W., Assemblyman, Mendocino, 1873–74. *Died, Mendocino County, May, 1876.*

McCallum, John G., Senator, El Dorado, 1856, 1857; Presidential Elector, 1864; Member Second Constitutional Convention, 1878–79, Alameda District.

McCandless, A. G., Assemblyman, Shasta, 1851; Sutter, 1853.

McCann, F. J., Superior Judge, Santa Cruz County, elected 1884, 1890.

McCarthy, D. J., Senator, San Francisco, 1887.

McCarthy, J. J., Assemblyman, San Francisco, 1880.

McCarthy, John, Assemblyman, San Francisco, 1889.

McCarthy, John W., Clerk of the Supreme Court, 1883–85.

McCarthy, Michael, Assemblyman, San Francisco, 1875–76. *Died, San Francisco, October 30, 1884.*

McCarthy, Timothy, Senator, San Francisco, 1875–76, 1877–78, 1883.

McCarty, A. P., Assemblyman, Lake, 1880.

McCarver, M. M., Member First Constitutional Convention, 1849, Sacramento District.

McCauley, C. D., Assemblyman, Solano, 1893.

McClaskey, C., Assemblyman, Yuba, 1869–70.

McClaskey, Calvin, Assemblyman, Plumas and Lassen, 1883.

McClelland, J. A., Assemblyman, San Francisco, 1865–66. *Died, San Francisco, September 17, 1884.*

McClenahan, F. W., Assemblyman, Calaveras, 1887.

McClure, David, Assemblyman, San Francisco, 1881; Senator, San Francisco, 1883, 1885. *Died, San Francisco, December, 8, 1888.*

McClure, R. A., Assemblyman, Alameda, 1877–78. *Died, Mission San Jose, December 9, 1879.*

McColliam, T. W., Assemblyman, San Francisco, 1863-64.
McComas, J. E., Senator, Los Angeles, 1887, 1889, 1891.
McComas, Rush, Assemblyman, Santa Clara, 1877-78, 1880; Member Second Constitutional Convention, 1878-79, Santa Clara District.
McConaha, G. N., Assemblyman, Sacramento, 1852. *Drowned, Seattle, May 4, 1854.*
McConnell, H., Assemblyman, El Dorado, 1855.
McConnell, John R., Attorney-General, 1854-55; Assemblyman, Los Angeles, 1875-76; Trustee of State Library, 1861-63, 1870. *Died, Denver, Colorado, August 18, 1879.*
McConnell, Thomas, Member Second Constitutional Convention, 1878-79, Sacramento District.
McCoppin, Frank, Senator, San Francisco, 1875-76, 1877-78.
McCorkle, Joseph W., Assemblyman, Sutter, 1851; Representative to Congress, 1851-52; Judge Ninth Judicial District, appointed 1853. *Died, Maryland, March 30, 1884.*
McCoun, W. H., Senator, San Joaquin and Contra Costa, 1855, 1856. *Killed at Cavorca, Mexico, April 7, 1857.*
McCoy, James, Senator, San Diego, etc., 1871-72, 1873-74.
McCoy, John, Member Second Constitutional Convention, 1878-79, Nevada District.
McCoy, W. W., Assemblyman, Santa Clara, 1858.
McCudden, James, Senator, Solano, 1887.
McCullough, John G., Assemblyman, Mariposa, 1862; Senator, Mariposa, Merced, etc., 1863; Attorney-General, 1863-67.
McCullough, Samuel, Assemblyman, San Francisco, 1871-72. *Died, San Mateo County, June 11, 1890.*
McCune, H. E., Senator, Solano and Yolo, 1873-74; Trustee of State Library, 1891-
McCurdy, Samuel, Assemblyman, Tuolumne, 1855.
McCusick, H. J., Senator, El Dorado, 1871-72, 1873-74.
McCutcheon, J. L., Assemblyman, Colusa, 1855. *Died, Sandwich Islands, 1859.*
McDade, J. J., Assemblyman, San Francisco, 1880.
McDaniel, C. A., Assemblyman, Calaveras, 1854.
McDermit, Charles, Assemblyman, Siskiyou, 1860.
McDonald, F. G., Assemblyman, Calaveras, 1863.
McDonald, George, Assemblyman, El Dorado, 1854, 1857. *Died, Berkeley, March 19, 1885.*
McDonald, J. M., Senator, Sacramento, 1859, 1860.
McDonald, J. R., State Treasurer, 1891-
McDonald, J. W., Assemblyman, San Francsico, 1881.
McDonald, Thomas H., Assemblyman, San Francisco, 1883, 1885; Senator, San Francisco, 1887, 1889.
McDonald, Walter, Assemblyman, Klamath, 1856.
McDonnell, James, Jr., Assemblyman, Sonoma, 1887.
McDougal, F. A., Senator, Monterey and Santa Cruz, 1867-68, 1869-70.
McDougal, John, Member First Constitutional Convention, 1849, Sacramento District; Lieutenant-Governor, 1849-50; Governor, 1851. *Died, San Francisco, March 30, 1866.*
McDougall, James A., Attorney-General, 1850-51; Representative to Congress, 1853-54; United States Senator, 1861-66. *Died, Albany, New York, September 3, 1867.*
McDougall, William C., Assemblyman, San Joaquin, 1851.
McDuffie, James Y., Assemblyman, Yuba, 1854.
Mace, R. P., Assemblyman, Fresno, 1865-66, 1867-68, 1877-78.
McElhany, W. T., Assemblyman, Santa Barbara, etc., 1867-68.
McElroy, J. J., Assemblyman, Alameda, 1893.
McFarland, J. P., Assemblyman, Los Angeles, 1853; Senator, Los Angeles, etc., 1854, 1855.
McFarland, Thomas B., Assemblyman, Nevada, 1856; Judge Fourteenth Judicial District, elected 1861, 1863; Member Second Constitutional Convention, 1878-79, Sacramento District; Superior Judge, Sacramento County, appointed 1882, elected 1884; Supreme Justice, 1887-
McGarry, Edward, Assemblyman, Napa, 1853; Senator, Napa, Solano, and Yolo, 1854, 1855. *Died, San Francisco, December 31, 1867.*
McGarvey, Robert, Senator, Mendocino, etc., 1875-76, 1877-78; Superior Judge, Mendocino County, elected 1879, 1884, 1890.

McGee, John B., Assemblyman, Butte, 1854; Senator, Butte and Plumas 1856; 1857.
McGehee, M., Assemblyman, Tuolumne, 1856.
McGlashan, Charles F., Assemblyman, Nevada, 1885.
McGowan, James, Assemblyman, San Francisco, 1893.
McGowan, J. Frank, Assemblyman, Humboldt, 1887; Senator, Humboldt and Del Norte, 1889, 1891, 1893.
McHale, P., Assemblyman, Placer, 1883.
Machin, T. N., Assemblyman, Tuolumne and Mono, 1862, 1863; Speaker, 1863; Lieutenant-Governor, 1863–67.
McInerny, Thomas, Assemblyman, San Francisco, 1875–76.
McIntosh, E., Assemblyman, San Joaquin, 1880.
McJunkin, Hugh K., Assemblyman, San Francisco, 1885.
McKamy, J., Assemblyman, Napa, 1853.
McKee, Samuel Bell, Judge Third Judicial District, elected 1858, 1863, 1869, 1875; Supreme Justice, 1880–86. *Died, Oakland, March 2, 1887.*
McKenna, Joseph, Assemblyman, Solano, 1875–76; Representative to Congress, 1885–92; Commissioner to attend the Centennial Celebration of the Inauguration of George Washington as President of the United States, 1888; United States Circuit Judge, Ninth Circuit, March 18, 1892-
McKenzie, F. S., Assemblyman, Trinity, 1852.
McKeown, Joseph, Assemblyman, Alameda, 1889. *Died, Alameda, February 7, 1890.*
McKibben, Joseph C., Senator, Yuba, 1852, 1853; Representative to Congress, 1857–58.
McKim, W. S., Assemblyman, Calaveras, 1852.
McKinley, B. F., Assemblyman, San Francisco, 1883.
McKinley, D. A., Presidential Elector, 1876. *Died, San Francisco, September 20, 1892.*
McKinley, J. W., Superior Judge, Los Angeles County, appointed 1889, elected 1890.
McKinney, F. S., Assemblyman, Santa Clara, 1854. *Killed at Cavorca, Mexico, April 7, 1857.*
McKinstry, Elisha W., Assemblyman, Sacramento District, 1849–50; Adjutant-General, 1851–52; Judge Seventh and Twelfth Judicial Districts, elected 1852, 1858, 1869; Supreme Justice, 1874–88.
McKune, John H., Assemblyman, Sacramento, 1857; Judge Sixth Judicial District, elected, 1858, 1863.
Maclay, Charles, Assemblyman, Santa Clara, 1862; Presidential Elector, 1864; Senator, Santa Clara, 1867–68, 1869–70, 1871–72. *Died, San Fernando, July 19, 1890.*
McLean, Alexander, Assemblyman, Santa Barbara, 1885.
McMahon, James, Assemblyman, Klamath, 1853.
McMann, William, Assemblyman, San Francisco, 1875–76.
McMeans, S. A., Assemblyman, El Dorado, 1852, 1853; State Treasurer, 1854–55. *Died, Reno, Nevada, July 31, 1876.*
McMertry, Louis, Superior Judge, San Luis Obispo County, elected 1879. *Died, San Luis Obispo, February 11, 1883.*
McMilien, C. E., Assemblyman, San Francisco, 1869–70.
McMullin, George O., Assemblyman, Trinity, 1869–70. *Died, San Francisco, March 1, 1885.*
McMullin, John, Assemblyman, San Joaquin, 1889.
McMurray, James D., Assemblyman, El Dorado, 1869–70, *Died, Placerville, March 18, 1872.*
McMurray, John, Assemblyman, Trinity and Shasta, 1869–70, 1881; Senator, Shasta and Trinity, 1871–72, 1873–74.
McMurray, V. C., Assemblyman, San Francisco, 1885.
McMurtry, W. S., Senator, Santa Clara, 1863–64.
McNabb, James H., Senator, Sonoma, 1863.
McNealy, W. T., Judge Eighteenth Judicial District, elected 1873; Superior Judge, San Diego County, elected 1879, 1884.
McNeill, J. A., Senator, Mariposa, etc., 1855, 1856.
McNutt, John F., Member Second Constitutional Convention, 1878–79, Yuba District.
McRuer, D. C., Representative to Congress, 1865–66.
McVay, John, Assemblyman, Del Norte and Siskiyou, 1889.
Mack, P. H., Assemblyman, Alpine, Inyo, and Mono, 1893.
Maddox, C. H., Senator, Santa Clara, 1883.

Maddox, F. L., Senator, El Dorado, 1863-64, 1865-66. *Died, Georgetown, April 4, 1871.*
Magruder, Lloyd, Assemblyman, Yuba, 1861. *Died, Washington Territory, 1863.*
Maguire, A. B., Assemblyman, San Francisco, 1880.
Maguire, James G., Assemblyman, San Francisco, 1875-76; Superior Judge, San Francisco, elected 1882; Representative to Congress, 1893.
Maher, Thomas C., Assemblyman, San Francisco, 1889; Senator, San Francisco, 1891, 1893.
Mahler, Henry, Senator, El Dorado, 1885; Assemblyman, El Dorado, 1887, 1889.
Maholmb, J. B., Assemblyman, Sacramento, 1865-66.
Mahon, Frank, Assemblyman, San Francisco, 1867-68.
Mahon, E. B., Superior Judge, Marin County, elected 1884.
Mahoney, David, Senator, San Francisco, 1854, 1855. *Died, San Francisco, November 22, 1880.*
Mahoney, J. H., Senator, San Francisco, 1891, 1893.
Makins, J. M., Assemblyman, Placer, 1860.
Malarin, Mariano, Assemblyman, Monterey, 1859, 1860.
Mandeville, James W., Assemblyman, Tuolumne, 1853, 1854; Senator, Tuolumne, etc., 1855, 1856, 1857, 1867-68, 1869-70; State Controller, 1875. *Died, Sacramento, February 4, 1876.*
Mann, Henry R., Assemblyman, San Francisco, 1887.
Mansfield, John, Member Second Constitutional Convention, 1878-79, Fourth Congressional District; Lieutenant-Governor, 1880-82.
Mardis, B. A., Assemblyman, Tuolumne and Mono, 1867-68. *Died, Sacramento, February 7, 1873.*
Marion, F. W., Assemblyman, Los Angeles, 1891.
Markham, H. H., Representative to Congress, 1885-87; Governor, 1891–
Markley, John, Member of State Board of Equalization, 1883-86; Private Secretary to Governor Washington Bartlett.
Markley, William J., Assemblyman, Tuolumne, 1858.
Marks, Charles H., Superior Judge, Merced County, elected 1879, 1884.
Marks, J. M., Assemblyman, San Francisco, 1893.
Marlette, S. H., Surveyor-General, 1854-55.
Marshall, B. F., Assemblyman, Calaveras, 1858.
Marshall, E. C., Representative to Congress, 1851-52; Attorney-General, 1883-86.
Marsteller, M., Superior Judge, Lassen County, elected 1884.
Marston, B. O., Assemblyman, Tuolumne and Mariposa, 1893.
Martin, Andrew J., Assemblyman, San Francisco, 1887.
Martin, Edward, Member Second Constitutional Convention, 1878-79, Fourth Congressional District.
Martin, J. W., Member Second Constitutional Convention, 1878-79, Second Congressional District.
Martin, James C., Assemblyman, Butte, 1869-70.
Martin, Montgomery, Assemblyman, Los Angeles District, 1849-50.
Martin, Noble, Assemblyman, Placer, 1891; Senator, Placer, 1873-74, 1875-76; El Dorado and Placer, 1893.
Martin, R. M., Assemblyman, Siskiyou, 1869-70.
Martin, S. M., Assemblyman, Sonoma, 1867-68, 1883.
Martin, Seth, Assemblyman, Nevada, 1863, 1863-64.
Martin, W. C., Assemblyman, Trinity, 1853.
Marvin, John G., State Superintendent of Public Instruction, 1851-53. *Died, Honolulu, December 10, 1857.*
Maslin, E. W., Private Secretary to Governor William Irwin; Trustee of State Library, 1878-82, 1884-85; Secretary of the State Board of Equalization, 1869-71, 1880-91.
Mason, W. B., Assemblyman, Del Norte, 1881.
Masten, W. T., Superior Judge, Lassen County, elected 1890.
Mathers, George B., Assemblyman, Mendocino, 1871-72.
Mathews, W. P., Assemblyman, Tehama. Colusa, etc., 1880, 1881, 1887, 1889, 1893.
Matlock, James T., Assemblyman, Tehama, 1891.
Matthews, J. H., Assemblyman, Trinity, 1862; San Benito, 1881, 1883, 1887, 1893.
Matthews, J. R., Assemblyman, Los Angeles, 1891; Senator, 1893.

41

Matthews, R. L., Assemblyman, Monterey, 1856.
Matthews, William R., Assemblyman, Napa, 1859.
Mattingly, R. L., Assemblyman, San Mateo, 1867-68.
Maxson, W. B., Assemblyman, San Mateo, 1860.
May, W. B., Assemblyman, San Francisco, 1877-78, 1880, 1881, 1885; Senator, Trinity, Klamath, etc., 1854, 1855.
Maybell, Stephen, Assemblyman, San Francisco, 1880.
Mayfield, J. M., Assemblyman, Napa, 1877-78.
Mayhew, H. A., Superior Jndge, Tehama County, appointed 1881.
Mead, M. H., Senator, Modoc, Lassen, etc., 1889, 1891.
Meagher, Michael, Assemblyman, Tuolumne and Mono, 1867-68.
Meany, A. J., Senator, Merced, Stanislaus, etc., 1889, 1891. *Died, Merced, November 25, 1891.*
Mears, William T., Assemblyman, Sonoma, 1885.
Mebius, C. F., Assemblyman, San Francisco, 1863-64.
Meeker, David, Assemblyman, San Francisco, 1871-72. *Died, San Francisco, May 21, 1891.*
Mein, Thomas, Assemblyman, Nevada, 1881.
Mellus, Francis, Assemblyman, Los Angeles, 1855.
Melone, Drury, Secretary of State, 1871-75.
Meloney, A. R., Assemblyman, Contra Costa, 1856; State Controller, 1858-59; Senator, San Joaquin and Contra Costa, 1857, 1858. *Died, Lafayette, Contra Costa County, March 1, 1861.*
Mentzel, Otto, Assemblyman. Calaveras, 1867-68.
Meredith, G., Assemblyman, Sierra, 1865-66. *Died, St. Helena, July 13, 1892.*
Meredith, H. B., Assemblyman, Sacramento, 1855.
Meridith, W., Assemblyman, Tuolumne, 1853.
Merrit, George, Assemblyman, Yuba, 1869-70.
Merritt, Samuel A., Assemblyman, Mariposa, 1851, 1852; Senator, Mariposa, etc., 1857, 1858; President pro tem., 1858.
Merry, T. H., Assemblyman, San Francisco, 1880.
Mesick, R. S., Senator, Yuba, 1857, 1858.
Messenger, H. A., Assemblyman, Calaveras, 1880.
Meyers, Samuel, Assemblyman, San Joaquin, 1862, 1863, 1873-74, 1877-78.
Micheltorena, Manuel, Governor under Mexican rule, 1842-45. *Died, Mexico, September 7, 1853.*
Middleton, John, Assemblyman, San Francisco, 1867-68.
Miles, Benjamin H., Assemblyman, Santa Cruz, 1857. *Died, Arizona, 1858.*
Miles, S. M., Assemblyman, Sierra, 1857. *Died, Sierra County, May 8, 1869.*
Miller, E. O., Register United States Land Office, 1888-1889; Trustee of State Library, 1891-
Miller, H. B. M., Assemblyman, Alameda, 1893.
Miller, James, Senator, Mariposa, 1851, 1852.
Miller, James H., Assemblyman, El Dorado, 1869-70, 1877-78.
Miller, John F., Presidential Elector, 1872, 1876; Member Second Constitutional Convention, 1878-79, First Congressional District; United States Senator, 1881-86. *Died, Washington, D. C., March 8, 1886.*
Miller, L., Assemblyman, Amador and Alpine, 1873-74.
Miller, N. C., Assemblyman, Nevada, 1861.
Miller, William J., Assemblyman, Marin, 1869-70.
Millington, Seth, Superior Judge, Glenn County, elected 1891.
Mills, Hiram, Member Second Constitutional Convention, 1878-79, Contra Costa District.
Minis, William, Assemblyman, Yolo, 1858; Senator, Yolo and Solano, 1869-70, 1871-72; Surveyor-General, 1875-79.
Minor, W. O., Superior Judge, Stanislaus County, elected 1884, 1890.
Miro, Emanuel, Assemblyman, San Francisco, 1857.
Mitchell, A. H., Assemblyman, Fresno and Tulare, 1858.
Mitchell, E. F., Assemblyman, Tuolumne and Mono, 1863-64.
Mitchell, M. N., Assemblyman, El Dorado, 1857.
Mitchell, T. F., Senator, San Francisco, 1893.
Mitchell, Thomas, Assemblyman, San Francisco, 1887.
Mizner, Lansing B., Private Secretary to Governor John Bigler, first term; Senator, Yolo and Solano, 1865-66, 1867-1868; President pro tem., 1867-68; Presidential Elector, 1888; Minister to Central American States, March 30, 1889-December 31, 1890.
Moffat, S. P., Assemblyman, Inyo and Mono, 1877-78. *Died, San Francisco, 1883.*

Moffatt, William S., Member Second Constitutional Convention, 1878-79, San Mateo District.

Moffitt, A. B., Assemblyman, Los Angeles, 1883. *Died, San Fernando, June 10, 1884.*

Moffitt, Frank J., Assemblyman, Alameda, 1885; Senator, Alameda, 1887, 1889.

Monson, A. C., Judge Sixth Judicial District, appointed 1852, elected 1852.

Montague, J. C., Assemblyman, Trinity and Shasta, 1877-78.

Montgomery, J. M., Senator, Mariposa and Merced, 1875-76, 1877-78.

Montgomery, W. S., Senator, Mariposa and Merced, 1863-64, 1865-66.

Montgomery, Zach., Assemblyman, Sutter, 1861.

Mooney, J. S., Assemblyman, Tuolumne and Mono, 1869-70.

Moore, Benjamin F., Member First Constitutional Convention, 1849, San Joaquin District; Assemblyman, San Joaquin District, 1849-50, Tuolumne, 1851. *Dead.*

Moore, E. J., Senator, San Francisco, 1854, 1855.

Moore, George, Superior Judge, Amador County, elected 1879. *Died, Jackson, September 8, 1884.*

Moore, J. G., Assemblyman, Butte, 1863. *Dead.*

Moore, J. M., Assemblyman, Alameda, 1862.

Moore, Jacob B., Assemblyman, San Francisco, 1858, 1859. *Died, San Francisco, August 31, 1885.*

Moore, John H., Assemblyman, Santa Clara, 1867-68.

Moore, Philip, Assemblyman, Nevada, 1853, 1857, 1859, 1860; Speaker, 1860. *Dead.*

Mordecai, G. W., Assemblyman, Fresno, 1891, 1893.

Morehead, James C., Assemblyman, San Joaquin District, 1849-50.

Morehouse, L. C., Member of State Board of Equalization, 1883-86, 1887-90, 1891-

Moreland, Thomas, Assemblyman, Placer, 1855. *Dead.*

Moreland, W. W., Member Second Constitutional Convention, 1878-79, Sonoma District; Senator, Sonoma, 1880, 1881; Private Secretary to Governor George Stoneman; Bank Commissioner, 1886-1890.

Morgan, G. W., Assemblyman, Sonoma, 1887.

Morgan, James H., Assemblyman, Santa Clara, 1861. *Died, San Jose, March 27, 1883.*

Morgan, W. R., Assemblyman, Sierra, 1873-74.

Morrill, D. L., Senator, Calaveras, 1867-68, 1869-70.

Morris, Thomas, Member Second Constitutional Convention, 1878-79, San Francisco District.

Morris, Thomas C., Assemblyman, Alameda, 1885.

Morris, W. D., Assemblyman, Modoc and Lassen, 1887.

Morrison, H. J., Assemblyman, Butte, 1857.

Morrison, Murray, Assemblyman, Los Angeles, 1861, 1862; Judge Seventeenth Judicial District, appointed 1868, elected 1869. *Died, Los Angeles, December 18, 1871.*

Morrison, Robert F., Judge Fourth Judicial District, elected 1869, 1875; Chief Justice Supreme Court, 1880-87. *Died, San Francisco, March 2, 1887.*

Morrow, L. J., Assemblyman, San Joaquin, 1867-68.

Morrow, William W., Representative to Congress, 1885-90; Commissioner to attend the Centennial Celebration of the Inauguration of George Washington as President of the United States, 1888; District Judge, Northern District of California, September 18, 1891-

Morse, John F., Trustee of State Library, 1863-64. *Died, San Francisco, De-30, 1874.*

Morse, L. G., Assemblyman, Mendocino, 1880.

Morse, Lucius D., Member Second Constitutional Convention, 1878-79, San Francisco and San Mateo District.

Morse, Nelson D., Assemblyman, Butte, 1852.

Morton, W. L., Assemblyman, Tulare and Kern, 1883 (elected 1882, died before qualifying). *Died, Grangeville, December 29, 1882.*

Moses, H. A., Assemblyman, El Dorado, 1858. *Died, Sacramento, May, 1890.*

Mott, E. B., Jr., Assemblyman, Sacramento, 1871-72; Trustee of State Library, 1872-78. *Died, Sacramento, April 4, 1882.*

Mott, Gordon M., Judge Tenth Judicial District, appointed 1851. *Died, San Francisco, April 27, 1887.*

Mott, T. D., Assemblyman, Los Angeles, 1871-72.

Moulder, Andrew J., State Superintendent of Public Instruction, 1857-62.

Moulthrop, E. W., Assemblyman, San Francisco, 1856.
Mount, Charles E., Assemblyman, Calaveras, 1859.
Moyle, J. W., Senator, Sierra, 1863-64.
Moynihan, T. J., Assemblyman, San Francisco, 1869-70.
Mudgett, G. C., Assemblyman, Humboldt, 1881.
Mulgrew, F. B., Assemblyman, Sonoma, 1889.
Mulholland, Charles, Assemblyman, Plumas and Lassen, 1880.
Mullaney, J. A., Assemblyman, Solano, 1889.
Mulvey, Thomas, Assemblyman, San Francisco, 1889.
Munday, B. B., Assemblyman, Sonoma, 1869-70, 1871-72. *Died, Sonoma County, 1873.*
Munday, M. E. C., Assemblyman, Sonoma, 1885.
Munday, Patrick, Assemblyman, Placer, 1861. *Died, Cisco, October 14, 1872.*
Murch, L. H., Assemblyman, Klamath and Del Norte, 1865-66; Senator, Del Norte, etc., 1867-68, 1869-70. *Died, Oakland, June 24, 1885.*
Murdock, A. H., Assemblyman, Humboldt, 1855. *Dead.*
Murdock, Charles A., Assemblyman, San Francisco, 1883.
Murnan, Frank T., Assemblyman, Tuolumne, 1891.
Murphy, B. D., Assemblyman, Santa Clara, 1869-70; Senator, Santa Clara, 1877-78, 1883; Trustee (Chairman) of the State Insane Asylum at Agnews, 1890-
Murphy, D. J., Superior Judge, San Francisco, elected 1884, 1890.
Murphy, D. W., Assemblyman, Calaveras, 1851.
Murphy, Frank J., Assemblyman, Sonoma. 1891.
Murphy, James E., Assemblyman. Del Norte, 1869-70, 1873-74, 1875-76, 1877-78; Speaker pro tem., 1875-76; Member Second Constitutional Convention, 1878-79, Del Norte District; Superior Judge, Del Norte County, elected 1879, 1884, 1890.
Murphy, James T., Bank Commissioner, 1878-79.
Murphy, John C., Assemblyman, San Francisco, 1875-76; Senator, San Francisco, 1877-78. *Died, San Francisco, June 16, 1887.*
Murphy, P. J., Senator, San Francisco, 1887, 1889.
Murphy, P. W., Assemblyman, San Luis Obispo, 1881; Senator, Santa Barbara, 1865-66, 1867-68, 1877-78.
Murphy, R., Assemblyman, San Francisco, 1857.
Murphy, R. W., Assemblyman, San Francisco, 1877-78.
Murphy, Thomas H., Assemblyman, San Francisco, 1883.
Murray, Edward, Assemblyman, San Francisco, 1889.
Murray, Hugh C., Chief Justice, 1852-57. *Died, Sacramento, September 18, 1857.*
Murray, J. G., Assemblyman, Humboldt, 1889.
Murray, Walter, Assemblyman, San Luis Obispo, 1859; Judge First Judicial District, appointed 1873. *Died, San Luis Obispo, October 5, 1875.*
Musser, John, Assemblyman, Trinity, 1854.
Myers, B. F., Assemblyman, Placer, 1853, 1854; Judge Eleventh Judicial District, appointed 1858, elected 1858; Superior Judge, Placer County, elected 1879, 1884.
Myers, S., Senator, San Joaquin, 1863-64, 1865-66.
Myrick, M. H., Supreme Justice, 1880-86.
Naphtaly, Joseph, Assemblyman, San Francisco, 1869-70.
Nason, Edmund, Member Second Constitutional Convention, 1878-79, San Benito District.
Nealley, Gilbert H., Assemblyman, Butte, 1877-78.
Neblett, E., Assemblyman, Trinity, 1858.
Neff, Jacob H., Senator, Placer, 1871-72, 1873-74; State Prison Director, 1880-83, 1891-
Nelson, James, Assemblyman, Sierra, 1880.
Nelson, Thorwald K., Senator, San Francisco, 1880, 1881; Member Second Constitutional Convention, 1878-79, San Francisco District. *Died, Santa Barbara, March 5, 1888.*
Neuman, Paul, Senator, San Francisco, 1880, 1881.
Neunaber, Henry, Member Second Constitutional Convention, 1878-79, San Francisco District.
Neve, Felipe de, Governor under Spanish rule, 1774-82.
Newell, H. B., Assemblyman, El Dorado, 1867-68, 1869-70.
Newson, J. M., Assemblyman, Stanislaus and Merced, 1867-68.
Nichols, Elijah, Assemblyman, San Francisco, 1854. *Died, Sacramento, March 11, 1888.*
Nichols, H. L., Secretary of State, 1867-71; Trustee of State Library, 1871-72.

Nicol, F. D., Assemblyman, Tuolumne, 1883.

Nicol, G. W., Superior Judge, Tuolumne County, elected 1890.

Niles, Addison C., Supreme Justice, 1872–79. *Died, San Francisco, January 17, 1890.*

Nixon, A. B., Senator, Sacramento, 1862, 1863. *Died, Sacramento, November 2, 1889.*

Noel, Alonzo E., Member Second Constitutional Convention, 1878–79, Lake District.

Noel, Charles P., Assemblyman, San Diego, 1854.

Noonan, J. G., Assemblyman, San Francisco, 1881.

Norman, W. B., Senator, Calaveras and Amador, 1855, 1856, 1857. *Died Stockton, August 26, 1880.*

Northcutt, W. H., Assemblyman, Sonoma, 1873–74.

Northup, B. C., Assemblyman, Nevada, 1873–74.

Norton, Edward, Judge Twelfth Judicial District, appointed 1854, elected 1854; Supreme Justice, 1862–63. *Died, London, England, May 12, 1872.*

Norton, Myron, Member First Constitutional Convention, 1849, San Francisco District.

Norton, Wilham C., Assemblyman, Placer, 1873–74; Senator, Placer, 1877–78. *Died, Auburn, May 11, 1890.*

Nott, S. A., Assemblyman, Amador and Alpine, 1875–76, 1877–78. *Died, on the Cosumnes River, February 27, 1880.*

Nunan, Edward, Senator, San Francisco, 1875–76, 1877–78.

Nye, Stephen G., Senator, Alameda, 1880, 1881.

Oates, S. T., Assemblyman, Nevada, 1869–70.

O'Brien, Thomas, Assemblyman, Calaveras, 1858, 1861, 1862.

O'Connell, W., Assemblyman, San Francisco, 1869–70, 1875–76.

O'Conner, E. J., Assemblyman, San Francisco, 1883.

O'Conner, Miles P., Assemblyman, Nevada, 1860; Senator, Nevada, 1869–70, 1871–72, 1873–74, 1875–76.

O'Conner, Timothy, Assemblyman, San Francisco, 1881.

Odell, John A., Assemblyman, Sacramento, 1869–70. *Died, Folsom, May 29, 1881.*

O'Donnell, Charles C., Member Second Constitutional Convention, 1878–79, San Francisco District.

O'Farrell, Jasper, Senator, Sonoma, etc., 1859, 1860. *Died, San Francisco, November 16, 1875.*

Ogier, I. S. K., Assemblyman, San Joaquin District, 1849–50. *Died, San Bernardino, May 21, 1861.*

O'Grady, Frank, Assemblyman, Solano, 1887.

Ohleyer, George, Member Second Constitutional Convention, 1878–79, Sutter District; Assemblyman, Sutter and Yuba, 1887.

Ohr, A. D., Private Secretary to Governor John McDougal.

O'Keefe, James T., Assemblyman, San Mateo, 1893.

Olds, D., Assemblyman, Marin, 1865–66.

Oliver, J. W., Assemblyman, El Dorado, 1856. *Dead.*

Oliver, W. A., Assemblyman, Calaveras, 1853.

Oliver, Warner, Presidential Elector, 1864; Assemblyman, San Joaquin, 1867–68.

Olvera, Augustin, Presidential Elector, 1856.

O'Malley, J. J., Assemblyman, San Francisco, 1867–68.

O'Meara, John, State Printer, 1858–59. *Died, New York, April 7, 1860.*

O,Melveny, H. K. S., Superior Judge, Los Angeles County, appointed 1887.

O'Neill, H. J., Assemblyman, Alameda, 1893.

O'Neill, James, Assemblyman, Placer, 1854, 1857; Speaker pro tem., 1857. *Died, San Francisco, September 5, 1876.*

Ord, Pacificus, Member First Constitutional Convention, 1849, Monterey District.

Ord, W. M., Assemblyman, Butte, 1867–68.

O'Rear, Benjamin T., Assemblyman, Yuba, 1860.

Ormsby, J. S., Assemblyman, Sonoma and Mendocino, 1858.

Orr, N. M., Senator, San Joaquin, 1869–70.

Orr, N. W., Assemblyman, Tuolumne, etc., 1857.

Orr, Orestes, Senator, Santa Barbara and Ventura, 1893.

Orrick, Benjamin, Assemblyman, San Francisco, 1852.

Orton, Richard H., Adjutant-General, 1887–90.

Orvis, Charles, Assemblyman, El Dorado, 1857.

Osgood, H. P., Assemblyman, Yolo, 1851.

Osgood, Henry M., Assemblyman, San Luis Obispo, 1858.
Ostrander, H. J., Presidential Elector, 1876.
Ostrom, D. A., Assemblyman, Yuba, 1875-76, 1877-78, 1889; Senator, Yuba and Sutter, 1891, 1893.
O'Sullivan, James, Member Second Constitutional Convention. 1878-79, San Francisco District. *Died, Sacramento, March 12, 1889.*
Otis, George E., Superior Judge, San Bernardino County, elected 1890.
Otis, James, Assemblyman, San Francisco, 1862.
Oullahan, D. J., State Treasurer, 1884-87. *Died, San Francisco, November 5, 1889.*
Oulton, George, Senator, Siskiyou, 1862, 1863; State Controller, 1863-67; Senator, San Francisco, 1871-72, 1873-74.
Overton, A. P., Member Second Constitutional Convention, 1878-79, Third Congressional District.
Owen, Eben B., Assemblyman, Sacramento, 1893.
Owen, J. J., Assemblyman, Santa Clara, 1863, 1863-64; Trustee of State Library, 1882-85.
Owen, J. W., Assemblyman, Santa Clara, 1863. *Dead.*
Owen, T. H., Assemblyman, Solano, 1853.
Oxley, Thomas J., Assemblyman, Tuolumne, 1855, 1856. *Died, Cavorca, Mexico, April 7, 1857.*
Pace, George, Assemblyman, Santa Cruz, 1877-78. *Died, Watsonville, May 8, 1881.*
Pacheco, M. G., Assemblyman, San Luis Obispo, 1852, 1853. *Died, San Luis Obispo, January 27, 1865.*
Pacheco, Romualdo, Senator, Santa Barbara, etc., 1858, 1859, 1862, 1863, 1869-70; State Treasurer, 1863-67; Lieutenant-Governor, 1871-75; Governor, 1875; Representative to Congress, 1877, 1879-82; Minister to · Central American States, appointed December 11, 1890.
Page, Horace F., Representative to Congress, 1873-82. *Died, San Francisco, August 23, 1890.*
Palmer, Cyrus, Assemblyman, San Francisco, 1857, 1858, 1863. *Dead.*
Palmer, J. W. D., Assemblyman, Amador, 1855.
Palmer, Noah, Assemblyman, Santa Clara, 1857.
Palmieri, Egisto, Senator, San Francisco, 1885.
Papy, J. J., Assemblyman, San Francisco, 1867-68.
Pardee, E. H., Assemblyman, Alameda, 1871-72; Senator, Alameda, 1880, 1881.
Pardee, George, Assemblyman, Santa Cruz, 1867-68.
Park, F. A., Assemblyman, Sacramento, 1854. *Died, San Francisco, November 13, 1870.*
Park, J. W., Assemblyman, Sacramento, 1854.
Parker, Edwin, Assemblyman, San Diego, 1883; Superior Judge, San Diego County, appointed 1887.
Parker, Eustace, Assemblyman, Calaveras, 1858. *Died, Mazatlan, November 4, 1865.*
Parker, H. G., Assemblyman, El Dorado, 1862.
Parker, J. E., Assemblyman, Tuolumne, Mono, etc., 1873-74.
Parker, S. H., Senator, San Francisco, etc., 1859, 1860. *Died, San Francisco, March 14, 1866.*
Parker, S. N., Assemblyman, Calaveras, 1863-64.
Parker, W. B., Senator, Solano, 1885.
Parkinson, George C., Senator, San Francisco, 1885.
Parks, William H., Senator, Sutter and Yuba, 1859, 1860, 1861, 1862, 1863; Assemblyman, Yuba (Speaker), 1881, 1885. *Died, Marysville, July 23, 1887.*
Parrish, E. C., Assemblyman, Los Angeles, 1865-66.
Parrish, John G., Assemblyman, Yolo, 1852.
Parsons, Levi, Judge Fourth Judicial District, elected by Legislature, 1850. *Died, New York, October 23, 1887.*
Pate, B. T., Assemblyman, San Francisco, 1860. *Died, San Francisco, March 1, 1862.*
Paterson, A. Van R., Superior Judge, San Joaquin County, elected 1879, 1884; Supreme Justice, 1887-
Patrick, G. W., Assemblyman, Tuolumne, 1857, 1861.
Patten, Edmund, Assemblyman, Yolo, 1863.
Patterson, A. D., Assemblyman, Sacramento, 1875-76. *Died, Routier's Station, December 4, 1884.*
Patterson, Alexander, Assemblyman, San Francisco District, 1849-50.

Patterson, J. A., Assemblyman, Kern and Tulare, 1875–76.
Patterson, J. B., Assemblyman, Nevada, 1881.
Patterson, James, Assemblyman, San Francisco, 1873–74.
Patterson, John, Assemblyman, San Joaquin, 1875–76, 1881.
Patterson, W. F., Assemblyman, Santa Clara, 1885.
Patterson, W. H., Senator, Modoc, Lassen, etc., 1887.
Pattison, John, Assemblyman, Nevada, 1865–66.
Patton, D. C., Assemblyman, El Dorado, 1860.
Paulk, C. C., Assemblyman, San Joaquin, 1881. *Died, Oakland, January 29, 1884.*
Paulsell, A. C., Assemblyman, San Joaquin, 1873–74; Member Board of State Harbor Commissioners, 1883–89.
Pauly, Frederick N., Assemblyman, San Diego, 1877–78.
Paxton, John A., Assemblyman, Yuba, 1852.
Payne, George M., Assemblyman, Amador and Alpine, 1867–68.
Peachy, Archibald C., Assemblyman, San Francisco, 1852; Senator, San Francisco, 1860. *Died, San Francisco, April 17, 1883.*
Pearce, E. D., Assemblyman, Shasta, 1852.
Pearce, George, Senator, Sonoma, 1863–64, 1865–66, 1867–68.
Pearis, C. W., Assemblyman, El Dorado, 1858.
Pearson, James, Assemblyman, Calaveras, 1855, 1856.
Peck, E. T., Senator, Butte, 1854, 1855.
Peck, George, Assemblyman, Santa Clara, 1856.
Pedrorena, Miguel D., Member First Constitutional Convention, 1849, San Diego District.
Peek, W. P., Assemblyman, Calaveras, 1873–74.
Pelham, A. J., Assemblyman, Nevada, 1873–74. *Died, Nevada County, August 26, 1881.*
Pellet, H. A., Assemblyman, Napa, 1885.
Pemberton, James C., Assemblyman, Tulare, 1862. *Died, Bakersfield, August 16, 1879.*
Pendegast, William W., Senator, Napa, Lake, etc., 1867–68, 1869–70, 1871–72, 1873–74. *Died, Santa Rosa, February 29, 1876.*
Pendleton, C. W., Assemblyman, Los Angeles, 1893.
Perkins, D. T., Assemblyman, Ventura, 1893.
Perkins, George C., Senator, Butte, Lassen, etc., 1869–70, 1871–72, 1873–74; Director Napa State Insane Asylum, 1876–79; Governor, 1880–83; Director Deaf and Dumb and Blind Asylum, Berkeley, 1888–91, 1891– Trustee of State Mining Bureau, 1889–
Perkins, R., F. Senator, San Francisco, 1862, 1863. *Died, at sea, October 13, 1868.*
Perkins, William Dana, Sergeant-at-Arms of the Assembly, 1869–70, 1875–76; Member State Board of Agriculture, 1877–79, 1888; Member Board of Agriculture, District No, 20, Placer County, 1889–; State Librarian, 1890–
Per Lee, T. R., Assemblyman, Monterey District, 1849–50; Adjutant-General, 1850.
Perley, James E., Assemblyman, San Joaquin, 1863–64; Senator, San Joaquin, 1867–68. *Died, Woodstock, New Brunswick, June 17, 1868.*
Perrin, O., Assemblyman, Tuolumne and Mono, 1863–64, 1865–66.
Perry, George H., Senator, San Francisco, 1883, 1885.
Personette, M. W., Assemblyman, Trinity, 1863, 1863–64,
Peters, J. M., Judge Eighth Judicial District, elected 1852.
Peterson, Peter, Assemblyman, Siskiyou and Modoc, 1883.
Peterson, William H., Assemblyman, Los Angeles, 1865–66.
Petrie, W. M., Assemblyman, Sacramento, 1889.
Phelps, Abner, Assemblyman, San Francisco, 1860.
Phelps, J., Assemblyman, Nevada, 1855.
Phelps, Timothy Guy, Assemblyman, San Francisco, 1857; Senator, San Francisco, 1858, 1859, 1860, 1861; Representative to Congress, 1861–63; Collector of Port of San Francisco, 1889–; Regent of State University.
Phillips, Louis A., Assemblyman, San Francisco, 1891.
Pickett, G., Assemblyman, San Francisco, 1880.
Pico, Andres, Assemblyman, Los Angeles, 1851, 1852, 1858, 1859; Presidential Elector, 1852; Senator, Los Angeles, 1860, 1861. *Died, Los Angeles, February 14, 1876.*
Pico, Antonio M., Member First Constitutional Convention, 1849, Pueblo de San Jose District; Presidential Elector, 1860. *Died, San Jose, May 23, 1869.*
Pico, Pio, Governor under Mexican Rule, 1832–33, 1845–46.

Pierce, J. M., Assemblyman, San Diego, 1875–76.   Died, San Diego, August 6, 1887.
Pierce, Parker H., Assemblyman, Nevada, 1857.
Pierce, W. L., Superior Judge, San Diego County, appointed 1889, elected 1890.
Pierce, Winslow S., State Controller, 1852–53.   Died, Brooklyn, New York, July 29, 1888.
Piercy, Charles W., Assemblyman, San Bernardino, 1861.   Died, Marin County, May 25, 1861.
Pierson, William M., Senator, San Francisco, 1875–76, 1877–78.
Pinder, Thomas J., Assemblyman, San Francisco, 1881; Senator, San Francisco, 1887, 1889.
Piper, W. A., Representative to Congress, 1875–77.
Pishon, N. J., Assemblyman, San Bernardino, 1873–74.
Pitzer, J. S., Assemblyman, Trinity, 1853; Judge Fifteenth Judicial District, elected 1855.
Pixley, Frank M., Assemblyman, San Francisco, 1859; Attorney–General, 1862–63; Park Commissioner, San Francisco, 1882–86.
Platt, Horace G., Assemblyman, San Francisco, 1881.
Plover, P., Assemblyman, San Francisco, 1883.
Pool, D. M., Assemblyman, Mariposa, 1869–70; Senator, Mariposa, Merced, etc., 1880, 1881.
Portala, Gaspar de, Governor under Spanish Rule, 1767–71.
Porter, Arza, Assemblyman, San Luis Obispo, 1885.
Porter, C. H., Assemblyman, Butte, 1889.
Porter, Charles B., Assemblyman, Contra Costa, 1861, 1862; Senator, Contra Costa and Marin, 1863, 1863–64, 1865–66.
Porter, George K., Senator, Santa Cruz and Monterey, 1862, 1863.
Porter, J, M., Member Second Constitutional Convention, 1878–79, Second Congressional District.
Porter, Nathan, Senator, Alameda, 1877–78.   Died, Sacramento, June 5, 1878.
Post, G. B., Senator, San Francisco, 1849–50,   Died, San Francisco, February 26, 1861.
Potts, A. W., Bank Commissioner, 1886–90.
Powell, Joseph, Assemblyman, Sacramento, 1861.   Died, Folsom, November 27, 1869.
Power, M. H., Assemblyman, Placer, 1869–70.   Died, Auburn, July 17, 1885.
Powers, O. B., Senator, Solano and Yolo, 1862, 1863.
Pratt, J. D., Assemblyman, Placer, 1863–64.
Pratt, L. E., Senator, Sierra, 1865–66, 1867–68; Judge Seventeenth Judicial District, appointed 1862, elected 1862.   Died, San Francisco, October 25, 1886.
Pratt, O. C., Judge Twelfth Judicial District, elected 1863.   Died, San Francisco, October 24, 1891.
Pratt, William C., Assemblyman, Calaveras, 1854.
Pressley, J. G., Superior Judge, Sonoma County, elected 1879, 1884.
Preston, E. M., Senator, Nevada, 1889, 1891.
Preston, R. M., Assemblyman, San Luis Obispo, 1875–76.   Died, Santa Rosa, March 22, 1882.
Prewitt, J. E., Superior Judge, Placer County, elected 1890.
Price, E. B., Assemblyman, Butte, 1893.
Price, Johnson, Senator, Sacramento, 1859; Secretary of State, 1860–61.   Died, San Francisco, February 8, 1868.
Price, Rodman M., Member First Constitutional Convention, 1849, San Francisco District.
Price, W. Z., Assemblyman, San Mateo, 1887.
Printy, George W., Assemblyman, Butte, 1862.
Proctor, W. G., Assemblyman, Siskiyou, 1853.
Prouty, William H., Member Second Constitutional Convention, 1878–79, Amador District.
Pueschel, E. A., Assemblyman, Kern, 1893.
Pugh, J. W., Assemblyman, Sacramento, 1856.
Pullen, F. A., Assemblyman, San Francisco, 1875–76.
Pulliam, Mark R. C., Member Second Constitutional Convention; 1878–79, Butte District.   Died, San Francisco. January 28, 1883.
Purdy, Edwin B., Assemblyman, San Francisco, 1854.
Purdy, Samuel, Lieutenant-Governor, 1852–56.   Died, San Francisco, February 17, 1882.

Puterbaugh, George, Superior Judge, San Diego County, appointed 1889, elected 1890.
Pyle, D. M., Assemblyman, Santa Clara, 1885.
Quigley, R. V. S., Assemblyman, Lake, 1875–76.
Quimby, J. A., Assemblyman, Santa Clara, 1857.
Quin, J. M., Assemblyman, Tuolumne, 1855.
Quinn, I. N., Senator, Stanislaus, etc., 1859, 1860; President pro tem., 1860; Lieutenant-Governor, 1860. *Died, San Rafael, June 26, 1865.*
Quint, Leander, Senator, Tuolumne and Mono, 1862, 1863. ' *Died, San Francisco, March 28, 1890.*
Ragsdale, J. W., Assemblyman, Sonoma, 1889; Senator, Sonoma, 1891, 1893.
Raisch, Frederick, Assemblyman. San Francisco, 1875–76.
Ralston, James H., Senator, Sacramento, 1852, 1853. *Died, near Austin, Nevada, May, 1864.*
Ramage, Lewis, Judge Sixth Judicial District, elected 1869. *Died; Kansas City, February 14, 1879.*
Randall, A., Assemblyman, Monterey, 1851. *Died, San Francisco, January 13, 1869.*
Randolph, Edmund, Assemblyman, San Francisco District. 1849–50. *Died, San Francisco, September 8, 1861.*
Rankin, H., Assemblyman, San Francisco, 1875–76.
Rathburn, J. S., Assemblyman, Sonoma, 1856.
Raw, R. S., Assemblyman, El Dorado, 1893.
Rawle, Bernard, Assemblyman, San Francisco, 1883.
Rea, James W., Railroad Commissioner, Third District, 1887–90, 1891–
Rea, Thomas, Assemblyman, Santa Clara, 1873–74.
Reading, R. G., Assemblyman, Trinity, 1853.
Ream, Daniel, Senator, Siskiyou, etc., 1877–78.
Rearden, Timothy H., Superior Judge, San Francisco, appointed 1883, elected 1884. *Died, San Francisco, May 10, 1892.*
Reardon, T. B., Judge Fourteenth Judicial District, elected 1869, 1875. *Died, Oroville, August 4, 1885.*
Reavey, James, Assemblyman, San Francisco, 1889.
Reavis, J. J., Assemblyman, Modoc and Lassen, 1889.
Rector, T. H., Assemblyman, Klamath, etc., 1867–68, 1871–72.
Reddick, John Burke, Assemblyman, Calaveras, 1875–76, 1881; Presidential Elector, 1884; Lieutenant-Governor, 1891–
Redding, Benjamin B., Assemblyman. Yuba and Sierra, 1853; State Printer, 1854–55; Mayor of Sacramento, 1856; Secretary of State, 1863–67; Trustee of State Library, 1864–66. *Died, San Francisco, August 21, 1882.*
Reddington, J. H., Senator, San Francisco, 1863–64.
Reddy, Patrick, Member Second Constitutional Convention, 1878–79, Mono and Inyo District; Senator, Tulare, Fresno, etc., 1883, 1885.
Redfield, O. F., Assemblyman. Yuba, 1863, 1863–64.
Redington, Alfred, Presidential Elector, 1868. *Died, Sacramento, May 22, 1875.*
Redman, R. A., Senator, Alameda and Santa Clara, 1859, 1860.
Reed, Charles F., Assemblyman, Yolo, 1865–66; Member Second Constitutional Convention, 1878–79, Solano and Yolo District; Presidential Elector, 1884.
Reed, G. W., Assemblyman, Sonoma, 1862. *Died, Petaluma, 1868.*
Reed, H. R., Assemblyman, San Francisco, 1871–72.
Reed, T. H., Assemblyman. Placer, 1856.
Reed, Theron, Judge Sixteenth Judicial District, appointed 1866, elected 1867, 1873.
Reese, William S., Assemblyman, San Francisco, 1862.
Reeve, George B., Assemblyman, San Francisco, 1862.
Reeves, Truman, Assemblyman, San Bernardino, 1883, 1885.
Regan, Daniel S., Assemblyman, San Francisco, 1887, 1889.
Reichert, Theodore, Surveyor-General, 1887–91, 1891–
Reid, Hugo, Member First Constitutional Convention, 1849, Los Angeles District. *Died, Los Angeles, December 12, 1852.*
Renfro, James H., Assemblyman, Lake, 1891.
Renison, Thomas, Assemblyman, Monterey, 1887, 1889.
Reynolds, C. D., Senator, Calaveras and Tuolumne, 1883.
Reynolds, E. J., Assemblyman, San Francisco, 1889.
Reynolds, G. A. F., Assemblyman, Nevada, 1856.
Reynolds, James S., Member Second Constitutional Convention, 1878–79, San Francisco District.

Reynolds, John, Assemblyman, Santa Clara, 1881; Superior Judge, Santa. Clara County, appointed 1888, elected 1888, 1890.
Reynolds, S. F., Judge Fourth Judicial District, elected 1861.
Rhiel, Adam, Assemblyman, Santa Clara, 1883.
Rhoades, G. H., Assemblyman, Mariposa, 1856. *Died, Cavorca, Mexico, April" 7, 1857.*
Rhoads, John P., Assemblyman, Sacramento, 1863–64. *Died, Sacramento County, December 20, 1866.*
Rhodes, A. L., Senator, Alameda and Santa Clara, 1861, 1862; Supreme Justice, 1864–79; Chief Justice, 1870–72.
Rhodes, John M., Member Second Constitutional Convention, 1878–79, Yolo District.
Rhodes, W. H., Private Secretary to Governor J. Neely Johnson.
Rice, D. W. C., Assemblyman, Yuba, 1857. *Died, San Francisco, August 3, 1870.*
Rice, Henry, Assemblyman, Santa Cruz, 1875–76. *Died, Santa Cruz, September 29, 1889.*
Rice, J. B., Assemblyman, Marin, 1871–72.
Rice, T. H., Assemblyman, Kern and Ventura, 1891.
Richardson, H. S., Assemblyman, Mariposa, 1851.
Ricks, C. S., Assemblyman, Humboldt, 1856, 1857. *Died, Eureka, California, June, 1888.*
Rider, W. M., Assemblyman, Sonoma, 1863.
Ridley, Thomas E., Assemblyman, Mariposa, 1852.
Ring, John A., Assemblyman, Shasta, 1854.
Ringgold, Charles S., Member Second Constitutional Convention, 1878–79,.. San Francisco District.
Roach, Philip A., Senator, Monterey and Santa Cruz, 1852, 1853; San Francisco, 1873–74, 1875–76. *Died, San Francisco, April 27, 1889.*
Roane, James M., Assemblyman, Fresno, Tulare, etc., 1859.
Robberson, John S., Assemblyman, Sonoma and Mendocino, 1859.
Roberts, E. W., Senator, Nevada, 1863–64, 1867–68, 1869–70; Register United States Land Office, Sacramento District, 1890–92. *Died, Sacramento, July 13, 1892.*
Roberts, George M., Assemblyman, San Benito, 1875–76.
Robertson, George B., Assemblyman, Del Norte and Siskiyou, 1891.
Robertson, J. W., Assemblyman, Stanislaus and Merced, 1863.
Robertson, P. C., Assemblyman, Siskiyou and Modoc, 1877–78.
Robinson, Charles, Assemblyman, Sacramento, 1851.
Robinson, H. E., Senator, Sacramento, 1849–50, 1851, 1852. *Died, Norwalk,. Connecticut, January 9, 1880.*
Robinson, Henry, Assemblyman, Alameda, 1863; Senator, Alameda, 1865–66,. 1867–68.
Robinson, Henry H., State Printer, 1850.
Robinson, Robert, Assemblyman, Sacramento, 1853; Adjutant-General, 1865–66.
Robinson, Tod, Judge Sixth Judicial District, appointed 1851; Supreme Court Reporter, 1870. *Died, San Mateo County, October 27, 1870.*
Robinson, W. N., Assemblyman, San Diego, 1869–70.
Rockwell, E. A., Assemblyman, San Francisco, 1869–70. *Died, Sacramento,. November 16, 1877.*
Rodgers, E. A., Assemblyman, Tuolumne, 1860.
Rodgers, Robert C., Assemblyman, San Francisco, 1855.
Rodgers, William P., Assemblyman, Alameda, 1859.
Rodriguez, Jacinto, Member First Constitutional Convention, 1849, Monterey District. *Died, Monterey, December 14, 1878.*
Rogers, Daniel, Assemblyman, San Francisco, 1860, 1873–74.
Rogers, George H., Assemblyman, Tuolumne, 1857; San Francisco, 1869–70; Speaker, 1869–70; Senator, Tuolumne and Stanislaus, 1858; San Francisco, etc., 1875–76, 1877–78.
Rogers, W. M., Assemblyman, Calaveras, 1853.
Rolfe, Horace C., Judge Eighteenth Judicial District, appointed 1872; Member Second Constitutional Convention, 1878–79, San Diego and San Bernardino District; Superior Judge, San Bernardino County, elected 1879.-
Rollins, H. G., Assemblyman, Nevada, 1867–68.
Roman, Richard, State Treasurer, 1849–53. *Died, San Francisco, December 22,. 1875.*

Romea, Jose Antonio, Governor under Spanish rule, 1790-92. *Died, April 9, 1792.*
Romer, J. L., Assemblyman, San Francisco, 1869-70.
Rooney, J. F., Superior Judge, Tuolumne County, elected 1879, 1884.
Rosborough, A. M., Judge Ninth Judicial District, elected 1869, 1875.
Rose, A. H., Senator, Amador and Alpine, 1865-66, 1867-68.
Rose, L. J., Senator, Los Angeles, 1887.
Rose, T. H., Presidential Elector, 1872.
Roseberry, Thomas A., Assemblyman, Modoc and Lassen, 1885.
Rosecrans, William S., Representative to Congress, 1881-85; Register of United States Treasury, 1885-
Rosenthal, M., Presidential Elector, 1893.
Ross, Erskine M., Supreme Justice, 1880-86.
Ross, William, Assemblyman, Sonoma, 1861. *Died, Santa Rosa, April 10, 1874.*
Roth, John, Senator, Tulare and Kern, 1887, 1889.
Rousch, William, Assemblyman, Placer, 1873-74.
Routier, Joseph, Assemblyman, Sacramento, 1877-78; Senator, Sacramento, 1883, 1885; Fish Commissioner, 1887-89.
Rowan, Martin, Assemblyman, Calaveras, 1854. *Died, Sacramento, September 23, 1872.*
Rowe, E. A., Assemblyman, Trinity, 1855. *Dead.*
Rowell, C. W. C., Superior Judge, San Bernardino County, appointed 1889, elected 1890.
Rowell, Chester, Senator, Tulare, Kern, etc., 1880, 1881; Presidential Elector, 1884; Regent of State University.
Rowland, Thomas B., Assemblyman, El Dorado and Alpine, 1883. *Died, Lake Tahoe September 5, 1883.*
Rucker, Samuel, Assemblyman, Santa Clara, 1887.
Ruggles, E. S., Assemblyman, Butte, 1875-76.
Rule, J. W., Assemblyman, Nevada, 1863, 1863-64.
Rundell, William M., Assemblyman, Merced and Mariposa, 1889.
Rush, J. A., Senator, Colusa and Tehama, 1863-64, 1865-66.
Russ, A. G., Assemblyman, San Francisco, 1869.
Russ, Joseph, Assemblyman, Humboldt, 1871-72, 1877-78, 1885. *Died, Alameda, October 8, 1886.*
Russell, P. H., Assemblyman, Sacramento, 1873-74.
Rust, P. C., Senator, Yuba and Sutter, 1855, 1856.
Rutledge, Thomas, Superior Judge, Sonoma County, appointed 1886.
Ryan, Frank D., Assemblyman, Sacramento, 1883; Chief Clerk of the Assembly, twenty-sixth and twenty-seventh sessions; Member of Board of Trustees of Sutter's Fort, 1891-
Ryan, James T., Senator, Trinity and Humboldt, 1860, 1861.
Ryan, P. H., Senator, Humboldt, etc., 1880, 1881, 1883.
Ryan, Thomas P., Assemblyman, San Francisco, 1869-70.
Ryland, C. T., Private Secretary to Governor Peter H. Burnett; Assemblyman, Santa Clara, 1855, 1867-68; Speaker, 1867-68.
Safford, A. P. K., Assemblyman, Placer, 1857, 1858. *Died, Florida, December 16, 1891.*
Salomon, E. S., Assemblyman, San Francisco, 1889.
Sammons, B. J., Assemblyman, Sierra, 1869-70, 1871-72.
Samuels, James, Assemblyman, Sonoma, 1875-76, 1881.
Sanderson, A. A., Superior Judge, San Francisco, elected 1890.
Sanderson, Silas W., Assemblyman, El Dorado, 1863; Supreme Justice, 1864-70; Chief Justice, 1864-66. *Died, San Francisco, June 24, 1886.*
Sansevaine, Pedro, Member First Constitutional Convention, 1849, San Jose District.
Sargent, Aaron A., Representative to Congress, 1861-63, 1869-71; United States Senator, 1873-79. *Died, San Francisco, August 14, 1887.*
Sargent, B. V., Senator, Monterey and San Benito, 1887.
Sargent, J. C., Assemblyman, Yuba, 1862, 1863. *Dead.*
Sargent, J. L., Assemblyman, Amador, 1893.
Sargent, J. P., Assemblyman, Santa Clara, 1871-72.
Sargent, R. C., Assemblyman, San Joaquin, 1871-72, 1875-76, 1877-78, 1881.
Satterwhite, J. W., Assemblyman, San Bernardino, 1865-66, 1869-70; Senator, San Diego, etc., 1875-76, 1877-78, 1880, 1881. *Died, San Bernardino, February 16, 1885.*
Saul, James B., Assemblyman, Sacramento, 1862. *Died, Davisville, October 30, 1881.*

Saunders, J. H., Asssemblyman, San Francisco, 1853; Senator, San Francisco, 1867–68, 1869–70.
Saunders, R. F., Assemblyman, Butte, 1851.
Sawyer, E. D., Senator, Calaveras, 1854; Judge Fourth Judicial District, elected 1863.
Sawyer, F. A., Assemblyman, San Francisco, 1860.
Sawyer, Lorenzo, Judge Twelfth Judicial District, appointed 1862, elected 1862; Supreme Justice, 1864–70; Chief Justice, 1868–69; United States Circuit Judge, Ninth Circuit, 1869–91. *Died, San Francisco, September 7, 1891.*
Sawyer, N. G., Assemblyman, Calaveras, 1865–66.
Sayle, C. G., Assemblyman, Fresno, 1880.
Saxe, A. W., Senator, Santa Clara, 1885.
Saxton, A. H., Senator, El Dorado, 1863. *Died, Tahoe City, August 19, 1886.*
Scarce, L., Assemblyman, Colusa and Tehama, 1869–70.
Scellen, John D., Senator, Sierra, 1855, 1856. *Dead.*
Schell, George W., Member Second Constitutional Convention, 1878–79, Fourth Congressional District; Prison Director, 1880–83; Presidential Elector, 1888.
Schlesinger, Bert, Assemblyman, San Francisco, 1893.
Schmidt, John C., Assemblyman, San Francisco, 1860.
Schomp, Justus, Member Second Constitutional Convention, 1878–79, San Joaquin District.
Schrack, L. M., Assemblyman, Calaveras, 1871–72. *Died, Calaveras County, February 7, 1883.*
Schroebel, D. J. B., Assemblyman, Calaveras, 1893.
Scott, Charles L., Representative to Congress, 1857–59.
Scott, J., Assemblyman, Santa Barbara District, 1849–50.
Scott, John B., Assemblyman, Napa, 1861. *Died, San Francisco, June 30, 1890.*
Scott, R. C., Assemblyman, Siskiyou, 1863–64.
Scott, Thomas, Assemblyman, Alameda, 1863, 1863–64.
Scrivner, J. J., Assemblyman, Stanislaus, 1875–76; State Prison Director, 1887–89.
Scudder, Frank V., Assemblyman, San Francisco, 1867–68. *Died, San Francisco, June 17, 1877.*
Searey, Thomas M., Assemblyman, San Francisco, 1887, 1889.
Searls, Niles, Senator, Nevada and Sierra, 1877–78; Judge Fourteenth Judicial District, elected 1855, 1858; Supreme Court Commissioner, 1884–87; Chief Justice of the Supreme Court, 1887–88.
Sears, William H., Assemblyman, Nevada, 1862, 1863, 1863–64; Speaker, 1863–64; Senator, Contra Costa and Marin, 1880, 1881. *Died, San Francisco, February 27, 1891.*
Seaton, G. W., Assemblyman, Amador, 1862. *Died, Yosemite, October 13, 1865.*
Seawell, J. H., Assemblyman, Mendocino, 1889; Senator, Mendocino and and Lake, 1891, 1893; Director Mendocino State Insane Asylum, 1891–
Seawell, W. M., Assemblyman, Amador, 1857.
Seckel, George, Clerk of the Supreme Court, 1867–71.
Seibe, John, Assemblyman, San Francisco, 1871–72.
Selleck, Silas, Assemblyman, Placer, 1856. *Died, Sacramento, June 17, 1878.*
Semple, Robert, Member First Constitutional Convention, 1849, Sonoma District. *Died, near Colusa, October 25, 1854.*
Sensabaugh, J. B., Assemblyman, Merced, 1871–72.
Sepulveda, Ygnacio, Assemblyman, Los Angeles, 1863–64; Judge Seventeenth Judicial District, elected 1873; Superior Judge, Los Angeles County, elected 1879.
Sexton, Warren T., Judge Second and Thirteenth Judicial Districts, elected 1857, 1863, 1875. *Died, Oroville, April 14, 1878.*
Sexton, William, Assemblyman, Placer, 1865–66.
Seymour, E. C., Senator, San Bernardino and Orange, 1893.
Shafter, James McMillan, Senator, San Francisco, 1861, 1862, 1863–64; President pro tem., 1862; Member Second Constitutional Convention, 1878–79, Third Congressional District; Superior Judge, San Francisco, appointed 1889, elected 1890. *Died, San Francisco, August 29, 1892.*
Shafter, Oscar L., Supreme Justice, 1864–67. *Died, Florence, Italy, January 22, 1873.*

Shanahan, T. W. H., Assemblyman, Trinity and Shasta, 1887, 1889, 1891; Shasta and Modoc, 1893; Member Board of Agriculture, District No. 27, Shasta County, 1889-

Shanklin, James W., Surveyor-General, 1880-83.

Shannon, Thomas B., Assemblyman, Plumas, 1859, 1860, 1862; San Francisco, 1871-72; Speaker, 1871-72; Senator, Plumas, 1863; Representative to Congress, 1863-65.

Shannon, W. E., Member First Constitutional Convention, 1849, Sacramento District. *Died, Sacramento, November 3, 1850.*

Sharp, Sol. A., Assemblyman, San Francisco, 1856; Senator, San Francisco, etc., 1860. *Died, San Francisco, June 8, 1878.*

Sharpstein, John R., Judge Twelfth Judicial District, appointed 1874; Supreme Justice, 1880-82, 1882-92. *Died, San Francisco, December 28, 1892.*

Shattuck, F. K., Assemblyman, Alameda, 1860.

Shaw, Lucien, Superior Judge, Los Angeles County, appointed 1889, elected 1890.

Shaw, William J., Senator, San Francisco, 1856, 1857, 1865-66, 1867-68.

Shearer, Edwin, Superior Judge, Siskiyou County, appointed 1883, elected 1884.

Shearer, Jacob, Assemblyman, Yuba, 1856.

Sheehan, John F., Adjutant-General, 1882-83; Bank Commissioner, 1882.

Shelton, H. A., Assemblyman, Calaveras, 1860.

Shepard, Joseph, Senator, Calaveras, 1863-64.

Shepard, William W., Assemblyman, San Francisco, 1857, 1858, 1859. *Dead.*

Shepherd, W. M., Assemblyman, San Joaquin District, 1849-50.

Sherburne, D. N., Assemblyman, Contra Costa, 1880, 1887.

Sheridan, James E., Assemblyman, Sacramento, 1858, 1859. *Died, Sacramento County, October 12, 1872.*

Sherman, Caleb, Assemblyman, Santa Barbara, 1877-78.

Sherrard, Robert B., Assemblyman, Sutter, 1855, 1856. *Died, Winchester, Virginia, 1860.*

Sherwin, J. L. C., Assemblyman, Plumas, 1858.

Sherwood, T. J., Assemblyman, Yuba, 1865-66.

Sherwood, Winfield S., Member First Constitutional Convention, 1849, Sacramento District; Judge Ninth Judicial District, elected by Legislature, 1850; Presidential Elector, 1852. *Died, Allegany, Sierra County, California, June 25, 1870.*

Shields, P. J., Trustee of State Library, 1887-89.

Shippee, W. A., Senator, Butte, 1891, 1893.

Shirley, Paul, Senator, Contra Costa and Marin, 1875-76, 1877-78.

Shoaff, Philip L., State Printer, 1887.

Shoemaker, Rufus, Member Second Constitutional Convention, 1878-79, Second Congressional District.

Shoemaker, W. B., Assemblyman, Santa Clara, 1869-70.

Shorb, J. Campbell, Presidential Elector, 1880. *Died, San Francisco, October 1, 1889.*

Shores, William, Assemblyman, Siskiyou, 1869-70.

Shortridge, Samuel M., Presidential Elector, 1888.

Showalter, Daniel, Assemblyman, Mariposa and Merced, 1857, 1861; Speaker pro tem., 1861. *Died, Mazatlan, Mexico, February 4, 1866.*

Shuler, George L., Assemblyman, Calaveras, 1857.

Shurtleff, Benjamin, Senator, Shasta and Trinity, 1862, 1863; Member Second Constitutional Convention, 1878-79, Third Congressional District; President of the Board of Trustees of the Napa State Asylum for the Insane, 1888-

Siebe, John D., Assemblyman, San Francisco, 1881.

Silman, W. L., Presidential Elector, 1893.

Sime, John, Assemblyman, San Francisco, 1853. *Died, San Francisco, October 13, 1871.*

Simons, Solon S., Assemblyman, Santa Clara, 1858.

Simpers, G. W., Assemblyman, El Dorado, 1873-74.

Simpson, C. M., Assemblyman, Los Angeles, 1893.

Simpson, E. M., Assemblyman, Amador, 1863.

Simpson, John, Assemblyman, Colusa and Tehama, 1873-74.

Simpson, William, Assemblyman, Alameda, 1889; Senator, Alameda, 1891, 1893.

Sims, J. C., Assemblyman, Sonoma, 1893.

Sims, Josiah, Assemblyman, Nevada, 1887, 1889.

Singleton, M. A., Assemblyman, Sierra, 1865-66.
Singley, James, Assemblyman, Sonoma, 1855.
Sinon, W. J., Assemblyman, San Francisco, 1880, 1883.
Slack, Chas. W., Superior Judge, San Francisco, appointed 1891, elected 1892.
Slaughter, F. M., Assemblyman, San Bernardino, 1871-72.
Slicer, T. A., Assemblyman, Nevada, 1869-70.
Slingerland, James S., Assemblyman, Yuba, 1859.
Sloss, Gordon E., Member of State Board of Equalization, 1887-90. *Dead.*
Sloss, H. C., Assemblyman, El Dorado, 1859. *Died, Placerville, March 11, 1864.*
Smith, A. A., Assemblyman, Nevada, 1863-64.
Smith, A. Guy, Assemblyman, Los Angeles and Orange, 1891.
Smith, Ansel, Superior Judge, San Joaquin Couuty, elected 1890.
Smith, B. N., Superior Judge, Los Angeles County, elected 1890.
Smith, C. F., Assemblyman, Nevada, 1860.
Smith, E. B., Assemblyman, Sierra, 1862, 1863.
Smith, E. L., Assemblyman, El Dorado, 1865-66.
Smith, E. O., Member Second Constitutional Convention, 1878-79, Santa
    Clara District.
Smith, F. M., Assemblyman, Butte, 1863; Senator, Butte, Plumas, etc.,
    1863-64, 1865-66. *Died, Tucson, Arizona, April 21, 1884.*
Smith, George A., Judge Ninth Judicial District, elected 1852. *Died, Hamil-*
    ton, August 26, 1853.
Smith, George E., Assemblyman, Butte, 1865-66.
Smith, George H., Senator, Los Angeles, 1877-78.
Smith, George V., Member Second Constitutional Convention, 1878-79,
    Fourth Congressional District.
Smith, H. P. A., Assemblyman, Marin, 1855.
Smith, Henry C., Assemblyman, Santa Clara, 1853. *Died, Livermore, Novem-*
    ber 24, 1875.
Smith, Henry M., Superior Judge, Los Angeles County, appointed 1884.
Smith, Henry W., Member Second Constitutional Convention, 1878-79, San
    Francisco District.
Smith, Isaac W., Assemblyman, San Bernardino, 1858.
Smith, J., Assemblyman, Sonoma, 1863-64.
Smith, J. J., Assemblyman, Butte. 1891.
Smith, J. Langdon, Assemblyman, Sutter, 1860.
Smith, James, Assemblyman, Fresno, 1862. *Died, King's River, December 17,*
    1862.
Smith, James K., Assemblyman, Nevada, 1858; Yuba, 1867-68.
Smith, L. G., Assemblyman, Placer, 1861.
Smith, N. T., Assemblyman, El Dorado, 1855.
Smith, Napoleon B., Assemblyman, Contra Costa, 1852.
Smith, O. K., Assemblyman, Tulare and Fresno, 1857, 1861. *Died, San Luis*
    Obispo, February. 1871.
Smith, Samuel B., Senator, Sutter, 1853, 1854.
Smith, Stanley A., Superior Judge, Sierra County, elected 1890.
Smith, W. L., Assemblyman, Mariposa and Merced, 1883.
Smyth, Edward, Assemblyman, Tuolumne, 1877-78, 1887.
Snyder, E. H., Assemblyman, Placer, 1863-64.
Snyder, Frederick A., Assemblyman, San Francisco, 1853. *Died, July 23,*
    1854, while on his way to Lake Bigler.
Snyder, J. W., Assemblyman, Mariposa, 1873-74.
Snyder, Jacob R., Member First Constitutional Convention, 1849, Sacra-
    mento District; Senator, San Francisco, 1852, 1853. *Died, Sonoma, April*
    29, 1878.
Sola, Pablo Vincente de, Governor under Spanish rule, 1815-22; Governor
    under Mexican rule, 1822-23. *Died, Mexico, 1827.*
Sorrell, F., Assemblyman, Siskiyou, 1861.
Soule, Ezra P., Member Second Constitutional Convention, 1878-79, Plumas
    and Lassen District.
Soulé, Frank, Senator, San Francisco, 1852. *Died, San Francisco, July 3, 1882.*
Soulé, Samuel, Senator, San Francisco, 1858, 1862. *Died, San Francisco, No-*
    vember 18, 1889.
Southard, James B., Judge Seventh Judicial District, appointed 1862, elected
    1863.
Soward, F. D., Superior Judge, Sierra County, elected 1884.
Spect, Jonas, Senator, Sonoma District, 1849-50. *Died, Colusa, July 3, 1883.*
Spellacy, L., Senator San Francisco, 1887, 1889.

:Spence, E. F., Assemblyman, Nevada, 1861. Died, *Los Angeles, September 19, 1892.*

Spencer, C. G., Assemblyman, Placer, 1867–68.

.Spencer, Dennis, Senator, Napa, Sonoma, etc., 1883, 1885.

.Spencer, F. E., Assemblyman, Santa Clara, 1871–72; Superior Judge, Santa Clara County, elected 1879, 1884.

.Spencer, J. D., Assemblyman, Stanislaus, 1880; Senator, Mariposa, etc., 1883, 1885; Clerk of the Supreme Court, 1886–90.

.Spencer, M., Assemblyman, Humboldt, 1854.

.Spencer, S., Senator, Yuba and Sutter, 1873–74, 1875–76.

.Spillman, B. R., Assemblyman, Yuba, 1858; Sutter, 1867–68. Died, *Marysville, October 14, 1888.*

Splivalo, A. D., Assemblyman, San Francisco, 1871–72.

Sprague, F. S., Senator, Yolo and Napa, 1889, 1891.

.Sprague, Royal T., Senator, Shasta, etc., 1852, 1853, 1854, 1855; President pro tem. Senate, 1855; Supreme Justice, 1868–72; Chief Justice, 1872. Died, *Sacramento, February 24, 1872.*

Spreckels, Claus, Presidential Elector, 1872.

.Springer, E. C., Assemblyman, El Dorado, 1854.

Springer, Grant H., State Printer, 1874–75.

Springer, James P., Assemblyman, Santa Clara, 1859. Died, *Santa Clara County, June 2, 1861.*

.Springer, Thomas A., State Printer, 1871–74. Died, *San Francisco, February 25, 1874.*

Spurgeon, W. H., Assemblyman, Los Angeles, 1887.

:Squires, Ogden, Assemblyman, El Dorado, 1869.

Stabler, H. P., Assemblyman, Sutter and Yuba, 1891.

Stakes, A. G., Assemblyman, San Joaquin, 1858. Dead.

.Standart, George, Assemblyman, Lassen, Plumas, and Sierra, 1893.

.Stanford, Leland, Governor, 1862–63; United States Senator, 1885–90, 1891–; Commissioner to attend the Centennial Celebration of the Inauguration of George Washington as President of the United States, 1888.

Stanley, H. Y., Assemblyman, San Luis Obispo, 1880.

Stark, John S., Assemblyman, Napa, 1852.

:Starr, Henry, Assemblyman, Sacramento, 1860.

.Staude, John, Assemblyman, San Francisco, 1889.

.Stearns, Abel, Member First Constitutional Convention, 1849, Los Angeles District; Assemblyman, Los Angeles, 1851, 1861. Died, *San Francisco, August 23, 1871.*

Stebbins, James G., Senator, Yuba and Sutter, 1854, 1855.

.Stedman, John C., Member Second Constitutional Convention, 1878–79, San Francisco District.

.Steele, D. M., Assemblyman, Colusa and Tehama, 1857.

Steele, Elijah, Assemblyman, Siskiyou, 1867–68; Superior Judge, Siskiyou County, elected 1879. Died, *Yreka, June 27, 1883.*

:Steele, George, Member Second Constitutional Convention, 1878–79, San Luis Obispo District; Senator, San Luis Obispo, etc., 1885, 1887.

Steele, Thomas H., Assemblyman, Siskiyou, 1865–66.

Steltz, John T., Assemblyman, San Francisco, 1891.

.Stemmons, John, Assemblyman, San Joaquin, 1854. Died, *San Francisco, May 26, 1856.*

Stephens, C. S., Assemblyman, San Joaquin, 1883.

:Stephens, J. F., Assemblyman, San Joaquin District, 1849–50.

:Stephens, Russell D., Assemblyman, Sacramento, 1869–70; Postmaster, Sacramento, 1885–90; Trustee of State Library, 1889–90, 1891–; Viticultural Commissioner, 1890–; Alternate Commissioner to World's Fair, 1890–

Stephens, S. B., Assemblyman, Calaveras, 1855.

.Stephenson, C. B., Assemblyman, Santa Cruz, 1852,

:Stephenson, E. A., Assemblyman, El Dorado, 1854, 1855; Tehama and Colusa, 1860; Speaker pro tem., 1860.

:Sterritt, John M., Assemblyman, Yuba, 1856.

:Steuart, William M., Member First Constitutional Convention, 1849, San Francisco District.

Stevenson, A. M., Assemblyman, Solano, 1856, 1857.

:Stevenson, D. C., Member Second Constitutional Convention, 1878–79, Siskiyon, Modoc, Trinity, and Shasta District. Died, *Millville, April, 1883.*

:Stewart, J., Assemblyman, San Joaquin District, 1849–50.

.Stewart, James S., Assemblyman, Sonoma, 1855.

Stewart, Orrin, Assemblyman, Yuba, 1865–66.
Stewart, Robert, Assemblyman, Amador, 1883.
Stewart, William M., Attorney-General, 1854.
Stillwagon, W. W., Assemblyman, Napa and Lake, 1871–72. *Died, Napa, July 12, 1884.*
Stocker, J. T., Assemblyman, Marin, 1858.
Stoddard, C. L., Assemblyman, Humboldt, 1880.
Stone, W. H., Assemblyman, El Dorado, 1860.
Stoneman, George, Railroad Commissioner, appointed 1876–79, Third District, elected 1880–82; Governor, 1883–86.
Storke, C. A., Assemblyman, Santa Barbara and Ventura, 1883, 1889.
Stout, Lansing, Assemblyman, Placer, 1856. *Died, Oregon, March 17, 1871.*
Stout, Moses, Assemblyman, Sacramento, 1858. *Died, Sacramento County, December 20, 1879.*
Stow, W. W., Assemblyman, Santa Cruz, 1854, 1855; Speaker of the House, 1855; Park Commissioner, San Francisco, 1890–
Stowell, Levi, Assemblyman, San Francisco, 1849–50. *Died, San Francisco, May 18, 1855.*
Stowers, W. H., Assemblyman, Amador, 1873–74.
Stratton, W. C., Assemblyman, Placer, 1858, 1859; Speaker, 1859; State Librarian, 1861–69.
Street, Charles R., Assemblyman, Shasta, 1858, 1859.
Streeter, Henry M., Assemblyman, Santa Barbara, 1880, 1881; Presidential Elector, 1888; Senator, San Diego and San Bernardino, 1891, 1893.
Strong, J. M., Member Second Constitutional Convention, 1878–79, Mariposa and Merced District. *Died, Sacramento, November 19, 1878.*
Strother, Fleet F., Trustee of State Library, 1891–
Stuart, C. V., Member Second Constitutional Convention, 1878–79, Sonoma District.
Sturtevant, George, Assemblyman, Mendocino, 1891.
Sullivan, D. C., Assemblyman, San Francisco, 1875–76.
Sullivan, E. L., Senator, San Francisco, 1857, 1858. *Died, San Francisco, March 26, 1885.*
Sullivan, F. J., Senator, San Francisco, 1883.
Sullivan, J. F., Superior Judge, San Francisco, elected 1879, 1884.
Sullivan, J. J., Senator, San Francisco, 1887.
Sullivan, M. J., Assemblyman, San Francisco, 1885.
Summers, James W., Assemblyman, Tuolumne, Mono, etc., 1873–74 *Died, Bridgeport, April 26, 1877.*
Sumner, Charles A., Representative to Congress, 1883–85.
Sumner, George S., Assemblyman, Butte, 1863–64.
Sutter, John A., Member First Constitutional Convention, 1849, Sacramento District. *Died, Washington, District of Columbia, June 18, 1880.*
Sutton, O. P., Assemblyman, San Francisco, 1863. *Died, San Francisco, September 1, 1881.*
Suverkrup, Henry, Assemblyman, San Bernardino, 1875–76. *Dead.*
Swan, J. S., Member of State Board of Equalization, 1891–
Swan, Thomas M., Assemblyman, Solano, 1860, 1875–76. *Died, Suisun, August 29, 1885.*
Swan, Robert R., Assemblyman, Tulare, 1856.
Swayne, T. J., Assemblyman, San Diego, 1885.
Sweasey, W. J., Assemblyman, San Francisco, 1854; Member Second Constitutional Convention, 1878–79, Humboldt District. *Dead.*
Sweeney, Edward, Superior Judge, Shasta County, elected 1890.
Sweetland, H. P., Assemblyman, Nevada, 1854. *Dead.*
Sweetland, J. O., Assemblyman, Nevada, 1880, 1883.
Swenson, Charles, Member Second Constitutional Convention, 1878–79, San Francisco District.
Swett, John, State Superintendent of Public Instruction, 1863–67.
Swezy, G. N., Assemblyman, Yuba, 1857. *Died, August 29, 1876.*
Swift, C. B., Assemblyman, Amador, 1881.
Swift, John F., Assemblyman, San Francisco, 1863, 1873–74, 1877–78; Presidential Elector, 1888; Minister to Japan, 1889–91. *Died, Yokohama, March 10, 1891.*
Swinnerton, J. G., Superior Judge, San Joaquin County, elected 1884.
Swing, Randolph S., Member Second Constitutional Convention, 1878–79, San Bernardino District.
Sykes, J. I., Assemblyman, Nevada, 1887, 1889.

Taggart, Grant I., Clerk of the Supreme Court, 1871-75; Assemblyman, Alameda, 1893.
Talbott, W. L., Assemblyman, Santa Barbara, 1893.
Taliaferro, Alfred W., Assemblyman, Marin, 1852; Senator, Sonoma and Marin, 1857, 1858. *Died, San Rafael, December 9, 1885.*
Taliaferro, T. W., Assemblyman, Calaveras, 1855, 1856. *Died, San Francisco, December 6, 1889.*
Tallmadge, D. P., Assemblyman, El Dorado, 1854. *Died, New York, 1858.*
Tallman, John H., Assemblyman, Mariposa, 1858.
Taylor, Clay W., Senator, Shasta, Modoc, etc., 1883, 1885.
Taylor, E. W., Assemblyman, San Francisco, 1855.
Taylor, Edward F., Assemblyman, El Dorado, 1865-66.
Taylor, Edward R., Private Secretary to Governor Henry H. Haight.
Taylor, James I., Assemblyman, Marin, 1893.
Taylor, James M., Assemblyman, San Francisco, 1853, 1859.
Taylor, L. S., Assemblyman, Sacramento, 1887.
Taylor, Nelson, Senator, San Joaquin District, 1849-50.
Taylor, R. H., Judge Seventeenth Judicial District, elected 1859.
Taylor, W. H., Assemblyman, El Dorado, 1856.
Teare, P., Assemblyman, El Dorado, 1863-64.
Teegarden, Eli, Assemblyman, Yuba, 1862; Senator, Sutter and Yuba, 1865-66, 1867-68. *Died, Marysville, June 14, 1884.*
Tefft, Henry A., Member First Constitutional Convention, 1849, San Luis Obispo District; Assemblyman, San Luis Obispo District, 1849-50; Judge Second Judicial District, elected by Legislature, 1850. *Drowned at San Luis Obispo, February 6, 1852.*
Temple, Jackson, Judge Twenty-second Judicial District, appointed 1876, elected 1877; Supreme Justice, 1870-71, 1887-89; Superior Judge, Sonoma County, elected 1879, 1884; Supreme Court Commissioner, 1891-
Ten Broeck, George W., Assemblyman, San Francisco, 1852.
Tennis, William E., Assemblyman, San Francisco, 1891.
Terrill, C. C., Assemblyman, San Francisco, 1873-74.
Terry, David S., Member Second Constitutional Convention, 1878-79, San Joaquin District; Supreme Justice, 1855-59; Chief Justice, 1857-59. *Died, Lathrop, August 14, 1889.*
Terry, Samuel L., Assemblyman, San Joaquin, 1883. *Died, Stockton, April 1, 1885.*
Tharp, E. H., Clerk of the Supreme Court, 1850-52.
Theller, Samuel L., Assemblyman, San Francisco, 1860.
Thom, Cameron E., Senator, Los Angeles, San Diego, etc., 1858, 1859.
Thomas, C. C., Assemblyman, Butte, 1853.
Thomas, C. L., Assemblyman, Santa Cruz, 1873-74.
Thomas, George W., Assemblyman, Stanislaus, 1858, 1859.
Thomas, James S., Judge Sixth Judicial District, elected by Legislature, 1850. *Died, St. Louis, 1857.*
Thomas, Massey, Assemblyman, Santa Clara, 1893.
Thomas, Philip W., Senator, Placer, 1861, 1862. *Died, Auburn, October 24, 1871.*
Thomas, R. I., Assemblyman, Nevada, 1893.
Thomas, T. R., Assemblyman, Santa Clara, 1869-70. *Died, Gilroy, July 3, 1885.*
Thompson, Frank P., State Printer, 1875-79.
Thompson, James A., Bank Commissioner, 1887-89.
Thompson, James T., Assemblyman, Santa Clara, 1852.
Thompson, John, Assemblyman, San Joaquin, 1862.
Thompson, Joseph W., Assemblyman, Tehama and Colusa, 1862.
Thompson, R. B., Assemblyman, San Joaquin, 1877-78.
Thompson, S. B., Member Second Constitutional Convention, 1878-79, San Francisco District.
Thompson, Thomas L., Secretary of State, 1883-87; Representative to Congress, 1887-89; Commissioner to attend the Centennial Celebration of the Inauguration of George Washington as President of the United States, 1888.
Thornbury, Caleb N., Assemblyman, Siskiyou, 1862.
Thorne, Isaac N., Assemblyman, San Francisco, 1851.
Thornton, Harry I., Senator, Sierra, 1861.

42

Thornton, J. D.; Judge Twenty-third Judicial District, appointed 1878; Supreme Justice, 1880–91.
Thurston, J. S., Assemblyman, San Joaquin, 1869–70.
Tilden, William P., Assemblyman, Butte, 1861, 1865–66.
Tilford, Frank, Senator, San Francisco, 1856, 1857. *Died, Denver, Colorado, June 2, 1886.*
Tilghman, T. W., Assemblyman, San Diego, 1853.
Tilton, S., Assemblyman, San Mateo, 1862.
Tilton, S. S., Assemblyman, San Francisco, 1860, 1861, 1862.
Tindall, C. W., Assemblyman, Mendocino, 1893.
Tingley, George B., Assemblyman, Sacramento District, 1849–50; Senator, Santa Clara, 1851, 1852. *Died, San Francisco, August 3, 1862.*
Tinnin, W. J., Assemblyman, Trinity, 1871–72, 1873–74; Senator, Shasta, Trinity, etc., 1875–76; Member Second Constitutional Convention, 1878–79, Third Congressional District; United States Surveyor of Port of San Francisco, 1885–89.
Tipton, J. S., Assemblyman, El Dorado, 1858, 1859.
Tittle, F. G. E., Assemblyman, San Francisco, 1861. *Died, San Francisco, October 20, 1877.*
Tivy, John T., Assemblyman, Tulare, 1854.
Titus, Isaac S., Senator, El Dorado, 1859, 1860. *Died, Prescott, Arizona, April 22, 1892.*
Tobin, John J., Assemblyman, San Francisco, 1877–78; Assistant Adjutant-General, 1883–86; Private Secretary to Governor George Stoneman; Commissioner of the Bureau of Labor Statistics, 1887–91.
Tompkins, Edward, Senator, Alameda, 1869–70, 1871–72. *Died, Oakland, November 14, 1872.*
Toner, Hugh, Assemblyman, San Francisco, 1887.
Toohy, D. J., Superior Judge, San Francisco, elected 1882.
Torrance, E. S., Superior Judge, San Diego County, elected 1890.
Torrence, R. B., Assemblyman, Marin, 1863.
Torres, Manuel, Assemblyman, Marin, 1859,
Torrey, Mark S., Assemblyman, Calaveras, 1885.
Towner, J. W., Superior Judge, Orange County, elected 1889, 1890.
Townsend, F. O., Member Second Constitutional Convention, 1878–79, Mendocino District.
Townsend, J. H. M., Assemblyman, Santa Clara, 1883.
Traylor, W. W., Senator, San Francisco, 1880, 1881. *Died, San Francisco, January 18, 1883.*
Troutt, J. M., Superior Judge, San Francisco, elected 1890.
Tubbs, A. L., Senator, San Francisco, 1865–66, 1867–68.
Tucker, E. H., Assemblyman, Fresno, 1889.
Tucker, Joseph C., Assemblyman, Sacramento, 1852. *Died, Oakland, December 22, 1891.*
Tukey, Francis, Assemblyman, Sacramento, 1863–64. *Died, Sacramento County, November 23, 1867.*
Tullock, L. R., Assemblyman, Tuolumne, 1889.
Tully, E. C., Assemblyman, Monterey and Santa Clara, 1859, 1867–68, 1873–74; Assemblyman, San Benito, 1889.
Tully, P. B., Member Second Constitutional Convention, 1878–79, Fourth Congressional District; Representative to Congress, 1883–85.
Tully, Thomas J., Assemblyman, San Francisco, 1891.
Turner, Henry K., Senator, Nevada and Sierra, 1869–70, 1871–72, 1873–74, 1875–76; Member Second Constitutional Convention, 1878–79, Sierra District; Assemblyman, Plumas and Sierra, 1889.
Turner, J., Assemblyman, El Dorado, 1857.
Turner, J. N., Assemblyman, Nevada, 1852; Butte, 1871–72. *Died, Oroville, April 10, 1884.*
Turner, R. M., Assemblyman, Yuba, 1856.
Turner, William R., Judge Eighth Judicial District, elected by the Legislature 1850, elected 1863. *Died, Jacksonville, Oregon, August 6, 1869.*
Tuttle, A. A. H., Assemblyman, Tuolumne, 1858; Secretary of State, 1863. *Died, Donner Lake, September 7, 1866.*
Tuttle, B. F., Senator, Sonoma, 1871–72, 1873–74, 1875–76; President pro tem., 1875–76; Assemblyman, Sonoma, 1877–78.
Tuttle, Charles A., Senator, Placer, 1854, 1855; Presidential Elector, 1860; Assemblyman, Placer, 1867–68. *Died, Auburn, June 24, 1888.*

Tuttle, Daniel, Member Second Constitutional Convention, 1878–79, Santa Cruz District.

Tttle, M. C., Senator, San Diego, 1863–64, 1865–66. *Died, San Bernardino, March, 10, 1867.*

Tweed, Charles A., Senator, Placer, 1867–68, 1869–70. *Died, San Francisco, July 22, 1887.*

Tyler, George W., Assemblyman, Alameda, 1880.

Underwood, J. K., Assemblyman, Tuolumne, 1857.

Updegraff, J· H., Assemblyman, Yolo, 1855. *Died, Knights Landing, May 9, 1860.*

Upton, Clarence W., Assemblyman, Santa Clara, 1877–78. *Died, February 5, 1878.*

Upton, W. W., Assemblyman, Trinity, 1856.

Vacquerel, Alphonse P., Member Second Constitutional Convention, 1878–79, San Francisco District. *Died, San Francisco, February 21, 1883.*

Vallejo, M. G., Member First Constitutional Convention, 1849, Sonoma District; Senator, Sonoma District, 1849–50. *Died, Sonoma, January 18, 1890.*

Van Benschoten, J· W., Assemblyman, San Joaquin District, 1849–50.

Van Buren, Thomas B., Senator, San Joaquin, 1851, 1852. *Died, San Francisco, October 13, 1889.*

Vance, J. M., Senator, Butte and Plumas, 1860, 1861.

Van Cleft, G. H., Assemblyman, Placer, 1854.

Van Chef, Peter, Judge Seventeenth Judicial District, appointed 1859; Supreme Court Commissioner, 1888–

Vandall, B. C., Assemblyman, San Francisco, 1873–74.

Vandever, William, Representative to Congress, 1887–91; Commissioner to attend the Centennial Celebration of the Inauguration of George Washington as President of the United States, 1888.

Van Dusen, J. T., Assemblyman, Tuolumne, 1856.

Van Dyke, Walter, Assemblyman, Klamath, 1853; Senator, Humboldt, etc., 1862, 1863; Member Second Constitutional Convention, 1878–79, Second Congressional District; Superior Judge, Los Angeles County, elected 1888.

Van Fleet, W. C., Assemblyman, Sacramento, 1881; Prison Director, 1883–84; Superior Judge, Sacramento County, elected 1884, 1890.

Van Leuven, A., Assemblyman, San Bernardino, 1863–64.

Vann, W. A., Assemblyman, Colusa and Lake, 1893.

Van Ness, James, Senator, Santa Barbara and San Luis Obispo, 1871–72; Mayor of San Francisco, 1855. *Died, San Luis Obispo, December 28, 1872.*

Van Reynegom, F. W., Superior Judge, San Francisco, appointed 1889.

Van Schaick, H. D., Assemblyman, Santa Clara, 1863–64.

Van Voorhies, R. J. Assemblyman, Alpine, Mono, etc., 1885.

Van Voorhies, William, Assemblyman, San Francisco District, 1849–50; Secretary of State, 1849–52; Member Second Constitutional Convention, 1878–79, Alameda District. *Died, Eureka, California, September 6, 1884.*

Van Zant, John W., Assemblyman, San Francisco, 1862.

Variel, R. H. F., Assemblyman, Plumas and Sierra, 1887.

Varney, B. F., Assemblyman, Siskiyou, 1857, 1863.

Vaughn, C. L. N., Assemblyman, Sutter, 1859.

Venable, J. W., Assemblyman, Los Angeles, 1873–74.

Venable, McD. R., Assemblyman, San Luis Obispo, 1887.

Vermeule, Thomas L., Member First Constitutional Convention, 1849, San Joaquin District; Senator, San Joaquin District, 1849–50. *Died, Stockton, May 7, 1856.*

Victoria, Manuel, Governor under Mexican rule, 1831–32.

Vincent, J. P., Assemblyman, Fresno, 1887.

Vineyard, J. R., Assemblyman, Sacramento, 1855; Senator, Los Angeles, 1862, 1863. *Died, Los Angeles, August 30, 1863.*

Virden, W. H., Superior Judge, Mono County, elected 1890.

Voorhies, E. C., Senator, Amador and Calaveras, 1891, 1893.

Vrooman, Henry, Senator, Alameda, 1883, 1885, 1887. *Died, Oakland, April 8, 1889.*

Waddell, William, Assemblyman, Amador, 1862.

Wade, James H., Senator, Mariposa and Tulare, 1853, 1854. *Died, San Francisco, October 8, 1867.*

Wade, Owen, Assemblyman, Napa, 1893.

Wade, W. P., Superior Judge, Los Angeles County, elected 1888.

Wadsworth, E., Senator, Siskiyou, 1865–66, 1867–68.

Wagner, George W., Assemblyman, Amador, 1856.   *Died, Jackson, March 2, 1874.*

Waite, E. G., Assemblyman, Nevada, 1855; Senator, Nevada, 1856, 1857; Secretary of State, 1891–

Walden, Minor, Assemblyman, Stanislaus and Merced, 1860, 1861, 1869–70.

Waldron, Mahlon, Assemblyman, Placer, 1867–68, 1869–70.

Walker, A. B., Assemblyman, Siskiyou, 1858.

Walker, A. M., Assemblyman, Nevada, 1880.   *Died, Truckee, November 14, 1882.*

Walker, Asa, Assemblyman, Alameda, 1863–64.   *Died, Brooklyn, Alameda County, May 12, 1869.*

Walker, Hugh, Member Second Constitutional Convention, 1878–79, Marin District.

Walker, I. N., Assemblyman, Fresno, 1863–64, 1871–72.

Walker, J. P., Member First Constitutional Convention, 1849, Sonoma District.

Walker, James M., Assemblyman, Fresno, 1863.

Walker, Thomas R., Assemblyman, Marin, 1853.

Walkup, Joseph, Senator, Placer, 1853, 1854, 1857; Lieutenant-Governor, 1858–59.   *Died, Auburn, October 15, 1873.*

Wall, Isaac B., Assemblyman, Monterey, 1852, 1853; Speaker of the House, 1853.   *Died, Monterey, November 9, 1855.*

Wallace, George, Private Secretary to Governors Milton S. Latham and John G. Downey.

Wallace, William C., Judge Seventh Judicial District, elected, 1869, 1875; Superior Judge, Napa County, elected 1879.

Wallace, William T., Attorney-General, 1856–57; Supreme Justice, 1870–79; Chief Justice, 1872–79; Presidential Elector, 1880; Assemblyman, San Francisco, 1883; Superior Judge, San Francisco, elected 1886, 1892; Regent of State University.

Walling, J. M., Superior Judge, Nevada County, elected 1884.

Wallis, H. W., Senator, Nevada and Sierra, 1883, 1885.   *Died, Forest City, June 9, 1887.*

Wallis, J. S., Senator, Santa Clara, 1863.

Wallis, Talbot H., State Librarian, 1882–90.

Walrath, Austin, Assemblyman, Nevada, 1883, 1885; Senator, Nevada, 1887.

Walsh, James, Senator, Nevada, 1852.

Walsh, P. F., Adjutant-General, 1875–80; Registrar of Voters, San Francisco, 1885–87.

Walter, F., Assemblyman, Trinity, 1861.

Walthall, Madison, Assemblyman, Sacramento District, 1849–50.   *Died, Stockton, April 28, 1873.*

Walton, John, Senator, El Dorado, 1852, 1853.

Wand, Thomas N., Assemblyman, San Francisco, 1867–68; Senator, San Francisco, 1869–70, 1871–72.

Ward, Charles H., Assemblyman, San Francisco, 1885.

Ward, J. B., Assemblyman, San Francisco, 1880.

Ward, J. M., Assemblyman, Butte, 1885.

Ward, J. N., Assemblyman, Mariposa and Merced, 1858.

Ward, Loomis, Assemblyman, Colusa, 1871–72.

Ward, R. H., Assemblyman, Merced and Stanislaus, 1865–66.

Warden, L. M., Assemblyman, San Luis Obispo, 1877–78.

Warfield, J. B., Assemblyman, Nevada, 1858; Sonoma, 1867–68.   *Died, San Francisco, November 19, 1878.*

Warkins, Chapman, Assemblyman, Amador, 1881.

Warmcastle, F. M., Assemblyman, Contra Costa, 1854 1858; Senator, San Joaquin, etc., 1861, 1862; Superior Judge, Contra Costa County, appointed 1886,

Warner, J. J., Senator, San Diego, 1851, 1852; Assemblyman, Los Angeles, 1860.

Warren, G. R., State Controller, 1862–63.

Warrington, Samuel R., Assemblyman, Sutter, 1857.

Warwick, J. H., Assemblyman, Sacramento, 1862, 1863.

Washburn, C. A., Presidential Elector, 1860.   *Died, New York, January 28, 1889.*

Wason, Milton, Assemblyman, Solano, 1863–64; Santa Barbara, etc., 1880, 1881.

Wasson, Joseph, *April 18, 1883.*Assemblyman, Mono and Inyo, 1880, 1881. *Died, San Blas,*

Waterman, R. W., Lieutenant-Governor, 1887; Governor, 1887-90. *Died, San Diego, April 12, 1891.*

Waters, Byron, Assemblyman, San Bernardino, 1877-78; Member Second Constitutional Convention, 1878-79. Fourth Congressional District.

Watkins, H. P., Senator, Yuba, 1860, 1851.

Watkins, Jason, Assemblyman, Yolo, 1875-76.

Watkins, Joseph S., Assemblyman, Alameda, 1854, 1855; Calaveras, 1857.

Watkins, William F., Assemblyman, Siskiyou, 1859. *Died, Panama, January 26, 1878.*

Watson, B. J.. Senator, Nevada and Sierra, 1880, 1881.

Watson, E. H., Assemblyman, El Dorado, 1885.

Watson, George W., Assemblyman, Alameda, 1885.

Watson, J. H., Assemblyman, El Dorado, 1860.

Watson John A., Assemblyman, Los Angeles, 1862, 1863, 1867-68. *Died, Los Angeles, September 16, 1869.*

Watson, John H., Judge Third Judicial District, elected by the Legislature, 1850.

Watson, John H., Assemblyman, San Francisco District, 1849-50; Senator, Monterey and Santa Cruz, 1860, 1861.

Watson, J. R., Assemblyman, Sacramento, 1863-64. *Died, Sacramento, September 11, 1889.*

Watt, Robert, State Controller, 1867-71; Bank Commissioner, 1878-82; President of the Board of Directors of Stockton Insane Asylum, 1889-

Watt, William, Senator, Nevada, 1861. *Died, North Bloomfield, July 6, 1878.*

Wattson, C. C., Assemblyman, San Diego, 1880.

Waymire, James A., Superior Judge, San Francisco, appointed 1881.

Wear, G. W.. Assemblyman, Kern and Ventura, 1889.

Weaver, J. H. G., Assemblyman, Humboldt, 1883, 1885; Speaker pro tem., 1885.

Weber, C. N., Assemblyman, Santa Clara, 1887.

Webster, Jonathan V., Member Second Constitutional Convention, 1878-79, Alameda District.

Weeks, J. E. P., Trustee of State Library, 1872-73. *Died, Sacramento, August 28, 1877.*

Weeks, William H., Presidential Elector, 1860; Secretary of State, 1862-63. *Died, Sacramento, August 16, 1863.*

Weil, John, State Treasurer, 1880-82.

Weinstock, Harris, Trustee of State Library, 1887-89.

Weir, B. G., Assemblyman, San Joaquin, 1856. *Died, Tuolumne City, November 19, 1886.*

Welch, J. W., Senator, San Francisco, 1887, 1889, 1891.

Welch, S. K., Assemblyman, Napa and Lake, 1873-74, 1877-78.

Welcker, W. T., State Superintendent of Public Instruction, 1883-86.

Weller, John B., United States Senator, 1851-56; Governor, 1858-59. *Died, New Orleans August 17, 1875.*

Weller, Joseph R., Member Second Constitutional Convention, 1878-79, Santa Clara District.

Wellin, Patrick M., Member Second Constitutional Convention, 1878-79, San Francisco District.

Wells, Alexander, Attorney-General. 1852; Supreme Justice, 1853-54. *Died, San Jose, October 31, 1854.*

Wells, Thomas, Assemblyman. Butte. 1853, 1855. *Dead.*

Welsh, L. S., Assemblyman, El Dorado, 1856,

Welty, Daniel W., Assemblyman, Sacramento, 1860. *Died, Chehalis, Washington, March 24, 1891.*

Welty, Jacob, Assemblyman, Placer, 1871-72. *Died, Lincoln, November 17, 1879.*

Wendell, J. T.. Senator, Solano and Yolo, 1880, 1881. *Died, San Francisco, February 16, 1891.*

Wentworth, George A., Assemblyman, San Francisco, 1891.

Wentz, Christian, Assemblyman, Santa Clara, 1881.

Werk, G. W., Assemblyman, Humboldt, 1862.

Wertsbaugher, Joseph C., Assemblyman, Butte, 1881. *Died, Chico, August 1, 1884.*

Wescott, Jonas, Assemblyman, Yuba, 1860.

West. John P., Member Second Constitutional Convention, 1878-79, Los Angeles District; Senator, Los Angeles, 1880, 1881.

Westmoreland, Charles, Assemblyman; Humboldt, 1867–68; Senator, Placer, 1856, 1857; Presidential Elector, 1868. *Died, Panama, December 23, 1868.*
Weston, H. L., Assemblyman, Sonoma, 1891.
Weston, R. S., Assemblyman, Sierra, 1863–64.
Wethered, James S., Assemblyman, San Francisco, 1851.
Wetherill, S. E., Assemblyman, San Francisco, 1875–76. *Died, San Francisco, January 7, 1885.*
Whalen, Peter, Assemblyman, San Francisco, 1883.
Whallon, M., Assemblyman, Sonoma, 1863–64.
Wharton, J. F., Assemblyman, Fresno, 1883. *Died, Fresno, March 17, 1889.*
Wheadon, John, Assemblyman, Yuba, 1859.
Wheat, A. R., Assemblyman, Calaveras, 1877–78, 1883.
Wheaton, William R., Assemblyman, San Francisco, 1863, 1871–72. *Died, Oakland, September 11, 1888.*
Wheeler, Alfred, Assemblyman, San Francisco District, 1849–50.
Wheeler, E. D., Senator, Yuba, etc., 1859, 1860; Judge Nineteenth Judicial District, appointed 1872, elected 1873.
Whipple, E. L., Assemblyman, Sonoma, 1881. *Died, Santa Rosa, December 8, 1882.*
Whipple, S. G., Assemblyman, Klamath, 1854, 1857; Humboldt, 1863.
Whitcomb, N. T., Assemblyman, San Francisco, 1885.
White, James D., Assemblyman, El Dorado, 1856; Nevada, 1867–68. *Died, Nevada City, December 19, 1883.*
White, John, Assemblyman, Shasta, 1860, 1861. *Died, England, February 23, 1871.*
White, P. J., Railroad Commissioner, Second District, 1887–90.
White, Stephen M., Senator, Los Angeles, 1887, 1889; President pro tem., 1887, 1889; Lieutenant-Governor, 1887–90; Trustee State Normal School at Los Angeles, 1887–91, 1891–; United States Senator, 1893–
White, Thomas J., Assemblyman (Speaker), Sacramento, 1849–50. *Died, Los Angeles, December, 1861.*
White, William F., Member Second Constitutional Convention, 1878–79, Santa Cruz, Monterey, and San Benito District: Bank Commissioner, 1879–87. *Died, Los Angeles, May 13, 1890.*
Whitehurst, L. A., Assemblyman, Santa Clara, 1889; Senator, Santa Clara, 1893.
Whiteside, N. E., Assemblyman (Speaker), Yuba, 1858. *Died, Marysville, September 1, 1876.*
Whiting, B. C., Senator, Monterey, etc., 1854, 1855. *Died, Los Angeles, June 7, 1881.*
Whiting, Charles J., Surveyor-General, 1849–51.
Whiting, G. A., Assemblyman, Tuolumne, Mono, etc., 1871–72.
Whiting, M, S., Senator, San Francisco, 1863.
Whitlock, J. H., Assemblyman, Plumas and Lassen, 1877–78.
Whitman, B. C., Assemblyman, Solano, 1854. *Died, San Francisco, August 5, 1885.*
Whitman, G. N., Assemblyman, San Bernardino, 1859.
Whitman, George W., State Controller, 1856–57.
Whitney, A. P., Senator, Sonoma, 1877–78. *Died, San Francisco, February 10, 1884.*
Whitney, D. L., Assemblyman, Sierra, 1871–72.
Whitney, G. W., Assemblyman, Tuolumne, 1859.
Whitney, George E., Senator, Alameda, 1883, 1885.
Whitney, William, Assemblyman, San Francisco, 1855. *Died, Nevada County, June 18, 1872.*
Wickes, John T., Member Second Constitutional Convention, 1878–79, Nevada District.
Wickware, G. C., Assemblyman, San Francisco, 1873–74.
Widney, Robert M., Judge Seventeenth Judicial District, appointed 1871.
Wiggin, C. L., Assemblyman, San Francisco, 1865–66. *Died, San Francisco, March 29, 1891.*
Wiggin, Marcus P., Superior Judge, Mono County, appointed 1880, elected 1880.
Wigginton, P. D., Representative to Congress, 1875–77, 1878. *Died, Oakland, July 7, 1890.*
Wilcox, I. A., Assemblyman, Santa Clara, 1887.
Wilcox, John W., Assemblyman, Mariposa and Merced, 1863, 1863–64, 1865–66, 1871–72, 1873–74.

Wilcoxon, C. E., Assemblyman, Sutter, 1862; Member of State Board of
    Equalization, 1883-86, 1887-90.
Wiley, A., Assemblyman, Humboldt, 1863-64.
Wilkins, Charles P., Assemblyman, Sonoma, 1860. *Died, Santa Rosa, August 1, 1864.*
Wilkins, W. W., Assemblyman, Tuolumne, 1851.
Willets, Stephen, Assemblyman, El Dorado, 1867-68.
Willey, Henry I., Surveyor-General, 1883-86.
Willey, O. F., Assemblyman, San Francisco, 1861.
Williams, A. P., United States Senator, 1886.
Williams, B. T., Superior Judge, Ventura County, elected 1884, 1890.
Williams, C. E., Judge Fifteenth Judicial District, appointed 1856.
Williams, C. H. S., Senator, San Francisco, etc., 1859. *Died, San Francisco, January 4, 1867.*
Williams, George, Assemblyman, Humboldt, 1887, 1889.
Williams, George E., Assemblyman, El Dorado, 1873-74; Judge Eleventh
    Judicial District, elected 1875; Superior Judge, El Dorado County, elected
    1879, 1884.
Williams, George H., Senator, San Francisco, 1891, 1893.
Williams, J. M., Assemblyman, Santa Clara, 1860.
Williams, John F., Assemblyman, Sacramento District, 1849-50.
Williams, L. S., Senator, Trinity and Klamath, 1853. *Died, San Francisco, October 16, 1860.*
Williams, R. L., Assemblyman, Placer, 1856.
Williams, Thomas H., Attorney-General, 1858-61. *Died, San Francisco, February 28, 1886.*
Williams, W. H., Senator, San Francisco, 1889, 1891.
Williams, W. S., Assemblyman, Calaveras, 1869-70.
Williamson, C. V., Senator, Tuolumne, 1861, 1862.
Willis, Henry N., Superior Judge, San Bernardino County, appointed 1887.
Willson, Israel C., Assemblyman, Santa Cruz, 1858, 1863. *Died, Santa Cruz, December 30, 1869.*
Wilsey, Levi, Assemblyman, Mendocino, 1863-64. *Dead.*
Wilson, B. D., Senator, Los Angeles, San Diego, etc., 1856, 1857, 1869-70, 1871-72. *Died, Los Angeles, March 11, 1878.*
Wilson, H. C., Member Second Constitutional Convention, 1878-79, Tehama
    District; Senator, Tehama and Colusa, 1891, 1893.
Wilson, J. L., Assemblyman, Alameda, 1865-66.
Wilson, J. M., Assemblyman, Tuolumne, 1853.
Wilson, J. N. E., Senator, San Francisco, 1887, 1889; Insurance Commissioner, 1889-
Wilson, M. W., Assemblyman, Placer, 1877-78.
Wilson, Samuel, Assemblyman, Calaveras, 1860.
Wilson, Samuel M., Member Second Constitutional Convention, 1878-79,
    First Congressional District. *Died, San Francisco, June 4, 1892.*
Wilson, T. K., Senator, San Francisco, 1883; Superior Judge, San
    Francisco, elected 1879, 1880, 1886.
Winans, Joseph W., Trustee of State Library, 1861-70; Member Second
    Constitutional Convention, 1878-79, First Congressional District. *Died,
    San Francisco, March 31, 1887.*
Winchell, G., Assemblyman, Sierra, 1873-74.
Winchester, Jonas, State Printer, 1850-51. *Died, Columbia, February 23, 1887.*
Winchester, M. C., Assemblyman, Placer, 1863-64.
Windrow, Joseph, Assemblyman, San Francisco, 1887, 1891.
Wing, Austin, Assemblyman, El Dorado, 1852, 1853.
Wing, Stephen, Senator, Tuolumne, etc., 1869-70, 1871-72.
Wing, W. P., Assemblyman, Placer. 1859.
Winsor, W. B., Assemblyman, Yuba, 1856.
Winston, Joseph, Assemblyman, Plumas, 1856.
Witherby, O. S., Assemblyman, San Diego District, 1849-50; Judge First
    Judicial District, elected by Legislature 1850.
Wohler, Herman, Assemblyman, San Francisco, 1852, 1856. *Died, San Francisco, June 2, 1877.*
Wolcott, Oliver, Senator, Tuolumne, etc., 1865, 1867-68.
Wolfskill, J. C., Assemblyman, Solano, 1891.
Wolfskill, John, Senator, San Diego and San Bernardino, 1883.
Wolleb, Charles, Assemblyman, Sacramento, 1867-68. *Died, Fruitvale, December 21, 1883.*

Wombough, M. M., Senator, Yolo and Colusa, 1852, 1853.
Wood, A., Assemblyman, Plumas, 1861.
Wood, Charles, Assemblyman, Contra Costa, 1875–76.
Wood, George, Assemblyman, Plumas and Sierra, 1881, 1885.
Wood, Joseph, Assemblyman, San Francisco, 1863–64.
Wood, Joseph C., Assemblyman, Nevada, 1857; Yolo, 1861.
Wood, R. N., Assemblyman, San Francisco, 1852. *Died, Cavorca, Mexico, April 7, 1857.*
Wood, William G., Clerk of the Supreme Court, 1867. *Died, Brooklyn, New York, April 20, 1869.*
Woodman, George W., Assemblyman, Shasta, 1862.
Woodside, P. K., Clerk of the Supreme Court, 1853–54.
Woodward, F. J., Assemblyman, San Joaquin, 1871–72, 1885.
Woodworth, F. A., Senator, San Francisco, 1857. *Dead.*
Woodworth, S. E., Senator, Monterey, 1849–50, 1851. *Died, San Francisco, January 29, 1871.*
Woolf, D. B., Clerk of the Supreme Court, 1875–80; Secretary of Supreme Court Commission, 1885–
Works, John D., Superior Judge, San Diego County, appointed 1886, elected 1886; Supreme Justice, 1888–1890.
Worthington, Henry G., Assemblyman, San Francisco, 1862.
Wozencraft, O. M., Member First Constitutional Convention, 1849–50, San Joaquin District. *Died, New York, November 22, 1887.*
Wright, C. C., Assemblyman, Stanislaus, 1887.
Wright, George W., Representative to Congress, 1849–51.
Wright, M. J., Assemblyman, Solano, 1871–72; Senator, Solano, 1885.
Wright, S. P., Assemblyman, Klamath and Del Norte, 1862, 1863; Senator, Del Norte, Klamath, etc., 1863–64, 1865–66; President pro tem., 1865–66.
Wright, T. J., Assemblyman, Contra Costa, 1863, 1863–64.
Wright, Thomas, Assemblyman, Sierra, 1861.
Wright, W. S. M., Assemblyman, Sonoma, 1873–74.
Wyatt, N. G., Member Second Constitutional Convention, 1878–79, Monterey District.
Wyman, S. B., Assemblyman, Placer, 1857.
Yager, Cornelius, Assemblyman, Contra Costa, 1860.
Yancey, F., Assemblyman, Tuolumne, 1860.
Yell, Archibald, Assemblyman, Mendocino, 1883; Senator, Mendocino and Lake, 1887, 1889; Director Mendocino State Insane Asylum, 1889–91.
Yeiser, Frederick, Assemblyman, San Joaquin, 1851, 1852, 1853.
York, Frank, Assemblyman, Tuolumne, Mono, etc., 1869–70.
York, J. L., Assemblyman, Santa Clara, 1880.
Young, A. R., Assemblyman, Calaveras, 1869–70.
Young, Albert J., Assemblyman, Contra Costa, 1877–78.
Young, George A., Assemblyman, Nevada, 1858, 1859; San Francisco, 1875–76.
Young, George E., Assemblyman, Calaveras, 1852. *Died, Arizona, 1877.*
Young, J. D., Assemblyman, San Joaquin, 1887.
Young, John D., State Printer, 1880–82, 1887–90,
Young, John N., Assemblyman, Sacramento, 1880, 1881.
Young, Nestor A., Assemblyman, San Diego, 1887, 1889, 1891.
Yule, John, Assemblyman, Placer, 1862, 1863, 1865–66; Trinity and Shasta 1885; Speaker of the House, 1865–66; Senator, Placer, 1863–64. *Died, El Dorado County, March, 1888.*
Zuck, J. C., Senator, Santa Clara, 1880, 1881.
Zuck, John, Assemblyman, Santa Clara, 1862, 1865–66.

INDEX.

44

45

Lightning Source UK Ltd.
Milton Keynes UK
UKHW040851070119

335137UK00011B/302/P